# THE BURNS MANTLE
## THEATER YEARBOOK 1989–1990

FEATURING
THE TEN BEST PLAYS
OF THE SEASON

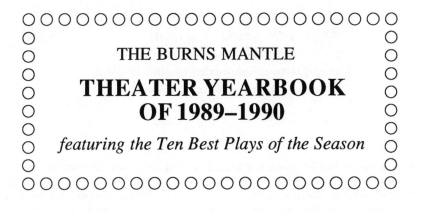

THE BURNS MANTLE

# THEATER YEARBOOK
## OF 1989–1990

*featuring the Ten Best Plays of the Season*

# EDITED BY OTIS L. GUERNSEY JR.
# AND JEFFREY SWEET

*Illustrated with photographs and
with drawings by* HIRSCHFELD

○○○○○○

**APPLAUSE**
THEATRE BOOK PUBLISHERS
211 West 71 St. New York, N.Y. 10023

*Copyright © 1990  by Applause Theatre Book Publishers*
*ISBN: 1–55783–091–6 (cloth)*
*ISBN: 1–55783–090–8 (paper)*
*Library of Congress Catalog Card Number: 20–21432*
*Printed in the United States of America*

# EDITOR'S NOTE

WONDERS never cease—not in the theater, anyhow. As the 1989–90 sea-son paraded through our playhouses from river to river and from coast to coast, the type and volume of new shows remained fairly steady—but wasn't New York's most lavish, eight-a-week, do-or-die commercial theater an ex-ception? As the decade turned, as production and ticket costs continued to rise while recessionistic rumbles were being heard in the economic distance, sad Broadway was carrying its slow attenuation of the 1980s over into the 1990s—wasn't it? It was *not*! The number of Broadway shows offered in 1989–90 rose almost 20 percent above last year by our count (see details in our review of The Season On and Off Broadway), and that included an increase in both new-play and new-musical production.

And the 1989–90 season on Broadway didn't show any signs of weakening with the onset of summer. It passed its formal May 31 milestone at full speed, with two shows selling out, ten more doing better than 90 percent of capacity business and a half a dozen or so others going along with the leaders. "The best season in years for dramatic shows," trumpeted *Variety*, while the New York *Times* admitted, "The state of the art seems to be healthy." And this more fabulous than invalid Broadway was already getting ready for another upbeat year with a decamillion-plus advance sale for a musical that isn't ex-pected to open until April 1991.

In this 1989–90 *Best Plays* volume we follow the theater, the wonder medium, wherever it leads—even to Broadway—with the same attention to small detail and wide-ranging trend as in the past 70 volumes of this long-run-ning series of yearbooks, and with the same dedicated personnel as in recent years. Jonathan Dodd manages the publication as usual, for Glenn Young's Applause Theater Books, publisher of the series. Associate Editor Jeffrey Sweet—critic, Tony nominator, playwright, teacher of playwrights, screen writer—covers and reports on the Broadway and off-Broadway scene, from which he makes his Best Play selections, with minor input from the editor-in-chief. (And under our two-seasons-old policy of expanding Best Play eligibil-ity, we include an occasional new off-off-Broadway script, such as Athol Fugard's latest, which made the Best Plays list in this volume.)

The editor's diligent wife continues to scrutinize and improve the accuracy of our listings, while the associate editor's equally diligent helpmeet, Sheridan

Sweet, prepares the comprehensive listings of new plays in first class mainstage or experimental production across the United States. A major asset in this section of each volume continues to be the American Theater Critics Association's selection of a sample of outstanding scripts in cross-country theater (including the recipient of its annual New Play Award) by a committee headed this year by T. H. McCulloh of the Los Angeles *Times*.

Highlights of the off-off-Broadway year are identified and reviewed by Mel Gussow, distinguished theater critic of the New York *Times*. In our summary of the Circle's voting in last year's volume, we stated correctly that the *Times*'s executive editor had directed all the paper's critics to refrain from consensual procedures such as the Critics' balloting for bests; but we added, incorrectly, that the *Times* drama critics had therefore resigned from the Circle. Not so. They remain non-voting members, and, Gussow tells us, "Last year and this year I have been the president of the Circle and presided over the meetings. I plan to remain a member after my term in office."

No worthy off-off-Broadway offering escapes the notice of Mr. Gussow, nor do its smallest efforts escape their appearance in our record of the OOB season, scrupulously compiled by Camille Croce. The usefulness and enjoyment of this volume is further enhanced for our readers by Rue E. Canvin (play publications and necrology), Stanley Green (major cast replacements on and off Broadway), Sally Dixon Wiener (three Best Play synopses), William Schelble (Tony Awards listing), Thomas T. Foose (historical footnotes), Henry Hewes (a previous Best Plays editor whose advice continues to abet this enterprise), Ossia Trilling (Our Man in London), Michael Kuchwara (Critics Circle voting), Gary Denys (for his photo handling), Dorothy Swerdlove of the Lincoln Center Library and Ralph Newman of the Drama Book Shop—and most of all, the men and women of the Broadway, off-Broadway, off-off-Broadway and cross-country press offices whose willing, generous and knowledgeable assistance make the *Best Plays* coverage possible in its broad-based 1990s form.

And these yearbooks are perennially favored with the flowering elan of Al Hirschfeld revealing in his wonderful caricatures a whole season's worth of the exuberant personalities who stand and deliver at the footlighted edge of the stage. We are very grateful, likewise, to Santo Loquasto for providing us with examples of his costume designs, the best of the year; to Martha Swope and her Associates (including Carol Rosegg) for the photos synopsizing *Once on This Island* and other illustrations in these pages; and for the graphic photo coverage of New York and cross-country stages by Bert Andrews, Chris Bennion, Tom Brazil, Marc Bryan-Brown, Kyle Chepulis, Paula Court, Peter Cunningham, Zoe Dominic, Dalia Studios, Lisa Ebright, Chris Fessler, Gelfand-Piper, Gerry Goodstein, Irene Haupt, John Haynes, Martha Holmes, Bob Hsiang, Joan Marcus, Bob Marshak, Anita and Steve Shevett, Megan Terry, Michael Tighe, Richard Trigg and Sandy Underwood.

Reflecting on the 1989–90 season with its newfound Broadway momentum, we can't help applauding the participation of such organizations as AT&T and Suntory, who have joined the professional producers in supporting shows—Suntory prestigiously with *A Few Good Men, The Circle, Tru* and both Tony winners (*City of Angels* and *The Grapes of Wrath*); and AT&T: OnStage adventurously in the farther reaches of Manhattan including, this season, the Shakespeare revivals in Central Park and the Playwrights Horizons Best Play *Once on This Island.* We admire their sense of values, and we value their good sense in taking a constructive part in one of the world's greatest art forms in one of the world's greatest concentrations of it. This object of their attention and support, a New York theater season, is annually renewed and invigorated by the efforts of gallant playwrights, composers, lyricists and librettists, who are never discouraged by failure or lulled into complacency by success, but who, year after year, put forth a collective creative effort the equal of any on this planet. To AT&T, Suntory and all comers, welcome aboard their bandwagon as closely described and delineated in this *Best Plays* volume. It will parade as proudly in this new decade as it did in the last one. It has never stopped calling a lively tune for living theater, and it never will.

OTIS L. GUERNSEY Jr.

September 1, 1990                                                                      Editor

# CONTENTS

EDITOR'S NOTE                                                          vii

THE SEASON ON AND OFF BROADWAY                                           1
  Broadway and Off Broadway, by Jeffrey Sweet        3
    One-page summary of the Broadway Season        4
    One-page summary of the Off-Broadway Season        11

A GRAPHIC GLANCE BY HIRSCHFELD                                          63

THE TEN BEST PLAYS: SYNOPSES AND EXCERPTS                              129
  The Loman Family Picnic        131
  Love Letters        151
  Grand Hotel, The Musical        166
  My Children! My Africa!        193
  City of Angels        220
  Sex, Drugs, Rock & Roll        258
  Prelude to a Kiss        269
  The Grapes of Wrath        293
  The Piano Lesson        313
  Once on This Island        344

PLAYS PRODUCED IN NEW YORK                                            357
  Plays Produced on Broadway        359
  Plays Which Closed Prior to Broadway Opening        393
  Plays Produced Off Broadway        398
  Cast Replacements and Touring Companies        432

THE SEASON OFF OFF BROADWAY                                           447
  Off Off Broadway, by Mel Gussow        449
  Plays Produced Off Off Broadway        454

THE SEASON AROUND THE UNITED STATES                                  481
  Outstanding New Plays Cited by American
    Theater Critics Association        483
  A Directory of New-Play Productions        503

FACTS AND FIGURES                                                                543
    Long Runs on Broadway       545
    Long Runs Off Broadway       549
    New York Drama Critics Circle Awards        550
    Pulitzer Prize Winners       553
    The Tony Awards       554
    The Obie Awards       557
    Additional Prizes and Awards        558
    1989-1990 Publication of Recently-Produced Plays        561
    Necrology       564
    The Best Plays, 1894-1989       575

INDEX                                                                            597

## *Drawings by* HIRSCHFELD

Rachel York, Rene Auberjonois, Randy Graff, Scott Waara, Dee
    Hoty, James Naughton and Gregg Edelman in *City of Angels*      64–65
Randy Graff in *City of Angels*                                            66
James Naughton in *City of Angels*                                         67
Terry Kinney, Lois Smith, Gary Sinise in *The Grapes of Wrath*      68–69
Lois Smith in *The Grapes of Wrath*                                        70
Bob Gunton in *Sweeney Todd*                                               71
Jim Walton, Gretchen Kingsley, Michael McCarty, Bill Nabel, Bob
    Gunton, David Barron, Beth Fowler and Eddie Korbich in
    *Sweeney Todd*                                                      72–73
Kathleen Turner in *Cat on a Hot Tin Roof*                                 74
Mandy Patinkin in *Mandy Patinkin in Concert: Dress Casual*                75
Nathan Lane in *The Lisbon Traviata*                                       76
Andy Halliday in *The Lady in Question*                                    77
Jonathan Hadary in *Gypsy*                                                 78
Crista Moore, Tyne Daly, Jonathan Hadary, Jana Robbins, Barbara
    Erwin and Anna McNeeley in *Gypsy*                                     79
Stewart Granger in *The Circle*                                            80
Rex Harrison in *The Circle*                                               81
Rex D. Hays, Karen Akers, David Carroll, John Wylie, Liliane
    Motevecchi, Jane Krakowski, Yvonne Marceau and Pierre
    Dulaine, Michael Jeter and Kathi Moss in *Grand Hotel*             82–83
Michael Jeter in *Grand Hotel*                                             84
Jace Alexander in *Heart of a Dog*                                         85
Joseph Daly in *Mastergate*                                                86

Ann McDonough, John Dossett, Zach Grenier, Jeff Weiss, Joseph
    Daly, Tom McDermott, Melinda Mullins, Jerome Kilty, Wayne
    Knight, Daniel von Bargen and Steve Hofvendahl in *Mastergate*    87
Eric Bogosian in *Sex, Drugs, Rock & Roll*    88
Stephan Lang in *A Few Good Men*    89
Lisa Gay Hamilton, S. Epatha Merkerson, Lou Myers, Charles S.
    Dutton, Carl Gordon, Tommy Hollis and Rocky Carroll in *The
    Piano Lesson*    90–91
Mo Gaffney and Kathy Najimy in *The Kathy and Mo Show*    92
Robert Morse in *Tru*    93
Rita McKenzie in *Call Me Ethel!*    94
Sophie Maletsky in *Der Ring Gott Farblonjet*    95
Everett Quinton in *Dr. Jekyll and Mr. Hyde*    96
Sloane Shelton in *Orpheus Descending*    97
Frances Conroy, Stephen Vinovich, Jennifer Van Dyck, Mary Beth
    Hurt, Michael Wincott and Blair Brown in *The Secret Rapture*    98–99
Vanessa Redgrave, Anne Twomey, Tammy Grimes and Kevin
    Anderson in *Orpheus Descending*    100
Michael Siberry in *The Merchant of Venice*    101
Jean Stapleton in *Mountain Language*    102
Barnard Hughes in *Prelude to a Kiss*    103
Ellen Burstyn in *Shirley Valentine*    104
Nathaniel Parker, Geraldine James, Leigh Lawson and Dustin
    Hoffman in *The Merchant of Venice*    105
Maggie Smith and Margaret Tyzack in *Lettice & Lovage*    106
Christine Lahti in *The Heidi Chronicles*    107
Simon Jones in *Privates on Parade*    108
Maureen McGovern, Suzzanne Douglas, Sting, Alvin Epstein,
    Georgia Brown, Ethyl Eichelberger and Josh Mostel in
    *3 Penny Opera*    109
Michael Cumpsty, Harold Gould, Stephanie Roth, Paxton Whitehead,
    Jim Fyfe, Michael Winther and John McMartin in *Artist
    Descending a Staircase*    110
James DeMarse in *Cahoots*    111
Kevin Colson, Ann Crumb, Michael Ball and Kathleen Rowe
    McAllen in *Aspects of Love*    112
Henderson Forsythe in *Some Americans Abroad*    113
Diane Venora, Peter Francis James, Josef Sommer, Dana Ivey,
    Michael Cumpsty, Kevin Kline and Brian Murray in *Hamlet*    114
Len Cariou in *Mountain*    115
Jerome Kilty in *The Doctor's Dilemma*    116
Polly Holliday in *Cat on a Hot Tin Roof*    117
Betty Garrett in *Meet Me in St. Louis*    118

Calista Flockhart in *Beside Herself*                                        119
Faith Prince in *Jerome Robbins' Broadway*                                  120
Sally Mayes in *Closer Than Ever*                                           121
Mary-Louise Parker in *The Art of Success*                                  122
John Curless in *Progress*                                                  123
Mike Burstyn in *The Rothschilds*                                           124
Paul Provenza in *Only Kidding!*                                            125
Tony Roberts in *Jerome Robbins' Broadway*                                  126
Marcia Jean Kurtz in *When She Danced*                                      127
George Abbott, author and director of *Frankie*                             128

# THE SEASON
# ON AND OFF
# BROADWAY

CITY OF ANGELS—A detective-fiction author (Gregg Edelman as Stine, *above left*) is confronted by his imaginary private eye (James Naughton as Stone); *below*, the finale of the Larry Gelbart-Cy Coleman-David Zippel musical is set on a Hollywood movie sound stage

# BROADWAY AND OFF BROADWAY

O    *By Jeffrey Sweet*

*LARGO Desolato*, one of the Best Plays of 1985–86, is a dark comedy about a professor named Leopold Kopriva who, awaiting imprisonment for having offended a totalitarian state in a philosophical work, finds himself the object of adoration by those who consider him a hero. Kopriva is embarrassed by and uncomfortable with this attention; the actions he took had nothing to do with any desire to be a hero, and he seems as much beleaguered by the adulation of his admirers and their attendant expectation of further deeds of valor as by the persecution of his enemies.

During the 1988–89 season, the author of that play was in prison for having offended the authorities in Czechoslovakia. In the middle of the 1989–90 season, having been in the forefront of the nonviolent "Velvet Revolution" which brought down the Communist government of his country, that author, Vaclav Havel, was installed by acclamation as Czechoslovakia's president.

On Feb. 22, 1990, during a visit to the United States, President Havel was honored by a special program at the Cathedral of St. John the Divine in Manhattan. What distinguished this salute from the many others celebrating his courage and integrity was that it was by his fellow artists. One after another, leading figures from the performing and literary arts rose to speak in his praise or perform for him—Saul Bellow, Elie Wiesel, Arthur Miller, Paul Simon, Milos Forman, Roberta Flack, Dizzy Gillespie, Mikhail Barishnikov, Lukas Foss, James Taylor, Placido Domingo, Ellen Burstyn, Paul Newman, Spike Lee, Ron Silver, Harry Belafonte, Joseph Papp and many others.

Watching him being so honored, I couldn't help wondering if, as pleased as he evidently was, his ironically-inclined mind occasionally turned to Dr. Kopriva, his inadvertent hero.

Given the fact that so much of his art has been the product of conflict with the state, I also wondered how, if he succeeds in his stated desire to return to playwriting, having been the *head* of that state will affect his work.

The adversarial relationship between the artist and his society has often been the catalyst for art, particularly in the theater, which, being a social form,

3

# The 1989–90 Season on Broadway

**PLAYS (10)**

Mastergate
**LOVE LETTERS**
(transfer)
A Few Good Men
Tru
THE GRAPES OF WRATH
THE PIANO LESSON
Accomplice
PRELUDE TO A KISS
(transfer)
Some Americans Abroad
(transfer)
The Cemetery Club

**MUSICALS (8)**

Dangerous Games
Meet Me in St. Louis
Prince of Central Park
GRAND HOTEL
CITY OF ANGELS
Aspects of Love
Truly Blessed
A Change in the Heir

**REVUES (2)**

Sid Caesar & Company
(transfer)
Oba Oba '90

**FOREIGN PLAYS IN ENGLISH (4)**

The Secret Rapture
Artist Descending a Staircase
Lettice & Lovage
Zoya's Apartment

**HOLDOVER WHICH BECAME A HIT IN 1989–90**

**The Heidi Chronicles**

**REVIVALS (11)**

Shenandoah
Sweeney Todd
Orpheus Descending
3 Penny Opera
Gypsy
The Circle
The Tenth Man
**The Merchant of Venice**
Miss Margarida's Way
The Sound of Music
Cat on a Hot Tin Roof

**SPECIALTIES (4)**

**Mandy Patinkin**
Radio City Music Hall:
Takarazuka
Christmas Spectacular
Easter Extravaganza

**FOREIGN-LANGUAGE PLAY (1)**

Junon and Avos: The Hope

Categorized above are all the new productions listed in the Plays Produced on Broadway section of this volume.
Plays listed in CAPITAL LETTERS have been designated Best Plays of 1989–90.
Plays listed in italics were still running June 1, 1990.
Plays listed in bold face type were classified as successes in Variety's annual estimate published June 6, 1990.

so easily lends itself to the exploration of social issues. But, while a playwright was a central actor in a great drama played on the stage of Europe, most of the playwrights produced on New York stages this year did little to engage the issues of the day. At a time when the world was turned on its ear, there was scant representation of the forces behind these events on or off Broadway.

So what *were* the plays of the year about? In the main, art, artists and non-artists who were obsessed with or affected by art and artists. Leading characters in show after show were writers, actors, singers, dancers, directors, painters, musicians, or people who wanted to be writers, actors, etc., or adulated those who were. Case by case, several of these shows were works of value, as can be gleaned from the many cited in this volume as Best Plays. But I must confess to being troubled by the state of an art so thoroughly dominated by narcissism.

The good news is that this year the editors of this series had a longer list than usual of creditable choices from which to select the Best Plays. Though we saw the premiere of no play or musical of the overwhelming caliber of, say, *A Streetcar Named Desire* or *West Side Story*, still there was a continuous parade of impressive work by talented people.

One index of good tidings can be seen in the fact that, for the first time since the 1966–67 volume of this series, three musicals have been cited as Best Plays—*City of Angels, Grand Hotel* and *Once on This Island*. (The three from the 1966–67 season were *The Apple Tree, Cabaret* and *You're a Good Man, Charlie Brown*.) Wonder of wonders, in these days of Andrew Lloyd Webber and Cameron Mackintosh, none of these is a British creation (though *City of Angels*'s director, Michael Blakemore, does hail from England). Of the musicals, only *Once on This Island* was written without a contribution from a dramatist previously represented in past Best Play citations.

Among the straight Best Plays, again veterans of previous volumes are well represented—August Wilson (*The Piano Lesson*), Eric Bogosian (*Sex, Drugs, Rock & Roll*), A.R. Gurney (*Love Letters*), Athol Fugard (*My Children! My Africa!*), and Craig Lucas (*Prelude to a Kiss*). The newcomers to the circle are Donald Margulies (*The Loman Family Picnic*) and Frank Galati, though the adaptation for which the latter is cited, *The Grapes of Wrath*, is of a novel written by the late John Steinbeck, whose *Of Mice and Men* was a Best Play of the 1937–38 season.

As usual, most of the Best Plays originated in non-commercial arenas. *The Grapes of Wrath* began at Chicago's Steppenwolf Theater, *The Loman Family Picnic* at the Manhattan Theater Club, *Love Letters* at Long Wharf, *My Children! My Africa!* at Johannesburg's Market Theater, *Once on This Island* at Playwrights Horizons, *The Piano Lesson* at Yale (in association with several other regional managements) and *Prelude to a Kiss* at South Coast Repertory followed by a revised version at Circle Rep.

Several other works were also received enthusiastically by sizable proportions of the press and the public, among them Terrence McNally's *The Lisbon Traviata*, Jay Presson Allen's *Tru*, Peter Nichols's *Privates on Parade*, Peter Shaffer's *Lettice & Lovage*, Aaron Sorkin's *A Few Good Men*, George C. Wolfe's adaptation of Zora Neale Hurston's *Spunk* and Richard Nelson's *Some Americans Abroad*—all in all, an impressive showing.

Impressive, too, was the star power. Well-known movie actors, always helpful in luring a general audience, lent their talents to a variety of productions. Among them were an unusually large contingent of those who had either won or been nominated for Oscars—Dustin Hoffman, Kathleen Turner, William Hurt, Kevin Kline, Rex Harrison, Maggie Smith, Vanessa Redgrave, Tom Hulce, Charles Durning, Jason Robards, Mary Elizabeth Mastrantonio, Michelle Pfeiffer and Timothy Hutton.

And, as always, there were performers, some of whom have been on the scene for years, who rose to sudden prominence in roles that showed their abilities to special advantage—Michael Jeter and Jane Krakowski in *Grand Hotel*, Marcia Jean Kurtz in *The Loman Family Picnic* and *When She Danced*, La Chanze in *Once on This Island*, Mary-Louise Parker in *Prelude to a Kiss*.

An unusually large percentage of this year's directors were British, among them Michael Blakemore (*City of Angels* and *Lettice & Lovage*), Peter Hall (*Orpheus Descending* and *The Merchant of Venice*), Trevor Nunn (*Aspects of Love*), Howard Davies (*Cat on a Hot Tin Roof*), Les Waters (*Ice Cream With Hot Fudge*), Roger Michell (*Some Americans Abroad*), Adrian Hall (*The Art of Success*), Tim Luscombe (*Artist Descending a Staircase* and *When She Danced*), the late John Dexter (*3 Penny Opera*) and David Hare, who directed his own play, *The Secret Rapture*. Among the other dramatists who directed their own work were Jay Presson Allen (*Tru*), Frank Galati (*The Grapes of Wrath*), Arthur Laurents (*Gypsy*), Richard Maltby Jr. (*Closer Than Ever*), Tim Robbins (*Carnage, a Comedy*), George C. Wolfe (*Spunk*), Vernel Bagneris (*Further Mo'*), Stuart Ross (*Forever Plaid*) and Israel Horovitz (*The Widow's Blind Date*). There were also a number of familiar writer-director partnerships—August Wilson and Lloyd Richards (*The Piano Lesson*), Craig Lucas and Norman Rene (*Prelude to a Kiss*), William Mastrosimone and Marshall W. Mason (*Sunshine*), David Mamet and Gregory Mosher (*Bobby Gould in Hell*, part of a bill under the title *Oh, Hell*), Terrence McNally and Paul Benedict (*Bad Habits*) Terrence McNally and John Tillinger (*The Lisbon Traviata*), and A.R. Gurney and John Tillinger (*Love Letters*).

It was a good season to appreciate the handiwork of designers, the flashiest as usual in the service of the musicals. *Aspects of Love*'s Maria Bjornson, in collaboration with lighting designer Andrew Bridge, offered a Cook's tour of European imagery. For *City of Angels*, Robin Wagner created two sets of sets, one batch to depict Hollywood in the 1940s, the other to

OUTSTANDING MUSICAL DESIGNS—*above*, a photo of Tony Walton's setting for *Grand Hotel*; *below*, examples of Santo Loquasto's costume design sketches for the same Broadway musical

parody Hollywood film design of detective movies of the time. Tony Walton did more with less with an elegant evocation of Berlin's Grand Hotel of the 1920s, brilliantly lit by Jules Fisher and filled with an ensemble stylishly dressed by Santo Loquasto. Among the straight plays, Kevin Rigdon employed fire, water and lots of wood in his virtuosic scenic and lighting design for *The Grapes of Wrath*. Among the more realistic designs which afforded special pleasure were David Mitchell's version of Truman Capote's apartment at United Nations Plaza, David Jenkins's witty takeoff of the conventions of murder mystery design for *Accomplice* and Alan Tagg's trio of designs contrasting a stately home of Britain's past with the more modest accomodations of the present in *Lettice & Lovage*.

The criteria for selection as a Best Play remain constant. To quote Otis L. Guernsey Jr. in past volumes, "The choice is made without any regard whatever to the play's type—musical, comedy or drama—or origin on or off Broadway, or popularity at the box office or lack of same.

"We don't take the scripts of bygone eras into consideration for Best Play citation in this one, whatever their technical status as American or New York 'premieres' which didn't have a previous production of record. We draw the line between adaptations and revivals, the former eligible for Best Play selection but the latter not, on a case-by-case basis. If a script influences the character of a season, or by some function of consensus wins the Critics, Pulitzer or Tony Awards, we take into account its future historical as well as present esthetic importance. This is the only special consideration we give, and we don't always tilt in its direction, as the record shows."

Our choices for the Best Plays of 1989–90 are listed below in the order in which they opened in New York (a plus sign + with the performance number signifies that the play was still running on June 1, 1990).

*The Loman Family Picnic*
(Off B'way, 16 perfs.)

*Sex, Drugs, Rock & Roll*
(Off B'way, 103 perfs.)

*Love Letters*
(Off B'way, 64 perfs.;
B'way, 96 perfs.)

*Prelude to a Kiss*
(Off B'way, 33 perfs.;
B'way, 36+ perfs.)

*Grand Hotel*
(B'way, 229+ perfs.)

*The Grapes of Wrath*
(B'way, 81+ perfs.)

*My Children! My Africa!*
(Off Off B'way, 28 perfs.)

*The Piano Lesson*
(B'way, 52+ perfs.)

*City of Angels*
(B'way, 214+ perfs.)

*Once on This Island*
(Off B'way, 24 perfs.)

*A FEW GOOD MEN*—Stephen Lang *(left)* as Lt. Col. Nathan Jessep and *(above)* Tom Hulce as Lt. j.g. Daniel A. Kaffee with Megan Gallagher as Lt. Cmdr. Joanne Galloway in Aaron Sorkin's drama of a court martial

## New Plays

The staging of A.R. Gurney's Best Play *Love Letters* could hardly be simpler—two actors emerge from the wings, take their places behind a desk, open their scripts and, with scarcely a look at each other, read the lifelong correspondence between Andrew Makepeace Ladd III and Melissa Gardner. The letters tell of their childhood as neighbors, their sexual fumblings as teens, their disappointing marriages to others, their careers (his in politics, hers in art), their affair and, finally, his effort to come to terms with her death. The script offers the rare opportunity to watch the metamorphosis of character over decades, observing the relationship between the endearing quirks of childhood and the ingrained habits and compulsions of adulthood. An epic for two people requiring only a day or two to rehearse (the script is read, not memorized), it understandably attracted some of the stage's leading actors to alternate in the parts under John Tillinger's direction, among them, Jason Robards, Elaine Stritch, Edward Herrmann, Stockard Channing, Richard Thomas, Swoosie Kurtz, John Rubinstein and Kathleen Turner. I had the pleasure of seeing it played by Treat Williams and Kate Nelligan. Williams's work was arguably among the best of his career, particularly sensitive to the passionate private man behind the picture-perfect public image. Nelligan was stunning, contrasting the often bawdy, free-spirited young girl with the desperate and disintegrating older woman. The script has the earmarks of a theatrical perennial which will doubtless enrich the seasons of many stages in the years to come.

As previously mentioned, *Love Letters*'s Melissa Gardner was but one of many artist characters—painters, performers, writers and directors—whose travails were the stuff of drama this season. Several other plays were concerned with the related subject of those who, though not artists themselves, to a greater or lesser degree are defined by their relationship to the arts—scholars, fans and one boy who, in his imagination, transforms his family's pain into musical comedy.

Tom Stoppard's *Artist Descending a Staircase*, which was first presented as a radio play by the BBC in 1972, begins with the death of Donner, one of a trio of artists who have known each other more than 50 years. Each subsequent scene skips backward in time (in a manner reminiscent of Harold Pinter's *Betrayal*) till we see the three as young men in 1914, inadvertently caught in the middle of a battle at the beginning of World War I. Then Stoppard returns, in chronological order, to all of the previous scenes, completing the action of each. Initially, one believes that the time-travelling is designed to reveal clues to Donner's death, but Stoppard has other things on his mind. He is particularly interested in a young blind woman named Sophie who, in the early 1920s, was the mistress of one of the artists and for whom Donner felt the pangs of unrequited love which haunted his life years after her death. The friend who accompanied me to the play saw in this a bittersweet love story, but, for my taste, Stoppard doesn't individualize the characters sufficiently or write them with enough depth for one to care much about them. Stoppard mocks the artists' attempts at avant-garde art so relentlessly it is hard to take anything about them seriously, including their emotional lives. What is left is the expected cascade of Stoppardian wit interlaced with a few ironic observations about lives built on and destroyed by misperception. Under Tim Luscombe's brisk direction, Paxton Whitehead, John McMartin and Harold Gould distinguished themselves as the artists, but the final impression was of a beguiling doodle from this gifted playwright, rather than a work that merited a full Broadway staging.

Off Broadway, Luscombe also directed Martin Sherman's *When She Danced*, a script which bears more than a casual resemblance to Kaufman and Hart's *You Can't Take It With You*. Both concern a household filled with eccentrics noisily expressing themselves, and both portray disastrous dinner parties in which the eccentrics try to make good impressions on visiting bourgeois. The chief eccentrics in Sherman's play, set in Paris in 1923, are Isadora Duncan, the legendary modern dancer, and her alcoholic, suicidal Russian poet husband Sergei, with whom she shares passion but no common language. To facilitate communication, Isadora hires Miss Belzer, a quiet little Russian whose tragic past is only implied. Much of the play juxtaposes the self-dramatizing temperaments of the artists with the self-effacement of non-

# The 1989–90 Season Off Broadway

## PLAYS (38)

Circle Repertory:
Florida Crackers
Beside Herself
Sunshine
Imagining Brad
PRELUDE TO A KISS
*Each Day Dies With Sleep*

MTC:
The Lisbon Traviata
THE LOMAN FAMILY PICNIC
The Talented Tenth
The Lady in Question
LOVE LETTERS

N.Y. Shakespeare:
Carnage, a Comedy
Kate's Diary
Kingfish
A Mom's Life
*Spunk*

The Man Who Shot Lincoln

Playwrights Horizons:
Young Playwrights Festival
Hyde in Hollywood
When She Danced
The Aunts
All God's Dangers
The Widow's Blind Date

Lincoln Center:
Oh, Hell
Some Americans Abroad
MY CHILDREN! MY AFRICA! (OOB production)

Negro Ensemble:
Jonquil
Burner's Frolic
Lifetimes on the Streets

American Place:
Zora Neale Hurston
Neddy
Ground People
Come as You Are
Spare Parts
Making Movies
Mountain
*Talking Things Over With Chekhov*
*The Grand Guignol*

## REVUES (3)

Sid Caesar & Company
*Closer Than Ever*
*Forbidden Broadway 1990*

## FOREIGN PLAYS IN ENGLISH (3)

Privates on Parade
The Art of Success
Ice Cream With Hot Fudge

## MUSICALS (8)

Songs of Paradise
 (return engagement)

N.Y. Shakespeare:
Up Against It
Romance in Hard Times
Jonah
A Spinning Tale
ONCE ON THIS ISLAND
*Further Mo'*
*Forever Plaid*

## REVIVALS (14)

Ubu

Shakespeare Marathon:
Twelfth Night
Titus Andronicus
Macbeth
Hamlet

Roundabout:
The Tempest
The Doctor's Dilemma
The Crucible
Juan Darién
Bad Habits
St. Mark's Gospel
*By and for Havel*
*The Rothschilds*
*The B. Beaver Animation*

## SPECIALTIES (3)

The People Who Could Fly
SEX, DRUGS, ROCK & ROLL
Feast of Fools

## FOREIGN-LANGUAGE PLAY (1)

King Lear

Categorized above are all the new productions listed in the Plays Produced Off Broadway section of this volume.
Plays listed in CAPITAL LETTERS have been designated Best Plays of 1989–90.
Plays listed in *italics* were still running June 1, 1990.

artist Belzer; as the evening progresses, one comes to appreciate that Belzer's pain is no less real just because it hasn't provided fodder for art. But Belzer doesn't resent Isadora for the showiness of her grief. The translator speaks movingly of her memory of one of Isadora's performances, and one gets the idea that Sherman is saying that artists are elected by their audience to give public expression to that which the audience is unable to express for itself. Luscombe orchestrated the chaos coherently and elicited an appropriately bravura performance from Elizabeth Ashley as Isadora. In intended contrast to Miss Ashley's flamboyance was Marcia Jean Kurtz's understated but enormously affecting portrayal of the translator, her every gesture informed by a history of pain survived.

The Roundabout Theater Company's production of Peter Nichols's *Privates on Parade* was technically a New York premiere, but it was written in 1977 and already appeared in a film version some years ago. Set in 1948 during the British Malayan Emergency, it deals with a ragtag entertainment troupe assigned to amuse soldiers with the unhappy luck to be stationed in Singapore and Malaya. The show they perform is largely made up of English music hall-style numbers with some cross-dressing tossed in. (The authorship credits were billed as "book, music and lyrics" in the playbill, but this is clearly a play with music, not a musical.) The naivete underlying the cheerful cheesiness of their show is intended to echo the naivete of the British military effort there. But, whereas the only risk a naive show biz turn runs is of being the cause of modest embarrassment, a naive military action can have deadly consequences. Indeed, Nichols's play progresses to the point at which some of his hapless and amateurish entertainer-soldiers find themselves touring a risky area and are wounded or killed. Nichols is making an interesting point here about the relationship between the values which support English popular culture and the values which led to Britain's decline as a power, but the play doesn't have the kick it ought to have. Written with a revisionist perspective by now so familiar from countless other "outrageous" plays, the script provides little by way of surprise. As usual, the commanding officer is characterized as a dim, jingoistic idiot, so his leading the troupe into disaster is expected. It is similarly expected that Terri Dennis, the gay civilian female impersonator who directs and stars in the entertainments, will turn out to be the most morally courageous character on the stage.

Jim Dale created the role of Terri Dennis in the play's London premiere a decade ago, and he reprised it here with brio. Simon Jones and Jim Fyfe distinguished themselves as, respectively, the commanding officer and the troupe's newest and most innocent member, and Donna Murphy did well as the pragmatic Sylvia Morgan, the product of a British father and an Asian mother with illusions about what she believes to be her British heritage. Despite their contributions, a large dose of obscenity, some unnecessary nudity (making the title a pun) and a brisk staging by director Larry Carpenter, the play registered as being rather tame, though it did win the Critics Circle's citation as best foreign play of the season.

There was more cross-dressing and more toying with popular culture in *The Lady in Question*, a parody of World War II movie melodramas about strong-willed Americans battling aristocratic Nazis. Author Charles Busch played Gertrude Garnet, a self-centered concert pianist who becomes politicized when she comes face-to-face with the German menace. There is much to-do about spies, secret passages and the like. On the *Carol Burnett Show*, this would have made for a lively 15-minute skit. There were 15 minutes' worth of genuinely funny bits here, but they were surrounded by another hour and half of fairly pedestrian sketch comedy. Much of the press, however, had a higher opinion of it than mine, and *The Lady in Question* ran for several months off Broadway.

Terrence McNally's *The Lisbon Traviata* dealt with another nexus of homosexuality and culture, the obsession of two of its four gay characters with grand opera. In the first act, Mendy, an opera enthusiast who is gay, plays host to his friend Stephen. Mendy has had no success finding sustained romantic interest in his real life, so he submerges himself in the lush romanticism of grand opera with a particular obsession for pirated recordings of Maria Callas. Stephen's romantic life has hit a dip, too. His roommate-lover, Paul, is spending an increasing amount of time with another partner, and Stephen is preparing himself (and not terribly well) for the imminent confrontation. The confrontation, set in Stephen and Paul's apartment, comprises the second act.

*THE LISBON TRAVIATA*—Nathan Lane, Dan Butler and Anthony Heald in Terrence McNally's play at Manhattan Theater Club

The first act is McNally at his extraordinary best, dramatizing the contrasting characters of his principals with wit and the verbal equivalents of arias. The second act begins promisingly, but deteriorates midway. McNally apparently sensed he had a problem. The first version of the play, presented at the Manhattan Theater Club, ended with a murder. The second version, the one on view in the production which played the Promenade Theater, avoided this violence. But the problem with the second act was not so much a question of the ending as the shift in McNally's writing. The remarkable first act is written in an implicit manner, our understanding of Mendy and Stephen emerging as a byproduct of their wranglings over opera and related topics. In the second act, McNally gives Stephen speech after speech explicitly articulating his pain. As heartfelt as these speeches are, they offer no unanticipated ideas or insights and consequently make little emotional impact. (The Council of the Dramatists Guild did not share my reservations and gave *The Lisbon Traviata* its Hull-Warriner award, the third time McNally has been so honored.) Anthony Heald, so delightful a few seasons back as a foppish British lord in *Anything Goes*, excelled as the embittered Stephen. Nathan Lane gave a tour de force performance as Mendy, veering brilliantly between bursts of flamboyant comedy to wrenching despair under John Tillinger's direction.

Homosexuality again is a major element of Peter Parnell's *Hyde in Hollywood*, the tale of Julian Hyde, an actor-director in the 1930s, who locks horns with a gossip columnist writing under the name Hollywood Confidential. The columnist has discovered that Hyde is a "homosexualist" and uses the threat of revealing this to the public in order to blackmail Hyde into giving him inside tips on the private lives of other stars. Hyde counters by undertaking a film whose leading character bears the same relation to the columnist as did Orson Welles's Charles Foster Kane to William Randolph Hearst. A mysterious death, a suicide, and various betrayals also figure in the intricate plot. Parnell here addresses a provocative subject—the way in which film makers had to deny "unacceptable" aspects of their identities in order to work in Hollywood; homosexuals hiding their homosexuality, Jews hiding their Jewishness, left-wing sympathizers hiding their politics. Parnell wishes to dramatize how this institutionalized hypocrisy behind the scenes came to shape what appeared on the screen and consequently to influence American values.

The execution is not on a par with the aspiration. The play wavers uneasily between parody and pastiche. The sections making fun of movie cliches and conventions undermine belief in the characters necessary to take their problems seriously; the sections in which Parnell attempts to match the ominous tone of the wonderfully murky RKO movies which exemplify *film noir* simply haven't the intensity of the originals he invokes. The casting of the lead part didn't help matters. Robert Joy has proven himself to be a fine character actor in dozens of roles on stage and on screen, but despite the energy and intelligence with which he addressed the role of Hyde, he simply did not convince as a charismatic matinee idol. Keith Szarabajka as the columnist, Fran Brill as his lovelorn assistant and Stephen Pearlman as a studio executive all essayed their parts with the requisite snap, but the evening remained more interesting for the ideas raised than for what was brought to the stage.

The movies also figure in Larry Gelbart's *Mastergate*, a satire on a Congressional hearing of a Washington scandal. The testimonies of a series of witnesses uncover an elaborate scheme under which the U.S. government appropriated the assets of a failing Hollywood studio in order to produce a movie about Vietnam. When pressed, the witnesses reveal that this scheme was designed to funnel government monies into the Central American country where it was being filmed, said monies mostly going not to film an account of an old American foreign policy debacle but to finance a new one, the attack on a Nicaraguan-like government by U.S.-backed contras.

Gelbart's avowed subject is how the decay of language mirrors the decay of ethics. The play begins with a flurry of nimble one-liners and polished vaudeville-style routines, but it soon becomes repetitive. Every third joke is based on a ludicrous mixed metaphor, and much of the script's meat and manner seem recycled from Joseph Heller's ground-breaking 1955 satire of military doublespeak, *Catch-22*. All of Gelbart's dramatis personae are pure caricatures, and familiar caricatures at that. His Major Manley Battle is substantially the same as the macho Oliver North that has appeared in editorial page cartoons for the past two years, the doodle of George Bush seemed almost affectionate given some of the satire fresh in memory from the previous year's election, and the fatuous, self-important TV reporters and their pet experts have been subjects of regular skewering since the days of *That Was the Week That Was* and the young Mort Sahl. Despite Michael Engler's zippy direction of a nimble cast of comic actors and the quotable jokes, *Mastergate* was a clever premise unrealized in execution. Off Broadway, the New York Shakespeare Festival's production of *Carnage, a Comedy* by Adam Simon and Tim Robbins, took more theatrical risks in its satire on television evangelism, but its script, too, is defeated by the familiarity of the characterization of its targets.

*The Loman Family Picnic*, a Best Play by Donald Margulies, again deals with the relationship between culture and life. An 11-year-old boy named Mitchell, living in Coney Island in 1965 with his father, mother and brother, is studying Arthur Miller's *Death of a Salesman* in school. Much of *The Loman Family Picnic* mines the similarities and the contrasts between the clan author Margulies has created and Miller's, but there are some telling differences. In Margulies's play, both parents—not just the salesman father—seem to be cracking up. Instead of Miller's Uncle Ben enticing Billy from beyond the grave, it's dead Aunt Marsha who fills the mother's head with questionable advice. In Miller's work, before Willy drove off to his death he had the comfort of knowing he had Biff's love; Margulies's father, Herbie, gets no such emotional protestations from his family; and when he leaves, it is not to suicide but to a temporary retreat in a local movie house showing *Born Free*.

*Born Free* is an ironic choice, for much of Margulies's play concerns the family's lack of freedom—the ways in which they chain themselves to familial, economic and cultural expectations. Herbie finances a bar mitzvah he can't afford for his son Stewie because he is afraid it would look wrong to neighbors and relatives if he didn't. Doris throws herself into the part of a devoted, encouraging mother with manic energy, even though half of the time she doesn't hear, much less understand, what her children say to her. Stewie rehearses his bar mitzvah routine, though the words have no meaning for him.

The preparations for, reception after and fallout from the bar mitzvah form the structure of the play. The bar mitzvah, of course, is a ritual to symbolize Stewie's entrance into manhood. The ceremony itself goes smoothly. That night, however, Herbie is forced to break the news to Stewie that the cash gifts his son has received must all be used to help defray the expenses of the day. Initially, Herbie is embarrassed, but in the face of his son's resistance he explodes. In the explosion, the anger, frustration and humiliation of Herbie's life come spilling out. It is more than Stewie wants to know. "I'm just a kid!" he cries. In a sense, this is his *real* bar mitzvah, a painful introduction into not the idealized adulthood invoked in the ceremony, but the terrors of real grown-up existence. The scene is among the most original and horrifying in recent American drama.

The play benefitted from a near-ideal production under the direction of Barnet Kellman, with Larry Block and (again) Marcia Jean Kurtz giving performances poignantly balancing comedy and pain. The overwhelming majority of the press welcomed both play and production; the sole significant exception being the notice in the New York *Times*. One hopes that one dissenting review in a prominent forum will not prevent the play from reaching the wide audience it so richly deserves.

Richard Wesley also dealt with the issue of an ethnic group confronting its image in the media. In *The Talented Tenth*, the leading character is pushed to crisis when the black radio station he has helped manage is sold to a white-owned corporation. His concern about the future integrity of the station's programming—specifically how much play the new white owners will allow him to give to black political issues—echoes his doubts about the professional and personal choices he has made as one of the minority of black Americans to achieve some measure of economic success. He is part of a circle who have been friendly since student days at Howard University and who each, in his or her own way, has dealt with the question of a successful black's responsibility to the 90 percent of their race who don't enjoy similar prosperity. The script has fascinating patches—particularly a dialogue in which a dark-skinned black woman confronts her resentment of a light-skinned friend—but Wesley spends too much time having his stand-in explicitly moralize about the issues of the play rather than implying them through dramatic action.

In *The Secret Rapture*, David Hare hoped to dramatize the state of England under Margaret Thatcher through a confrontation between two sisters in the wake of their father's death. The "good" sister, Isobel, meaning well, takes into her design firm her father's alcoholic second wife, Katherine. The "bad" sister, Marion, and her husband Tom prevail upon Isobel to accept an investment in the firm which, naturally, leads to its destruction and ultimately that of Isobel. The first act is filled with tartly-written social comedy on a level with Hare's best. The second act, however, goes haywire, lurching unconvincingly into violent melodrama. Isobel is a large part of the problem—she is virtuous, yes, but she also initiates little action. With a central character who refuses to drive the play, Hare must depend on his other characters to inflict woes on her to generate some sort of plot. Hare also insists on having all of his characters Represent Viewpoints, which undercuts belief in them as human beings.

The single figure who is not so easily pigeonholed, Katherine, is sufficiently ambiguous to fascinate. As she did in Michael Frayn's *Benefactors* a few seasons back, Mary Beth Hurt played this, the script's wild card character, with jaw-jutting vigor. The talented Blair Brown seemed stymied by Isobel; Frances Conroy—coiffed to look like Margaret Thatcher—had great fun saying Marion's outrageously insensitive lines, and Stephen Vinovich gave her Christian businessman husband a genuine sweetness.

Hare also directed; much of his staging employed devices he used to better effect in his production of his Best Play *Plenty*, e.g., backlit figures framed in doorways, rooms denuded of furniture. Disconcertingly, he underscored the archness of his own work by having his actors pose rigidly in position as they articulated their creeds at each other. No Hare play can be without interest, but, between a wayward second act, a passive protagonist and stiff staging, the evening had to be counted a disappointment.

Playwright Nick Dear employs historical figures for *his* attack on Thatcherism, *The Art of Success*. Artist William Hogarth is the central figure here, trying to reconcile his independent spirit as an artist with his attempt to curry favor with Robert Walpole in order to get copyright legislation passed so that he can make a living at his art. This is contrasted with the trials of his friend, dramatist Henry Fielding, who is driven from the theater by Walpole because of attacks on Walpole in his satiric plays. Dear has engaged an intriguing subject here, the relationship between artists and the state they alternately attack and appeal to for protection and support. But much of the play is a muddle of juvenile attitudinizing and by-the-numbers revisionist raunch (particularly a scene depicting Walpole playing childish sexual games in bed with Queen Caroline). The production design by the monomial Ultz reflected both the play's aspirations and limitations. The centerpiece of the in-the-round set, moored by cables in the middle of the audience, was a platform wrapped in white paper; scenes played upon it conveyed the impression of figures springing to life on a giant sketch pad. Surrounding this impressive conceit was a good deal of straw liberally distributed among which were realistic-looking plastic turds (I suppose to underline that this was not a sanitized view of history). Director Adrian Noble staged it with the requisite high spirits; he and the author were fortunate in having Tim Curry and Daniel Benzali as Hogarth and Walpole, supported by the ever-marvelous Suzanne Bertish.

Caryl Churchill offered two more views of contemporary England in *Ice Cream With Hot Fudge*. The shorter piece, *Hot Fudge* ("fudge" as in "to fudge" or lie), concerns the beginning of a romance between a man and a woman who, though from different classes, share backgrounds of equivalent crookedness and attendant prevarication. *Ice Cream* tells of a pair of naive Americans tourists disabused of their kneejerk Anglophilia when British relatives they unearth make them complicit in a murder. Both plays showcase Churchill's frequently dazzling technique—overlapping speeches, startling imagery, a breathtaking theatrical swiftness. Fine performances were forthcoming from an impressive cast including John Pankow, Margaret Whitton, Jane Kaczmarek, Robert Knepper, James Rebhorn and Julianne Moore in multiple roles, in a bill which impressed more as sketches than fully realized pieces.

More American Anglophiles were featured in Richard Nelson's *Some Americans Abroad*. In his similarly-titled *The Innocents Abroad*, Mark Twain spunkily announced that a distinctive American consciousness had come into being and that he was not automatically in thrall of every European cultural artifact just because it had dust on it. The group of American academics making the tour of British literary and theatrical monuments in Nelson's play don't have the same cheerful skepticism as did Twain. Nelson's Americans ooh and ahh and make appreciatively learned pronouncements over everything British. Though they parade their insight when it comes to mining art for hours of animated discussions of structure and symbols and so forth, they betray very little insight when dealing with personal issues.

Nelson gets a good deal of pointed humor out of their posturings, but, despite many bright patches, for me the play falls short of its promise. Suspense resides in wondering how a play's protagonists will deal with the choices which confront them. Since Nelson establishes early on that his characters are various stripes of hypocrites and brown-nosers and thus constitutionally incapable of courage and honesty, there is very little doubt as to how they will choose when put to ethical tests. The only question posed in each scene is whose turn it will be to behave badly, and, as the evening goes on, this lack of variety grows wearing. Still, it isn't often that a new play featuring so much genuine wit comes along. Roger Michell's finely-tuned production showed

Colin Stinton, Frances Conroy and Jane Hoffman to particular advantage, supported by some of Nelson's tartest lines. Henderson Forsythe was a standout as a retired academic entirely devoid of tact. (The production began its life in Lincoln Center's Mitzi Newhouse Theater and was sufficiently successful there to be transferred, with substantially the same cast, to the larger Vivian Beaumont Theater upstairs.)

*The Grapes of Wrath,* drawn from John Steinbeck's novel, suffers from a similar structural problem as does Nelson's play. Steinbeck told of the Joads, a family of Oklahoma farmers who lose their land in the Depression and, lured by false promises of prosperity in California, head west only to find a life of poverty and exploitation as migrant workers in the orchards. Steinbeck's novel was a tapestry of the time, short on psychological detail but rich in descriptive passages and imbued with an arresting combination of the journalistic and the mythic. In the condensing necessary to make a play of manageable length out of a fat novel, writer-director Frank Galati, collaborating with the Steppenwolf Theater Company, had to do away with most of the description and anything that didn't relate directly to the Joads. Despite Galati's always evident taste and intelligence, what is left tends toward narrative monotony.

As each sequence begins, we are aware that, by its end, the Joads will suffer another loss and further disillusionment. This is certainly faithful to Steinbeck and, God knows, true to the real-life experiences of the people from whose misery Steinbeck derived his novel, but as scene after scene of similar shape and effect rolls out the repetition begins to numb. At any rate, that was my reaction. That a sizable proportion of the audience felt otherwise may be gleaned by the fact that it won the Tony Award for the year's best play. So, with a nod to the considerable many who embraced it, Mr. Galati's adaptation is here cited as a Best Play. Even with my reservations, I was glad to see a work of this scope and seriousness thrive on a Broadway stage, especially given the fine efforts by Lois Smith as Ma Joad, Gary Sinise as Tom, Terry Kinney as the Preacher and Jeff Perry as Noah among the generally excellent 35-member cast, supported by the lean and suggestive scenery and lighting by Kevin Rigdon.

I was more impressed with another adaptation, *Spunk,* derived from the work of Zora Neale Hurston, a leading figure of the Harlem Renaissance. The evening was made up of three contrasting tales—the first dealing with a wife avenging herself on a murderous mate, the second concerning two comical zoot-suited characters trying to outdo each other and the third about a loving marriage threatened by a lapse in judgement. Adaptor-director George C. Wolfe employed story theater techniques pioneered by Paul Sills, calling for the actors to alternate between playing roles and narrating their characters' actions in the third person. Between the vitality of Hurston's language and the unceasing invention of Wolfe's staging, it was arguably the most satisfying transfer to the stage from literature since the David Edgar-Trevor Nunn adaptation of Charles Dickens's *Nicholas Nickleby*. In a generally splendid cast, Danitra Vance shone as the tales' three very different leading women.

Pulitzer Prize-winner Charles Fuller returned with the third and fourth plays of *We*, his six-play cycle derived from chapters of black history. *Jonquil*, the third, shared the weaknesses of its predecessors, *Sally* and *Prince*, being diffuse, under-characterized and sketchy. Set in 1876, the fourth, *Burner's Frolic*, while not wholly successful, was a significant improvement. Certainly this script was more tightly focussed than the ones that came before, the bulk of its action taking place in one day. The "frolic" of the title is a party organized by the leading black businessman of a Virginia town at which he announces his political candidacy in defiance of the local white politicos. A gang of white hooligans lays siege to Burner's land in an attempt to intimidate his supporters. Under the pressure of this threatened violence, Fuller explores the conflicting philosophies in the black community—who is for undertaking the challenge, who counsels tactical retreat and who urges capitulation in the face of the daunting odds. With further exploration and development, this could be a major play.

*SPUNK*—K. Todd Freeman, Reggie Montgomery and Danitra Vance in a scene from George C. Wolfe's adaptation of Zora Neale Hurston tales at the Public Theater

Another Pulitzer Prize-winner, August Wilson, has also been writing a cycle of plays dramatizing aspects of black American history. *The Piano Lesson*, a Best Play and winner of this season's Pulitzer Prize for drama and Critics Circle best-play citation, is the latest in a remarkable string of works brought to acclaim on Broadway under the direction of Lloyd Richards (the others being *Ma Rainey's Black Bottom, Fences* and *Joe Turner's Come and Gone*—all also cited as Best Plays). The piano in question was acquired in 1856 by a plantation owner who traded a slave woman and her son for it. The woman's grieving husband carved into the instrument images of his lost family and his ancestors. At the cost of lives, the carver's family managed to spirit the piano away; at rise, it sits in a Pittsburgh living room in 1936, co-owned by the carver's great-grandchildren, Boy Willie and Berniece. Boy Willie wants to sell the piano and use the money to be the first in his family to own the land he farms. This puts him at loggerheads with Berniece, who refuses to countenance securing the future by the sale of such an important part of the family's past.

As in his other plays, Wilson surrounds his central characters with several secondary characters, each of whom offers a view of another aspect of black life at the time. Boy Willie and Berniece's two uncles, Doaker and Wining Boy, share their respective experiences working for the railroad and leading the life of an itinerant piano player. Berniece's beau, Avery, a preacher aspiring for his own pulpit, speaks for the role of religion in providing a sense of community. Willie's friend Lymon offers a view of a young and somewhat naive Southern sharecropper plunging unprepared into the urban North. A lesser dramatist might have fallen into the trap of having these characters merely serve as mouthpieces for their contrasting perspectives, but Wilson seems constitutionally incapable of writing a role without size and dimension. Each character is a fully-developed person in his or her own right. In production, the cast—led by Charles S. Dutton as Boy Willie, S. Epatha Merkerson as Berniece, Carl Gordon as Doaker, Lou Myers as Wining Boy and Rocky Carroll as Lymon—met the challenge with some of the season's most stirring ensemble work.

This is by no means a flawless play, however. Wilson has imposed on it a confusing and metaphorically muddled ghost story involving the haunting of the family's house by a descendent of the slavemaster, building to a flashy but none-too-convincing climactic battle between Boy Willie and the spirit. Wilson is also unpersuasive in conveying the logic behind Berniece's insistence that her daughter take piano lessons, given her own refusal to touch the instrument on point of principle.

Even when the flaws are most apparent, however, the largeness of spirit in Wilson's work stands in dramatic contrast to the anecdotal tendencies of most contemporary drama. Ferociously gifted as a portraitist, a storyteller and a dialogist, if Wilson can only come to grips with the structural problems which tend to weaken his second acts, he will surely earn a place as one of the foremost dramatists in American theatrical history.

Courtney Vance, who was so impressive as the son in Wilson's *Fences*, returned this season in Athol Fugard's Best Play *My Children! My Africa!* (an off-off-Broadway production by New York Theater Workshop but eligible for Best Play citation under our policy of considering any such work which has already made its mark in world theater and thus can in no way be labeled an "experimental" offering). Fugard tells of a liberal white South African girl named Isabel Dyson who, through an extramural debate at the black Zolile High School, gets to know a black teacher named Mr. Myalatya, commonly known as Mr. M, and Thami Mbikwana, a black youth, one of Mr. M's best student's. Mr. M—who believes that his pupils' best hope for achieving parity with whites in South Africa is through education—conceives the idea of having Isabel and Thami join forces as the team for an inter-school English literature quiz. Isabel and Thami begin to spend a lot of time together, preparing for the quiz and becoming close friends. Ultimately, however, Thami rejects his teacher's moderate doctrine of change through reform, withdraws from the competition and allies himself with a boycott against the South African school system. Seeing the school which is the center of his life threatened, Mr. M makes the fatal mistake of assisting the police in dealing with the boycott. Identified as an informer, he is marked for death by a mob who march on Zolile High. Thami hopes to shield his former teacher by vouching for Mr. M's innocence, even though he knows Mr. M to be guilty. Mr. M refuses to accept the protection of a lie and is killed standing his ground in his beloved school. In a wrenching scene, Thami visits Isabel one last time before fleeing the country to join with rebels, the two forced to accept that their different places in their troubled world make their continued friendship impossible.

As is true of most tragedies—and *My Children! My Africa!* is most definitely a tragedy—Fugard's play deals with characters who find themselves torn between two or more deeply-held but mutually exclusive roles. Thami has to decide which is more important to him, his growing friendship with Isabel and his unspoken but abiding love for his teacher, or what be believes to be his proper role in the fight for freedom. Mr. M is similarly torn—in his own way he is as fiercely committed as Thami to his people's struggle, but his view of appropriate methods takes him on a different path than his student, and ultimately this difference brings about his destruction. The conflict between private affections and public responsibilities has seldom been so effectively dramatized.

*My Children! My Africa!* strikes me as being a significant step forward in Fugard's craft as a dramatist. Usually the first halves of his plays require a great deal of patience as heavy chunks of exposition are laboriously carted out. Here, instead of straining to incorporate necessary information into dialogue, he simply allows his characters license to address the audience directly

*LETTICE & LOVAGE*—Maggie Smith as Lettice Douffet (*left*) and Margaret Tyzack as Lotte Schoen in a scene from the play by Peter Shaffer, both 1989-90 Tony Award-winning performances, the former for best leading actress in a play and the latter for best supporting actress in a play

in a series of well-composed monologues. Relieved of the responsibility to brief the audience on given circumstances, the scenes between the characters are consistently dynamic and purposeful. All in all, I think this to be his most impressive dramatic writing since *Sizwi Banzi Is Dead.*

Fugard also staged the play, eliciting from his daughter Lisa a promising debut as Isabel. Vance as Thami and Fugard's frequent collaborator John Kani as Mr. M were extraordinary, Vance carefully detailing the transition from soft-spoken schoolboy to formidable activist, Kani immensely touching in his dismay as Mr. M's world falls apart.

Aaron Sorkin's *A Few Good Men* puts on the airs of being a play about issues, specifically about the importance of keeping the military subordinate to the interests of the democratic society it is supposed to protect; but what it really is about is giving actors the opportunity to play their favorite scenes from old movies. A lot of those scenes are here—the wise-cracking underdog attorney tripping up the wily antagonist, the wise-cracking female associate putting male chauvinists in their place, the wise-cracking sidekick tossing off one ironic quip after another when faced with a team of macho bullies. Under Don Scardino's direction, Tom Hulce, Megan Gallagher and Mark Nelson, as attorneys assigned to defend a couple of uncooperative soldiers charged with killing a fellow soldier, batted Sorkin's snappy patter back and forth with great elan, and Stephen Lang snarled memorably as the principled villain, a role he reportedly helped write. If the play has less substance than it affects, it introduces in Sorkin a writer with the welcome ability to spin a full-length yarn. It was an ability, alas, not in much evidence in his off-Broadway collaboration with Don Scardino, *Making Movies*, a slight and unfunny comedy about friends and lovers at odds during the production of a film.

Israel Horovitz's *The Widow's Blind Date* concerns a woman returning to her home town to confront two of the men who gang-raped her some years before. Though Horovitz makes an effort to explore the sociological roots of his characters' repellant behavior, ultimately the play feels hyped, ostensibly condemning violence but depending on a trumped-up violent confrontation to generate enough theatrical heat for a climax.

Over at Circle Rep, William S. Leavengood's *Florida Crackers* concerned a pair of brothers involved in drug trafficking. It was dismissed by most of the press as an evening of unappealing people cussing a lot. For my part, I was fascinated by Leavengood's portrait of the elder brother—a man who hews to rigid ethical precepts when it comes to family matters and simultaneously, in his "professional" life, has no compunction about embracing the skuzzy practices endemic to the drug trade.

Three of Circle Rep's other plays were variations on the familiar pattern of two wounded people reaching out to each other. Joe Pintauro's *Beside Herself* was of interest chiefly in that it gave Lois Smith and William Hurt (in a charmingly self-effacing performance) the chance to do affecting moment-to-moment work as an eccentric widow and a younger delivery man beginning an awkward relationship. Despite a graphic masturbation scene set in an X-rated emporium, William Mastrosimone's *Sunshine* was essentially a sentimental tale of an encounter between an emotionally-wounded ambulance attendant and a peep-show girl with a pure soul, film actress Jennifer Jason Leigh bringing some freshness to the stock character of the latter. In Peter Hedges's *Imagining Brad*, the leading characters are a pair of women—Dana Sue and Valerie—who meet in a Nashville church and compare husbands. It is gradually revealed that Dana Sue's husband is a prototypical macho S.O.B. and the injuries she initially claims to have received in an auto accident have really been at his abusive hands. The hands of Brad, Valerie's husband, are not abusive; they are nonexistent, Brad having been born without limbs and suffering from a catalogue of afflictions. The play's very black joke is that his physical inability to batter makes Dana Sue come to see Brad as the superior spouse and to yearn for a Brad of her own. The combination of this piece and a brief curtain-raiser depicting Valerie at a younger age barely occupied 75 minutes and seemed attenuated even at that, much time given over to teasing out Valerie's secret; but Erin Cressida Wilson was arrestingly creepy as the older Valerie.

Circle Rep's most successful offering of this season, and indeed of several seasons, was Craig Lucas's Best Play, *Prelude to a Kiss*. Its success was all the more impressive in that it relied on a gimmick overly familiar from several movies of recent vintage—the switching of souls in bodies. In all the previous entries in this genre with which I'm familiar, the audience shared the perspectives of the souls being switched as they tried to cope inside their new bodies without being detected by family and acquaintances (*e.g.*, the film of Mary Rodgers's *Freaky Friday*, in which Barbara Harris and Jodie Foster played mother and daughter with teenage Foster trying to counterfeit adulthood inside her mother's body and mother Harris trying to recall teenage logic inside her daughter's). In Lucas's play, however, the perspective the audience shares is not of those who switch but that of a young man who senses disturbing shifts in his wife's values and behavior after she is kissed by an old man who has wandered into their wedding reception. The old man, we subsequently learn, is terminally ill, and the sight of the young woman at the beginning of her adult life excited such yearning that, when he had the opportunity to kiss her, the swap came about without any conscious effort on his part. The scenes in which the young husband recognizes the soul of his bride inside the old man's body are particularly affecting. Initially, he is put off by the vessel which contains his love, but ultimately it is the attraction of the soul rather than the distraction of the body which is the more important. Their encounter leads to a kiss which confirms the full intention of the marriage vows they made before the switch.

There are one or two regrettable lapses of logic and plotting sleights-of-hand, but in the main *Prelude to a Kiss* is a delicate and resonant modern fairy tale which acknowledges that "happily ever after," while a nice sentiment, must give way to an appreciation of the transient nature of life. The production, under the direction of Lucas's longtime collaborator Norman Rene, managed to maintain the delicacy necessary for fantasy without succumbing to the cutes. The excellent cast included Alec Baldwin as the perplexed husband, Mary-Louise Parker as his wife and Barnard Hughes as the old man. (A film commitment necessitated Alec Baldwin's departure from the cast when the play was transferred to Broadway; Timothy Hutton took his place offering an intelligent but a shade more reserved interpretation than Baldwin's.)

Circle Rep's final production, *Each Day Dies With Sleep*, was written by Jose Rivera, a writer whose work I usually admire. This play, however, a surreal tale concerning a woman whose husband and father are both macho cretins, left me blinking with bewilderment.

*Lettice & Lovage* was conceived by Peter Shaffer as a star vehicle for Maggie Smith and, as such, served admirably, giving her fans ample opportunity to enjoy her under full sail. Her role, Lettice Douffet, is a romanticist. When hired to guide tours through an unremarkable building, in order to keep herself and her listeners interested, she concocts an elaborate presentation full of tales of passion and heroism bearing little relationship to historical fact. A representative of the agency employing her, a starchy bureaucrat named Lotte Schoen, calls her onto the carpet for these embellishments. A skirmish ensues in Lotte's office, during which Lettice defiantly proclaims her mission to "enlarge, enlighten and entertain," even at the expense of accuracy. Lotte fires her. In the second act, Lotte, feeling somewhat guilty, drops by Lettice's flat with a recommendation for a job for which Lettice would be better suited. The two women open up to each other and begin a friendship.

The two acts which contain these events are not high-powered drama, but they are filled with graceful and witty reflections on the loss of elegance in a world obsessed with utility. One might also see in Lettice's character some parallels to the playwright; as the author of *Amadeus* and *The Royal Hunt of the Sun*, he himself has been accused of Lettice-like embellishments of historical events in the name of enlarging, enlightening and entertaining.

*SOME AMERICANS ABROAD*—Kate Burton, Nathan Lane, Colin Stinton and Frances Conroy in the Lincoln Center production of Richard Nelson's comedy

Unfortunately, Shaffer has appended to these two happy acts a silly third. What begins as a comedy of character shifts gears into farcical contrivance, with Lettice charged with Lotte's attempted murder and her lawyer trying to pry the truth out of the two. After a lot of labored comic business, during which the lawyer turns out to have a childlike heart akin to his client's, it is revealed that the two ladies have gotten into the habit of re-enacting famous executions, and Lotte's injury was the result of a mishap involving a headsman's axe while essaying the demise of Charles I.

Though Shaffer slips in the third act, the cast, under Michael Blakemore's meticulously-timed staging, did not. Smith was a constant delight in a role which licenses shameless extravagance. Margaret Tyzack had the more challenging job of playing Lotte so as to simultaneously maintain her integrity and yet engage the audience's affection. In the supporting parts, Bette Henritze was the essence of tremulousness as Lotte's bullied receptionist, and Paxton Whitehead's comic skills made the preposterous lawyer's scene less trying than it might otherwise have been. Anthony Powell got separate credit for the design of Miss Smith's very funny costumes recalling Mary, Queen of Scots.

There were several works for solo performers this season. *A Bronx Tale*, written by and starring Chazz Palminteri, related his relationship with a local Mafia figure. Palminteri was adept at evoking his neighborhood's conflicting values and peopling the stage with colorful hoods. The vigor of his performance went a long way toward offsetting the string of coincidences which brought his narrative to its close. Kathryn Grody's autobiographic solo piece, *A Mom's Life*, concerned the trials of motherhood on the Upper West Side. It was filled with wise observations on the deterioration an adult sensibility undergoes when the majority of its time is devoted to coping with child care. Despite Grody's appealing and resourceful performance, after the first half hour the piece became repetitious. Cleavon Little was stirring as Nate Shaw, a member of the Alabama Sharecroppers Union who was railroaded into prison for standing up to white landlords, in *All God's Dangers*. Adapted by Theodore Rosengarten, Michael Hadley and Jennifer Hadley from Rosengarten's book of the same title, (which, in turn was based on a series of interviews Rosengarten recorded with the real-life Shaw, Ned Cobb), the script is a valuable reminder that individuals of courage made significant contributions decades before Martin Luther King galvanized the civil rights movement.

*Tru*, Jay Presson Allen's portrait of the late Truman Capote, manages to avoid most of the pitfalls one generally encounters in solo plays about writers. The usual structure of a one-person show about a celebrated person has the subject speaking in retrospect, moving through autobiography chronologically, rarely with any pressing reason to do so. In contrast, Allen motivates Capote's monologue, setting it at a time when Capote was in crisis. In late 1975, Capote published in *Esquire* an excerpt from *Answered Prayers*, a novel-in-progress intended as an epic expose of the values and habits of the super-rich. The excerpt made it clear that Capote was drawing for inspiration on the private lives of many of the people with whom he'd socialized for years. Outraged by what they saw as his violation of their rules, much of society, including some of his close friends, closed ranks and ostracized him. The play takes place in Capote's apartment at the United Nations Plaza on two successive nights in late December. As the celebrations of the holiday season—including parties to which he has conspicuously not been invited—whirl around him, Capote parades his defiance. A writer can only write from his experience, he states, so why should these people be shocked when he writes of his experiences with them? What did they *think* he was doing hanging around with them? He goes on to trumpet how valuable it is for an artist to be an outsider. But as much as he claims to rejoice in his outsider status—both as an author and as a short, openly gay man with the piping, lisping voice of a child—his pain at being *pushed* further outside is palpable. His roles as writer and as friend of the rich and famous have come into collision, leaving him stunned and, for all of his wit and insight, uncomprehending.

The action of the play is the result of his effort to understand how he has come to this pass. Instead of autobiography, Allen, drawing on Capote's writings, offers fragments of memories, a cascade of frequently bitterly funny jokes and, in a penultimate passage arranged around Cole Porter's song "At Long Last Love," a Faulknerian stream-of-consciousness. The play assumes the audience knows who Truman Capote was and has a familiarity with the contours of his career, so the piece probably is less effective for the uninitiated. Anyone looking for an "and-then-I-wrote" chronicle would be better advised to read a biography. But as a portrait of an artist in extremis, *Tru* has few rivals.

The production could hardly have been more impressive. Serving as her own director, Allen guided Robert Morse through the challenging evening. Morse, best-known for a series of juvenile roles in *Take Me Along, Say, Darling, How to Succeed in Business Without Really Trying* and *Sugar*, had not been seen on a Broadway stage for the better part of two decades. His return, physically transformed to the point of unrecognizability, was a triumph. The illusion of being the much-exposed Capote was complete. But the performance went beyond the extraordinary make-up job by Kevin Haney and wigmaker Paul Huntley. Morse hauntingly conveyed Capote's quicksilver quality, the abrupt shifts between impishness and despair, the turmoil in the soul of this man who suffered for being perceived as a figure of peculiarity and outrageousness despite the fact he was the conscious architect of this image. How poignant that Morse should have a triumphant comeback portraying the beginning of another artist's sad decline!

*Sex, Drugs, Rock & Roll* was performer-author Eric Bogosian's second Best Play and fourth solo show made up of cameos of people one would not like to be too close to in real life. The wonder of it was how little repetition there was from his previous work. While this is good news artistically, it gives one pause to realize that this society produces so many different strains of desperate and off-putting characters as to populate Bogosian's rogue's gallery prolifically. As was the case with his Best Play *Drinking in America*, Bogosian presents his characters without special pleading or hinting at his own judgements about them. His skills as an actor have grown in the intervening seasons; the verbal specificity of his portraits was always impressive, now it is rivalled by the subtlety of his performance skills. To watch him switch from an aggressive subway beggar, to a laid-back 40-ish British rock 'n' roll star bragging about having kicked drugs (even as he continues to romanticize them), to a swaggering jerk reveling in the abundance of his penis is to be reminded again that much of the magic of theater resides in the actor's transformational abilities. Bogosian has announced that after finishing with this show he doesn't intend to return to the solo form. If so, he leaves it at the peak of his powers.

Shel Silverstein contributed another solo piece, *The Devil and Billy Markham* to a double bill of thematically-related one-acts under the title of *Oh, Hell*. In an exuberant performance, Dennis Locorriere recited Silverstein's rhymed poem about a songwriter's epic battle with the devil. Fifteen minutes of pure, vulgar storytelling was great fun, but it went on for nearly an hour; evidently, the author mistook length for development. The delight of the evening was a 45-minute theatrical jape by David Mamet called *Bobby Gould in Hell*, in which the producer familiar from Mamet's Best Play *Speed-the-Plow* finds himself hauled down to the nether world to answer to Satan—here called the Interrogator—for various ethical offenses. The Interrogator is particularly exercised over Gould's treatment of a young woman named Glenna whom Gould had casually bedded and ditched. Failing to get an admission of culpability out of Gould, the Interrogator calls Glenna down to testify against Gould. But Glenna is not content to indict Gould; she's not too crazy about the chauvinism implicit in the Interrogator's dealings, and soon she has *him* nearly at wit's end. Under the direction of Mamet's longtime collaborator Gregory Mosher, Treat Williams as Gould, Felicity Huffman as Glenna, Steven Goldstein as the devil's assistant and, particularly, W.H. Macy as the Interrogator made Mamet's sketch fly.

Douglas Scott's *Mountain* was not a one-man play, but, despite protean work by supporting players Heather Summerhayes and John C. Vennema, the evening rested almost entirely on the shoulders of Len Cariou as controversial Supreme Court Justice William O. Douglas. Cariou was impressive as ever, but the play was to be valued more for the information it conveyed than for drama.

The season had its usual quotient of productions with minor felicities, usually the contributions of valiant performers: writer Buck Henry showing unforeseen acting skill as a beleaguered homosexual in a threatening absurdist world in Marlane Meyer's *Kingfish*; Eileen Heckart, Elizabeth Franz and Doris Belack demonstrating their flair for banter as Jewish widows in Ivan Menchell's audience-pleasing sentimental comedy, *The Cemetery Club*; Reed Birney and Robin Groves as a gay man and woman offering each other consolation in Elizabeth Page's illogical *Spare Parts*; Natalia Nogulich as a possibly murderous leading lady in Rupert Holmes's shotgun marriage of Ira Levin and Pirandello, *Accomplice*; Lizbeth Mackay as yet another troubled writer in Kathleen Tolan's *Kate's Diary*; Ron Richardson as the head of a black vaudeville troupe in the Mississippi Delta of 1920 in Leslie Lee's *Ground People*; and the remarkable group of Negro Ensemble Company actors led by Peggy Alston and Douglas Turner Ward assembled to deliver Gus Edwards's uneven collection of monologues of contemporary Harlem life, *Lifetimes on the Streets*. The Circle in the Square production of Bulgakov's *Zoya's Apartment*, staged by Soviet director Boris A. Morozov, a tale of corruption in 1926 Moscow, frustrated the best efforts of its talented cast to hold the interest.

Here's where we list the Best Plays choices for the outstanding straight-play achievements of 1989–90 in New York, on and off Broadway. In the acting categories, clear distinction among "starring," "featured" or "supporting" players can't be made on the basis of official billing, which is as much a matter of contracts as of esthetics. Here in these volumes we divide acting into "primary" or "secondary" roles, a primary role being one which might some day cause a star to inspire a revival in order to appear in that character. All others, be they vivid as Mercutio, are classed as secondary. Furthermore, our list of individual standouts makes room for more than a single choice when appropriate. We believe that no useful purpose is served by forcing ourselves into an arbitrary selection of a single best when we come upon multiple examples of equal distinction.

# PLAYS

BEST PLAY: *The Piano Lesson* by August Wilson

BEST FOREIGN PLAY: *My Children! My Africa!* by Athol Fugard

BEST REVIVAL: *Cat on a Hot Tin Roof; The Merchant of Venice*

BEST ACTOR IN A PRIMARY ROLE: Eric Bogosian in *Sex, Drugs, Rock & Roll*; Nathan Lane as Mendy in *The Lisbon Traviata*; Robert Morse as Truman Capote in *Tru*

BEST ACTRESS IN A PRIMARY ROLE: Kate Nelligan as Melissa Gardner in *Love Letters*; Maggie Smith as Lettice Douffet in *Lettice & Lovage*; Kathleen Turner as Maggie in *Cat on a Hot Tin Roof*

BEST ACTOR IN A SECONDARY ROLE:  Carl Gordon as Doaker in *The Piano Lesson*; Terry Kinney as the Preacher in *The Grapes of Wrath*; Josef Sommer as Polonius in *Hamlet*

BEST ACTRESS IN A SECONDARY ROLE:  Polly Holliday as Big Mama in *Cat on a Hot Tin Roof*; Marcia Jean Kurtz as Miss Belzer in *When She Danced*; S. Epatha Merkerson as Berniece in *The Piano Lesson*

BEST DIRECTOR:  Peter Hall for *The Merchant of Venice*; George C. Wolfe for *Spunk*

BEST SCENERY:  Kevin Rigdon for *The Grapes of Wrath*; Ultz for *The Art of Success*

BEST COSTUMES:  Toni-Leslie James for *Spunk*

BEST LIGHTING:  Kevin Rigdon for *The Grapes of Wrath*

*ASPECTS OF LOVE*—Ann Crumb, Danielle Du Clos and Kevin Colson in
a scene from the Andrew Lloyd Webber-Don Black-Charles Hart musical

## Musicals and Special Attractions

The show concerns a mystery novelist who, in the middle of a personal
crisis, spins a tale in which his detective alter ego takes on a case. Many of
the members of the show's cast double as people in the novelist's real life and
as characters encountered during the detective's investigation, implicitly
charting the links between the novelist's reality and his fiction. Ultimately, the
detective comes to the novelist's aid, helping to resolve his creator's real-life
problems.

The above is a brief description of *City of Angels*. It is a description which
applies equally to Dennis Potter's landmark 1986 TV drama, *The Singing Detective*. I probably would be more enthusiastic about the former had I not
seen the latter. In Potter's version, the conventions of gumshoe fiction were
engaged for serious and disturbing purpose, the central character being a
bedridden author who employs his fictional counterpart as a kind of
psychological investigator, the most private of private eyes, who ultimately
brings about catharsis and healing. The result was arguably the best dramatic
writing for the stage or screen of the 1980s.

In *City of Angels*, book-writer Larry Gelbart, composer Cy Coleman and lyricist David Zippel display more modest ambitions. The bulk of the show consists of straightforward parody of the sort which has been common on-stage, on TV and in movies for years. Even the idea of a musical treatment of the hardboiled detective genre isn't new, as those familiar with the *Girl Hunt* ballet in the 1953 film *The Band Wagon* can attest. The non-parodistic section of the story isn't any fresher. Set in postwar Hollywood, it recounts the usual travails of the idealistic artist battling studio Philistines, this time in the form of a novelist's fight with an arrogant producer-director over the screen adaptation of his book. The authors intend us to view the novelist's battle for artistic integrity with sympathy, but protestations of moral superiority and integrity ring hollow from a character who jumps into the sack with the first (well, maybe the second) available female as soon as the wife he professes to love turns her back.

Still, there is no denying that the show is very entertaining. Though parodying detective stories isn't an original concept, Gelbart's line-by-line writing maintains a high level of wit; it may be the funniest musical book since he and the late Burt Shevelove collaborated on the script of *A Funny Thing Happened on the Way to the Forum*. Composer Cy Coleman is near the peak of his form here, the jazz-flavored score (smartly orchestrated by Billy Byers) registering as his best work since *Sweet Charity*. In half the songs lyricist David Zippel aims to be clever and mostly succeeds, but when it comes to songs aspiring to more than cleverness, Zippel is somewhat hampered by the parameters Gelbart has set up. As Gelbart has written none of the characters with much depth—they are as much types as were the characters in *A Funny Thing*—the lyrics which attempt to put passionate statements into their mouths seem to be cranked up to meet formal necessities rather than organic extensions of the book. Zippel's work is interesting primarily for the promise it shows—he obviously has an understanding of what theater lyrics are supposed to accomplish, an understanding which the pop-oriented lyricists of most of the recent British imports patently lack. I look forward to seeing what he comes up with in a show which allows him more latitude.

The writers were well-served by the production. Michael Blakemore, in collaboration with set designer Robin Wagner, costume designer Florence Klotz and lighting designer Paul Gallo, adroitly invoked the parallel worlds of black-and-white movies and sun-bleached Hollywood, getting particular mileage out of instances when the two overlapped. James Naughton knocked out the Raymond Chandler-esque overheated similes with appealing authority as the detective, Rene Auberjonois gave another of his nimble performances as two slimy producers with a more than incidental resemblance to each other, and Randy Graff, Dee Hoty, Kay McClelland and Rachel York played an assortment of vamps, bimbos, wives and fallen women with slam-bang musical comedy showmanship. Graff did especially well with one of the best

Coleman-Zippel numbers, "You Can Always Count on Me," a wryly comedic plaint on the plight of the eternal other woman, sung first from the perspective of the detective's Gal Friday and then from the writer's assistant and casual bedmate. Gregg Edelman made the most of the limited opportunities available to him as the novelist (writers almost always come across as passive characters onstage), projecting a sense of rumpled irony and singing well. On balance, we cite *City of Angels* as a Best Play of 1989–90.

Old Hollywood was invoked again in the form of a stage adaptation of the M-G-M musical *Meet Me in St. Louis*. The original film had little by way of plot. The "boy next door" was such a square-jawed stick that it was hard to care if dewy-eyed Esther landed him or not, and the father's threat to move his family from their beloved home to New York was introduced so late that it created no suspense whatever. What put the film over were its art direction, three lovely Hugh Martin-Ralph Blane songs, and Judy Garland. Onstage, the sets were handsome, the three songs were still lovely but were joined by several undistinguished new ones, and Donna Kane sang beautifully but couldn't manage the impossible job of replacing her predecessor. The lack of plot was felt even more keenly in the theater than in the movie house. The first act curtain arrived without offering a compelling dramatic reason to return after the intermission. While George Hearn, Milo O'Shea, Charlotte Moore and Betty Garrett are always welcome company, I yearned to see their talents put to better use.

Andrew Lloyd Webber's reputation has been built on shows with an emphasis on spectacle—most notably and successfully *Cats* and *The Phantom of the Opera*. With *Aspects of Love*, he aimed for the Continental elan Stephen Sondheim and Hugh Wheeler realized so adroitly in *A Little Night Music*. In fact, aspects of *Aspects* are reminiscent of *Night Music*—the leading female character is an actress with a history of liaisons, much of the action takes place in and around a romantic chateau, youthful idealism is juxtaposed with the bemused wisdom of the mature, etc. For all the effort Lloyd Webber and his librettists Don Black and Charles Hart put into it, *Aspects* reminds me of nothing so much as the high school kids I knew in the 1960s who thought that sneaking sips of Cinzano, seeing movies with subtitles, and smirking at bourgeois (that is, their parents') values were all that it took to be soulmates of Truffaut and Fellini. Similarly, Lloyd Webber and his collaborators seem to think that introducing their dramatis personae as artists with Bohemian sexual habits automatically makes their work sophisticated.

But there is a difference between invoking a milieu and making it credible—proving it in dramatic terms—onstage. The authors of *Aspects* have not made the world in which the action is set or the characters who are supposed to people this world believable. Oh, dressed up with Maria Bjornson's luxurious sets and elegant costumes, it all *looks* right, but every time a character opens his or her mouth, all that emerges are banalities, homilies and generalizations.  This is disastrous for what is intended to be a grand, romantic musical as it precludes establishing the emotional logic necessary to support two and a half hours of musical beds.  Rather than being rooted in persuasive human connections, the attractions seem to be merely functions of proximity—if any pair of male and female (or female and female) principals find themselves onstage at the same time, they instantly switch into seduction mode.  Rather than appearing worldly, the characters seem silly and shallow, and their authors consequently naive.

Generally speaking, the artistic level of a musical is set by the most powerful collaborator on the project.  Being producer as well as composer (and, in this case, credited with the book adaptation), Lloyd Webber is the most powerful figure on his shows.  My hunch is that he might do the work of which he is palpably capable if he were to abdicate some of that power to a collaborator who would hold him to a standard higher than the one he currently sets for himself.  In any case, this score struck me as being one of his weaker efforts, full of strained musical devices and coercive in its attempts to wrench emotional responses out of the listener.  Black and Hart's lyrics don't help matters, being characterized by the relentless and deadening articulation of the self-evident which seems common to the majority of British theater lyrics.

The most notable work in *Aspects* was the aforementioned production design by Maria Bjornson, which moved one swiftly through a variety of European scenes—an outdoor cafe, an artist's studio, a vineyard, a circus, a fair, and so forth, and so ceaselessly on.  While dazzling, the scenic abundance juxtaposed with the slightness of many of the episodes made the design seem profligate—the display of too much effect for too little purpose.

Bjornson's apparent intention was to create theatrical equivalents of cinematic conventions—pans, optical wipes and jump cuts.  The designers of *Grand Hotel* achieved similar goals without shifting flats and travellers or enlisting treadmills and turntables.  Instead, set designer Tony Walton provided an evocative but spare skeleton composed primarily of transparent pillars implying the character of the hotel in the Berlin of 1928.  The specific rooms were suggested by the constantly-shifting arrangements of chairs, telling props and Jules Fisher's virtuosic lighting.  At times, the transitions were as astonishing as a magician's prestidigitation; one especially startling segue, accomplished with an abrupt light cue, moved from a ballroom in full motion to a conference room filled with agitated stockholders with a swiftness that put the audience at risk of whiplash.

*Grand Hotel* (subtitled *The Musical*), a Best Play, was a good deal more than a technical tour de force.  Derived from Vicki Baum's novel (which was also the basis of the famous film), the show offers several variations on the theme of bankruptcy; each of the major characters is brought to crisis over the imminent exhaustion of some crucial resource—a ballerina facing the loss of her ability, an aristocrat floundering in a world in which aristocratic privileges are shrinking, an accountant with a terminal illness, a would-be actress on the brink of prostitution because of grinding poverty and an unforeseen pregnancy, the general director of a company who has played out the string of his authority. They and the many concisely delineated supporting characters are observed as if the hotel were an ecosystem—a world of predators, victims, parasites and the occasional flash of beauty. The book, credited to Luther Davis with the unofficial but widely-known assist of Peter Stone, contains some unintentionally funny lines, but these count for little when weighed against its organizational brilliance. At times, as many as five scenes play in counterpoint, simultaneous actions on various parts of the stage informing and commenting on each other. The songs are credited primarily to the team of Robert Wright and George Forrest with augmentations, revisions and additional material by Maury Yeston. The result is uneven—the music sometimes soaringly melodic (as in the Baron's "Life as It Should Be") or jazzy ("Maybe My Baby Loves Me"), sometimes bogged in uninspired pastiche ("Bonjour Amour," which sounds like an unintentional parody of Edith Piaf songs). The lyrics are more consistent, for the most part holding to a solid, if unexciting level of functionality.

The unevenness of the score, however, is offset by the gallery of fine performances and Tommy Tune's astonishing staging. In his previous shows, such as *Nine* and *My One and Only*, Tune charmed with cleverness; his work on *Grand Hotel* was the most impressive musical staging I can recall since the heyday of Jerome Robbins. The stage teemed with constant life, each character's personality made distinct by his or her own choreographic grammar. Much of this reportedly was derived from Tune's painstaking analysis of each cast member's potential. In the case of Michael Jeter, a fine and versatile actor who had never danced in a musical before, Tune uncovered a talent for eccentric dancing the actor himself had no idea was there. The resulting number in which Jeter was transformed from an awkward, stumbling and pitiable creature into a high-kicking marionette possessed by the spirit of the Charleston brought the audience to the point of show-stopping cheers. Yvonne Marceau and Pierre Dulaine's erotic and acrobatic tango of love and death (which they choreographed under Tune's supervision) was similarly thrilling, as was Jane Krakowski in a brief but spectacular flurry of syncopation shared with bartenders David Jackson and Danny Strayhorn. Jeter and Krakowski's acting skills were on a par with their dancing, both giving subtle and affecting performances as the dying accountant and would-be movie actress. There was solid work, too, from Karen Akers, David Carroll, Timothy Jerome and Liliane Montevecchi in the other leading roles, and the entire supporting ensemble. All in all, despite the occasional infelicities, this was the most satisfying new musical I've seen on Broadway since the original production of *Sweeney Todd*.

For a full measure of traditional Broadway songwriting craftsmanship at its best, one had to go off Broadway to *Closer Than Ever*. Over the course of two acts, various combinations of the four talented performers—Brent Barrett, Sally Mayes, Richard Muenz and Lynne Wintersteller—stepped out to sing songs by lyricist Richard Maltby Jr. and composer David Shire. Some of these were originally written for but cut from their one Broadway collaboration, *Baby*. A few others were written for Manhattan Theater Club's 1988 revue *Urban Blight*, and others made their first appearance with this production. Whatever their points of origin, sharing an evening they comprised a convincing whole, treating with humor and sensitivity various aspects of contemporary urban life with a particular emphasis on those reluctantly coming to terms with middle age.

Being a collection of songs, *Closer Than Ever* does not lend itself to selection as one of the Best Plays, but in a volume devoted to saluting the high points of the season, it seems appropriate to include a sample. So, with the kind permission of Richard Maltby Jr., below is the lyric of "Life Story," sung by a middle-aged woman.

It was a liberated marriage
We shared the household chores, of course
We understood each other's feelings
Right down to the day of
    our sensible divorce
I didn't ask him for a penny
I'd had my "liberated" training
So off he went with his hair of bronze
To find a life like Kahlil Gibran's
I got my rest from the drugs he did
He got his quest, I got the kid
And oh
I'm not complaining

So I set off to be a writer
A modern mother on her own
I wrote up happenings at gall'ries
Turned down jobs with sal'ries,
    stayed free-lance and alone
I fought the battles of the Sixties

Which you recall were rather draining
When men were thick, I hit the fray
Became a prick, got equal pay
I faced down chauvinistic slobs
I won the fights, improved the jobs
And oh
I'm not complaining

*CLOSER THAN EVER*—Sally Mayes (*foreground*) with Lynne Wintersteller, Brent Barrett and Richard Muenz in the off-Broadway revue of Richard Maltby Jr.-David Shire numbers

My husband found himself his ashram
Lost forty pounds and went through hell
Then one day he came back from limbo
Found himself some bimbo
    and moved to New Rochelle
I raised my son, and I had lovers
My choices sometimes take explaining
I'd meet some jock, my friends would scoff
He'd stay a while, I'd drive him off
I kept my space, preserved my turf
Six months—I'd send him back to surf
And ohh
I was not complaining

So now my son's halfway through college
I pay tuition like a fine
I'm still this feisty free-lance writer
Resume well-honed
    at a well-toned forty-nine
I find that getting work is harder
Each job I want takes more campaigning
And those sweet young things who hire me now
Those M.B.A.s making fifty thou
Who smile and ask me what I have done
When they got their jobs from the fights I won
(They should all stay home and have babies)
But I'm not complaining

And in the evening at my window
As I watch Jersey growing dim
I feel a troubling emotion
Summed up in this notion
    I wish I'd stayed with him
Lord knows each day with him was madness
As I have spent my life maintaining
But more and more I recall the joy
My golden dreamer, my lost boy
Our life was in the "twilight zone"
But no worse than a life alone
And oohh—

Well, I chose my way
And I'm not complaining

Having inveighed at length against the deficiencies of most contemporary lyric writing, I would like to explain why I think this to be a superior example of the craft. What makes this—and so many of the other lyrics in *Closer Than Ever*—remarkable is the degree to which Maltby allows the *audience* to complete the images and come to its own conclusions. For instance, in the lines referring to her husband, the woman refers to them sharing chores in a "liberated" marriage, him leaving her "to find a life like Kahlil Gibran's" and so giving her a "rest from the drugs he did." He reappears in a later verse, the veteran of an ashram and a crash diet, suddenly married to "some bimbo" and settled in New Rochelle. From these shards of information we arrive at our own evaluation of him. If Maltby had had her explicitly characterize him as a rather pitiful character blown hither and yon by the changing trends and values of the past couple of decades, the portrait would have been ruined. This restraint stimulates the audience to collaborate with the lyric, to supply from their own understanding the final bit of meaning. The process is rather analogous to a circuit, with the audience throwing the switch which closes it and so provides electricity with a path. If more of the lyricists attempting to write for the theater were to study Maltby's craft seriously, the American musical would be in a lot better shape.

Graciela Daniele's *Dangerous Games*, a double bill of dance pieces augmented by a few lyrics and even fewer spoken lines, was met with a nearly universal derision I didn't think it quite deserved. The second piece, *Orfeo*, a retelling of the Orpheus myth set during the military dictatorship in Argentina under which thousands "disappeared," undoubtedly was intended as a stirring political statement; but when an evil commandant started singing a song called "The Joys of Torture," it was hard not to laugh. The opening piece, *Tango*, described the activities of an unsavory pair of brothers in an Argentine brothel. Avowedly an exposé of machismo, it was overwrought to the point of silliness, but it was the occasion for some of Ms. Daniele's most arresting choreography danced with great verve by John Mineo and Gregory Mitchell, as the brothers, and Tina Paul, as the virginal whore they woo, compete for and abuse. Two hours of tango-flavored music would normally be a good hour more than I would care to sit through, but Astor Piazzolla composed a score of remarkable variety within those narrow stylistic confines.

The author of the few and disappointing lyrics in *Dangerous Games*, William Finn, was also the author of book, music and lyrics of *Romance in Hard Times*, a would-be fable set during the Depression. Part of the plot deals with Eleanor Roosevelt taking up residence in a soup kitchen to help the mostly black patrons. Though the whimsy is labored, there are enough sparkling songs in the score to remind one of Finn's genuine and considerable gifts.

*Romance in Hard Times* was one of three musicals presented by Joseph Papp's Public Theater, the other being *Up Against It*, adapted from a Joe Orton screenplay originally designed for the Beatles in the 1960s, and *Jonah*, adapted by Elizabeth Swados from a Robert Nathan novel. The plot of *Romance in Hard Times* concerns some young men facing a society in which very militant women have taken over the government. Whatever satiric point stereotyping women as mostly shrill Amazons might have made two decades ago is hard to fathom now, and even then it is hard to see how a political assassination was calculated to raise lighthearted guffaws. There were some compensations. If Todd Rundgren's lyrics were uninteresting, much of his music was beguiling, particularly a ballad called "Parallel Lines." Philip Casnoff reinforced the impression he made in *Chess* of being a gifted singer, and Alison Fraser was an Edward Gorey cartoon brought to life as the long-suffering female lead.

*Prince of Central Park* deals with a runaway foster child who lives in a tree house in Central Park and befriends a 50-ish lady depressed by an impending divorce. Reportedly the original novel by Evan H. Rhodes has enjoyed a fair amount of popularity over the years, but whatever qualities have endeared it to its readers have been obscured by Rhodes's adaptation. The songs, by composer Don Sebesky and lyricist Gloria Nissenson, are relentlessly obvious, as were Tony Tanner's direction and choreography for the production. In the midst of the coyness and staleness, Richard H. Blake, as the title character, managed to muster some real feeling and sang with a clear, impassioned voice. Jo Anne Worley deserved more credit than she got for the gameness with which she tackled the material she was assigned.

*A Change in the Heir*, a fairy tale musical patterned after *Once Upon a Mattress*, concerns a prince and princess who, for reasons too complicated to go into here, are forced to assume opposite sexual identities from infancy. When they meet, of course, they fall in love and sort out who and what they are. The work was clearly not appropriate for the Broadway arena, as the New York press confirmed with withering notices. Still, underneath the heavy-handed and cutesy anachronisms and the slavish imitations of Sondheim, there is reason to believe that librettist George H. Gorham and composer Dan Sticco might be capable of more substantial work.

Gorham and Sticco might take heart from the fortunes of Lynn Ahrens, Stephen Flaherty and Graciela Daniele. Ahrens and Flaherty had been worked over by much of the critical fraternity for their promising but unsuccessful off-Broadway musical *Lucky Stiff* a few seasons ago, and Graciela Daniele suffered an even more rigorous drubbing on the aforementioned *Dangerous Games*. Toward the close of this season, however, Daniele's staging of Ahrens and Flaherty's *Once on This Island* provided vindication of their gifts. The story, which, as widely noted, bears a strong resemblance to Hans Christian Andersen's *The Little Mermaid*, is set against the backdrop of divided black society on an island in the French Antilles. Out joy-riding one night, Armand, the rich, light-skinned young scion of one of the island's "grands hommes," crashes his sports car. Near death, he is found by Ti Moune, a beautiful young peasant girl, who saves his life. The boy is retrieved by his wealthy family, and Ti Moune journeys across the island to the family's hotel to be reunited with and begin a romance with Armand. But, being a peasant, Ti Moune is not considered an appropriate wife for Armand, and she refuses to stay on as his mistress when he marries one from his own social set. She dies of heartbreak and, in death, is transformed into a tree whose fruit helps bring conciliation to the island.

The show brings to mind an old Second City sketch in which a cultural maven commented on some examples of primitive sculpture. "Have you seen them?" he says. "My *God*, they're sophisticated!" *Once on This Island*, too, could be described as sophisticated primitive art. The cast of characters in Ahrens's book includes four island gods. Flaherty's music draws its inspirations from native rhythms and harmonies and Daniele's choreography from island dances. Though the elements have folk roots, the skill with which they have been interpreted, augmented and blended bespeaks theatrical craft of a high order. The result is a happy integration of virtually nonstop song and dance featuring the best sustained score for a book musical this season, brilliantly orchestrated for a small ensemble by Michael Starobin. The enchanting La Chanze starred as Ti Moune and was supported by a remarkable ensemble of ten.

*Truly Blessed*, a musical biography of gospel-singing great Mahalia Jackson, starred Queen Esther Marrow, who was also responsible for the show's conception, book, and much of its original music and lyrics. The script consisted of the sketchiest outline of Jackson's life and career, offering little by way of psychological depth or drama. But one doesn't go to a gospel musical for drama; the music and the singers are everything, and, in the case of *Truly Blessed*, they were more than sufficient. Ms. Marrow didn't seem to be in full voice the night I saw the show, but her supporting company—Carl Hall, Lynette G. DuPre, Doug Eskew and Gwen Stewart—were all stirring singers and had energy and enthusiasm to spare.

The score of *Truly Blessed* is made up of both original material and gospel standards. The scores of two other musical offerings, *Further Mo'* and *Forever Plaid*, are completely drawn from pre-existing material. A sequel to *One Mo' Time, Further Mo'* made me regret having missed its predecessor. An evocation of the world of black vaudeville in St. Louis of the 1920s, the production at the Village Gate offered one winning number after another by four vibrant performers: Vernel Bagneris (who played Papa Du, the leader of the troupe), Topsy Chapman, Frozine Thomas and Sandra Reaves-Phillips. Bagneris also directed and wrote the agreeably featherweight book concerning the backstage lives of the four and their relationship with the racist theater owner, played by James "Red" Wilcher. Much credit for the success of the enterprise was also due to choreographer Pepsi Bethel and arrangers Lars Edegran, Orange Kellin and Topsy Chapman.

In *Forever Plaid*, a quartet of semi-pro singers called the Plaids, having died in a traffic accident in 1964, are allowed to return to earth to give one performance. In 90 minutes, the four run through a program of closely-harmonized arrangements of pop music from the 1950s and early 1960s. The humor of the evening derives from the quartet's blithe ignorance of how profoundly the popular culture has changed since their demise. Unaware of their squareness and desperately eager to please, they cheerfully subvert everything they sing. At one point, in a salute to the Beatles, they launch into an arrangement of "She Loves You" which converts "Yeah, yeah, yeah!" to "Yessiree," in the process hilariously neutralizing those very elements which identify it as a Beatles song. The winningly daffy evening was conceived and staged by Stuart Ross, and James Raitt's arrangements managed the neat trick of both satirizing the music and allowing its genuine charms to come through.

Mandy Patinkin hasn't created a musical role since *The Knife*, a short lived effort of the 1986-87 season. In lieu of this, at the Helen Hayes Theater he offered an evening entitled *Mandy Patinkin In Concert: Dress Casual* in which he harnessed his manic intensity to a varied program of songs, most tantalizing a medley from *Pal Joey* and "Soliloquy" from *Carousel*.

Another attraction was *Sid Caesar & Company: Does Anybody Know What I'm Talking About?* in which the comic reprised several of his better-known bits. There were a few songs that seemed to be there only to give the star a chance to change backstage, and, of the supporting players, only Linda Hart seemed to enter fully into the logic of his humor. Nevertheless, Caesar himself proved he could still seduce an audience with his graceful silliness, and his show deserved to run longer than it did.

To sum up on the most positive note, here's where we list the *Best Plays* choices for the musical and revue bests of 1989–90.

## MUSICALS AND REVUES

BEST MUSICAL OR REVUE: *Grand Hotel*

BEST BOOK: Lynn Ahrens for *Once on This Island;* Luther Davis for *Grand Hotel*

BEST MUSIC: Cy Coleman for *City of Angels*; David Shire for *Closer Than Ever*

BEST LYRICS: Richard Maltby Jr. for *Closer Than Ever*

BEST ACTOR IN A PRIMARY ROLE: Bob Gunton as Sweeney Todd in *Sweeney Todd*; James Naughton as Stone in *City of Angels*

BEST ACTRESS IN A PRIMARY ROLE: La Chanze as Ti Moune in *Once on This Island*; Tyne Daly as Mama Rose in *Gypsy*

BEST ACTOR IN A SECONDARY ROLE: Michael Jeter as Otto Kringelein in *Grand Hotel*; Jonathan Hadary as Herbie in *Gypsy*

BEST ACTRESS IN A SECONDARY ROLE: Jane Krakowski as Flaemmchen in *Grand Hotel*

BEST DIRECTOR: Tommy Tune for *Grand Hotel*

BEST CHOREOGRAPHY: Tommy Tune for *Grand Hotel*

BEST SCENERY: Tony Walton for *Grand Hotel*

BEST LIGHTING: Jules Fisher for *Grand Hotel*; Andrew Bridge for *Aspects of Love*

BEST COSTUMES: Santo Loquasto for *Grand Hotel*

SPECIAL CITATIONS: Billy Byers for orchestrations for *City of Angels*; Wally Harper for music supervision for *Grand Hotel*; Michael Starobin for orchestrations for *Once on This Island*

*CAT ON A HOT TIN ROOF*—Kathleen Turner as Maggie and Charles Durning as Big Daddy in the revival of Tennessee Williams's drama

## Revivals

Upon resigning from the stewardship of London's National Theater, director Peter Hall established a commercial producing organization to mount plays in the West End and in New York. The first production to arrive on these shores was of Tennessee Williams's *Orpheus Descending*, starring Vanessa Redgrave as Lady Torrance, the brutalized Italian-American wife of a dying Southern merchant. The play tells of her life-restoring affair with a sensitive young guitar-playing stranger named Valentine Xavier and of their destruction at the hands of the town's bigots.

Even in its most successful incarnation—the Sidney Lumet film *The Fugitive Kind* (which featured Anna Magnani and Marlon Brando)—this was never top-grade Williams, loaded as it is with melodramatic contrivance and heavy-handed symbolism, stumbling again and again over the line into unintended absurdity. Hall's production aggravated the text's flaws, ominous rumblings from synthesizers and portentous lighting effects underscoring every other gesture.

Vanessa Redgrave's appearance as Lady Torrance was the raison d'etre of the production, and audiences were divided in their opinion of it. A sizable contingent marvelled at her bravura turn. Though I normally number myself as one of her enthusiastic admirers (her Mrs. Alving in *Ghosts* in London a few seasons back is certainly among the great performances of my theater-going career), I thought her work here spectacularly wrong-headed. It was as if she had found five good ideas for every moment and, instead of choosing between them, was determined to play all simultaneously—the kind of bad performance that only a great actress could give. Generally, the supporting cast, too, disappointed. Kevin Anderson seemed too lightweight a partner for Redgrave, Anne Twomey was directed to act relentlessly eccentric in Kabuki-like makeup as a disturbed free spirit, and most of the townspeople were played as simple-minded goons. In sharp and happy contrast were Tammy Grimes, who gave a restrained and disciplined performance as an eccentric barely tolerated by her husband and neighbors, and Sloane Shelton, who managed to bring dramatic life to a gossip whose only function was to spiel exposition.

The other Williams of the season was a revival which was, paradoxically, a partial premiere. When *Cat on a Hot Tin Roof* was given its initial production, director Elia Kazan prevailed upon the author to rewrite the third act. Kazan asserted that the audience would be upset if Big Daddy, who dominates the second act, didn't figure in the play's closing action. So Williams rewrote to prescription, brought back Big Daddy, and the show was a hit. But, hit or no, Williams still had his doubts. In the published text, he included both his original and the revised versions. It is his original that finally made it to the Broadway stage this season. And, to my mind, this production proved it to be the superior of the two.

In the version Kazan directed, Big Daddy was reconciled with Brick, he chose to believe Maggie's lie about being pregnant, and he offered a passive indication that he wasn't entirely unwilling to accept Big Mama's company again. Also, Brick gave signs that he would soon relent in his resistance to Maggie and live with her once more as husband and wife—all in all, upbeat and comforting resolutions to the problems posed in the first two acts.

In Williams's original version, however, Big Daddy makes peace with nobody. He stalks offstage in a fury on learning that his cancer is indeed inoperable, and all we hear of him thereafter are howls of agony as the disease gnaws into him. As for Brick, when push comes to shove he agrees to go along with Maggie's plan to impregnate her but otherwise offers scant cause for hope that he will return to her emotionally. Instead of catering to audience sentiment, the original has the courage to portray the harder truth that hearts don't change overnight.

In addition to offering the text as originally written, this production went a long way toward correcting what I believe to be a common misreading of the play. Perhaps because of wide familiarity with Paul Newman's interpretation in the film version, there has been a tendency to view Brick as a noble figure, a prince full of potential in temporary retreat. Daniel Hugh Kelly's performance struck me as being closer to Williams's intentions, showing Brick to be, at heart, a weak man whose greatest insight is into his own essential mediocrity. From all of the evidence Williams gives us, Brick could do one thing well in his life—play football. His playing days behind him now, he hasn't learned to do anything else and so has been unable to make the transition to full adulthood. He's a Peter Pan without a Never-Never Land, and the world shows no interest in continuing to support his post-pubescent yearnings. His reaction is petulant—to blame everyone else for failures originating in his own character. He drinks to avoid the pain of the truth, an avoidance strategy which makes his famous speech about mendacity all the more ironic. The news of his father's imminent death brings him to crisis because it puts pressure on him to make choices required of an adult.

As for Big Daddy, between Charles Durning's justifiably acclaimed performance and his excision from the third act, he is a good deal less the curmudgeon lovable in spite of himself than was Burl Ives (or, for that matter, Laurence Olivier, who twinkled inappropriately in a misbegotten TV adaptation). One of the revelations of this production is how little regard the old man has for Maggie or, for that matter, for most women, except insofar as they might offer sexual gratification. Both Big Daddy and Brick indulge their adolescent impulses—Brick by drinking and sulking when life turns out to be more complicated then his childish illusions have prepared him to handle, and Big Daddy by making plans to spend in hedonistic abandon the extra 20 years he initially believes the doctors have given him. If Big Daddy is more engaging than Brick, it is because we see less of his self-pity, and he is more entertaining in his vulgarity. But, in truth, neither father nor son is a particularly attractive character.

It is Maggie who excites admiration because, rather than trying to escape through drinking and bedhopping, she has the guts to face up to the imperatives of time. Loving Brick despite his weaknesses, she takes those actions necessary to defend what she clearsightedly sees as his genuine interests and her own. In her first major role on the Broadway stage, Kathleen Turner was a valiant Maggie, giving full expression to her humor and resilience without soft-pedaling her malice. The production also benefited from Polly Holliday's Big Mama, most arresting when she put aside flibbertigibbet surface behavior to reveal the bedrock of courage underneath.

If director Howard Davies deserves credit for this quartet of remarkable performances, he also deserves criticism, as did Peter Hall, for succumbing to the temptation to caricature the supporting roles. Kevin O'Rourke, Debra Jo Rupp and Jerome Dempsey have all done impressive work in the past; here they seemed to be constrained by an imposed interpretation that denied them the opportunity to find some point of sympathy with their characters. Even with these reservations, however, this production of *Cat* was easily the most satisfying Williams to appear in New York in the past decade.

Another American classic, Arthur Miller's *The Crucible*, received a strong staging this season under the direction of Gerald Freedman. Justine Bateman and Vicki Lewis were properly terrifying as two of the girls bringing accusations of witchcraft, and Randle Mell and Harriet Harris were poignant as the besieged Proctors. The only serious problem with the production had to do with the acoustical deficiencies of the Christian C. Yegen Theater, in which the Roundabout Theater Company presents its plays. There is a dome in the auditorium, and unless a play's design team provides some kind of baffle in the set to compensate, the sound flies up into it, and the audience below misses a good deal. From where I sat in an aisle seat close to the front of the house, a good third of the production was inaudible. (It was a good season for *The Crucible*; Arvin Brown staged an exemplary production at Long Wharf in his three-quarters round space. The Brown production also included a riveting scene between John Proctor and Abigail not included in the Freedman production.)

The revival of W. Somerset Maugham's comedy *The Circle* proved to be the occasion of Rex Harrison's last stage appearance. His role as Lord Porteous, a man who gave up a brilliant political career in favor of running off with a friend's wife many years ago, was essentially to chime in with tart comments. I understand that his performance varied from show to show depending on how he felt, but when I saw him he was at the top of his game, his wry inflections perfectly supporting Maugham's wit. Glynis Johns and Stewart Granger, too, as the other sides of the aged triangle, played with great elan. Unfortunately, the script devotes most of its attention to a parallel triangle among a younger generation. These passages contain the play's most pedestrian writing, and the trio of younger players—Roma Downey, Robin Chadwick and Harley Venton—for all of their evident talent and intelligence could do little with this recalcitrant stuff. Our historian, Thomas T. Foose, reminds us that *The Circle* hasn't been seen often in New York, and working backward in time he reports, "There was an off-Broadway staging in 1985-86, with Geraldine Page. In 1973-74 the play was offered by the Roundabout. (One might add here that in 1965-66 Helen Hayes played Lady Kitty in a very short-lived road tour production.) Before that there were only two productions in New York: A 1937-38 staging at the Playhouse with Tallulah Bankhead and Grace George, and the original 1921-22 New York staging with Estelle Winwood, Mrs. Leslie Carter and John Drew. Burns Mantle chose this play as one of his Best Plays for the 1921-22 season."

The two revivals produced by Lincoln Center this season were both unsatisfying. Larry Sloan's direction of his and Doug Wright's adaptation of *Ubu* offered little indication of why Alfred Jarry's play occupies an important place in the literature of modern theater. Ulu Grosbard's revival of Paddy Chayefsky's *The Tenth Man* similarly made me wonder why this muddled and inconsistent version of the dybbuk legend had been such a substantial hit on

Broadway in the 1959–60 season. Meanwhile, at the Manhattan Theater Club, despite the spirited work of Kate Nelligan, Nathan Lane and Faith Prince, time also was not kind to Terrence McNally's *Bad Habits*, which I remember enjoying enormously in its initial run in the mid-1970s. Perhaps, as I've observed in reaction to some revivals of Joe Orton's work, society has changed so much that what impressed as outrageous satire before appears comparatively mild now.

On Broadway, the much-anticipated revival of the Bertolt Brecht-Kurt Weill *Threepenny Opera* (for some reason retitled *3 Penny Opera*) was rejected with nearly unanimous critical swats. I thought that most of what was wrong with John Dexter's production (which proved to be the last of his distinguished career) had to do with the inappropriateness of the house in which it played. I doubt that there is any dramatic work so hardy that it can survive being given in the wrong theater, and it would be hard to think of a theater less suitable for this work than the one into which it was booked. *Threepenny* is designed to be done in an intimate environment, a description which in no way captures the dubious charm of the cavernous Lunt-Fontanne. In a smaller space, I think Sting's cunning and acrobatic Macheath would have found more admirers. (But then, in a smaller space, the producers could not have hoped to make enough money to pay Sting's salary.) Georgia Brown was a wonderfully dangerous Mrs. Peachum, and Kim Criswell gave a fine account of Lucy, making "Lucy's Aria" a highlight of the score. The production also did a great service in introducing Michael Feingold's translation, as singable as Marc Blitzstein's popular version but eschewing the bowdlerization Blitzstein apparently felt was required for the audiences of the 1950s.

Speaking of the Lunt-Fontanne, it was the original home of *The Rothschilds* when it opened in the 1970–1971 season. At the time, I thought the musical too diffuse, the constant shifts in location making for a dramatic breathlessness as the action dashed from one European capital to another to another, often skipping decades in seconds. This year's revival, which moved up from OOB late in the season to an off-Broadway production, directed by Lonny Price, made an asset of limited resources. The downtown Circle-in-the-Square space, in which the audience is positioned on three sides of the stage, mandates that scenery must be very sparse in order to keep sightlines clear. Instead of the parade of sets which characterized the Lunt-Fontanne production, Price, in collaboration with designer Russell Metheny, staged his version on a unit set slightly modified from scene to scene. This scenic unity conferred upon the action the impression of greater dramatic unity. The score remains one of Jerry Bock's and Sheldon Harnick's less memorable collaborations, but their craftsmanship and that of the book's author, Sherman Yellen, gracefully meets the considerable challenge of relaying a huge chunk of 19th century European history in a coherent and entertaining way. Mike Burstyn, the show's star, was an engagingly tenacious Mayer Rothschild, who par-

*GYPSY*—Tyne Daly as Rose, Crista Moore as Louise and
Jonathan Hadary as Herbie in the revival of the musical

layed a rare coin business into a vast family fortune and used his economic influence as leverage in the struggle against anti-Semitism. The only substantial
loss from the Broadway edition was in the necessary adaptation of the
orchestration to a pair of synthesizers. Much of the transcription, under the
musical direction of Grant Sturiale, was done with ingenuity, but inevitably
what were intended to be grander passages sounded tinny.

Such was also the case with David Krane's synthesizer transcription of
Stephen Sondheim's score for *Sweeney Todd, the Demon Barber of Fleet
Street*, which opened earlier in the season. In Jonathan Tunick's stunning orchestrations for the original, the orchestra seemed to represent London itself.
One could almost hear bells pealing in support of the sailor's hopes at the end
of "Johanna" or the grinding of massive factory machinery behind Sweeney's
aria, "Epiphany." Krane's work, done in close consultation with the composer, was resourceful, but much of the score's epic sweep was lost.

The original production of *Sweeney Todd* opened in the 1978–79 season
under Harold Prince's direction at the Uris (now the Gershwin) Theater on a
massive set by Eugene Lee which included elements of a real foundry. This
season's Broadway revival was staged in the smaller theater in the same

building, the uptown Circle in the Square. Whereas Prince's production had been a spectacular Brechtian epic with images of humanity being crushed by the industrial revolution, Susan H. Schulman's production necessarily had a narrower focus. Designer James Morgan faced essentially the same challenge in the uptown Circle in the Square as Metheney did later downtown with *The Rothschilds*. Morgan's solution was to turn the entire theater into the world of Fleet Street and its environs, an impression reinforced by drab laundry hanging on lines over the audience's heads.

The intimate playing area also made for a shift in the scale of the performances. Upstairs, in the huge Uris, Len Cariou and Angela Lansbury were compelled to paint in broad strokes in order to register, and they did so brilliantly. Downstairs, the cast had the freedom to work more subtly. Bob Gunton and Beth Fowler took full advantage of their opportunity, with the result that one better understood the chemistry of Sweeney and Mrs. Lovett's bizarre relationship. Gunton was equally as effective as Cariou and George Hearn in capturing Sweeney's obsessiveness, with the added benefit that we saw more traces of the virtues the barber had possessed before persecution drove him mad. Fowler didn't attempt to challenge Lansbury's comedic elan, but her singing voice is more musical than her predecessor's and so revealed more of the beauty of the scoring for Mrs. Lovett's songs and, by extension, more of the demented pie-maker's heart. Some of Schulman's staging harkened back to elements of Prince's production; but she was ingenious in fashioning new devices when adaptation of the original wasn't possible. All things considered, this was a valuable production of a Broadway classic. It is sobering to note, however, that, in the decade since *Sweeney*'s premiere, Broadway hasn't seen a new musical of comparable stature.

Another compelling leading musical performance was given in the revival of another Sondheim musical in which Angela Lansbury had previously triumphed, *Gypsy*. Tyne Daly had the challenge of going up against not only the memory of Lansbury's acclaimed interpretation but, of course, that of Ethel Merman, for whom the show was written in the first place. Ms. Daly did just fine. Having been a schoolchild when I saw Merman on tour in Chicago, I'm not going to pretend to be able to make a detailed comparison; but Daly projected not only Rose's determination (which one can hear blasting out of Merman in the original cast album) but a vulnerability I don't associate with Merman. For the first time in my experience, Rose and Herbie's affair made real emotional sense, no small part of this due to Jonathan Hadary's immensely appealing Herbie. As Hadary is more musically confident than was Jack Klugman (the original Herbie), some of the songs which were solos in the Merman *Gypsy* were shared between Daly and Hadary, which reinforced belief in them as a couple. Crista Moore was appropriately vulnerable as Louise, but her second act transition into the poised and self-possessed Gypsy Rose Lee was not persuasive. This undermined the penultimate dressing room confrontation scene in which the daughter is supposed to prove as tenacious as her mother. To be fair, Gypsy's transformation from ugly duckling to confident star is difficult to pull off. In fact, the only time I've seen it work was in the late Natalie Wood's performance in the much-reviled film version.

Arthur Laurents, who wrote the book and had directed the Lansbury revival, also staged this edition with great distinction, and the Jule Styne-Stephen Sondheim score reaffirmed its ability to unleash the audience's adrenalin at will. The production was the enormous success it fully deserved to be.

Ironically, of the three actresses nominated for Tony Awards for playing Rose, only the original, Merman, didn't win. She lost to Mary Martin for her performance as Maria in *The Sound of Music*. The Richard Rodgers-Oscar Hammerstein II-Howard Lindsay-Russel Crouse musical of the Trapp Family Singers also returned this season in an extended run at Lincoln Center. Though it was presented by the New York City Opera, the production was cast primarily from the non-operatic world, Debby Boone making a spirited Maria, solidly supported by Laurence Guittard as Captain von Trapp and Werner Klemperer as their pragmatic friend Max. James Hammerstein's direction underscored the juxtaposition of the moral choices the adults faced in the wake of the Anschluss with the upbringing of the children under their care.

The other Broadway musical revival was *Shenandoah*, which concerns a family caught up in the Civil War against its will. John Cullum recreated his Tony-winning performance as the family patriarch and was as impressive as before. But the material itself struck me then and strikes me now as awkward and simplistic. (I took my 9-year-old son to this show. At the end, he turned to me and said, "Dad, *West Side Story* is better than this, right?")

This season's Shakespeare productions ran the gamut of quality. Most disappointing was Richard Jordan's mild staging of *Macbeth* for the New York Shakespeare Festival with Raul Julia in the lead. The sole distinguishing aspect of the Roundabout's production of *The Tempest* was the passionate and extremely well-spoken performance of Frank Langella as Prospero.

In Central Park, the Shakespeare Festival's *Twelfth Night* was loaded with stars. Jeff Goldblum and John Amos seemed stymied by the roles of Malvolio and Sir Toby. Michelle Pfeiffer and Mary Elizabeth Mastrantonio couldn't work up the chemistry necessary to make the scenes between Olivia and Viola play. But the chemistry between Mastrantonio and Stephen Collins's Duke was very affecting; and, although Gregory Hines went overboard as Feste (at one point mooning Malvolio), he made me laugh as few Festes have.

Central Park also hosted *Titus Andronicus*, which was filled with imaginative staging ideas by Michael Maggio, a Chicago director making his New York debut. Unfortunately, that fine actor Donald Madden could not break free from the moderating bonds of rationality as Titus, and a moderate Titus is as dramatically frustrating as a mild Macbeth. Kate Mulgrew, however, as the vicious Queen Tamora threw herself wholeheartedly into the excesses of this most ludicrously excessive of Shakespeare's plays. Our Mr. Foose reminds us, "Prior to 1989–90, *Titus Andronicus* had been twice produced by Joseph Papp. The more recent of these was at the Delacorte in 1967. Olympia Dukakis was Tamora, Moses Gunn was Aaron, and in the title role was Jack Hollander; Gerald Freedman directed. Papp's earlier bout with *Titus Andronicus* was in 1956–57 when he was operating in the upstairs auditorium of the Emanuel Presbyterian Church at 729 E. 6th Street. There Mr. Papp gave what the New York *Times* and *Herald Tribune* described as the first New York professional performance of this play, opening Nov. 27, 1956. Colleen Dewhurst was Tamora, Roscoe Brown was Aaron and Frederick Rolfe directed."

The best of the Shakespeare Festival's offerings was the *Hamlet* starring and directed by Kevin Kline. Though still very strong, Kline's performance as the Prince has lost some of the edge I so admired when he performed it under Liviu Ciulei's direction a few season's back. Whereas Ciulei's production was very definitely a director's *Hamlet*, full of startling and illuminating stage pictures, Kline's de-emphasized design elements (there was very little use of furniture or set pieces) and was focussed on the company, an entirely appropriate choice given the powerhouse cast he enlisted. Most impressive in an ensemble without a weak link were Diane Venora's Ophelia and Josef Sommer's Polonius. Sommer managed the neat trick of making Polonius both an intelligent man on whom someone as shrewd as Claudius would rely and a man of limited humor and imagination who would naturally be a foil for Hamlet. He was also a figure of sufficient warmth as to make Ophelia's and Laertes's reactions to his death believably heartfelt. Venora's Ophelia was particularly strong in dramatizing the degree to which the character is a reflection of Hamlet—both vulnerable in their uninsulated honesty, both devastated by the loss of their fathers. Hamlet feigns madness; Ophelia genuinely goes mad. Kline and Venora's "nunnery" scene was thrillingly intense and provided the production with its most memorable passage.

Having begun this section critical of Peter Hall's work on *Orpheus Descending*, it is a pleasure to be able to end by praising his staging of *The Merchant of Venice*. Again, the production came about because of the participation of a star, in this case Dustin Hoffman, making his first performance on a New York stage since his well-received Willy Loman in *Death of a Salesman* in 1984. Hoffman evidently worked hard technically, and the work paid off; here he spoke with a clarity and a musicality new to him. The production was predicated upon making the most positive case possible for Shylock, and Hoffman was particularly strong in exploring Shylock the ironist. His was not a Shylock to rage, but one who saw injustices clearly and commented on them with a disarming humor. Only with the betrayal of Jessica—and, in this production, Jessica's elopement was very definitely played as a betrayal and the prologue to an unhappy life with her Christian husband—did one get the feeling that Shylock's heart was resolved for Antonio's blood.

Yet another landmark performance from one of America's most adventuresome actors, Hoffman's Shylock was the production's chief attraction, though it shared the stage with a number of other very strong performances. Leigh Lawson was an unusually bold Antonio, rescuing him from the passivity which has often characterized the interpretation of this part in the past. In a particularly controversial moment, so that Shylock will make no mistake about his unchanged antipathy, Lawson spat upon Hoffman even as he asked for his loan. It was a moment that was tellingly echoed when Hoffman turned on Lawson in the courtroom scene. Geraldine James, too, was outstanding as Portia, making of her a woman of spirit fighting against the constraints of a world ordered by men.

Hall's direction was marked by a bracing clarity of purpose, for the most part avoiding the fussy frills in which less confident directors dress up the classics. *Merchant* is a gripping if disquieting story, and he was intent on letting nothing get in the way of its telling. The result was, without a doubt, the year's best production of Shakespeare.

## Offstage

The upswing in this Broadway season's quality was mirrored by an upswing in income, according to the League of American Theaters and Producers. Their figures, covering the period of May 29, 1989 through June 3, 1990 aver a box office record of $283 million in ticket sales, an 8 percent increase over last season's $262 million. (One can only speculate how much higher that figure might have been if two eagerly-anticipated shows, *Annie 2* and Neil Simon's *Jake's Women*, had fared better in their out-of-town tryouts and come into New York.) By our own count, Broadway production in 1989–90 amounted to 14 new plays (3 more than last season) including 3 transfers from off Broadway and 4 foreign scripts, 8 new musicals (double last year's production), 2 revues, 5 musical and 6 play revivals, 4 specialties and a foreign-language play, a total of 40 offerings as compared with last season's 34. Off Broadway by our count, production of new work continued in slight decline, with 41 new plays, 8 musicals and 3 revues, as compared with 44–7–6 last year and 47–6–7 the year before.

The League also reported a dramatic increase in touring income, a record $367 million, 43 percent more than last season's $256 million. Part of the Broadway increase was fueled by an increase in ticket prices, last season's *Jerome Robbins' Broadway* leading the way by pushing the top to $60. According to *Variety*, the average Broadway ticket price escalated to $35.24 from the previous season's average of $32.88.

Though no show this season broke the Robbins show's record capitalization of $8.8 million, substantial sums still had to be committed to launch a major enterprise. *City of Angels*, for example, cost approximately $5 million to open, and *Annie 2* spent about that much before it died in Washington. (Had it continued on to New York, it would have cost an estimated $7 million total.)

This is not to say that it still wasn't possible to launch Broadway productions for substantially less. On the low end, the unsuccessful revival of *Miss Margarida's Way* cost only $180,000 and *Love Letters*, with its rotating cast, $200,000. The larger-scaled productions required sums in the high six or low seven figures, *Cat on a Hot Tin Roof* requiring $829,000, *Lettice & Lovage* $1.2 million, and the large-cast *The Grapes of Wrath* $1.75 million. (One of the primary attractions of off Broadway, of course, is the lower cost. Eric Bogosian's *Sex, Drugs, Rock & Roll* opened for an estimated $100,000, and Terrence McNally's *The Lisbon Traviata* for a sum reportedly under $200,000.)

*A Few Good Men* began its production life at the University of Virginia in Charlottesville, then moved to the Kennedy Center before playing Broadway. The Charlottesville production made it possible to try out the play with less financial pressure than if it had gone straight to New York. The capitalization for the University of Virginia-Kennedy Center leg of the venture was $180,000, with the university kicking in $25,000. The Broadway capitalization was estimated at $600,000. The University of Virginia has become a frequent host for Broadway-bound productions, providing an educated and enthusiastic audience as well as an economic guarantee for such other productions as this season's revival of *The Circle* and last season's *Metamorphosis*.

An off-Broadway company also gave a boost to an incoming Broadway production. The Manhattan Theater Club purchased 12,000 tickets for August Wilson's *The Piano Lesson*, distributing them to its subscribers in fulfillment of one of the offerings it was obliged to present during the season. The purchase of such a large block of tickets gave the production a $210,000 advance, providing its producers a substantial hedge at a time when a serious work with no box office-enhancing stars is by definition a doubtful financial proposition. The significance of this arrangement goes beyond the dynamics of the specific deal, in that it establishes yet another way in which non-profit theaters may be linked to the commercial arena. (Some observers, such as artistic director-critic Robert Brustein, contend that such linkage threatens to obliterate the distinctions between the non-commercial and profit-oriented producers, further homogenizing the American theater.)

Of the shows to open this season, *Variety* estimated that five (three of them revivals) could be designated financial successes by the close of the season—*Gypsy, Cat on a Hot Tin Roof, The Merchant of Venice,* Mandy Patinkin's solo evening and *Love Letters. Lettice & Lovage* and *City of Angels* were expected to reach hit status, however, and, in the wake of an impressive showing on the Tony Awards broadcast, the box office for *Grand Hotel* zoomed to near-capacity business giving that show a better shot at breaking even.

The reason producers continue to gamble large sums of money in a game in which profit is so unlikely lies in the hope that their shows will be among the select few to go on to money-making multi-year runs. This season, the two shows with the multiest of multi-year runs in Broadway history finally closed, *A Chorus Line* (6,137 performances, not counting the 101 performances it played in its off-Broadway engagement at the Public Theater) and the Broadway revival run of *Oh! Calcutta!* (5,959 performances). In neither case was its chief creator around to enjoy the glory. Kenneth Tynan, who conceived the latter, died in 1980. The key figure behind *A Chorus Line*, director-choreographer Michael Bennett, as well as its lyricist, Ed Kleban, and the co-author of the book, James Kirkwood, also died well before the last curtain of the show which confirmed their places in American theatrical history.

As noted previously, a large proportion of the American plays which arrive in New York each season begin their lives in regional theaters. This season, after two years of research and development, the Dramatists Guild announced a standardized contract for use in productions of its members' plays at theaters affiliated with the League of Resident Theaters. It provided for a minimum author's royalty of 5 percent of the gross and established rules about management's participation in subsidiary rights of new plays. The contract was not a product of negotiation between the Guild and LORT, as LORT refused to negotiate. The theaters' management insisted that, as the relationship between a theater and a playwright is not technically that of employer to employee (playwrights retain ownership of their scripts which they merely lease to producers), the Guild could not undertake a union-like function of collective bargaining on behalf of its 7,500 members. Theater representatives announced that their managements would ignore the contract and continue making individual deals with authors. At a party in the Dramatists Guild's offices marking the end of the season, the organization's president, Peter Stone, acknowledged that the contract was not yet in wide use and urged the membership to fight harder for it.

The LORT managements proved also to be formidable opponents of the Society of Stage Directors and Choreographers, beating back most of that union's demands in a rancorous confrontation.

In contrast, Broadway labor relations were fairly placid. The contract covering Equity actors on Broadway was settled without public contention, the terms calling for increases of 5, 4 and 6 percent over the next three years. Also, producers and union representatives made headway on the formulation of a plan to encourage the Broadway production of serious plays. Under the proposal, plays produced in designated houses—probably the Nederlander, the Walter Kerr and the Belasco or Lyceum—would be allowed to operate under modified salaries and royalties. Actors' salaries would be limited to a top of $2,000, budgets to a top of $350,000 and ticket prices to no more than $24.

The aforementioned Walter Kerr Theater is one of two older Broadway theaters that were refurbished and rechristened this season, the Kerr (formerly the Ritz) so designated in honor of the former drama critic of the *Herald Tribune* and the *Times*, who expressed his pleasure at a ceremony featuring excerpts from his writing and highlights from shows he had covered. Two blocks south, the 46th Street Theater was renamed the Richard Rodgers, its lobby decorated with a permanent exhibit devoted to the composer's many accomplishments.

As previously mentioned, David Hare was represented on Broadway this year with *The Secret Rapture*; but the most-discussed piece he produced this season was a letter to *Times* critic Frank Rich. Rich had praised *The Secret Rapture* in its London production under the direction of Howard Davies, but he wrote at length on his belief that the dramatist had hurt his own play by directing it in New York. In response, Hare fired off a letter to Rich which, in this day of fax and copying machines, received wide circulation though Hare refused to authorize its publication. In it, Hare alluded to a recent conversation with *Newsweek* critic Jack Kroll, paraphrasing Kroll's assertion that Rich was writing as if he were simply the critic for some small-town paper, expressing opinions without regard for their consequences. Hare expressed his view that it was wrong for Rich to write without acknowledging that, as first-string critic for the *Times*, his notices have a determining impact on the lives of the shows covered. Specifically, Hare objected to the way Rich phrased his review of *The Secret Rapture*. As Hare saw it, Rich had two options in reviewing the show: to emphasize what was good about the *play*, or to emphasize what was lacking in the *production*. By choosing the latter, Hare insisted, Rich knew he was dooming the show. He further claimed that what he viewed as the consistently bitter temper of Rich's criticism was discouraging theater artists from attempting to produce serious work for Broadway.

Rich wrote a letter in reply which was published without his authorization by a New York weekly named *Seven Days* (which itself folded this season). He insisted that *he* didn't close *The Secret Rapture*, the show's producer did, and went on to point out the fact that he was hardly alone in not writing favorably about it. He also challenged Hare's assertion that his tenure was discouraging serious artists by pointing to a roster of distinguished writers who had recently or would soon see their work on Broadway. Further, he questioned Jack Kroll's judgement in having a conversation with a playwright whose work he was scheduled to review, adding that Hare did no favor to Kroll by making that conversation public.

*THE SECRET RAPTURE*—Blair Brown and Michael Wincott in a scene from David Hare's play, produced on Broadway by New York Shakespeare Festival and the subject of one of the season's major controversies

There were a number of aftershocks to this correspondence, one of which hit Kroll, whose editor at *Newsweek* called him into his office to discuss the appropriateness of criticizing a fellow critic. Kroll was suspended from the magazine for several weeks.

Others also chimed in. Under the classic *Variety* headline, "Ruffled Hare Airs Rich Bitch," theater correspondent Richard Hummler went beyond reporting on the Hare-Rich confrontation to write a sharply-worded attack both on Rich's writing and what Hummler saw as the *Times*'s abuse of its power. Charles Marowitz, a Los Angeles-based playwright-critic (whose play *Sherlock's Last Case* Rich had panned in its Broadway run) continued the attack in *TheaterWeek*, which was in turn rebutted by former New York *Post* critic Martin Gottfried in a subsequent issue. The subject continued to be debated in a variety of symposia and a number of periodicals—except, that is, in the *Times*, which published nothing concerning the controversy in its pages.

Further controversy centered around another member of the *Times* critical staff. Laurie Winer, who had published a number of pieces for the *Wall Street Journal*, was added to the roster of *Times* theater critics. She began by re-reviewing Wendy Wasserstein's *The Heidi Chronicles* on the occasion of the introduction of a new cast, panning a script which the *Times*'s Mel Gussow and almost all of the rest of the critical community (including the Pulitzer Prize judges) had praised. A series of other negative notices under her byline followed. After three months, Miss Winer resigned, though her byline later appeared in the Sunday section with a free-lance piece on Caryl Churchill.

The Tony Awards decision to drop the categories of Best Book and Best Score for 1988–89 was a public concession on the part of the theater establishment that the musical as a form was in trouble. This season, members of this establishment took steps to address the problem. Cameron Mackintosh, the British impresario best known for producing *Les Misérables*, gave the University of Oxford an endowment for the study and development of the form. Stephen Sondheim, the dominant musical dramatist of the post-Rodgers-and-Hammerstein era, was named a visiting professor and travelled to St. Catherine's College to lecture and counsel writers in an advanced workshop.

In the meantime, producer Marty Bell inaugurated New Musicals, a venture designed to offer the creators of works-in-progress the kind of opportunity to revise and adjust their projects that the road offered in days of yore. Based at the Purchase campus of the State University of New York, the announced plan was to present laboratory productions of four shows a year for the next four years. The first four scheduled, collectively budgeted at $9.5 million, were adaptations of the film *My Favorite Year* and the novels *Kiss of the Spider Woman, The Secret Garden* and *Fanny Hackabout Jones*. Among the talents involved were John Kander, Fred Ebb, Terrence McNally, Marsha Norman, Susan Birkenhead, Erica Jong and Harold Prince. Artistic director

Bell conceived the enterprise as a commercial venture, figuring that if one out of every eight shows he produced were a substantial hit, the project would pay for itself. The various unions and guilds negotiated special agreements with the producers in order to keep costs down. As Bell was quoted in *Variety*, "This is truly a partnership among the unions and guilds, the shops, the creators, the financial backers and SUNY-Purchase, who have all agreed that the way to revitalize the American musical theater is to rethink the process." Series tickets were sold to the public, but critics were not invited.

Which brings us to another controversy in which the *Times* figured. When the first offering, *Kiss of the Spider Woman*, began its run, *Times* editors Warren Hogue and Marvin Siegel announced their intention to send critic Frank Rich to evaluate it. Bell and many other members of the theatrical community descended on the *Times* offices to protest, saying that such coverage would frustrate the purpose of the New Musicals project. Hogue and Siegel were not convinced. "This is a show involving some very prominent and interesting people in the American musical theater. It is presented to the public as a commercial enterprise, charging a competitive price, and it's playing in our town," said Hogue. Rich trekked to Purchase and returned with a pan. Several other reviewers followed his lead and came back with mostly negative reports. The future of *Spider Woman* was uncertain at season's end, as was the future of New Musicals. "If the *Times* policy stands," said Bell, "I would recommend to a writer or a director that they do a show right on Broadway instead of coming here. What they did was invade the work process here." Bell let it be known he was considering moving the project to a location outside of the *Times*'s primary market.

All of the above fracases were eclipsed by the battle over the National Endowment for the Arts. Money from the government-funded NEA has to some degree supported most of the major and many of the minor artistic institutions in this country, including a great many theaters. The NEA has never been popular with figures of the religious right such as Pat Robertson and political conservatives such as Sen. Jesse Helms, who believe either that the public till should not support any arts, or that it should support only works which do not offend their sensibilities. The fuss began when Robertson, Helms, *et. al.* discovered that an exhibit of the late photographer Robert Mapplethorpe's work—some of it including graphic homoerotic imagery—was supported in part by the NEA, as was a controversially-titled photograph by Andres Serrano, "Piss Christ." Armed with copies of these provocative works, the NEA's opponents began rallying support for the office's reorganization or dismantlement.

Under pressure from Helms, Congress passed the following amendment: "For Fiscal 1990, none of the funds authorized for the National Endowment for the Arts may be used to promote, disseminate, or produce material which in the judgement of the National Endowment for the Arts may be considered obscene, including but not limited to depictions of sadomasochism, homo-eroticism, the sexual exploitation of children, or individuals engaged in sex acts and which, when taken as a whole, do not have serious literary, artistic, political, or scientific value." Recipients of grants were required to sign pledges agreeing to abide by the amendment's prescriptions. Joseph Papp refused to cash the check for $50,000 allotted to the New York Shakespeare Festival under those restrictions. Similarly, Terrence McNally, in a letter to fellow members of the Dramatists Guild, urged his colleagues not to apply for or accept money on these terms. (Accepting the Hull-Warriner Award for *The Lisbon Traviata*, he observed that both that play and his popular *Frankie and Johnny in the Clair de Lune* might well be considered in violation of the pledge.) Others urged artists to accept the money but to append the phrase "signed under protest" to their signatures. Some also warned that if artists refused to accept the money, this might give ammunition to those who claim that the arts don't need subsidizing.

As the season progressed, the battle intensified. With a vote pending in Congress on whether appropriations for the agency should continue, theater artists joined with artists from other fields in trying to gain public support. Activists distributed petitions, set up special phone numbers and spoke out publicly. Among the more controversial gestures was that of actor Ron Silver, who irritated the Tony Awards television producers by making a speech in the middle of the broadcast in which he reminded the audience that many of the works being honored began their lives in theaters supported by NEA funds.

To turn to less weighty matters, there was the usual crop of squabbles around the Tony Awards, most centering around the nomination of actors in inappropriate categories. What logic, for instance, could support the nomination of Margaret Tyzack in the featured category when her part in *Lettice & Lovage* is substantially longer than that of Mary-Louise Parker in *Prelude to a Kiss*, who was nominated in the leading actress category? Similarly, even with his part in the third act cut, the role of Big Daddy clearly is one of *Cat on a Hot Tin Roof*'s starring roles, and it attracted a name in Charles Durning. The placement of these actors in featured categories may have been urged by their shows' producers so as to give them a better chance at winning. But, being larger roles, they made larger impressions and so put others nominated in their categories at an unfair disadvantage when voting time came. For that matter, such nominations rob actors in genuine supporting roles of the chance of nomination. Had Durning been nominated appropriately in the leading actor category, Larry Bryggman in *Prelude to a Kiss*, Henderson Forsythe in *Some Americans Abroad* or Carl Gordon in *The Piano Lesson* might well have had a shot at the honor. It is also unfortunate, though more understandable, that the rotating repertory nature of *Love Letters*'s run led the Tony Administration Committee to determine that none of its performers would be eligible for nomination. As a member of the Tony Nominating Committee, I would certainly have cast a vote for Kate Nelligan.

The Tony results themselves provided no surprises. Indeed, in a piece in *Newsday* Allan Wallach correctly predicted all of them. The closest thing to an upset was the award for best play to *The Grapes of Wrath*; this may well have been in reaction to the fact that August Wilson had previously won a Tony for *Fences* and that *The Piano Lesson* had already been rewarded with the Pulitzer Prize. Despite the richness of the season, the major prizes from the various organizations tended to cluster around the same recipients. *City of Angels* picked up most of the awards for best musical, *The Grapes of Wrath* and *The Piano Lesson* picked up most of the best-play citations, Tommy Tune and Michael Jeter won everything possible for their work in *Grand Hotel*, Tyne Daly cleaned up similarly for her work in *Gypsy* and Robert Morse collected enough honors to crowd a mantle for his tour de force in *Tru*. The only award that caused me to blink was that for best foreign play given by the New York Drama Critics Circle to Peter Nichols's *Privates on Parade*.

So, yes, I grumble about the narcissism. Still, especially in contrast to the thin season which preceded it, this year must be counted as one filled with memorable performances in the service of adventurous work. May Congress have the wisdom not to cripple the NEA, from whence so many of these good things have flowed.

# A GRAPHIC GLANCE

(*Clockwise from upper left*) Rachel York, Rene Auberjonois, Randy Graff, Scott Waara, Dee Hoty, James Naughton and Gregg Edelman (*on telephone*) in *City of Angels*

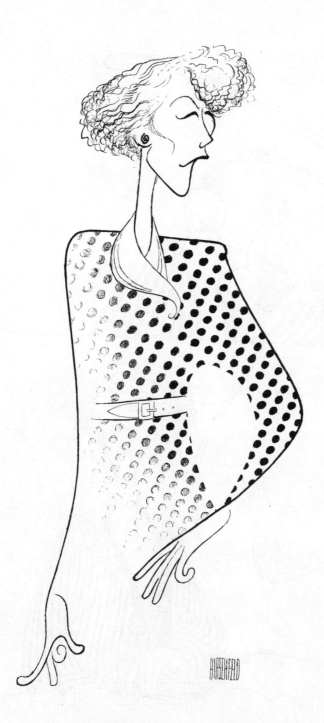

Randy Graff in *City of Angels*

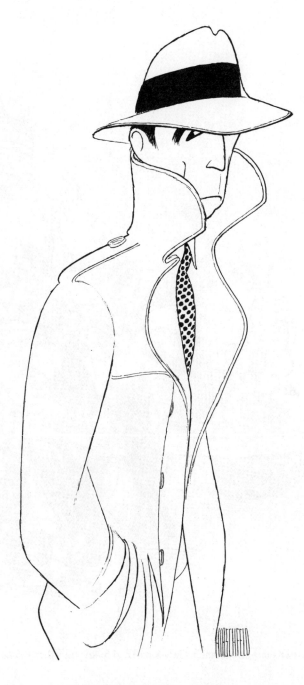

James Naughton in *City of Angels*

Terry Kinney, Lois Smith, Gary Sinise and fellow travellers in *The Grapes of Wrath*

HIRSCHFELD 3

Lois Smith in *The Grapes of Wrath*

Bob Gunton in *Sweeney Todd*

(*Lower left*) Jim Walton and Gretchen Kingsley (*clockwise from upper left*) Michael McCarty,
Bill Nabel, Bob Gunton, David Barron, Beth Fowler and Eddie Korbich in *Sweeney Todd*

Kathleen Turner in *Cat on a Hot Tin Roof*

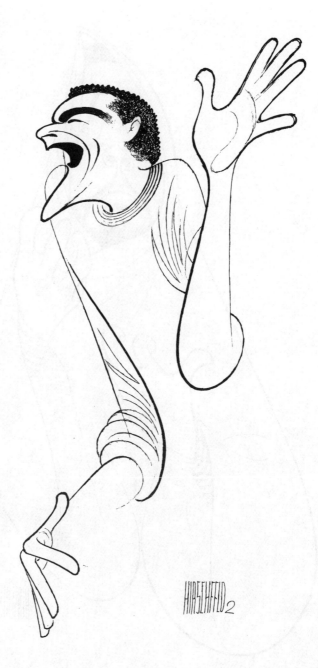

Mandy Patinkin in *Mandy Patinkin in Concert: Dress Casual*

Nathan Lane in *The Lisbon Traviata*

Andy Halliday in *The Lady in Question*

Jonathan Hadary in *Gypsy*

Crista Moore, Tyne Daly, Jonathan Hadary and the three strippers—
Jana Robbins, Barbara Erwin and Anna McNeely—in *Gypsy*

Stewart Granger in *The Circle*

Rex Harrison in *The Circle*

Rex D. Hays, Karen Akers, David Carroll, John Wylie, Liliane Montevecchi,
Jane Krakowski, Yvonne Marceau and Pierre Dulaine, Michael Jeter and Kathi Moss in *Grand Hotel*

Michael Jeter in *Grand Hotel*

Jace Alexander in *Heart of a Dog*

Joseph Daly in *Mastergate*

Ann McDonough, John Dossett, Zach Grenier, Jeff Weiss, Joseph
Daly, Tom McDermott, Melinda Mullins, Jerome Kilty, Wayne
Knight, Daniel von Bargen and Steve Hofvendahl in *Mastergate*

Eric Bogosian in *Sex, Drugs, Rock & Roll*

Stephen Lang in *A Few Good Men*

Lisa Gay Hamilton, S. Epatha Merkerson, Lou Myers, Charles S. Dutton, Carl Gordon, Tommy Hollis and Rocky Carroll (*kneeling*) in *The Piano Lesson*

Mo Gaffney (*top*) and Kathy Najimy in *The Kathy and Mo Show*

Robert Morse in *Tru*

Rita McKenzie in *Call Me Ethel*!

Sophie Maletsky in *Der Ring Gott Farblonjet*

Everett Quinton in *Dr. Jekyll and Mr. Hyde*

Sloane Shelton in *Orpheus Descending*

Frances Conroy, Stephen Vinovich, Jennifer Van Dyck, Mary Beth
Hurt, Michael Wincott and Blair Brown in *The Secret Rapture*

Vanessa Redgrave, Anne Twomey, Tammy Grimes and Kevin Anderson
in *Orpheus Descending*

Michael Siberry in *The Merchant of Venice*

Jean Stapleton in *Mountain Language*

Barnard Hughes in *Prelude to a Kiss*

Ellen Burstyn in *Shirley Valentine*

Nathaniel Parker, Geraldine James, Leigh Lawson and Dustin Hoffman
in *The Merchant of Venice*

Maggie Smith and Margaret Tyzack in *Lettice & Lovage*

Simon Jones in *Privates on Parade*

Maureen McGovern, Suzzanne Douglas, Sting, Alvin Epstein, Georgia
Brown, Ethyl Eichelberger and Josh Mostel in *3 Penny Opera*

Michael Cumpsty, Harold Gould, Stephanie Roth, Paxton Whitehead, Jim Fyfe, Michael Winther and John McMartin in *Artist Descending a Staircase*

James DeMarse in *Cahoots*

Kevin Colson, Ann Crumb, Michael Ball and Kathleen Rowe McAllen in *Aspects of Love*

Henderson Forsythe in *Some Americans Abroad*

(*Clockwise from upper left*) Diane Venora, Peter Francis James, Josef Sommer,
Dana Ivey, Michael Cumpsty, Kevin Kline and Brian Murray in *Hamlet*

Len Cariou in *Mountain*

Jerome Kilty in *The Doctor's Dilemma*

Polly Holliday in *Cat on a Hot Tin Roof*

Betty Garrett in *Meet Me in St. Louis*

Calista Flockhart in *Beside Herself*

Faith Prince in *Jerome Robbins' Broadway*

Sally Mayes in *Closer Than Ever*

Mary-Louise Parker in *The Art of Success*

John Curless in *Progress*

Mike Burstyn in *The Rothschilds*

Paul Provenza in *Only Kidding!*

Tony Roberts in *Jerome Robbins' Broadway*

Marcia Jean Kurtz in *When She Danced*

George Abbott, author and director of *Frankie*

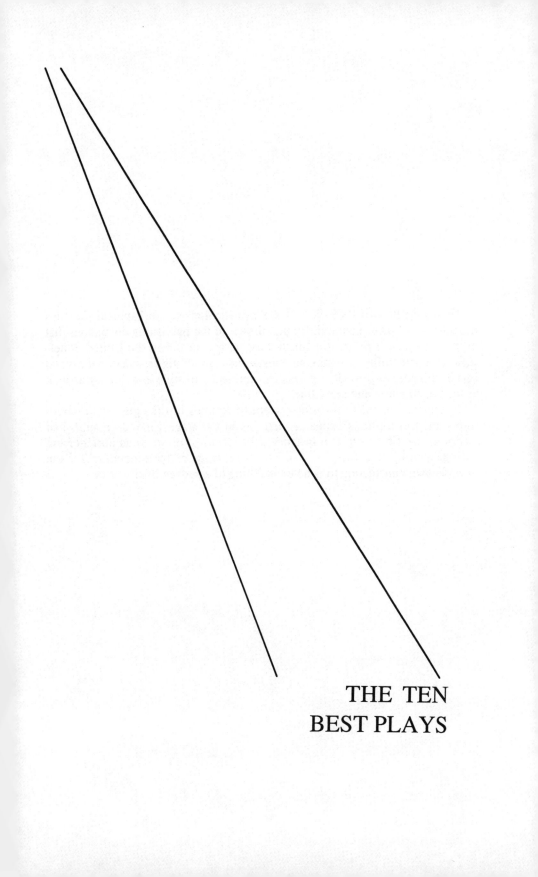

**THE TEN
BEST PLAYS**

Here are details of 1989–90's Best Plays—synopses, biographical sketches of authors and other material. By permission of the publishing companies that own the exclusive rights to publish these scripts in full in the United States, most of our continuities include substantial quotations from crucial/pivotal scenes in order to provide a permanent reference to style and quality as well as theme, structure and story line.

In the case of such quotations, scenes and lines of dialogue, stage directions and descriptions appear *exactly* as in the stage version or published script unless (in a very few instances, for technical reasons) an abridgement is indicated by five dots (. . . . .). The appearance of three dots (. . .) is the script's own punctuation to denote the timing of a spoken line.

# THE LOMAN FAMILY PICNIC

*A Play in Two Acts*

BY DONALD MARGULIES

Cast and credits appear on pages 400–401

*DONALD MARGULIES was born in Brooklyn Sept. 2, 1954. His father was a salesman in a store selling wallpaper, and the future playwright showed an early interest, not in writing, but in the visual arts. After attending public school and John Dewey High School he studied graphic design at Pratt Institute and proceeded to SUNY Purchase where he received his B.F.A. in 1977. But at SUNY he began to take an interest in playwriting—for no particular reason he can put his finger on now—and approached Julius Novick, who was teaching the subject there. Novick asked Margulies if he'd ever written a play, and Margulies replied frankly, "No." Novick nevertheless agreed to sponsor the young man in a playwriting tutorial, "a life-changing event," as Margulies looks back on it now.*

*The first Margulies scripts were put on at SUNY, and in New York he first surfaced OOB with* Luna Park, *a one-act adaptation of a Delmore Schwartz short story, commissioned by Jewish Repertory Theater and staged by them Feb. 5, 1982. There followed* Resting Place *at Theater for the New City (1982),* Gifted Children *at JRT (1983) and finally the full-fledged off-Broadway production of* Found a Peanut *at New York Shakespeare Festival for 33 performances in June 1984.*

*Later that season Margulies was represented at the Quaigh Theater Dramathon with* Who's Holding the Elevator *co-authored with Tony DeNonno; and Manhattan Theater Club produced his* What's Wrong With This Picture? *in previews, but this one was withdrawn before opening and wasn't officially presented until 1988 in a revised version at the Back Alley Theater in Los Angeles, a city which also witnessed the premiere of his* The Model Apartment *at Los Angeles Theater Center in 1989. Meanwhile, in 1987, his* Zimmer *appeared on a program at JRT. His first Best Play,* The Loman Family Picnic, *was produced by MTC on June 20, 1989, for 16 performances.*

*At this writing, Margulies is preparing two commissioned playscripts, one for MTC and one for South Coast Repertory in Costa Mesa, Calif. He is married to a doctor now serving her residence at Bellevue, and they divide their time between New York and New Haven, where Margulies is a visiting lecturer in playwriting at Yale.*

*The following synopsis of* The Loman Family Picnic *was prepared by Jeffrey Sweet.*

*Time: Around 1965*

*Place: Coney Island, Brooklyn, N.Y.*

### ACT I

*Scene 1*

SYNOPSIS: It's three o'clock in the afternoon of a day in October 1965. A 38-year-old woman named Doris sits in the living room of her high-rise Coney Island apartment with a pair of scissors in her hand. Surrounded by her Spanish Provincial furnishings, wearing a housecoat over her pajamas, she is cutting her wedding dress to shreds as she addresses the audience.

"On the day I was married the world showed every sign of coming to an end." Rain, thunder, lightning, hail, "Pearl S. Buck tidal waves." Her mother insisted it was a good sign. But then her mother said sunshine would also have been a good sign. "I began to distrust her." She points to the damage her wedding dress sustained from that day. "Look at this: ruined. From day one. I should've known." Still, she protests, as she continues to shred the dress, she's *very* happy with the way her life has turned out. Two sons. Mitchell, 11, reads way above his grade level. Stewie, also smart, is preparing himself for his bar mitzvah this Saturday, after which there will be "a gala affair starring me." She insists that her husband, Herbie, is not at all threatened by his sons' intelligence. "They aren't showoffs. I don't like showoffs. I raised my boys to stand out but not too much, you know?, otherwise people won't like you any more. Look what happened to the Jews in Europe. Better you should have friends and be popular than be showy and alone. My Aunt Marsha, may she rest in peace, taught me that. She was very popular."

Doris and Herbie's 18th wedding anniversary was yesterday. They didn't celebrate last night. "Herbie had to work, what else is new. I love the way my life has turned out. Did I say that already? On the day I was married the world showed every sign of coming to an end . . . "

Mitchell arrives home from school, surprising Doris, who has lost track of time. She tells him that she's redoing her wedding gown for a Halloween costume; she'll be the Bride of Frankenstein. "You're gonna tear up your wedding gown for a costume?" "I'm not disenchanted with my marriage," she insists, adding that she still loves and is not at all bored by his father, then wanders into speculations as to which parent Mitchell would live with if she and Herbie divorced. Mitchell takes these and his mother's other distracted musings in stride. He has news: the poster he drew for Brotherhood Week— showing a rabbi and a priest and black and white hands shaking—has been selected as one of the finalists for a city-wide competition. It's going to hang in a display at the Lincoln Savings Bank. If his poster wins, he'll get to meet Mayor Lindsay, and his picture will appear in the *Daily News*.

His teacher, Miss Schoenberg, has been very encouraging, saying that he has the potential to go to an Ivy League school—maybe Harvard, Princeton. Doris does not greet this news with enthusiasm.

DORIS: Tell Miss Schoenberg *she* can put you through college.

MITCHELL: She says there are scholarships.

DORIS: Look, sweetheart, we are not Ivy League. We are City College. We are not like those people. City College was invented for people like us. You get a perfectly decent education.

MITCHELL: Whatever happened to the immigrant ideal of education or death?

DORIS: It died in the Depression. Miss Schoenberg is a troublemaker.

MITCHELL: Don't you want me to fulfill my potential? Don't you want me to continue getting "excellents?"

DORIS: Of course I do. But don't let your head get too big, it's unseemly. To be excellent is one thing; to be outstanding is another. We aren't fancy people, we're hand to mouth. We are middle-middle class, smack in the middle.

MITCHELL: But, Mom—

DORIS: Do you want to kill your father completely? He's half-dead just treading water. How would we explain Ivy League to the relatives? They think we're rich already, because we live in this luxurious high-rise; then they'd *really* despise us. We want everyone to love us. Remember what my Aunt Marsha always said, may she rest in peace: Don't go around thinking you're better than everyone else 'cause you'll be alone in the end. Dream, my son, but not too big.

Stewie arrives home now, agitated over this afternoon's session with Mr. Shlosh, the rabbi who is preparing him for his bar mitzvah. He's been working with the rabbi for years without ever having had a conversation with him, so today he decided to try to make human contact. He asked Shlosh what these symbols he's learned to read right to left actually *mean*. Shlosh replied that they mean he will be bar mitzvahed. But Stewie pressed him. "You taught me how to *read* but you didn't teach me how to *understand*! What kind of Jew is that?!" Stewie reports that Shlosh practically had a fit. Stewie tells his mother he's decided he wants out of this bar mitzvah business. Doris doesn't take this well.

DORIS (*infuriated, through gritted teeth*): How dare you do this to me!

STEWIE (*his teeth also gritted*): What?, what am I doing to you?!

DORIS: You know how hard I've been working to make you a beautiful party?!

STEWIE: Me? It's not for me. *Make* your beautiful party! I just won't be there. Tell everybody I got the runs!

DORIS: Don't do this to me, Stewie! Don't make me cancel! We'll lose all our deposits! Is that what you want?! Hm?! Your father's blood money down the drain?! The hall, the band, the flowers?! The caterers?! I already bought my dress, what do you want me to do with it?, hock it? I've spent *days* laying out response cards like solitaire and clipping tables together! This is no time to be a prima donna, Stewie. One more week. That's all I ask. Give me the nachas, then you can do whatever the hell you want. You want to re-nounce Judaism?, renounce Judaism. Become a monk, I don't care.

   *A beat.*

STEWIE (*teeth gritted again*): Remember, Ma, I'm doing this for you. I'll go through with it, and sing nice, and make you proud, and make the relatives cry, but once I'm bar mitzvahed, that's it, Ma. I'm never stepping foot in that place. Never again.

DORIS: Thank you, darling, thank you.

   *She kisses and tickles Stewie; he squeals with delight.*

Mitchell chimes in to tell Stewie about being a finalist in the poster contest. Stewie doesn't bother to fake excitement. Doris turns to the audience and says, "Isn't it wonderful how my boys get along?"

Marcia Jean Kurtz as Doris and Larry Block as Herbie
in Donald Margulies's *The Loman Family Picnic*

*Scene 2*

Around midnight, Herbie, "*a burly 40-year-old, enters wearily, a shopping bag in each hand and newspapers tucked under his arm.*" His family is asleep in the living room in front of a TV set tuned to a station that is signing off. Sarcastically, Herbie announces his return and pretends that they have all rushed to him to shower him with love and appreciation for the day he has spent busting his balls for them. They snore on as he talks about what a madhouse it was at work; he was so busy selling lighting fixtures he didn't have time to go to the bathroom all day. "I wouldn't be surprised if my bladder just *exploded* one of these days, pshhhoo, like a water balloon!" He takes off his shoes, revolted by the smell of his own feet.

It is this smell which finally rouses Doris, who in turn rouses her sons and encourages them to greet their father. Mitchell obeys orders to kiss him, and

Stewie raises an accordion to rush through a rendition of "Lady of Spain." Doris urges Mitchell to tell about his poster being a finalist. Herbie is unable to take in the implications of this great honor. "Tell him about Mayor Lindsay," says Doris. Mitchell repeats that if he wins, he gets to meet Lindsay. "Oh," says Herbie, adding, "I didn't vote for him."

Herbie wearily sits down at the kitchen table as Doris places in front of him his dinner—a dietetic tuna dish Herbie obviously loathes. They make brief, exhausted small talk. *"She sighs; her boredom and despair are palpable but she continues to sit in silence, struggling to stay awake while watching him eat . . . . ."*

A shift in the lighting signals that the play has moved into a fantasy zone. Suddenly, the two are speaking animatedly and with enormous affection, *". . . . . relating to one another, as old friends, stories they've never before shared, each telling how the other died."* Herbie's version of Doris's death has her having a heart attack while she lies next to him in bed. He calls the emergency number, paramedics arrive with red lights flashing, they open her top ("and I wasn't even embarrassed 'cause these guys are professionals, I thought, they do this all the time"). He hovers, waiting for her to come to and say, "What the hell happened, Herbie?" Only she doesn't. Doris listens to his story raptly, appreciating his obvious concern.

And now it's her turn. "Well, *you*," she says, "you took forever." Herbie laughs as she narrates his end, the "longest deathbed scene in history." He was in the hospital a long time, hooked up to all sorts of things. The waiting took its toll on her. "I thought I myself would die of exposure to weeks of fluorescent lighting and hospital food." "You're funny," says Herbie with affection, and she continues, telling how she asked him, in his hospital bed, if he wanted to die. He nodded.

HERBIE: I did?
DORIS: Yes, and then something remarkable happened to your face.
HERBIE: What.
DORIS: It lost all the tensed-up lines in your forehead and round your mouth. And your features looked young and smooth, like when you were a G.I. You were Claude Rains turning visible again, for the last time, before my very eyes. The old Herbie came back, the *young* Herbie, the Herbie before *everything*, *my* Herbie, smooth of brow and cute of nose . . . The face of my oldest of friends came into focus out of the fog of machines and sour odors . . . I got you back for a second, Herbie, so letting you go wasn't so bad.
        *Herbie holds her hand; they look at one another for a beat. He remembers something.*
HERBIE: Oh, and the part I thought you'd love:
DORIS: What.
HERBIE: While they were pumping away at you?

DORIS: Uh huh . . . ?

HERBIE: The doorbell rang. The schmuck from downstairs.

DORIS: Friedberg?

HERBIE: The schmuck, right?

DORIS: Yeah. What did *he* want?

HERBIE: Wait. "What the hell kind of racket's going on up here," he says, "you know what time it is?!!" Look, I said, my wife just passed away.

DORIS (*amused*): Uy vey.

HERBIE: "Oh yeah?," the schmuck says, "Oh yeah? Well you should hear what it sounds like downstairs!"

They howl with laughter, sharing the joke. Now the lights change. They are back in reality. Doris yawns. She gets up, prodding Stewie to bed, and tells Mitchell to keep Herbie company. They sit quietly for a second, then Herbie suggests they go out and toss around a football. Mitchell looks at him with disbelief. Herbie tells him it was a joke.

Mitchell turns to the audience to tell us how Miss Schoenberg had the class read *Death of a Salesman*, this play Arthur Miller wrote about a family that took place in this very neighborhood "a long time ago." The family had two sons, a mother and a salesman father. "I read it really fast to see if there were any real similarities, but no: Willy Loman doesn't sell lighting fixtures." Instead of writing a conventional book report, Mitchell was motivated to do a special project—a musical comedy version of *Death of a Salesman* called *Willy!* "With an exclamation point. You know, like *Fiorello! Oliver!*" He's finished some of the songs, including one for Biff and Happy called "Dad's a Little Weird." Mitchell sings some of it to us. "Well, it's a start. What do you think?"

## Scene 3

Doris is up in the middle of the night, fretting, smoking a cigarette, complaining about Herbie's snoring. The thought of leaving him tantalizes. But no, they have to stay together at least till the bar mitzvah is over. She drifts into her obsession with *A Star Is Born*, how she would love to have the opportunity to show the nobility Judy Garland did at the end, after James Mason walked into the ocean. "Now, if *Herbie* walked into the waves at Coney Island . . . If he walked into the ocean à la James Mason and made me a widow, there's no question I'd go through with the bar mitzvah. I'd wear black sequins and clutch my boys to me with my head held high like Jackie Kennedy in the rotunda. *Then* I'd go through with it solo. But a divorce?"

Fantasy again as Doris's dead Aunt Marsha, a 23-year-old beauty with a page-boy cut, climbs down onto the terrace outside Doris's apartment. Marsha looks around, noticing the Spanish decor with some irony. Doris tells

Marsha that Marsha's taste and ideas have continued to influence her. Always the question—what would Aunt Marsha think of this? "You never liked it when I went too fancy. Not too fancy, you don't want to be too fancy. You taught me that." Doris confesses that she's 38 now. Marsha would have *hated* 38. Maybe Marsha had the right idea to check out young.

Marsha changes the subject. She wants to see the bar mitzvah dress. Doris hesitates at first, but when Doris displays it, Marsha likes it very much. Doris is overjoyed. Marsha isn't entirely thrilled with where Doris is living, however. She always imagined for Doris a place with trees. Doris insists she's very happy to be here in this high-rise apartment. She and Herbie were the first ones in this building.

DORIS: You should've seen the place we lived *before*. I don't know how we did it. A slum; the neighborhood was going to hell. But *here*! Hot water always. Rec room. Elevators that work. Security patrolled by German shepherds. A Waldbaum's that delivers. This is a big step for us. *Luxury*. I'm *telling* you. Like fancy people. I hope not *too* fancy.

MARSHA: To think this is Brooklyn . . .

DORIS: Oh, we worked very hard for all this, Marsh, you don't know. This is progress. I love our high-rise ghetto. *Look* out there. I can't wait for Hannukah; Hannukah looks like Kristalnacht here: a bonfire of orange-red menorah bulbs burning in thousands of windows. A brick wall of electric flame! We're not alone. You know how good that feels? They moved us up, closer to heaven. Jews upon Jews who are glad to be here, who came as far as we did, from Flatbush, from Williamsburg, from East New York. Jews who escaped the Nazis, who escaped their relatives, who fled the schvartzes. Millions of miles of wall-to-wall carpeting that, if placed end to end, would reach from here to Jupiter and back. Instead of stoops they built these little terraces. Sometimes I have to restrain myself from doing the cha-cha over the edge just to see what it would feel like going down. (*A beat; a confession.*) I hung my last sconce today. I'm done decorating, Marsh. I bought my last tschatchke. My life is over.

Marsha tries to comfort Doris, remembering her when she was a baby. Marsha was about to turn eight when Doris was born. She thought of Doris as a little sister. She taught her everything she knew. "You ruined me, Marsh," says Doris. "Just myself," says Marsha. "I ruined myself." She partied on the wrong side of the tracks, enjoying the fast life, enjoying the succession of men and enjoying the heartache she gave her mother. "I ruined *myself*, kiddo. Nobody did me in but me. I didn't mean to take no casualties."

Doris tells her that she compensated for Marsha's bad ways by being very, very good. And here she is, married, in a room she decorated Spanish herself.

"I want you to be proud of me," she tells Marsha. "I love my life, I love my life . . . " Marsha holds Doris, rocks her gently as the lights dim.

*Scene 4*

An alarm clock wakes Mitchell and Stewie in their bedroom (suggested by a bunk bed behind a scrim). Mitchell looks into the living room and sees his father, stopped in the middle of dressing for work, sitting with one sock on and the other in his hand. "He's staring again," he tells Stewie. And now they hear him talking. To no one. Stewie complains that every morning lately Mitchell has been getting up to watch his father in this state, waking Stewie in the process. "I'm sorry . . . I thought you were interested . . . " says Mitchell.

Herbie begins to talk. Something has happened to his memory. He can't remember what dreams he had. He can't remember the names of the buddies he had in the army. Family dates are a muddle—when his kids were born, how many years he's been married. Details from old movies—these remain vivid, " . . . but I don't remember my father even shaking my hand." He remembers being poor. He remembers the Depression and thinking that the Army in wartime was an improvement. After the Army came marriage, kids, his job. " . . . And I go through every day with my eyes shut tight and holding my breath, till the day is over and I can come home. To what? What kind of home is left to come home to by the time I come home?" He knows he's drifting, and he's fearful of saying something stupid. Mitchell asks Stewie, "Was he always like this? Did he ever have anything to say?"

HERBIE: . . . . . It seems to me, in the days when I *would* say what was on my mind, I'd be shot down an awful lot. The more shot down you get, the less likely you are to say what's on your mind . . . It kills you after a while, thinking all the time how . . . (*A beat.*) You don't even pay attention what's being said any more 'cause you're too busy worrying how you might come off.

MITCHELL (*sighs*): Boy . . . (*He gathers his schoolbooks.*)

HERBIE (*to us*): So I shut up a long time ago. It was a decision I made after something happened, something I don't remember what. I remember deciding well, fuck-'em-all one day, and Doris has handled it ever since. I let her do the talking. What the hell, I save my breath.

STEWIE (*to Mitchell*): Where you going?

MITCHELL: In.

STEWIE: Well . . . might as well practice . . . (*Stewie picks up his Haftarah books and sings softly through the rest of the scene.*)

HERBIE (*to us*): I'm still waiting for her, for somebody, to notice and ask: What's up, Herbie? We'll all drop dead first.

    *Mitchell, schoolbooks in hand, tentatively enters the living room. Herbie senses his presence and looks up and sees him. Pause.*

MITCHELL (*in explanation*):  Cereal.
>*Pause. They continue to look at one another.*
HERBIE (*finally*):  That's *good*. It's *good* you eat breakfast.
>*A beat. Mitchell nods, starts for the kitchen, but stops.*
MITCHELL:  Um . . . Dad?
HERBIE (*turns; expectantly*):  Yeah, son?
>*A beat. Mitchell, shakes his head "nothing," shrugs and exits to the kitchen. Herbie watches him go. We hear Stewie practicing his Hebrew as Herbie finishes dressing. Lights fade to black.*

*Scene 5*

Halloween night.  Mitchell is dressed in a skeleton costume.  Stewie is made up as the Hunchback of Notre Dame à la Charles Laughton.  The two are eager to go.  Doris yells from offstage, "You will *wait* for your mother!!  I gave you life!!"  Herbie enters, home early from work for once.  He looks at the boys' costumes, and the fact that it's Halloween registers.  They tell him that Doris is going to join them.  "You're going trick-or-treating, Doris?" he calls to her.  "So?" she responds from the next room.  Herbie doesn't pursue the topic.

He has news.  He tells Mitchell that today a man came into the lighting fixtures room, asked him all kinds of questions.  Herbie told this man—a Mr. Fred Werner of House and Home Stores, Incorporated—about his philosophy regarding how to lay out a lighting fixture showroom.  He and Mr. Werner got along very well together.  Werner was impressed by Herbie's ideas; so impressed, in fact, that Werner wants Herbie to relocate to Albuquerque and manage all four of the House and Home showrooms there.  "Is that a compliment or what?  You see what he thinks of your dad?  That's a big responsibility."  Mitchell offers him restrained congratulations.  All Stewie can hear is the possibility of having to go elsewhere.

HERBIE:  I didn't say yes. I said I would think about it.
STEWIE (*calls*):  Ma, Daddy wants us to move to New Mexico.
HERBIE:  I didn't say that, I said I would think about it.
DORIS (*off; overlap*):  Not New Mexico. There are no Jewish people in New Mexico.
HERBIE (*calls*):  This guy Fred Werner says the climate's gorgeous, year round.
DORIS (*off*):  Werner? That's a German name, Werner. There are Indians in New Mexico. And Germans.
HERBIE (*calls*):  But isn't it nice he wants me?
DORIS (*off*):  We just furnished, Herbie. We're throwing a bar mitzvah. We have *people* here, our people are *here*.

HERBIE (*calls*): But isn't it nice he wants me to think about it?

DORIS (*off*): Very nice.

> *Doris enters dressed in her tattered wedding gown, her hair teased wildly, her face monstrous with makeup. She presents herself with a flourish, laughing madly.*

Ta dahhh!

> *The boys love it and clamor around her.*

STEWIE: Ma! Wow!

MITCHELL: You look great! Boy, everybody's gonna flip!

DORIS (*to us*): I'm telling you, this is inspired. I'll go around with the boys to all the neighbors, and they won't know who I am. They'll think I'm just another crazy kid out trick-or-treating. People always mistake me for their older sister, that's how young I look. When I take the boys to the movies, the matron makes us sit in the children's section; I don't even bother to argue. I was married young. Eighteen. Well, twenty. I'm not obsessed with age. (*To Herbie.*) Would you've recognized me on the street? I bet not.

Herbie recognizes the wedding dress. He is hurt, incredulous. How could she do this? "The dress you wore to your wedding. It's supposed to mean so much. How does a girl rip—" She doesn't understand why he's upset. They have no daughter, so there was nobody to pass it along to. Besides, it was ruined the day of the wedding. She thinks he's lost his sense of humor. Can't he see what a good joke this is?

Herbie is stunned, overcome with sadness. Doris is puzzled by his attitude. Stewie goes into the hall to ring for the elevator, but Mitchell stays behind to watch his parents. Doris reminds Herbie to eat the dietetic tuna dish she left for him. She is about to leave for her Halloween romp when she turns and asks him to sing "Autumn Leaves" for her. "What?" says Herbie. Stewie calls out to her to get a move on. On her way to the door, she seeks reassurance from Herbie. "You were only kidding about New Mexico. Right?" "Sure," says Herbie quietly. Doris says goodbye and exits.

Herbie goes to the kitchen and finds the tuna dish. He toys with it a bit, then pushes it away, disgusted, turning for comfort instead to a half gallon of fudge-swirl ice cream which he consumes with a vengeance as he watches TV.

Mitchell steps into a light and addresses the audience. He's been thinking more about his musical. It needs an up number in the second act—maybe a scene with all of the Lomans on a picnic in Prospect Park. "Everybody's young and happy." Most of the supporting characters will frolic there, too— Charley, Bernard, the woman from Boston (in disguise), even Willy's dead brother Ben. And Willy will be making franks on a barbecue and singing a song about what a great day it is for a picnic. It will be a number about the Loman family having a perfect day, singing in harmony, suffused with the joy of being alive. Mitchell is very happy about having come up with this picnic idea. He loves picnics. "We never go on any picnics," he says.

*Curtain.*


## ACT II

*Scene 1*

In "*the suggestion of a room in a fancy catering establishment,*" the family is posing for a series of photographs; Herbie and the boys wearing rented tuxes and yarmulkes. Doris in a chiffon dress with a fur wrap. Between the unseen photographer's flash shots are vignettes in which members of the family either confide in the audience or trade comments with each other:

Doris exults in how good she looks. It's not only a rite-of-passage for Stewie, it's one for her—today she becomes a middle-aged lady. "I'll show them middle-aged!" she says. "I'm not in the least concerned with getting older."

Herbie has his concerns. Taking the day off is costing him a day's pay at the store. "I take off enough Saturdays, they could fire me." As they smile for a pose, Doris tells Herbie not to worry. Herbie continues to worry.

Stewie confides in us his relief that the ceremony is over. Now that he doesn't have to go to Hebrew school any more, he can play after school with his friends.

Doris gives us a detailed summary of the party—the dance band, the open bar, the clever food. "A hundred and sixty-seven people, including four of Stewie's closest friends." Also a lot of relatives, some of whom she hasn't seen since she got married. "Now they're seeing my son bar mitzvahed. Isn't it beautiful how life goes on?"

Mitchell tells us he's nervous at the prospect of having to sing in front of so many people when it's time for his bar mitzvah. Stewie tells us he did real well. "My voice cracked only once, but it sounded like I did it for effect. I brought down the house."

Herbie remembers that his bar mitzvah was paltry in comparison.

Stewie thinks about all the loot he's going to clear in bar mitzvah gifts. He knows what he's going to spend it on—an electric guitar, an amplifier and a lot of phonograph records.

Herbie wonders if maybe they haven't gone overboard on the party. Doris tells him it looks bad to cut corners on something like this. Looking around the room, she gets excited about the people beginning to arrive. Some of them only she can see—relatives who died in Germany during the war, a cousin who died in the Triangle Factory Fire. And, of course, Aunt Marsha. "Boy," she says, "they're really coming out for Stewie's bar mitzvah!"

*Scene 2*

That night, in their living room, the family is still high from the excitement of the bar mitzvah. Stewie opens the envelopes, and he and Mitchell cheer as they count the checks and savings bonds. Herbie eats chopped liver he brought home from the party. Doris continues to exult in how well everything went and what a good impression she believes she made. She tries to distract Herbie from the chopped liver (which he insists is the *best* he's ever tasted). She wants him to get up and dance with her. He doesn't want to. Hurt, she turns to Stewie, trying to tickle him into agreeing to dance. A giggling Stewie resists; he's still concentrating on his haul. Mitchell steps forward. *He'll* dance with Doris. They take position. "Ready?" asks Doris.

> *Mitchell nods shyly; while looking down at their feet, Doris leads him in a cha-cha. She occasionally offers words of encouragement ("Good . . . Watch . . .") Herbie and Stewie, pretending not to care, soon find themselves looking at Mitchell and Doris with growing resentment; their eyes meet for a moment, but they look away in embarrassment. Doris playfully sticks her tongue out at Herbie. Fade out.*

*Scene 3*

Some time later, Herbie and Stewie are alone. Herbie wants to know how much Stewie cleared. $2,375. Herbie's impressed. And proud. Stewie did well. Not just in the money department. "You were proud? Of me?" Stewie asks. Of course, says Herbie. A son becoming a man. Makes you feel things. Herbie can't quite describe what. But it's something to do with Herbie being in the middle of his own life, looking at Stewie entering adulthood. Something about being aware that life doesn't go on forever. "This creates a feeling in you," says Herbie. "You wish . . ." But he can't put it into words.

Herbie wants to look at Stewie's stack of checks, cash and savings bonds. Stewie holds it up and waves it in display. Herbie asks what his plans are. Stewie talks about records and an electric guitar. No, specifically Herbie wants to know where he's going to *put* the money now. The bank doesn't open till Monday. Stewie figures he'll keep it in his room. Herbie doesn't think this is a good idea. Something could *happen* to it. Stewie doesn't understand why Herbie is worried. Herbie puts out his hand. He wants to *feel* the money.

Stewie reluctantly gives Herbie the stack. Herbie muses on it. "I don't think I ever in my life held this much money at once. Except for maybe a day's receipts." Stewie wants his money back. Herbie continues: "You know how many weeks it would take me to make that? *Weeks*. I take home a hundred and fourteen bucks a week. *You* figure it out. One-fourteen. Figure it out; you're smart." Stewie doesn't want to figure. Herbie tells him: this much money would take him almost half a year to make. Stewie wants to go to his room.

> *Stewie extends his hand for the money. Pause; they look at one another for a long time.*

HERBIE: No, son.

STEWIE: *No?*

HERBIE: I'm gonna put it in my drawer.

STEWIE: Why?

HERBIE: It'll be safe there. You know my drawer, I got all my valuables.

STEWIE: Daddy . . .

HERBIE: What, you don't trust me? It'll be safe in my drawer, believe me. Safer in my drawer than under your *pillow.*

STEWIE: I wasn't gonna put it under my pillow . . .

HERBIE: Whatever.

STEWIE: It's my money.

HERBIE: It's not yours.

STEWIE: What do you mean not mine? It's my bar mitzvah! All the cards say my name!

HERBIE: I mean it's not yours to *spend.*

STEWIE (*going through discarded envelopes*): "For Stewie," "For Stewie on his bar mitzvah."

HERBIE (*overlap*): I know, I know. I mean it's not *your* money, it's *our* money.

STEWIE: How is it ours? It's my bar mitzvah!

HERBIE: What we have to do: sign the checks and I'll countersign them.

STEWIE: *How is it ours?*

HERBIE: You're a minor. A kid.

STEWIE: Today I am a man! You even said!

HERBIE: You don't understand something, son.

STEWIE: No, I understand.

HERBIE: We got a misunderstanding.

STEWIE: YOU'RE TAKING MY MONEY!

HERBIE: Oh, shut up. Who the hell you think is *paying* for this thing? Hm? You think Rockefeller?

> *Mitchell, in his pajamas, watches from the foyer.*

STEWIE: I thought *you.*

HERBIE: *Me?* With *what?*

STEWIE: I don't know. You're the father.

HERBIE: With what am I supposed to be paying for this with? Hm? Do I have the money for this kind of thing?

STEWIE: I don't know.

HERBIE: How would I have that kind of money? Schmuck. Think about it. I told you what I take home.

STEWIE: Yeah ...

HERBIE: So where am I getting the money to throw *you* a fancy party? (*Stewie shrugs. A beat.*) The gifts!

STEWIE: You mean with the *gifts*?

HERBIE: Yeah. That's how we have to do it: what comes in has to go right out again. Didn't you *know* that?

STEWIE: No.

Now Herbie goes through the bills for the party. Even including the gift money, Herbie will still have to come up with another two grand. Stewie offers to loan him some of the money. This infuriates Herbie. Who's the father, after all?

STEWIE: Why didn't you tell me this before?! Why didn't you tell me I'd have to pay for my own bar mitzvah?!

HERBIE: Why didn't I *tell* you? I thought you'd figure it out for yourself.

STEWIE: So why did we do this? I didn't want it.

HERBIE: Why do we *do* this?, everybody does it.

STEWIE: My friend Jeffrey ...

HERBIE: How would it look if we didn't throw you a bar mitzvah?

STEWIE: I don't know.

HERBIE: It would look very funny. Like something was wrong.

STEWIE: Isn't something wrong?

HERBIE: Hm?

STEWIE: You mean it would've looked like we couldn't afford it, so you made one anyway, even though we couldn't afford it?

HERBIE: Don't open a mouth like that to me.

STEWIE: But isn't it true?

HERBIE: Don't open a mouth.

STEWIE (*overlap*): We couldn't afford it. Say it. We couldn't afford it but you did it anyway and *I* have to pay for something I didn't ask for in the first place!

HERBIE (*enraged, he shakes Stewie violently*): YOU THINK I WANT YOUR MONEY?!!

MITCHELL (*approaches timidly*): Daddy ...

HERBIE (*to Mitchell*): Get outta here. (*To Stewie, while shaking him.*) YOU THINK I LIKE HAVING TO DO THIS?!!

DORIS (*calls from offstage*): I hear body-drops in there!

STEWIE (*overlap*): YOU MADE A MISTAKE AND *I* HAVE TO PAY FOR IT!

MITCHELL: Daddy, stop ...

HERBIE (*to Mitchell*):  Get *away* I said.

STEWIE (*overlap*):   WHY SHOULD I HAVE TO PAY FOR YOUR MISTAKES?  IT ISN'T FAIR!—

DORIS (*off*):  I hear body-drops!

STEWIE:  —I'M JUST A KID!

HERBIE:  UH!  *NOW* YOU'RE A KID!  *NOW* YOU'RE A KID!

MITCHELL (*tugging on Herbie*):  Daddy . . .

HERBIE (*to Mitchell*):  I TOLD YOU—(*Pushes him.*)

STEWIE (*adrenalin rushing madly*):  HEY!  DON'T YOU TOUCH *HIM.* YOU HEAR ME?  (*Swipes at Herbie with his fist.*)  DON'T YOU TOUCH MY BROTHER!

HERBIE:  YOU WANT TO FIGHT?  HM?  YOU WANT TO KILL ME?

> *Stewie and Herbie are throwing punches; Doris comes in.*

DORIS:  Boys!  What the—Herbie!  Stop that!

HERBIE (*still sparring*):  *I* should stop?!  He started!

DORIS:  Herbie!  What's the matter with you?!

STEWIE (*throwing punches; nearly hysterical*):  HE HATES US, MOMMY!  HE HATES US!

HERBIE (*that did it; he's going berserk*):  YOU THINK I DON'T LOVE YOU?!!  YOU THINK I DON'T *LOVE* YOU?!!!

> *Doris puts her arms protectively around the shaken boys.*

DORIS:  Herbie, shush!  The house is shaking!

HERBIE (*jabbing at Stewie*):  I DON'T LOVE YOU?!!

DORIS (*shielding Stewie*):  DON'T HURT HIM!

HERBIE:  LOOK AT YOU WITH YOUR PRECIOUS BOYS!  WHAT DO *I* GET, HM?!  (*Storms off to bedroom, screaming.*)  WHO DO *I* HAVE! WHAT DO *I* HAVE!

> *Doris has her arms around both whimpering boys when Herbie re-*
> *turns carrying a dresser drawer.*

(*Now at a terrifying pitch.*)  EVERYTHING I HAVE IS HERE IN THIS DRAWER!  EVERYTHING I OWN IS RIGHT HERE!  I COULD GET THE HELL OUT OF HERE LIKE *THAT!*

DORIS:  Herbie, shhh . . .

HERBIE (*overlap*):  WHAT DO I *HAVE*?!  WHAT'S *MINE*?!  THIS MUCH SPACE IN THE CLOSET?!  One suit?!  You can *keep* the suit; I don't give a damn about that suit; I hate suits; you made me buy that suit.

DORIS (*quietly*):  I thought you needed—

HERBIE:  DONATE IT TO GOODWILL!  MAKE BELIEVE I DIED! WEAR IT FOR HALLOWEEN!  WHAT DO I *HAVE!*  I HAVE NOTHING! I HAVE SHIT!  I HAVE THE TOILET FOR TEN MINUTES IN THE MORNING!  I DON'T EVEN HAVE *YOU!*

DORIS:  Herbie . . .

HERBIE:  LOOK AT YOU!  LOOK WHO GETS *YOU!*

Marcia Jean Kurtz as Doris and Michael Miceli
as Mitchell in *The Loman Family Picnic*

Herbie tears through the dresser drawer. *This* is all he has. Old under-
wear, socks with holes in them, cufflinks. "THIS IS ME?! THIS IS MY
LIFE! THIS DRAWER IS MY WHOLE LIFE RIGHT HERE; THIS
DRAWER!" He hurls the drawer down and slams out of the apartment.

And suddenly—a change. A painted backdrop falls, lights shift, music begins. Mitchell is alone and starts to sing. And quickly it becomes apparent
that he's singing from his musical version of *Death of a Salesman*—the picnic
scene. His song is an up-tempo ode to what fun they could all have in the
park. (This and all the songs are colored by an 11-year-old's grasp of the
conventions of musical comedy circa the late 1950s and early 1960s.)

Now Stewie enters *"wearing a yarmulke, a varsity sweater over his
tuxedo and reading his Haftarah booklet."* He sings of his bad fortune, how
nothing turns out right. Then the music shifts to a soft-shoe as Stewie sings,
"Something funny's going on/Something funny with our dad/I don't mean
something funny ha-ha/I mean it's something funny-sad." Mitchell, trying to
keep up with Stewie's dance, joins in and they continue to sing about their

worry for their father's mental condition. Mitchell wonders if maybe they should take away from Dad stuff with which he could do himself injury.

Doris has entered during this, and she sails into her musical contribution.

DORIS (*sings*):
  Attention!
  Attention!
  You must pay attention
  To such a man as your dad.
  In his soul I know where
  Ev'ry nook and cranny is.
  You just don't understand
  The sort of man
  He is.

  He's not a bad man
  He's not a great man.
  Yes, he may even be a truly
  Second-rate man.
  Call him good, call him bad.
  That's just fine—
  He's mine.

Herbie enters, carrying the Willy Loman trademark valises. He sets them down and begins a frenetic vaudeville turn about what a great day he had at the store, singing about "shaking all those clammy hands and cracking bad jokes." His forced bouyancy gives way to a confession of desperation and exhaustion. He collapses in the middle of his song. Doris goes to him and sings a song which owes more than a little to Rodgers and Hammerstein.

DORIS (*sings*):
  Give me your feet,
  I'll rub them.
  Hand me your feet,
  I'll soothe your aching soles.
  I promise I'll rid
  Your socks of their holes,
  Put your feet in my hands,
  With your feet in my hands,
  You'll never walk alone.

Mitchell returns to a reprise of the picnic song, joined by the others singing fragments of their songs until the effect is one of numbing cacophony. With some effort (this is his fantasy after all), Mitchell stills the others' voices, and they exit. Alone on the stage, he sings a bittersweet little reprise of the picnic song.

MITCHELL (*sings*):
    It was a perfect day
    For a picnic,
    Till the clouds made the sky turn dark.
    There'll be another day
    We'll have our chance to play.
    Hey, folks, what do you say?
    Maybe some other day
    I'll take us all away
    To a picnic
    In the
    Park!

*Scene 4*

Late at night, Doris is having another fantasy conversation with Aunt Marsha. Marsha knows what Doris should do: "You gotta leave the bum." Life is too short to waste on Herbie, who is obviously "a dead-end proposition." Doris is doubtful. Divorce? That's not something that their people do. "Jewish people don't go their separate ways, they stick it out even if they're miserable." Marsha continues to insist that Doris should grab the kids and walk. The sound of the key turning in the front door hastens Marsha's exit.

Herbie enters. He and Doris look at each other. Then Herbie tells her where he's been since he stormed out. The movies. *Born Free*, to be specific. "About lions yearning to breathe free, or something." He didn't think much of the picture. He feel asleep. He ate Bon Bons.

And now Doris unloads her bomb. She's finished. The marriage is over. She's all used up.

DORIS: . . . . . I can't prop you up and make you feel good when you should feel lousy. I can't cover for you and make excuses. I can't run your public relations any more, Herbie. Eighteen years; that's not so bad. Nothing to be ashamed of. Who *says* you have to be married to just one person your whole life? Yeah, at this rate you still have time to squeeze in another couple of eighteen-year marriages. You and the *next* eighteen-year lady, the two of you'll have a great time, I promise, Herbie. She'll either pick up where I left off and be your mother all over again or, if you're lucky . . . I can't make up for your childhood any more. And neither can the boys. I'm sorry, my job is done. I quit. (*A beat.*) I packed up your drawer in the American Tourister like I'm sending you off to camp for the last time. Kiss the boys goodbye. We'll be in touch.

The lights shift. In a moment, we're back at Herbie's entrance again. He repeats his *Born Free* speech. Only this time, instead of pushing Herbie out of her life, Doris is determined to check out of life itself. "It's the going *on* that's painful, not the going," she says. She'd just as soon be like Marsha—living in people's memories as a tragic, gorgeous figure who never had the chance to fulfill the enormous promise of her life. This apartment on the tenth floor of the high-rise "is as far as they'll let us go," says Doris. She feels stuck, trapped. "There's nowhere to go but out the window." So saying, she walks onto the terrace, climbs over the railing and leaps.

The lights shift. Herbie's entrance again. *Born Free* and Bon Bons again. Doris's reaction this time is one of enormous relief.

DORIS (*runs into his arms; tearfully*): Don't ever run out on me like that again, you hear me?! I never felt so lonely in my life! How dare you do that to me?! When I married you I thought, here is a man who'll never leave me, and when you did, it was like a part of me was stolen, my leg, my child. I need you to take care of. Who'm I going to take care of if you leave me? The boys need me less and less; what happens when they don't need me at all? I need you, Herbie. Don't let me go. Please don't let me go.

They sway together, and Herbie begins to sing "Autumn Leaves" to her. The two boys rush in now and throw their arms around him—a picture of family reconciliation and harmony.

The lights shift again. And again it's Herbie, *Born Free* and Bon Bons.

And now, after the three "dramatic" possibilities that have just been enacted, we get reality:

DORIS: Bon Bons? That's why I bust my chops making you Weight Watchers? I made you a tuna plate for when you got home. Eat it and eliminate your fruit today and tomorrow. Bon Bons! (*As she goes to the kitchen.*) Sit.

> Herbie does; Doris returns with his tuna plate, sets it down in front of him and sits beside him as he begins to eat. Finally, he speaks.

HERBIE (*sheepishly*): Doris, look, I'm sorry about—
DORIS: Don't. (*A beat. Quietly.*) Don't.

> A beat. Herbie resumes eating, and Doris watches in silence, as the lights fade very slowly. Curtain.

# LOVE LETTERS

## A Play in Two Acts

## BY A. R. GURNEY

Cast and credits appear on pages 369, 405–406

*A.R. GURNEY (who recently dropped "Jr." from his byline) was born Nov. 1, 1930 in Buffalo, N.Y., the son of a realtor. He was educated at St. Paul's School and Williams College, where he received his B.A. in 1952. After a stint in the Navy, he entered Yale Drama School in 1956 and emerged with an M.F.A. after studying playwriting in seminars conducted by Lemist Esler, Robert Penn Warren and John Gassner. His first production, the musical* Love in Buffalo, *took place at Yale in 1958.*

*"Pete" Gurney's first New York production of record was the short-lived* The David Show *off Broadway in 1968, repeated in an off-Broadway program with his* The Golden Fleece *the following season. His* Scenes From American Life *premiered in Buffalo in 1970, then was produced by Repertory Theater of Lincoln Center for 30 performances in 1971, winning its author Drama Desk and Variety poll citations as a most promising playwright and achieving many subsequent productions at home and abroad.*

*Gurney next made the off-Broadway scene with* Who Killed Richard Corey? *for 31 performances at Circle Repertory in 1976, the same year that his* Children *premiered in Richmond, Va. and his* The Rape of Bunny Stunte *was done OOB. The next year,* Children *appeared at Manhattan Theater Club,* The Love Course *was produced OOB and* The Middle Ages *had its premiere at the Mark Taper Forum in Los Angeles. Gurney's* The Problem *and* The Wayside Motor Inn *were done OOB in the 1977–78 season. In 1981– 82* The Middle Ages *came to New York OOB and Circle Rep workshopped* What I Did Last Summer.

*In that same season, Gurney's first Best Play,* The Dining Room, *began a 583-performance run at Playwrights Horizons on Feb. 24. His second Best Play,* The Perfect Party, *opened a 238-performance run April 2, 1986, also at Playwrights Horizons. His third Best Play,* The Cocktail Hour, *reached independent off-Broadway production last season Oct. 20. While it was chalking up 351 performances at the Promenade Theater, another Gurney script that had been staged at the Long Wharf Theater in New Haven in November 1988,* Love Letters, *was being put on in staged readings March 6–April 10 on Monday evenings at the Promenade, when* The Cocktail Hour *had the night off.* Love Letters *reopened this season as a full off-Broadway offering for 64 performances Aug. 22–Oct. 15, after which, on Oct. 31, it moved to Broadway, its author's fourth Best Play.*

*New York has also seen Gurney's* What I Did Last Summer *for 31 performances in full production at Circle Rep and* The Middle Ages *for 110 off-Broadway performances, both in 1983;* The Golden Age, *suggested by Henry James's* The Aspern Papers, *on Broadway April 12, 1984 for 29 performances;* Sweet Sue *on Broadway January 8, 1987 for 164 performances; and* Another Antigone *at Playwrights Horizons Jan. 11, 1988 for 30 performances.*

*Gurney is also the author of the TV adaptation from John Cheever's* O Youth and Beauty! *and of three novels:* The Gospel According to Joe, Entertaining Strangers *and* The Snow Ball. *He has been the recipient of Rockefeller and National Endowment Awards, an Old Dominion Fellowship, an honorary degree from Williams, a New England Theater Conference citation for outstanding creative achievement and an Award of Merit from the American Academy and Institute of Arts and Letters. He has taught literature at M.I.T. for 25 years. He is married, with four children, and lives in New York City, where he serves on the artistic board of Playwrights Horizons and as secretary and council member of the Dramatists Guild.*

*In the following synopsis of* Love Letters, *the three-asterisk dashes* (\*      \*      \*) *appear as they do in the script to indicate major transitions of time, place or subject.*

PART I

SYNOPSIS: An author's note describes the staged-reading form of this presentation as follows: *"This is a play, or rather a sort of play, which needs no theater, no lengthy rehearsal, no special set, no memorization of lines and no commitment from its two actors beyond the night of performance. It is de-signed simply to be read aloud by an actor and an actress of roughly the same age, sitting side by side at a table, in front of a group of people of any size. The actor might wear a dark gray suit, the actress a simple, expensive-look-ing dress . . . . . In performance, the piece would seem to work best if the ac-tors didn't look at each other until the end, when Melissa might watch Andy as he reads his final letter. They listen eagerly and actively to each other along the way, however, much as we might listen to an urgent voice on a one-way radio, coming from far, far away."*

In the first letter, the child Andrew Makepeace Ladd III formally accepts Mr. and Mrs. Channing Garner's invitation to their daughter Melissa's birth-day party. As a present, he is bringing her a copy of *The Lost Princess of Oz,* appropriate because "When you came into second grade with that stuck-up nurse, you looked like a lost princess." But in her thank-you note Melissa doesn't seem to appreciate Andy's gift.

They continue corresponding on such children's occasions as Valentine's Day, Christmas, Halloween, tonsillectomy, etc.—and later, Andy's apology for sneaking into the girls' bathhouse to spy on Melissa and her nurse, Miss Hawthorne, while they were changing. Andy writes that his parents have sent him to summer camp, "so that I can be with all boys." Melissa, whose parents are now divorced, writes, "Here's some bad news. My mother's gotten married again to a man named Hooper McPhail. HELP! LEMME OUTA HERE!"

Josef Sommer and Colleen Dewhurst

As Andy and Melissa grow older, they find themselves attending the same dancing school.

ANDY: Dear Mrs. McPhail. I want to apologize to you for my behavior in the back of your car coming home last night from dancing school. Charlie and I were just goofing around, and I guess it just got out of hand. I'm sorry you had to pull over to the curb, and I'm sorry we tore Melissa's dress. My father says you should send me the bill and I'll pay for it out of my allowance.

MELISSA: Dear Andy. Mummy brought your letter up here to Lake Placid. She thought it was cute. I thought it was dumb. I could tell your father made you write it. You and I both know that the fight in the car was really Charlie's fault. And Charlie never apologized, thank God. That's why I like him, actually. As for you, you shouldn't always do what your parents WANT, Andy. Even at dancing school you're always doing just the RIGHT THING all the time . . . . .

ANDY: I know it seems jerky, but I like writing, actually. I like writing compositions in English. I like writing letters, I like writing you. I wanted to write that letter to your mother because I knew you'd see it, so it was like talking to you when you weren't here. And when you couldn't *interrupt* . . . . .

Andy writes his formal acceptance of an invitation by Melissa's grandmother to a dinner before a ball. Melissa's next letter is a reproach to Andy for not having danced with his dinner hostess (herself) at least twice. Andy attributes this to a hockey injury which limited his activity.

Melissa is now seeing a psychiatrist and is becoming very interested in sex. She believes her attraction for Andy consists only in the luxurious lifestyle her family can afford. Andy replies, "All I know is, my mother keeps saying you'd make a good match. She says if I ever married you, I'd be set up for life. But I think it's really just physical attraction. That's why I liked going into the elevator with you at your grandmother's that time. Want to try it again?"

Melissa is shipped off to boarding school and hates it. Ditto Andy, again to be with all boys, but he seems to be managing to adapt to its demands. He tells her of his social, athletic and academic victories, but she'd rather he wrote her about feelings (he admits that he missed his dog Porgy dreadfully). Melissa can't go home for Thanksgiving because she is being disciplined for smoking, but she's happy to inform Andy that her mother is going to Reno to divorce Hooper McPhail, "a jerk and a pill, and he used to bother me in bed, if you must know."

After spending some time together during Christmas vacation, Andy invites Melissa to go steady, but she declines. Besides, she hates coming home—"My mother gets drunk a lot"—and plans to spend spring vacation with her grandmother in Palm Beach. "You may not have as much money as

we have," Melissa observes, "but you've got a better family." A boy Melissa
met in Palm Beach is now boasting about his prowess with her, but Melissa
writes Andy that he's "a lying son of a bitch."

Andy plans to stay home this summer, caddying. Melissa will visit her
father in California in hopes of finding a new family.

ANDY:  Write me about California. How's your second family?

\*        \*        \*

Did you get my letters? I checked with your mother, and I had the correct address. How come you haven't answered me all summer?

\*        \*        \*

Back at school now. Hope everything's O.K. with you. Did you get my letters
out in California, or did you have a wicked stepmother who confiscated them?

MELISSA:  I don't want to talk about California. Ever. For a while I thought
I had two families, but now I know I really don't have any. You're very lucky,
Andy. You don't know it, but you are. But maybe I'm lucky, too. In another
way. I was talking to Mrs. Wadsworth who comes in from Hartford to teach
us art. She says I have a real talent both in drawing and in painting, and she's
going to try me out in pottery as well . . . . .

Timothy Hutton and Elizabeth McGovern

Andy invites Melissa to his school's midwinter dance. His subsequent letter to her reproaches her bitterly for having "sneaked off" during the waltz with one Bob Bartram who has since been boasting of the extent of their kisses and fondling.

MELISSA: Sorry, sorry, sorry. I AM! I HATE that Bob Bartram. I hated him even when I necked with him. I know you won't believe that, but it's true. You can be attracted to someone you hate. Well, maybe *you* can't, but I can . . . . .

And besides, Andy. Gulp. Er. Ah. Um. How do I say this? With you it's different. You're like a friend to me. You're like a brother. I've never had a brother, and I don't have too many friends, so you're both, Andy. You're it. My mother says you must never say that to a man, but I'm saying it anyway, and it's true. Maybe if I didn't know you so well, maybe if I hadn't grown up with you, maybe if we hadn't written all these goddamn LETTERS all the time, I could have kissed you the way I kissed Bob Bartram.

Oh, but PLEASE let's see each other spring vacation. Please. I count on you, Andy. I NEED you. I think sometimes I'd go stark raving mad if I didn't have you to hold onto. I really think that sometimes. Much love.

\*　　　　\*　　　　\*

Happy Easter! I know no one sends Easter cards except maids, but here's mine anyway, drawn with my own hot little hands. I drew those tears on that corny bunny on the left because it misses you so much, but maybe I've just made it all the cornier.

\*　　　　\*　　　　\*

Greetings from Palm Beach. Decided to visit my grandmother. Yawn, yawn. I'm a whiz at backgammon and gin rummy. Hear you took Gretchen Lascelles to see *Quo Vadis* and sat in the *loges* and put your arm around her and smoked! Naughty, naughty!

\*　　　　\*　　　　\*

Back at school, but not for long, that's for sure. Caught nipping gin in the woods with Bubbles Harriman. Have to pack my trunk by tonight and be out tomorrow. Mummy's frantically pulling strings all over the Eastern Seaboard for another school. Mrs. Wadsworth, my art teacher, thinks I should chuck it all and go to Italy and study art. What do you think? Oh, please write, Andy, PLEASE. I need your advice, or are you too busy thinking about Gretchen Lascelles?

Andy thinks Melissa should finish school (she's been admitted to another one) and college before going to Italy. He has given up Gretchen Lascelles but won't see Melissa in June because he has a summer job as a counselor in a camp for slum children. Hearing that Melissa has behaved outrageously at a

Cliff Robertson and Elaine Stritch

party, he likens her to Gretchen Lascelles and addresses her angrily: "Don't you care about anything in this world except hacking around? Don't you feel any obligation to help poor people, for example? Sometimes I think your big problem is you don't have enough to do, and so you start playing grab-ass with people."

Understandably, Melissa doesn't answer Andy's next few letters, but gradually their correspondence resumes: a letter of condolence on the death of Melissa's grandmother; letters on Melissa's entry into Briarcliff College, Andy's into Yale and Andy's inviting Melissa to a football weekend in New Haven—and then, after the weekend, the recriminations.

ANDY: . . . . . We didn't really click, did we? I always had the sense that you were looking over my shoulder, looking for someone else, and ditto with me. Both of us seemed to be expecting something different from what was there.

As for the Hotel Duncan, I don't know. Maybe I had too many Sea-Breezes. Maybe you did. But what I really think is that there were too many people in that hotel room. Besides you and me, it seemed my mother was there, egging us on, and my father, shaking his head, and *your* mother zonked out on the couch, and Miss Hawthorne and your *grand*mother, sitting on the sidelines, watching us like hawks. Anyway, I was a dud. I admit it. I'm sorry.

I went to the Infirmary on Monday and talked to the doctor about it, and he said these things happen all the time. Particularly when there's a lot of pressure involved. The woman doesn't have to worry about it so much, but the man does. Anyway, it didn't happen with Gretchen Lascelles. You can write her and ask her if you want.

MELISSA: You know what I think is wrong? These letters. These goddamn letters. That's what's wrong with us, in my humble opinion. I know you more from your LETTERS than I do in person. Maybe that's why I was looking over your shoulder. I was looking for the person who's been in these letters all these years. Or for the person who's NOT in these letters. I don't know. All I know is, you're not quite the same when I see you, Andy. You're really not. I'm not saying you're a jerk in person. I'm not saying that at all. I'm just saying that all this letter-writing has messed us up. It's a bad habit. It's made us seem like people we're not. So maybe what was wrong was that there were two people *missing* in the Hotel Duncan that night: namely, the real you and the real me.

Melissa suggests that they talk on the telephone instead of writing letters, but Andy finds either that Melissa's phone is busy or she hangs up on him. She hears that he has been writing two long letters a week to another girl, and he admits it. He feels that he is at his best when writing a letter, and "I feel like a true lover when I'm writing you." He gives himself totally to the person he is writing.

Andy remembers "all those dumb things which were done to us when we were young. We had absent parents, slapping nurses, stupid rules, obsolete schooling, empty rituals, hopelessly confusing sexual customs . . . oh my God, when I think about it now, it's almost unbelievable, it's a fantasy, it's like back in the Oz books, the way we grew up." But he found that learning how to write, learning how to organize his thoughts and put them down on paper, saved him in some way.

ANDY: . . . . . Won't you please escape from that suburban Sing-Sing and come down here and see me? I wrote my way into this problem, and goddamn it, I'm writing my way out. I'll make another reservation at the Hotel Duncan, and I promise I'll put down my pen and give you a better time.

MELISSA: Dear Andy: Guess what? Right while I was in the middle of reading your letter, Jack Duffield telephoned from Amherst and asked me for a weekend up there. So I said yes before I got to where you asked me. Sorry, sweetie, but it looks like the telephone wins in the end.

ANDY: Dear Melissa: Somehow I don't think this is the end. It could be, but I don't really think it is. At least I hope it isn't. Love, Andy.

*End of Part I.*

## PART II

Melissa has gone to Florence to concentrate on her painting, while Andy has graduated from college summa cum laude and is doing a hitch in the Navy. His ship will be stationed in the Mediterranean in spring, but by then Melissa will be on the move. Soon Andy is seeing the world—Manila, Hong Kong, Japan—and Melissa hears that he has taken up with a Japanese woman. His only reply to her letters is one noncommittal card. Finally she decides to marry Darwin H. Cobb, a Wall Streeter. Andy's reply to her wedding invitation is a formal regret that he cannot attend. Then Melissa writes to thank him for his wedding present of a Japanese bowl.

MELISSA: . . . . . I know you'll like Darwin. When he laughs, it's like Pinocchio turning into a donkey. We're living in a carriage house in New Canaan close to the train station, and I've got a studio all of my own. P.S. Won't you PLEASE write me about your big romance? Mother says your parents won't even talk about it any more.

ANDY: Dear Melissa: I'm writing to tell you this. Outside of you, and I *mean* outside of you, this was probably the most important thing that ever happened to me. And I mean *was*. Because it's over, it's gone, and I'm coming home, and that's all I ever want to say about it, ever again.

Richard Thomas and Swoosie Kurtz

Melissa announces the birth of a daughter, Francesca, and Andy makes the review at Harvard Law School. She has a show of her paintings, in Stamford, and her second baby; he takes a position as clerk for a Supreme Court Justice. She sends him her condolences on the death of his father—"I know you loved him very much. I also know he didn't like *me*"—and Andy replies with thanks, commenting, "He was a classy guy, the best of his breed . . . . . All my life he taught me that those born to privilege have special responsibilities, which is, I suppose, why I came home alone from Japan, why I chose the law and why I'll probably enter politics at some level, some time on down the line."

Soon Andy gets a card from Reno, where Melissa has gone for the usual reason. In the meantime Andy has met "a great girl named Jane." Melissa regrets Andy's wedding invitation and sends the happy couple a tray handpainted by herself.

Andy lands a job with a big New York City law firm. He hears that Melissa has been ailing and sends her flowers. At first he gets no response but finally hears from her.

MELISSA: Dear Andy. Yes, I'm all right. Yes, I got your flowers. Yes, I'm fine. No, actually, I'm not fine, and they tell me I've got to stop running around saying I am. I am here at this posh joint outside Boston, drying out for one hundred and fifty-five dollars a day. One of my problems is that I got slightly too dependent on the Kickapoo Joy Juice, a habit which they tell me I picked up during the party days back in Our Town. Another is that I slide into these terrible lows. Mummy says I drag everybody down, and I guess she's right. Aaaanyway, the result is that my Ex has taken over custody of the girls, and I'm holed up here, popping tranquillizers, talking my head off in single and group psychiatric sessions and turning into probably the biggest bore in the Greater Boston area.

ANDY: Have you thought about doing some painting again? That might help.

*          *          *

Did you get my note about taking up art? You were good, and you know it. You should keep it up.

MELISSA: I *did* get your note, I *have* taken it up, and it *helps*. Really. Thank you. I'm channeling my rage, enlarging my vision, all that. I hope all goes well with you and—wait, hold it. I'm looking it up in my little black book . . . ah, hah! Jane! It's Jane. Hmmmm. I hope all's well with you and Jane.

ANDY: Merry Christmas from Andy and Jane Ladd. And Andrew the Fourth! . . . . .

Melissa is married and divorced again and moves all over the world while Andy is made a partner of his firm.  She moves to New York just as the Ladds move out to suburbia.  Describing himself as "a liberal Republican with a strong commitment to women's rights," Andy enters politics.  Melissa has a show in New York, about which the critics say she's "dancing on the edge of an abyss."

ANDY:  Dear friends.  Jane tells me that it's about time I took a crack at the annual Christmas letter, so here goes.  Let's start at the top with our quarterback, Jane herself, who never ceases to amaze us all.  Not only has she continued to be a superb mother to our three sons, but she has also managed to commute into the city and hold down a part-time job in the gift shop at the Metropolitan Museum of Art.  Furthermore, she is now well on her way to completing a full-fledged master's degree in Arts Administration at SUNY Purchase.  More power to Jane, so say we all.

We are also proud of all three boys.  Young Drew was soccer captain at Exeter last fall and hopes to go on to Yale.  Nicholas, our rebel in residence, has become a computer genius in high school and has already received several tantalizing offers for summer jobs from local electronics firms.  We all know that it's tougher to place our youngsters in meaningful summer employment than to get them into Harvard, so we're very proud of how far Nick has come.  Ted, our last but in no way our least, now plays the clarinet in the school band at Dickinson Country Day . . . . .

Edward Herrmann and Jane Curtin

I've enjoyed very much serving on the State Legislature. We've proposed and written a number of bills, and we've won some and lost some. All my life I've had the wish to do something in the way of public service, and it has been a great pleasure to put that wish into practice. For those of my friends who have urged me to seek higher office, let me simply say that I have more than enough challenges right here where I am.

Jane and the boys join me in wishing each and all of you a Happy Holiday season.

MELISSA: Dear Andy. If I ever get another one of those drippy Xeroxed Christmas letters from you, I think I'll invite myself out to your ducky little house for dinner, and when you're all sitting there eating terribly healthy food and discussing terribly important things and generally congratulating yourselves on all your accomplishments, I think I'll stand up on my chair, and turn around, and moon the whole fucking family!

ANDY: You're right. It was a smug dumb letter, and I apologize for it. Jane normally writes it, and it sounds better when she does. I always felt better writing to just one person at a time, such as to you. I guess what I was really saying is that as far as my family is concerned, we're all managing to hold our heads above water in this tricky world. Jane and I have had our problems, but we're comfortable with each other now, and the boys, for the moment, are out of trouble. Nicky seems to be off drugs now, and Ted is getting help on his stammer. Porgy Jr., my old cocker, died, and I miss him too much to get a replacement. I'm thinking of running for the Senate next fall if O'Hara retires. What do you think? I'd really like your opinion. If you decide to answer this, you might write care of my office address. Jane has a slight tendency toward melodrama, particularly after she got ahold of your last little note.

Melissa advises Andy to go for it and contributes to his campaign. But soon she is back in the sanatarium after another alcoholic lapse during which her ex-husband managed to reduce her visitation rights to her children. A series of Christmas card exchanges as the years pass inform each other that Andy made the Senate and Melissa is living alone in New York and modeling clay animals the way they used to do it in fourth grade. After a while she has a show, which Andy can't attend because he's abroad on an official visit. At first Melissa doesn't answer when he writes to ask her how the show went, but finally she reveals, "The show stank. The crowd hated it, the critics hated it. I hated it. It was nostalgic shit. You can't go home again, and you can quote me on that. I'm turning to photography now. Realism! That's my bag. The present tense. Look at the modern world squarely in the face, and don't blink . . . Oh Andy, couldn't I see you? You're all I have left."

Andy agrees to stop by Melissa's place after a fund-raising dinner. Their meeting is apparently a great success, because Melissa begs to see him again. Andy asks her not to phone him, because a record is made of all his incoming calls, but to write to the attention of Mrs. Walpole, his private secretary, so that his staff won't read the letters.  But he agrees to see her again at the next opportunity, and soon their letters echo with the resonances of love.

MELISSA:  . . .Did you ever *dream* we'd be so good at sex?

ANDY:  . . . Two uptight old Wasps going at it like a sale at Brooks Brothers . . .

MELISSA:  . . . I figure fifty years went into last night . . .

ANDY:  . . . Let's go for a hundred . . .

MELISSA:  . . . Oh my God, come again soon, or sooner . . .

ANDY:  . . . I'm already making plans . . .

MELISSA:  . . . have to go to San Francisco to visit the girls.  Couldn't we meet somewhere on the way?

ANDY:  . . . I don't see how we can possibly go public.

As Melissa becomes more and more desirous of an open, permanent relationship with Andy, the latter becomes more and more reluctant to risk public disapproval—and maybe lose an election—by disrupting his home life.  Soon the press picks up the story, and they decide to "lie low for a while," though they miss each other terribly.  Melissa feels that her whole life is now wrapped up in Andy, but Andy is beginning to concentrate on getting re-elected and stops even communicating with Melissa.  Just as she is becoming desperate, writing "Is this it, Andy?", he arranges a meeting for the next Sunday night, "to talk"—which she dreads, and rightfully so.

Treat Williams and Kate Nelligan

ANDY: Dearest Melissa: Are you all right? That was a heavy scene last Sunday, but I know I'm right. We've got to go one way or the other, and the other leads nowhere. I know I sound like a stuffy prick, but I do feel I have a responsibility to Jane, and the boys, and now, after the election, to my constituency, which had enough faith and trust in me to vote me back in, despite all that crap in the newspapers. And it wouldn't work with us anyway, in the long run, sweetheart. We're too old. We're carrying too much old baggage on our backs. We'd last about a week if we got married. But we can still write letters, darling. We can always do that. Letters are still our strength and our salvation. Mrs. Walpole is still with us, and there's no reason why we can't continue to keep in touch with each other in this wonderful old way. I count on your letters, darling. I always have. And I hope you will count on mine . . .

Andy gets no reply to this letter, but later he gets a response to his Christmas card in which Melissa writes, "We who are about to die salute you." This alarms him, but he gets no response to his immediate inquiries until Melissa's mother lets him know that Melissa is back in the sanitarium. Andy writes to Melissa about a plan to visit her right away, but Melissa begs him not to come and see her like this, fat and ugly.

MELISSA: . . . . . My girls won't even *talk* to me on the telephone now. They say I upset them too much. Oh, I've made a mess of things, Andy. I've made a total, ghastly mess. I don't like life any more. I hate it. Sometimes I think that if you and I had just . . . if we had just . . . oh but just stay away, Andy. Please.

ANDY: Arriving Saturday morning. Will meet you at your mother's.

MELISSA: DON'T! I don't want to see you! I won't be there! I'll be GONE, Andy! I swear. I'll be gone.

Andy's next letter is addressed, not to Melissa, but to her mother—a letter of condolence on Melissa's death. He feels that, in writing to her mother, in a way he is continuing to write to Melissa. Indeed, she seems to be commenting on each of his sentences as he writes about their "complicated relationship" in which they were opposites attracting each other—Melissa the rebel and Andy the balance.

ANDY: Most of the things I did in life I did with her partly in mind. And if I said or did an inauthentic thing, I could almost hear her groaning over my shoulder. But now she's gone I really don't know how I'll get along without her.

MELISSA (*looking at him for the first time*): You'll survive, Andy.

ANDY: I have a wonderful wife, fine children, and a place in the world I feel proud of, but the death of Melissa suddenly leaves a huge gap in my life . . .

MELISSA:  Oh now, Andy . . .

ANDY:  The thought of never again being able to write to her, to connect to her, to get some signal back from her, fills me with an emptiness which is hard to describe.

MELISSA:  Now Andy, stop . . .

ANDY:  I don't think there are many men in this world who have had the benefit of such a friendship with such a woman. But it was more than friendship, too. I know now that I loved her. I loved her even from the day I met her, when she walked into second grade, looking like the lost princess of Oz.

MELISSA:  Oh, Andy, PLEASE. I can't bear it.

ANDY:  I don't think I've ever loved anyone the way I loved her, and I know I never will again. She was at the heart of my life, and already I miss her desperately. I just wanted to say this to you and to her. Sincerely, Andy Ladd.

MELISSA:  Thank you, Andy.

*End of Part II*

○○○
○○○
○○○
○○○
○○○
○○○
○○○ GRAND HOTEL, The Musical

*A Full-Length Musical in One Act*

BOOK BY LUTHER DAVIS

SONGS BY ROBERT WRIGHT
AND GEORGE FORREST

ADDITIONAL MUSIC AND LYRICS BY MAURY YESTON

BASED ON VICKI BAUM'S *GRAND HOTEL*

Cast and credits appear on pages 374–376

*LUTHER DAVIS (book) was born in Brooklyn Heights, where his father was a manufacturer of surgical sutures. He was educated at Brooklyn Poly Prep, Culver Military Academy and Yale University, and it was while a Yale undergrad that his writing career took shape. He was one of the editors of the Yale Lit (the college literary magazine) and was permitted to take Walter Pritchard Eaton's graduate course in playwriting at Yale Drama School for two years. He tried to start a musical comedy club to be called "The Lily Gilders," but the dean turned it down because of its potentially high cost. Even more significantly, while still at Yale he managed to place some sketches with Leonard Sillman's Broadway revue* Who's Who *in 1937, giving him an infatuation with musical shows from which, he says, he has never recovered: "All those girls on the fire stairs . . . "*

*After active service with the U.S. Air Corps in World War II, Davis re-sumed his writing career.  His first stage credit was* Kiss Them for Me, *based on Frederic Wakeman's novel* Shore Leave *about Navy fliers on a troubled four-day leave in San Francisco, on Broadway March 20, 1945 for 103 per-formances.  His first collaboration on a musical with the songwriters Robert Wright and George Forrest was the co-authorship (with Charles Lederer) of* Kismet *which opened on Broadway Dec. 3, 1953, ran for 583 performances, won a Tony, was revived in a major production at Lincoln Center June 22, 1965 for 48 performances and reappeared in a new musical version, a kind of Broadway remake, entitled* Timbuktu, *with a revised book and produced by Davis March 1, 1978 for 221 performances.  Off Broadway he co-produced* Eden Court *May 14, 1965 for 15 performances and the Obie-winning* Not About Heroes *Oct. 21, 1985 for 24 performances.  His book for* Grand Hotel, *which opened on Broadway Nov. 12, is his first Best Play citation.*

*Davis is also the author of 15 screen plays (including the movie version of* Kismet *and* Lady in a Cage, *for which he won one of his two Mystery Writers of America Awards) and numerous contributions to major series and other TV entertainments.  He is divorced, with two daughters, and lives in New York City.*

*ROBERT WRIGHT and GEORGE FORREST (songs).  Robert Wright was born in Daytona Beach, Florida in 1914 and George Forrest was born in Brooklyn in 1915—and it's lucky for us all that Forrest's aunt was in the real estate business in Palm Beach in the early 1930s, because that's why Forrest's mother brought him to Florida and at age 15 he and Wright met in the sophomore class at Miami Senior High School.  From then on—except that Wright went to the University of Miami for two years and Forrest eschewed college—they have worked together as songwriters, musicians and even as teachers in one of American show business's most fruitful collaborations: 2,000 music-and-lyrics compositions for 16 produced stage musicals, 18 stage revues, 58 motion pictures, countless cabaret acts, thousands of single recordings and 30 albums.*

*At college, Wright was studying journalism but soon found himself deeply and profitably involved on the side in the music world, where Forrest was already a success as a musician. They began writing songs, yes, songs—each of them is composer, lyricist and musician in a collaboration which is seamless as to who creates what. In 1935 they had a portfolio of 88 songs and persuaded M-G-M to give them an audition. They had played 11 of them when they were hired. One of their biggest hits was "The Donkey Serenade"* in The Firefly *(1937), and the roster of their movies includes* Maytime, Sweethearts, Broadway Serenade, I Married an Angel, Saratoga, Music in My Heart; Dance, Girl, Dance *and the film versions of their own* Kismet *and* Song of Norway. *Their Academy Award nominations were for "Always and Always," "It's a Blue World" and "Pennies for Peppino."*

*Three of the best-known Wright & Forrest songs are "Stranger in Paradise," "And This Is My Beloved" and "Baubles, Bangles and Beads," all from their Broadway hit* Kismet, *which won its songwriters Tony Awards. Their* Song of Norway *(1944) ran even longer—860 performances—and their Broadway credits have included* Magdalena, Gypsy Lady, Kean, Anya, Timbuktu *and now the musical version of* Grand Hotel, *their first Best Play. At present they are working on a musical version of* The Ponder Heart, *with book by Jerome Chodorov, to be called* Uncle Daniel. *They have often served as adjunct professors and/or artists-in-residence at such educational institutions as Boston University, Hope College in Holland, Mich., the University of Alabama and the University of Miami—always as a team, never separately. Their home base continues to be in Florida.*

MAURY YESTON *(additional music and lyrics) was born Oct. 23, 1945 in Jersey City, N.J. He received his B.A. at Yale in 1967, his M.A. at Clare College, Cambridge, England in 1969 and his Ph.D. in 1976 at Yale, whose music faculty he joined as Associate Professor of Music Theory in 1974 and as Director of Undergraduate Studies in Music in 1976, remaining at Yale until 1982. It was as a Yale undergraduate that he started writing music, contributing to college shows and composing* Movement for Cellos and Orchestra *which was given its premiere performance by the Norwalk Symphony Orchestra with Yo Yo Ma as guest soloist.*

*Yeston had written a children's musical, based on* Alice in Wonderland *and produced at the Long Wharf Theater in New Haven in 1970, but his first credit in the New York theater was the incidental music for the Best Play*

Cloud 9 *off Broadway in 1981. He had begun writing songs for a musical at the Lehman Engel BMI workshop in 1973, which later were part of his music and lyrics for the Broadway musical* Nine, *which opened May 9, 1982, ran for 739 performances and won Yeston a Best Play citation and the Tony and Drama Desk Awards for the best score of a musical. He has rounded out the 1980s with his contributions to* Grand Hotel.

*Yeston's other activities have included the authorship of two textbooks—* The Stratification of Musical Rhythm *(1975) and* Readings in Schenker Analysis *(1977)—the score to the movie* Ripe Strawberries, *songs for albums (the most recent being* Goya . . . A Life in Song*) and a musical in Japanese,* Nukata No Okime, *recently produced in Tokyo. He now presides over the BMI Workshop, teaches at Yale occasionally and lives in Woodbridge, Conn. with his wife and two sons.*

## The Presentation of the Company

SYNOPSIS: In a show played in one set with musicians visible onstage, a doorman stands by the hotel's revolving door, as the sounds of hotel life begin to build in the background—guests phoning the operators and asking for ice water, hangers, a barber's appointment, a taxi, etc. Overlapping, these sounds segue into music, and the Colonel-Doctor Otternschlag, "*enters desperately, prepares a hypodermic needle and injects himself with morphine . . . . . the Grand Parade begins, as the revolving door begins to turn upstage. The characters in the play (Chauffeur, Zinnowitz, Sandor, Witt, Madame Peepee, General Director Preysing, Flaemmchen, Otto Kringelein, Baron Felix Von Gaigern, Raffaela, Elizaveta Grushinskaya) enter one by one through the door.*" The Doctor begins the song "The Grand Parade."

DOCTOR (*sings*):
   Velvet stairs
   Easy chairs
   Perfumed air gently blowing

   Chandeliers
   Light appears
   Burning bright, crystal glowing

   People come, people go
   Wave of life overflowing
   Come . . . begin . . .
   In old Berlin
   You're in
   The Grand Hotel.

The others pick up the song, after which the Doctor comments, "Grand Hotel, Berlin. Always the same. People come. People go. Look at them— living the high life! But time is running out." He introduces some of the characters, including the Baron, Felix, whom he calls "a nobleman. And a thief."

The Chauffeur demands a payment for his "boss" from Felix, who brushes him off. The music changes "*and takes on an angry beat; the angry faces of scullery workers appear amid steam.*"

*Scene 1: The Grand Hotel lobby and far below in the scullery*

The scullery workers complain, "Some Have, Some Have Not," in song, adding "Every bum and bitch in all Berlin is rich except for us." Upstairs, the hotel staff joins their song.

> HOTEL STAFF (*sing*):
>     Some have, some have not!  Why?
>     They're in here spending money,
>     A million marks a day.
>     We're one step from the street
>     Making just enough to eat
>     For a day,
>     Week,
>     Month,
>     Year . . .
>     With a thousand bills to pay!
>     They have us run to hail their cabs
>     While they're running up their tabs . . . . .

Among those who join the scullery workers and hotel staff in song is Felix, who sings in "As It Should Be" that he loves to live dangerously: "Give me the thrill/Of a careless existence . . . . . I want the height/And romance of adventure/Cooled by the chill/Of the danger I'm in."

Erik at the front desk answers the phone and learns that his wife, in labor, is having a hard time and asking for him—but he can't leave his post.

Elizaveta Grushinskaya enters with her entourage, instructing her company manager, Witt, to cancel tonight's booking because, contract or no contract, she is resolved never to dance again, after a poor audience turnout and a poor performance in Amsterdam. Felix regards her admiringly as she goes off to her room. Felix ignores Rohna, the grand concierge, when he reminds the Baron that his bill is six months in arrears.

The Chauffeur approaches Felix again and insists that he come to the phone to talk to his boss. On the phone, Felix assures a "Mister S." that he

Rex D. Hays (Rohna), John Wylie (Col. Dr. Otternschlag), Michael Jeter (Kringelein), Jane Krakowski (Flaemmchen), Charles Mandracchia (Doorman), Liliane Montevecchi (Grushinskaya), Karen Akers (Raffaela), Timothy Jerome (Preysing), David Carroll (Felix) and Kathi Moss (Mme. Peepee) in *Grand Hotel*

will soon pay him back in full with the proceeds of a "reliable tip on a sure thing" on the New York Stock Exchange.

In another phone booth, a young girl who has adopted the stage name "Flaemmchen" tells a friend that she is here at the Grand Hotel on a secretarial assignment but hopes to become a big movie star like Theda Bara.

In another booth, General Director Preysing of Saxonia Mills is inquiring about a radiogram he's expecting from America, concerning a Boston merger essential to his company's survival.

In another booth, Raffaela, the ballerina's attendant and companion, is inquiring on Grushinskaya's behalf about selling some jewelry "she has grown tired of."

And in another booth Otto Kringelein is telling his doctor that he has received very bad news from the specialist but is not coming back to end his days in the hospital. He has cashed in his life's savings and means to stay here, in "the most expensive hotel in Europe," where even his old boss,

Preysing, is a fellow guest. Felix and the staff finish with the song "At the Grand Hotel."

FELIX (*sings*):
Let me walk tall

And be all that I could be,

Never to fall,

Ever up, never down,

At the top of the town!

SCULLERY WORKERS (*sing*):
Some have, some have not!
Some have, some have not!
If only I were smarter
I wouldn't have to sweat so much!
To have that fellow's bankroll
I would wheel, deal,
Cheat, steal, whatever
He did to get so much!
It's the din of old Berlin
It's the din of old Berlin

ALL (*sing*):
It's the din of the old Berlin
You're in the Grand Hotel!

Erik approaches the Doctor with an offer of a box at the Theater Royale for Grushinskaya's performance.

DOCTOR: So Grushinskaya doesn't sell out any more. I'm not surprised. Dances about dying swans in an age where an entire generation of young men was wiped out—no thanks.

ERIK: Colonel-Doctor—I need your help. I talked to the hospital—my wife is in terrible pain.

DOCTOR: Pain? They call that pain? What does anyone know about pain who hasn't danced with mustard gas and shrapnel?

ERIK: Some people say you have something that kills pain—

DOCTOR: Yes—something they give you when you need it that still sings to you when you don't.

ERIK: Maybe you could prescribe some of it for my wife—

DOCTOR: Don't be a fool! Morphine is for field hospitals, not maternity wards. It would harm the baby. Go hold her hand.

ERIK: Oh, I wish I could—but I have to be here. We need this job! God, how we need it!

*Doctor nods and Erik goes off.*

DOCTOR: Poor women, what a price they pay. (*To a reigning beauty as she passes—but not so she can hear.*) Hold your head high while you can, you arrogant bitch—

*Beckons to Bellboy, who approaches.*

See if there's any mail for me. Or messages. And tell Reception I may be checking out today.

BELLBOY:  What, again?
> *The Doctor gives him a sharp look.*
Yes, Colonel-Doctor.
> *Otto Kringelein comes in carrying all his worldly belongings.*
OTTO:  No! Please! I have a reservation! Please! I'm going to be a guest at the Grand Hotel! My name is Kringelein, Otto Kringelein—
ROHNA:  I'm afraid there isn't a thing today.

Rohna insists that the hotel is full. Otto suffers some kind of fainting seizure and is helped to a chair by Erik and attended by the Doctor, who assures the others that Otto is all right, for the moment—but only for the moment, as Otto well knows. In the meantime, he has come to the Grand Hotel to grasp at an experience in life: "It went by while I wasn't looking. I've quite entirely missed it!", Otto confesses.

OTTO:  . . . . . I'm feeling much, much better. Thank you, Doctor.
DOCTOR (*to Erik*): I'll stay. One more day.
OTTO (*to Erik*): Please, young man . . . I don't have these spells very often. Really, they're extremely rare. Please tell me: I see people leaving with their bags. Why is it you have no room for *me*? Is it possible the Grand Hotel does not take Jews?
ROHNA (*overhearing*): I assure you, Baron Rothschild is even now upstairs in the Prince Albert Suite.
OTTO:  Sir, there are Jews . . . and there are *Jews* . . . . .
FELIX (*coming over*): Excuse me—(*To Rohna.*) Baron Rothschild's an old friend of my family's. Would it be helpful if I were to ask him to intercede for this gentleman?
ROHNA:  No! Do not disturb the baron, Baron.
OTTO:  You, you're a baron? You see? I was right about the Grand Hotel! Already I've met my first baron, and I'm only in the lobby!
FELIX (*to Rohna*): I really think I should call him.
ROHNA:  Perhaps I could check the register one more time. (*Goes.*)
FELIX:  Brilliant. Why didn't I think of that? (*To Otto.*) Hasn't anyone warned you that everything here costs double?
OTTO:  I don't have to worry about money any more.
FELIX:  Ah, I see! Made your pile, now wine and women?
OTTO:  Not so fast. I don't even have a room.
FELIX:  I'll just go and see how he's doing. (*Crosses to join Rohna.*) . . . . .
OTTO (*sings "At the Grand Hotel" and "Table With a View"*):
> . . . . . I want to know that I once was here
> While all my faculties still are clear
> And check into my room
> As I've planned

At the Grand Hotel

I want to sit where I can sit
And stare life in the eye!
I want to go to the Grand Cafe
Where life begins at the end of the day
And have them show me to
A little table with a view!

The sleek young men,
The slender girls,
They please my eyes!
Perfumes from France
And tropic plants
Around me rise!

I listen to the swish of the silk and
The tune the fiddle plays
And I feel gay and warm and free! . . . . .

Felix comes over and hands Otto a room key, while Erik attends to Otto's luggage. Otto is deeply grateful.

### Scene 2: *The Moroccan Coffee Bar*

The Jimmys, black Americans in Moroccan costume, are rehearsing their act, chatting with each other in French. Flaemmchen enters and uses the phone to leave word that the typist General Director Preysing wanted is here. She orders a cup of coffee, and the Jimmys sing their duet of "Maybe My Baby Loves Me." They are from the Carolinas and scoff at Flaemmchen's delusion that in America the streets are paved with gold: "Honey, where I come from they ain't even paved!" But they support Flaemmchen's fantasy that she ought to be in the movies—she's obviously pretty enough. Flaemmchen joins them in their song.

THE JIMMYS AND FLAEMMCHEN (*sing*):
. . . . . Maybe my baby loves me,
But oh, if so,
Why does my baby leave me
Cryin' alone in my cot?
Maybe my lovin' baby loves me,
Maybe my lovin' baby loves me,
Maybe my baby loves me—
Not!

*Scene 3: A corner of the Grand Ballroom*

Grushinskaya, in tutu and toe shoes, insists that she means to retire, over the protests of Witt and the impresario, Sandor, who remind her of a reviewer's opinion that "She is fire and ice: fire in the passion she brings to her roles, and ice in her technical perfection." Grushinskaya mocks this praise because she feels she no longer deserves it: "The world has grown old . . . . . the theaters are old, the ballets are old—even the audience is old. One must feel *young* to dance."

Sandor persuades her that she must dance tonight, because the house is sold out. But as they leave, Sandor confides to Witt that this is a lie—he can't give the tickets away.

Raffaela joins Grushinskaya and pleads with her not to sell jewelry, though the appraiser was much impressed by it. Raffaela reminds her, "It is all you have left from him."

GRUSHINSKAYA: Prince Sergei is dead, Raffaela. This is from another age. Just like me.

RAFFAELA: I remember the night he gave it to you. In St. Petersburg. He called it "frozen applause" . . . . .

GRUSHINSKAYA (*examines the necklace*): Will it bring enough to pay everybody?

RAFFAELA: Madame, listen. I have saved a great deal of money. Let me help!

GRUSHINSKAYA: Dear Raffaela—how kind you are. I am glad you have saved your pennies. But no, absolutely no. Raffaela—why have you put up with me all these years? My tempers, my tears, my vanity, my thoughtlessness—(*Smiles.*)—Even my laundry. I've asked so much and paid so little. Why Raffaela?

RAFFAELA: Madame is a great artist.

GRUSHINSKAYA: *Was.* What is it you want?

RAFFAELA: Madame needs me.

GRUSHINSKAYA: But what is it *you* need?

    *A pause.*

RAFFAELA: I need to change the ribbons on your shoes, or they won't be ready for tonight.

GRUSHINSKAYA: And I need to practice. Grazie, Raffaela. Grazie.

RAFFAELA: Prego.

The ensemble takes up the song "Fire and Ice," picked up by Grushinskaya and then taken forward by Raffaela, alone in her room, in "Twenty-Two Years" and then "Villa on a Hill."

GRUSHINSKAYA (*sings*):
  Were those years
  Worth all that I gave up?
  How was I to save up
  The life I let go
  In order to dance?
ENSEMBLE (*sings*):
  Fire and ice!
  Passion and sheer perfection
  In the wings quietly sighing . . . . .
RAFFAELA (*sings*):
  For twenty-two years
  I have kept secrets from you.
  Twenty-two years
  I've protected you
  From the harshness of life . . .

  Always feeling for you
  A kind of love.

  Dear one,
  Come where the pines grow,
  Come, come and we'll find
  A villa on a hill
  In Positano . . . . .

Felix comes through the Grand Ballroom, and his eyes fix on Grushinskaya as she departs.

*Scene 4: The ladies powder room*

In the lobby outside the powder room, Flaemmchen is still trying to reach Preysing on the phone, unsuccessfully. Felix notices her and follows her into the powder room, guarded by Madame Peepee. He arranges a rendezvous for that afternoon at the Yellow Pavilion. After he goes, Flaemmchen looks in the mirror where she sees herself as a glamorous movie star and confides to the mirror image, "I Want to Go to Hollywood."

FLAEMMCHEN (*sings*):
  I wanna be that girl in the mirror there.
  I wanna be that girl with golden hair
  Up on a silver screen
  Most ev'rywhere in the world

  I want to go to Hollywood!

Talkies!
I mean the pictures.
I wanna have a hot time ev'ry night
Get out and raise a little fahrenheit
Knock ev'ry duke and count and baron right off his feet!
I'll be that girl that's understood, oh!
I want to go to Hollywood . . . . .

Hollywood would be a great improvement over Friedrichstrasse where she lives in a cold water flat (Flaemmchen continues in song), and she is bound and determined to get away.

*Scene 5: Men's washroom and hotel bar*

Preysing comes into the washroom with a colleague, Zinnowitz, who warns Preysing that the stockholders are ready to replace him as general director of the company unless he can pull off the Boston merger.

ZINNOWITZ: . . . . . Is the Boston merger on or not?
PREYSING: I'm not sure. I'm still waiting for a radiogram.
ZINNOWITZ: We've got to buy time. At the meeting today you'll have to tell them the merger is on.
PREYSING: You mean *lie* to them? My God, I couldn't do that!
ZINNOWITZ: Don't be a fool! (*Sings.*)
    You want to put a lock
    On the company stock
    It's a block of twenty thousand
    You're already in the red
    And you won't tell a little bitty lie
    To get ahead?
    Everybody's doing it . . .
    Everybody's doing it.
PREYSING: You shouldn't even suggest such a thing! You, a lawyer—
ZINNOWITZ: Oh, I forgot. You're the very model of an honest business man.
PREYSING: Yes, I am!
ZINNOWITZ: Well, wake up, for God's sake! This is 1928!

Zinnowitz sings another couple of choruses of "Everybody's Doing It" and brings up the fact that Preysing has sunk a lot of his wife's money into his effort to stabilize the company's shares. Preysing had better "fib a little" or lose everything, Zinnowitz warns, exiting as Flaemmchen enters with her typewriter. She's ready to go to work—with the understanding that "I don't go to rooms." "Of course not," Preysing agrees, "I have rented a conference room. I'm a married man."

A page enters with a radiogram for Preysing—bad news, the Boston merger is off. He reconsiders his precarious position.

PREYSING (*sings*):
    Once upon a time, a lad,
    Out upon a stroll,
    Came upon an old crow
    Perched upon a pole.
    The pole stood at a crossroads.
    Which could the right road be?
    "Caw Caw,"
    Said the crow,
    And then, whaddaya know?
    He blinked and muttered Mephistophically:

    "Take the crooked path, lad,
    Walk the crooked mile!
    Skip the straight and narrow,
    It is out of style!
    Take the crooked path, boy,
    Give yourself a break:
    No one ever made a living
    Giving
    When he had the chance to take!"

Preysing concludes in this song, "The Crooked Path," that he can't decide which way to go, and then the scullery workers join him in a chorus of their "Some Have, Some Have Not."

*Scene 6: The Baron's room*

While Felix is dressing, the Chauffeur lounges on a chaise, insolently reminding the Baron that the time for paying his debt is running out. The Chauffeur knows of a diamond and ruby necklace right here in the hotel and ripe for the taking, suggesting to Felix that it might solve his financial problem. The Chauffeur produces a pistol, points it at the Baron and orders him to have the money by midnight, or else—and then he exits.

FELIX (*smiles and sings a reprise of "As It Should Be"*):
    Dangerous game
    And a carefree existence,

Only for those
With the courage to play
And the money to pay,
Buying life
As it should be!
*Will* be!

## Scene 7:  The Yellow Pavilion

Flaemmchen runs into an old friend, Trude, and they great each other cordially.

FLAEMMCHEN: . . . . . How's your mother?

TRUDE: Still whoring for American officers.  How's yours?

FLAEMMCHEN: Still dead.

TRUDE: Jesus, I forgot.  I'm sorry.  Guess what—I'm saving up to take the Graf Zeppelin to America.  Chicago, maybe.  I want to go to a speakeasy (*Miming peephole.*) Jack sent me.

FLAEMMCHEN: . . . . . It's Hollywood, California for me.  I want to be in the talkies!—all singing, all dancing—no typing!

TRUDE: Good luck.  Where did you get the money?

FLAEMMCHEN: I haven't yet.  Trude, I think I may be pregnant.

TRUDE: So—who isn't.

Trude leaves when Felix comes in, keeping the date he made with Flaemmchen previously.  As they dance, Otto greets them and describes his room with great enthusiasm and gratitude to Felix for arranging it for him.

Flaemmchen learns that Felix is a real baron—Baron Felix Amadeus Benvenuto Von Gaigern, to be exact.  Flaemmchen comments that he dances like a prince and adds in the song "Who Couldn't Dance With You?" that he gives her the confidence she needs on the dance floor.

Felix asks her as a favor to dance with Otto Kringelein, who is making a determined effort to get a share of enjoyment out of life.  They join Otto.  He is sampling something called a Louisiana Flip and offers the young couple a round.

FELIX: I'm afraid I can't, Old Socks, the New York Stock Exchange will be opening in minutes.  Are you interested in the stock market, Mister Kringelein?

OTTO: Oh no, I never gamble.

FELIX: Pity.

OTTO: Pity?

FELIX: That's how all these people can afford to spend all their days "making pleasure," as you put it.

OTTO (*light going on*): Oh! So that's how they do it.

FLAEMMCHEN: Mister Kringelein—

OTTO: No, Otto.

FLAEMMCHEN: —Otto, could I please have the next dance?

OTTO: With me?

FLAEMMCHEN: Yes, with you.

> *Otto stands up—and his pants droop severely; he has to stop to hitch them up.*

OTTO: Oh, excuse me—I've been reducing lately . . .

FELIX: I'll introduce you to my tailor. And if you like, the stock ticker.

OTTO: Yes, please.

FELIX (*to Flaemmchen*): The American Bar. Five o'clock tomorrow.

FLAEMMCHEN: Oh, yes. (*To Otto, as Felix goes.*) Let's go shake a wicked leg!

OTTO: I've never danced before. Since my uncle died, I'm the only Jew in Fredersdorf. Who'd dance with me?

> *They dance; Otto is helpless at first, then slowly begins getting the hang of it.*

FLAEMMCHEN (*sings*):
> Well, who couldn't dance with you?
> You sweep a lady off her feet, Mister!
> Who couldn't dance with you?
> You are so beautifully on the beat—

You're doing very, very well—

OTTO: I hope I haven't stepped on your feet, Miss Flaemmchen.

FLAEMMCHEN: Don't worry, Otto—you're light as a feather.

OTTO: I am? Oh, yes. I am. (*As he gains confidence, sings.*)
> Well, who couldn't dance with you?
> You sweep a person off his feet, lady!
> Who couldn't dance with you?
> You are so beautifully on the beat, lady!
> The band is playing,
> We're on the floor,
> The music's there to be shared!
> I used to be nervous before
> But here in your arms, I'm not scared!

Who wouldn't waltz through space?

FLAEMMCHEN (*sings*):
> We'll dance to Jupiter and Mars!

Two couples join the dance in *Grand Hotel*: Flaemmchen and
Kringelein (Jane Krakowski and Michael Jeter, *left*) and Grushinskaya
and Baron Felix (Liliane Montevecchi and David Carroll, *right*)

OTTO (*sings*):
    You make a man feel ten feet tall, lady!
    I may be short on grace—
FLAEMMCHEN (*sings*):
    We'll put our footprints on the stars . . . . .

Preysing interrupts them, wishing to get to work with the secretary. Otto,
recognizing Preysing as a former employer, greets him, but Preysing doesn't
recognize "the bookkeeper who saved you one hundred and four thousand
marks in that Estonian error . . . . . and I thank you for the raise I didn't get—
and for remembering my name, I don't think!" Preysing departs, giving
Flaemmchen five minutes to join him.

*Scene 8: The hotel conference room*

Preysing and Zinnowitz face a group of stockholders to whom Flaemmchen is passing out statements. It is clear that they are going to fire Preysing if the Boston merger falls through. They repeat "The Boston Merger" in chorus, while Zinnowitz sings confidingly to Preysing of "The Crooked Path." Preysing makes up his mind.

PREYSING: Ladies and gentlemen, I have just received a cablegram from America—the Boston merger is *on!*
COMPANY (*sings*):
    The Boston merger! The Boston merger!
PREYSING: That was easier than I thought . . . . .

*Scene 9: Backstage at the Opera House*

Not having received adequate applause from a sparse and unresponsive audience, Grushinskaya refuses to do an encore. "No Encore" the ensemble echoes in song. Despite Raffaela's assurance, "You danced *magnificently!*", Grushinskaya departs for her hotel much earlier than expected.

*Scene 10: The financial corner of the hotel lobby*

Felix is showing the ticker tape to Otto and suggesting that if he bought the right American stocks he'd soon be able to get himself a new wardrobe. The Chauffeur comes up to Felix and informs him, "The necklace belongs to that ballerina in room 510. Get it while she's at the theater!"

*Scene 11: The roof of the Grand Hotel*

*"Felix climbs along the outside of the hotel and gains the balcony of Grushinskaya's room,"* to the accompaniment of the ensemble's "Fire and Ice" in the background.

*Scene 12: Grushinskaya's suite*

Felix finds the necklace on Grushinskaya's makeup table and slips it into his pocket. Grushinskaya comes into the suite, discovering and challenging Felix, who presents himself as an ardent fan who has invaded her privacy "to breathe the air you breathe." His lavish compliments persuade her to half-believe him.

GRUSHINSKAYA: When did you first see me dance?
FELIX: Monte Carlo. You danced *Romeo and Juliet.*
GRUSHINSKAYA: My God! That was my *first* farewell tour. How old are you? If you don't mind my asking.

FELIX: The truth? I am twenty-nine years—(*A beat.*)—and twenty-nine months. And you, Madame?

GRUSHINSKAYA: And me what? My age? Are you crazy?

FELIX: If you don't mind my asking.

GRUSHINSKAYA (*pause, then smiling*): Why not? I am forty-nine years— (*A beat.*)—and forty-nine months.

> *They laugh.*

So. Now that we have been honest with each other, I presume our evening has concluded.

FELIX: On the contrary, Madame. Our evening has not yet even begun.

GRUSHINSKAYA (*sings, to herself*):
> What is this? Who can this be?
> My God! But this is charming!
> Suddenly a young and handsome stranger in my room . . .
> Why is it, in spite of that, he doesn't seem
> Alarming? But
> Charming! Charming.

(*To Felix*): Where else have you seen me dance?

Felix has followed Grushinskaya throughout her career (he sings, in "Love Can't Happen"), but he never imagined she would be so beautiful in person.

FELIX (*sings to himself*):
> Why am I talking this way?
> Can this be real to me?
> Nonsense, my boy . . .
> You knew she was beautiful
> But not so beautiful . . .
> (*To her.*) Love can't happen quite so quickly
> Not unless I dreamed you
> Beautifully and sweetly . . .
>
> No, don't look through me so clearly
> I might very nearly lose myself
> Completely
>
> Who could ever have suspected
> You would make me tremble so?
> I can't think of any answer
> Other than, if love comes . . .
> When love comes
> You know . . . . .

"Age has nothing to do with beauty," Felix declares, and orders Grushinskaya to leave the lights on so that he can look into her face. Together, they sing "Love Can't Happen," with Felix finishing, "When love comes/You know/And I know!"

### Scene 13: Raffaela's room

The Doctor comments that after most of the lights go out in the evening there is always one that burns late—Raffaela's. In her room, Raffaela soliloquizes in the song "What She Needs:" ". . . . . I will be/With her close to me/A person somehow strong/In some way wise . . . . ."

### Scene 14: The Hotel conference room and just inside the ever-revolving door

In the conference room Preysing is talking to Flaemmchen, and at the same time in the lobby Rohna is talking to Erik. Preysing is explaining that he must go to Boston on a very big deal, while Rohna reminds Erik that he gives him the best assignments, yet Erik sent a substitute on an errand to the Baron Rothschild. Erik protests that he's been working double shifts and is very worried about his wife. "Damn your wife!" exclaims Rohna with a fervor that indicates his interest in Erik may be more than merely a professional one.

In the other room, Preysing asks Flaemmchen to accompany him to Boston, someone to . . . to take care of him on the trip . . . to be nice to him. "I understand you perfectly, sir," Flaemmchen answers, and Preysing invites her to name her price.

And meanwhile Rohna tries to stroke Erik's cheek, telling Erik, "I thought I saw a certain—fineness in you—," but Erik flinches away.

### Scene 15: Raffaela's room

Raffaela continues with her song, "What She Needs." In the lobby, the Doctor comments: "Sometimes the touch of strangers triggers a passion which penetrates to the spine and echoes through the soul. But in the morning? Lovers are strangers again."

### Scene 16: Grushinskaya's suite

Felix leaves the bed to return the necklace to the night table. Grushinskaya awakens and sees him, and he pretends merely to be admiring her jewels. He tells her, "I've known many girls. I've never known a woman until last night," and then is moved to make a voluntary confession.

FELIX: . . . . . I came here to steal your necklace.
GRUSHINSKAYA: Ah. Really. Why are you telling me this now?
FELIX: Because until I did, you would never completely believe me when I say "I love you." (A beat.) And besides, you already knew it.

GRUSHINSKAYA: Then say you love me—*now.*
FELIX: I love you—
GRUSHINSKAYA: Yes, I believe it!
  *Kisses him.*
And now I must confess something to you—I want to dance again! I *have* to dance—you have made me young again.  Yesterday I canceled my performance in Vienna, but now I'm going there.  And you're going with me!
FELIX: To Vienna? When?
GRUSHINSKAYA: Tomorrow morning, very early . . . . .
FELIX: . . . . . I haven't any money. I must raise some first.
GRUSHINSKAYA: I'll give you money.
FELIX: Elizaveta! I am not a gigolo!
GRUSHINSKAYA: Of course not, I'm sorry.  Come to Vienna, *please*—I need you. I cannot dance without you! I need you.
FELIX (*figuring*): Vienna. Yes! Why not? I'll find a way. Of course I'll come with you! I'll manage somehow. I'll meet you at the railway station with my arms full of roses! Red roses for passion, Elizaveta—it's morning, bonjour!

Felix departs, leaving an ecstatic Grushinskaya to sing to herself, "Bonjour Amour."

GRUSHINSKAYA (*sings*):
  . . . . . This boy! This man!
  He makes me feel a girl again
  Bonjour!
  My joy! My fan!
  He puts me in a whirl again
  Bonjour! . . . . .

*Scene 17: The hotel bar*

The Jimmys sing "Happy," about the exhilarating new Charleston rhythm that is sweeping the world, as Flaemmchen enters and is joined by Felix. To her dismay, Flaemmchen learns that Felix has now fallen in love with another woman.

Otto enters and reveals that he took Felix's advice and bought radio stock which rose 16 points overnight (and when he removes his overcoat he is wearing a brand new tuxedo and waving a bulging wallet): "I made more last night than I ever made in a year!  . . . . . All this money, and all I did was sleep!"

As Otto prepares to buy champagne to celebrate, Flaemmchen drifts over toward Preysing, seeing where her best advantage now lies.

PREYSING: Do you like the idea of going to America?

FLAEMMCHEN: Yes, sir, very much . . . . .

PREYSING: All right, then. Run home and get your things. I'm going to get you a room, and then we'll go to the theater.

FLAEMMCHEN: Yes, sir.

Preysing and Flaemmchen exit in opposite directions. The Jimmys take up a rhythmic chant "Rub-a-dub/Rub-a-dub,/Rub-a-dub," and the others, celebrating Otto's good fortune, break into the song "We'll Take a Glass Together."

THE JIMMYS (*sing*):
. . . . . Rub-a-dub-a-dub-a-dub

OTTO (*sings*):
Friendly,

FELIX (*sings*):
Civilized,

FELIX and OTTO (*sing*):
Members of the race.

FELIX (*sings*):
I'll drink to you!

OTTO (*sings*):
No, I to you!

FELIX (*sings*):
You'll drink to me!

OTTO (*sings*):
*Then* you to me!

FELIX (*sings*):
I'm sure we two,

OTTO (*sings*):
I know we two

FELIX (*sings*):
Could find no finer company! . . . . .

A few drinks and choruses later, "*Otto and Felix dance a wild, and as Otto gets drunker, out-of-control Charleston . . . . . Exhausted, Otto nearly collapses; he accidentally drops his wallet. Felix picks it up, ponders its possibilities, then surreptitiously pockets it.*"

Scene 18:    *A cross corridor upstairs in the hotel; the Doctor's room; Preysing's room; Flaemmchen's adjoining room; Kringelein's room; the bedchamber of the Countess and the Gigolo.*

The Doctor has just injected himself with morphine and sings an occasional bar or two of "I Waltz Alone," punctuating the events which take place around him. Preysing escorts Flaemmchen to her room, adjoining his, while Felix helps a now-staggering Otto to his room. Preysing asks Flaemmchen if he can stay and watch her undress—"You said you'd be nice to me." Flaemmchen assures him, "I'm not a cheat or a tease."

In the other room, Felix is curious about whether Otto is afraid of dying. Not as long as he doesn't die penniless, Otto declares, patting the pocket where his fat wallet should be.

OTTO: My pocketbook! Where's my pocketbook? My *pocketbook*!

FELIX: Lie back! Forget your damn pocketbook! Lie back!

OTTO: You don't understand! Everything's in it: my savings, my winnings, my burial insurance . . . everything! They'll throw me out onto the street!

FELIX: Listen, Old Socks—I absolutely forgot—remember, you gave it to me to hold?

*He hands the wallet to Otto.*

OTTO: I did?—

DOCTOR (*sings*):
That's a neatly-done turn!

OTTO: Oh, yes. I quite remember now. I gave it to you to hold, and you said, "If you insist, Old Socks." Thank you, my friend. I knew I could depend on you.

DOCTOR (*sings*):
Your room grows dark,
It almost seems you're flying!
Are you flying?

PREYSING: Couldn't you call me something sweet? Maybe, "darling," like people do in films?

FLAEMMCHEN: But suppose I got in the habit and some time in the future I see you and I call out, "Hello, darling"—and your wife is with you? Or your children? How many do you have?

PREYSING: Now you're talking too much. Dance for me. Will you dance for me?

*She does, nervously.*

DOCTOR (*sings*):
Two and three and one,
Two and three and one, turn . . . . .

Otto gives Felix a fistful of money as his share of the stock deal. Felix accepts it only as a loan and gives Otto his cigarette case as collateral.

The Chauffeur accosts Felix in the hall and suggests that Preysing's well-filled wallet is unguarded while Preysing visits his secretary in another room.

Felix refuses the pistol the Chauffeur offers, but the Chauffeur presses it on him and departs. Meanwhile, the ensemble sings a chorus of "Happy."

Felix can been seen going into Preysing's room, as Preysing coaxes Flaemmchen to take off her dress and sit in his lap. Finally, Flaemmchen decides she is making a mistake, but Preysing holds onto her and prevents her from leaving until Felix steps into the room.

FELIX: Flaemmchen, get your things and go home.

PREYSING (*wheeling, furious*): What are you doing here?

FELIX: It's all right, Flaemmchen. He won't bother you any more.

PREYSING: What business is this of yours? Get out of my room!

FELIX: But this isn't exactly your room, is it? You're in no position to be giving orders, Mr. General Director Preysing.

PREYSING (*looks at them both*): Of course—I understand now. This is some sort of blackmail. I've seen you two dancing—you're in this together, aren't you?

FLAEMMCHEN: He had nothing to do with this—

PREYSING: Wait a minute—that's *my* room you came out of—what were you doing in there?

FELIX: Nothing. The night clerk must have let me into the wrong room.

PREYSING: No—no one let you in—my money is in there—let's see what you were doing—

> Moving quickly, he crosses to Felix and pushes him out, into his room. Their voices are heard.

FELIX (*offstage*): Let go of me—I wasn't doing anything!

PREYSING (*offstage*): Look at my room! You've been into everything. You're nothing but a common thief!

FLAEMMCHEN: No—he isn't a thief! He's a baron!

> The following lines overlap.

PREYSING (*offstage*): I'm calling the police!

FELIX (*offstage*): No! Take your hands off me! Stop!

FLAEMMCHEN: For God's sake, Mr. Preysing—don't—

FELIX (*offstage*): Good God, man!

> A shot rings out . . . . . Now everything breaks up, as Felix appears, rushing forward, as railroad passengers, as if at a station, form eerily around him.

FELIX (*sings "Roses at the Station"*):

. . . . . I'm here, Elizaveta, at the station
Here with the roses at the station

Here in my mind
With the seconds running out on my life
With the seconds running out on my life

I'm as close as I'll ever get to you
At the station . . .

Preysing, why did you struggle for the gun?
Why did you need to have your wallet?
Why did you need to keep your wallet?
Why did you kill me for your wallet?
Why?
> *The passengers begin to disperse . . . . . Blood appears on Felix's*
> *shirt-front—enough to run down and turn his shirt red.*

Elizaveta,
Love can't happen quite so quickly
Not unless I dreamed you
Beautifully and sweetly

I'm here, Elizaveta, at the station
Here with the roses at the station
Red roses
For passion
At the station
> *Growing faint.*

Where are you?
Where are you?

I can't see you
I can't see you . . .
> *He backs up, weakly. A shot rings out, and he staggers back and*
> *falls.*

DOCTOR:  And once again, those two sworn enemies, love and death, come
face to face and join hands.
> *A bolero begins, and the two dancers (Countess and Gigolo)*
> *perform their dance, as the dead Felix remains visible in the*
> *background."*

*Scene 19:  Grushinskaya's suite; Kringelein's room; Preysing's room*

As Raffaela sings "How Can I Tell Her?", others react to Felix's demise.
Zinnowitz tries to explain to a detective that Preysing was merely acting in
self-defense against a thief, but the detective scoffs, "Thief?  The deceased
was a baron."  Flaemmchen calls Preysing "a complete swine," and explains
to Otto that she direly needed the money Preysing was going to pay her to
accompany him.

OTTO:  I never realized how important money was until I saw what it could
buy.

FLAEMMCHEN: Do you mean me, by any chance?

OTTO: What? Oh, no, I didn't—

FLAEMMCHEN: Well, people come to that. When you've been without a job, and your clothes are out of date, and you can't bear where you live any more—

OTTO: If you could go away with him, hating him—

FLAEMMCHEN: You're right, Mister Kringelein—I've just got to find something else.

> *She goes.*

OTTO (*alone, he finishes the sentence, without realizing she's gone*): —I have money—

> *He turns and sees he's alone.*

RAFFAELA (*sings*):
> Is it wiser she not know?
> How can I tell her
> This tale so heavy with heartbreak?
> Her new-found lover
> So soon is gone?

> *Behind them, the police cover Felix and carry him out on a litter. Only the phone operators are there to mourn.*

OTTO: He was so young—so handsome—

RAFFAELA (*sings*):
> How can I tell her?
> I can't!

*Scene 20: The lobby of the Grand Hotel*

It is morning. *"The operators are at their switchboard,"* and Erik receives the news that he is the father of a boy, with mother and child doing fine. He sings "As It Should Be" while detectives escort Preysing, handcuffed, across the lobby and out.

Otto comes to settle his bill and leave, carrying his own luggage and confiding to the Doctor that "life resides in people, not buildings," so he will go elsewhere to enjoy his last days.

Rohna is warned that Grushinskaya, on her way down, knows nothing about what has happened to the Baron. Flaemmchen comes in to get her typewriter, and Otto invites her to come to Paris with him, but warning her that he's a dying man.

Grushinskaya appears—her car has been ordered, but she insists that she won't go without saying goodbye to Felix. Then she remembers that he has promised to meet her at the railroad station with red roses for passion. Raffaela assures her that the Baron will keep the appointment (and calls her "Elizaveta" for the first time, by mistake on purpose), and they depart.

The doctor warns Kringelein against Flaemmchen.

DOCTOR: . . . . . She'd leave you the minute your money ran out. Then where will life be?

OTTO: Where it's never been before. Behind me. Excuse me, my friend—
*He sees Flaemmchen returning with her typewriter and runs to meet her halfway.*

Miss Flaemmchen—*will* you come with me to Paris?

FLAEMMCHEN (*taken aback*): Good Lord, you've got a way with you. Good Lord.

OTTO: But will you come?

FLAEMMCHEN: You're awfully sweet, Otto—but I have to tell you the truth. I'm afraid I'm pregnant.

OTTO: Really?
*Takes her typewriter.*
But that's wonderful! I've never seen a newborn baby—that's certainly something to look forward to. So I'll ask you again—will you come to Paris?

FLAEMMCHEN: Don't ask me, Otto—*tell* me.

OTTO (*looks around, straightens his shoulders, sings*):
Fraulein Flaemmchen
You will come to Paree
You'll be taking the train there
Next to me

FLAEMMCHEN: Oh, Otto, how can I refuse?

Otto tips Erik handsomely on behalf of the Baron and goes off to his taxi with Flaemmchen.

"Arbeit!" exclaims Kohl, and the scullery workers respond by singing their song. The Doctor comments, "Grand Hotel, Berlin . . . . . One man goes to jail while another goes to Paris—always the same. Nothing ever happens . . . . . The revolving door turns and turns—swings and swings and swings—and life goes on. I'll stay one more day."

And the company sings "The Grand Parade."

GROUP 1 (*sing*):
Grand Hotel
Grand Hotel
Music constantly playing
Grand Hotel
Living well
Where the wealthy are staying

It's the din
Of old Berlin
You're in the Grand Hotel . . . . .

GROUP 2 (*sing*):
At the Grand
You are at the Grand
At the Grand
You are at the Grand
At the Grand
You are at the Grand Hotel

At the Grand
You are at the Grand
At the Grand . . . . .

*The Grand Finale (Curtain Calls)*

ENSEMBLE (*sings "The Grand Waltz"*):
   And life goes on,
   Round 'n' round,
   Back 'n' forth,
   On and on!
   We and you parading through the Grand Cafe
   Nonchalantly table-hopping life away?
   Day to night
   Dark to dawn
   Come 'n' gone
   Back 'n' forth
   East 'n' west
   South 'n' north
   Life goes on.
      *Curtain.*

# MY CHILDREN! MY AFRICA!

*A Play in Two Acts*

BY ATHOL FUGARD

Cast and credits appear on page 422

*ATHOL FUGARD was born June 11, 1932 in Middelburg in the semi-desert Karoo country of South Africa. His mother was an Afrikaner, his father of Irish and Huguenot descent. He studied motor mechanics at Port Elizabeth Technical College and philosophy at the University of Cape Town and spent three years in the Merchant Marine, mostly in the Far East. He married an actress, Sheila Meiring, and for a time they ran an experimental theater in Cape Town. His first play,* No-Good Friday, *was produced in 1959 with an all-black cast, and his* Nogogo *(also 1959) had an American premiere in 1978 for 20 performances at Manhattan Theater Club.*

*Fugard's* The Blood Knot *premiered in Sophiatown, near Johannesburg, Sept. 3, 1961 and won him an international reputation extending to these shores in an off-Broadway production starring James Earl Jones, March 1, 1964 for 240 performances (it is about two black half-brothers, one light-skinned and one dark). His next play,* People Are Living There, *was done in Glasgow in 1968 and then in London during the 1971–72 season. His* Hello and Goodbye, *first produced in 1965, appeared off Broadway with Martin*

*Sheen and Colleen Dewhurst Sept. 18, 1969 for 45 performances and was produced in London in 1972–73. His next,* Mille Miglia *(1968) was aired on BBC-TV (as was* The Blood Knot*). It was followed by* Boesman and Lena *(1969), done off Broadway with James Earl Jones, Ruby Dee and Zakes Mokae, June 22, 1970 for 205 performances and named a Best Play of its season, a year before its London premiere.*

*Fugard's second Best Play,* The Island, *had strong mimetic as well as literary elements and is credited as a collaboration "devised" by the author and the actors who appeared in it, John Kani and Winston Ntshona. It reversed the direction of the previous Fugard Best Play by stopping in London before coming to New York, appearing under the auspices of the Royal Court Theater on a two-play program with* Sizwe Banzi Is Dead *by the same authors. These two plays then had their American premiere in tandem, first at the Long Wharf Theater in New Haven, Conn. in October 1974 and then in alternating repertory (*Sizwe *for 159 performances,* Island *for 52) beginning Nov. 13, 1974 in mini-Broadway productions at the Edison Theater, receiving Tony nominations for best play and for Fugard's direction.*

*Fugard's third Best Play,* A Lesson From Aloes, *first appeared on this side of the Atlantic at the Centaur Theater in Montreal Jan. 1, 1980; then was produced at the Yale Repertory Theater in New Haven March 26 and finally on Broadway Nov. 17 for 96 performances, winning the Critics Award as the best play of the season and Tony-nominated for best play, in all three cases under the author's direction. Fugard's fourth Best Play was* Master Harold . . . and the Boys, *which premiered at Yale Rep under its author's direction, in a production brought to Broadway May 4, 1982 for 344 performances, again Tony-nominated for both best play and direction; and a London production received the Evening Standard best-play citation.*

*Fugard's fifth Best Play,* The Road to Mecca, *took the same route under its author's direction through Yale Rep production in May 1984 to New York, opening off Broadway April 12, 1988 and playing for 172 performances. Ineligible for Tony consideration under a system that still stubbornly refuses to recognize that much of the theater's very best work appears in the smaller context of off Broadway,* The *Road to Mecca nevertheless won the broader-visioned citation of the Critics Circle as the best foreign play of the season (and* The Blood Knot *had emphasized the fallacy of the Tony policy when, in a 1986 Broadway revival, it was nominated for a Tony as best "new" play because it hadn't previously appeared uptown).* The Road to Mecca *has also been produced in London, by the National Theater.*

*Fugard's* My Children! My Africa! *was originally produced by the Market Theater in Johannesburg in June 1989. It made its U.S. debut Dec. 18 in an off-off-Broadway production by New York Theater Workshop, in a run limited to 28 performances by its production contract. It is enthusiastically cited as Fugard's sixth Best Play, in accordance with our new policy (established last season with* Emerald City) *of widening Best Play eligibility to include special cases of OOB production (i.e.: modern scripts which have already made their esthetic mark outside New York but for commercial reasons appear outside the defined limits of Broadway and off Broadway).*

*Other Fugard works appearing on our record of U.S. production have included* Statements After an Arrest Under the Immorality Act *November 1978 for 35 performances at Manhattan Theater Club;* The Drummer *at Actors Theater of Louisville in the 1979–80 season;* A Place With the Pigs *March 1987 premiering at Yale Rep. Fugard has also acted in many of his own works including* The Road to Mecca *and the movies* The Guest *and* Marigolds in August. *He has received honorary degrees from Yale, Natal and Georgetown Universities and the Universities of Rhodes and Cape Town, and he is an honorary member of the American Institute of Arts and Letters.*

*Some of Fugard's training for what has turned out to be his triple profession of actor-director-writer was acquired in Rehearsal Room in Johannesburg's Dorkay House (the headquarters of South Africa's Union Artists, the organization that cares for the cultural interests of non-Europeans in the Transvaal). Later, as resident director of Dorkay House, he staged the work of many modern playwrights such as John Steinbeck and Harold Pinter. Since the mid-1960s he has been closely associated with Serpent Players of New Brighton, Port Elizabeth, a theater workshop for black Africans experimenting in collaborative "play-making" of works dealing with the contemporary South African scene. Rehearsals and performances of Serpent Players are customarily carried on after hours, with black participants sometimes classified technically as "household employees" of their white colleague Athol Fugard because "artist" has not been an accepted employment category for South African blacks.*

*Fugard lives near Port Elizabeth with his wife, and they have a daughter, Lisa-Maria. He has often been a focal point of controversy in his politically controversial land and was once denied a passport by his government when he wanted to come to New York for rehearsals of* Boesman and Lena *in the spring of 1970.*

*The following synopsis of* My Children! My Africa! *was prepared by Sally Dixon Wiener.*

*Time: The autumn of 1984*

*Place: A small Eastern Cape Karoo town*

## ACT I

*Scene 1*

SYNOPSIS: The play is minimally-staged and the action takes place in a number of locales in or near the town. It begins in a Zolile High School class-room with Mr. M, a black teacher, middle-aged, goateed and bespectacled, seated at a table upon which there are some books, the class register, his straw boater and a large school bell. Two chairs flank the table. *"A lively inter-school debate is in progress."* The debaters onstage are Thami Mbik-wana, a neatly-dressed black student at the Zolile school, and Isabel Dyson, a white student in the uniform and blazer of her school.

Isabel is arguing with Thami about whether women are more intuitive than men or more emotional. Mr. M, trying to re-establish order, rings the school bell vehemently to silence them. He reads them the definition of a debate from his worn dictionary. Although commending their enthusiasm, he points out that without discipline "it is as useless as having a good donkey and a good cart but no harness." Time is growing short, and he gives them each three minutes to sum up.

Thami is to go first and is roundly applauded as he stands to speak, confi-dent in front of the audience of his fellow students, whom he asks to think of his words as those of the ancestors of the culture on which they shouldn't turn their back.

THAMI: The opposition has spoken about sexual exploitation and the need for women's liberation. Brothers and sisters, these are foreign ideas. Do not listen to them. They come from a culture, the so-called Western Civilization, that has meant only misery to Africa and its people. It is the same culture that shipped away thousands of our ancestors as slaves, the same culture that has exploited Africa with the greed of a vulture during the period of colonialism and the same culture which continues to exploit us in the twentieth century under the disguise of concern for our future. The opposition has not been able to refute my claim that women cannot do the same jobs as men because they are not equals of us physically, and that a woman's role in the family, in soci-ety, is totally different to that of a man's. These facts taken together reinforce what our fathers, and our grandfathers knew: namely, that happiness and prosperity for the tribe and the nation is achieved when education of the little ladies takes these facts into consideration. Would it be right for a woman to go to war while man sits at the sewing machine? I do not have milk in my breasts to feed the baby while my wife is out digging up roads for the Divisional Council.

*Wild laughter.*

Thami expresses his belief that his schoolmates feel as he does about the issue and hopes the vote will indicate this. Again there is applause, and whistling as well, and then Isabel, the captain of the visiting team from Camdeboo Girls High, stands to make her last statement, to "polite applause," but is not going to let herself be intimidated by the audience.

She opens by assuring them of her respect for their history and traditions and for their values and principles that might be studied profitably by the Western Civilization that's been derided by her opponent. She believes, however, that Africa doesn't live in the past; that it's the 20th century, and the continent is trying hard to come to grips with that; and that the old arguments are being used in an effort to hold back progress.

ISABEL: Maybe there was a time in the past when a woman's life consisted of bearing children and hoeing the fields while men sharpened their spears and sat around waiting for another war to start. But it is a silly argument that relies on that old image of primitive Africa for its strength. It is an argument that insults your intelligence. Times have changed. Sheer brute strength is not the determining factor any more. You do not need the muscles of a prize fighter when you sit down to operate the computers that control today's world. The American space program now has women astronauts on board the space shuttles, doing the same jobs as men. As for the difference in the emotional and intellectual qualities of men and women, remember that it is a question of difference and not inferiority, and that with those differences go strengths which compensate for weaknesses in the opposite sex. And lastly, a word of warning. The argument against equality for women, in education or any other field, based on alleged "differences" between the two sexes, is an argument that can very easily be used against any other "different" group. It is an argument based on prejudice, not fact. I ask you not to give it your support. Thank you.

*She sits. Polite applause.*

MR. M: Thank you, Miss Dyson. We come now to the vote. But before we do that, a word of caution. We have had a wonderful experience this afternoon. Don't let it end on a frivolous and irresponsible note. Serious issues have been debated. Vote accordingly. To borrow a phrase from Mr. Mbikwana, forget the faces, remember the words. If you believe that we have the right to vote out there in the big world, then show it here in the classroom, that you know how to use it. We'll take it on a count of hands, and for the benefit of any over-enthusiastic supporters, only one hand per person please. Let me read the proposal once again: "That in view of the essential physical and psychological differences between men and women, there should be correspondingly different educational syllabuses for the two sexes."

The three of them count hands. There are 17 in favor, and 24 against. Isabel has won. Thami admits afterwards to her that her concluding statement was "a knockout." Mr. M tells Thami he did well also. Thami got her angry, Isabel confesses, and she'd begun to think he believed what he'd said. He assures her he did, but she doesn't believe him. Mr. M congratulates Isabel and twits Thami on his shamelessness in attempting to exploit the loyalty of his classmates. Thami laughs and asks if that was wrong. Mr. M admits it wasn't, but he was pleased with the decision and believes the audience members were the "real winners," that Isabel and Thami only had to talk, whereas the audience had to listen carefully.

Mr. M's due at a staff meeting, and he leaves the two young people, who are "a little self-conscious" at being on their own. As they pack up their papers and books, Isabel remarks that she wishes she had a teacher like Mr. Myalatya, struggling to pronounce Mr. M's name properly. She thinks he is wonderful; Thami allows that he is all right. They both agree they enjoyed the experience of the debate, then both confess they hadn't expected to. Thami again tells Isabel she was good, and Isabel explains it was because she felt strongly about the subject. And she liked the atmosphere, too. The debates at her school are usually unexciting. "This was a riot!" she says.

THAMI (*finger to his lips*): Be careful.
ISABEL: Of what?
THAMI: That word.
ISABEL: Which one?
THAMI: Riot! Don't say it in a black township. Police start shooting as soon as they hear it.
ISABEL: Oh . . .
THAMI (*having a good laugh*): I'm sorry. It's a joke, Isabel.
ISABEL: Oh . . . you caught me off guard. I didn't think you would joke about those things.
THAMI: Riots and police? Oh yes, we joke about them. We joke about everything.
ISABEL: Okay, then I'll say it again: this afternoon was a riot.
THAMI: Good! Try that one on your folks when you get home tonight. Say the newspapers have got it all wrong. You had a wonderful time taking part in a little township riot.
    *This time Isabel does get the joke. A good laugh.*
ISABEL: Oh ja, I can just see my mom and dad cracking up at that one.
THAMI: They wouldn't think it was funny?

*The subject of white reaction . . . . . amuses him enormously.*

ISABEL: Are you kidding? They even take the Marx Brothers seriously. I can just hear my Mom: "Isabel, I think it is very wrong to joke about those things!"

Thami notes that Dyson is an English name, and Isabel says she's third-generation English-speaking South African. He questions her about her family—her father has a chemist's shop, the Karoo Pharmacy, where her mother and sister work. She does, too, on Saturdays—except when she has a hockey match. "A happy family," Thami remarks. Isabel agrees, but her older sister would prefer it if Isabel weren't the family rebel. Isabel is 18, and thinks she wants to be a writer. English is her favorite subject, hockey her favorite sport. She'll answer any other questions Thami has.

THAMI: . . . . . What did you have for breakfast this morning?

ISABEL: Auntie, our maid, put down in front of me a plate of steaming, delicious jungle oats over which I sprinkled a crust of golden brown sugar, and while that was melting on top I added a little moat of chilled milk all around the side. That was followed by brown-bread toast, quince jam and lots and lots of tea.

THAMI: Yes, you're a writer.

ISABEL: You think so?

THAMI: You made me hungry.

ISABEL: My turn now?

THAMI: Yep.

ISABEL: Let's start with your family.

THAMI: Mbikwana! (*He clears his throat.*) Mbikwana is an old Bantu name, and my mother and my father are good, reliable, ordinary, hardworking Bantu-speaking black South African natives. I am the one hundred thousandth generation.

ISABEL: You really like teasing, don't you.

THAMI: Amos and Lilian Mbikwana. They're in Cape Town. My mother is a domestic, and my father works for the railways. I stay here with my grandmother and married sister. I was sent to school in the peaceful platteland because it is so much safer, you see, than the big city with all its temptations and troubles. (*Thami laughs.*) Another Bantu joke.

ISABEL: You're impossible.

They are much more at ease with each other now. Isabel is looking at the class register and wants to know which desk is Thami's. She sits down at it, notices the names carved into it and looks for his. It's not there. Thami doesn't want any part of himself left in that classroom. Isabel is surprised, as she assumes he has no trouble with exams. It's not that simple to Thami.

School doesn't mean to him and his fellow students what it means to her. He had liked it when he was younger and wished he could have gone to school on Saturdays and Sundays, too, but he'd changed, everything had changed. He is reticent about discussing it any further, she realizes.

Isabel (who plans to take journalism at Rhodes University) asks him what he's going to do when he's finished school, won't he want to go on with his studies? Thami isn't sure. Isabel supposes Mr. M must have plans for him, but Thami vehemently remarks that he doesn't listen to Mr. M or do what he says. She apologizes for interfering, and Thami explains that Mr. M seems to think he knows what's best for him, but never asks him what his own feelings are. And Thami has ideas of his own. The sound of the bell, off, ends their conversation, and they hurry off with their schoolcases.

*Scene 2*

Isabel, alone and speaking to the audience, is describing what everybody calls "the Location," although its real name is Brakwater, from a farm once there. It's regrettable that it's the first thing people see when they're visiting Camdeboo, which she says is a pretty town. The Location has houses of corrugated iron, or whatever else could make walls and a roof, and no gardens. Isabel's been there with her mother to visit Auntie, when the maid was ill, and with her father, when he took medicines to the clinic. The Location lacks electricity, running water, and privacy—nine people sleep in Auntie's two-room house. But the Location is just there, "on the edge of my life, the way it is out there on the edge of the town," so when the principal of her school said the black school had invited them to have a debate with its students she hadn't objected. Her principal, Miss Brockway, had called it a pioneering educational opportunity, and even though there'd been a little trouble in the Location, the police had considered it safe if they were driven to the school and back. Two other girls were on the team besides Isabel, and one of them had said, "We must remember English isn't their home language. So don't use too many big words and speak slowly and carefully."

When they got to the classroom, which she'd thought too depressing a place to study in, there were 40 or so students, the preponderance of them boys, and "not one welcoming smile." They weren't going to be grateful to her; they were waiting to judge her on a basis of equality, she was forced to realize, and she hadn't ever confronted that situation before, not just in debates, but in her life. She's had the average amount of cross-color contact as any young white South African, gossiping with Auntie in the kitchen at breakfast time, and talking with Samuel, her father's delivery man. But then she was "the baas's daughter." In that classroom it was different. "It was *their* school. It was *their* world." She was an outsider.

One member of her team said she'd started very badly but finished very strongly. Isabel recalls the moment she'd realized the audience was understanding her: "They were staring and listening so hard I could feel it on my skin!" The experience was so real, and it gave her such an exciting sense of herself. But that's what she wants—doesn't everyone?—she asks. She had found another world in the place that she'd just regarded as embarrassing, a new world with a life of its own, and the discovery was disconcerting to her. What she'd been brought up to believe was available—ideas, chances, especially people—is just a small part of what could be. Isabel wants more.

## Scene 3

Mr. M has come to Isabel's school to discuss a proposition with her. She is happy to see him and calls him "Mr. M," which pleases him and makes him feel as if she, as well as Thami, is a member of his extended family. He hopes she'd still like to return to his school, that "the unruly behavior of my young family" didn't put her off. Isabel says she was a bit unruly herself when there, and they agree she likes a good fight.

He tells her he's spoken to her principal about a prospect he's excited about. The principal has given it her blessing. The idea had come to him during the debate that it was a waste because the two (Isabel and Thami) ought not to be fighting each other, but fighting as allies. "They could take on anybody . . . and win!" he had thought. And, as a teacher, the thought that these two students would be just two more victims of the problems of the country nearly overcame him.

But now he has in hand an answer to his worries. The bank is to sponsor a new event at the Grahamstown Schools Festival, an inter-school English literature quiz. Each team will have two members, and it's Mr. M's idea that Zolile High and Camdeboo High enter a combined team, Isabel and Thami. Isabel is ecstatic and calls him a genius, but he warns her it will involve a lot of work. He will be the team coach and "can be a very hard taskmaster."

Mr. M is delighted Isabel has taken to his idea. She tells him her visit to Zolile had been very important to her, that she'd like to know them all better, and this provides the opportunity. She'd been feeling frustrated about the situation but hadn't been able to make her parents understand how she felt about it, especially her mother, who was frightened. Isabel isn't frightened any more, she says, and he realizes she had been. She had thought that everyone there would be "nice and polite and very, very grateful." Mr. M had been, but not Thami and the others. But making friends with Thami had made a difference. "Knowledge has banished fear," Mr. M remarks. He tells her the competition's first prize is five thousand rand, and the bank said it's to be spent on books for the school library; so when she and Thami are the winners, it will be divided between the schools.

ISABEL: Yes, what about my team mate? What does he say? Have you asked him yet?

MR. M: No, I haven't *asked* him, Isabel, and I won't. I will *tell* him, and when I do I trust he will express as much enthusiasm for the idea as you have. I am an old fashioned traditionalist in most things, young lady, and my class-room is certainly no exception. I teach, Thami learns. He understands and accepts that that is the way it should be. You don't like the sound of that, do you?

ISABEL: Does sound a bit dictatorial, you know.

MR. M: It might sound that way, but I assure you it isn't. We do not blur the difference between the generations in the way that you white people do. Respect for authority, right authority, is deeply ingrained in the African soul. It's all I've got when I stand there . . . . . Respect for my authority is my only teaching aid. If I ever lost it, those young people will abandon their desks and take to the streets. I expect Thami to trust my judgement of what is best for him, and he does. That trust is the most sacred responsibility in my life.

ISABEL: He's your favorite, isn't he?

MR. M: Good heavens! A good teacher doesn't have favorites! Are you suggesting that I might be a bad one? Because if you are . . . (*Looking around.*) you would be right, young lady. Measured by that yardstick I am a very bad teacher indeed. He *is* my favorite. Thami Mbikwana! Yes, I have waited a long time for him. To tell you the truth, I had given up all hope of him ever coming along. Any teacher who takes his calling seriously dreams about that one special pupil, that one eager and gifted young head into which he can pour all that he knows and loves, and who will justify all the years of frustration in the classroom . . . . . If he looks after himself he'll go far and do big things. He's a born leader, Isabel, and that is what your generation needs. Powerful forces are fighting for the souls of you young people. You need *real* leaders. Not rabble-rousers. I know Thami is meant to be one. I know it with such certainty it makes me frightened. Because it is a responsibility. Mine and mine alone.

If Isabel and Thami win at the Festival, Mr. M means to insist that Thami be given a university scholarship. Isabel assures him they'll win.

*Scene 4*

*Mr. M alone. He talks directly to the audience.*

MR. M: "I am a man who in the eager pursuit of knowledge forgets his food and in the joy of its attainment forgets his sorrows, and who does not perceive that old age is coming on." (*He shakes his head.*) No. As I'm sure you have already guessed, that is not me. My pursuit of knowledge is eager, but I do perceive, and only too clearly, that old age is coming on, and at the best of times I do a bad job of forgetting my sorrows. Those wonderful words come from the finest teacher I have ever had, that most wise of all the ancient philosophers ... Confucius! Yes. I am a Confucian. A black Confucian! There are not many of us. In fact, I think there's a good chance that the only one in the country is talking to you at this moment. I claim him as my teacher because I have read very carefully, and many times, and I will read it many more times, a little book I have about him, his life, his thoughts and utterances. Truly, they *are* wonderful words, my friends, wonderful, wonderful words! My classroom motto comes from its pages: "Learning undigested by thought is labor lost, thought unassisted by learning is perilous!" But the words that challenge me most these days is something he said towards the end of his life. At the age of seventy he turned to his pupils one day and said that he could do whatever his heart prompted, without transgressing what was right. What do you say to that? . . . . . Imagine being able to wake up in the morning in your little room, yawn and stretch, scratch a few fleabites and then jump out of your bed and eat your bowl of mealie-pap and sour milk with a happy heart because you know that when you walk out into the world you will be free to obey and act out, with a clear conscience, all the promptings of your heart. No matter what you see out there . . . . . no matter what stories of hardship and suffering you hear, or how bad the news you read in the newspapers, knowing that the whole truth, which can't be printed, is even worse . . . . . (*Another shake of his head, another rueful smile.*) No yet again. Not in this life . . . . . Not even if I lived to be one hundred and seventy, will I end up a calm, gentle Chinese heart like his. I wish I could . . . . . Because I am frightened of the one I've got. I don't get gentle promptings from it, my friends. I get heart attacks. When I walk out into those streets, and I see what is happening to my people, it jumps out and savages me like a wild beast. (*Thumping his chest with a clenched fist.*) I've got a whole zoo in here, a mad zoo of hungry animals ... and the keeper is frightened! All of them. Mad and savage! Look at me! I'm sweating today. I've been sweating for a week. Why? Because one of those animals, the one called Hope, has broken loose and is looking for food . . . . . You think I'm exaggerating? . . . . . Then I'd like to put you inside a black skin and ask you to keep Hope alive, find food for it on these streets where our children, our loved and precious children go hungry and die of malnutrition. No, believe me, it is a dangerous animal for a black man to have prowling around in his heart . . . . . That is why I am a teacher . . . . . The truth is that I am worse than Nero feeding Christians to the lions. I feed young people to my Hope. Every young body behind a school desk keeps it alive. So you've been warned! . . . . . That is the monster that stands here before you. Full name: Anela Myalatya. Age: Fifty-seven. Marital status: Bachelor. Occupation: Teacher. Address: The back room of the Reverend Mbopa's house next to the Anglican Church of St. Mark. It's a little on the small side. You know those big kitchen-size boxes of matches they sell these days . . . well if you imagine one of those as Number One Classroom at Zolile High, then the little matchbox you put in your pocket is my room at the Reverend Mbopa's. But I'm not complaining. It has got all I need . . . a table and chair where I correct homework and prepare lessons, a comfortable bed for a good night's insomnia and a reserved space for my chair in front of the television set in the Reverend Mbopa's lounge. So there you have it. What I call my life rattles around in these two matchboxes . . . the classroom and the back room. If you see me hurrying along the streets you can be reasonably certain that one of those two is my urgent destination. The people tease me. "Faster, Mr. M," they shout to me from their front door. "You'll be late" . . . . . They don't know how close they are to a terrible truth . . . . . The clocks are ticking, my friends. History has got a strict timetable. If we're not careful we might be remembered as the country where everybody arrived too late.

## Scene 5

Mr. M is waiting for Isabel, who comes on with her schoolcase and hockey stick, tired and disappointed at losing a game to the other team. Admitting to being a bad loser, she asks Mr. M if he has advice on how to be a dignified, gracious loser. He admits that he, too, is a bad loser, and, like Isabel, wants to take the hockey stick and hit somebody. Thami wouldn't, though, Isabel opines.

Mr. M is glad Isabel and Thami have gotten to be good friends. Isabel says the recent weeks have been "quite an education" for her and that she owes Mr. M a lot. She believes Thami would say so, too, if Mr. M gave him the opportunity. He bristles, but she points out that he is *always* the teacher" and Thami's *always* the pupil." She wishes Mr. M could just talk to him as a friend, as she has.

He's curious as to whether or not Thami seems happy, and Isabel wonders whether he means happy with them, with the competition. That, and his schoolwork, "and . . . everything else," he says. Why doesn't he ask Thami, Isabel retorts. Mr. M says he'll only get a "Yes, Teacher." Isabel believes Thami is happy, though he doesn't let out much about himself. She adds that being 18 is not a simple matter, and being happy doesn't mean she hasn't any problems, nor does she think Thami doesn't have any problems.

Thami isn't in trouble yet, but Mr. M believes he and his friends will be, if Thami isn't careful, because there's something going on in the Location, particularly among the younger people. There's whispering, and he asks Isabel if Thami has mentioned what it's about. It turns out Thami hasn't, but Isabel is shocked at Mr. M's question. It wouldn't be right for her to tell him if Thami had, but he claims "it would be for his own good." He admits to his mistake, but he's been very anxious about Thami. He asks Isabel not to mention anything about his questioning her and says he'll speak with Thami himself. Thami finally arrives, his game having gone into overtime.

ISABEL: Did you win?

THAMI: No. We lost one-nil.

ISABEL: Good.

THAMI: But it was a good game. We're trying out some new combinations and they nearly worked. The chaps are really starting to come together as a team. A little more practice, that's all we need.

ISABEL: Hear that, Mr. M? What did I tell you? And look at him. Smiling! Happy! Even in defeat, a generous word for his team mates.

THAMI: What's going on?

ISABEL: Don't try to look innocent, Mbikwana. Your secret is out. Your true identity has been revealed. You are a good loser, and don't try to deny it.

THAMI: Me? You're wrong. I don't like losing.

ISABEL: It's not a question of liking or not liking, but of being able to do so without a crooked smile on your face, a knot in your stomach and murder in your heart.

THAMI: You lost your game this afternoon.

ISABEL: Whatever made you guess! We were trounced. So be careful. I'm looking for revenge.

MR. M: Good! Then let's see if you can get it in the arena of English literature. What do we deal with today?

THAMI: Nineteenth century poetry.

MR. M (*with relish*): Beautiful! Beautiful! Beautiful! (*Making himself comfortable.*) Whose service?

> *Thami picks up a stone, hands behind his back, then clenched fists for Isabel to guess. She does. She wins. Their relationship is now obviously very relaxed and easy.*

ISABEL: Gird your loins, Mbikwana. I want blood.

THAMI: I wish you the very best of luck.

ISABEL: God, I hate you.

MR. M: First service, please.

Isabel begins with a question about the Lake poets, and the back-and-forth session continues with a great deal of good-natured bantering as Mr. M umpires. They have been reciting *Ozymandias* when Isabel takes out her notebook and remarks that Ozymandias was actually an Egyptian king who "erected many monuments . . . . . but his oppressive rule left Egypt impoverished and suffering from an incurable decline." Thami wonders what happened to the statue, how it was toppled. Isabel supposes it was weather and time but is curious to know why he is thinking about it. Thami recalls having a

Bible storybook when he was little and trying to count all the slaves pulling the stone blocks with ropes in a picture in the book, and that the slaves seemed to have "outnumbered the soldiers one hundred to one." She teasingly asks him if he's attempting to stir up ancient trouble. It's not a joking matter, Thami says, there are a number of Ozymandiases in this country, and *"We* won't leave it to time to bring them down."

MR. M (*trying to put a smile on it*): Who is the *we* you speak for with such authority, Thami?

THAMI: The People.

MR. M (*recognition*): Yes, yes, yes, of course . . . I should have known. The People . . . with a capital P. Does that include me? Am I one of The People?

THAMI: If you choose to be.

MR. M: I've got to choose, have I? My black skin doesn't confer automatic membership. So how do I go about choosing?

THAMI: By identifying with the fight for our freedom.

MR. M: As simple as that? I want our freedom as much as any of you. In fact, I was fighting for it in my small way long before you were born! But I've got a small problem. Does that noble fight of ours really have to stoop to pulling down a few silly statues? Where do you get the idea that we, The People, want you to do that for us?

THAMI (*trying*): They are not our heroes, teacher.

MR. M: They are not our statues, Thami! Wouldn't it be better for us to rather put our energies into erecting a few of our own? We've also got heroes, you know.

THAMI: Like who, Mr. M? Nelson Mandela? (*Shaking his head with disbelief.*) Hey! *They* would pull *that* statue down so fast . . .

MR. M (*cutting him*): In which case they would be just as guilty of gross vandalism . . . because that is what it will be, regardless of who does it to whom. Destroying somebody else's property is inexcusable behaviour! No, Thami. As one of The People you claim to be acting for, I raise my hand in protest. Please don't pull down any statues on my behalf. Don't use me as an excuse for an act of lawlessness. If you want to do something "revolutionary" for me, let us sit down and discuss it, because I have a few constructive alternatives I would like to suggest. Do I make myself clear?

THAMI: Yes, teacher.

MR. M: Good. I'm glad we understand each other.

Isabel intervenes by asking if they shouldn't pick out certain authors, such as Dickens, that are bound to come up at the competition, and Mr. M suggests she and Thami make a list of 20 novelists. Before Mr. M leaves, Isabel invites both of them to tea at her home. She and Mr. M set the date for the following

Sunday. Thami has not participated in the discussion, during which Mr. M has spoken for both of them. Finally Mr. M departs.

ISABEL (*sensitive to a change of mood in Thami*): . . . . . You will come, won't you?

THAMI (*edge to his voice*): Didn't you hear Mr. M? "A delight and a privilege! We accept most gratefully." (*Writing in his notebook.*) Charles Dickens . . . Thomas Hardy . . . Jane Austen . . .

ISABEL: Was he speaking for you as well?

THAMI: He speaks for me on nothing!

ISABEL: Relax. I know that. That's why I tried to ask you separately and why I'll ask you again. Would you like to come to tea next Sunday to meet my family? It's not a polite invitation. They really want to meet you.

THAMI: Me? Why? Are they starting to get nervous?

ISABEL: Oh come off it, Thami. Don't be like that. They're always nervous when it comes to me. But this time it happens to be genuine interest. I've told you. I talk about you at home. They know I have a good time with you . . . that we're a team . . . which they are now very proud of, incidentally . . . and that we're cramming like lunatics so that we can put up a good show at the Festival. Is it so strange that they want to meet you after all that? Honestly, sometimes dealing with the two of you is like walking on a tightrope. I'm always scared I'm going to put a foot wrong and . . . well, I just *hate* being scared like that.

*A few seconds of truculent silence between the two of them.*

What's going on, Thami? Between you two? There's something very wrong, isn't there?

THAMI: No more than usual.

ISABEL: No you don't! A hell of a lot more than usual, and don't deny it, because it's getting to be pretty obvious. I mean, I know he gets on your nerves. I knew that the first day we met. But it's more than that now. These past couple of meetings I've caught you looking at him, watching him in a . . . I don't know . . . in a sort of hard way. Very critical. Not just once. Many times. Do you know you're doing it?

*Shrug of the shoulders from Thami.*

Well, if you know it or not, you are. And now he's started as well.

THAMI: What do you mean?

ISABEL: He's watching you.

THAMI: So? He can watch me as much as he likes. I've got nothing to hide. Even if I had, he'd be the last person to find out. He sees nothing, Isabel.

Isabel disagrees, but Thami insists Mr. M doesn't see or hear anything and doesn't realize what's happening to blacks or understand the way they feel.

It's not the same as it was when Mr. M was young. People are impatient, want change and want it now, he tells Isabel. Mr. M has old-fashioned ideas about change, and they haven't achieved anything. "The people don't want to listen to his kind of talk any more," he insists. Isabel is confused about what kind of talk he's referring to, and Thami impatiently points out she has just been listening to it, Mr. M's calling their struggle "vandalism and lawless behavior," expecting them just to wait for white South Africa to awaken.

ISABEL: And those old fashioned ideas of his . . . are we one of them?
THAMI: What do you mean?
ISABEL: You and me. The competition.
THAMI: Let's change the subject, Isabel. (*His notebook.*) Charles Dickens . . . Thomas Hardy . . . Jane Austen . . .
ISABEL: No! You can't do that! I'm involved. I've got a right to know. Are we an old fashioned idea?
THAMI: Not our friendship. That is our decision, our choice.
ISABEL: And the competition?
THAMI (*uncertain of himself*): Maybe . . . I'm not sure. I need time to think about it.
ISABEL (*foreboding*): Oh boy. This doesn't sound so good. You've got to talk to him, Thami.
THAMI: He won't listen.
ISABEL: Make him listen!
THAMI: It doesn't work that way with us, Isabel. You can't just stand up and tell your teacher he's got the wrong ideas.
ISABEL: Well that's just your bad luck, because you are going to have to do it. Even if it means breaking sacred rules and traditions, you have got to stand up and have it out with him. I don't think you realize what all of this means to him. It's a hell of a lot more than just an old-fashioned idea as far as he's concerned. This competition, you and me, but especially you, Thami Mbikwana, have become a sort of crowning achievement to his life as a teacher. It's become a sort of symbol for him, and if it were to all suddenly collapse . . . ! No. I don't want to think about it.
THAMI (*flash of anger and impatience*): Then don't! Please leave it alone now, and just let's get on with whatever it is we've got to do.

Thami realizes Isabel means to be helpful, but the issue between himself and Mr. M is not just personal, it's political. The classroom is part of the whole system they're against and with which Mr. M has identified himself. Isabel accepts this, but argues that it is important that Thami and Mr. M begin talking. She's sure Mr. M wants to but doesn't know how to, and she urges Thami to take the first step. She's worried that things could go wrong between them and points out that they all need each other.

Courtney Vance as Thami Mbikwana in *My Children! My Africa!*

Thami claims Isabel doesn't know what his life is like and should keep her advice to herself, deeply hurting her. Since they were a team, she'd thought that what involved the two of them was also of concern to her. She is about to leave but comes back to remark that he had used the word "friendship" shortly before. If there is not openness and honesty between them, it's not right to use that word.

*Scene 6*

  THAMI (*sings*):
    Gonqo Gonqo
    The bell is calling!
Singing that at the top of his voice and holding his slate under his arm, seven-year-old Thami Mbikwana marched proudly with the other children every morning into his classroom. (*Sings.*)
    Gonqo Gonqo

The schoolbell is ringing!
And what a wonderful sound that was for me. Starting with the little farm
school, I remember my school bells like beautiful voices calling to me all
through my childhood . . . and I came running when they did. You should have
seen me, man. In junior school I was the first one at the gates every morning.
I was waiting there when the caretaker came to unlock them. Oh yes! Young
Thami was a very eager scholar. And what made it even better, he was also
one of the clever ones. "A most particularly promising pupil" is how one of
my school reports described me. My first real scholastic achievement was a
composition I wrote about myself in Standard Two. Not only did it get me top
marks in the class, the teacher was so proud of me, she made me read it out to
the whole school at assembly. (*His composition.*) "The story of my life so far.
By Thami Mbikwana. The story of my life so far is not yet finished because I
am only ten years old, and I am going to live a long, long time. I come from
King William's Town. My father is Amos Mbikwana, and he works very hard
for the baas on the railway. I am also going to work very hard and get good
marks in all my classes and make my teacher very happy. The story of my life
so far has also got a very happy ending, because when I am big I am going to
be a doctor so that I can help my people. I will drive to the hospital every day
in a big, white ambulance full of nurses. I will make black people better, free
of charge. The white people must pay for my medicine because they have got
lots of money. That way I will also get lots of money. My mother and my
father will stop working and come and live with me in a big house. That is the
story of my life up to where I am in Standard Two."

It's been eight years since "little Thami" wrote that, however, and to up-
date his story Thami says he's doubtful about becoming a doctor now, even
though the suffering of his people does disturb him. He's unsure of his future,
as it's difficult to have dreams of a career as a doctor or a lawyer in a world
that forbids most of his people to dream. Back then he did continue to be a
good pupil. Now, he regrets, he can't any more. The classroom full of
promises is a place he can't trust now. He doesn't feel safe there; he senses
danger and feels he must be careful.
He talks about the visit of the school inspector, who, at the start of the
school year, came as he always does to give the Standard Tens a pep talk.
They're supposed to call him Oom Dawie. He takes off his jacket and rolls up
his sleeves, tells them to sit down and calls them special, "the elite" who are
supposed to be "major shareholders in the future of this wonderful Republic of
ours. In fact, we want *all* the peoples of South Africa to share in that future
. . . black, white, brown, yellow, and if there are some green ones out there,
then them as well," Oom Dawie told them.
Thami doesn't recall much more about what Oom Dawie said because he
just kept thinking about the word "future." When Thami looks around at the

men and women who preceded him into the future, he sees only defeated people going back to their wretched homes at the end of the day after working for the white baas or madam. And they are lucky. They have work. For most, lives are wasting away as they helplessly await a miracle that would enable them to feed their families. And Thami and his classmates have grown up observing the humiliation of these people, their parents, watching them beg for food in the land in which they were born, and their parents before them, all the way back to the proud ancestors who lived there centuries before the white settlers.

THAMI: Does Oom Dawie think we are blind? That when we walk through the streets of the white town we do not see the big houses and the beautiful gardens with their swimming pools full of laughing people, and compare it with what we've got, what we have to call home? Or does Oom Dawie just think we are very stupid? That in spite of the wonderful education he has given us, we can't use the simple arithmetic of add and subtract, multiply and divide to work out the rightful share of twenty-five million black people? Do you understand me, good people? Do you understand now why it is not as easy as it used to be to sit behind that desk and learn only what Oom Dawie has decided I must know? My head is rebellious. It refuses now to remember when the Dutch landed, and the Huguenots landed, and the British landed. It has already forgotten when the old Union became the proud young Republic. But it does know what happened in Kliptown in 1955, in Sharpville on twenty-first March, 1960 and in Soweto on the sixteenth of June, 1976. Do you? Better find out, because those are dates your children will have to learn one day . . . . . We have found another school . . . the streets, the little rooms, the funeral parlors of the Location . . . anywhere the people meet and whisper names we have been told to forget, the dates of events they try to tell us never happened, and the speeches they try to say were never made. Those are the lessons we are eager and proud to learn, because they are lessons about *our* history, about *our* heroes. But the time for whispering them is past. Tomorrow we start shouting. AMANDLA! (*Curtain.*)

# ACT II

*Scene 1*

Isabel, alone with Thami, is telling him about the biographical material on the novelists that's she's brought, but Thami is inattentive. He has to talk to her and is unsure of how to begin. He's not going to be in the competition. She's not terribly surprised. She felt something would go wrong. Things everywhere have been strange recently, she muses. Her father thinks she's changed, but all she's sure of is that she doesn't like the way things seem now, herself included. She asks Thami if he's told Mr. M of his decision. He hasn't.

During their conversation, Thami reveals that at a meeting the previous evening in the Location a general stay-at-home was called for. As of the next day, classes are to be boycotted. He supposed Mr. M knows about this, but he had not been at the Comrades' meeting. He was not welcome there. "Because his ideas are old-fashioned" Isabel surmises. Thami admits that's why.

Thami has no idea how long it will all go on, but at the meeting it was resolved that they won't return to school until Bantu Education is "scrapped" and there is recognition of student committees. If it's over in time, could they still go on with the competition?, Isabel wonders. Thami doesn't want to commit himself. She wonders, too, if they can go on being friends. "When?" he asks, warily. Isabel, disgusted and disappointed, doesn't understand what is wrong about their friendship. What Thami's really worried about is the way the others would see it. Even this visit is "dangerous." And Isabel's family's maid has seen him and might mention that. There's to be no mixing with whites, and Thami's not going to go against the orders.

Isabel doesn't think much of this freedom he's talked about if others decide for him who his friends can be and what he should or shouldn't do. Mr. M has come in, not his usual ebullient self, hears this and is interested in how Thami sees it. Thami's attitude is that discipline is necessary only until the struggle is over and isn't comparable to the government's denying him and his people their freedom, keeping them suppressed by forcing inferior education on them.

MR. M (*grudging admiration*): Oh, Thami . . . you learn your lessons so well! The "revolution" has only just begun, and you are already word perfect. So then tell me, do you think I agree with this inferior Bantu Education that is being forced on you?

THAMI: You teach it.

MR. M: But unhappily so! Most unhappily, unhappily so! Don't you know that? Did you have your fingers in your ears the thousand times I've said so in the classroom? Where were you when I stood there and said I regarded it as my duty, my deepest obligation to you young men and women, to sabotage it, and that my conscience would not let me rest until I had succeeded. And I have! Yes, I have succeeded! I have got irrefutable proof of my success. You! Yes. You can stand here and accuse me, unjustly because I have also had a struggle, and I have won mine. I have liberated your mind in spite of what the Bantu Education was trying to do to it. Your mouthful of big words and long sentences which the not-so-clever comrades are asking you to speak and write for them, your wonderful eloquence at last night's meeting which got them all so excited—yes, I heard about it!—you must thank me for all of that, Thami.

THAMI: No, I don't. You never taught me those lessons.

MR. M: Oh I see. You have got other teachers, have you?

THAMI: Yes. Yours were lessons in whispering. There are men now who are teaching us to shout. Those little tricks and jokes of yours in the classroom liberated nothing. The struggle doesn't need the big English words you taught me how to spell.

Mr. M warns Thami to take care, that words are not to be scorned, they are "sacred" and "magical," that man thinks with words, and that is what separates men and animals. Words are the weapons the struggle needs, not stones and bombs, because words can get inside heads, and words alone can right wrongs.

MR. M: Talk to others. Bring them back into the classroom. They will listen to you. They look up to you as a leader.

THAMI: No, I won't. You talk about them as if they were a lot of sheep waiting to be led. They know what they are doing. They'd call me a traitor if I tried to persuade them otherwise.

MR. M: Then listen carefully, Thami. I have received instructions from the department to make a list of all those who take part in the boycott. Do you know what they will do with that list when all this is over . . . because don't fool yourself, Thami, it will be. When your boycott comes to an inglorious end like all the others . . . they will make all of you apply for re-admission, and if your name is on that list . . . (*He leaves the rest unspoken.*)

THAMI: Will you do it? Will you make that list for them?

MR. M: That is none of your business.

THAMI: Then don't ask me questions about mine.

MR. M (*his control finally snaps. He explodes with anger and bitterness*): Yes, I will! I will ask you all the questions I like. And you know why? Because I am a man and you are a boy. And if you are not in that classroom tomorrow you will be a very, very silly boy.

THAMI: Then don't call me names, Mr. M.

MR. M: No? Then what must I call you? Comrade Thami? Never! You are a silly boy now, and without an education you will grow up to be a stupid man!

> For a moment it looks as if Thami is going to leave without saying anything more, but he changes his mind and confronts Mr. M for the last time.

THAMI: The others called *you* names at the meeting last night. Did your spies tell you that? Government stooge, sellout, collaborator. They said you licked the white man's arse and would even eat his shit if it meant keeping your job. Did your spies tell you that I tried to stop them saying those things?

Before Thami departs, he tells Mr. M that he can begin to make his list now and to put Thami Mbikwana down as the first name. Afterward, Isabel starts to go to Mr. M, but he holds up his hand to warn her to keep her distance. "This fucking country!" Isabel despairs as she leaves.

*Scene 2*

> *Mr. M alone. To start with, his mood is one of quiet, vacant disbelief.*

MR. M: It was like being in a nightmare. I was trying to get to the school. I knew that if I didn't hurry I was going to be late so I *had to get to the school* ... but every road I took was blocked by policemen and soldiers with their guns ready, or Comrades building barricades. First I tried Jabulani Street, then I turned in Kwaza Road and then Lamini Street ... and then I gave up and just wandered around aimlessly, helplessly, watching my world go mad and set itself on fire. Everywhere I went ... overturned buses, looted bread vans, the government offices ... everything burning and the children dancing around rattling boxes of matches and shouting ..... and then running for their lives when the police armored cars appeared. They were everywhere, crawling around in the smoke like giant dung-beetles looking for shit to eat. I ended up on the corner where Mrs. Makatini always sits selling vetkoek and prickly pears to people waiting for the bus. The only person there was little Shipho Fondini from Standard Six, writing on the wall: "Liberation First, Then Education." He saw me and he called out: "Is the spelling right Mr. M?" ..... Somewhere else a police van raced past me, crowded with children who should also have been in their desks in school. Their hands waved desperately through the bars, their voices called out: "Teacher! Teacher! Help us! Tell our mothers. Tell our fathers." "No, Anela," I said. "This is too much now. Just stand here and close your eyes and wait until you wake up and find your world the way it was." But that didn't happen. A police car came around the corner, and suddenly there were children everywhere throwing stones, and tear gas bombs falling all around, and I knew that I wasn't dreaming, that I was coughing and choking and hanging onto a lamppost in the real world. No! No! Do something, Anela. Do something. Stop the madness! Stop the madness.

*Scene 3*

Mr. M is in his classroom ringing the school bell and calling "Come to School! Come to School! Before they kill you all, come to school!" The room is empty, but he begins to read the names from the class register as he usually does, but this time wondering which of his students are alive, which dead. His lessons were meant to help them, but now he has none that are useful to them.

A stone crashes through the glass. Reassured that at least one of his students must be alive, he is ringing the bell again when Thami enters and tells him to stop. Mr. M is defying the boycott by his presence and provoking the Comrades by ringing the bell. Mr. M retorts he will ring it as he always has.

In answer to Mr. M's questions, Thami admits he hasn't come just about the bell, and he hasn't come for a lesson, either. Nor does he need lessons in stone-throwing, Mr. M remarks. Mr. M has the stone in one hand and his dictionary in the other and comments that they probably weigh about the same. "But in this hand I am holding the whole English language. This . . . (*The stone.*) . . . is just *one* word in that language." He reads from the fly-leaf of the dictionary: "Anela Myalatya. Cookhouse. 1947." On impulse he offers it to Thami, who ignores the offer.

He has come to warn Mr. M, he says. At the meeting last night Mr. M had been denounced as an informer, as having given names to the police, and Thami wants him to know so that he can save himself. There's to be a march on the school. It's to be burned, and if Mr. M is there he'll be killed.

Mr. M says Thami was right to put it in words, straight out, but wonders what he ought to do. Ought he to hide? They would only find him, Thami believes. What he must do is join in the boycott. Thami will tell them they've talked, that Mr. M has realized he was wrong and is joining them. Mr. M questions their acceptance of him, but Thami plans to tell them he's not guilty, that he confronted Mr. M with the charge, that he denied it, and that Thami believes him.

MR. M: I see. (*Studying Thami intently.*) *You* don't believe that I am an informer.

THAMI: No.

MR. M: Won't you be taking a chance in defending me like that? Mightn't they end up suspecting you?

THAMI: They'll believe me I'll make them believe me.

MR. M: You can't be sure. Mobs don't listen to reason, Thami. Hasn't your revolution already taught you that? Why take a chance like that to save a collaborator? Why do you want to do all this for me?

THAMI (*avoiding Mr. M's eyes*): I'm not doing it for you. I'm doing it for the Struggle. Our Cause will suffer if we falsely accuse and hurt innocent people.

MR. M: I see. My "execution" would be an embarrassment to the Cause. I apologize, Thami. For a moment I allowed myself to think that you were doing it because we were . . . who we are . . . the "all-knowing Mr. M and his brilliant protege Thami!" I was so proud of us when Isabel called us that. Well, young Comrade, you have got nothing to worry about. Let them come and do whatever it is they want to. Your Cause won't be embarrassed, because you see, they won't be "hurting" an innocent man. (*He makes his confession simply and truthfully.*) That's right, Thami. I am guilty. I did go to the police. I sat down in Captain Lategan's office and told him I felt it was my duty to report the presence in our community of strangers from the north. I told him that I had reason to believe that they were behind the present unrest. I gave the Captain names and addresses. He thanked me and offered me money for the information, which I refused. (*Pause.*) Why do you look at me like that? Isn't that what you expected from me? ... a government stooge, a sellout, an arse-licker? Isn't that what you were all secretly hoping I would do ... so that you could be proved right? (*Appalled.*) Is that why I did it? Out of spite? Can a man destroy himself, his life for a reason as petty as that? I sat here before going to the police station, saying to myself that it was my duty, to my conscience, to you, to the whole community, to do whatever I could to put an end to this madness of boycotts and arson, mob violence and lawlessness ... and maybe that is true ... but only maybe ... because Thami, the truth is that I was so lonely! You had deserted me. I was so jealous of those who had taken you away. *Now*, I've *really* lost you, haven't I? Yes. I can see it in your eyes. You'll never forgive me for doing that, will you?

Mr. M also confesses he would sell his soul to the devil in exchange for one last time in the classroom with all of his students there. But everything is over now, he realizes, because teaching was everything to him. It all began when he was a ten-year-old member of a rugby team en route to a game in a lorry. They'd stopped to relieve themselves at the top of Wapadsberg Pass. When he saw the view, the vast beautiful stretches, he'd asked the teacher where he would end up if he started walking north. He would see all Africa, he was told—the rivers, the mountains, and "all our brothers," the pygmies, the Masai, the Watusi, the Kikuyu. The teacher had not seen it all, no, but it was all in the books he'd read. And it was, Mr. M marveled. For forty years it's all been there for him to conjure up, to make him proud to be an African. Then he'd seen something on television that made him not want to take the trip again. It was an Ethiopian tribesman carrying a small child, dead of famine, to a mass grave, and too weak to put the body down, he had simply let it fall into the grave. And nobody told what the man's name was, or that of the child being "thrown away."

MR. M: ..... What is wrong with this world that it wants to waste you all like that ... my children ... my Africa!
    *Holding out a hand as if he wanted to touch Thami's face.*
My beautiful and proud young Africa!
    *More breaking glass and stones and the sound of a crowd outside the school. Mr. M starts to move, Thami stops him.*

THAMI: No! Don't go out there. Let me speak to them first. Listen to me! I will tell them I have confronted you with the charges and that you have denied them and that I believe you. I will tell them you are innocent.

MR. M:  You will lie for me, Thami?

THAMI:  Yes.

MR. M (*desperate to hear the truth*):  Why?
        *Thami can't speak.*
Why will you lie for me Thami?

THAMI:  I've told you before.

MR. M:  The Cause?"

THAMI:  Yes.

MR. M:  Then I do not need to hide behind your lies.

THAMI:  They will kill you.

MR. M:  Do you think I'm frightened of them. Do you think I'm frightened of dying?

*Mr. M breaks away from Thami. Ringing his bell furiously he goes outside and confronts the mob. They kill him.*

*Scene 4*

Isabel has reluctantly come to meet Thami, who sent her a note saying he must see her. He wants to say good-bye to her. She thought he'd already done so the last time they'd met, three weeks ago. He explains that he's leaving for good. Isabel had assumed he had wanted to say something about the attack on Mr. M—hit in the head with a metal rod and set afire. She desperately needs to know why. He was an informer, Thami explains, he had given the police the names and addresses of the political action committee. Isabel doesn't believe it. Thami hadn't either until Mr. M had told him so himself. Mr. M had gone to the police, just that once, because he thought it was his duty. Isabel is outraged. "It was an act of self-defense," Thami insists. Mr. M had betrayed them. Five of them are in detention now, and there are other arrests and more to come. "Why do you think I'm running away?" he asks; and how was anyone to know whether Mr. M had not been a paid informer before and might have been again?

THAMI: . . . . . Try to understand, Isabel. Try to imagine what it is like to be a black person, choking inside with rage and frustration, bitterness, and then to discover that one of your own kind is a traitor, has betrayed you to those responsible for the suffering and misery of your family, of your people. What would you do? Remember there is no magistrate or court you can drag him to and demand that he be tried for that crime. There is no justice for black people in this country other than what we make for ourselves. When you judge us for what happened in front of the school four days ago, just remember that you carry a share of the responsibility for it. It is your laws that have made simple, decent black people so desperate that they turn into "mad mobs."

*Isabel has been listening and watching intently. It looks as if she is going to say something, but she stops herself.*

Say it, Isabel.

ISABEL: No.

THAMI: This is your last chance. You once challenged me to be honest with you. I'm challenging you now.

ISABEL (*she faces him*): Where were you when it happened, Thami? (*Pause.*) And if you were there, did you try to stop them?

THAMI: Isn't there a third question, Isabel? Was I one of the mob that killed him?

ISABEL: Yes. Forgive me, Thami . . . please forgive me! . . . but there is that question as well. Only once! Believe me, only once . . . late at night when I couldn't sleep. I couldn't believe it was there in my head, but I heard the words . . . "Was Thami one of the ones who did it?"

THAMI: If the police catch me, that's the question they will ask.

ISABEL: I'm asking you because . . . (*An open, helpless gesture.*) . . . I'm lost! I don't know what to think or feel any more. Help me. Please. You're the only one who can. Nobody else seems to understand that I loved him.

*This final confrontation is steady and unflinching on both sides.*

THAMI: Yes, I was there. Yes, I did try to stop it. (*Thami gives Isabel the time to deal with this answer.*) I knew how angry the people were. I went to warn him. If he had listened to me, he would still be alive, but he wouldn't. It was almost as if he wanted it to happen. I think he hated himself very much for what he had done, Isabel. He kept saying to me that it was all over. He was right. There was nothing left for him. That visit to the police station had finished everything. Nobody would have ever spoken to him again or let him teach their children.

Thami confesses he loved Mr. M, too, and realizes he ought to have tried more to get Mr. M to understand why he was doing what he had to do. Nor will he forgive himself for never letting Mr. M know his true feelings for him. Now Thami is going north, leaving the country, in fact, to join the movement. Isabel is despairing, only after a few days, of losing Mr. M, and there isn't any way to get close to him again. Thami tells her to get somebody to take her up to the Wapadsberg Pass, it was the special place where Mr. M first knew he would be a teacher. They exchange farewells in the Xhosa language.

*Scene 5*

*Isabel alone. She stands quietly, examining the silence. After a few seconds she nods her head slowly.*

ISABEL: Yes! Thami was right, Mr. M. He said I'd feel near you up here. He's out there somewhere, Mr. M . . . traveling north. He didn't say where exactly he was going, but I think we can guess, can't we? I'm here for a very "old fashioned" reason, so I know you'll approve. I've come to pay my last respects to Anela Myalatya. I know the old fashioned way of doing that is to bring flowers, lay them on the grave, say a quiet prayer and then go back to your life. But that seemed sort of silly this time. You'll have enough flowers around here when the spring comes . . . which it will. So instead, I've brought you something which I know will mean more to you than flowers or prayers ever could. A promise.

Isabel's promise to him is that she will try her best to ensure that her life is not a wasted one, but a useful one, as his was. She wants Mr. M to be proud of her because she is one of his children. He had welcomed her to his family. "The future is still ours, Mr. M." She goes off. *Curtain.*

# CITY OF ANGELS

*A Musical in Two Acts*

BOOK BY LARRY GELBART

MUSIC BY CY COLEMAN

LYRICS BY DAVID ZIPPEL

Cast and credits appear on pages 379–381

*LARRY GELBART (book) was born in Chicago Feb. 28, 1928 and did his first radio writing at 16, just before his two years service in the Army in 1945–46. He contributed to* Duffy's Tavern, Jack Paar, Jack Carson *and* Bob Hope *on radio, 1945–51, and to* Hope, Red Buttons, Sid Caesar *and* Art Carney *on TV, 1949–1960. He developed and co-produced the TV version of the movie* M*A*S*H *in the 1970s. It was one of the small screen's most successful, long-running, Emmy, Peabody, Humanitas and Writer's Guild Award-winning shows, and his work with* The Danny Kaye Show *won him another Peabody. Among the films he has provided for the large screen have been* The

220

Notorious Landlady *(1960)*, The Wrong Box *(1966)*, Movie, Movie *(1981)*, Oh, God! *(1977, an Oscar best-screen-play nominee) and* Tootsie *(1982, a New York, Los Angeles and National Film Critics Award-winner)*.

*Gelbart's stage writing career began in 1950 with* My L.A. *and has continued with the book for the musical* The Conquering Hero *(based on Preston Sturges's movie* Hail the Conquering Hero*) for 8 Broadway performances in 1961; the book (in collaboration with Burt Shevelove) of* A Funny Thing Happened on the Way to the Forum, *based on works of Plautus, a 964-performance smash Broadway hit and Tony Award-winner for its authors, beginning May 2, 1962; a straight-play adaptation of Ben Johnson's* Volpone *entitled* Sly Fox *which opened on Broadway Dec. 14, 1976, ran for 495 performances and won its author his first Best Play citation; and in the meantime, another of his plays,* Jump, *was produced in England. This season, Broadway audiences were treated to two Gelbart offerings:* Mastergate, *a straight-play satire on Senate hearings and other Washington doings, Oct. 12 for 68 performances; and the ongoing musical* City of Angels *on Dec. 11, the second Best Play of his career.*

*Gelbart is also a composer of songs, and his list of memberships in professional associations reflects his many accomplishments: the Dramatists Guild, the Writers Guild of America, the Writers Guild of Great Britain, ASCAP and the Directors Guild. He is married, with five children, and lives in Los Angeles.*

*CY COLEMAN (music) was born in New York City June 14, 1929 and was a concert pianist by age 6, playing at Carnegie, Town and Steinway Halls between the ages of 6 and 9. He received his diploma from the New York College of Music in 1948 and immediately set out on a career of night club and symphony orchestra bookings from coast to beyond coast (in Honolulu), and appearances on the Kate Smith show 1951–52.*

*As a composer, Coleman was writing popular songs ("Why Try to Change Me Now," 1952, is the first one he cares to mention) including many standard hits, and he contributed to the revues* John Murray Anderson's Almanac *and* The Ziegfeld Follies *(the latter starring Tallulah Bankhead). His first full Broadway show was the 171-performance* Wildcat *(starring Lucille Ball) opening Dec. 16, 1960. There followed* Little Me *(1962),* Sweet Charity *(1963, revived in 1986 and won the best-revival Tony),* Seesaw *(1973),* I Love My Wife *(1977, Drama Desk Award),* On the Twentieth Century *(1978, Tony and Drama Desk Awards for best score),* Barnum *(1980, an 854-performance hit which he also produced) and now* City of Angels *which brings its composer his first Best Play citation.*

*Coleman has won 12 Grammys for his song recordings, three Emmies, an Oscar nomination (for the score of the movie version of* Sweet Charity*),* *seven Tony nominations and the Irving Feld Humanitarian Award of the National Conference of Christians and Jews. He is a director of ASCAP, a member of the Dramatists Guild and lives in New York City.*

DAVID ZIPPEL *(lyrics) was born in 1954 in Easton, Pa., where his father was a toy distributor. He was already trying his hand at writing lyrics when he attended the University of Pennsylvania and contributed some lyrics to a show in a pre-Broadway tryout in Washington (it never got to New York). He graduated B.A. and Phi Beta Kappa in 1976 and went on to Harvard Law School, getting his degree in 1979, but is now delighted (a* Playbill *program note states) not to practice law.*

Zippel *wrote all of the lyrics for the revue* It's Better With a Band *(also the title of one of his song hits) which was produced off off Broadway and then moved to Sardi's in 1983 and to the West End in London in 1986. His off-Broadway credits include contributions to* Diamonds *and* A . . . My Name Is Alice *in 1984 and all of the lyrics for* Just So *in 1985.* City of Angels *is his first Broadway show and Best Play.*

With Wally Harper, *Zippel has written numerous songs for Barbara Cook concerts, including* Barbara Cook: A Concert for the Theater *booked recently in New York and the West End. They also contributed the original songs to Sandy Duncan's* Five, Six Seven, Eight . . . Dance! *at Radio City Music Hall in 1983. Zippel now makes his home in Manhattan.*

*Place: Los Angeles*

*Time: The late 1940s*

## ACT I

*Scene 1: L.A. County Hospital*

SYNOPSIS: The scenes of this musical shift among various locales and occasionally back and forth between the "real" life of a detective story writer named Stine who has been hired to write a movie based on the adventures of his private-eye hero, Stone. Scenes of the movie Stine is writing are played with sets, costumes, props, etc. limited to shades of black and white, with the sole exception of the actors' skin coloring. The scenes of the author's "real" life are of course in living color.

The opening scene is a "fictional" scene from Stine's script, with his hero, Stone, wheeled in on a gurney by a couple of hospital orderlies, with a bullet in his shoulder. As he lies there, Stone remembers how it was last Monday in his office with his secretary, Oolie, answering the phone. "Can your whole life roll over and play dead, turn bad-side out in just seven days?" Stone asks himself as he lets his memory (and the movie action) flash back to that day.

*Scene 2: Stone's office, one week earlier*

The movie continues, flashing back to Oolie in the outer office reading a newspaper and answering phone queries about her boss's services ("It's a flat rate. Twenty-five dollars a day plus eight cents a mile"). Stone enters and hangs up his coat and hat.

STONE:  Did I hear a phone?

OOLIE:  Some clown hoping for a few snaps of the little woman getting floor burns in the back of the family Chevvy. I think he used a slug to pay for the call.

STONE:  We get any busier, you can start reading *two* newspapers.

OOLIE:  Yesterday's lies with today's date on 'em. Happy Monday.

STONE:  No such animal.

Randy Graff as Oolie with James Naughton as Stone in *City of Angels*

Stone goes through into his inner office, shuts the door, opens the window, pours himself a drink from a bottle of whiskey, tears a page from his desk calendar and throws it into the waste basket, as his voice is heard over the action: "Three million people in the City of Angels according to the last census, easily half of them up to something they don't want the other half to know. We all get sucked in by the lobby. Palm trees finger the sky, and there's enough sunshine to lay some off on Pittsburgh. But that's all on top. L.A., truth to tell's, not much different than a pretty girl with the clap.

"Monday. What other day works so hard at reminding you not to get your hopes up, 'cause it's gonna be coming around again real soon?"

Oolie comes in to report that a client has just arrived, "wearing a whole year's salary," and wants to see him. Oolie ushers in Alaura Kingsley, "*a vision all in white*," and exits. Stone, all too aware of her femme-fatale attractions, lights her cigarette and asks what he can do for her. Her lips move, speaking words we can't hear, while Stone makes an audible comment with the song "Double Talk."

STONE (*sings*):
    Just watch her dodge the truth like a runaway streetcar
    This role she plays could win her a prize
    Each gesture is correct
    Well chosen for effect
    And it would be wiser if I kept my eyes off her thighs.
ALAURA: Mr. Stone? Are you listening to me?
STONE: I will, if you will—start leveling.
ALAURA: I beg your pardon?
STONE: Telling the truth. From the minute you walked in here, every time our eyes meet, you look like a deer caught in my headlights.
ALAURA: Let's just say I've been sizing you up.
STONE: All the measurements fit?
ALAURA: This is a very delicate situation, Mr. Stone. Reputations are at stake.
STONE: We don't share that problem.

Alaura finally describes hers: her stepdaughter Mallory—her 75-year-old husband's child—is missing. She hands him a snapshot of Mallory when she was 16. Stone senses that this is apt to bring him nothing but trouble, and explains why he'd rather not take it on. His lips move soundlessly as Alaura in her turn sizes him up in song.

ALAURA (*sings*):
    This song and dance of his is most unconvincing

He has that hungry look in his eye
He needs the work and soon
Some cash'll change his tune
He'll hop to the task
I'll say jump and he'll
Ask me how high.

Alaura is right—when she offers him a hundred bucks, Stone grabs the check and the case, even though he doesn't believe her story and senses big trouble ahead. He tries to get her phone number as he ushers her through the outer office. She says she'll call him, wishes Stone and Oolie "Good day" and exits.

## Scene 3: Writer's cell, Master Pictures Studio

Now the sound of typing is heard, and the "real" world appears onstage beside the movie scene, in the person of the author, Stine, working on his script. As he X's out a few lines, Stone and Oolie reverse their dialogue and gestures to a point three or four lines back (and Alaura reverses her exit, backing into the office; her "Good day" now comes out as "Yad doog"). The characters freeze while Stine ponders, then they replay the scene with minor dialogue changes.

A ringing telephone interrupts Stine's work. He stops typing and lifts the receiver. The detective's office disappears and is replaced by another flesh-and-blood Hollywood setting, with Stine's cell still visible alongside it.

## Scene 4: Buddy Fidler's office

Buddy Fidler, director/producer, is having his shoes shined and talking to Stine about the script on one of his three phones. As Stine rummages for some script pages Fidler wants to discuss, Fidler makes his own comment in "Double Talk."

FIDLER (sings):
    I buy a book and I get stuck with the author
    You buy a rose you're stuck with a thorn
    It's undeniable
    The guy is pliable
    And Shakespeare and Dickens were washed up before I was born.
STINE (on the phone in his office, having found the pages): Buddy? Shoot.
BUDDY: All right, all right, I gotta be honest, no matter how much it hurts me. I just didn't expect you to go into business for yourself, y'know what I mean? Those three shots in the dark, then opening in the hospital, Stone being wheeled in. We never said the rest of the picture was going to be a flashback.

Not once in all these weeks. I mean, the main titles, then boom! right into a flashback? That's kicked. It's tired. Flashbacks are a thing of the past. Anyway, we're gonna do one later, when we show Stone with his girl, the night club singer . . .

STINE: Bobbi.

BUDDY: Bobbi, right, back in their early days, aren't we?
*Another of his phones rings.*

STINE: But the book started with a flashback.

BUDDY: Don't go 'way. (*Picking up second phone.*) Yeah, put him on. (*Hanging up second phone, picking up third.*) Henry? Henry, look, never mind it's perfect. We gotta take out four minutes.
*As Stine pours a whiskey.*

Nothing any good's ever hurt by cutting—circumcisions to one side, of course.
*Shoeshine Boy laughs, Buddy joins in.*

(*Into third phone.*) It's all in how who does it. I could take ten seconds out of "The Minute Waltz," and nobody'd ever know.

Buddy continues giving orders into the two phones and to the shoeshine boy, ordering Stine to cut the flashback and open right in the office scene. And Buddy's car will pick up Stine and his wife Gabby a little early today to attend a screening of two movies. Stine explains that Gabby, who is also a writer, can't come. Her publisher wants her in New York.

BUDDY: That's all I need, you missing her right now. You're not the same when your wife's not around, you know that? (*Glancing at Stine's pages.*) It's like part of you's gone off somewhere. The secret, tender part. Tell her to haul her fanny back here soon. I'm the only one gets to make you unhappy, right? I need the new pages first thing yesterday. I'm going to open my window—I want to see some fingers flying. Stine? Let me hear a smile.
*Stine smiles despite himself.*

Louder! (*A laugh from Stine.*) That's my boy!
*Lights down on Buddy.*

STINE (*hangs up, sings "Double Talk"*):
This job is not to be believed
And I cannot believe my luck
I'm at the literary prime of my life
And I'm about to have the time of my life
Unless I'm easily deceived
Though Buddy doesn't tend to sugarcoat his comments
He's all right
All bark, no bite . . . . .

For making movies out of books

They say that Buddy wrote the book
I can depend on him to give me some lip
But you can trust a guy who shoots from the hip
Out here where nothing's how it looks
It's hard to disregard a candid stand-up guy
Who skips the double talk
And lets you know exactly what he's thinking about you
And I can beat the odds
And meet his demands
Though I'm a stranger in
This strangest of lands.

This mad adventure I've begun
Is unlike anything I know
It's gonna be a lotta work
And lots of fun
And pots of dough.
> *He resumes typing, reactivating Stone and Oolie.*

## Scene 5: Stone's office

In the movie Stine is writing, Stone and Oolie are admiring Alaura's check and discussing the case. Examining the photo of the missing girl, Mallory, Stone comments, "Young and ripe." Stone moves to exit and freezes in the doorway as the lights go down and the scene changes.

## Scene 6: Stine's bedroom, the Garden of Allah

Back in the "real" world, Gabby is packing for her trip to New York, and Stine believes she's looking forward to getting back there. And one of the things Gabby objects to out here is her husband's contract with the studio.

STINE: Gabby, it's a standard clause.

GABBY: That the *studio* is the author of the screen play? That after writing the script you're writing, it turns out you never wrote it at all?

STINE: If it's good enough for Faulkner and Fitzgerald . . .

GABBY: Then it's bad enough for you. Darling, for five thousand a week, you're willing to be as much of a hired hand as Stone is. You really should ask for eight cents a mile, too.

STINE: Five times ten weeks is fifty thousand dollars. Fifty thousand times three pictures is a *hundred* and fifty thousand dollars.

GABBY: Is there *ever* a conversation out here where anyone's at a loss for numbers? Do you have any idea what all that money is costing you? He thinks of writers as overpaid typists, Buddy does.

STINE: You've got him wrong, Gab.

GABBY:  You see the glass half full.
STINE:  And you see him peeing into it.

A car horn is heard—it's the studio car come for Stine, who declares he's going to miss Gabby, kisses her and exits, at which point Stone also finishes his exit from his office.  Alone without their men, Gabby and Oolie reflect in song, each in her separate set, "What You Don't Know About Women."

BOTH (*sing*):
      . . . . . A women needs to be assured
    That she remains alluring
    To now and then be reassured
    Your passion is enduring.

| GABBY (*sings*): | OOLIE (*sings*): |
|---|---|
| It's not enough to know your line | And heaven knows I know your line |
| To polish and routine it | The whole routine, I've seen it |

BOTH (*sing*):
    Ya gotta mean it.
GABBY (*sings*):
    What you don't know about women
OOLIE (*sings*):
    What you don't know about women
BOTH (*sing*):
    Is what we need to hear.
GABBY (*sings*):
    You think if you can sound sincere
    Then we'll come running to you.
OOLIE (*sings*):
    Throw in some truth for atmosphere
    But we can see right through you
GABBY (*sings*):
    And ev'ry hollow compliment and phrase defines
OOLIE (*sings*):
    And underlines
BOTH (*sing*):
    What you don't know about women . . . . .

    You are in need of
    A little enlight'ning
    On ladies in love
    But you can't see

    What you don't know about women
    Is fright'ning

And you don't know nothin' about me.
   *Blackout.*

*Scene 7: Stone's bungalow*

In the dreary little cubbyhole where he lives (in the screen play), the private eye is preparing a can of food while listening to a radio program called the "Hour of Powers," starring a singer named Jimmy Powers. As Stone studies Mallory's photo, the radio goes into a song number entitled "You Gotta Look Out for Yourself." There is a knock on Stone's door: "Special delivery for Mr. Stone." The detective opens the door to Big Six ("*a mountain of a man*") and Sonny ("*small, but just as menacing*"). As Sonny turns up the volume on the radio so that no one will hear the sounds of the beating they're about to give Stone, the radio station set with Jimmy Powers and his quartet appears and obscures the action so that the beating is seen only in shadows on the ceiling of Stone's room. Meanwhile, the radio performers deliver their song.

JIMMY and QUARTET (*sing*):
   Ya gotta look out for yourself
   If you're hoping to be first
   Then ya better think "Me first"
   Or you're gonna be last . . . . .

   Ya gotta look out for yourself
   If you're planning to do good
   Then be sure it does you good
   You don't wanna be too good
   You gotta look out for yourself
   Ya know the score when you adore yourself
   When you're in danger you can count on me to shout
   Look out for yourself.
SONNY (*to the barely conscious Stone*): Lemme give you a message, Mr. Stone: Drop the Kingsley case, y'unnerstan'? Drop it, or next time we'll have to get rough.

The hoodlums depart, Big Six taking with him Stone's radio as a birthday present for his girl. Stone lies crumpled, as we hear his voice over the scene: "It was as though I'd been hit by a wrecking ball wearing a pinkie ring. Some part of me that still seemed to be functioning was watching the other part of me, that wasn't, fall. Then that part started falling too, and the race began to see which part could hit bottom first . . . " The scene fades out with Stone's voice, which fades into Buddy's voice in the "real" world of Hollywood.

*Scene 8: Buddy's office*

Buddy is having his hair cut and is reading pages of Stine's screen play aloud to his barber Gilbert, quoting from the private eye's dialogue.

BUDDY: " . . . Somehow I was getting the idea that this was God's way of punishing me for having a hundred dollars all at once."

GILBERT: Is that supposed to be funny?

BUDDY: Half-and-half.

GILBERT: It's about right, then.

BUDDY: Donna! Waiting is expensive.

    *Donna enters. She is played by the same actress who plays Oolie.*

DONNA: He's on his way.

BUDDY: Here would be even better. That dress is half an inch too long. It'll photograph even longer.

DONNA: I'm not in a movie.

BUDDY: Everybody's in a movie. Sometimes we just turn the camera on.

Buddy orders Donna to call his wife and cancel their lunch date, admires his completed haircut and continues reading Stine's script. "The man of my dreams," Buddy comments, as Stine arrives and Gilbert exits.

BUDDY: I just got the pages where Stone gets beat up.

STINE: You like em?

BUDDY: Like is for pishers. These are to love. They're perfect. (*Laughs.*) But we'll fix 'em.

STINE: Can't I finish the script before we fix it?

BUDDY: Sure, you can finish it, but first, we'll fix.

STINE: What is it, you want new words?

BUDDY: No, no, no. There're too many words now. Give me pictures. Paint me scenes. Movies are shadows. They're light, they're dark. They're faces ten feet high. Close-up of him! Close-up of her! Cut to close-up of husband watching close-up of her watching close-up of him! (*Beat.*) You'll get it, you'll see. Sweetheart, nobody gets a hole-in-one their first time at bat. There's people make a fortune writing movies, and *they* don't know how. I mean, no offense, everybody and his brother writes books, but a screen play . . .

STINE: That's a ballgame of a different color, right?

BUDDY: When Buddy Fidler talks, you're not listening to someone else.

    *Sings "The Buddy System."*

      . . . . . I zipped through your book

And the characters jumped to life on the page

Now we're at the stage

Where I bring them to life on the screen
Don't cling to the words to which you gave birth
Remember how many a picture is worth
The odds are a thousand to one so get used to it Stine
The book may be yours baby trust me the movie is mine . . . . .

Authors unprepared to take
A stab at this collab'rative art
Must suppress their egos and part
With the notion that in motion pictures
Words are carved in marble
Donna darling get this on a pad
And type it up for next week
I have an engagement to speak
At the Writers Guild . . . . .

Buddy warns Stine in song not to cross him but to take advantage of his friendship and collaborative skill which Stine needs. He ushers Stine across the office and out, crying "Next!" to Donna. *Blackout.*

Rene Auberjonois as Buddy Fidler in *City of Angels*

*Scene 9: Stone's bungalow*

In the movie, the private eye is still lying on top of his bed, unconscious from the beating, while a plainclothes police detective, Lt. Munoz, and his uniformed assistant, Pasco, look the place over. The phone rings—it's Oolie, and Munoz puts her off. Pasco arouses Stone by dashing a glass of water onto his bruised face. Stone immediately challenges them.

STONE: You got a warrant?
MUNOZ: Don't need one when the peace gets this disturbed. Who did it?
STONE: Did what?
MUNOZ: Rearranged your furniture.
STONE: Interior decorator.
MUNOZ: He do your face, too? Neighbors said the whole place shook.
STONE: Must've been an earthquake.
MUNOZ: In just your bungalow?
STONE: Nature's funny. Which one of you stole my radio?
MUNOZ: What case you working on?
STONE: Who says I am?

A routine job, Stone tells the policeman, who has noticed the photo of Mallory and is sure there must be a woman in the case. They depart, leaving Stone alone to consider the situation, and his thoughts become audible in a voice over: "Munoz was right. Me and dames. Shorthand for trouble. Beginning with Bobbi. (*Beat.*) Bobbi. (*The name still hurts.*) Whoever said 'Time heals all wounds' never knew anyone like Bobbi."

*Scene 10: The Blue Note*

As Stone remembers the past, the movie flashes back to a cocktail lounge where Miss Bobbi Edwards (played by the same actress who plays Stine's wife Gabby) is singing "With Every Breath I Take."

BOBBI (*sings*):
There's not a morning that I open up my eyes
And find I didn't dream of you
Without a warning, though it's never a surprise
Soon as I awake
Thoughts of you arise
With ev'ry breath I take . . . . .

Darling,
You were the one who said forever from the start
And I've been drifting since you've gone

Out on a lonely sea that only you can chart
I've been going on
Knowing that my heart will break
With ev'ry breath I take.

Stone and Munoz, young police officers, come into the lounge. Munoz goes to the bar while Stone approaches Bobbi, slips a ring on her finger and, as they dance, begs Bobbi to consider them engaged. But Bobbi knows that Irwin S. Irving, "nobody bigger in the business," is coming by to check out her act, and this may be the career opportunity she's been working for. She returns to the mike and her song as the scene fades out.

*Scene 11: Bobbi's dressing room*

The flashback in Stone's memory continues, but the movie scene changes to another night when Stone goes to Bobbi's dressing room and finds the door locked. He breaks in to find Bobbi in a compromising embrace with Irwin S. Irving. Stone draws his gun in anger, and Irving (played by the same actor who plays Buddy Fidler) offers him money and a job in pictures if he'll just go away and forget the whole thing. Bobbi tries to restrain a furious Stone, and a scuffle ensues in which the light is knocked over, plunging the scene into darkness. Two shots are heard, followed by a cry from Irving and a scream from Bobbi.

*Scene 12: Writer's cell*

In the "real" world, Stine is on the phone to Gabby in New York, telling her, "Buddy's teaching me to write with guns instead of words." As he hangs up, Buddy's secretary Donna comes in with the latest script pages and the news that Buddy doesn't like the idea of his counterpart, Irwin S. Irving, getting shot.

> *Stine crumples the pages into a ball.*
> DONNA: I don't think the scene's dead; he just wants to fix it.
> STINE: Funny, how he can keep doing this to people without taking his pants down.
> *He tosses her the balled paper.*
> DONNA: You're wicked. He has to recognize himself in Irwin S. Irving.
> STINE: People never see themselves as others write them. You see any of you in Oolie's character?
> DONNA: Me? Never!
> STINE: I rest my case.
> *Donna puts the ball of paper on his desk and starts to go.*
> Donna.

*He tosses her the ball.*
Thanks for breaking the fall.
  DONNA: Just trying to be the best Oolie I can.
    *She starts to go once more.*
  STINE: Either of you ladies free for dinner tonight?
  DONNA (*exiting, smiling*): Donna might be.

Stine goes to his typewriter and starts writing a scene (which is acted out as he writes) in which Oolie goes to a phone booth and calls her boss to tell him that a teller at the bank recognized Alaura's signature on the $100 check and knows where she lives: "Try the top of Paso Robles Drive, right where it overlooks Arroyo Seco Canyon . . . I know. It doesn't get much more Pasadena than that . . . Looks like Mrs. Kingsley's not just any old Mrs. Kingsley, huh? Be careful. I'm getting that funny feeling I get in my bones, when people want to start breaking yours . . . Stone?" But he has hung up, as the movie cuts to the next scene.

*Scene 13: The Kingsley mansion*

The movie's action switches to the terrace of the Kingsley mansion where Alaura, in tennis clothes, is having her legs oiled by her 20-year-old stepson, Peter Kingsley. A maid enters to announce Stone. Peter is alarmed, but Alaura promises to handle the detective and urges Peter to act natural and keep on oiling her legs.
  Stone enters, "*a strip of adhesive over one eye, another on the bridge of his nose.*" Alaura sends Peter off to the tennis court to warm up.

  STONE: I don't know much about tennis, but how much more warming up do you figure he needs?
  ALAURA: You don't play?
  STONE: Too hard at my place. I keep breaking the lamps.
  ALAURA: I didn't expect to see you so soon, Mr. Stone. Any leads on Mallory? Isn't that what you call them?
  STONE: I'm not here to teach you my business, Mrs. Kingsley. Just to tell you I don't want yours. I don't suppose you'd know why two trained apes showed up at my place last night to give me a crash course in bleeding?
  ALAURA: Your face—
  STONE: It'll live. (*Handing her the cash.*) That's your deposit, Mrs. Kingsley, minus twenty-five dollars. I'm keeping a day's pay for the pounding. Only my friends beat me up for nothing.
  ALAURA: I don't understand. Why would anyone not want Mallory found? I have no idea. That's the truth.

Alaura informs Stone that her husband Luther Kingsley would not permit him to quit. She moves to escort him to her husband, and Stone's voice is heard over the action as they change scenes: "Luther Kingsley. 'The Widow Maker.' Half the planes and tanks in World War Two were built by Luther Kingsley. There weren't too many stray millions the man didn't own . . . . . "

*Scene 14: The solarium*

In the Kingsley solarium, Luther Kingsley, encased in an iron lung wheeled in by Dr. Mandril, is visible to Alaura and Stone only as a face reflected in the machine's mirror. Kingsley can barely get out the words "Stone! Find Mallory!" in a whisper. Stone refuses to go on with the case after the beating he took last night, and with the one word "Mandril!" Kingsley orders Dr. Mandril, his "spiritual advisor," to speak for him.

MANDRIL: Mr. Stone! If you do not agree to find Mallory, Mr. Kingsley will see to it that your investigator's license is held over a very slow flame at City Hall. You will be finished in this state.

STONE: The country's got one or two more.

MANDRIL: You can't see them, Mr. Stone—(*Re iron lung.*)—but there are some very long fingers in there. Fingers that can reach wherever you go. Lest you feel Mr. Kingsley does not appreciate your possible jeopardy, Mrs. Kingsley spoke to you of a bonus? That figure is ten thousand dollars. We trust that won't take too much thinking about.

STONE'S VOICE (*over, as Mandril wheels Luther out of the room*): Ten thousand dollars. Next to Mrs. Kingsley, that was the best figure in the room.

STONE (*to Alaura*): When was the last time you didn't get your way?

ALAURA (*smiles*): You'll be the first to know.

*Taking the cigarette from his lips, she takes a drag.*

STONE: Nasty habit.

ALAURA: Only kind to have.

*She returns the cigarette to his lips.*

STONE: Well, don't let me keep you. (*Reminding her.*) Your tennis game.

*Sings "The Tennis Song."*

You seem at home on the court.

ALAURA (*sings*):

Let's say that I've played around.

STONE (*sings*):

Well you don't look like the sort.

ALAURA (*sings*):

My hidden talents abound

A competitor hasn't been found to defeat me.

STONE (*sings*):
    I'll bet you're a real good sport.
ALAURA (*sings*):
    Shall we say the ball is in your court.
STONE (*sings*):
    I'll bet you like to play rough.
ALAURA (*sings*):
    I like to work up a sweat.
STONE (*sings*):
    And you just can't get enough.
ALAURA (*sings*):
    I'm good for more than one set
    But I promise I'll show no regret
    If you beat me.
STONE (*sings*):
    My backhand is clearly my forte
BOTH (*sing*):
    Shall we say the ball is in your court . . . . .

At the end of the song, the butler hands Stone his hat. Alaura will withhold her favors until after Stone finds Mallory. "Shall we say the ball is in your court," Alaura sings as the scene fades out.

*Scene 15: The search*

The movie continues with Stone looking for Mallory through a series of locales established by rear projection. It begins with Stone's voice over: "One more for the rule of thumb department: poor girls run away from home looking for something better, rich girls can't wait to find anything worse. With ten thousand and one new reasons to look for Mallory Kingsley, I started at the top, by going right to the bottom of the barrel." The Quartet, shabbily costumed, enters and goes into the song "Ev'rybody's Gotta Be Somewhere."

QUARTET (*sings*):
    . . . . . Try to track her down
    Go over the whole darn town
    Go on a fishin'
    Expedition
    Ev'rybody's gotta be somewhere . . . . .
STONE (*sings*):
    Where, I wonder, am I gonna find this chick?
    It's quite a blunder to underestimate her
    She's a sty in the eye of a private dick
    She look familiar?

PORNO VENDOR (*sings*):
    You don't know how many women I see each day
    Beneath innumerable guys
    Yours would be hard to forget I regret to say
    She's one I never laid my eyes on . . . . .
TWO B GIRLS (*sing*):
    You're quite a masterful detective
    And it's your lucky day to stumble on us
    (You'll find us a plus)
    It hardly seems at random
    You're wise to scrutinize us
    We won't refuse
    So take off your shoes
    We'll search for clues in tandem.
QUARTET (*sings*):
    Try to track her down
    Go over the whole town
    Better have hope and both eyes open
    Ev'rybody's gotta be somewhere . . . . .

*Scene 16: Stone's bungalow*

It's dark inside the bungalow when Stone comes home from his so-far-fruitless search. But there is movement under the bed sheet. *"Stone draws his gun, whips the sheet aside to reveal a naked, cheerful Mallory Kingsley."* Mallory says, "Hi!"; the Quartet reappears to sing the emphatic one-liner, "Everybody's gotta be somewhere!" and then exits, and Stone covers the girl with a sheet and turns on the lights as Mallory goes into the song "Lost and Found."

MALLORY (*sings*):
    Lost and found
    Lost and found
    You've earned your salary
    Searching for Mallory
    Wanna play lost and found?
    Well, then, here I am
    On the lam
    You've been assigned to find out where I've been
    And now you've found me in your bed
    And though my daddy said to turn me in
    Why don't I turn you on instead?

    . . . . . You'll never tame me

But you can claim me
At the lost and found.
*Fade out.*

## Scene 17: Donna's bedroom

In Stine's flesh-and-blood Hollywood, he is in Donna's bedroom letting her tie his tie. She invites him to spend the night, but he declines.

DONNA: You love your wife, you know that, don't you?

STINE: I do. (*On reflection.*) Strange phrase in this context.

DONNA: Then how do you explain being here?

STINE: Hate doing my tie alone, I guess. Or at least without someone I care about.

DONNA: Right. What's your line? "Some guys'll crawl out of the grave to cheat?"

STINE: It's Oolie's.

DONNA: You wrote it.

STINE: I just put down what my characters tell me. I'm nowhere as smart as they are.

*He is ready to go.*

DONNA: Which one of them's telling you to leave?

STINE: Stone. (*Kisses her brow.*) He's got a streak of morality that somehow eludes me.

*Lights fade.*

## Scene 18: Stone's bungalow

As the movie scene in Stone's place continues, Mallory is *un*doing Stone's tie and asking him to give her half the offered $10,000 bonus which he will earn so easily because she turned herself in to him.

STONE: And why does baby have to go through all this for what has to be petty cash in your family?

MALLORY: Don't let Luther Kingsley's condition fool you, just 'cause he looks like a hot dog on a roll. He wants to know what the score is all the time. I can't tell him why I need the money.

STONE: Blackmail?

MALLORY: How did you guess?

STONE: This is my room; I do very well here.

MALLORY: I kind of had a thing with my tennis teacher last year. A couple of other people, too. We all kind of had a thing together. Sort of mixed doubles. Manuelo took some pictures. *I* love how they came out, but I don't think Daddy would. (*Getting physical again.*) He thinks I'm a good girl. He just doesn't know *how* good.

Mallory assures him that she cooked up this disappearance with Peter, and her stepmother thinks it's the real thing. Stone tries to resist her blandishments, but she pulls him down onto the bed. At that moment a man appears in the door to take a flash picture, then he vanishes. When Stone runs out after him, Mallory picks up Stone's gun and runs off in the opposite direction. As Stone comments in voice over, "Another dame. Another gun. Will I ever learn? Will I ever forget? Is my life going to be one long flashback?", the movie goes into still another flashback into Stone's past.

## Scene 19: L.A. County Morgue

In the flashback to the morgue, the coroner, Harlan Yamato, wheels in the body of Irwin S. Irving on a gurney. Also present are Police Commissioner Gaines and a reporter, Mahoney. Irwin was shot in the thorax and the right kidney, so obviously (Yamato tells the reporter and the commissioner) the movie mogul died of a heart attack. All agree, and Gaines signs a paper to that effect.

Stone enters in his policeman's uniform (and minus the scars of his beating, of course). Coroner and reporter leave, but Commissioner Gaines remains to strip Stone of badge and gun. Bobbi enters just after Gaines exits, and Stone is able to reassure her that the shooting of Irwin S. Irving has now been covered up and no one will ever know the truth about it.

BOBBI (*a rueful glance at Irving's body on the gurney*): My chance to be somebody. Somebody I can't stand to be.
STONE: Time, Bobbi. Give it time.
BOBBI: That's one thing I've had enough of.
*She give him a kiss full of longing and despair, then steps back from him.*
Forget me.
STONE: The minute I die.

So Bobbi departs from Stone's life just as Munoz re-enters it and accuses Stone of getting away with murder because "you people" have "the right color skin . . . . . Kicked off the force. That don't even muss your hair," Munoz complains, noting that if this had happened to him, a non-gringo, they'd "hang me by my clockweights." From now on, Stone had better be extra careful because Munoz intends to watch his every move and catch him if he makes a false one: "I'll bust you for a bad haircut . . . . . Give me one more chance and I'll personally strap you into the gas chamber chair, sweetheart." Stone walks away from Munoz as the movie scene ends.

*Scene 20: Buddy's office*

Stine and Donna are watching Anna give Buddy a massage, while Buddy is complaining about the morgue scene showing the body of Irwin S. Irving. Stine argues that he needs the scene to establish Munoz's anger at Stone. Buddy refers to another scene in which Dr. Mandril is shot and killed by an unknown woman. He tells Stine: "After he's murdered and they wheel him into the morgue, you can establish whatever you want about Munoz there."

Buddy gets off the gurney, which is wheeled offstage by Anna, and continues his criticism of the script, complaining about "that 'my' people, 'your' people, social crap." Stone points out that it was that "social crap" which made his book more than just another private eye adventure.

BUDDY: Stine, Stine. Guy's sitting in the movies, right? Fifty cents to get in. The balcony's comfy, all nice and dark. He's got his hand between somebody's legs next to him. It might even be somebody he knows. We all of a sudden gonna remind him that he's white and that the Pachuco usher might try to stab him in his throat on the way out? What made your book was how good you write. I'm not asking you to write bad.

STINE: Just safe.

BUDDY: You bet your ass! The town's crawling with Congressmen. The last thing I need is for you to get blacklisted. You got any messages, put 'em in a letter. Then don't mail it. You got any idea how many close friends, how many personal relatives I can't have to my house for a bagel, just 'cause they mighta bought a Henry Wallace button at a rally?

STINE: But how do I fuel Munoz? Without the racial angle, what makes him hate Stone so? Why his compulsion to see Stone punished?

BUDDY: I don't care what it is, just change all that brown, black and yellow to red, white and blue. (*Beat.*) I know. Writing books is easier. But that way you don't get to see me naked, right?
*Opens his robe, flashes himself.*

STINE: Sure wish I'd brought my magnifying glass.

BUDDY (*a pained expression*): Oooooh. (*To Donna.*) The boy is not happy. (*To Stine.*) Okay, okay, wait! I knew if you gave it enough thought I'd come up with it. You ready? Munoz was *jealous of Stone*! He loved Bobbi, too. Almost went nuts when they got engaged. He *did* go nuts! It made him psycho! *That* gives him his heat! That gives Munoz his anger!

STINE: That's garbage!

BUDDY: Polish it! Make it shine! You like working in this town? You like having lunch ten feet from Betty Grable? Kill the politics. These guys from Washington aren't kidding around. They don't even want to get laid out here! Don't do anything to make the studio replace you.

STINE: They'd only do that if you asked.

BUDDY: Don't make me ask is what I'm asking. I can only protect you until I hafta start protecting myself. You wanna go down the toilet with your three-picture deal, I'm not going along for the ride sitting in your lap.

Stine departs with Buddy's "notes" about his script, but not before Buddy has a chance to add that he doesn't like the detective calling Irwin S. Irving a son-of-a-bitch, which wouldn't be allowed in a movie—and besides, Irving is his favorite character.

## Scene 21: The Morgue

In another morgue scene Stine has now written for the movie, it's the body of Dr. Mandril that Yamoto wheels in on his gurney, informing Munoz that the deceased was killed by a bullet in the larynx. Pasco brings in Stone, and Munoz confronts the private eye with questions about where he was between 7 and 9 p.m. tonight. Stone says he was at home, accompanied by a young lady—who unfortunately for Stone seems to be missing at the moment. Triumphantly, Munoz orders Pasco to put the cuffs on Stone and crows in the song "All Ya Have to Do Is Wait."

MUNOZ (*sings*):
      There's no sun up in the sky
      And the birds forgot to sing
      But you're headed for a cell
      Then to die and rot in hell
      So it might as well be spring
      I'll be singing like a bird
      When the jury sets the date
      And this capital event
      Proves revenge is heaven sent
      All ya have to do is wait . . . . .

When Munoz is finished relishing the details of Stone in the gas chamber in his song, Stone declares, "You got nothing on me." Munoz dots the i's and crosses the t's of his case: "Sebastian Mandril knew you and the Kingsley girl were playing footsies, way above the ankles, and he had the pictures to prove it. Afraid her old man'd find out, tired of being blackmailed, she begged you to get him off her back. Mandril goes through some kind of mumbo-jumbo meditation every night at the edge of the Kingsley estate, where it overlooks the canyon. You went there to try to pay him off, knock him off, finish it any way you could. There was a 'discussion,' the kind that always ends in a shot. If you hadn't panicked 'cause the staff came running, you'd've climbed down to get the pictures—(*Producing Stone's revolver.*)—and your gun. It took only one bullet. We found it in Mandril's voicebox. Even though he couldn't talk, it named you loud and clear."

Stone claims it's an obvious frame and tries to behave in friendly fashion to Munoz, as in the old days. But Munoz will have none of it. Munoz makes a resentful comment about Stone having "the right color skin," and at that moment the lights come up on Stine at the typewriter, writing this scene. Stine types X's across what he has just written, causing Munoz to move backward to the beginning of a revision in which Munoz mentions Bobbi and says, "Seeing what she saw in you, that was hard enough. What killed me was the way she looked right through me to see it."

At this point, Stone, the private eye, turns from Munoz to Stine, his creator, and asks, "You really going to do this?", as though the line between the movie scene and the "live" action were finally crossed in Stine's imagination. Stine tries to ignore Stone and keeps on typing dialogue for Munoz. But Stone persists.

STONE (*to Stine*): You're going to cave in? Just like that? (*Beat.*) I wouldn't have believed it.

STINE: You wouldn't've believed it? Is that what you said? *You* wouldn't've believed it? You?
> *Sings "You're Nothing Without Me."*
You are some gumshoe
You just don't think well
Get this, dumb gumshoe,
You come from my inkwell.

Is your mouth lonely
With one foot in there?
Stone, your brain only
Holds thoughts I put in there.

Just what you are I'll spell out
You are a novel pain
One speck of lint that fell out
The last time that I picked my brain.
STONE (*sings*):
You are so jealous
Of my track record
Tolstoy, do tell us
Your feeble hack record.

Your week-knees brand you
Soft and unstable
One small threat and you

Fold like a card table.

You drool at my adventures
Your broads in bed are bored
Go home and soak your dentures
Your pen is no match for my sword.
BOTH (*sing*):
    You're nothin' without me
    A no one who'd go undefined
    You wouldn't exist
    You'd never be missed.
STINE (*sings*):
    I tell you you're out of my mind.
BOTH (*sing*):
    A show off, a blowhard
    You're equal parts hot air and gall
    And no one would doubt me
    Without me you're nothin' at all . . . . .
        *To prove his dominance over Stone, Stine resumes typing, reactivating Munoz.*
MUNOZ (*to Stone*): Let's go!
STONE: Manny, wait!
MUNOZ: I said, keep my name out of your mouth!
        *He punches Stone hard, in the stomach, sending Stone to his knees.*
STONE (*stares at Stine, a character betrayed*): You bastard!
STINE (*ignoring him, types four letters*): "Fade . . . " (*Types three more letters.*) "Out."
        *And the lights do just that, on Munoz and Stone.*
STINE (*sings, triumphantly*):
    You're nothin' without me
    Without me you're nothin' at all.
        *Curtain.*

# ACT II

*Scene 1: A recording studio*

Jimmy Powers and his quartet are working on the 36th take of the song "Stay With Me."

JIMMY and QUARTET (*sing*):
    I'm in a sentimental way

So stay with me
I'll ask the orchestra to play
Your fav'rite song.

Thoughts that we would blush to say
Come easily in song
So why the rush to say so long?

There's no one calling you away
So stay with me
What say we while away the day
And pay the price?
For just this once
Let's not think twice . . . . .
> *The quality of the sound of the music changes, as lights fade on*
> *Jimmy and the quartet.*

## Scene 2: *A Bel-Air bedroom*

The tune is the same but the music loses sound quality, as though heard on a phonograph. In Buddy's bedroom his wife, Carla (an actress who is going to play Alaura Kingsley in Buddy's movie), is reading Stine's *City of Angels* script, which she likes. But Buddy doesn't want to talk about any of the six pictures he's working on simultaneously, he has other ideas and joins his wife on the bed, telling the phonograph "Sing it, Jimmy, sing it." The music comes up as the scene fades out.

## Scene 3: *L.A. County Jail*

In the movie, Stone is in jail for want of $100,000 bail and is being visited by Oolie. He instructs Oolie to do some digging in the back newspaper files to see what she might come up with. Oolie departs as the guard leads Stone off to his cell.

## Scene 4: *Oolie's bedroom*

Oolie comes in and hangs up her raincoat and scarf (under which she's wearing a nightgown; she was roused from bed to visit Stone in jail). She gets into bed and sings "You Can Always Count on Me."

OOLIE (*sings*):
     . . . . . If you need a gal
     To go without sal'ry and work too hard
     You can always count on me
     The kind of a pal

Who'd sneak you a file past the prison guard
Loyal to the nth degree
The boss is quite the ladies man
And that's my biggest gripe
Till I showed up he's never hired a girl 'cause she could type.
I'm no femme fatale
But faithful and true as a Saint Bernard
Barking up the wrong damn tree
You can always count on me.

Oolie winds and sets her alarm clock and turns out the light. The music continues, as the alarm clock rings and a lamp goes on.

## Scene 5: Donna's bedroom

When the lamp is turned on, it reveals the "real" world of Donna's bedroom where Stine, in pajamas, opens the blinds, waking Donna. Stine still feels so guilty about the script changes that he shrinks from the thought of looking at himself in the mirror while shaving, but Donna assures him that the Munoz rewrite is fine.

STINE: If you don't know what was there before. If you don't know I caved in.
DONNA: Collaborating is not caving in.
STINE: Collaborating is working with the enemy.
DONNA: You're too tough on yourself.
STINE: There're some who're tougher.
DONNA: You wake up with her, no matter who you go to sleep with, don't you?
STINE: All she asks is that I be the best possible me. I keep settling for being a first draft.
DONNA: I don't have any problem with that.
STINE: Don't make it easy. I need the pain.
        *Exits.*
DONNA: It's a big club.
        *Sings "You Can Always Count on Me."*
    I don't need a map
    I nat'rally head for the dead end street
    You can always count on me
    I'm caught in a trap
    When joy is approaching then I retreat
    I'm at home with misery
    I've been "the other women" since my puberty began

I crashed the junior prom
And met the only married man
I'm always on tap
For romance or choc'late that's bitter sweet
You can always count on me . . . . .
One Joe who swore he's single
Got me sorta crocked, the beast
I woke up only slightly shocked that I'd defrocked a priest.

Or else I attract
The guys who are longing to do my hair
You can always count on me.

Stine re-enters, dressing, headed for a party at Buddy's, to which Donna hasn't been invited. She tells him to notice Buddy acting as though he doesn't know about the affair between his wife and Jimmy Powers, an affair which Buddy himself seems to have engineered. Stine gives Donna the key to his hotel room so she can meet him there later, and he exits. Donna ends the scene alone with more of "You Can Always Count on Me."

Gregg Edelman as Stine, Deé Hoty as Carla Haywood and
Rachel York as Avril Raines in a scene from *City of Angels*

*Scene 6:  A Bel-Air garden*

At Buddy's garden party Del DaCosta, composer, enters and chats with the other guests (before taking over at the piano).  The conversation becomes inaudible, and we hear Buddy's thoughts about this latest arrival at his party.

> BUDDY (*sings*):
>     This tin pan putz is not the pick of the litter
>     There's not a clever note in his head
>     But what's so invaluable
>     Is he's so malleable
>     And Steiner's at Warner's
>     And Mozart and Gershwin are dead.

The guests, in their turn, are having private thoughts about their host.

> GUESTS (*sing*):
>     This pompous schmuck is making me nauseous
>     Somebody ought to set him on fire
>     I know where he can go
>     And I would tell him so
>     Except the day that I do is the day that I retire.

Buddy greets the actor who will play Munoz, as the scene changes to Stine alone on the phone.

*Scene 7:  Buddy's study*

In the study at Buddy's house, Stine is talking on the phone to his wife Gabby in New York.  After telling her about the party, he listens, growing more and more concerned, and then says, "You called the hotel? . . . My hotel? When? . . . Five minutes ago?  Look, hold on, will you?  I can explain.  She was there to—"  But Gabby has hung up on him.

*Scene 8:  The jail*

In the movie, some unknown person has put up bail for Stone, and Munoz is handing the private eye his belongings.  After gestures of hostility between the two, Stone signs for his things and departs.

*Scene 9:  Buddy's study*

Stine is trying to get Gabby back on the phone, but there is no answer in New York.  Avril Raines—a starlet played by the same actress as Mallory

Kingsley—enters and informs Stine that she's going to play Mallory in the movie.

AVRIL: I read every word of the book. From cover to cover.

STINE: It tends to make more sense that way.

AVRIL: I was so shocked when Mallory gets killed, I started crying. And I was all alone in bed, can you believe that? I mean, she was only what, at the most? Twenty-one?

STINE: Ah, well, the good die young. The naughty, even younger.

AVRIL: Mr. Fidler said it was going to be different in the movie. He said Mallory was going to be in it right up to the end.

STINE: I'm afraid Mr. Fidler's wrong.

AVRIL: How can he be? He's the producer-director. It's *his* movie.

STINE: His movie, *my* script.

AVRIL: I'd do anything for Mallory not to die, Mr. Stine. I mean, anything you could possibly think of.

Buddy's wife Carla enters, bringing Stine a drink he had requested and sending Avril away. They discuss the casting of their movie and then the script. As they are talking, the lights come up on one of the movie scenes: a cluttered shed with Big Six tying a trussed-up Stone to an overhead rail and Sonny wiring a complicated device to the telephone. The two scenes—movie and "real"—are simultaneously visible and play alternately.

At the party, Carla continues discussing the script while "You Gotta Look Out for Yourself" is the piano background. Carla doesn't like the two hoodlums being allied with Mandril, it seems contrived. But Stine has given them another motivation (as we hear from Big Six taunting Stone in the movie scene): Mandril had paid the hoodlums in advance to take revenge if anything happened to him—a kind of posthumous insurance policy.

Sonny has finally gotten the device working, and over the sound of its ticking he explains to Stone, "First time the phone rings, the cap gets snapped. Second ring, the fuse is exposed. The third ring ignites it an' then you an' this warehouse are somewhere over the Rockies."

The hoodlums exit on the way to making their lethal phone call, leaving Stone tied up and at their mercy. But as the phone rings once, he manages to get his bound hands loose from the rail, then turn on a nearby buzz saw; as it rings a second time, he cuts the bonds around his wrists with the buzz saw and picks up the receiver before the phone can ring for the third time. "Sorry, I'm just on my way out!" Stone says into the phone and exits.

Carla loves the scene, but there's more, Stine tells her: the hoodlums rush back into the empty shed with guns drawn and turn off the buzz saw. Big Six puts the phone receiver back on its cradle. The phone rings at once, and Big Six barely has time to get out, "Who knows to call us here?" before the shed disappears in a blinding explosion.

"Wonderful!" Carla applauds, but she rushes off when she hears Jimmy Powers singing "Stay With Me" to Del DaCosta's piano accompaniment out in the garden. Following the song, Buddy gives DaCosta instructions about composing a theme for Alaura in the movie, humming a few bars that sound very much like the beginning of "Tara's Theme" in *Gone With the Wind*.

### Scene 10: *Alaura's bedroom*

In the movie, Alaura is sitting on her bed, dressed in a satin nightgown and brushing her hair, when Stone bursts through the window, gun in hand, holding his hand over her mouth to keep her from crying out and then taking it away after demanding that she now tell him the truth about this case. Alaura calls it part of Peter Kingsley's plan to inherit as much of his father's money as possible. Mandril had to be eliminated, with Mallory stealing Stone's gun to leave at the murder scene, because Mandril seemed to be gaining an increasing influence over Luther. Alaura admits to being afraid now because she stands between Peter and some of the money.

> STONE: Where is he now?
> ALAURA: I don't know.
> *He grabs her, forcefully.*
> I don't! (*Beat.*) Without even touching, I felt this close the first time we met. Tell me you didn't know it, too.
> STONE: You've got a way of feeling close even when you're not there.
> *She kisses him hard.*
> Why me? Of all the poor suckers who could've taken the rap, why me?
> ALAURA: Only Peter can tell you. Find him and you'll know.
> STONE: Got any idea which part of the haystack?
> ALAURA: There's a place he goes. One place more than any other. I'll tell you where. Just promise me you'll do one thing when you find him. (*Her hand to his gun.*) Shoot first!
> *They fall to the bed in an embrace. Fade out.*

### Scene 11: *Buddy's office*

In his office, Buddy is on the phone to Stine because he's heard Stine is leaving to visit his wife in New York over the weekend. Buddy orders Stine not go, there's too much left to do on the movie script. Stine hangs up on him, leaving Buddy furious.

*Scene 12: Stine's apartment, New York*

It is immediately obvious that relations between Stine and his wife have been greatly strained by Donna's visit to Stine's Hollywood hotel room. Gabby reads from a letter of explanation Stine had sent her, claiming that his typewriter had been broken, so Buddy sent Donna with another typewriter to make sure the pages were typed on time. The letter also points out that Stine wasn't there with Donna in the hotel room, but at Buddy's party. Gabby doesn't buy this explanation, as she tells Stine in the song "It Needs Work."

GABBY (*sings*):
    No lack of alibis
    Your knack for the spectacular is still intact
    I like the tone of it
    It rings sincere and pretty near succeeds
    It's just the narrative
    Is like a sieve and cloudy as a cataract
    There's not a trace of honesty so face the fact
    It needs . . . work.

    . . . . . Your fiction always had
    A little grit in it
    A little heart in it
    A little wit in it
    It used to be so clear
    That there was art in it
    If you had written it
    What makes you go and spit in it?

    And come to think of it
    Your writing always mirrors our relationship
    With dangers cropping up
    And sweet young strangers popping up like weeds
    So if you wish official pardoning
    You better do a little gardening
    Ya know ya needn't be so generous with your seeds
    Your fertile lies don't fertilize
    It needs work . . . . .
        *By the finish of the song, she has handed him his hat and suitcase,*
        *Stine has exited and Gabby is alone.*

*Scene 13: The Red Room*

In the movie, Stone is searching for Peter Kingsley in a place run by cigar-smoking Margie and filled with obliging girls. Margie recognizes Kingsley from Stone's description and, persuaded by money changing hands, sends

Stone to the establishment's Red Room to talk to Kingsley's regular, "the only one he ever asks for."

The whore who enters the Red Room and pours herself a whiskey, offering one to Stone, is Stone's old flame, the former night club singer Bobbi. After a moment, she recognizes him.

BOBBI (*shocked, turning to face him*): Why did I know this would happen sooner or later?

STONE: Haven't I always been the answer to all your bad dreams?

BOBBI: How'd you find me?

STONE: The easiest way. By not looking.

BOBBI: I never figured you for a place like this.

STONE: Still able to read my mind.

BOBBI (*at the door*): I'll get you someone else.

STONE: Stay. You're paid for.

BOBBI (*properly stung*): Beatings cost extra.

What Stone wants from her is information about Peter Kingsley. Did she tell him about the shooting of Irwin S. Irving? Yes, but only the official version, not the truth. She is sorry that Stone had to suffer all the dire consequences of that incident, but Stone observes, "Looks to me like we're about even." Together they sing a reprise of Bobbi's song "With Every Breath I Take," after which Stone exits, leaving Bobbi to her fate.

## Scene 14: The Kingsley solarium

As the movie continues, when Stone enters the solarium of the Kingsley mansion, Alaura is spoon-feeding her husband his dinner. Stone hints that Alaura means Luther harm. He's learned in a phone call from Oolie that Alaura poisoned a previous ailing husband for his money and was prevented from collecting it when the deceased's children found out and blackmailed her into giving it up.

There is a storm outside—wind, thunder, lightning—as Stone outlines Alaura's misdeeds for Luther's benefit: she was going to be sure this time that there were no other heirs, not even Dr. Mandril whom she arranged to have Peter kill. Stone wonders out loud how she plans to kill her husband.

STONE (*re iron lung*): Were you going to arrange for this to have a head-on collision with a streetcar? Or were you just going to pull the plug on your married appliance here?

ALAURA: No, Mr. Stone. (*Producing a gun.*) *You* unhooked the machine; then you came at me. If I hadn't lost time shooting you in self-defense, I might have been able to get it started again.

*More thunder, more lightning.*

STONE: And my motive?

ALAURA: You knew that when my husband learned you'd murdered Dr. Mandril *and* that you were having an affair with Mallory, he'd have used his influence to put you in the gas chamber—for a whole week running. Isn't that true, Luther?

*Luther can only gasp pathetically.*

(*Calmly, reminding him*): Measured breaths, darling, measured breaths.

STONE: You're going to kill him before Peter and Mallory are safely out of the way?

ALAURA: By now, Peter will have killed Mallory and be heading to the beach house to meet me.

And on the way to the beach house (Alaura informs Stone), the brakes on Peter's car will fail on one of the many precipitous curves leading to it. "Which must have been just minutes ago," she concludes, then waves the gun and orders Stone to pull the plug on the respirator. Luther protests, and Stone doesn't move, but Peter Kingsley bursts into the room, followed by Mallory; Stone has arranged for Oolie to tip them off to come here, and they both now know all about Alaura's murderous intentions toward them. All eyes turn accusingly on Alaura—who is still holding the gun—and Alaura tries one more move.

ALAURA (*to Stone*): We can do it together! The two of us! (*Re Peter and Mallory*): And then them! You don't know how much there is! We deserve it all! We've both gotten rotten deals out of life! Peter only had to tell me about you and that singer for me to know you took the blame for her.

STONE: Believe what you want. Your past and mine don't add up to the same future.

ALAURA (*re gun*): Don't make me use this.

STONE (*moving toward her*): That's the last thing I had in mind.

PETER: Stone!

MALLORY: Don't!

*Stone puts his hand on Alaura's gun. She does not let go. His body is close to hers, the weapon pressed between them. Three gun shots rend the air. Mallory screams.*

STONE (*voice over*): Three gunshots rang out. (*Falls to the floor.*) Three shots, divided by two people . . .

*Alaura, still holding the gun, watches Stone fall, a look of victory on her face.*

(*Voice over continuing*): Somebody figures to die.

*A red stain appears beneath Alaura's heart. She falls to the floor—dead—as Stone, wounded, reaches to Peter for help.*

(*Voice over continuing*):  You can count it one of your better days if that someone doesn't turn out to be you.
> *Iris out.*

*Scene 15: Writer's cell*

Back in the "real" world of Hollywood, Stine is complaining to Donna about Buddy's interference in every aspect of the process: "So much to do before he shoots a movie, redesigning all the set designer's sets, personally biting off all the loose threads on the costumes, inventing the camera. It must kill him when a picture opens and someone else gets to butter the popcorn." And as for script revisions, Buddy riddled theirs while Stine was away for the weekend, changing lines in the final scene which Buddy plans to shoot first. Stine doesn't see how he can do this with all the adjustments to Buddy's changes that have to be made in the script—Mallory dead, Mallory living, etc. And Donna too tried to help with script input while Stine was away, suggesting lines that would sound as though Stine wrote them.

STINE:  . . . . . Jesus, where the hell is everybody when they first deliver the typing paper?  Where are all the "helpers" when those boxes full of silence come in?  Blank.  Both sides.  No clue, no directions enclosed on how to take just twenty-six letters and endlessly rearrange them so that you can turn them into a mirror of a part of our lives.  Try it sometime.  Try doing what I do before *I* do it.

DONNA:  You don't mind including *her* in your work.

STINE:  Her involvement's aimed at getting *me* to be the best possible me. She doesn't want to be me herself.  What's left?  Any other surprises?  Any more little changes?  Stone going to be played by Betty Hutton?

DONNA:  I'll tell him you want to see him.

STINE:  But in your own words.  I'm sure they'll sound just like me.  Maybe better.

> *Donna turns to go, stops.*

Donna.  I thought we meant something to each other.

DONNA (*before exiting*):  Funny.  I never got that impression.

STINE (*sings "Funny"*):
> Funny, how'd I fail to see this little bedtime tale was
> Funny
> I could cry to think of all the irony I've missed
> What an unusual twist
> Right at the end of it.
>
> . . . . . Just deserts
> We can laugh till it hurts
> At my expense

I'm accustomed to working on spec
I always pick up the check.

..... You'd have us all on the floor
That would be roaringly funny
Sad enough my life's a joke that suffers in the telling
Just another hoary chestnut from the bottom drawer
I've heard so often before
That I can't laugh any more.

*Scene 16: A studio sound stage*

Everyone on the set is busy preparing the scenery, props and actors for the shooting of Stine's movie script, beginning with the final scene in the Kingsley solarium. Buddy, director as well as producer of the film, is checking the setup with the cinematographer and a stand-in. Stine enters, furious, carrying a copy of the script.

STINE (*to Buddy, re script*): What is this shit?
BUDDY (*to Donna*): Donna, don't just sit there helping. Do something.
     *Donna exits.*
(*To Stine*): We haven't even started shooting, and already you're reviewing it?
STINE (*showing the cover page*): Screen play by the two of us?
BUDDY: Take it easy.
STINE: *We* wrote this? With *your* name on top?
BUDDY: Take it easy. It's studio policy. They automatically put my name on everything. We'll fix it.
STINE: Why don't I believe you?
BUDDY: Why? Because you're honest. Because you know in your heart-of-hearts that I was with you page-for-page; you *know* my name belongs there. On top, underneath, wherever. (*An arm around him.*) Stine, Stine, let's not spoil the first day. It's a wonderful script. Who cares who wrote what? Together, we made a beautiful child. We'll let the lawyers work everything out.

Buddy checks other details with Gene, his assistant director, as Avril comes onto the set, followed by Carla costumed as Alaura. Buddy orders the actor playing Luther into his iron lung and looks around for the actor who is to play the private eye. A voice singing "You Gotta Look Out for Yourself" is heard, and sure enough on comes Jimmy Powers costumed as Stone.
And once again we see imagination personified in "reality" as Stone him-self, now a magic presence in his own right, joins Stine on the set and com-plains bitterly about the crooner Jimmy Powers playing him in the movie:

"Guess they couldn't get Betty Hutton, right?" Stone reminds Stine that Jimmy and his recordings are so universally popular, *"That's* why Buddy doesn't care what Powers is doing to his wife. *Arranged* for him to do what he's doing to her."

The Clapperboy announces *"City of Angels,* Scene 93, Take 1," and the cameras roll on Alaura spoon-feeding Luther and "Stone" entering the solarium in the bland and grinning person of Jimmy Powers (and the "real" Stone asks Stine, in disgust, "Ever have anybody puke inside your head?") At last Stine can stand this travesty no longer and shouts "Cut!!", throwing everyone into confusion and bringing the action to a halt.

BUDDY (*to Stine*): Are you crazy? Nobody says "Cut" on a sound stage but me! If this building's on fire and everyone inside's drowning, nobody yells "Cut" but the director. It's the eleventh God damn commandment! It's an unwritten law—in letters twenty feet high!

STINE (*quietly, provocatively*): Cut.

BUDDY: What're you, looking to get thrown off the set? Is that what you want? Is this some kind of New York, snot-nose revenge?

    *Stine crosses to Buddy and hands him an object from his jacket pocket.*

What's this?

STINE: My pencil. Now, you don't have to envy it any more.

STONE (*to Stine*): I like that. Remember it.

Buddy orders a flunky to call the police to throw Stine out of the studio and out of movies. He's only too glad to go and return to the "reality of fiction," but the cops (played by the same actors who played Big Six and Sonny in the movie scenes) come on and start giving Stine a beating. Stone cheers Stine on, declaring, "Belt 'em! They're not tough." The private eye then sits down at Stine's typewriter and starts using it to manipulate Stine as Stine routinely uses it to manipulate Stone.

    *Stine, thus activated, dispatches the Cops using his fists, feet, the clapperboard and makeup powder puffs, relieving one of the Cops of his gun in the process. Stine turns to the crowd, holding the gun in innocent triumph, throwing them all into a panic.*

BUDDY (*starting to leave*): Somebody get this crazy maniac out of here.

    *Stine raises his hands, freezing Buddy. Stone strikes the typewriter's X key several times. Buddy walks and talks himself backwards to his starting point. Stine takes the screen play from Buddy and throws it into the air. As the pages flutter down, the entire company moves toward him, muttering angrily.*

GENE: Hey, get offa Buddy's set, Buster!

HAIRDRESSER: The very idea!
> *Stine raises his arms, freezing them. Stone X's the typewriter.*
> *All move and speak backwards to their previous positions.*

STINE (*to Stone*): You did it!

STONE: *You* did!

STINE and STONE: *We* did! (*Sing reprise of "You're Nothing Without Me"*):

I'm nothing without you
Without you I lack what it takes
Unless we're combined
I have half a mind
To blow all my chances and breaks.
> *Stine hands Stone the gun. Stone hands Stine a pencil.*

Without you I'm bupkis
A flop who keeps dropping the ball
It's time to stop quaking
Start taking the lead
And you are the singular buddy I need.

I'm nothing without you
Without you I'm nothing ...
> *Stone gestures "Wait!", crosses to the desk and sits at the*
> *typewriter.*

STONE (*to Stine*): A Hollywood ending!
> *He strikes a few keys on the typewriter, and the giant doors at*
> *the back of the sound stage open to admit Gabby, who joins them,*
> *to the delight of the company, now unfrozen.*

STINE, STONE and GABBY (*sing*):

I'm nothing without you

STONE (*sings*):

No hero

STINE (*sings*):

A zero

STINE and STONE (*sing*):

That's me

STINE, STONE and GABBY (*sing*):

With you by my side
There's no better guide
On how to be all I can be.

I'm nowhere without you
To doubt you is where I went wrong.

The script calls for fusing and using our smarts

*As Stine, Stone and Gabby get on the crane platform.*
And greatness can come from the sum of our parts
ALL (*sing*):
From now on I'm with you
And with you is where I belong.
> *They finish singing joyously, looking up, as Stine, Stone and Gabby atop the camera crane are raised high above the stage. Curtain.*

# SEX, DRUGS, ROCK & ROLL

*A Monologue of 12 Characters*

BY ERIC BOGOSIAN

Credits appear on page 425

*ERIC BOGOSIAN was born in Boston April 24, 1953, the son of an accoun-
tant. His college years were equally divided between the University of
Chicago and Oberlin, to which he transferred after two years and from which
he received his B.A. in theater in 1976. A year later, in New York City, he
founded the dance program known as The Kitchen, which he ran until 1981.
He had always wanted to write, however, and he kept at it with stage
vehicles for his own performances. In July 1982, New York Shakespeare
Festival workshopped Bogosian's* Men Inside *and* Voices of America, *solo
pieces which he performed and which were repeated in September of that
year. His next, a collection of mostly sinister characters written and acted
by Bogosian and entitled* Fun House, *was put on in workshop by New York
Shakespeare, then moved to full off-Broadway independent production Sept.
29, 1983 for 70 performances.*

*From then on, every Bogosian project has made an exceptional mark. His
fourth writing-and-solo-performing presentation of a variegated assortment
of characters,* Drinking in America, *became his first Best Play in American*

*Place production Jan. 19, 1986 for 94 performances and winning both Drama Desk and Obie Awards. His first conventionally constructed play,* Talk Radio, *was one of the highlights of its season in New York Shakespeare production May 28, 1987 for 210 performances and later won the Berlin Film Festival's Silver Bear after it was made into a motion picture starring its author. His fifth writing-and-solo-performing collection of characters,* Sex, Drugs, Rock & Roll, *presented Feb. 8 in independent off-Broadway production, collects his second Best Play citation.*

*Bogosian has been the recipient of National Endowment and New York State arts council grants. He is married, lives in New Jersey, is at work on a new play entitled* Suburbia *and once described his ambition as "to continue writing, for actors other than myself."*

*As in the case of his previous Best Play,* Drinking in America, *our method of representing* Sex, Drugs, Rock & Roll *differs from that of the other Best Plays. Instead of trying to precis all 12 of the distinct characterizations, we note nine of them briefly and present three in their entirety as prime examples of the style and quality of Bogosian's work.*

## Time: Tonight

SYNOPSIS: As the lights go down, the voice of *"a raucous D.J."* is heard exhorting the audience to get ready for a hard-rock evening. The audience is being inundated with hard rock music, when *"A man appears in silhouette, holding a stick. He begins a frenzied 'air guitar' mime to the music. The lights change. The man is hobbling toward the audience on the stick."* He is carrying a cup and speaks to the audience.

## 1. Grace of God

MAN: Good afternoon, ladies and gentlemen. I only want a few minutes of your time. It doesn't cost you anything to listen. Please be patient with me.

I just got released from Riker's Island where I was unjustly incarcerated for thirty days for acts I committed during a nervous breakdown due to a situation beyond my control. I am not a drug addict.

This is the situation. I need your money. I could be out mugging or stealing right now, but I don't want to be doing that. I could be holding a knife up to your throat right now, but I don't want to be doing that. And I'm sure you don't want that either.

I didn't choose this life. I want to work. But I can't. My medication costs over two thousand dollars a week of which Medicaid only pays one-third. I am forced to go down to the Lower East Side and buy illegal drugs to stop the pain. I am not a drug addict.

If you give me money, if you help me out I might be able to get someplace to live and get my life together. It's really all up to you.

*Drops cup.*

Bad things happen to good people. Bad situations beyond my control forced me on to the streets to a life of crime. I won't bore you with the details right now. But if you don't believe me, you can call my parole officer, Mr. Vincent Gardello, his home number is 555-1768.

The only difference between you and me is that you're on the ups and I'm on the downs. Underneath it all, we're exactly the same. We're both human beings. I'm a human being.

I'm a victim of a sick society. I come from a dysfunctional family. My father was an alcoholic. My mother tried to control me. My sister thinks she's an artist. You wouldn't want the childhood that I had.

The world is really screwed up. Things get worse every day. Now is your chance to help out somebody standing right in front of you instead of worrying about South fuckin' Africa ten thousand miles away. Believe me when I tell you God is watching you when you help someone less fortunate than you, a human being, like me.

I'm sorry I am homeless. I'm sorry I don't have a job. I am sorry that my clothes aren't clean. I'm sorry I have to interrupt your afternoon. But I have no choice, I have to ask for help. I can't change my life, you can. Please, please look into your hearts and do the right thing! . . . thank you.

*With his cup, he works the audience with "God bless you's," ad libs, etc. To people in audience who don't move: "I really feel sorry for you, man."*

Thank you. Thank you.

## 2. Benefit

Reformed addict, a musician, addresses a benefit gathering and describes the variety and intensity of the drugs he and his friends used to abuse almost continuously. When he suddenly realized from something an ex-addict said on a Donahue TV show that his life was meaningless, he abjured drugs entirely and is now trying to justify himself by helping the benighted Amazonian Indians in a misdirected way, raising funds to buy them presents like a Sony walkman—and cigarettes—supposedly to improve the quality of their lives.

## 3. Dirt

A derelict complains of the dirt and pollution which is befouling the whole world, from a hiker urinating in the mountains to the huge outpouring of sewage and chemicals into the sea.

Eric Bogosian in his *Sex, Drugs, Rock & Roll*

## 4. The Stud

A man drinking from a long-necked beer bottle self-satisfiedly claims that he has an edge on other men because he is "endowed." He describes some of the typical advantages of having "a long, thick, well-shaped prick" and admits to being sorry for just about everybody who lacks his special gift.

## 5. Stag

A friend describes a surprise party thrown for a bridegroom-to-be the night before his wedding: girls, booze, cocaine, even a run-in with Hell's Angels bikers. It turned into an all-night session so boisterous that the groom missed the wedding and the narrator remembers, "In my life it was a high point." There's even time for another such party before the postponed wedding, but this time without girls: "They cause too much trouble."

## 6. *Bottleman*

One of the street people tells (rapidly and with nervous mannerisms) how it is to live as he does: collecting cans and bottles to redeem them for sandwich money, sleeping wherever he can find a niche that nobody else tries to take away from him, damaged in mind and battered in body but managing to keep his spirits "on the sunny side of the street."

## 7. *Phone Sex*

"Candy" is providing sexual titillation over the phone, telling callers she's about to take a "really, really erotic bath" and suggesting provocatively that the caller should remain on the line while she does it.

## 8. *Rock Law*

> *Lights up on a man skidding across the stage in an office chair, yelling at someone on a portable phone. He paces, yelling.*

Frank, Frank, Frank . . . what did he say? HE'S GONNA SUE ME?! Wait a second, wait a second, no Frank, Frank, Frank, don't tell me that, I don't want to hear that. That's not what I want to hear! SUE ME? SUE ME?! Did you tell him who he's messing with here, Frank? Did you tell him who's SCREWING WITH? HE'S SCREWING WITH GOD, FRANK, DID YOU TELL HIM THAT?

Ever hear of Nagasaki, Frank? Ever hear of Sodom and Gomorrah? That's what I'm gonna do to his face! After I'm done with him he's gonna be declared a disaster area. I'm gonna blow him away. I'm gonna peel his skin off, I'm gonna chew his bones, I'm gonna drink his blood, I'm gonna eat his children, Frank . . . and you know something, Frank? I'm gonna enjoy myself. I'm gonna have a good time, because he is a schmuck, a shithead and a schlemiel for messing with me. He should know better. The world, Frank, the world is going to stand up and applaud me for removing this jerk from its midst . . .

No, no . . . Frank . . . SUE ME?! Frank, you keep an eye on where that guy is standing, because when I'm done with him there's gonna be a scorched spot there.

Sue me? Sue me? You tell him, you call him, Frank, and you tell him . . . no, no, don't call him, call his children. Call his children, Frank, and tell them to get ready to be eaten . . . G'bye.

> *Goes to intercom.*

DIANE! Who's on line one? She can wait . . . I'm hungry, where's my lunch? I don't care, Diane, anything, I don't care, Diane, I'm starving to death . . . I don't want that, I don't want that either, I don't want that either. No, no monkfish. No monkfish, no arugula, no sun-dried tomatoes, no Perrier. I want

FOOD!  Unlike you, Diane, I am a human being, and to survive I need food and coffee.  Get me some.  Now!  ... Call Jeff Cavanaugh, put him on line two, call Dave Simpson, put him on line three.  Thank you.

*On phone, pacing, more slowly now.*

Hi hon ... I tell her again and again, don't put my wife on hold, she puts you on hold.  What did you do today?  Oh really, that's nice, how much did that cost?  No, that's great, spend the money, that's what it's for ...

How's Jeremy?  How did he do that?  What do you mean he bit the kid?  Why would be bite another kid?  He says I told him to do it?  I did not tell him to do it, I told him ... Sonia, don't tell me what I tell him.  I told him that if a little boy does something to you, do twice as much back, that's all ...

I don't care what his therapist says ... His therapist is a ... he should bite his therapist.  I'm gonna tell him to bite his therapist!

What else?  How did she do that?  How did she get it in the microwave, Sonia?  That's what, three microwave ovens in two years.  You know, Sonia, if you hired somebody who came from a country where they had electricity, we wouldn't have this problem ... Well, you gotta tell her ... What do you mean she'll quit.  She won't quit, where's she gonna go?  She can't even speak English, what's she gonna do?  Sell crack?  Sonia, she has it great, she spends more time in our apartment than we do!

I'm not shouting, I'm not shouting.  I'm discussing.  We'll talk about it when I get home ...

Listen, I got a million people on hold, I just called to tell you I'll be a little late tonight.  Around nine—Sonia, do you think I like slaving all hours of the day so that you and Jeremy can be safe and warm?  Do you?

It hasn't been two weeks ... We'll have sex tomorrow night, I'll put it in my book.  Sonia, Sonia ... no don't read me your diary, I believe you ... it's been two weeks.

Listen Sonia, next month we'll go down to Saint Bart's for two weeks, we'll make love every day on the beach ... You won't get sand in your crotch ... Look, honey, I gotta get off ... No, don't do that.  Don't do that, don't cut your hair, I don't want any different hair ... Don't blackmail me with your hair, Sonia ...

We'll talk about it when I get home ... listen, honey, give Jeremy a kiss from me, alright?  Yeah, give your mother my love.  Yup.  I love you too ... O.K.  Alright.  Alright ... I'll be home around ten thirty.

*Intercom.*

Coffee, Diane, what are you doing in there, picking the beans?  Come on!  And food!  I feel like a poster child for Ethiopian relief.

*Continues on the phone, sits in his office chair.*

Yeah?  Jeff?  HEY.  Hey man, how they hanging?  Not bad, not bad ... yeah, I finished that deal yesterday morning ... I made twenty grand ... chump change.  Listen to this, I took in seventy-five this morning ... a hundred grand here, a hundred grand there, pretty soon you're talking real money . . . I don't know, maybe I'll buy a new Porsche for the country house, park it in front of the tennis court, piss off my neighbors . . . They have to pay me, Jeff, they have to pay me, they don't pay me I go next door, I get twice as much . . . Jeff, it's only rock and roll, like Bruce says, "No surrender!"

Nothing. I just called so you could tell me how great I am . . . thank you . . .

Nah, I can't tonight, I'm doin' something . . . Who am I doing? I'm not telling you. You'll tell Nadine, and she'll tell Sonia. Very beautiful . . . better . . . better . . . better than her . . . yeah she has breasts, yeah she has legs, she has arms, she has a head, I got the whole package . . . Jeff, let me put it to you this way, the closest you ever came to a girl this beautiful is that time you bought the scratch and sniff picture of Vanna White . . . hah-hah . . . And get this, she's an artist. She's very, very sensitive. She picked me up in a bar, how could I say no? Jeff, unlike you I have not forgotten my sixties roots, I am still committed to exploring and experience. When I cut off my hair I didn't cut off my dick . . .

Listen, I'll tell you about it tomorrow night, O.K., why don't we get together, play a little handball over at my club and uh, have a couple of pops afterwards, O.K.? No, my club, Jeff, my club, my club is nicer than your club, it's cleaner, it's more sanitary, it has no diseases . . . O.K.? They don't let those people in they let in at your club.

Jeff, I gotta get off, I got a million things to do, I can't spend all day goofing off the way you do . . . (*Laughs.*) Thank you, thank you very much, I deserve it because I'm the best. I'm a genius. No one can get close to me. I'll let you get close to me, you can blow me . . . Bye!

*Pushes buttons on phone.*

Dave! I'm so glad you called . . . I agree with you completely, he's a wonderful man, a real mensch. A human being. I felt terrible having to let him go . . . Yeah, yeah, I know he's got his pension coming up, I understand that, but Dave . . . Dave, can I just say something? I love that man. When I first came to this company, he was like a father to me. Our kids play together. And I hated to fire him . . . Yeah . . . yeah . . . Dave, I know he's going in for surgery next week. But Dave, I'm not his doctor, I'm his boss. My problem is not this guy's health, it's the health of this company!

But Dave, Dave . . . Dave may I say something please? Dave, Dave, Dave . . . now you've had your say, I've been listening very patiently to you now for five minutes. May I say something, please? Now, this guy is not performing any more. He's not hustling any more. He's easy listening, and this place is rock and roll! We can't have that . . . no, DAVE, DAVE, DAVE!

Let me make it a little clearer for you: You like your Mercedes station wagon? You like your country house? You like your swimming pool? You like skiing in Aspen? What pays for those things, Dave? Profits, that's what . . . say "profits," Dave! Say "profits" . . . Say it! Thank you . . .

Now, now, now, Dave, wait a minute ... When the profit axe comes down, anybody's head can roll. I could lose my job tomorrow, you could lose your job tomorrow. You could lose your job today, you could lose your job in the next five minutes if we keep this conversation up much longer. Because to tell you the truth, Dave, I want to get rid of the guy even more now, because now he's wasting your time as well as mine. And when all these people are wasting their time around here, I think, "What are we doing anyway?" What are we doing?

*Screaming.*

WHAT'S YOUR POINT, DAVE? Dave? ... You'll have to think about it? O.K., while you're doing that, let me just ask you this? Are you happy with our company? No, I mean are you happy with this company, because if you're not ... Good, well if you're happy, go back to work and stop wasting time ...

*Suddenly laughs.*

O.K. ... Alright ... no, no ... no hard feelings ... We've all been working hard ... O.K. ... Alright, I understand ... call any time ... Say hi to Judy for me ... Janet ... say hi to Janet ... O.K. ... Alright ... Take care ...

*Intercom.*

Diane, food ... Listen, I'll make it easy for you, put your hand in the microwave, grill it and bring it in to me.

*Continues on the phone.*

Hey ... how you doin'? Not bad ... I'm making money, what else do I do? I'm working hard, it's getting harder and harder every minute ... You being a good girl? Of course I got you something, don't I always get you something? What have you been doing? Oh, that's interesting, you made a sculpture of a horse and you wrote the word "horse" on it. That's nice. What do you mean I sound bored? I'm not bored, Yvette. Yvette, I spend all day thinking about your art. Come on. I was just telling somebody how nice your art is. Yvette, if you were ninety-five years old and in a wheelchair I would still love you, and you want to know why? Because I love your art, that's why.

You know when you say these things to me you make me angry, I'm gonna have to come over there and give you a little spanking. Huh? What? You are? And then what are you gonna do? Oh yeah? The whole thing? The phone is heating up. What did I do to deserve all this attention? I am wonderful, aren't I? ...

Um-hm ... I love you too. I love you too. Of course I mean it, and you know when I say I love you I mean I love you. No one else in the whole world knows what love means the way that I know what love means when I say from me to you, "I love you." No one was ever loved before the way that I love when I love you. Because my life would have no meaning without you. Of course I mean it, of course I mean it, would I lie to you? ... Yvette, the boss just walked in, I gotta get off ... I'll see you around six, O.K.? O.K. Me too ... keep making those sculptures ... Ciao to you too.

*Intercom.*

Diane, forget the food, forget the coffee. Send in a bottle of Maalox, the shoeshine boy and hold my calls. Thank you.

## 9. *X-Blow*

> I'm a child of nature, born to lose,
> people call me "Poison" but that's no news.
> When I wake up in the morning, I see what I see,
> I look into the mirror, what I see is me:
> A player, a winner, an unrepentant sinner—
> if you mess with me, I'll eat you for dinner.
> There are those that rule and those that serve,
> I'm the boss baby cause I got the nerve
> to take what I want, take what I need
> cut you first sucker and make you bleed.
> Cause life's a bitch, that I know.
> Don't misunderstand me or then you'll go
> To your grave in a rocket, nothing in your pocket,
> if you got a gun, you better not cock it,
> cause then you'll die, that I know
> the rest of you away will blow
> and you will spend eternity
> praying to God you never met me!

He dissed my ass, he dissed my ass! I had no choice. I walked up to him, I stuck my screwdriver into his stomach and I ran it right true his heart. He look surprised, man. Skinny kid like me, killing him like dat. Hah. Didn't even bleed.

Felt good man, felt better than gettin' laid on a sunny day. And I like to feel good, know what I'm saying? Feeling good makes me feel good. Don't need no sucker drugs to feel good.

'Fore they locked me up I used to get up every morning and I had me two problems, how to find money and how to spend it. All the rest was gravy. Like the guy says, "Don't worry, be happy."

But you know that was the Reagan years, and the Reagan years is over, man, and I miss 'em! Ronnie Reagan, he was my main man. He had that cowboys and Indians shit down solid. But now he's out in L.A. sitting on a horse and we're sitting in the shit he left behind. But it's O.K., he's gone. Now a new man's in charge! BATMAN! Batman is my man!

We gonna fly now, get into outer space like Kirk and Scotty, like the Jetsons, man! Just beaming around, beaming around. Be fine! Jump into my Batmobile, get behind some smoked bullet-proof windshield, pop in the CD and flip the dial to ten, rock the engine, burn the brakes . . . man that's living . . . You can smoke that shit! You only live once, you gotta grab that gusto shit.

A guy I knew in school, he went to work at McDonald's and he worked real hard, became 'sistant manager, and then he became a manager. I guess he figured if he worked hard enough, one day he's gonna be the president of McDonald's. He was making four-fifty a week, had himself a duplex rental apartment and a Ford Escort when one Friday night some Homeboys came in with a thirty-eight and greased him for the receipts, man . . . Bang . . . bang in the face . . . execution style!

Sucker missed the whole point! He's standing on that platform and that train be gone!

See, you wanna play the game, you gotta think about the big guy, you gotta look at the way He be doing things. God made man the same as hisself and check the big guy out! God, man, he gets up every morning and he don't smoke no crack, he don't shoot no dope. No man, he gets up and he looks down on the world and he says, "World, what am I gonna do with you today? . . . Oh how about this, I will make an earthquake . . . or I will make a tidal wave. Or I will smash two trains together in India, kill me some dot heads . . . or I will sprinkle some disease on some faggots, mess 'em up some!"

God likes the action! He's a player. He likes to rock, wants to get high. But he don't shoot no dope. He lets the dopes shoot each other! . . . Man, I know how he feels!

Before I was in the joint, I used to get me a nice ten gauge, go down in the sewer and shoot me some sewer rats. You hit one square, they just vaporize. Like with a ray gun! Makes a nice sound too! Boom! That must be what it's like to be God, lots of noise and destruction!

Lots of people they don't understand God. Last summer I was evading this perpetrator. Trying to put a bullet into me, so I'm running down the street and I jumped into this church, middle of the day. And there be this bunch a little kids in there with their teacher. Prayin'. In the middle of the day. Little tiny heads, little tiny butts. I said, "Yo teacher, whatchoo be doin in this here church for in the middle of the day?" She says, "Boy, we's in here prayin', we's prayin' for peace, we's prayin' against the nuclear bomb."

I starts laughin'. I says, "Baby, you be prayin' in the wrong place. This here's God's house. You better go pray someplace else. Who you think make all the war up in the first place? Who you think make that nuclear bomb up, sucker?" I's laughin' so hard, I fell right down on the floor of the church, my gun fell outta my pocket, went off, shot a hole right true the cross on the altar!

See, you gotta figure you wanna run with the big guy you gotta think big. Cause God, that's where all the power is. I want to get closer to the power, I want to get more and more spiritual, get closer to God.

That's when I gets out, I'm gonna get me some new wheels and an Uzi, man. I want to connect.

Peoples, they gotta wake up and smell the coffee. What goes around comes around. If you can't dig that, you just better get out of Gotham City.

## 10. Live

"Take care of the luxuries and the necessities will take care of themselves," is the motto of one who explains why he buys the best of everything from cigars to vacations, no matter the cost. This is the way to feel most intensely alive, he believes, and "Everybody else is sleepwalkin'!"

## 11. Dog Chameleon

The anger of a man talking to a recording machine is barely under control, as he pleads that all he wants is to be "normal"; that is, to live an Ozzie-and-Harriet sort of life. But he is continually frustrated by big and little things and people, and he gradually lets it be known that what he really longs for is enormous riches and exalting fame so that he can revenge all the slights he has accumulated and lord it over his persecutors: "I hate people . . . . . But I want you all to love ME."

## 12. Artist

Sitting with his legs crossed, puffing on a joint until he is stoned, an artist complains that the human world has been mechanized and is now controlled by unfeeling machines—TV, microwave, fax, computer, etc. Even the once-vital musicians seem to have turned into a collection of robots, and the life of the average individual is an automation of repetitious daily chores. There's no point in trying to create art under these soul-stultifying circumstances: "You write a book and it's a best seller, everybody reads it and a week later it's old news. You sing a song, it goes top forty, then it's a jingle on a beer ad. You paint a picture and a millionaire hangs it on a wall.

"Rich people used to take lions' heads and tigers' heads and hang 'em on the wall. Made 'em feel powerful, made 'em feel safe. Now they collect artists' minds. Lets 'em sleep better, knowing the best and brightest are dead from the neck up.

"So I don't give 'em the satisfaction. I keep my mind inside my head where they can't get at it, man. See, everything becomes part of the system, the only way to escape the system is to not do anything. That's what I do. If I want to paint something or write something, I just do it in my head, man, where they can't see it. (*Looks around.*) If they ever knew what I was thinking, man, I'd be dead."

# ⃝⃝⃝ PRELUDE TO A KISS

*A Play in Two Acts*

BY CRAIG LUCAS

Cast and credits appear on pages 392, 416–417

*CRAIG LUCAS was born in 1951 in Atlanta, Ga., the son of an F.B.I. agent. He was educated at Devon, Pa. and at Boston University, where his interest in writing intensified as he studied with the poets Anne Sexton and George Starbuck, and from which he graduated.*

*Lucas first came to the attention of New York theater audiences as a musical theater performer in the role of Confederate Sniper in* Shenandoah *in 1975. After an appearance in* Sweeney Todd, the Demon Barber of Fleet Street *in 1979, he joined with Norman Rene in the conception and development of* Marry Me a Little, *the collection of Stephen Sondheim songs which opened off off Broadway at The Production Company in November 1980 and moved up to off Broadway March 12, 1981 for 96 performances. Lucas's first fully scripted play was* Blue Window, *which also began at The Production Company under Rene's direction, opening June 12, 1984 and then rising to full off-Broadway status Dec. 9 of that year, also for a run of 96 performances.* Blue Window *won him the George and Elisabeth Marton Award "to recognize and encourage a new American playwright" and the 1985–86 Los Angeles Drama Critics Award for outstanding writing.*

*Lucas's first Best Play was the musical* Three Postcards, *with music and lyrics by Craig Carnelia, of far greater innovative and imaginative consequence than its short 22-performance run beginning May 14, 1987 at Playwrights Horizons (following production at South Coast Repertory, Costa Mesa, Calif. in January of that year) would seem to suggest. South Coast also commissioned his* Prelude to a Kiss, *which premiered there in January 1988 before coming to New York at Circle Repertory (both stagings under Norman Rene's direction) March 14 for a 33-performance off-Broadway run—and its author's second Best Play citation—before moving to Broadway May 1.*

*Lucas's other works for the stage include* Missing Persons *and* Reckless, *the latter produced off Broadway by Circle Rep Sept. 25, 1988 for 113 performances; and for American Playhouse on TV his own adaptation of* Blue Window *and* Longtime Companion *which won him the Audience Award for best dramatic film at this year's Sundance USA festival. In collaboration with Gerald Busby he has written the chamber opera* Orpheus in Love, *as well as many performance pieces. He is the recipient of Guggenheim and Rockefeller grants and three Drama-Logue Awards, is a member of the Dramatists Guild and lives in New York City.*

*The following synopsis of* Prelude to a Kiss *was prepared by Sally Dixon Weiner.*

## ACT I

SYNOPSIS: The basic set is simply a bare stage with a wide upstage window. Alongside it there is a molded tracery of a trunk and branches, one of which protrudes slightly into an upper corner of the seemingly limitless view of the sky. The effect is one of openness and of possibilities and complements the dream-like quality of the play. Props appear and disappear as required during the action, which is continuous within each of the two acts. Peter, one of the characters, occasionally speaks as narrator directly to the audience.

VOCALIST (*as the lights go down, sings*):
    If you hear a song in blue,
    Like a flower crying for the dew,
    That was my heart serenading you,
    My prelude to a kiss.

The play begins at a party where Peter, a handsome young man who is about to leave, is introduced to Rita, a wide-eyed, beautiful and appealing young woman, a neighbor of Taylor, the party's host. She tells Peter she's an insomniac and hasn't slept since she was 14. Peter thinks she looks very well considering that, and as they talk their attraction to each other becomes almost immediately obvious.

Taylor, a business associate of Peter's, brings Rita a Dewars and then leaves them again. Peter wonders what Rita does when she's awake. She writes in her journal, and, to make a living, she tends bar at the Tin Market, a place Peter knows.

PETER: I guess it's a good place for an insomniac to work. You work Saturdays?
    *She nods.*
Well, you must make good money. Well, so you hate it, I'm sorry, I can't help that. What are your aspirations, in that case?
RITA: I'm like a graphic designer.
PETER: Oh, great.
RITA: I studied at Parsons.
PETER: This is good.
RITA: What do you do?
PETER: I make little tiny, transparent photographs of scientific articles which are rolled on film like microfilm only smaller. You'd like it. It's really interesting.
RITA: What are your aspirations in that case?
PETER: I should have some, shouldn't I? No, I I I I I I, uh, can't think of the answer, I'm sorry.
RITA: That's okay! . . . . .
PETER: It was nice talking to you.
RITA: You, too.
PETER: Get some sleep.
RITA: I'll try.

"The spell was cast," Peter tells the audience. He hopes Rita doesn't mind that he's come to the bar where she's working the next night. She teases him, "No, I'm sorry, you can never come in here." He's having a Molson and has read *The White Hotel* during the day. Rita hasn't read it, but she's read some of Freud's case histories that the novel was based on, much to Peter's surprise. The book begins with a "high-falutin' sexual dream thing" he reports. It's a depressing book about a woman in therapy who a few years later is killed by Nazis.

Rita's apparently asked Taylor about Peter and is curious as to why Peter spent ten years in Europe. He's delighted she's interested in him and explains that when he was 4 his parents separated and he'd lived with his grandparents. (He wants to make the story as short as he can, but Rita urges him not to rush, adding that they could go to her apartment when she gets off duty.) It seems Peter's grandparents had both become ill by the time he was 11, and he went to live with his mother who had remarried and had had two more children. That not working out well for him, he then went to live with his father, also remarried, and having had three other children. And his father's wife disliked him even more than his mother's husband. "This is like Dickens," Rita comments. His stepmother had made spaetzles for him because he liked them, Peter admits. (Rita can't believe the serendipitousness of this. It seems she loves spaetzles, too.) But things were not happy for Peter, and one evening he left, announcing he was going to the movies. Instead, he went to Europe. "What movie?" Rita wants to know. *The Wild Bunch*, he thinks. She seems to know that he'd lived in Amsterdam when he was over there, and Peter suggests she's been spying on him.

As they leave the bar and stroll toward Rita's place, she tells him she was once a Socialist (she never told her family) for about two months but supposes she's a Democrat now. (So is Peter.) But she believes Democrats "under the skin" are really Republicans.

Peter asks about her family. Rita's from New Jersey, from Englewood Cliffs, and her father's a dentist. She's an only child.

Rita asks Peter to say something in Dutch, and he says "Uh . . . Je hebt erg witte tanden," which translates as "You have very white teeth." He wants her to say something in Dutch to him: "Om je better mee op te eten." He coaches her until she's got it right but won't tell her what it means. He will some day, he promises. As for his life in Amsterdam, he was a caterer, making sandwiches, for a while, and then became a tutor and attended school at night. When his father died he came home, but he never sees or calls his mother or his family. In answer to Rita's question as to whether or not he misses them, he just shakes his head.

At Rita's apartment she offers Peter a Molson. He again is pleasantly surprised at this further example of their mutual tastes, but what he really is concerned about is her insomnia. She claims to have been to all the doctors, every kind, taken endless pills and liquids, and even been to an acupuncturist. And, yes, sometimes it did hurt. He tells her she's beautiful, and she laughs, and after they kiss she laughs again.

PETER: This is not supposed to be the funny part.
RITA: No, I know, I'm sorry . . . I'm, I guess I'm nervous.
PETER: Why are you nervous? Don't be nervous.
RITA: All right.
    *He approaches to kiss her.*
PETER: Don't laugh . . . All right, you can laugh.
    *They kiss.*
Am I going too fast?
    *She shakes her head.*
Is this tacky of me?

*Headshake.*

Oh good.

*They kiss.*

This is definitely the highlight of my weekend.

*She smiles.*

So maybe we should just, you know, watch some TV, have happy memories of this and anticipate the future—

*She is shaking her head.*

—we shouldn't?

*They kiss.*

I would really, really like to see you with all of your clothes off and stuff like that.

RITA: I would really, really like to see you with all of your clothes off and . . .

PETER: Stuff like that?

*To us.*

When you're first getting to know someone and in that blissful, psychotic first flush of love, it seems like every aspect of their personality, their whole demeanor, the simple, lovely twist of their earlobes and their marvelous phone voice and their soft, dark wet whatever is somehow imbued with an extra push of color, an intensity heretofore . . . you know. *Unknown.*

Later, Peter compares sex to a drug. Rita says it *is* one, meant to snare them into mating. Her remark strikes him as cynical, and he suspects she doesn't like children. Rita denies this but admits she doesn't want to have any. She doesn't think it would be fair "to raise them in the world. The way it is now." Peter wonders where else you could raise children.

RITA: People do die in lime pits, in the real world, not just in books. Women go blind from watching their children being murdered.

PETER: Not in this country, they don't. Do they?

RITA: What—I mean, your grandparents getting sick and dying and you being passed from one . . . I don't know.

PETER: I survived. You know?

RITA: I don't have a choice about already being here, but I do have a choice about bringing more children into a world where they have to live with the constant fear of being blown up. I mean, I'll be like . . . or I'll be lying in bed late at night, and I'll look at the light in the room and suddenly see it all go up in a blinding flash, in flames, and I'm the only one left alive . . .

PETER: No wonder you can't sleep.

RITA: The world's a really terrible place. It's too precarious.

*Pause.*

You want kids, obviously. I wish I could say I did.

PETER: It's okay.

It is six weeks later. Peter and Rita have seen each other every night, Peter tells the audience. He's been by his apartment occasionally, but his clothes are at Rita's, and his books.

Peter has cooked dinner and serves it, and while they are eating Rita reveals that she's told her parents about Peter, and that she and her parents talk very openly about sex. She's described him as always bringing protection and paying attention to whether or not she's had an orgasm. Peter claims this is "bullshit," and she backs down but admits that she has said to them that they should meet Peter. Peter agrees to meet them on the weekend. Rita has told her mother about Peter and his family.

PETER: Will you marry me?
RITA: Uh-huh.
PETER: You will?
RITA: Uh-huh.
    *Beat.*
PETER: I just wanted to see how it sounds.
RITA: It sounds great.
PETER: This is too fast. Isn't it?
RITA: Is it?
PETER: I don't think so.
RITA: Neither do I.
PETER: You'll marry me?
RITA: Uh-huh.
PETER: You will?
RITA: Uh-huh.

The scene changes as Rita and Peter have just arrived at the Boyle home in New Jersey, and she has introduced him to her parents.

MRS. BOYLE: So I understand you're a manager in a publishing firm.
PETER: That's correct. Yes.
DR. BOYLE: That must be, uh . . . What kind of firm is it?
MRS. BOYLE: Publishing.
DR. BOYLE: What kind—Don't belittle me in front of new people.
MRS. BOYLE: Belittle?
RITA: Dad, please.
DR. BOYLE: What kind of publishing firm is it? I was asking.
PETER: It's uh, scientific publishing. They publish, you know, scientific publishing—things—journals! I knew I knew that.
RITA (*to Peter*): You want a beer?

John Dossett (Taylor), Kimberley Dudwitt, L. Peter Callender, Barnard Hughes (Old Man), Mary-Louise Parker (Rita), Debra Monk (Mrs. Boyle) and Alec Baldwin (Peter) in the off-Broadway cast of Craig Lucas's *Prelude to a Kiss*

MRS. BOYLE: In the morning, Rita?

RITA: Yes, mother, we have been drinking non-stop for weeks, it's time you knew this about us.

MRS. BOYLE: I'll have one too, then.

RITA: You will?

DR. BOYLE: Me, too.

PETER: A bunch of lushes here, Rita, you didn't tell me.

DR. BOYLE: Oh, I can pull out four wisdom teeth on a fifth of Stoly.

PETER: You can?

MRS. BOYLE: He's teasing you.

DR. BOYLE: Scien—What kind of scientific?

PETER: Abstracting and indexing. It's a service.

DR. BOYLE: Like a database.

PETER: It is a database.

Rita brings the beers, and the discussion about Peter's job continues in great detail until Dr. Boyle has gotten it clearly in mind exactly what he does.

Eventually he grants his and his wife's approval of the young man. Dr. Boyle is hopeful also that perhaps Rita will be getting some sleep at last.

Mrs. Boyle mentions that Marshall, her husband, had been in Korea (as a serviceman), and much to Rita's chagrin, Dr. Boyle starts to pull his shirt tail out of his pants. He's bound and determined that, if Peter is going to be joining the family, he's got to see his scar because it's the only one he's ever going to see that's shaped like a saxophone.

A month later at the Boyle home, it's the day of Peter and Rita's wedding. Taylor has brought two beers and helps Peter dress, all the while assuring him he has nothing to worry about. Peter should regard it as just another little skirmish in the "struggle against mediocrity and decay." The music is beginning. Taylor has the ring, he assures Peter, and he kisses Peter on the cheek and departs.

The outdoor wedding is beginning, and the minister is admonishing Peter and Rita to "live with tender consideration for each other." After conducting the formal ceremony and pronouncing them man and wife, the minister opines that applause is in order. " . . . . . As if we'd made a good putt or something, and we all made a beeline for the champagne with the strawberries in it," Peter tells the audience.

The reception is in full swing when Peter becomes aware of an Old Man in a green jacket. Rita doesn't know who he is, nor does Mrs. Boyle. The picture-taking subsides and Rita and the Old Man toast each other with their glasses of champagne. Mrs. Boyle had assumed the Old Man was from Peter's office. She comments to Dr. Boyle, who doesn't know who he is either, that the Old Man seems "peculiar."

The Old Man congratulates Rita and Peter, remarking on what a lovely couple they make and what a wonderful day it is for a wedding. Rita seems mesmerized by him. Taylor, in an effort to find out the Old Man's name, attempts to introduce himself to him, but he seems unaware of Taylor.

OLD MAN: How precious the time is . . . How little we realize 'til it's almost gone.

DR. BOYLE: You'll have to forgive us, but none of us seems to remember who you are.

RITA: It's all right, Daddy.

OLD MAN: I only wanted to wish the two young people well. And perhaps to kiss the bride. Before I'm on my way.

DR. BOYLE: Well—

RITA: I'd be flattered. Thank you.

TAYLOR: Some angle this guy's got.

RITA: My blessings to you.

*The Old Man takes Rita's face in his hands. There is a low rumble which grows in volume as they begin to kiss. Wind rushes through the trees, leaves fall, no one moves except for Rita who loses hold of her bridal bouquet as it slips to the ground. The Old Man and Rita separate and the wind and rumble die down.*

And you.

*The Old Man seems off balance; Dr. Boyle steadies him.*

DR. BOYLE: Do you want to sit down?

AUNT DOROTHY: Get him a chair, Fred.

TAYLOR: Too much blood rushing to the wrong place, I guess.

*The Old Man stares at Peter and Rita.*

DR. BOYLE: Are you dizzy?

OLD MAN: Peter? . . .

*Uncle Fred brings a chair.*

DR. BOYLE: Here you go now.

*He eases the Old Man into the chair, takes his pulse. Peter remains fixated on the Old Man. Rita has withdrawn from the crowd; she examines her dress, her hands, the air around her, as if it were all new, miraculous.*

MRS. BOYLE: I thought you said you didn't know him.

*Peter is mystified.*

Peter?

DR. BOYLE: Take it easy now.

OLD MAN (*to Peter*): Honey? . . . It's me. What's happening? . . . Why is everybody . . . ?

DR. BOYLE (*overlapping*): You're okay now, just breathe for me, nice and easy.

OLD MAN (*staring at Dr. Boyle*): Daddy, it's me.

AUNT DOROTHY: Ohhhh, he thinks Marshall's his father.

TAYLOR: Where do you live, can you tell us?

DR. BOYLE: Okay. He's doing fine. Everybody relax.

Mrs. Boyle wonders if they should call an ambulance, but Dr. Boyle thinks it isn't necessary. "I've had too much to drink," the Old Man says. Uncle Fred, arriving with a glass of water, is sent back for coffee instead. Meanwhile, the Old Man refuses to answer their questions about where he lives, or if there is anyone that could be called. He's sorry for any trouble he's caused, he tells them, and he begins to stand up. He doesn't want any coffee and backs away. Mrs. Boyle is concerned about him, and Dr. Boyle and Taylor follow him off.

Aunt Dorothy is convinced he is a neighbor or someone's gardener, but Mrs. Boyle claims to know everyone and believes he isn't from the area. Peter asks Rita if she's all right, and she nods. Peter remarks to Rita about the strangeness of the Old Man calling him "honey" and how vulnerable he had seemed. Again he wants to know if Rita is really all right. Others come in to

report that the Old Man has just gone off, down the street. Mrs. Boyle is upset
to think that Rita and Peter's wedding has been spoiled.

MRS. BOYLE:  . . . . . Your father thinks that's the Evans's gardener, but I
don't think it is, do you, Rita? . . .

DR. BOYLE (*overlapping*): Enough, Marion.

MRS. BOYLE: That's not the Evans's gardener, is it? . . . Rita?
>    *All eyes on Rita; she turns to look over her shoulder before turn-*
>    *ing back and smiling.*

RITA: Must have been my kiss is all.

AUNT DOROTHY: That's right.

DR. BOYLE (*overlapping*): That's right.

UNCLE FRED (*overlapping*): There you go.

RITA: Drives the men wild.

UNCLE FRED: Hear, hear!

TAYLOR: This is a party, come on!

DR. BOYLE (*overlapping, to Mrs. Boyle*): Come on, give me a kiss.

MINISTER (*overlapping*): A toast!

AUNT DOROTHY: Here's to the lucky couple!

TAYLOR (*overlapping, singing*): Celebrate, celebrate! Dance to the music!

UNCLE FRED (*overlapping*): Hear, hear!

MINISTER (*overlapping*): To the lucky couple!
>    *Someone starts to sing "For they're a jolly good couple!" Every-*
>    *one joins in, then singing fades.*

PETER (*to us*): And there was a toast to us and to love and to Jamaica and
to our plane flight and to airline safety and to the old drunk, whoever he was.
Whoever he was. I was completely trashed by the time the limo pulled up to
take us to the airport. Dr. Boyle told us to sign anything we wanted onto the
hotel bill, his treat, and off we went . . . The whole way down on the plane and
straight through that first night in the hotel, Rita slept like a baby I couldn't.
For some reason. I kept hearing that poor old guy calling me "Honey."
"Honey, it's me." Who's "me?" And I'd wanted to protect him.

Peter and Rita are on chaise longues next to the pool. A waiter is at hand.

PETER (*to Rita*): Don't you want to try one?

RITA (*to the waiter*): Just a seltzer water.

PETER: Okay. (*To the waiter.*) I'll take another, thanks.
>    *The waiter retreats. Beat. Peter notices something on Rita's*
>    *wrist.*

What's that?

RITA: You like?

PETER: Well . . . sure, where'd you get it?

RITA: Just now.

PETER: In the shop? Here? It's not gold, is it?

RITA: Fourteen carat.

PETER: You're kidding. How much was it?

RITA: Fifteen hundred or so.

PETER: Dollars?

RITA: Why? He said to charge anything.

PETER: You charged fifteen hundred dollars on your dad's bill?

RITA: I like it.

PETER: Well . . . you do? It's sort of like a . . . it's like a charm bracelet, isn't it?

RITA: It is a charm bracelet.

PETER: Like old women wear? I'm sorry. Look, if you like it, I think it's great. And he did say . . . You're right, he's your dad.

RITA: Relax, we're on vacation.

PETER: I know.

RITA: And you're my puppy puppy.

PETER: Your puppy puppy?

RITA: And the world is a wonderful place to live, admit it!

Peter picks up the sunscreen, noting the unusually high degree of protectiveness, 25, and applies it to Rita's back as she's requested. He's still thinking about the Old Man at the wedding and wondering who he was. "My fairy godfather come to sprinkle the fairy dust on us," Rita suggests, but she isn't curious about him. She runs off to swim, and Peter muses about her. Rita seems like a different person to him. He assumes it's only normal to ask himself, since it's for the rest of his life, if this is the right person for him.

She returns in high spirits. She loves the place and looks forward to jet-skiing, scuba-diving, going up to the mountains to see the monkeys, going to a soccer game, all with Peter. Peter, feeling more sentimental, is concerned because he won't ever be able to share her past, no matter how close they are. Rita tells him not to worry, that he should take things "as they come and enjoy them".

There's something Peter wants to suggest to her even though he's sure of her reaction, but he wants her to consider it, at least. What he'd like is for her to stop tending bar and let him support her so she could work on her portfolio. He is vastly surprised when she agrees. He asks her, as he has before, if she's sorry she married him, and says he means it seriously this time. She tells him not to be a silly. "Okay," he says.

But it's *not* okay, he tells the audience. Time's gone by. They've gone to see a soccer game, windsurfed, eaten, snorkeled, walked on the beach. Rita's been tireless and afraid of nothing, and she's been sleeping. Nothing wrong with that, he admits. "But nothing felt . . . nothing *felt*."

The waiter comes in, and Peter orders a Long Island Ice Tea, while Rita orders a seltzer. Peter brings up the subject of racist repression and the uneven distribution of wealth, but Rita doesn't seem interested and advises him just to be happy. But Peter had been thinking about the people who live in abandoned cars and refrigerators near the airport. Rita agrees it's awful, but insists he doesn't have to look at it. She changes the subject by asking him what he's reading. It's Freud's case histories. Rita remarks that it sounds "interesting" and wants to have the book when he's finished. *"Peter stares at her."*

The waiter comes back to report that the bartender doesn't know how to make a Long Island Ice Tea. Peter asks Rita. She claims she's forgotten, that she's on vacation. He's disappointed in her, and she takes umbrage. "It's a real busman's holiday with you around, you know? You could fuck up a wet dream!" she tells him before she goes off.

Forgetting a drink recipe or that you'd read a book a long time ago is possible, Peter considers, but what about ideals? He has the feeling Rita has "switched channels, switched . . . *something."*

On their last evening in Jamaica they are walking on the beach, and Rita is exclaiming about how beautiful it is, how great it is to be alive and young, and how there won't ever be a better opportunity for "two people to love each other. If they don't try so hard." And she's remembered the recipe for Long Island Ice Tea.

Rita does not have to prove anything to him, Peter tells her. He wonders how it was having a surgeon for a father. Rita always thought of him as helping people. But as for how her brothers and sisters felt about it, Peter would have to ask them, she answers him.

Rita wants Peter to make love to her, there on the beach, and tells him she wants to have his baby. Already concerned enough about her memory, and worried that something might be very wrong, he reminds her that she hadn't wanted babies, and that she's already read Freud's case histories, that her father is a dentist, not a surgeon, and that she doesn't have any siblings.

RITA: Why are you telling me all this . . . ?

PETER: What, you were teasing me?

RITA: Of course I was teasing you. Did you think I didn't know those things? . . . Sweetie?

PETER: You never call me that or "Puppy puppy," you never say "Don't be a silly" or "Bring home the bacon" or pull the skin off your chicken. You're not drinking, you're not using salt, Rita, you're suddenly—

RITA: I want to have your baby. I'm taking better care of myself. Now, please darling, relax. You're having some kind of a—

PETER: No. No! You're a Communist, Rita, or Socialist, Democrat, what-ever you are, you don't defend the social order in Jamaica or anywhere, you have . . . You're just not . . . It's like you don't even need me any more.
     *Beat.*
RITA: You need . . . *need* to see someone as soon as we get back to New York, Peter. And I'm going to insist on it. And you *need* to take a hot bath and look at the moon and breathe life in, Peter.
PETER: Rita is afraid of life, she doesn't drink it in.
RITA: Grow up.
PETER: Je hebt erg witte tanden.
RITA: Thanks.
PETER: What did I say?
RITA: You said my teeth are white, you know what you said.
PETER (*embracing her*): Yes! Thank you. My baby. What do you say?
RITA: What do you mean?
PETER: What's your line? What do you say? Your line, you memorized it.
RITA: I'm sorry, Peter—
PETER (*overlapping*): In Dutch! Rita, what do you say?
RITA: I say goodnight.
     *She turns, starts to walk off; he grabs her.*
PETER: No, please! Rita!
RITA (*overlapping*): Watch it, pal!
PETER: I want you to be you, Rita, I want you!
RITA: I am me. This is all I am. I'm sorry I can't be whatever you want me to be. This is me. And maybe what you saw wasn't here at all.
     *She walks off. Pause. Peter looks at us. The sound of surf breaking. Curtain.*

## ACT II

Peter and Rita, back from Jamaica, are visiting her parents who are pleased to see them looking so well and delighted that Rita's been sleeping. Peter would like a beer, yes, but Rita's not drinking, he tells them. Both Peter and Rita assure her parents the trip was very good and the weather was, too. Dr. Boyle wonders if they played golf. It's the one thing they didn't do, Rita admits. Mrs. Boyle explains to Peter that her husband is teasing Rita because they had taken her for golf lessons for several years and it just hadn't worked out. Now Rita says she might try it again, that she's serious.

Rita reports that Peter was disturbed by the poverty on the island, which Dr. Boyle says is inescapable wherever one goes. Peter suggests Rita show them the bracelet she bought, but she hasn't brought it with her.

Her husband hadn't wanted her to bring up the subject, but Mrs. Boyle feels she must tell Rita that the man at the wedding was not the Evans's gardener. Again Peter asks who they thought he was. Rita repeats what she'd told Peter before, that she thought he was her fairy godfather.

When Rita goes off with her mother to set the table, Peter asks her father if she seems all right to him. It's just that she seems changed, Peter explains. Rita has always had very high expectations of everyone, herself included, Dr. Boyle states, but he admits that "in some way she's always been . . . uncertain." He's sure Peter will become accustomed to her, however. Peter mentions her forgetfulness. Dr. Boyle assures him he is aware of that. Peter also apprises him of the fact that she's given up salt and takes the skin off her chicken. "Watching out for her old age already," Dr. Boyle comments. When Peter tells him Rita may be giving up her job and letting him support her, Dr. Boyle is pleased, convinced that Peter's making Rita happy, and congratulates him.

The next day Peter is back on the job and is welcomed by Taylor who briefly discusses some business matter with him and then starts to leave, but Peter detains him.

PETER: Listen, Tay?

TAYLOR: Yeah.

PETER: If you could switch souls with somebody? . . . like go inside their body and they go inside yours? . . . You know? Switch?

TAYLOR: . . . Yeeaaaaah?

PETER: Do you think it would be possible, if you didn't know someone, to impersonate them, by just being inside them and . . . looking like them?

TAYLOR: Where are they?

PETER: Inside you.

TAYLOR: And you're inside them?

PETER: Right.

TAYLOR: Why would you go inside another person's body if you didn't know them?

PETER: It's conjecture.

TAYLOR: I think I know that, Peter. But wouldn't you do better to pick someone you knew, a particular person you envied—

PETER: Right.

TAYLOR: —or admired so that you could do or be or have the things this other person did or be'd or had?

PETER: Maybe. Yes.

TAYLOR: Are you Rita now? Is that what you're telling me? You two have merged?

PETER: All right, here's another question. Have you ever . . . This is sort of a bizarre question. Have you ever been having sex with somebody . . . ?

TAYLOR: Nope.

PETER: And they're doing everything, you know, right more or less.

TAYLOR: Oh, right, sex, I remember, go ahead.

PETER: And you just get the feeling that . . . something is wrong? I mean, they pretty much stop doing some of the things they used to do—

TAYLOR: Ohhhh.

PETER: —and only do certain other things now, more . . .

TAYLOR: Right.

PETER: . . . traditional sorts of things.

Taylor jumps to the conclusion Peter's talking about blow jobs. Peter isn't referring to a specific thing, he insists, but Taylor goes off on a minor diatribe about how women don't like doing that, which Peter denies. The argument dwindles with Taylor claiming he was only trying to help because Peter had asked him to, and Peter thanks him.

Peter tells the audience, "That night everything was miraculously restored . . . " He arrives home from work to find that Rita's having a Dewars and is making him a surprise and wants him to guess what it is.

> . . . . . *She sniffs the air; he does too.*

PETER: Spaetzles?

> *Rita smiles.*

You're kidding.

RITA: I'm sure they won't be anywhere near as good as Sophie's, but then I'm not such a cruel mama, either. You want a Molson?

PETER: Sure.

> *She goes off; he picks up a book.*

RITA (*from off*): So, I don't know, I made some calls about taking my portfolio around today, but the whole thing terrifies me . . .

> *She returns with his Molson.*

And I started reading that, finally.

PETER: *The White Hotel?*

RITA: Cheers.

PETER: Cheers.

RITA: You didn't call the doctor, did you?

PETER: No, I will.

RITA: No, I don't want you to . . . Oh, I know things were hard in Jamaica. Maybe it's taken me this time to get used to being married, but . . . I love you, Peter.

> *They kiss. He pulls away, holding onto her.*

PETER: You read her journal, didn't you? You figured out how to fix your hair from the pictures in the albums and what to wear, what she drinks . . . Where is she? Please. I won't be angry. You can go back wherever you came from, and I won't tell a soul, you don't have to tell me who you are.  Just tell me where Rita is, and we'll pretend this never took place.

    *Pause.*

Okay.  Play it your way.  But I'm onto you.

    *Peter walks out.*

At the Tin Market, the Old Man is seated at a table as Peter comes in.  The bartender recognizes Peter and asks about Rita.  Peter responds she isn't feeling well.  He has ordered a double vodka on the rocks when he spots the Old Man.  "Dewars?" he asks him.  He nods.  The bartender says the Old Man has been a regular here for a couple of weeks.

    *Peter crosses to the Old Man's table.*

PETER:  Have we . . . Have we met?

    *The Old Man nods.*

Mind if I sit?

    *He does.*

You were at my wedding, weren't you?

    *The Old Man nods. Beat.*

Do I know you?

    *The Old Man nods.*

What's my stepmother's name?

Timothy Hutton as Peter and Mary-Louise Parker
as Rita in the Broadway cast of *Prelude to a Kiss*

> *Pause.*

What's the movie I said I was going to see the night I left for Europe?

OLD MAN:  The *Wild Bunch*!

PETER:  Je hebt erg witte tanden.

OLD MAN:  Not any more.

> *He shows Peter his teeth.*

PETER:  What shape's your father's shrapnel scar?

OLD MAN:  He thinks it's shaped like a saxophone, but it's not.

PETER:  I knew it wasn't you! I *knew* it. Oh, I knew it! Oh my god, Rita.

> *They embrace.*

OLD MAN:  Baby.

Peter becomes flustered, draws back and asks the bartender for the bill. It's on the house, he's told. Peter goes off with the Old Man, saying to the bartender that he's going to walk him to the subway.

"How are you?" Peter asks as they are walking outside. "I've missed you," the Old Man says. The Old Man, it seems, has been staying with his family in Brooklyn. Julius Becker. There was a wallet. What else was there to do? "I couldn't call my mother or go to the police . . . . . I didn't even have our keys. I had to pretend to be him until you figured it out. And I knew you would." It's like a dream in which you say to yourself to hang on, we'll all wake up, Peter opines. They are going to the apartment, and she will be there. "And it's gonna be okay, Rita" he tries to reassure the Old Man.

OLD MAN:  . . . . . When he leaned in to kiss me, I saw this look in his eye, you know? . . . . . I was holding your hand, and then I wasn't. I was turned all around. You were over there, and *I* was over there. I thought it was a mirror, that's why I reached out—to steady myself, and instead I saw his hand . . . this hand . . . on *me* . . . And then everybody was staring at me, and my dad was saying I'd had too much to drink, and I don't know, I thought I had salmonella.

PETER:  Really? That's great.

OLD MAN:  I thought if I went along with it, then you'd all come running out after me and say, "It's a joke, come on Rita, you're going on your honeymoon." And we'd laugh . . . I just kept walking, past all the cars parked for the wedding. I was afraid to look down at my shadow to see if it was true—my reflection in the windows . . . I found this card in his wallet.

> *He shows Peter the card.*

"In case of emergency please call Mr. and Mrs. Jerome Blier." His daughter and her husband. They came and picked me up . . .

> *Beat.*

So how was your honeymoon?

> *Peter does not laugh.*

PETER:  I'm fine.

OLD MAN: Does he know you know?
PETER: *He?* Yeah. He does.
OLD MAN: She. Whatever. He does?
PETER: Yes, I think so.

As they are looking up at the apartment, the Old Man wants to know if "he's" there. Peter nods, but he thinks it would be better for the Old Man to wait in the hall in the event "Rita" tries to get away. But when Peter enters the apartment, he finds Dr. Boyle coming out of the bedroom with a suitcase. Rita is not there. Dr. Boyle is sorry, he likes Peter, but Rita has gone to New Jersey with her mother, and it would be better if Peter doesn't come to the house or call until she's calmer.

Peter wants to know if something's happened and claims he had just gone for a walk. Dr. Boyle is distressed about "whatever personal turmoil" Peter is going through and offers to refer Peter to someone. It seems Rita had called them in a state of hysteria, claiming that Peter was suffering from delusions, convinced she is somebody else. Dr. Boyle is also to tell Peter she's considering getting a divorce or an annulment.

Peter is defensive; it was a difference of opinion, he insists, but Dr. Boyle says he practically had to carry her to get her to the car. He's sorry, but he's deferring to her wishes. Peter insists that Dr. Boyle doesn't really know her. Dr. Boyle is trying to leave, but Peter stops him to tell him that Rita is lying to him now. This false Rita knows "certain facts" from reading the real Rita's journals, but she isn't her, he insists. Peter gives every evidence of being irrational, and Dr. Boyle urges him to see a doctor and finally makes his way out of the apartment.

After Dr. Boyle has gone, the Old Man comes in.

PETER: Look . . . I like you very much. I'm not equipped for this. I'm sorry. I still like you.
OLD MAN: *Like* me?
PETER: I'm not . . . I don't feel the same way about you, I'm not attracted to you.
OLD MAN: What, are you nuts? I don't think that's the issue, Peter, have a seat, come on, you're . . . . . You're not imagining me. Or we're both insane . . .
PETER: All right, *think*. We've got to try to figure out how . . . This just does not happen.
OLD MAN: Tell me about it.
PETER: All right . . . let me see his wallet, please. May I?
*The Old Man hands over the wallet.*
Thank you. Becker? Is he Dutch, do you know?
OLD MAN: Is it a Dutch name?
PETER: You're the one who says you live there, Rita, Jesus!

OLD MAN: Well, they don't speak Dutch. I mean, I can't exactly ask. I'm trying to keep a low profile in case they find out I'm really a girl, okay?

Peter has located the card in the wallet and wants to know how to say the daughter's name. It's Leah Blier—the husband is Jerry. Peter dials their number, and Leah appears with the receiver. Determining that it is Becker's daughter, Peter introduces himself under an assumed name as someone from a Crisis Intervention Center and reports to Leah that her father is all right, that he'd asked two people what city he was in and they'd called the Center's hotline. Peter asks where her father was born. It was in Amsterdam, year uncertain, and she reveals that he's disappeared before. Recently they'd had to go to New Jersey to get him. Peter asks if her father has any mental or neurological disorders, and she admits he hasn't been himself since his wife died the previous fall, at which point he had moved in with them.

Leah is anxious to speak to her father, and Peter puts the Old Man on. They have a brief conversation, and then Peter takes the phone again. In the course of his further questioning she tells him her father has had cirrhosis for a long time and that three months ago they'd discovered he had lung cancer and has less than a year to live. She wants the address of where he is, but Peter says he's sorry, he'll have to call her back and Leah disappears as he hangs up the phone.

Peter repeats to the Old Man what Leah had said about him, including his being sick. There's a pause, and then the Old Man announces they need a plan. What does Peter think happened? Could it have been unintentional, or a form of hypnosis? If "Rita" wanted to disappear he would not have called the parents, the Old Man surmises: "He wants to be me." "Rita" doesn't know the Old Man and Peter have found each other. "Mom's the one who's going to want us back together . . . . . I say that our best bet is try and get her to bring him here," the Old Man decides. Peter's not sure.

For six strange days, the worst in his life (Peter tells the audience), they went back and forth in the apartment, playing cards, watching TV. Peter cooked, as if they'd been married for ages, but without sex. During the nights Peter could "feel the loneliness coming off both of us like heat". He kept calling Rita's parents and getting no answer. Peter called Rita's Aunt Dorothy in Cincinnati, who knew nothing about what had happened to them and was sorry to hear that Peter and Rita had broken up.

Meanwhile, Peter went on, they "kept up the pleasantries, the old married couple we'd become."

PETER: I miss your face.
OLD MAN: Don't think about it.
PETER: How soft it was.
   *Pause.*

OLD MAN: I miss it, too.

PETER: Your hair was so great.

OLD MAN: Oh, come on.

PETER: And your little white feet.

OLD MAN: What, you don't like these?

*Pause.*

You know . . . if you think how we're born and we go through all the struggle of growing up and learning the multiplication tables and the name for everything, the rules, how not to get run over, braid your hair, pig-Latin. Figuring out how to sneak out of the house late at night. Just all the ins and outs, the *effort*, and learning to accept all the flaws in everybody and everything. And then getting a job, probably something you don't even like doing for not enough money like tending bar, and that's if you're lucky. That's if you're not born in Calcutta or Ecuador or the U.S. without money. Then there's your marriage and raising your own kids if . . . you know. And they're going through the same struggle all over again, only worse, because somebody's trying to sell them crack in the first grade by now. And all this time you're paying taxes, and your hair starts to fall out, and you're wearing six pairs of glasses which you can never find, and you can't recognize yourself in the mirror, and your parents die and your friends, again if you're lucky it's not you first. And if you live long enough, you finally get to watch everybody die: all your loved ones, your wife, your husband and your kids, maybe, and you're totally alone. And as a final reward for all this . . . you disappear.

*Pause.*

No one knows where.

*Pause.*

So we might as well have a good time while we're here, don't you think?

PETER: I don't want you to die, Rita.

OLD MAN: I don't want me to die, either. And I'm going to. So are you. Hopefully later and not sooner. But we got to have this. I mean, what a trip! Meeting you and being in love. Falling. It was bitchin' for a while. And okay, so this isn't such a turn on, I admit. But . . .

PETER: I adore you.

OLD MAN: What? My hearing. No, I'm serious.

PETER: I said I ADORE YOU!

OLD MAN: That's what I thought.

PETER: For better or for worse.

OLD MAN: Huh?

PETER: I said: You would have hated Jamaica. Trust me.

The Old Man tells Peter to try telephoning once more. This time Mrs. Boyle, appearing with the receiver, answers. Rita had been so shaken up they'd taken her to London, it seems. Mrs. Boyle can only talk to him now because Rita and her father are out at the store, but she'd like to know what happened to the marriage. But Peter is unsure that he really knows. He supposes it was his telling Rita that she wasn't the same person.

Peter looks at the Old Man and he tells Mrs. Boyle he'd do anything to get Rita back, that he loves her very much. He's very anxious to see Rita. But Mrs. Boyle says he mustn't come there—they would be angry at her for even speaking to him. Peter suggests to Mrs. Boyle she might tell Rita he's going on a business trip (he isn't really) and that she could come to get her other things that are in storage there. If Mrs. Boyle came with her, they could talk. He must see her, he insists, even if she doesn't speak to him. Mrs. Boyle hesitates, then agrees to try. She suggests Monday and they agree on high noon.

MRS. BOYLE: What you said before about Rita not being the same person?
PETER: Uh-huh?
MRS. BOYLE: They never are, Peter. They're never Rita. They're never Dr. Marshall Boyle, not the way that you think they should be. They're always someone else. They're always changing.
PETER: Uh-huh.
MRS. BOYLE: That's life. That's marriage. They're always growing and shifting and so are you.
PETER: Right.

When the conversation ends Mrs. Boyle disappears, and Peter *"slowly kneels and kisses the Old Man tenderly on the mouth."*

When Mrs. Boyle and Rita arrive at the apartment and Rita realizes that Peter is there, her mother insists they talk. Afterward, if Rita doesn't want to stay, she'll be waiting in the car. And before she leaves she tells Rita the meeting was her idea.

As Peter and Rita begin a conciliatory discussion, *"The Old Man appears behind Rita; he carries a kitchen knife and a length of rope. She does not see him immediately."* When she turns and sees him, Peter grabs her from the rear and tells the Old Man, "Tie his feet." But Rita and the Old Man are staring at each other and cannot move, so Peter finally takes the rope and ties her himself. "It's not necessary, kids," Rita remarks. Then Peter demands the knife and takes it with one hand, meanwhile holding Rita's arm behind her with his other.

PETER: Now kiss him.
    *The Old Man kisses Rita on mouth. They separate. Peter releases Rita and wields the knife, particularly wary of the Old Man.*
Rita?
OLD MAN: No. It didn't work.

PETER (*to Rita*): Is it you?
>*Rita is shaking her head.*

OLD MAN: No!

PETER: Rita?

RITA: I don't know how it happened. I don't know what I did.

PETER (*to Rita*): I'll kill you, I swear to God.

OLD MAN: Peter.

PETER (*threatening Rita with the knife*): How did you do this? *How the hell did you do this?*

OLD MAN: Put the knife down, please.

PETER (*to the Old Man*): I'll take care of this, Rita! It's a trick, don't you know that much?

OLD MAN (*overlapping*): He doesn't know. Give it to me.
>*The Old Man is holding out his hand.*

Please. Peter.

Peter is still too *"paralyzed with doubt"* to hand the knife over, but finally he puts it down. Rita is asking the Old Man "Where'd you go?" "Twelve twenty-two Ocean Avenue," the Old Man answers. Rita inquires about Leah. The Old Man believes Leah misses her father. Leah watches wrestling on TV, and the Old Man has tried to seem interested. It's something they laugh at, Rita explains. And the Old Man complains that Leah keeps offering him soup all the time. Rita confesses it's fatty, but questions the Old Man about peanut butter and mayonnaise sandwiches. The Old Man claims he hasn't had one since grade school, but that they are good.

Peter is interrupting, impatient with their chatter; and after a beat, Rita attempts to explain what happened, but doesn't know how. It started with taking a walk, then taking a Port Authority bus at random. The bus went to Englewood Cliffs. When it stopped at the first corner there was a wedding. There was champagne. "I wished to God I were that young bridegroom starting out. Or the bride, for that matter." Rita recalls thinking, "If I could shine like the light of that girl . . . . . I'd never take a drink, I'd let my liver hang on another decade, stay out of the sun, eat right. This time I would floss." And the Old Man remembers, "It was your eyes I saw flashing back," and thinking, "If I could get inside that somehow."

RITA: Yes.

OLD MAN: If I could just know what it's like for one second of one day to have lived all that time, and be so alive, so sure of something, anything. Oh, please God, let me know what it is to have so little to lose. If I could just get inside.

RITA (*overlapping slightly*): I'll kiss the bride.

OLD MAN: So much past.

RITA: I'll be the bride. So much life inside.

OLD MAN (*overlapping slightly*): My whole life would be behind me.

RITA: My whole life again from the other side of the mirror. All ahead of me again.

OLD MAN: With nothing to lose.

OLD MAN and RITA (*simultaneously*): *At last.*

RITA: All you've got to do is—

RITA and OLD MAN (*simultaneously*): —want it. *Bad enough.*

> *Without touching, the Old Man and Rita switch souls; a wind passes through the room—a low rumble—as they speak.*

RITA: The soft arms.

OLD MAN: The strong arms.

RITA: The white teeth—

OLD MAN: The back.

RITA: The sweet smell of her breath.

OLD MAN: That smell.

RITA: Not like something rotting, coming up from your insides, but soft—

OLD MAN: Like a father—

RITA: Like a baby. And white.

OLD MAN: A man.

RITA: Clean.

OLD MAN: An old man.

> *Rita is now standing; the Old Man is now seated.*

RITA: My God.

OLD MAN: Like an old suit . . .

The Old Man continues talking to Rita, explaining about the strong bond between his wife and daughter, and how great his love for both of them was. Rita remembers seeing photographs of them and of his mother as well. When he turns to Peter, he lectures him briefly about how he made every effort to be patient with him, and about how he telephoned all the hotels in Kingston to find out the recipe for Long Island Ice Tea. Peter is "sweet," and "no hard feelings," but he's not the Old Man's type, he admits. He also admits that living forever is not such a good idea.

He pauses for a moment before adding that, as for Rita's parents, she can keep them. She thanks him, and the Old Man starts off, but before he leaves he turns back to give them a final admonition: "Do yourselves a favor: Floss."

PETER: Rita? . . . Oh, Rita . . . Oh my beautiful . . .

RITA: My body. My body.

> *He unties her feet.*

PETER: There they are. Look at those. Yes! Your hair.

RITA:  I'm here.  I'm not afraid.

PETER:  I know.

RITA:  I'm not afraid.

PETER:  Oh, I love you . . . Give me a smile.

> *She does.*

Je hebt erg witte tanden. Je hebt erg witte tanden.

RITA:  Ohhhhhh, I don't remember what I'm supposed to say, Peter, I know I memorized it.

PETER:  Om je better me op to eten.

RITA:  You promised you'd tell me.  What does it mean?

PETER:  The better to eat you with.  Oh, Rita.  Never to be squandered . . . the miracle of another human being.

RITA:  You're the miracle.

PETER:  No, you are.

RITA:  You.

PETER:  You.

> *They clasp one another.  Music plays.  Peter lifts Rita and carries her, finally, across the threshold.*

VOCALIST (*sings*):

How my lovesong gently cries
For the tenderness within your eyes.
My love is a prelude that never dies:
My prelude to a kiss.

> *Curtain.*

# THE GRAPES OF WRATH

*A Play in Two Acts*

BY FRANK GALATI

BASED ON THE NOVEL BY JOHN STEINBECK

Cast and credits appear on pages 386–387

*FRANK GALATI was born in Highland Park, Ill. on Nov. 29, 1943 and attended Northwestern University where he received his B.S. in 1965, his M.A. in 1966 and his Ph.D. in 1971. He embarked upon a teaching career in 1965 as an assistant professor of speech at the University of South Florida in Tampa, achieved his full professorship at Northwestern in 1983 and continues his teaching career there in the Department of Performance Studies.*

*Meanwhile, Galati gravitated toward the theater, teaching acting and other theater skills in Chicago in the 1970s and taking part in production there as director of the Chicago Opera Theater and associate director of the Goodman Theater. In 1986 he became a member of the Steppenwolf ensemble and in the years since then has received eight Joseph Jefferson Awards for writing, directing and acting.*

*Galati's authorship of record includes the plays* Winnebago *(1974),* Heart of a Dog *(1985, adapted from the Mikhail Bulgakov novel),* She Always Said

293

No, Pablo *(1987, conceived by Galati with words by Gertrude Stein, music by Virgil Thomson and Igor Stravinsky and images by Pablo Picasso) and now the adaptation, with Elaine Steinbeck's blessing, of her late husband John's great novel* The Grapes of Wrath *which premiered at Steppenwolf in Chicago on Sept. 18, 1988 and, after playing the La Jolla Playhouse in May and June 1989 and London's National Theater in June and July 1989, arrived on Broadway March 22, 1990 as its author's first Best Play and winner of the Tony Awards for the best play and its direction by Galati.*

*Galati is also the author of the screen plays* The Living End, There's No Tomorrow *and* The Accidental Tourist *(for which he received an Academy Award nomination) and co-author of the textbook* Oral Interpretation. *He lives in the Chicago area, in Evanston, Ill.*

*Our method of representing* The Grapes of Wrath *in this Best Plays section of our yearbook differs somewhat from that of most other selections. Instead of a detailed synopsis of the events of this already-familiar novel, we offer the sketchiest of summaries but several major episodes from the script to demonstrate fully the style, technique and matching eloquence of the original material and the adaptation.*

## Time: 1938

## Place: Oklahoma and then California

### ACT I

SYNOPSIS: In the feeble light of the dust-ridden air, two men—Tom Joad (*"in cheap new clothes"*) and Jim Casy (playing "Yes, Sir, That's My Baby" on a small harmonica and then singing a verse with new lyrics with the punch line "Jesus is my Saviour now")—encounter each other on opposite sides of a sagging barbed wire fence in an open expanse of parched and ruined farmland. Casy recognizes Tom and identifies himself as the preacher who baptized Tom in his farm's irrigation ditch.

Tom remembers that Casy "used to give a good meetin'" and offers him a drink of whiskey, which Casy gladly accepts. Casy doesn't call himself a preacher any more; the spirit doesn't seem to move in him or in the people the same as it used to.

CASY: . . . . . I went off alone, an' I sat and figured. The sperit's strong in me, only it ain't the same. I ain't so sure of a lot of things.

*Casy digs his bony hand into his pocket and brings out a black,
bitten plug of tobacco. He brushes it off, bites off a corner and
settles the quid into his cheek.*

I used to get the people jumpin' and talkin' in tongues and glory-shoutin' till
they just fell down an' passed out. And some I'd baptize to bring 'em to. An'
then—you know what I'd do? I'd take one of them girls out in the grass, an'
I'd lay with her. Done it ever' time. Then I'd feel bad, an' I'd pray an' pray,
but it didn't do no good. Come next time, them an' me was full of the sperit, I'd
do it again.

TOM: There ain't nothing like a good hot meetin' for pushin' 'em over. I
done that myself.

CASY: But you wasn't the preacher. A girl was just a girl to you. But to
me they was holy vessels.

TOM (*moves next to Casy*): You shoulda got a wife. Preacher an' his wife
stayed at our place one time. Jehovites they was. Slep' upstairs. Held
meetin's in our barnyard. Us kids would listen. That preacher's missus took a
godawful poundin' after ever' night meetin'.

CASY: I'm glad you tol' me. I used to think it was jus' me. Finally it give
me such pain I quit an' went off by myself an' give her a damn good thinkin'
about.

TOM: You give her a goin' over.

CASY: Well, I was layin' under a tree when I figured her out. Before I
knowed it, I was sayin', "The hell with it! There ain't no sin and there ain't no
virtue. There's just stuff people do."

TOM: You figured her out.

CASY: I says, "What's this call, this sperit?" An' I says, "It's love. I love
people so much I'm fit to bust, sometimes." An' I says, "Don't you love
Jesus?" Well, I thought and thought, an' finally I says, "No, I don't know nobody name' Jesus." I been talkin' a hell of a lot. Anyway, I'll tell you one
more thing I thought about: an' from a preacher it's the most unreligious thing,
and I can't be a preacher no more because I thought it an' I believe it.

TOM: What's that?

CASY (*looks at Tom shyly*): If it hits you wrong, don't take no offense at it,
will you?

TOM: I don't take no offense 'cept a bust in the nose. What did you figger?

CASY: I figgered about the Holy Spirit and the Jesus road. I figgered,
"Why do we got to hang it all on God or Jesus? Maybe," I figgered, "maybe
it's all men an' all women we love; maybe that's the Holy Sperit—the human
sperit—the whole shebang. Maybe all men got one big soul ever'body's a
part of." Now I sat there thinkin' it, an' all of a sudden—I knew it. I knew it
so deep down that it was true, and I still know it.

TOM (*his eyes drop to the ground*): You can't hold no church with idears
like that. People would drive you out of the country with idears like that.

Jumpin' and yellin'. That's what folks like. Makes 'em feel swell. When Granma got to talkin' in tongues, you couldn't tie her down.

CASY: I baptized you right when I was in the glory rooftree.

TOM: She could knock over a full-growed deacon with her fist.

CASY: Had little chunks of Jesus jumpin' outa my mouth that day.

TOM: Guess I'll mosey along.

Jim True (Al) and Gary Sinise (Tom Joad) *below*, with
Mark Deakins (Connie) and Sally Murphy (Rose of Sharon)
(*above*) in a scene from *The Grapes of Wrath*

CASY: It's a funny thing. I was thinkin' about ol' Tom Joad when you come along. Thinkin' I'd call on him. How is Tom?

TOM: I don't know how he is. I ain't been home in four years.

CASY: Been out travelin' around?

TOM (*suspiciously*): Didn't you hear about me? I was in the papers?

CASY: No—I never. What?

TOM: I been in McAlester them four years.

CASY: Ain't wantin' to talk about it, huh? I won't ask you no more questions, if you done something bad—

TOM: I'd do what I done—again. I killed a guy. In a fight. We was drunk at a dance. He got a knife in me, an' I killed him with a shovel that was layin' there. Knocked his head plumb to squash.

CASY: You ain't ashamed of nothin', then?

TOM: No, I ain't. I got seven years, account of he had a knife in me. Got out in four—parole. (*He shades his eyes.*) I hate to hit the sun, but it ain't so bad now.

CASY: I ain't seen ol' Tom in a bug's age.

TOM: Come along.

CASY: I was gonna look in on him anyways. I brang Jesus to your folks for a long time.

TOM: Pa'll be glad to see you. He always said you got too long a pecker for a preacher.

> *The two hesitate for a moment and then move off. The sky begins to darken. A cloud of black dust advances in the distance. In the near darkness, a Man with a Guitar appears.*

MAN WITH A GUITAR (*sings*):
Down in Oklahoma, my baby fainted in the rain
Down in Oklahoma, my baby fainted in the rain
Had to throw a bucket of dirt on her
To bring her back again.

> *The dust cloud swallows him in darkness, and the wind howls. Faint moonlight catches a broken porch column. The column and a few crates define the space that was the Joad house. Tom and Casy emerge in the distance and walk along the fence. A dog barks. Tom sees the fragment of house and stops.*

TOM: Somepin's happened. They ain't nobody here.

> *They climb under the fence and move into the dusty yard.*

Jesus! Hell musta popped here. There ain't nothin' left.

CASY: Le's look in the house. She's all pushed outa shape. Somethin' knocked the hell out of her.

TOM: They're gone—or Ma's dead. If Ma was anywhere about, that gate'd be shut and hooked. That's one thing she always done—seen that the gate was shut. Ever since the pig got in over to Jacobs' an' 'et the baby.

CASY: If I was still a preacher I'd say the arm of the Lord had struck. But now I don't know what happened.

> *Tom lights a match and slips cautiously into the shack. He stoops down, finds and lights the stub of a candle and then picks up a woman's high button shoe.*

TOM: I remember this. This was Ma's. It's all wore out now. Ma liked them shoes. Had 'em for years. No—they're gone—or dead.

> *A board creaks. Muley Graves suddenly appears in the shadows.*

MULEY: Tommy?

> *Tom turns and sees Muley.*

TOM: Muley!

MULEY: When'd you get out, Tommy?

TOM: Two days ago. Took a little time to hitchhike home. An' look here what I find. (*To Muley.*) Where's my folks, Muley?

MULEY: They're all at your Uncle John's. The whole brood. Gettin' money together so they can shove on west. Uncle John got *his* notice too.

TOM: You know this here preacher, don't you Muley? Rev. Casy.

MULEY: Why, sure, sure. Didn't look over. Remember him well.

TOM: What happened here?

MULEY: Well, your folks was gonna stick her out, when the bank come to tractorin' off the place. Bumped the hell outa the house, an' give her a shake like a dog shakes a rat.

CASY: Why they kickin' folks off the lan'?

MULEY: Bank can't afford to keep no tenants. Them sons-a-bitches. Them dirty sons-a-bitches. I tell ya, men, I'm stayin'. They ain't gettin' rid a me.

Muley's whole family went west, but Muley can't bear to abandon the ground soaked with his father's blood when his father was gored by a bull.

Used car salesmen are having a field day selling junk to the migrating Okie families. The Joads have decided to try for California and a better life, and their dilapidated truck is piled high with their belongings, ready to roll, as Tom and Casy meet up with them. Tom is greeted warmly by his family, especially his mother, who feared that she might never see her Tom again if they left for California and lost touch.

The Joads' wrenching departure is slowly, painfully but finally accomplished, with each finding a place in, on or clinging to the wheezing truck. This Joad migration includes Tom (on parole and not supposed to leave the state), Casy (invited to go along and accepts), Granma and Grandpa Joad (he refuses to leave and has to be pushed into his seat), Pa and Ma Joad (she won't look back when the time comes to move), Uncle John, Tom's siblings Noah (*"tall and strange, with a calm but puzzled look"*), 12-year old Ruthie, 10-year old Winfield and Rose of Sharon (now pregnant), with her 19-year-old husband Connie, and finally Al Joad, another brother of Tom's, can *"tinker an engine"* and picked out this truck for the journey.

When everybody and everything is loaded, including 13 people and enough pieces of salt pork to keep them going, Al persuades the truck's engine to move them slowly toward Route 66 and their 2,000-mile journey from Oklahoma to beckoning California.

The Joads' saga begins as a series of incidents in their struggle toward what they hope is a Promised Land; and, in California at last, continues with their attempt to find a place for themselves in a society that has little use and no comfortable place for these agrarian refugees. First to drop off is Granpa, who escapes into death before the first stop and is buried at once with a note in a bottle explaining that he died a natural death, in case his corpse is ever discovered by the authorities.

The straight line of the truck's journey is marked off by a line of episodes, bridged by the songs of a guitar player and band. Exploitation of these pilgrims begins when Tom, Al and Casy, who have been off getting a part for the truck, rejoin the rest of the Joads in a camping area. The Proprietor threatens a visit from the deputy sheriff if the three men try to camp out in open land instead of paying him a fifty-cent fee to bed down in his campground.

> *Tom's eyes glow angrily.*

TOM: Deputy sheriff ain't your brother-in-law by any chance?

PROPRIETOR (*leaning forward*): No, he ain't. An' the time ain't come yet when us local folks got to take no talk from you goddamn bums, neither.

TOM: It don't trouble you none to take our four bits. An' when'd we get to be bums? We ain't asked ya for nothin'. All of us bums, huh? Well, we ain't askin' no nickels from you for the chance to lay down and rest.

> *The men are rigid, motionless, quiet. Expressions are gone from their faces. Their eyes, in the shadows under their hats, move secretly to the face of the Proprietor.*

PA: Come off it, Tom.

TOM: Sure, I'll come off it. I don't wanta make no trouble. It's a hard thing to be named a bum. I ain't afraid. I'll go for you an' your deputy with my mitts—here now, or jump Jesus. But there ain't no good in it.

PROPRIETOR: Ain't you got half a buck?

TOM: Yeah, I got it. But I'm gonna need it. I can't set it out just for sleepin'.

PROPRIETOR: Well, we all got to make a livin'.

TOM: Yeah, on'y I wisht they was some way to make her 'thout takin' her away from somebody else.

PA: We'll get movin' smart early. Look, mister. We paid. These here fellas is part of our folks. Can't they stay? We paid a dollar and a half.

PROPRIETOR: For nine. Three more is another fifty cents.

TOM: We'll go along the road. Come for ya in the morning. (*To the Proprietor.*) That awright with you?

PROPRIETOR: If the same number stays that come and paid—that's awright.

TOM: We'll go along pretty soon.

> *Pa speaks generally. The men shift their positions.*

PA: It's dirt hard for folks to tear up an' go. Folks like us that had our place. We ain't shif'less. 'Till we got tractored off, we was people with a farm.

> *A young thin man turns his head slowly.*

YOUNG MAN: Croppin'?

PA: Sure we was sharecroppin'. Used ta own the place.

YOUNG MAN: Same as us.

PA: Lucky for us it ain't gonna las' long. We'll get out west, an' we'll get work, an' we'll get a piece of growin' land with water.

> *A man in a ragged coat, huddled in a corner, laughs and then moves out of the shadows.*

MAN GOING BACK: You folks must have a nice little pot of money.

PA: No, we ain't got no money. But they's plenty of us to work, an' we're all good men. Get good wages out there an' we'll put 'em together. We'll make out.

> *The Man Going Back laughs again. His laughter turns hysterical, a high whining giggle, then dissolves into a fit of coughing.*

MAN GOING BACK: You goin' out there—oh, Christ. You goin' out an' get—good wages—oh, Christ! Pickin' oranges, maybe? Gonna pick peaches?

TOM (*dignified*): We gonna take what they got. They got lots of stuff to work in.

> *The Man Going Back giggles under his breath.*

What's so goddamn funny about that?

MAN GOING BACK: You folks all goin' to California, I bet.

PA: I tol' you that. You didn' guess nothin'.

MAN GOING BACK: Me—I'm comin' back. I been there. I'm goin' back to starve. I'd ruther starve all over at once.

PA: What the hell you talkin' about? I got a han'bill says they got good wages, an' little while ago I seen a thing in the paper says they need folks to pick fruit.

MAN GOING BACK: I don' wanna fret you.

TOM: You ain't gonna fret us. You done some jackassin'. You ain't gonna shut up now. The han'bill says they need men.

MAN GOING BACK: You don't know what kind a men they need.

TOM: What you talkin' about?

MAN GOING BACK:  Look.  How many men they say they want on your han'bill?

PA:  Eight hunderd, an' that's in one little place.

MAN GOING BACK:  Orange color han'bill?

PA:  Why—yes.

MAN GOING BACK:  Give the name a the fella—says so-and-so, labor contractor?

*Pa reaches in his pocket and brings out a folded orange handbill.*

PA:  That's right.  How'd you know?

MAN GOING BACK:  Look.  It don't make no sense.  This fella wants eight hunderd men.  So he prints up five thousan' of them things an' maybe twenty thousan' people sees 'em.  An' maybe two-three thousan' folks get movin' account of this here han'bill.  Folks that's crazy with worry.

PA:  But it don't make no sense!

MAN GOING BACK:  Not till you see the fella that put out this here bill.  You'll see him, or somebody that's working for him.  You'll be a-campin' by a ditch, you an' fifty other families.  An' he'll look in your tent an' see if you got anything lef' to eat.  An' if you got nothin', he says, "Wanna job?"  An' you'll say, "I sure do, Mister.  I'll sure thank you for a chance to do some work."  An' he'll say, "I can use you."  An' you'll say, "When do I start?"  An' he'll tell you where to go, 'an what time, an' then he'll go on.  Maybe he needs two hunderd men, so he talks to five hunderd, an' they tell other folks, an' when you get to the place, they's a thousan' men.  This here fella says, "I'm payin' twenty cents an hour."  An' maybe half the men walk off.  But they's still five hunderd that's so goddamn hungry they'll work for nothin' but biscuits.

The Joads, persistently, move onward.  They get water for their car at a gas station whose owner and attendant clearly consider "Okies" a race of sub-humans.

They arrive at the Colorado River and revel in its waters.  Noah is captivated by the river and decides to stay here and live the rest of his life with its enjoyments.  He wanders away, leaving Tom to tell Ma he's gone.

The Joads proceed to cross the desert, at night.  They're stopped by two agricultural officers for inspection.  But when one of them shines his flashlight into the back of the truck and sees Granma, cradled in Ma's arms, looking appallingly ill, the Joads are waved on.

The First Narrator observes, "All night they bored through the hot darkness, and jackrabbits scuttled into the lights and dashed away in long, jolting leaps.  And the dawn came up behind them . . . and then—suddenly they saw the great valley below them . . . . . The vineyards, the orchards, the great flat valley, green and beautiful, the trees set in rows, and the farm houses."

The Joads look down, *"awestruck and embarrassed before the great valley."*  Ma is called out of the truck to see this wonderful sight; she seems at the point of collapse from fatigue. It turns out that Granma has died in the night, and Ma didn't tell anyone but stayed there with her, to prevent any delay in the family's progress. Granma's burial will cost just about everything the family has left, but they made it—they're in California. (*Curtain*).

## ACT II

It isn't long before the Joads realize what a fix they're in. They settle into a Hooverville, a shanty community of migrants like themselves, looking for work—300,000 of them in California by the latest estimate. Tom learns from an acquaintance, Floyd, about the system of employing very few men on the farms year round and thousands of desperate extras at harvest time for a mere pittance. Tom suggests getting together and organizing to force wages upward but is warned he'd merely be found dead in a ditch for his efforts.

Casy is considering going off on his own to give the group one less mouth to feed, but Tom asks him to stay for the time being.

Living this migrant life (Connie tells Rose of Sharon) is making him think better and better of the three dollars a day he could have earned fixing tractors back home.

A contractor comes into the Hooverville and asks if anybody wants work. Someone in the crowd of men says "Sure," but Floyd comes forward and intervenes.

FLOYD (*quietly*): I'll go, Mister. You're a contractor, an' you got a license. You jus' show your license, an' then you gives us an order to work, an' where, an' when, an' how much we'll get, an' you sign that, an' we'll all go.

CONTRACTOR (*turns*): You telling me how to run my own business?

FLOYD: 'F we're workin' for you, it's our business too.

CONTRACTOR: Well, you ain't telling me what to do. Fruits opening up. I need men.

FLOYD: But you ain't sayin' how many men, an' you ain't sayin' what you'd pay.

CONTRACTOR: Goddamn it, I don't know yet.

FLOYD: If you don' know, you got no right to hire men.

CONTRACTOR: I got a right to run my business my own way. If you men want to sit here on your ass, O.K. I'm getting men for Tulare County. Going to need a lot of men.

FLOYD (*turns to the crowd of men*): Twicet now I've fell for that. Maybe he needs a thousan' men. He'll get five thousan' there, an' he'll pay fifteen cents an hour. An' you poor bastards'll have to take it 'cause you'll be hungry. 'F he wants to hire men, let him hire 'em and write it out an' say what he's gonna pay. Ast ta see his license. He ain't allowed to contract without a license.

> *A man appears. On his leather jacket is pinned the star of the deputy sheriff. A heavy pistol holster hangs on his belt. He moves through the crowd.*

CONTRACTOR: Ever see this guy before, Joe?

DEPUTY SHERIFF: Which one?

CONTRACTOR (*indicating Floyd*): This fella.

DEPUTY SHERIFF: What'd he do?

CONTRACTOR: He's talking red, agitating trouble.

DEPUTY SHERIFF: Hm-m-m.

> *He moves slowly around Floyd.*

FLOYD: You see? If this guy's on the level, would he bring a cop along?

CONTRACTOR: Ever see 'im before?

DEPUTY SHERIFF: Hmmm, seems like I have. Las' week when that used-car lot was busted into. Seems like I seen this fella hangin' aroun'. Yep! I'd swear it's the same fella. You come on.

> *He unhooks the strap that covers the butt of his automatic.*

TOM: You got nothin' on him.

> *The Deputy swings around and moves slowly to Tom.*

DEPUTY SHERIFF: 'F you'd like to go in too, you jus' open your trap once more. They was two fellas hangin' around that lot.

TOM: I wasn't even in the state las' week.

DEPUTY SHERIFF: Well, maybe you're wanted someplace else. You keep your trap shut, Okie.

> *The Deputy gives Tom a sudden violent shove. The Contractor turns back to the men.*

CONTRACTOR: You fellas don't want to listen to these goddamn reds. Trouble-makers—they'll get you in trouble. Now I can use all of you in Tulare County.

> *The men are silent. The Deputy smiles.*

DEPUTY SHERIFF: Might be a good idear to go. Board of Health says we got to clean out this camp. An' if it gets around that you got reds out here—why, somebody might git hurt. Be a good idear if all you fellas moved on to Tulare. They isn't a thing to do around here. That's jus' a friendly way a tellin' you. Be a bunch of guys down here, maybe with pick handles, if you ain't gone.

> *Ma and Ruthie appear near the Joad camp.*

CONTRACTOR: I told you I need men. If you don't want to work—well, that's your business.

> *Floyd stands stiffly, his thumbs hooked over his belt. The Contractor moves away.*

DEPUTY SHERIFF (*moving to Floyd*):  Now c'mon, Hayseed, we're goin' for a ride.

> *Floyd's wife tries to intercede, but Al holds her back. The Deputy reaches a large hand up and takes hold of Floyd's left arm. Floyd pushes the hand away. The Deputy reaches again, and Floyd pushes the hand away again and swings with one movement. His fist splashes into the large face, and in the same motion he is away. The Deputy falls in a heap on the ground. Floyd bumps into Casy, who sends him off. The Deputy stands, draws his gun and moves after Floyd, who pushes through the crowd.*

AL:  He's got a gun!

> *Tom steps in and puts out his foot. The Deputy falls heavily and rolls, looking back at Tom. The crowd screams and parts at the sight of the Deputy's gun. Floyd trips and falls to the ground. The Deputy fires. A woman near Floyd screams and grabs her hand. Floyd stands and ducks out of sight. The Deputy, kneeling on the ground, raises his gun again, and then, suddenly, from the group of men, Casy steps in. He kicks the Deputy in the face and then stands back as the heavy man crumples. Most of the crowd flees. The Deputy is lying on his back, his mouth open. Tom picks up the automatic and pulls out the magazine. Casy kneels down and checks the Deputy.*

TOM:  Fella like that ain't got no right to a gun.

> *A small crowd gathers around the wounded woman. Ma moves to her. Casy moves close to Tom, takes the gun and places it next to the Deputy.*

CASY:  You got to git out. You go down in the willas an' wait. He didn't see me kick 'im, but he seen you stick out your foot.

TOM:  I don't want ta go.

CASY:  They'll fingerprint you. You broke parole. They'll send you back.

TOM:  Jesus! I forgot.

CASY:  Go quick. Fore he comes to.

> *Tom runs away. Al steps over to the fallen Deputy, then turns to Casy admiringly.*

AL:  Jesus, you sure flagged him down!

CASY (*to Al*):  Get out. Go on, get out—to the fambly. You don't know nothin'.

AL:  Yeah? How 'bout you?

CASY (*to the family*):  Somebody got to take the blame. I got no kids. They'll just put me in jail, an' I ain't doin' nothin' but set aroun'.

AL:  Ain't no reason for—

Gary Sinise as Tom Joad and Terry Kinney as Jim Casy in the
Hooverville scene of Frank Galati's adaptation of *The Grapes of Wrath*

CASY: Go on now. You get outa this.

AL (*bristling*): I ain't takin' orders.

CASY (*softly*): If you mess in this, your whole fambly, all your folks, gonna
get in trouble. I don' care about you. But your ma and your pa, they'll get in
trouble. Maybe they'll send Tom back to McAlester.

AL: O.K. I think you're a damn fool, though.

CASY: Sure. Why not?

The authorities arrive and haul Casy off to jail. After they've left, Tom returns to the family. They pack up, knowing that the camp will be burned out
tonight in revenge for the attack on the officer.

As they leave Hooverville, they realize that the hardships have been too
much for Connie, who has deserted them, probably to make his way back
home. As they drive off they can see the shantytown burning in the distance.

Tom's anger at the illegal and unwarranted harassment by the police is sim-
mering, close to the boiling point.

The Joads' luck seems to be changing with their arrival at Weedpatch
Camp, run by the U.S. Government, policeless, clean, charging $1 a week
which can be earned by doing camp chores. They even have occasional entertainment for the campers. Ma has the leisure to pierce Rose of Sharon's
ears for earrings, and Al indulges in his favorite diversion, the pursuit of femi-
nine happiness. But, as the Third Narrator observes, "The moving, questing
people were migrants now. Those families which had lived on a little piece of
land, who had lived and died on forty acres, had now the whole West to rove.
And they scampered about, looking for work; and the highways were streams
of people, and the ditch banks were lines of people. Behind them more were
coming."

Food and money having run out, the Joads move north looking for work
picking peaches. They arrive at the Hooper Ranch, where armed guards prevent an animated crowd, *"yelling and taunting,"* from coming any closer to an
iron fence, behind which a Bookkeeper is hiring pickers. He hires all the
Joads—four men, two women and two children—to work picking peaches for
five cents a box and sends them to a numbered shelter.

As the family settles in, Tom wanders off to find out what all the commo-
tion is about. He is intercepted by a ranch guard with a flashlight who warns
him away from "the crazy pickets ... them Goddamn reds!" As Tom moves
off, the Man With a Guitar is heard singing: "In the souls of the people/The
grapes of wrath are filling/And growing heavy, growing heavy/For the
vintage."

In the darkness, Tom creeps along the ground toward a campfire. He is
challenged by a sentry but is immediately recognized and embraced by one of
the campers. It is none other than Casy, asking after the Joad family, out of
jail, explaining what it was like.

CASY: . . . . . Some a them fellas in the tank was drunks, but mostly they
was there 'cause they stole stuff; an' mostly it was stuff they needed an'
couldn' get no other way. Ya see?

TOM: No.

CASY: Well, they was nice fellas, ya see. What made 'em bad was they
needed stuff. An' I began to see, then. It's need that makes all the trouble. I
ain't got it worked out. Well, one day they give us some beans that was sour.
One fella started yellin', an' nothin' happened. He yelled his head off. Trusty
come along an' looked in an' went on. Then another fella yelled. Well, sir,
then we all got yellin'. An' we all got on the same tone, an' I tell ya, it jus'
seemed like that tank bulged an' give an' swelled up. By God! Then somepin'
happened! They come a-runnin', an' they give us some other stuff to eat—
give it to us. Ya see?

TOM: No.

CASY: Maybe I can't tell you. Maybe you got to find out. Where's your cap?

TOM: I come out without it.

CASY: How's your sister?

TOM: Hell, she's big as a cow. I bet she got twins. You ain' tol' me what's goin' on.

OLD MAN: We struck. This here's a strike.

TOM: Well, fi' cents a box ain't much, but a fella can eat.

OLD MAN: Fi' cents? Fi' cents? They payin' you fi' cents?

TOM: Sure.

> *A heavy silence falls. Casy stares out into the dark night, his face bright in the firelight.*

CASY: Look, Tom. We come to work there. They says it's gonna be fi' cents. They was a hell of a lot of us. We got there an' they says they're payin' two an' a half cents. A fella can't eat on that, an' if he got kids—so we says we won't take it. So they druv us off. An' all the cops in the worl' come down on us. Now they're payin' you five. When they bust this here strike—ya think they'll pay five?

TOM: I dunno. Payin' five now.

CASY: Look. We tried to camp together, an' they druv us like pigs. Scattered us. Beat the hell outa fellas. Druv us like pigs. They run you in like pigs too. We can't las' much longer. Some people ain' et for two days. You goin' back tonight?

TOM: Aim to.

CASY: Well—tell the folks in there how it is, Tom. Tell 'em they're starvin' us an' stabbin' theirself in the back. 'Cause sure as cowflops she'll drop to two and a half jus' as soon as they clear us out.

TOM: I'll tell 'em. I don' know how. Never seen so many guys with guns. Don' know if they'll even let a fella talk.

CASY: Try an' tell 'em, Tom. They'll get two an' a half, jus' the minute we're gone. You know what two and a half is—that's one ton of peaches picked and carried for a dollar.

OLD MAN: You can't do it, Tom.

CASY: No—you can't do it. You can't get your food for that. Can't eat for that. (*He drops his head.*)

TOM: I'll try to get to tell the folks.

CASY: Look, Tom. Try an' get the folks in there to come on out. They can do it in a couple days. Them peaches is ripe. Tell 'em.

TOM: They won't.

CASY: But jus' the minute they ain't strikebreakin' they won't get no five.

TOM: I don't think they'll swalla that.

CASY: Well, tell 'em anyways.

TOM: Pa wouldn't do it. I know 'im. He'd say it wasn't none of his business.

CASY: Yes. I guess that's right. Have to take a beatin' fore he'll know.

TOM: Think Pa's gonna give up his meat on account of other fellas? An' Rosasharn ought to get milk. Think Ma's gonna wanta starve that baby jus' cause a bunch a fellas is yellin' outside a gate?

CASY: I wisht they could see it.

TOM (*exploding*): Talkin'! Always talkin'!

*The other men freeze and listen. Tom calms himself.*

Take my brother Al. He's out lookin' for a girl. He don' care 'bout nothin' else. Couple days he'll get him a girl. Think about it all day and do it all night. He don't give a damn.

CASY: Sure. Sure. He's jus' doin' what he's got to do. All of us like that.

*The man standing guard approaches.*

MAN WHO SEES TOM: Goddamn it, I don't like it.

*The men put out the fire and separate, straining to hear.*

CASY: What's the matter?

MAN WHO SEES TOM: I don't know. I jus' itch all over. Nervous as a cat.

CASY: Well, what's the matter?

MAN WHO SEES TOM: I don't know. Seems like I hear somepin', an' then I listen an' they ain't nothin' to hear.

OLD MAN: You're jus' jumpy. They's a cloud a-sailin' over. Bet she's got thunder. That's what's itchin' him—'lectricity.

CASY (*softly*): All of 'em itchy. Them cops been sayin' how they're gonna beat the hell outa us an' turn us outa the county. They figger I'm a leader 'cause I talk so much.

OLD MAN: Wait a minute. Listen!

CASY: What is it?

OLD MAN: I dunno.

CASY: Can't really tell if you hear it. Fools you. Get nervous. We're all nervous. Can't really tell. You hear it, Tom?

TOM: I hear it. Yeah, I hear it. I think they's guys comin' from ever' which way. We better get outa here.

OLD MAN (*whispering*): Under the bridge span—out that way. Hate to leave my tent.

CASY: Le's go.

> *The men begin to scatter. Suddenly, dozens of flashlight beams slice through the dark. White luminous blades slash moving fig- ures, and human voices bark and growl and whisper from the shadows. Suddenly Tom's face is frozen in a sword point of light. They start to move quietly away.*

FIRST MAN WITH CLUB: There they are!

SECOND MAN WITH CLUB: Stand where you are.

*One of the flashlight beams finds Casy.*

FIRST MAN WITH CLUB: That's him. That shiny bastard. That's him.

*Casy stares blindly at the light. More lights move to Casy. Some flashlights stay pointed at Tom. Casy breathes heavily.*

CASY (*moving toward the first man*): Listen. You fellas don' know what you're doin'. You're helpin' to starve kids.

*The first man, short and heavy, steps into the light. He carries a pick handle.*

FIRST MAN WITH CLUB: Shut up, you red son-of-a-bitch.

CASY: You don' know what you're a-doin'.

*The First Man swings with the pick handle. Casy dodges down into the swing. The heavy club crashes into the side of his head with a dull crunch of bone, and Casy falls sideways out of the light. The Second Man dashes over and shines his light on Casy's face. The preacher's eyes are wide. His mouth is open in surprise as if drawing in air. Suddenly, blood gurgles up and spills onto his chin.*

SECOND MAN WITH CLUB: Jesus, George. I think you killed him.

FIRST MAN WITH CLUB: Serve the son-of-a-bitch right.

*Tom is frozen in horror, looking down at Casy. A bellow of rage escapes from him as he leaps at the First Man and throws him to the ground. The Second Man rushes in, but Tom wrenches his pick handle away, swings wildly and begins beating the fallen First Man about the head and shoulders. The Second Man fumbles in the dark, grabs up a club and rushes for Tom with a glancing blow to his head. Tom staggers out of the cross-hatching of flashlight beams and disappears in the shadows. The other men dash about searching and calling. Many run off. Two or three beams of light remain in the foreground shining out.*

HOOPER RANCH GUARD: Who's there?

*The light beams snap off . . . . . Light reveals Ma near a wooden bench leaning over a bundle. Tom crawls in the circle of light. One side of his face is caked with blood.*

MA: Tom, what's the matter?

TOM: Sh! Don't talk loud. I got in a fight.

*He stumbles closer to Ma.*

MA: Tom!

TOM: I couldn' help it, Ma.

MA: You in trouble?

TOM: Yeah. In trouble. I can't go out to work. I got to hide.

*Tom sits on the bench.*

MA: Is it bad?

TOM: Nose busted.

MA: I mean the trouble.

TOM: Yeah, bad! I went out to see what all the yellin' was about. An' I come on Casy.

MA: The preacher?

TOM: Yeah, the preacher, on'y he was a-leadin' the strike. They come for him.

MA: Who come for him?

TOM: I dunno. Had pick handles. They killed 'im. Busted his head. I was standin' there. I went nuts. Grabbed the pick handle. I—I clubbed a guy.

MA: Kill 'im?

TOM: I dunno. I was nuts. Tried to.

MA: Was you saw?

TOM: I guess so. They had the lights on us.

MA: Tom, you got to go away.

TOM: I know, Ma.

MA: You gonna have a bad scar, Tom. An' your nose is all crooked.

TOM: Maybe tha's a good thing. Nobody wouldn't know me, maybe. If my prints wasn't on record, I'd be glad.

MA: I want you should go a long ways off.

TOM: Hm-m. Lookie, Ma. I been all night hidin' alone. I been thinkin' about Casy. He talked a lot. Use' ta bother me. But now I been thinkin' what he said, 'an I can remember—all of it.

MA: He was a good man.

*A dog barks in the distance.*

Hush—listen.

TOM: On'y the wind, Ma. I know the wind.

*Ma sits next to Tom.*

MA: Tom, what you aimin' to do?

TOM: What Casy done.

MA: But they killed him!

TOM: Yeah. He didn't duck quick enough. He wasn't doin' nothin' against the law, Ma. I been thinkin' a hell of a lot, thinkin' about our people livin' like pigs, an' the good rich lan' layin' fallow, or maybe one fella with a million acres, while a hunderd thousan' good farmers is starvin'. An' I been wonderin' if all our folks got together an' yelled, like them fellas yelled, only a few of 'em outside the gate—

MA: Tom, they'll drive you, an' cut you down.

TOM: They gonna drive me anyways. They drivin' all our people.

MA: How'm I gonna know 'bout you? They might kill ya an' I wouldn' know. They might hurt ya. How'm I gonna know?

TOM: Well, maybe like Casy says, a fella ain't got a soul of his own, but on'y a piece of a big one—an' then—

MA: Then what, Tom?

TOM: Then it don' matter. Then I'll be all aroun' in the dark. I'll be ever'where—wherever you look. Wherever they's a fight so hungry people can eat. I'll be there. Wherever they's a cop beatin' up a guy, I'll be there. An' when our folks eat the stuff they raise an' live in the houses they build— why, I'll be there. See? God, I'm talkin' like Casy.

MA: I don' un'erstan'. I don' really know.

TOM: Me neither. It's jus' stuff I been thinkin' about.

MA: Tom, later—when it's blowed over, you'll come back? You'll find us?

TOM: Sure. Now I better go.

MA: Goodbye.

*Ma takes his head in her hands and kisses him on the brow. Tom stands up and starts to leave. Ma's arms thrust out, but when Tom turns around she pulls them back suddenly.*

TOM: Goodbye.

*Tom ducks and crawls away. Ma's eyes are wet and burning, but she does not cry. Darkness engulfs her . . . . .*

The lights come up on the side of a rusty boxcar which the Joads now call home—a better one than they've had for some time. They are just about out of food, money and patience.

Al and a neighbor's daughter, Aggie Wainwright, have decided to get married and move into town looking for a garage job. The two families start to organize a little celebration, but the sound of thunder warns them there's a storm coming. The men grab shovels and try to keep the nearby creek from flooding.

Meanwhile, Rose of Sharon's baby is coming, creating a second emergency with the women coping. The intensity of the storm increases until the bank gives way and the workers flee the rising water. So does the intensity of Rose of Sharon's pain, as her baby is born dead. Uncle John floats the little box containing the corpse onto the swelling creek, hoping it will bear witness downstream to their misery.

The Joads decide to go for higher ground, all except Al, who will stay here with Aggie. They find a dry barn, and Ma makes Rose of Sharon take off her wet clothes and wrap herself in a blanket. Soon they also find that they have company. A boy and his father have taken refuge here in the barn, the father collapsed and near death from starvation.

*Ma looks at Pa and Uncle John. She turns to Rose of Sharon now wrapped in the blanket. The two women look deep into each other. The girl's eyes widen.*

ROSE OF SHARON: Yes.

MA: I knowed you would. I knowed!

ROSE OF SHARON (*whispering*): Will—will you all go out?

*Ma brushes the hair from her daughter's eyes and kisses her on the forehead.*

MA: Come on, you fellows. You come out in the shed.

*The boy opens his mouth to speak.*

Hush. Hush and git.

*Ma helps the boy up and leads him to the open door. Uncle John, Pa and the children leave. The boy looks back after his father and then goes out. Ma stands in the door for a few moments, looking back at Rose of Sharon, and then goes. Rose of Sharon stands still in the whispering barn. Then she draws the comfort about her and moves slowly to the man and stands looking down at the wasted face, into the wide frightened eyes. She slowly kneels down beside him, loosens one side of the blanket and bares her breast. He shakes his head feebly from side to side.*

ROSE OF SHARON: You got to.

*She bends low. Her hand moves behind his head and pulls him up gently.*

There. (*Her eyes gleam.*) There.

*A violin plays in the distance. As the lights fade slowly, Rose of Sharon looks up and across the barn. Her lips come together and smile mysteriously. Curtain.*

○○○
○○○
○○○
○○○
○○○
○○○
○○○ # THE PIANO LESSON

*A Play in Two Acts*

BY AUGUST WILSON

Cast and credits appear on page 389

*AUGUST WILSON was born in 1945 in Pittsburgh, where his father worked as a baker and his mother determinedly introduced her son to the written word and had him reading at 4 years old. Despite his early acquaintance and continuing fascination with words, he didn't long pursue formal education, leaving Central Catholic High School before graduating. He can clearly remember when he began to approach writing as a profession: it was April 1, 1965; he had just earned $20 writing a term paper for his sister, and he bought a typewriter which, he remembers, "represented my total commitment" because it took every penny he had. Lacking bus fare, he carried it home.*

*Wilson started with poetry. By 1972 he was writing one-acts. His first production was* Jitney, *staged in 1978 by Black Horizons Theater, a group which he himself had founded in 1968.* Jitney *was repeated in 1982 by Allegheny Repertory Theater; meanwhile his* Black Bart and the Sacred Hills *was produced in 1981 by Penumbra Theater in St. Paul. After a staged reading at the O'Neill Theater Center in Waterford, Conn. in 1982 and production by Yale Repertory Theater April 3, 1984 (both organizations and the play itself being directed by Lloyd Richards), Wilson's* Ma Rainey's Black Bottom *was brought to Broadway Oct. 11, 1984 for 275 performances, becoming its*

*author's first full New York production, first Best Play, first Tony nominee
and the winner of the New York Drama Critics Circle citation as the season's
best play.*

*All four of Wilson's New York productions have been named Best Plays
and all have been directed by Richards. The second,* Fences, *was also developed at the O'Neill and premiered at Yale Rep on April 25, 1985, receiving
the first annual American Theater Critics Association New Play Award, as
recorded in* The Best Plays of 1985–86. *It was produced on Broadway March
26, 1987 and carried off its author's second Critics citation, the Pulitzer
Prize and the Tony Awards for both best play and direction. Fences was still
running on Broadway a year later when Wilson's* Joe Turner's Come and
Gone *opened March 27, 1988 after previous productions at Yale Rep and at
the Huntington Theater, Boston (two groups which also presented Wilson's*
The Piano Lesson *in regional theater productions during the 1987–88 season
after an O'Neill tryout, then followed by a Goodman Theater, Chicago production cited by the American Theater Critics Association for its fourth annual New Play Award).* Joe Turner *won Wilson his third Best Play citation,
third New York Drama Critics Circle Award and third Tony nomination.
When it finally arrived on Broadway this season on April 16,* The Piano
Lesson *won Wilson his fourth round of kudos in all three of these categories,
plus the Pulitzer Prize.*

*Wilson is a member of New Dramatists (which presented his* The Mill
Hand's Lunch Bucket *in staged readings in 1983 and 1984), the Dramatists
Guild and the Playwrights' Center in Minneapolis. He has been a recipient
of Bush, McKnight, Rockefeller and Guggenheim fellowships in playwriting
and a Whiting Writer's Award. He is married, with one daughter, and lives in
St. Paul.*

*The following synopsis of* The Piano Lesson *was prepared by Sally Dixon
Wiener.*

## *Time: 1936*

## *Place: Pittsburgh*

### ACT I

*Scene 1*

SYNOPSIS: The play takes place in the kitchen and parlor of the house in
which Doaker Charles lives with Berniece, his niece, and her daughter

Maretha, 11. Berniece and Maretha have the upstairs rooms. Doaker's room opens onto the kitchen, which is stage left. Upstage of the adjoining parlor, stage right, a long staircase leading to the second floor is clearly in view.

"The house is sparsely furnished, and although there is evidence of a woman's touch, there is a lack of warmth and vigor." The centerpiece of the parlor, as well as of the play, is a massive old upright piano. On top of it a piano scarf and a scattering of framed family photographs look almost doll-like in contrast to the large portraits carved into the wood on each side of the front of the piano. Scenes are carved on each end of the piano, and the legs are also carved. The sound of the piano frames a number of portions of the play; it is not so much a player-piano sound as it is a haunting sound from bygone days. Within the context of the play there are also haunting sounds, like rushes of wind, with perhaps lightning as well, and a billowing of curtains at a window suddenly spotlit somewhere at the top of the stairway, indicating the periodic presence of Sutter's ghost.

> *The lights come up on the Charles household. It is 5 o'clock in the morning. The dawn is beginning to announce itself, but there is still something in the air that belongs to the night. A stillness that is a portent, a gathering, a coming together of something akin to a storm. There is a loud knock at the door.*

BOY WILLIE (*offstage, calling*): Hey, Doaker . . . Doaker!
> *He knocks again and calls.*

Hey, Doaker! Hey Berniece! Berniece!
> *Doaker enters from his room. He is a tall, thin man of 47, with severe features, who has for all intents and purposes retired from the world, though he works full-time as a railroad cook.*

DOAKER: Who is it?

BOY WILLIE: Open the door, nigger! It's me . . . Boy Willie!

DOAKER: Who?

BOY WILLIE: Boy Willie! Open the door!
> *Doaker opens the door, and Boy Willie and Lymon enter. Boy Willie is 30 years old. He has an infectious grin and a boyishness that is apt for his name. He is brash and impulsive, talkative and somewhat crude in speech and manner. Lymon is 29. Boy Willie's partner, he talks little, and then with a straightforwardness that is often disarming.*

DOAKER: What you doing up here?

BOY WILLIE: I told you, Lymon. Lymon talking about you might be sleep. This is Lymon. You remember Lymon Jackson from down home. This my Uncle Doaker.

DOAKER: What you doing up here? I couldn't figure out who that was. I thought you was in Mississippi.

BOY WILLIE: Me and Lymon selling watermelons. We got a truck out there. Got a whole truckload of watermelons. We brought them up here to sell. Where's Berniece?

Berniece is Boy Willie's sister. He hasn't seen her for three years, and now—at the end of the 1,800-mile journey with Lymon in the truck that's broken down three times on their way from Sunflower County—he wants her to get up and say hello to him. He keeps calling for her, despite Doaker's telling him she doesn't like "all that hollering," which she herself makes very clear to Boy Willie when she does appear. Berniece is 35, a pretty woman *"still in mourning for her husband after three years."* She is prim and proper, the antithesis of her brother, who is like a big, round, spinning, bouncing top, filling the place with his presence physically and vocally. Why can't he come "like normal folks," she complains, instead of "waking the neighbors with all that noise."

Boy Willie is ready to celebrate and wants Doaker to bring out a bottle because the Ghosts of the Yellow Dog got someone named Sutter. (He drowned in his well three weeks ago while he and Lymon were away working in Stoner County.) Berniece regards this ghost talk as nonsense—somebody is pushing people in their wells down there. She doesn't believe, either, that Lymon really bought the truck, and she is disturbed to hear that the sheriff was looking for Lymon. Lymon claims it was all a misunderstanding.

Doaker has brought out a bottle of good whiskey. Lymon isn't used to that, Boy Willie teases. It might make him sick. Berniece asks how long they'll be there. Boy Willie tells her that Lymon is staying up North, but he's leaving as soon as they sell the watermelons. "That's what you need to do. And you need to do it quick," she insists, as she starts to go upstairs, having refused to wake up Maretha so her uncle can see her. It's Boy Willie's opinion that "Berniece still try to be stuck up."

Boy Willie finds out from Doaker that Wining Boy had been there a year or so ago. He'd had a lot of money and stayed a couple of weeks but had gotten angry and left when Berniece had asked him for three dollars for food. Wining Boy is Boy Willie's uncle and Doaker's brother, Boy Willie explains to Lymon. He's a piano player as well and has made some records. That was a long time ago, Doaker comments.

Lymon notices the piano. Boy Willie talks admiringly about it, about how his mama polished it all the time and about what a good price it would sell for. Boy Willie reveals that Sutter's brother has offered to sell his land to him, and he needs to sell the piano now so he'll have enough money. Berniece won't sell it, Doaker points out, but Boy Willie is convinced he can talk her around when she realizes it will give him the chance to get the land. Berniece doesn't play the piano. She hasn't since their mother died seven years ago. "She say it got blood on it," Doaker says. But her daughter Maretha is playing the

Charles S. Dutton as Boy Willie and Rocky Carroll
as Lymon in August Wilson's *The Piano Lesson*

piano. Berniece takes her to the Irene Kaufman Settlement House school and hopes Maretha will become a teacher, perhaps even teach piano. Maretha could play the guitar instead, Boy Willie thinks.

DOAKER: How much land Sutter got left?

BOY WILLIE: Got a hundred acres. Good land. He done sold it piece by piece, he kept the good part for himself. Now he got to give that up. His brother come down from Chicago for the funeral . . . he up there in Chicago got some kind of business with soda fountain equipment. He anxious to sell the land. He don't want to be bothered with it. He called me to him and said cause of how long our families done known each other and how we been good friends and all, say he wanted to sell the land to me. Say he'd rather see me with it than Jim Stovall. Told me he'd let me have it for two thousand dollars cash money. He don't know I found out that most Stovall would give him for it was fifteen hundred dollars. He trying to get that extra five hundred out of me telling me he doing me a favor. I thanked him just as nice. Told him what a good man Sutter was and how he had my sympathy and all. Told him to give me two weeks. He said he'd wait on me. That's why I come up here. Sell them watermelons. Get Berniece to sell that piano. Put them two parts with the part I done saved. Walk in there, tip my hat. Lay my money down on the table. Get my deed and walk on out. This time I get to keep all the cotton.

Hire me some men to work it for me. Gin my cotton. Get my seed. And I'll see you again next year. Might even plant some tobacco and some oats.

DOAKER: You gonna have a hard time trying to get Berniece to sell that piano. You know Avery Brown from down there don't you? He up here now. He followed Berniece up here trying to get her to marry him after Crawley got killed. He been up here about two years. He call himself a preacher now.

BOY WILLIE: I know Avery. I know him from when he used to work on the Willshaw place. Lymon know him too.

DOAKER: He after Berniece to marry him. She keep telling him no, but he won't give up. He keep pressing her on it.

BOY WILLIE: Avery think all white men is bigshots. He don't know there some white men ain't got as much as he got.

DOAKER: He supposed to come past here this morning. Berniece going down to the bank with him to see if he can get a loan to start his church. That's why I know Berniece ain't gonna sell that piano. He tried to get her to sell it to help him start his church. . . . .

Avery had sent a white fellow over to see the piano, according to Doaker, a man who has been buying musical instruments. He'd offered Berniece a good price for it (Doaker doesn't know how much), but she wouldn't sell it. And he'd given her his number and asked her to call him if she changed her mind, promising to top anybody else's offer. Lymon figures Boy Willie should find the man and tell him someone's interested. It won't do any good, Doaker warns him, because she won't sell. She doesn't have to, Boy Willie claims, because he's going to. It's his as much as hers.

BERNIECE (*offstage, hollers*): Doaker! Go on get away. Doaker!
DOAKER (*calling*): Berniece?
> *Doaker and Boy Willie rush to the stairs, Boy Willie runs up the stairs, passing Berniece as she enters, running.*
DOAKER: Berniece, what's the matter? You all right? What's the matter?
> *Berniece tries to catch her breath. She is unable to speak.*
That's all right. Take your time. You all right. What's the matter? (*He calls.*) Hey Boy Willie?
BOY WILLIE (*offstage*): Ain't nobody up here.
BERNIECE: Sutter . . . Sutter's standing at the top of the steps.
DOAKER (*calls*): Boy Willie!
> *Lymon crosses to the stairs and looks up. Boy Willie enters from the stairs.*
BOY WILLIE: Hey Doaker, what's wrong with her? Berniece, what's wrong? Who was you talking to?
DOAKER: She say she seen Sutter's ghost standing at the top of the stairs.
BOY WILLIE: Seen what? Sutter? She ain't seen no Sutter.

BERNIECE:  He was standing right up there.

Boy Willie insists that it's all in Berniece's head, but Doaker doesn't believe she would make that up and wants her to tell them what happened.  She had come out of her room, and Sutter was standing there in the hall in a blue suit with his hand on the top of his head.  She'd told him to go away, but he just looked at her and called out Boy Willie's name.  Berniece thinks Boy Willie must have pushed him in the well.  But Boy Willie wasn't there—it was the Ghosts of the Yellow Dog that did it to Sutter and to a lot of others.

Berniece claims to know better.  She wants Boy Willie and Lymon to get out of her house.  They're trouble, and she believes if it weren't for them her husband Crawley would still be alive.  Boy Willie denies this and won't leave until the watermelons are sold.  He thinks Sutter wasn't looking for him; he was looking for the piano.  To get rid of his ghost, she should get rid of the piano.

It's time for them to get out and sell their watermelons, Berniece orders.  She asks Doaker to go upstairs with her, being still apprehensive about the ghost.  Lymon thinks Boy Willie should stay in Pittsburgh with him, that down home Sutter's ghost might look for him all the time.  That doesn't worry Boy Willie.  He's going to get the land and farm it.

Doaker has come back downstairs and is cooking his breakfast.  Boy Willie is teasing him about the women down home who wait for his visits there.  He only gets there once a month now, Doaker informs Boy Willie, but all those women want is "somebody with a steady payday," and they aren't going to get him tied up.  After Coreen he has no use for them.

BOY WILLIE:  Doaker can't turn that railroad loose.  He was working the railroad when I was walking around crying for sugartit.  My mama use to brag on him.

DOAKER:  I'm cooking now, but I used to line track.  I pieced together the Yellow Dog stitch by stitch.  Rail by rail.  Line track all up around there.  I lined track all up around Sunflower and Clarksdale.  Wining Boy worked with me.  He helped put in some of that track.  He'd work it for six months and quit.  Go back to playing piano and gambling.

BOY WILLIE:  How long you been with the railroad now?

DOAKER:  Twenty-seven years.  Now, I'll tell you something about the railroad.  What I done learned after twenty-seven years.  See, you got North.  You got West.  You look over here you got South.  Over there you got East.  Now, you can start from anywhere.  Don't care where you at.  You got to go one of them four ways.  And which ever way you decide to go they got a railroad that will take you there.  Now, that's something simple.  You think anybody would be able to understand that.  But you'd be surprised how many people trying to go North get on a train going West.  They think the train's supposed to go where they going rather than where it's going. Now, why people going? Their sister's sick. They getting away before they kill somebody . . . and they sitting across from somebody who's leaving to keep from getting killed. They leaving cause they can't get satisfied. They going to meet someone. I wish I had a dollar for every time that someone wasn't at the station to meet them. I done seen that a lot. In between the time they sent the telegram and the time the person get there . . . they done forgot all about them. They got so many trains out there they have a hard time keeping them from running into each other. Got trains going every whichaway. Got people on all of them. Somebody going where somebody just left. If everybody stay in one place I believe this would be a better world. Now what I done learned after twenty-seven years of railroading is this . . . if the train stays on the track . . . it's going to get where it's going. It might not be where you going. If it ain't then all you got to do is sit and wait cause the train's coming back to get you. The train don't never stop. It'll come back every time. . . . .

Maretha comes downstairs, and Boy Willie's good nature overcomes her shyness. She likes watermelon, and he promises her as many as she wants. She looks like her mother, he tells her. He hopes she'll come see him, and he'll teach her to ride a mule and kill a chicken. Throw the chicken in the pot then, and you'll have something good to eat. He wonders what kind of food she likes. She likes everything except black-eyed peas.

BOY WILLIE: Uncle Doaker tell me your mama got you playing that piano. Come on, play something for me.
*Boy Willie crosses over to the piano followed by Maretha.*
Show me what you can do. Come on now. Here . . . Uncle Boy Willie give you a dime . . . show me what you can do. Don't be bashful now. That dime say you can't be bashful.
*Maretha plays. It is something any beginner first learns.*
Here, let me show you something.
*Boy Willie sits and plays a simple Boogie Woogie.*
See that? See what I'm doing? That's what you call the Boogie Woogie. See now . . . you can get up and dance to that. That's how good it sound. It sound like you wanna dance. You can dance to that. It'll hold you up. Whatever kind of dance you wanna do you can dance to that right there. See that? See how it go? Ain't nothing to it. Go on, you do it.
MARETHA: I got to read it on the paper.
BOY WILLIE: You don't need no paper. Go on. Do just like that there.
BERNIECE: Maretha! You get up here and get ready to go so you be on time. Ain't no need you trying to take advantage of company.
MARETHA: I got to go.

BOY WILLIE: Uncle Boy Willie gonna get you a guitar. Let Uncle Doaker teach you how to play that. You don't need to read no paper to play the guitar. Your mama told you about that piano? You know how them pictures got on there?

MARETHA: She say, it just always been like that since she got it?

BOY WILLIE: You hear that, Doaker? And you sitting up here in the house with Berniece.

DOAKER: I ain't got nothing to do with that. I don't get in the way of Berniece's raising her.

BOY WILLIE: You tell your mama to tell you about that piano. You ask her how them pictures got on there. If she don't tell you I'll tell you.

Maretha has gone upstairs at Berniece's behest when Avery arrives. He is 38, *"honest and ambitious, he has taken to the city like a fish to water, finding in it opportunities for growth and advancement that did not exist for him in the rural South. He is dressed in a coat and tie."* He has come by for Berniece as planned and is surprised to find Boy Willie and Lymon. He assumes it must be their truck out in front. Boy Willie offers him as many watermelons as he wants. Avery has a half day off from his job running an elevator at the Gulf Building—"Got a pension and everything. They even give you a turkey on Thanksgiving."

Boy Willie remembers when Avery was planting cotton and seems intrigued with the fact that he's a preacher now. He wonders how he got to be one, because he might want to be one himself some day. God had called him in a dream, Avery admits, and Doaker urges him to tell about it. Avery doesn't think Boy Willie wants to hear about it, but Lymon does.

AVERY: Well, it come to me in a dream. See ... I was sitting out in this railroad yard watching the trains go by. The train stopped and these three hobos got off. They told me they had come from Nazareth and was on their way to Jerusalem. They had three candles. They gave me one and told me to light it ... but to be careful that it didn't go out. Next thing I knew I was standing in front of this house. Something told me to go knock on the door. This old woman opened the door and said they had been waiting on me. Then she led me into this room. It was a big room, and it was full of all kinds of different people. They looked like anybody else except they all had sheep heads and was making noise like sheep make. I heard somebody call my name. I looked around and there was these same three hobos. They told me to take off my clothes, and they give me a blue robe with gold thread. They washed my feet and combed my hair. Then they showed me these three doors and told me to pick one. I went through one of them doors, and that flame leapt off that candle, and it seemed like my whole head caught fire. I looked around, and there was four or five other men standing there with these same blue robes on. Then we heard a voice tell us to look out across this valley. We looked out and saw the valley was full of wolves. The voice told us that these sheep people that I had seen in the other room had to go over to the other side of this valley, and somebody had to take them. Then I heard another voice say, "Who shall I send?" Next thing I knew I said, "Here I am. Send me." That's when I met Jesus. He say, "If you go, I'll go with you." Something told me to say, "Come on. Let's go." That's when I woke up. My head still felt like it was on fire . . . but I had a peace about myself that was hard to explain. I knew right then that I had been filled with the Holy Ghost and called to be a servant of the Lord. It took me a while before I could accept that. But then a lot of little ways God showed me that it was true. So I became a preacher.

LYMON: I see why you gonna call it the Good Shepherd Church. You dreaming about them sheep people. I can see that easy.

Boy Willie tries to find out from Avery the name of the man who came to look at the piano, but Avery's forgotten. The man had given Berniece his card, but he thinks she threw it away. When Berniece comes downstairs with Maretha she's annoyed that Boy Willie and Lymon haven't gone off yet to sell watermelons, and Doaker agrees with her.

Doaker asks Berniece to pick up some ham hocks, turnip greens and cornmeal while she's downtown. Berniece prepares to leave with Avery and Maretha, who will be dropped off at Settlement House.

AVERY: I'll be seeing you again, Boy Willie.

BOY WILLIE: Hey Berniece . . . what's the name of that man Avery sent past say he want to buy the piano?

BERNIECE: I knew it. I knew it when I first seen you. I knew you was up to something.

BOY WILLIE: Sutter's brother say he selling the land to me. He waiting on me now. Told me he'd give me two weeks. I got one part. Sell them watermelons get me another part. Then we can sell that piano and I'll have the third part.

BERNIECE: I ain't selling that piano, Boy Willie. If that's why you come up here you can just forget it. (*To Doaker.*) Doaker, I'll see you later. Boy Willie ain't nothing but a whole lot of mouth. I ain't paying him no mind. If he come up here thinking he gonna sell that piano, then he done come up here for nothing.

*Berniece, Avery and Maretha exit the front door.*

BOY WILLIE: Hey Lymon! You ready to go sell these watermelons?

*Boy Willie and Lymon start to exit. At the door Boy Willie turns to Doaker.*

Hey, Doaker . . . if Berniece don't want to sell that piano . . . I'm gonna cut it in half and go on and sell my half.

    *Boy Willie and Lymon exit.*

## Scene 2

Three days later Wining Boy has appeared and is sitting at the kitchen table. He's 56 and *"tries to present the image of a successful musician and gambler, but his music, his clothes, and even his manner of presentation are old. He is a man who, looking back over his life, continues to live it with an odd mixture of zest and sorrow."* There's a bottle on the table, and from what Wining Boy is saying it's obvious Doaker has been telling him about the Ghosts of the Yellow Dog getting Sutter, about Boy Willie and Lymon and their truckload of watermelons, and about Sutter's ghost. Wining Boy wonders why Sutter's sons aren't going to farm his land. Doaker explains that one has come North to school and the other "ain't got as much sense as that frying pan over yonder. . . . . . He'd stand in the river and watch it rise till it drown him." Berniece is all right, Doaker informs Wining Boy, but she still hasn't gotten over Crawley's death. But she and Avery have something going, he tells Wining Boy, adding that Avery's a preacher now, and according to Avery "heaven opened up with thunder and lighting and God was calling his name."

Boy Willie and Lymon return, happy to see Wining Boy, who remembers Lymon's father. The truck's broken down again, and they have to wait until the next day to get it fixed. Boy Willie kids Wining Boy about how he'd left the last time after Berniece had asked him for three dollars. It wasn't the money, Wining Boy explains, it was the way she "try and rule over you too much." Boy Willie thinks Wining Boy still has money, but Wining Boy admits he was just about to ask Boy Willie for five dollars.

They all begin recounting the people the Ghosts of the Yellow Dog have gotten and think there may be as many as a dozen.

BOY WILLIE: Berniece say she don't believe all that about the Ghosts of the Yellow Dog.

WINING BOY: She ain't got to believe. You go ask them white folks in Sunflower County if they believe. You go ask Sutter if he believe. I don't care if Berniece believe or not. I done been to where the Southern cross the Yellow Dog and called out their names. They talk back to you too.

LYMON: What they sound like? The wind or something?

BOY WILLIE: You done been there for real, Wining Boy?

WINING BOY: Nineteen thirty. July of nineteen thirty I stood right there on that spot. It didn't look like nothing was going right in my life. I said everything can't go wrong all the time. Let me go down there and call on the Ghosts of the Yellow Dog, see if they can help me. I went down there, and right there where them two railroads cross each other ... I stood right there on that spot and called out their names. They talk back to you too.

LYMON: People say you can ask them questions. They talk to you like that?

WINING BOY: A lot of things you got to find out on your own. I can't say how they talked to nobody else. But to me it just filled me up in a strange sort of way to be standing there on that spot. I didn't want to leave. It felt like the longer I stood there the bigger I got. I seen the train coming, and it seem like I was bigger than the train. I started not to move. But something told me to go ahead and get on out the way. The train passed, and I started to go back up there and stand some more. But something told me not to do it. I walked away from there feeling like a king. Went on and had a stroke of luck that run on for three years. So I don't care if Berniece believe or not. Berniece ain't got to believe. I know cause I been there. Doaker'll tell you about the Ghosts of the Yellow Dog.

DOAKER: I don't try and talk that stuff with Berniece. Avery got her all tied up in that church. She just think it's a whole lot of nonsense.

BOY WILLIE: Berniece don't believe in nothing. She just think she believe. She believe in anything if it's convenient for her to believe. But when that convenience run out then she ain't got nothing to stand on.

Boy Willie announces he's gotten the name of the man who was interested in buying the piano from the man who fixed their truck. He explains to Wining Boy about his plans to buy Sutter's land.

Wining Boy has heard that Boy Willie and Lymon had been hauling wood for someone and keeping some aside to sell. They ran into trouble with the sheriff. They tried to get away, but Berniece's husband Crawley had his gun, fought back and was killed. Lymon was wounded and both Boy Willie and Lymon were sent to the penitentiary.

Lymon thinks they treat you better up here in the North. Boy Willie claims people treat you the way you let them and if he's mistreated, he'll mistreat back. He doesn't believe in any difference between himself and a white man. He begins a song, and they all join in, stamping and clapping to keep time, and singing in harmony.

BOY WILLIE: ..... Hey, Wining Boy, come on play some piano. You a piano player, play some piano. Lymon wanna hear you.

WINING BOY: I give that piano up. That was the best thing that ever happened to me, getting rid of that piano. That piano got so big and I'm carrying it around on my back. I don't wish that on nobody. See, you think it's all fun being a recording star. Got to carrying that piano around, and man did I get slow. Got just like molasses. The world just slipping by me, and I'm walking around with that piano. All right. Now, there ain't but so many places you can go. Only so many roads wide enough for you and that piano. And that piano get heavier and heavier. Go to a place, and they find out you play piano, the first thing they want to do is give you a drink, find you a piano and sit you right down. And that's where you gonna be for the next eight hours. They ain't gonna let you get up! Now, the first three or four years of that is fun. You can't get enough whiskey and you can't get enough women and you don't never get tired of playing that piano. But that only last so long. You look up one day, and you hate the whiskey, and you hate the women, and you hate the piano. But that's all you got. You can't do nothing else. All you know how to do is play that piano. Now, who am I? Am I me? Or am I the piano player? Sometime it seem like the only thing to do is shoot the piano player cause he the cause of all the trouble I'm having.

If Lymon knew how, he'd play it, but he doesn't, so he would sell it if he had it. Wining Boy knows Berniece won't sell it, and Doaker sets about to explain to Lymon why she won't. It goes back to the time of slavery, when Sutter's grandfather Robert owned the family. The piano belonged to a man named Nolander from down in Georgia. Sutter wanted to buy an anniversary present for his wife, Miss Ophelia, but he didn't have any money, so he offered to trade "one and a half niggers for it . . . . . one full grown and one half grown." Nolander agreed, if he could pick them out himself, and he chose Doaker's grandmother (for whom Berniece is named) and his father, who was 9. Miss Ophelia dressed up every day and was happy playing the piano, but as time went on she began to miss his grandmother, Doaker continues, and missed his daddy, too, "having him around the house to fetch things for her." She wanted to trade the piano back for them, but Nolander wouldn't agree, and Miss Ophelia took to her bed. "That's when Sutter called our grandaddy up to the house," Wining Boy puts it.

DOAKER: Now, our grandaddy's name was Boy Willie. That's who Boy Willie's named after . . . only they called him Willie Boy. Now, he was a worker of wood. He could make you anything you wanted out of wood. He'd make you a desk. A table. A lamp. Anything you wanted. Them white fellows around there used to come up to Mr. Sutter and get him to make all kinds of things for them. Then they'd pay Mr. Sutter a nice price. See, everything my grandaddy made Mr. Sutter owned cause he owned him. That's why when Mr. Nolander offered to buy him to keep the family together, Mr. Sutter wouldn't sell him. Told Mr. Nolander he didn't have enough money to buy him. Now . . . am I telling it right, Wining Boy?

WINING BOY: You telling it.

DOAKER: Sutter called him up to the house and told him to carve my grandmother and my daddy's picture on the piano for Miss Ophelia. And he took and carved this . . .

*Doaker crosses over to the piano.*

See that right there? That's my grandmother, Berniece. She looked just like that. And he put a picture of my daddy when he wasn't nothing but a little boy the way he remembered him. He made them up out of his memory. Only thing . . . he didn't stop there. He carved all this. He got a picture of his mama . . . Mama Ester . . . and his daddy, Boy Charles.

WINING BOY: That was the first Boy Charles.

DOAKER: Then he put on the side here all kinds of things. See that? That's when him and Mama Berniece got married. They called it jumping the broom. That's how you got married in them days. Then he got here when my daddy was born . . . and here he got Mama Ester's funeral . . . and down here he got Mr. Nolander taking Mama Berniece and my daddy away down to his place in Georgia. He got all kinds of things what happened with our family. When Mr. Sutter seen the piano with all them carvings on it, he got mad. He didn't ask for all that. But see . . . there wasn't nothing he could do about it. When Miss Ophelia seen it . . . she got excited. Now she had her piano and her niggers too. She took back to playing it and played on it right up till the day she died. . . . .

After that, Doaker's and Wining Boy's older brother, Boy Charles (Boy Willie's and Berniece's father) who would be 57 if he'd lived, talked about the piano all the time. It was always on his mind. "Say it was the story of our whole family, and as long as Sutter had it . . . he had us. Say we was still in slavery." Doaker and Wining Boy tried to dissuade him, but he was determined to get the piano. When Sutter was at the county's annual Fourth of July picnic in 1911, the three of them took the piano from Sutter's house and put it on a wagon to take to the next county to Mama Ola's people. But Boy Charles made the mistake of staying there until Sutter came home.

DOAKER: . . . . . Now, I don't know what happened when Sutter came home and found that piano gone. But somebody went up to Boy Charles' house and set it on fire. But he wasn't in there. He must have seen them coming cause he went down and hopped the 3:57 Yellow Dog. He didn't know they was gonna come down and stop the train. Stopped the train and found Boy Charles in the boxcar with four of them hobos. Must have got mad when they couldn't find the piano cause they set the boxcar afire and killed everybody. Now, nobody know who done that. Some people say it was Sutter cause it was his piano. Some people say it was Sheriff Carter. Some people say it was Robert Smith and Ed Saunders. But don't nobody know for sure. It was about two months after that that Ed Saunders fell down his well.

Just upped and fell down his well for no reason. People say it was the ghost of them men who burned up in the boxcar that pushed him in his well. They started calling them the Ghosts of the Yellow Dog. Now, that's how all that got started, and that why we say Berniece ain't gonna sell that piano. Cause her daddy died over it.

BOY WILLIE: All that's in the past. If my daddy had seen where he could have traded that piano in for some land of his own, it wouldn't be sitting up here now. He spent his whole life farming on somebody else's land. I ain't gonna do that. See, he couldn't do no better. When he come along he ain't had nothing he could build on. His daddy ain't had nothing to give him. The only thing my daddy had to give me was that piano. And he died over giving me that. I ain't gonna let it sit up there and rot without trying to do something with it. If Berniece can't see that, then I'm gonna go ahead and sell my half. And you and Wining Boy know I'm right.

DOAKER: Ain't nobody said nothing about who's right and who's wrong. I was just telling the man about the piano. I was telling him why we say Berniece ain't gonna sell it.

Lymon understands now and thinks Boy Willie ought to stay up North with him, but Boy Willie doesn't see why he should be up here trying to learn something else when farming is what he already knows.

Wining Boy goes to the piano, and Doaker encourages him to play. He sits and begins to play and sing. *"The song is one which has put many dimes and quarters in his pocket, long ago, in dimly remembered towns and way stations. He plays badly, without hesitation, and sings in a forceful voice."* His song is about a rambling, gambling traveling man and some bad jobs and times in the state of Arkansas, and as he's finishing it, Berniece comes in with Maretha. Berniece immediately assumes Wining Boy and Boy Willie had planned this out, but Wining Boy didn't know Boy Willie was going to be here. He'd just come by to see her and Doaker on his way down home.

Berniece didn't see the truck and is annoyed that Boy Willie isn't out selling melons. She's going to go change her clothes and then cook something for Wining Boy, something she hadn't offered to do for Boy Willie when he'd arrived.

When Berniece and Maretha have gone upstairs, Boy Willie wants Lymon to help him see if they can move the piano. As they try to move it and can move it only enough so that it's out of place a bit, there is the sound of Sutter's ghost again, but at first only Doaker hears it. Then there is the sound again, and everyone hears it, as Berniece comes on again, furious at their having moved the piano and threatening Boy Willie that he's going to play around with her once too often. She's not selling. He's trying to get some land, Boy Willie pleads with her: "Land the only thing God ain't making no more of."

She can get another piano. But "Money can't buy what that piano cost," she argues.

BOY WILLIE: . . . . . All right now if you say to me, Boy Willie, I'm using that piano, I give out lessons on it, and that help me make my rent or whatever. Then that be something else. I'd have to go and say, well, Berniece using that piano. She building on it. Let her go on and use it. I got to find another way to get Sutter's land. But Doaker say you ain't touched that piano the whole time it's been up here. So why you wanna stand in my way? See, you just looking at the sentimental value. See, that's good. That's all right. I take my hat off whenever somebody say my daddy's name. But I ain't gonna be no fool about no sentimental value. You can sit up here and look at the piano for the next hundred years, and it's just gonna be a piano. You can't make more than that. Now, I want to get Sutter's land with that piano . . . . . Cause that land give back to you. I can make me another crop and cash that in. I still got the land and the seed. But that piano don't put out nothing else. You ain't got nothing working for you. Now, the kind of man my daddy was he would have understood that. I'm sorry you can't see it that way. But that's why I'm gonna take that piano out of here and sell it.

BERNIECE: You ain't taking that piano out of my house.

*She crosses to the piano.*

Look at this piano. Look at it. Mama Ola polished this piano with her tears for seventeen years. For seventeen years she rubbed on it till her hands bled. Then she rubbed the blood in . . . mixed it up with the rest of the blood on it. Every day that God breathed life into her body she rubbed and cleaned and polished and prayed over it. "Play something for me, Berniece. Play something for me, Berniece." Every day. "I cleaned it up for you, play something for me, Berniece." You always talking about your daddy but you ain't never stopped to look at what his foolishness cost your mama. Seventeen years worth of cold nights and an empty bed. For what? For a piano? For a piece of wood? To get even with somebody. I look at you, and you're all the same. You, Papa Boy Charles, Wining Boy, Doaker, Crawley, . . . you're all alike. All this thieving and killing. And thieving and killing. And what it ever lead to? More killing and more thieving. I ain't never seen it come to nothing. People getting burned up. People getting shot. People falling down their wells. It don't never stop.

Boy Willie admits to a little stealing, not to killing anybody, but Berniece believes he killed Crawley as surely as if he'd pulled the trigger. Boy Willie swears Crawley knew what he was doing, and it was Crawley's getting his gun that was the cause of the trouble, not their offering to cut him in on making a little money on the wood they'd set aside. It was Crawley's own fault, he assures her. But all Berniece knows is that Crawley's dead and Boy Willie isn't. Crawley went off with them and never came back. Increasingly upset, she keeps on hitting Boy Willie. He doesn't try to defend himself. Doaker is still trying to stop her when they hear a terrified scream from upstairs and then Maretha is calling for her mother. *Curtain.*

## ACT II

*Scene 1*

> *The lights come up on the kitchen. It is the following morning. Doaker is ironing the pants to his uniform. He has a pot cooking on the stove at the same time. He is singing a song. The song provides him with the rhythm for his work, and he moves about the kitchen with the ease born of many years as a railroad cook.*

DOAKER (*sings*):
Gonna leave Jackson Mississippi
and go to Memphis
and double back to Jackson
Come on down to Hattiesburg
Change cars on the Y.D.
coming through the territory to
Meridian
and Meridian to Greenville
and Greenville to Memphis
I'm on my way and I know where

Change cars on the Katy
Leaving Jackson
and going through Clarksdale
Hello Winona!
Courtland!
Bateville!
Como!
Senitobia!
Lewisberg!
Sunflower!
Glendora!
Sharkey!
And double back to Jackson
Hello Greenwood
I'm on my way to Memphis
Clarksdale

Moorhead
Indianola
Can a highball pass through?
Highball on through sir
Grand Carson!
Thirty-First Street Depot
Fourth Street Depot
Memphis!

Wining Boy comes on carrying a silk suit. It is a bilious green. He's disgusted with the man at the pawnshop who claimed it was old and would only offer him three dollars for it. In Wining Boy's estimation, a silk suit can't get too old and ought to be worth five dollars anywhere. Berniece isn't there, Doaker tells Wining Boy, nor are Boy Willie and Lymon.

Doaker mentions that Maretha, who saw the ghost the night before, is frightened of sleeping upstairs. He admits that he hasn't told Berniece that he'd seen Sutter's ghost himself around three weeks before, shortly after Sutter died. Sutter had been sitting at the piano with his hand on his head. Doaker thinks he must have broken his neck. But the ghost hadn't said anything, hadn't called out Boy Willie's name, like Berniece had said he did when she saw him. Doaker doesn't think Boy Willie pushed Sutter in the well; he thinks Sutter's here because of the piano. In fact, Doaker's heard him playing it. He'd supposed it was Berniece, but it was not her type of music. He couldn't see anybody, but the keys were moving "a mile a minute." He believes the piano should be gotten rid of, it only causes trouble, but Wining Boy agrees with Berniece. He reasons that Boy Charles didn't plan on giving it back and felt he had a right to it, more than Sutter. Anyway, Sutter's dead and doesn't care.

Wining Boy wants to know when Berniece will be back because he missed seeing her in the morning. He was still asleep when Berniece left, Doaker explains, "She out there in Squirrel Hill cleaning house for some bigshot down there at the steel mill. They don't like you to come late. You come late they won't give you your carfare." He suspects Wining Boy is going to ask her for money and tells him she doesn't have any. Wining Boy asks Doaker for five dollars. Doaker gives in, but not to Wining Boy's fast follow-up request to make it seven instead.

Boy Willie and Lymon come in, jubilant, eager to count the earnings they've got in their pockets.

BOY WILLIE: They was lining up for them.
LYMON: Me and Boy Willie couldn't sell them fast enough. Time we got one sold we'd sell another.

Lou Myers as Wining Boy, Rocky Carroll as Lymon, Charles S. Dutton as
Boy Willie and Carl Gordon as Doaker in a scene from *The Piano Lesson*

BOY WILLIE: I seen what was happening and told Lymon to up the price on
them.

LYMON: Boy Willie say charge them a quarter more. They didn't care. A
couple of people give me a dollar and told me to keep the change.

BOY WILLIE: One fellow bought five. I say now what he gonna do with five
watermelons? He can't eat them all. I sold him they five and asked him did he
want to buy five more.

LYMON: I ain't never seen nobody snatch a dollar fast as Boy Willie.

BOY WILLIE: One lady asked me say, "Is they sweet?" I told her say,
"Lady where we grow these watermelons we put sugar in the ground." You
know, she believed me. Talking about she had never heard of that before.
Lymon was laughing his head off. I told her, "Oh, yeah, we put the sugar right
in the ground with the seed." She say, "Well, give me another one." Them
white folks is something else . . . ain't they Lymon?

LYMON: Soon as you holler watermelons they come right out their door.
Then they go and get their neighbors. Look like they having a contest to see
who can buy the most.

While they're counting their money, Wining Boy seizes the opportunity to
do a little business himself and brings his silk suit out for Lymon to try on.

Lymon puts on the jacket and is duly impressed. Clothes like that only come from New York and Chicago, Wining Boy assures him, and it's what big shots wear. It's a $55 suit, but he'll let Lymon buy it for three dollars. He sells him a shirt for another dollar and, for good measure, some "pointy toe" shoes, insisting they're size nine, Lymon's size. Lymon isn't too sure about the size when he tries them on, but Wining Boy says they are.

Boy Willie wonders if they've sold enough melons to have room in the truck yet for the piano. Lymon thinks so, and Boy Willie plans to call the man about the piano the next day.

Lymon's eager to go out on the town with Boy Willie, and he goes upstairs to get ready. Boy Willie is going to wear what he has on. Lymon would like to see a picture show, if they have one in Pittsburgh, and wants to find some women. While Lymon is dressing, Wining Boy tells a story about bribing the sheriff to keep Lymon's father out of jail after a tussle with a white man. Doaker, coming out of his room remembers that Lymon's father was an unlucky fellow. When Lymon comes out dressed in his new clothes Wining Boy suggests they play cards, but Boy Willie isn't going to fall for that. Wining Boy, even so, is pleased with Lymon's appearance.

WINING BOY (*to Lymon*): You got a magic suit there. You can get you a woman easy with that suit . . . but you got to know the magic words. You know the magic words to get you a woman?

LYMON: I just talk to them to see if I like them and they like me.

WINING BOY: You just walk right up to them and say "If you got the harbor I got the ship." If that don't work, ask them if you can put them in your pocket. The first thing they gonna say is "It's too small." That's when you look them dead in the eye and say, "Baby, ain't nothing small about me." If that don't work, then you move on to another one. Am I telling him right, Doaker?

DOAKER: That man don't need you to tell him nothing about no women. These women these days ain't gonna fall for that kind of stuff. You got to buy them a present. That's what they looking for these days.

BOY WILLIE: Come on, I'm ready. You ready, Lymon? Come on, let's go find some women.

WINING BOY: Here, let me walk out with you. I wanna see the women fall out their window when they see Lymon.

*They all exit and the lights go down on the scene.*

## Scene 2

Late that evening Berniece has put a tub in the kitchen and water is heating on the stove for her bath, when Avery comes by to tell her he's rented a place for $30 a month for his church. The congregation would be better if the preacher was married, he points out, but Berniece isn't interested in being courted at the moment. She isn't ready to marry, she insists.

AVERY: You too young a woman to close up, Berniece.

BERNIECE: I ain't said nothing about closing up. I got a lot of woman left in me.

AVERY: Where's it at? When's the last time you looked at it?

BERNIECE (*stunned by his remark*): That's a nasty thing to say. And you call yourself a preacher.

AVERY: Any time I get anywhere near you . . . you push me away.

BERNIECE: I got enough on my hands with Maretha. I got enough people to love and take care of.

AVERY: Who you got to love you? Can't nobody get close enough to you. Doaker can't half say nothing to you. You jump all over Boy Willie. Who you got to love you, Berniece?

BERNIECE: You trying to tell me a woman can't be nothing without a man. But you all right, huh? You can just walk out of here without me—without a woman—and still be a man. That's all right. Ain't nobody gonna ask you, "Avery, who you got to love you?" That's all right for you. But everybody gonna be worried about Berniece. "How Berniece gonna take care of herself? How she gonna raise that child without a man? Wonder what she do with herself. How she gonna live like that?" Everybody got all kinds of questions for Berniece. Everybody telling me I can't be a woman unless I got a man. Well, you tell me, Avery—you know—how much woman am I?

AVERY: It wasn't me, Berniece. You can't blame me for nobody else. I'll own up to my own shortcomings. But you can't blame me for Crawley or nobody else.

BERNIECE: I ain't blaming nobody for nothing. I'm just stating the facts.

The facts as far as Avery's concerned are that Berniece has got to let go—Crawley's been dead for three years—and life goes on. She's just drifting, and Avery isn't sure how long he'll be waiting for her. Berniece reminds him she'd agreed to talk about it when his church is all set up. For now, she has to deal with Boy Willie and the piano and the ghost.

Maretha's seen the ghost too and is frightened of sleeping upstairs, but Berniece has the idea that if Avery were to bless the house the ghost would disappear. He's dubious about getting into a thing like that. It might take "a special kind of preacher."

Berniece admits she'd been telling herself that when Boy Willie goes, so will the ghost, because she's convinced Boy Willie pushed Sutter in the well. Avery reminds her the Ghosts of the Yellow Dog have been pushing people in wells since before Boy Willie was even grown up. It's somebody, not just

wind, Berniece insists. But Avery's not sure, because God is the Great
Causer. A minister had even preached about the Ghosts of the Yellow Dog as
the hand of God, he recalls, but Berniece isn't buying it. She thinks Boy Willie
pushed Sutter to get that land.

As for talking to Boy Willie about anything, nobody can. Even Mama Ola
had trouble talking to him. He doesn't listen to anybody, any more than her
father did. Avery suggests that if Berniece were to put the piano in the church
and start a choir, Boy Willie might see the situation differently.

BERNIECE: . . . . . Ain't no need in you to keep talking this choir stuff. When
my mama died I shut the top on that piano, and I ain't never opened it since. I
was only playing it for her. When my daddy died, seem like all her life went
into that piano. She used to have me playing on it . . . had Miss Eula come in
and teach me . . . say when I played it she could hear my daddy talking to her.
I used to think them pictures came alive and walk through the house.
Sometimes late at night I could hear my mama talking to them. I said that
wasn't gonna happen to me. I don't play that piano cause I don't want to
wake them spirits. They never be walking around in this house.

AVERY: You got to put all that behind you, Berniece.

BERNIECE: I got Maretha playing on it. She don't know nothing about it.
Let her go on and be a school teacher or something. She don't have to carry
all of that with her. She got a chance I didn't have. I ain't gonna burden her
with that piano.

AVERY: . . . . . That's the same thing like Crawley. Everybody got stones in
their passway. You got to step over them or walk around them. You picking
them up and carrying them with you. All you got to do is set them down by the
side of the road. You ain't got to carry them with you. You can walk over
there right now and play that piano. You can walk over there right now, and
God will walk over there with you. Right now you can set that sack of stones
down by the side of the road and walk away from it. You don't have to carry it
with you. You can do it right now. (*Avery crosses over to the piano and
raises the lid.*) Come on, Berniece . . . set it down and walk away from it.
Come on, play "Old Ship of Zion." Walk over here and claim it as an
instrument of the Lord. You can walk over here right now and make it into a
celebration.

*Berniece moves toward the piano.*

BERNIECE: Avery . . . I done told you I don't want to play that piano. Now
or no other time.

With God's strength she can do anything, Avery exhorts, but all Berniece
would like to do is take her bath. Avery agrees to leave and return the next
day to bless the house, if the Lord gives him the strength.

*Scene 3*

Much later that night, after Berniece has retired, Boy Willie comes into the dark house with Grace, an attractive and affable young woman. It's his sister's house, he tells her, saying Berniece won't mind. Grace wants him to turn the light on, but he won't, and he tells her they're going to sleep on the couch. If Lymon comes back he'll have to sleep on the floor.

Grace is a bit put out about the couch, she had a bed in mind. Boy Willie claims she doesn't need one, and he brags about his grandfather who took women on the backs of horses. Grace is surprised at just how "country" he is, but Boy Willie says he can show her what a country boy can do.

She suggests they go back to her place where there's a bed. There's a slight catch to that, though, she confesses. Leroy, once her man, still has a key. Boy Willie isn't anxious to risk that and sets about persuading her to stay. In the course of their amorous tussling, a lamp is knocked over, and Berniece is awakened. She calls down, and Boy Willie assures her everything is all right, but she comes downstairs in her white nightgown and turns on the light. It was only the lamp that fell, Boy Willie explains, but that isn't what Berniece is so upset about. She insists he has to take his company somewhere else. She won't allow "that kind of stuff" in her house, there's an 11-year-old girl upstairs. Boy Willie is hurt and embarrassed in front of Grace, even though Berniece does say to Grace that she's sorry. Grace seems unflappable. They'll go to her place. She doesn't want to stay where she isn't wanted, and they leave.

Berniece goes to the kitchen and has put the tea kettle on the stove, when Lymon knocks on the door. She lets him in. He's just missed Boy Willie, she tells him. He'd been here with a woman and she'd sent them away. Lymon wonders if she was "about this high" and "with nice hips on her." She was wearing a red dress, Berniece states. That's the woman Lymon thought it was, and he'd liked her. He'd wanted to wait a little before he went to speak to her, but by the time he got around to it, Boy Willie had already begun talking to her. "She was talking to him, kept looking at me," Lymon relates. Then her friend Dolly came in, and Lymon asked Dolly to go to the picture show. She wanted to think about it over a drink, and after a few drinks he'd finally left and come back to see if Boy Willie was here.

Berniece claims Lymon doesn't need to be in those saloons. "You start out that fast life, you can't keep it up." And you can't tell what you're going to run into, she warns him, what with knives and guns.

BERNIECE: ..... I don't know what them women out there be thinking about.

LYMON: Mostly they be lonely and looking for somebody to spend the night with them. Sometimes it matters who it is, and sometimes it don't. I used to be the same way. Now it got to matter. That's why I'm here now. Dolly liable not to even recognize me if she sees me again. I don't like women like that. I like my women to be with me in a nice and easy way. That way we can both enjoy ourselves. The way I see it, we the only two people like us in the world. We got to see how we fit together. A woman that don't want to take the time to do that I don't bother with. Used to. Used to bother with all of them. Then I woked up one time with this woman, and I didn't know who she was. She was the prettiest woman I had ever seen in my life. I spent the whole night with her and didn't even know it. I had never taken the time to look at her. I guess she kinda knew I ain't never really looked at her. She must have known that cause she ain't wanted to see me no more. If she had wanted to see me I believe we might have got married. How come you ain't married? It seem like to me you would be married? I remember Avery from down home. I used to call him plain old Avery. Now he Reverend Avery. That's kinda funny about him becoming a preacher. I like when he told about how that come to him in a dream about them sheep people and them hobos. Nothing ever come to me in a dream like that. I just dream about women. Can't never seem to find the right one.

BERNIECE: She out there somewhere. You just got to get yourself ready to meet her. That's what I'm trying to do. Avery's alright. I ain't really got nobody in mind.

LYMON: I get me a job and a little place and get set up to where I can make a woman comfortable I might get married. Avery's nice. You ought to go ahead and get married. You be a preacher's wife you won't have to work. I hate living by myself. I didn't want to be no strain on my mama, so I left home when I was about sixteen. Everything I tried seem like it just didn't work out. Now I'm trying this.

BERNIECE: You keep trying it'll work out for you.

Lymon wonders if Berniece ever goes to the picture show (she doesn't). Mostly she's at home, caring for Maretha. His feet hurt, and he takes off his shoes and apologizes for keeping her up. She assures him she couldn't sleep after Boy Willie had awakened her.

LYMON: You got on that nightgown. I likes women when they wear them fancy night clothes and all. It makes their skin look real pretty.

BERNIECE: I got this at the five and ten cents store. It ain't so fancy.

LYMON: I don't too often get to see a woman dressed like that.

*There is a long pause. Lymon takes off his suit coat.*
Well, I'm gonna sleep here on the couch. I'm supposed to sleep on the floor but I don't reckon Boy Willie's coming back tonight. Wining Boy sold me this

suit. Told me it was a magic suit. I'm gonna put it on again tomorrow. Maybe it bring me a woman like he say.

> *He goes into his coat pocket and takes out a small bottle of perfume.*

I almost forgot I had this. Some man sold me this for a dollar. Say it come from Paris. This is the same kind of perfume the Queen of France wear. That's what he told me. I don't know if it's true or not. I smelled it. It smelled good to me. Here . . . smell it see if you like it. I was gonna give it to Dolly. But I didn't like her too much.

BERNIECE (*takes the bottle*): It smells nice.

LYMON: I was going to give it to Dolly if she had went to the picture with me. Go on, you take it.

BERNIECE: I can't take it. Here . . . go on, you keep it. You'll find somebody to give it to.

LYMON: I wanna give it to you. Make you smell nice.

> *He takes the bottle and puts perfume behind Berniece's ear.*

They tell me you supposed to put it right here behind your ear. Say if you put it there you smell nice all day.

> *Berniece stiffens at his touch. Lymon bends down to smell her.*

There . . . you smell real good now.

> *He kisses her neck.*

You smell real good for Lymon.

> *He kisses her again. Berniece returns the kiss, then breaks the embrace and crosses to the stairs. She turns and they look silently at each other. Berniece exits up the stairs. Lymon picks up his suit coat and strokes it lovingly with the full knowledge that it is indeed a magic suit. The lights go down on the scene.*

## Scene 4

Late the following morning, Lymon is still asleep on the sofa when Boy Willie comes in the front door. He tries to wake Lymon, finally dumping him off the sofa onto the floor. Lymon is annoyed that Boy Willie left him the night before. Boy Willie explains he came back here with Grace and was looking for Lymon later on, assuming Lymon was with Dolly. Boy Willie had been at Grace's house—until her old boy friend tried to get in.

Lymon mentions that Wining Boy saw the ghost last night. Boy Willie is surprised Wining Boy even found the house, but his mind is really on the piano. Boy Willie wants to get the piano on the truck to take it to the buyer before Berniece returns. He and Lymon each take an end. *"The sound of Sutter's ghost is heard. They do not hear it."* They each have a good grip on the piano, but now it won't even budge. Lymon doesn't think they can manage it, but Boy Willie's determined they can—they've carried cotton sacks. It seems as if it's stuck. They are still trying to move it, to no avail, when Doaker comes on from his room and tells them they're to leave it until Berniece comes home. "This is my business," Boy Willie claims, but Doaker says it's his house and Boy Willie isn't going to take anything out of it without permission. Boy Willie argues that the piano is his. Doaker says it's partly Berniece's, and they'll have to wait. They can cut it in two, but he won't let them take Berniece's half. Boy Willie and Lymon go off to get rope and a plank and wheels, telling Doaker they'll be back.

*Scene 5*

> *The lights come up. Boy Willie sits on the piano stool screwing casters on a wooden plank. Maretha is lying on the floor with a book. Doaker is cooking.*

BOY WILLIE (*to Maretha*): Then after that, them white folks down around there started falling down their wells. You ever seen a well? A well got a wall around it. It's hard to fall down a well. You got to be leaning way over. Couldn't nobody figure out too much what was making these fellows fall down their well . . . so everybody says the Ghosts of the Yellow Dog must have pushed them. That's what everybody called them four men what got burned up in the boxcar.

MARETHA: Why they call them that?

BOY WILLIE: Cause the Yazoo Delta railroad got yellow boxcars. Sometime the way the whistle blow sound like an old dog howling so the people call it the Yellow Dog.

MARETHA: Anybody ever see the Ghosts?

BOY WILLIE: I told you they like the wind. Can you see the wind?

MARETHA: No.

BOY WILLIE: They like the wind you can't see them. But sometimes you be in trouble they might be around to help you. They say if you go where the Southern cross the Yellow Dog . . . you go to where them two railroads cross each other . . . and call out their names . . . they say they talk back to you. I don't know, I ain't never done that. But Uncle Wining Boy he say he been down there and talked to them. You have to ask him about that part.

Berniece comes in the front door and wants Maretha to get ready for her to do her hair. Maretha is frightened of going upstairs, so Boy Willie accompanies her. Boy Willie and Lymon are trying to move the piano out of the house, Doaker explains to Berniece—Boy Willie got the board and wheels and Lymon's gone to get rope.

Berniece reminds him she has Crawley's gun upstairs. When Boy Willie comes back with Maretha, Berniece sends Maretha off to buy more hair grease and again tells Boy Willie to leave her house. He claims to be in Doaker's house, and Doaker'll have to ask him to leave. Doaker doesn't. Boy Willie *"draws a line across the floor with his foot,"* says she could consider him gone from her portion of the house and again claims he's going to take the piano.

Berniece threatens him, but Boy Willie isn't afraid of dying. He'd prayed so hard once when he had a puppy that died and nothing happened that he'd gone out and killed a cat and "discovered the power of death." His theory is that a white man isn't able to hold the power over "a nigger that isn't afraid to die."

The conversation continues as Maretha returns and sits on a kitchen chair near the stove for Berniece to do her hair with the hot comb. Boy Willie, on learning that Avery is coming to bless the house in the hope of getting rid of Sutter's ghost, claims Berniece and Avery "go at the Bible halfway" if they don't believe in "an eye for an eye." Maretha gives out a howl as Berniece continues her ministrations and comments, "If you was a boy I wouldn't be going through this." Boy Willie thinks she shouldn't talk that way: "How's that gonna make her feel?" If Berniece has to tell Maretha something, she should tell her all about the piano. And they ought to celebrate the date Papa Boy Charles got it. Then Maretha could hold her head up high and "know where she was at in the world."

When Boy Willie has a child of his own he can teach it what he wants, Berniece snaps. If he was rich he'd make a child every day, he says, but he doesn't have any advantages to offer anybody. He recalls seeing his daddy looking at his big capable hands and later realized what he'd been thinking about. Those hands were all he had, and the best he could do was make a 50-acre crop for Mr. Stovall. But if he'd had his own land he'd have felt differently. "If you teach that girl that she living at the bottom of life, she gonna grow up and hate you," he lectures Berniece.

Boy Willie claims he's living "at the top of life." Berniece denies this. Boy Willie doesn't think Crawley or Papa Boy Charles or Mama Ola lived at the bottom of life, either, but "if you act that way then that's where you gonna be." Doaker doesn't think about top or bottom. Boy Willie believes Berniece might have gotten this idea from Avery, who seems to be under the impression that getting a Thanksgiving turkey from a white man is going to get him out of the bottom of life. Boy Willie can get his own turkey.

BOY WILLIE: See now . . . I'll tell you something about me. I done strung along and strung along. Going this way and that. Whatever way would lead me to a moment of peace. That's all I want. To be as easy with everything.

But I wasn't born to that. I was born to a time of fire. The world ain't wanted no part of me. I could see that since I was about seven. The world say it's better off without me. See, Berniece accept that. She trying to come up to where she can prove something to the world. I look around and say you all got to come up a little ways to be where I am. That's the way I see it. Hell, the world a better place cause of me. I don't see it like Berniece. I got a heart that beats here and it beats just as loud as the next fellow's. Don't care if he black or white. Sometime it beats louder. When it beat louder then everybody can hear it. Some people get scared of that. Like Berniece. Some people get scared to hear a nigger's heart beating. They think you ought to lay low with that heart. Make it beat quiet and go along with everything the way it is. But my mama ain't birthed me for nothing. So what I got to do? I got to mark my passing on the road. Just like you write on a tree, "Boy Willie was here." That's all I'm trying to do with that piano. Trying to put my mark on the road. Like my daddy done. My heart say for me to sell that piano and get me some land so I can make a life for myself to live in my own way. Other than that, I ain't thinking about nothing Berniece got to say.

When Avery arrives with his Bible, Boy Willie starts in on him about trying to get into heaven with half of it. Doaker tells Avery to pay no attention to Berniece's and Boy Willie's ongoing arguing. Avery is hopeful of getting the loan, his congregation is increasing and Berniece is going to be the Deaconess, he informs Doaker, who hopes, along with Avery, that then the two of them will get married. Berniece is only thinking about it, she reminds him.

Avery found a portion in the Bible that he feels will make the ghost, if he's here, go away. Boy Willie's still sure it's all Berniece's imagination and doesn't think Avery has the power to do anything. Avery agrees, but he's sure that God has the power.

Lymon finally returns with the rope. He'd met Grace, and they'd had a drink, and she's going to the picture show with him. Boy Willie isn't interested in that; he's interested in getting the rope around the piano. Doaker tells him not to do it, but he and Lymon pay no attention. Berniece goes upstairs and returns. *"She has her hand in her pocket where she has Crawley's gun."* Avery wishes they'd sit down and talk about all this, but both Berniece and Boy Willie are through talking.

Avery and Doaker again try to intervene to get them to respect each other's wishes. Berniece's only wish is that Boy Willie would leave, and she warns them he will be leaving "one way or another." He's not scared of a gun, Boy Willie claims, but Lymon is convinced Berniece will shoot him. She'll have to, Boy Willie shrugs.

Berniece has told Doaker to put Maretha in his room, and Boy Willie and Lymon are trying to lift the piano when Wining Boy comes in, obviously having been drinking. He tries to interrupt Boy Willie's and Lymon's efforts by asking Boy Willie for the pint he knows he must have in his coat. Then he asks Doaker for a drink. They all try to convince him he's had enough to drink. Wining Boy's not trying to be disrespectful, he assures Berniece, he's trying to be nice: "I been with strangers all day and they treated me like family. I come in here to family and you treat me like a stranger." He doesn't need their whiskey. He can buy his own. He only wanted their company. And he doesn't want to lie down or sit down. He wants to party with Boy Willie, and he insists on sitting down at the piano and singing and playing a song he wrote. When he finishes the song they try to get him to get up, but he puts his arms out over the piano, saying they'll have to take him with it.

Berniece is trying to get Wining Boy away from the piano, too, when there's a knock at the door. It's Grace. She's been sitting in the truck waiting for Lymon, but she's not about to sit there much longer. She's surprised to see Boy Willie, because Lymon had told her he'd gone already. Berniece insists Lymon take his company some other place. *"Everybody but Grace suddenly senses Sutter's presence,"* and then she senses something as well: "Something ain't right here. I knew I shouldn't have come back up in this house." She goes off, and Lymon rushes after her, saying he'll take her home. Not until they've taken the piano out, Boy Willie orders, but Lymon says he'll return. *"Again the presence of Sutter is felt."*

Berniece urges Avery to begin blessing the house. It's the piano that needs blessing, Doaker argues, because it's caused the trouble. "Let him bless everything . . . . . Go on and bless it all," Wining Boy urges. Avery opts for blessing the piano. He has a small bottle with him that he asks Berniece to fill with water. He also has a candle in his pocket which he takes out and lights and gives to Berniece to hold and he begins praying.

"All this old preaching stuff. Hell, just tell him to leave," Boy Willie bursts out. Then, as Avery continues reading from the Bible, Boy Willie takes a pot of water that was on the stove and flings it all around the room in a frenzy calling Sutter's name, telling him "Get your ass out of this house!" He is a whirling dervish shouting and flinging water and is still calling to Sutter to come and get some water as he starts toward the stairs.

> *The sound of Sutter's ghost is heard. As Boy Willie approaches the steps, he is suddenly thrown back by the unseen force which is choking him. As he struggles, he frees himself, then dashes up the stairs.*

BOY WILLIE: Come on, Sutter!

AVERY: I will sprinkle clean water upon you and ye shall be clean; from all your uncleanliness, and from all your idols, will I cleanse you. A new heart also will I give you, and a new spirit will I put within you: and I will take out of your flesh the heart of stone, and I will give you a heart of flesh. And I will put my spirit within you, and cause you to walk in my statutes, and ye shall keep my judgements, and do them.

> *There are loud sounds heard from upstairs, as Boy Willie begins to wrestle with Sutter's ghost. It is a life-and-death struggle fraught with perils and . . . . . terror. Boy Willie is thrown down the stairs. Avery is stunned into silence. Boy Willie picks himself up and dashes back upstairs.*

Berniece, I can't do it.

> *There are more sounds heard from upstairs. Doaker and Wining Boy stare at one another in stunned disbelief. It is in this moment, from somewhere old, that Berniece realizes what she must do. She crosses to the piano. She begins to play. The song is found piece by piece. It is an old urge to song that is both a commandment and a plea. With each repetition it gains in strength. It is intended as an exorcism and a dressing for battle. A rustle of wind blowing across two continents.*

BERNIECE (*sings*):
I want you to help me
I want you to help me
I want you to help me
I want you to help me
I want you to help me
I want you to help me
Mama Berniece
I want you to help me
Mama Ester
I want you to help me
Papa Boy Charles
I want you to help me
Mama Ola
I want you to help me

> *Doaker and Wining Boy join in, calling the names of the people on the piano.*

I want you to help me
I want you to help me . . . . .

> *The sound of a train approaching is heard. It roars into the house and stops. The noise upstairs subsides.*

BOY WILLIE: Come on, Sutter!  Come back, Sutter!

> *Berniece, still playing the piano, begins to chant a simple thank you. She is joined by Doaker, Avery and Wining Boy.*

BERNIECE: Thank you. Thank you. Thank you.

> *A calm comes over the house. Boy Willie enters on the stairs. He pauses a moment to watch Berniece play the piano.*

As she continues the simple litany of thank you's, he goes to the piano, takes his dolly and goes into the kitchen. He asks Wining Boy if he's ready to go home. He asks Doaker what time the train leaves. Doaker says they've got time to catch it. Then he calls to Berniece, warning her that if she and Maretha don't both keep on playing the piano he and Sutter are both liable to return. *Curtain.*

# ONCE ON THIS ISLAND

*A Full-Length Musical in One Act*

BOOK AND LYRICS BY LYNN AHRENS

MUSIC BY STEPHEN FLAHERTY

BASED ON A NOVEL BY ROSA GUY

Cast and credits appear on pages 413, 415

*LYNN AHRENS (book and lyrics) was born in New York City in 1948. Her father was then and still is a professional photographer and has a school of photography in New Jersey. Ahrens was educated in New York schools, a Neptune, N.J. high school and Newhouse School of Syracuse University, where she majored in journalism and graduated with a B.A. in 1970. As long as she can remember, she's been writing songs (music as well as lyrics) and has always loved the theater but didn't approach it professionally until after the decade of the 1970s, when she was occupied in many other writing fields including children's TV and TV commercials. Four of the programs she has created and produced were nominated for Emmys (one of them, ABC-TV's H.E.L.P., won), and her songs have been heard often on* Schoolhouse Rock.

*In 1983, Ahrens met her* Once on This Island *collaborator, Stephen Flaherty, at the BMI Workshop, and by the following year they were working on a couple of shows—*Bedazzled *and* Antler*—that never got as far as production. But their Rodgers Award-winning musical* Lucky Stiff *did, beginning* *with a staged reading in November 1987, going into full production at Playwrights Horizons April 25, 1988 for 15 performances and taking its place on the national stage, receiving six Helen Hayes Award nominations for a 1990 production in Olney, Md.*

*Once on This Island is Ahren's second full production and first Best Play, with a planned move to Broadway in October. Ahrens has been the recipient of grants from the National Institute of Music Theater and the National Endowment for the Arts and is a member of the Dramatists Guild. She is married and lives in Manhattan.*

*STEPHEN FLAHERTY (music) was born Sept. 18, 1960 in Pittsburgh, where his father was a draftsman and his mother was a teacher in the University of Pittsburgh's nursing school. He was educated in the city's Catholic school system and, having focused his life on music at an early age after learning to play the piano, went on to the Cincinnati College-Conservatory of Music, from which he graduated in 1982 with a bachelor's degree in music composition.*

*While at college, Flaherty wrote three student shows (one of which,* The Carnival of Life, *went on to other amateur productions in the Midwest), and in 1983 he joined the BMI Workshop and began the collaboration with Lynn Ahrens which eventually won the 1988 Richard Rodgers Production Award for the musical* Lucky Stiff, *which was then produced. Flaherty places a special value on the workshop system, particularly in the development of* Once on This Island *in Playwrights Horizons workshop in October and November 1989 prior to its production and Best Play citation on May 6 for 24 performances leading to its scheduled move to Broadway in October 1990. He calls it "the ideal way to develop a show slowly," the authors working together with the director and choreographer, Graciela Daniele, and the designers.*

*Flaherty toured Eastern Europe in 1987 as a representative of the American musical theater, under the sponsorship of the International Theater Institute, exchanging views and ideas with other theater artists. Like his collaborator, he has received grants from NEA and NIMT and is a member of the Dramatists Guild. Flaherty lives in Manhattan.*

*Our method of synopsizing* Once on This Island *in these pages differs from that of other Best Plays. In order to illustrate the distinctive "look" of its characters, setting and choreography, the musical is represented here mostly in photographs, with excerpts from its all-sung text to portray its verbal style and flavor. These photographs of* Once on This Island *depict scenes as produced off Broadway May 6, 1990 by and at Playwrights Horizons (Andre Bishop artistic director, Paul S. Daniels executive director) in association with AT&T: OnStage, as directed and choreographed by Graciela*

*Daniele, with scenery by Loy Arcenas, costumes by Judy Dearing and lighting by Allen Lee Hughes.*

*Our special thanks are tendered to the producer and his press representative, Phil Rinaldi, and to Martha Swope Photography, Inc. for making available these excellent photographs of the show by Martha Swope.*

1. On an island in the French Antilles, the peasants are "black as night, eternally at the mercy of the wind and sea. . . . . 'We Dance,'" they sing, "to the music of the gods." And they labor, while across the island "The grands hommes, with their pale brown skin and their French ways, owners of the land, dance to a different tune" and drink their champagne.

The gods have sent a storm which frightens a small peasant girl. To comfort her, grownups gather round to tell her a story (*above*): "Once on this island," in a hurricane, floods orphaned "One Small Girl" (they sing). But she was caught in a tree and found alive (*below*) by Tonton Julian (Ellis E. Williams) and Mama Euralie (Sheila Gibbs, *below left*).

2. The parents name their adopted daughter Ti Moune. One day Ti Moune, now a young woman (La Chanze, *left*), watches a grand homme drive past in his car and (in "Waiting for Life") prays to the gods that one day she will have a romantic adventure with just such a glamorous stranger.

3. "And the Gods Heard Her Prayer," the Storytellers sing. Gods and Goddesses (*below*) of Love (Andrea Frierson), Death (Eric Riley), Water (Milton Craig Nealy) and Earth (Kecia Lewis-Evans) grant Ti Moune's wish, starting a contest of love vs. death.

4. Agwe sings "Rain" (*above*) and sends it in abundance to wreck the grand homme's car. Ti Moune finds Daniel (Jerry Dixon, *opposite page, top*) and takes him home with her to nurse him (*right*), as Villagers "Pray" in rhythmic song.

5. Tonton Julian goes to find Daniel's people, the Beauxhommes. Ti Moune defies the Villagers' warning that she is cheating Papa Ge, God of Death, by keeping Daniel alive. To still unconscious Daniel she sings "Forever Yours":

> Sure as a wave
> Needs to be near the shore
> You are the one
> I was intended for
> Deep in your eyes
> I saw the gods' design
> Now my life is forever yours
> And you are mine.

When Papa Ge comes to claim Daniel, Ti Moune puts Death off by pledging her soul for Daniel's. Others recount in "The Sad Tale of the Beauxhommes" how this family was founded long ago by a Frenchman and his peasant love, whom he refused to marry. He cursed his progeny when blacks rebelled and drove him from the island.

6. At the Beauxhommes', Tonton Julian is severely abused but brings back help to carry Daniel home. Fearing that Daniel will die without her care, Ti Moune begs to follow him. The parents object in the song "Ti Moune": "Who knows how high those mountains climb/Who knows how deep those rivers flow/Who knows how wrong a dream can go/Ti Moune." But finally they bid her farewell and let her go (*above*). "Mama Will Provide," sings Asaka the Earth Goddess (*below*), for Ti Moune's needs on the journey. Storytellers sing "Some Say" that she conquered all obstacles. They agree that she got past the guards and made her way to Daniel's bedroom.

7.  Daniel takes Ti Moune for an intruder, until she identifies herself: "I was the one who found you crushed inside your car. I watched over you when you nearly died. I bathed you. . . . . I have seen the scar on your chest. Like a half moon. (*Touching him.*) Here." Daniel replies, "So it was you." Ti Moune sees that he is still quite ill—his leg won't heal—and she assures him, "The gods have sent me to make you well." "You're very young. . . . . and so pretty," Daniel decides, "Come here, then. What harm can it do. Stay the night and show me your powers. Make me forget this pain. Who knows. Perhaps the gods did send me a gift, after all." (*She begins to stroke his head. Gradually she cradles him in her arms. . . . . Ti Moune lies down beside Daniel, and little by little they gently touch and discover one another.*)

8.  Erzulie the Love Goddess (*center, above*) and Storytellers gather at the bedside to sing "The Human Heart": "The hopes that make us happy/The hopes that don't come true/And all the love there ever was/I see all this in you." But Gossipers, reprising "Pray," tell a different tale in one-liners like "Now what can he want with a woman like that/Blacker than coal and low as dirt/He could have the world but takes a peasant/Perhaps his brain was hurt!" And as Daniel slowly recovers under Ti Moune's ministrations and begins moving around, his father warns him, "You'll do what must be done/No matter what you feel" about his peasant love.

9. Ti Moune dreams, "And our little house will have pink walls and a blue roof, and a beautiful tree in the garden just like the one that sheltered me as a child. And you and I will lie in the shade of the tree. And our children will climb in it." Daniel sings "Some Girls":

Some girls
Take courses
At all the best schools in France
Riding their horses
And learning their modern dance
They're clever and cultured and
    worldly wise
But you see the world through a
    child's wide eyes
While their dreams are grand ones
You want what's just in reach
Some girls you learn from
Some you teach

You are not small talk
Or shiny cars
Or mirrors
Or French cologne

You are the river
The moon and the stars
You're no one else
I've known. . . . .

Some girls
Take pleasure
In buying a fine trousseau
Counting each treasure
And tying each tiny bow
They fold up their futures
With perfumed hands
While you face the future
With no demands
Some girls expect things
Others think nothing of
Some girls you marry
Some you love.

Daniel carries Ti Moune offstage. Meanwhile, Daniel's fiancee, Andrea Devereaux, has been dressing for a ball which is soon in progress. Daniel enters, takes Andrea (Nikki Rene, *top of opposite page*) in his arms for the waltz. When Ti Moune enters, Daniel goes to greet her and then introduces Andrea, who asks Ti Moune to dance for them.

10. Ti Moune dances so joyously (*below*), Andrea easily perceives she's in love with Daniel. Setting things straight, Andrea tells Ti Moune (in the song "The Ball") "Something I fear was left unsaid": that Andrea and Daniel are to be married. Daniel explains further, "Andrea and I have been promised to each other since we were children. . . . . This is how things are done, Ti Moune. It's expected. . . . . I thought you understood. We could never marry."

Ti Moune cries out in despair to the gods. But Storytellers remind her, "There can never be anything between a peasant and a grand homme. They despise us for our blackness. Marry you! You are mad!"

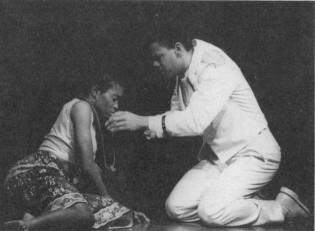

11. Papa Ge brandishes a knife at Ti Moune, then presses it upon her (*above*), demanding she redeem her promise to the gods and forfeit her life for Daniel's— or else "Prove that death is stronger than love" by killing the lover who betrayed her. She tries but cannot; she drops the knife and falls to the floor (*left*). Before casting her out of the Hotel Beauxhomme, Daniel asks her "Why? . . . Why?" Ti Moune replies, "I love you."

12. Outcast and scorned, Ti Moune waits helplessly by the gate while Daniel and Andrea are married. Mama sings that Ti Moune will always be "A Part of Us." Finally the gods take pity on the girl "Who proved that love could withstand the storm. . . . . and survive even in the face of death." The gods transform Ti Moune into a tree (*above*) whose roots "cracked the wall of the Hotel Beauxhomme" and sheltered Daniel and his children until one day Daniel's son found a peasant girl in its branches. "And the spirit of Ti Moune touched their hearts and set them free to love."

The Storytellers (*below*) explain "Why We Tell the Story" of Ti Moune: "Life is why . . . . . Pain . . . . . Love . . . . . Grief . . . . . Hope . . . . . Faith is why . . . . . It will help you feel the anger and the sorrow/And forgive/For out of what we live/And we believe/Our lives become/The stories that we weave." The stars come out, and the storm ends. *Curtain*.

PLAYS PRODUCED
IN NEW YORK

# PLAYS PRODUCED ON BROADWAY

Figures in parentheses following a play's title give number of performances. These figures are acquired directly from the production offices and do not include previews or extra non-profit performances. In the case of a transfer, the off-Broadway run is noted but not added to the figure in parentheses.

Plays marked with an asterisk (*) were still in a projected run on June 1, 1990. Their number of performances is figured through May 31, 1990.

In a listing of a show's numbers—dances, sketches, musical scenes, etc.— the titles of songs are identified wherever possible by their appearance in quotation marks (").

## HOLDOVERS FROM PREVIOUS SEASONS

Plays which were running on June 1, 1989 are listed below. More detailed information about them appears in previous *Best Plays* volumes of appropriate years. Important cast changes since opening night are recorded in the Cast Replacements section of this volume.

**A Chorus Line** (6,137; longest run in Broadway history). Transfer from off Broadway of the musical conceived by Michael Bennett; book by James Kirkwood and Nicholas Dante; music by Marvin Hamlisch; lyrics by Edward Kleban. Opened April 15, 1975 off Broadway where it played 101 performances through July 13, 1975; transferred to Broadway July 25, 1975. (Closed April 28, 1990)

**Oh! Calcutta!** (5,959; sometimes played 10 performances weekly, 2 more than regular Broadway productions, under a special "middle" contract). Revival of the musical devised by Kenneth Tynan; with contributions (in this version) by Jules Feiffer, Dan Greenberg, Lenore Kandel, John Lennon, Jacques Levy, Leonard Melfi, David Newman & Robert Benton, Sam Shepard, Clovis Trouille, Kenneth Tynan and Sherman Yellen; music and lyrics (in this version) by Robert Dennis, Peter Schickele and Stanley Walden; additional music by Stanley Walden and Jacques Levy. Opened September 24, 1976 in alternating performances with *Me and Bessie* through December 7, 1976, continuing alone thereafter. (Closed August 6, 1989)

***Cats** (3,193). Musical based on *Old Possum's Book of Practical Cats* by T. S. Eliot; music by Andrew Lloyd Webber; additional lyrics by Trevor Nunn and Richard Stilgoe. Opened October 7, 1982.

**Me and My Girl** (1,420). Revival of the musical with book and lyrics by L. Arthur Rose and Douglas Furber; music by Noel Gay; book revised by Stephen Fry; contributions to revisions by Mike Okrent. Opened August 10, 1986. (Closed December 31, 1989)

**\*Les Misérables** (1,285). Musical based on the novel by Victor Hugo; book by Alain Boublil and Claude-Michel Schönberg; music by Claude-Michel Schönberg; lyrics by Herbert Kretzmer; original French text by Alain Boublil and Jean-Marc Natel; additional material by James Fenton. Opened March 12, 1987.

**Anything Goes** (804). Revival of the musical with original book by Guy Bolton & P. G. Wodehouse and Howard Lindsay & Russel Crouse; new book by Timothy Crouse and John Weidman; music and lyrics by Cole Porter. Opened October 19, 1987. (Closed September 3, 1989)

**Into the Woods** (765). Musical with book by James Lapine; music and lyrics by Stephen Sondheim. Opened November 5, 1987. (Closed September 3, 1989)

**\*The Phantom of the Opera** (981). Musical adapted from the novel by Gaston Leroux; book by Richard Stilgoe and Andrew Lloyd Webber; music by Andrew Lloyd Webber; lyrics by Charles Hart; additional lyrics by Richard Stilgoe. Opened January 26, 1988.

**Sarafina!** (597). Transfer from off Broadway of the musical conceived and written by Mbongeni Ngema; music by Mbongeni Ngema and Hugh Masekela. Opened October 25, 1987 off Broadway where it played 81 performances through January 3, 1988; transferred to Broadway January 28, 1988. (Closed July 2, 1989)

**M. Butterfly** (777). By David Henry Hwang. Opened March 20, 1988. (Closed January 27, 1990)

**Rumors** (531). By Neil Simon. Opened November 17, 1988. (Closed February 24, 1990)

**\*Black and Blue** (564). Musical revue with musical numbers by various authors. Opened January 26, 1989.

**Born Yesterday** (153). Revival of the play by Garson Kanin. Opened January 29, 1989. (Closed June 11, 1989)

**Shirley Valentine** (324). One-character play by Willy Russell. Opened February 16, 1989. (Closed November 25, 1989)

**\*Jerome Robbins' Broadway** (527). Musical dance revue conceived, choreographed and directed by Jerome Robbins; music and lyrics by various authors. Opened February 26, 1989.

**Lend Me a Tenor** (481). By Ken Ludwig. Opened March 2, 1989. (Closed April 22, 1990)

**Metamorphosis** (96). By Steven Berkoff; adapted from a story by Franz Kafka. Opened March 6, 1989. (Recessed May 8, 1989 after 72 performances) Reopened June 12, 1989. (Closed July 1, 1989)

**\*The Heidi Chronicles** (514). Transfer from off Broadway of the play by Wendy Wasserstein. Opened December 11, 1988 off Broadway where it played 81 performances through February 19, 1989; transferred to Broadway March 9, 1989.

*ORPHEUS DESCENDING*—Vanessa Redgrave as Lady Torrance in the Peter Hall production of Tennessee Williams's play

**Barry Manilow at the Gershwin** (44). One-man performance by Barry Manilow; conceived by Ernie Chambers, Jack Feldman, Roberta Kent, Barry Manilow and Bruce Sussman; written by Ken & Mitzi Welch, Roberta Kent and Barry Manilow. Opened April 17, 1989. (Closed June 10, 1989)

**Starmites** (60). Musical with book by Stuart Ross and Barry Keating; music and lyrics by Barry Keating. Opened April 27, 1989. (Closed June 18, 1989)

**Largely New York** (152). Play in pantomime "written" by Bill Irwin. Opened May 1, 1989. (Closed September 2, 1989)

# PLAYS PRODUCED JUNE 1, 1989—MAY 31, 1990

**Mandy Patinkin in Concert: Dress Casual** (56). One-man performance by Mandy Patinkin. Produced by Ron Delsener at the Helen Hayes Theater. Opened July 25, 1989; see note. (Closed September 16, 1989)

Musical direction and piano accompaniment, Paul Ford; lighting, Richard Nelson; production stage manager, Brian A. Kaufman; press, PMK Public Relations, Jim Baldassare.

Informal concert-style presentation, presented without intermission and previously produced as *Mandy Patinkin: Dress Casual* for 6 performances at the Public Theater. Song numbers included "Soliloquy," a *Pal Joey* medley, "Buddy's Blues," "When the Red, Red Robin Comes Bob, Bob, Bobbin' Along," "And the Band Played On," "Over the Rainbow," "Pennies From Heaven," "Top Hat, White Tie and Tails," "Puttin' on the Ritz," "Alexander's Ragtime Band," "Sonny Boy," "No One Is Alone" and "No More" (from *Into the Woods*), "A Tisket, a Tasket" and "Coffee in a Cardboard Cup."

Note: Press date for *Mandy Patinkin in Concert: Dress Casual* was 8/1/89.

**Shenandoah** (31). Revival of the musical based on the screen play by James Lee Barrett; book by James Lee Barrett, Peter Udell and Philip Rose; music by Gary Geld; lyrics by Peter Udell. Produced by Howard Hurst, Sophie Hurst and Peter Ingster at the Virginia Theater. Opened August 8, 1989. (Closed September 2, 1989)

| | | | |
|---|---|---|---|
| Charlie Anderson | John Cullum | Rev. Byrd; Engineer | Donald Saunders |
| Jacob | Burke Lawrence | Sam | Thomas Cavanagh |
| James | Christopher Martin | Sgt. Johnson | Jim Selman |
| Nathan | Nigel Hamer | Lieutenant | Casper Roos |
| John | Stephen McIntyre | Tinkham | Richard Liss |
| Jenny | Tracey Moore | Carol | Jim Bearden |
| Henry | Robin Blake | Corporal | Stephen Simms |
| Robert | Jason Zimbler | Marauder | Sam Mancuso |
| Anne | Camilla Scott | Confederate Snipers | David Connolly, |
| Gabriel | Roy McKay | | Gerhard Kruschke |

Ensemble: Henry Alessan, Jim Bearden, Mark Bernkoff, David Connolly, Lesley Corne, Mark Ferguson, Brian Gow, Jennifer Griffin, Gerhard Kruschke, Richard Liss, Robert Longo, Sam Mancuso, Casper Roos, Fernando Santos, Jim Selman, Stephen Simms. Swing: Paul Mulloy.

Standbys/Understudies: Mr. Cullum—Casper Roos; Miss Scott—Lesley Corne; Miss Moore—Jennifer Griffin; Messrs. Lawrence, Hamer—Fernando Santos; Mr. Martin—Brian Gow; Mr. McIntyre—Mark Bernkoff; Messrs. Zimbler, Simms—David Connolly; Mr. McKay—Z Wright; Mr. Cavanagh—Robert Longo; Mr. Saunders—Richard Liss.

Directed by Philip Rose; choreography, Robert Tucker; musical direction, David Warrack; original scenery by Kert Lundell, adapted by Reginald Bronskill; costumes, Guy Geoly; lighting, Stephen Ross; production state manager, Mortimer Halpern; stage managers, Jim Roe, Amelia Linden; press, the Joshua Ellis Office, Jackie Green, Chris Boneau.

Orchestra: Barbara Ackerman, Robert Bonfiglio, John Bova, Lester Cantor, Lynn Crigler, William Ellison, Phil Granger, Charles Homewood, Susan Jolles, Janet Lantz, Martin Morell, Porter Poindexter, Robert Steen, Gregory Utzig, David Warrack, Roger Wendt.

Time: The Civil War. Place: The Shenandoah Valley, Virginia. Act I: Spring. Act II: Autumn.

*Shenandoah* was first produced on Broadway 1/7/75 for 1,050 performances. This production was previously presented at the Queen Elizabeth Theater in Toronto.

The list of musical numbers in *Shenandoah* appears on page 337 of *The Best Plays of* 1974–75.

**\*Circle in the Square Theater** 30th anniversary season. Schedule of two revivals. **Sweeney Todd** (189). Musical with music and lyrics by Stephen Sondheim; book by Hugh Wheeler; from an adaptation by Christopher Bond. Opened September 14, 1989. (Closed February 25, 1990) **\*Zoya's Apartment** (25). By Mikhail Bulgakov; translated by Nicholas Saunders and Frank Dwyer. Opened May 10, 1990. Produced by Circle in the Square Theater (sometimes listed as Circle in the Square), Theodore Mann artistic director, Paul Libin producing director, at Circle in the Square Theater.

## SWEENEY TODD

| | |
|---|---|
| Jonas Fogg ......................................... Tony Gilbert | Beggar Woman .............................SuEllen Estey |
| Policeman.....................................David E. Mallard | Mrs. Lovett................................... Beth Fowler |
| Bird Seller............................................ Ted Keegan | Judge Turpin ............................... David Barron |
| Dora ................................................. Sylvia Rhyne | Beadle ................................... Michael McCarty |
| Mrs. Mooney ..................................Mary Phillips | Johanna...............................Gretchen Kingsley |
| Anthony Hope......................................Jim Walton | Tobias Ragg................................Eddie Korbich |
| Sweeney Todd..................................... Bob Gunton | Pirelli ...............................................Bill Nabel |

Keyboards: Andrew Cooke, Stephen Marzullo.

Standbys: Misses Fowler, Estey—Anne McGreevey; Mr. Barron—Tony Gilbert; Beggar Woman (swings)—Rebecca Judd, Sylvia Rhyne; Miss Kingsley—Carol Logen, Sylvia Rhyne; Mr. Korbich—Franc D'Ambrosio, David E. Mallard; Mr. McCarty—Bill Nabel, David Vosburgh; Mr. Walton—Franc D'Ambrosio, Ted Keegan; Mr. Nabel—Franc D'Ambrosio, David Vosburgh.

Directed by Susan H. Schulman; musical direction and design, David Krane; choreography, Michael Lichtefeld; scenery, James Morgan; costumes, Beba Shamash; lighting, Mary Jo Dondlinger; assistant musical director, Jan Rosenberg; production stage manager, Perry Cline; stage manager, Trey Hunt; press, Merle Debuskey, Leo Stern.

Time: The 19th century. Place: London, Fleet Street and environs. The play was presented in two parts.

This is a somewhat shortened version of the Sondheim-Wheeler musical *Sweeney Todd, the Demon Barber of Fleet Street*, which was first produced on Broadway under the direction of Harold Prince 3/1/79 for 557 performances and was named a Best Play of its season and won the Critics Award for best musical and the Tony Awards for best musical, best musical score, best book and best direction.

## ACT I

(Musical numbers listed as "The Barber and His Wife" and "Quartet" in Act I of the original production did not appear in this revival. Numbers listed in *italics* below were not included in the original listing.)

| | |
|---|---|
| "The Ballad of Sweeney Todd" ...........................................................................................Company |
| "No Place Like London"................................................................... Anthony, Todd, Beggar Woman |
| "The Worst Pies in London".................................................................................................Mrs. Lovett |
| "Poor Thing"..........................................................................................................Mrs. Lovett, Company |
| "My Friends"............................................................................................................ Todd, Mrs. Lovett |
| "Green Finch and Linnet Bird" ...................................................................................................Johanna |
| "Ah, Miss" ................................................................................Anthony, Johanna, Beggar Woman |
| "Johanna" ...........................................................................................................................Anthony |
| "Pirelli's Miracle Elixir"................................................... Tobias, Todd, Mrs. Lovett, Company |
| "The Contest".............................................................................................................. Pirelli |
| *"Johanna" (Reprise)* ............................................................................................. Judge Turpin |
| "Wait"........................................................................................... Mrs. Lovett, Beggar Woman |
| "Kiss Me"..............................................................................................................Johanna, Anthony |
| "Ladies in Their Sensitivities" ...........................................................................Beadle, Judge Turpin |
| "Pretty Women"....................................................................................................................Judge, Todd |
| "Epiphany" ....................................................................................................................................... Todd |
| "A Little Priest"............................................................................................................ Mrs. Lovett, Todd |

## ACT II

| | |
|---|---|
| "God, That's Good" .................................................Tobias, Mrs. Lovett, Todd, Beggar Woman, Company |
| "Johanna" (Reprise) ...................................................................Anthony, Todd, Johanna, Beggar Woman |
| "By the Sea".......................................................................................................... Mrs. Lovett, Todd |
| *"Wigmaker Sequence"* ........................................................................................Todd, Anthony, Quintet |
| "Not While I'm Around"...................................................................................Tobias, Mrs. Lovett |
| "Parlor Songs"............................................................................................ Beadle, Mrs. Lovett, Tobias |
| "City on Fire".......................................................................................................................Company |
| *"The Judge's Return"* ...........................................................................................................Todd, Judge |
| Final Scene including "The Ballad of Sweeney Todd" (Reprise) ......................................................Company |

## ZOYA'S APARTMENT

Zoya Denisova Peltz........................Linda Thorson
Manyushka ......................................Chandra Lee
Anisim Zotikovich Aliluya................Ray DeMattis
Pavel Fyodorovich Abolyaninov .......Robert LuPone
Gandzalin.....................................Akira Takayama
Cherubim ............................................Ernest Abuba
Aleksander Tarasovich Ametistov....Bronson Pinchot
Agnes Nikolaevna ...........................Florence Rowe
Tailor, 3d Stranger..........................Kevin Crawford
Sepoorakhina....................................Fiona Davis

Shopping Lady ......................................Talia Paul
Alla Vadimovna................................Lauri Landry
Marya Nikiforovna ......................Colleen Gallagher
Lizanka ...........................................Holley Chant
Madame Ivanova .........................Careayre Rambeau
Boris Semyonovich Goose.................Robert Stattel
1st Stranger.......................................Dana Mills
2d Stranger........................................David Silber
Dead Body of Ivan Vasilyevich..............Joe Palmieri
Robert...................................Robertson Carricart

Directed by Boris A. Morozov; scenery, James Morgan, based on original designs by Josef Sumbatsivily; costumes, Cynthia Doty, based on original designs by Tatiana Gleboya; lighting, Mary Jo Dondlinger; music, Gregory Gobernik; stage movement, Mina Yakim; production stage manager, William Hare.

Time: 1926. Place: Moscow. Act I, Scene 1: An apartment, an evening in May. Scene 2: A laundry, later that evening. Scene 3: The apartment, soon after. Scene 4: The apartment, an afternoon in September. Scene 5: The apartment, that evening. Act II, Scene 1: The apartment, a day in October. Scene 2: That night. Scene 3: A few moments later.

A farcical struggle against the Russian bureaucracy of the 1920s, originally produced at the Vakhtangov Theater in Moscow in 1926 and previously produced off off Broadway at the Gene Frankel Theater 2/10/78 for 12 performances.

**Orpheus Descending** (97). Revival of the play by Tennessee Williams. Produced by James M. Nederlander, Elizabeth Ireland McCann and Duncan C. Weldon & Jerome Minskoff, in the Peter Hall Company production at the Neil Simon Theater. Opened September 24, 1989. (Closed December 17, 1989)

Dolly Hamma...................................Patti Allison
Beulah Binnings...........................Sloane Shelton
Pee Wee Binnings .........................Pat McNamara
Dog Hamma......................................Mitch Webb
Carol Cutrere.................................Anne Twomey
Eva Temple....................................Bette Henritze
Sister Temple.....................................Peg Small
Uncle Pleasant............................Doyle Richmond
Val Xavier ...................................Kevin Anderson
Vee Talbott...................................Tammy Grimes

Lady Torrance.............................Vanessa Redgrave
Jabe Torrance...................................Brad Sullivan
Sheriff Talbott..........................Manning Redwood
Mr. Dubinsky; 1st Man.................Thomas Kopache
Woman ...............................Constance Crawford
David Cutrere ........................................Lewis Arlt
Nurse Porter.....................................Marcia Lewis
Clown; 2d Man..........................Stephen Mendillo
Townspeople.......Lynn Cohen, Richard McWilliams

Understudies: Misses Redgrave, Twomey—Joan McIntosh; Messrs. Anderson, Kopache, Mendillo—Richard McWilliams; Misses Grimes, Shelton, Allison—Constance Crawford; Mr. Sullivan—Thomas Kopache; Mr. Redwood—Mitch Webb; Messrs. Webb, McNamara, Arlt—Stephen Mendillo; Misses Henritze, Small, Lewis—Lynn Cohen; Mr. Richmond—Fred Tyson; Miss Crawford—Peg Small.

Directed by Peter Hall; designed by Alison Chitty, American costumes in association with Richard Schurkamp; lighting, Paul Pyant with Neil Peter Jampolis; sound, Paul Arditti; electronic score, Stephen Edwards; associate producer, Nick Frei; production stage manager, William Dodds; stage manager, Steven Shaw; press, the Joshua Ellis Office, Adrian Bryan-Brown.

Time: During the rainy season, from January to Easter Sunday. Place: A general dry-goods store and part of the connecting "confectionary" in a small Southern town. The play was presented in two parts.

This revival of *Orpheus Descending* was first produced at the Haymarket in London 12/13/88. Tennessee Williams's first produced play (experimentally, under the title *Battle of Angels* in 1940 and 1941), it finally reached Broadway as *Orpheus Descending* 3/21/57 for 68 performances and was named a Best Play of its season. Its only previous New York revivals of record took place off Broadway in the seasons of 1958–59 and 1959–60.

**Mastergate** (68). By Larry Gelbart. Produced by Gene (Eugene V.) Wolsk at Criterion Center Stage Right. Opened October 12, 1989. (Closed December 10, 1989)

The Committee:
Sen. Bowman, Chairman................Jerome Kilty
Rep. Proctor............................Tom McDermott
Shepherd Hunter, Chief Counsel.......John Dossett
Rep. Byers; Sen. Knight...............Wayne Knight
Sen. Bunting; Rep. Sellers..................Jeff Weiss
The Witnesses:
Steward Butler ...........................Wayne Knight
Abel Lamb.............................Steve Hofvendahl
Maj. Manley Battle..................Daniel von Bargen
Sec. of State Bishop .................Tom McDermott
Vice Pres. Burden............................Joseph Daly
Wylie Slaughter...............................Jeff Weiss

The Lawyers:
Messrs. Child, Picker,
  Boyle, Carver ...............................Zach Grenier
For Total Network News:
Merry Chase............................ Melinda Mullins
Clay Fielder ..................................Joseph Daly
TNN Director ............................Katrina Stevens
TNN Cameramen ................... Merrill Holtzman,
                                                Harold Dean James
Senior Staffer ................................ William Cain
The Wives ................................ Ann McDonough
Pages...............Charles Geyer, Isaiah Whitlock Jr.,
                                                Priscilla C. Shanks

Directed by Michael Engler; scenery, Philipp Jung; costumes, Candice Donnelly; lighting, Stephen Strawbridge; sound, Marc Salzberg; video, Dennis Diamond; video music, Glen Roven; production stage manager, Cathy B. Blaser; stage manager, Pat Sosnow; press, Merle Debuskey, Bruce Campbell.

Time: The morning after. Place: Washington, D.C. The play was presented without intermission.

Satire on the style and substance of Congressional hearings, reminiscent of the Oliver North affair. Previously produced by American Repertory Theater, Cambridge, Mass.

**Dangerous Games** (4).   Musical conceived by Graciela Daniele; book by Jim Lewis and Graciela Daniele; music by Astor Piazzolla; lyrics by William Finn. Produced by Jules Fisher, James M. Nederlander and Arthur Rubin in association with Mary Kantor at the Nederlander Theater. Opened October 19, 1989. (Closed October 21, 1989)

## TANGO

Delia, the Madame............................ Dana Moore
The Men:
Felipe .....................................Philip Jerry
Ricardo....................................Richard Amaro
Carlos..............................................Ken Ard
The Women:
Renata....................................... Rene Ceballos
Diana.................................... Diana Laurenson

Maria.......................................Malinda Shaffer
Adriana...........................Adrienne Hurd-Sharlein
The Brothers:
Juan..............................................John Mineo
(Gregorio)................Gregory Mitchell, Luis Perez
(Christina, the New Whore)....................Tina Paul,
                                                Elizabeth Mozer

## ORFEO

(Orfeo) ......................Gregory Mitchell, Luis Perez
Dicha............................................ Rene Ceballos
Aurora....................................... Danyelle Weaver
Pluton...............................................Ken Ard
(Nora; Lascivia) .............Tina Paul, Elizabeth Mozer
Antares; Altivo.................................John Mineo
Mira; Codicia .................................. Dana Moore

Lyrae; LaGula...............................Malinda Shaffer
Cleo; Envidia ............................. Diana Laurenson
Alberio; Ira ......................................... Marc Villa
Ursula; Malicia....................Adrienne Hurd-Sharlein
Leon; Mentira.....................................Philip Jerry
Arturo; Charon; Perez ......................Richard Amaro
Bambo Player................................. Adrian Brito

(Parentheses indicate roles in which the actors alternated)

The Quintet: Rodolfo Alchourron guitar; Jorge Alfano Bass, bamboo flute; Miguel Arrabal bandoneon; Jon Kass violin; James Kowal piano, conductor; Rene Ceballos offstage vocals.

Understudies for *Tango*: Messrs. Amaro, Ard, Jerry—Marc Villa, Frank Cava; Misses Ceballos, Hurd-Sharlein, Moore—Mamie Duncan-Gibbs; Misses Laurenson, Shaffer—Adrienne Hurd-Sharlein; Mr. Mineo—Richard Amaro; Mr. Mitchell—Luis Perez, Philip Jerry; Miss Paul—Elizabeth Mozer, Diana Laurenson.

Understudies for *Orfeo*: Mr. Ard—Marc Villa; Miss Ceballos—Dana Moore; Messrs. Amaro, Jerry, Mineo, Villa—Frank Cava; Misses Hurd-Sharlein, Moore—Mamie Duncan-Gibbs; Misses Laurenson, Shaffer—Adrienne Hurd-Sharlein; Miss Paul—Elizabeth Mozer, Malinda Shaffer; Mr. Mitchell—Luis Perez, Philip Jerry; Miss Weaver—Nicole Leach.

Swings: Frank Cava, Mamie Duncan-Gibbs.

Directed and choreographed by Graciela Daniele; co-choreographed by Tina Paul; musical direction and arrangements, James Kowal; scenery, Tony Straiges; costumes, Patricia Zipprodt; lighting, Peggy Eisenhauer; sound, Otts Munderloh; musical consultant and arrangements, Rodolfo Alchourron; *Tango* fight direction, B. H. Barry; *Orfeo* fight direction, Luis Perez; music coordinator, John Monaco; production stage manager, Robert Mark Kalfin; stage manager, Paula Gray; press, Shirley Herz Associates, Robert W. Larkin.

Musical consisting largely of dances and dance characterizations, presented in two parts. *Tango* (previously produced OOB in 1987 as *Tango Apasionado*) is set in an Argentine brothel and concerns male sexuality in its rougher stages. *Orfeo* is a version of the Orpheus story, dedicated to the *desaparecidos*, those who vanished during the military rule of Argentina. Previously produced in regional theater at the La Jolla Playhouse, the Spoleto Festival in Charleston and the American Music Theater Festival in Philadelphia.

There were no song or other musical numbers listed in the program for *Dangerous Games.*

**Radio City Music Hall Productions.** Schedule of three programs. **Takarazuka** (6). Limited engagement of the Japanese revue, presented in the Takarazuka Revue Company production, Kohei Kobayashi producer, Haruhiko Saka president, as a Mitsubishi special event. Opened October 25, 1989. (Closed October 29, 1989) **Christmas Spectacular** (188). Return engagement of the spectacle originally conceived by Robert F. Jani. Opened November 10, 1989. (Closed January 3, 1990) **Easter Extravaganza** (26). Spectacle conceived and created by Patricia M. Morinelli and William Michael Maher. Opened April 11, 1990. (Closed April 23, 1990) Produced by Radio City Music Hall Productions, Patricia M. Morinelli and David J. Nash executive producers, at Radio City Music Hall.

*MASTERGATE*—Daniel von Bargen (*center*) as "Maj. Manley Battle," Ann McDonough as his wife and Zach Grenier as his lawyer in a scene from Larry Gelbart's satire on Senate hearings

## TAKARAZUKA

Flower Troupe: Mizuki Oura (male roles), Mito Hibiki (female roles) and 18 others.

Moon Troupe: Ai Kodama (female roles), Yuki Amami and nine others.

Show Troupe: Yu Asuka (male roles) and 12 others.

Star Troupe: Yu Shion (male roles), Yuka Shima (female roles) and 14 others.

Artistic directors, Shinji Ueda, Hirotoshi Ohara; composers and arrangers, Takio Terada, Kenji Yoshizaki, Kaoru Irie, Kazuakira Hashimoto, Toshiko Yonekawa; conductor, Kazuakira Hashimoto; choreography, Yoshijiro Hanayagi, Kiyomi Hayama, Taku Yamada, Roger Minami; scenery, Hideo Ishihama, Toshiaki Sekiya; costumes, Harumi Tokoro, Kikue Nakagawa, Ikuei Touda; lighting, Naoji Imai; lighting supervisor, Ken Billington; assistant directors, Masazumi Tani, Masaya Ishida; press, Jeffrey Richards Associates, Susan Chicoine.

The first American engagement of this large all-female revue company in 30 years, with its leading performers listed above, has a repertoire of traditional Japanese dance pieces, musical revue numbers, musical theater versions of Western literature and excerpts from Broadway musicals. A foreign show originating in Takarazuka City and Tokyo.

## CHRISTMAS SPECTACULAR

| | |
|---|---|
| Narrator; Scrooge; Santa............Charles Edward Hall | Belinda...............................................Amy Gear |
| Mr. Cratchit.........................Steven Edward Moore | Martha .......................................Christiane Farr |
| Mrs. Cratchit.............................Ann-Marie Blake | Coachman...............................Marty McDonough |
| Sarah Cratchit...............Stacy Latham, Amy Sanders | Poultry Man................................LeRoi Freeman |
| Peter Cratchit.................Bradley Latham, John Zisa | Mrs. Claus....................................Marty Simpson |
| Tiny Tim....................Alex Myers, Benjamin Mack | |

Skaters: Laurie Welch & Randy Coyne, Amy Tolbert & Keith Davis.

Elves: Jiggle—Scott Seidman; Squiggle—Lou Carry; Wiggle—John Edward Allen; Giggle—Michael J. Gilden; Bruce—Shari Weiser; Understudies—Elena Bertagnolli, Phil Fondacaro.

The New Yorkers: David Askler, Gina Biancardi, Ann-Marie Blake, Pamela Cecil, Keith Cromwell, John Dietrich, LeRoi Freeman, Deborah Geneviere, Peter Gregus, Andrea Hopkins, David Koch, Michelle Mallardi, John Curtis-Michael, Steven Edward Moore, Ryan Perry, Marty Simpson, Susan Streater, Mary Jayne Waddell.

Dancers: Robert Ashford, Jean Barber, Joseph Bowerman, Richard Costa, Teresa DeRose, Christiane Farr, Amy Gear, Jack Hayes, Edward Henkel, Terry Lacy, Marty McDonough, Joan Mirabella, Kevin Weldon, Taylor Wicker, Travis Wright.

Rockettes: Carol Beatty, Dottie Belle, Susan Boron, Katy Braff, Julie Branam, Janice Cavargna, Phyllis Frew Ceroni, Elizabeth Chanin, Stephanie Chase, Connie House Cittadino, Eileen M. Collins, Linda Deacon, Marylee Dewitt, Susanne Doris, Joyce Dwyer (Captain), Prudence Gray, Pam Kelleher Halpern, Susan Heart, Vickie Hickerson, Ginny Hounsell, Stephanie James, Jennifer Jones, Joan Peer Kelleher, Dee Dee Knapp, Judy Little, Sonya Livingston, Setsuko Maruhashi, Mary McNamara, Lori Mello, Laraine Memola, Lynn Newton, Rosemary Noviello, Carol Paracat, Pam Stacey Pasqualino, Kerri Pearsall, Maureen Stevens Pollack, Gerri Presky, Laureen Repp, Linda Riley, Mary Six Rupert, Jereme Sheehan, Terry Spano, Lynn Sullivan, Pauline Achillas Taikas, Scotti Tittle, Jill Turnbull, Darlene Wendy, Beth Woods, Eileen Woods, Phyliss Wujko.

Orchestra: Joseph Church conductor; Bradford P. Garside associate conductor; Katsuko Esaki concert master; Gilbert Bauer, Carmine Deleo, Howard Kaye, Joseph Kowalewski, Julius H. Kunstler, Nannette Levi, Samuel Marder, Holly Ovenden violin; Barbara Harrison, Andrea Andros viola; Frank Levy, Sarah Carter cello; Dean Crandall bass; Kenneth Emery flute; Gerard J. Niewood, Richard Oatts, John M. Cippola, Joshua Siegel, Kenneth Arzberger reeds; George Bartlett, Nancy Freimanis, French horn; Richard Raffio, Zachary Shnek, Norman Beatty trumpet; John Schnupp, Thomas B. Olcott, Mark Johansen trombone; John Bartlett tuba; Thomas J. Oldakowski drums; Mario DeCiutiis, Maya Gungi percussion; Anthony Cesarano guitar; Susanna Nason, Henry Aronson piano; Jeanne Maier harp; George Wesner, Robert Maidhoff, Paul Fleckenstein, Fred Davies organ.

Originally directed by Robert F. Jani; staging director, Frank Wagner; staging and choreography, Violet Holmes, Linda Lemac, Marianne Selbert; musical direction, Joseph Church; scenery, Charles Lisanby; costumes, Jose Lengson, Frank Spencer; lighting, Ken Billington; orchestrations, Elman Anderson, Robert M. Freedman, Michael Gibson, Don Harper, Arthur Harris, Bob Krogstad, Phillip J. Lang; musical routines,

Tony Fox, Bob Krogstad, Don Pippin, Don Smith; production stage manager, Howard Kolins; stage managers, Mimi Apfel, Travis DeCastro, Andy Feigin, Michael Harrod, Joseph A. Onorato; press, Sandra Manley.

The Music Hall's annual Christmas show with its famous Nativity pageant, last offered 11/11/88 for 166 performances.

SCENES: Overture, "We Wish You a Merry Christmas" (Radio City Music Hall Orchestra); Scene 1: The Nutcracker, A Teddy Bear's Dream; Scene 2: *A Christmas Carol*, adapted from Charles Dickens; Scene 3: Christmas in New York (New Yorkers, Rockettes, Orchestra, Entire Company); Scene 4: Ice Skating in the Plaza; Scene 5: "The Twelve Days of Christmas"; Scene 6: "They Can't Start Christmas Without Us" (Santa, Mrs. Claus, Elves); Scene 7: The Parade of the Wooden Soldiers (Rockettes); Scene 8: Beginning of Santa's Journey (Santa, Mrs. Claus, Elves); Scene 9: *The Night Before Christmas*, adapted from Clement C. Moore; Scene 10: "The Christmas Song" (New Yorkers); Scene 11: The Rockettes Christmas Carousel (Rockettes); Scene 12: The Living Nativity, includes "Silent Night," "O Little Town of Bethlehem," "Away in a Manger," "The First Noel," "We Three Kings," "O Come All Ye Faithful," "Hark, the Herald Angels Sing" and *One Solitary Life* (medieval poem, author anonymous); Jubilant: "Joy to the World" (Orchestra, Company).

ORIGINAL MUSIC: "T'was the Night Before Christmas" by Tom Bahler; "They Can't Start Christmas Without Us" music by Stan Lebowsky, lyrics by Fred Tobias; "My First Real Christmas" music by Don Pippin, lyrics by Nan Mason; "Christmas in New York" by Billy Butt.

SPECIAL MUSIC CREDITS: "Silent Night" arrangement by Percy Faith; "The Twelve Days of Christmas" arrangement by Tom Bahler and Don Dorsey; "The Christmas Song" by Mel Torme and Martin Wells, arrangement by Bob Krogstad.

## EASTER EXTRAVAGANZA

CAST: Wayne Cilento, Rockettes.

Directed and choreographed by Scott Salmon; scenery, Erté; costumes, Erté, Eduardo Sicangeo, Jose Lengson; lighting, Ken Billington, Jason Kantrowitz; orchestrations, Michael Gibson, Dick Lieb, Glenn Osser, Jim Tyler; musical direction and vocal arrangements, Don Pippin; dance music arrangements, Gordon Lowry Harrell, Mark Hummell, Marvin Laird, Ethyl Will; special musical material, Larry Grossman; special material, Hal Hackady; vocal solo recording "Glory of Easter," Marilyn Horne; production stage manager, Howard Kolins.

Spectacle in the traditional Music Hall style, including the pageant *Glory of Easter* produced by Leon Leonidoff from 1933 to 1979 but not seen since then. The show was presented without intermission.

**The Secret Rapture** (12). By David Hare. Produced by Joseph Papp and The Shubert Organization in the New York Shakespeare Festival production at the Ethel Barrymore Theater. Opened October 26, 1989; see note. (Closed November 4, 1989)

| | | | |
|---|---|---|---|
| Isobel Glass | Blair Brown | Katherine Glass | Mary Beth Hurt |
| Marion French | Frances Conroy | Irwin Posner | Michael Wincott |
| Tom French | Stephen Vinovich | Rhonda Milne | Jennifer Van Dyck |

Understudies: Misses Brown, Conroy—Alma Cuervo; Misses Hurt, Van Dyck—Joyce O'Connor; Messrs. Wincott, Vinovich—Armand Schultz.

Directed by David Hare; scenery, Santo Loquasto; costumes, Jane Greenwood; lighting, Richard Nelson; music, Nick Bicât; associate producer, Jason Steven Cohen; production stage manager, Karen Armstrong; stage manager, Buzz Cohen; press, Richard Kornberg, Barbara Carroll, Reva Cooper, Carol Fineman.

Time: The present day. Place: England. Act I, Scene I: Robert's bedroom. Scene 2: The lawn of Robert's house. Scene 3: Isobel's office. Scene 4: Robert's living room. Act II, Scene 1: Isobel's new offices. Scene 6: Tom's office. Scene 7: Robert's house. Scene 8: Robert's living room.

Black comedy, two sisters react to the death of their father, with overtones of the sociopolitical situation in modern England. A foreign play previously produced at the Royal National Theater, London.

Note: This production of *The Secret Rapture* was presented in 22 tryout performances off Broadway at the Public Theater 9/8/89–9/27/89.

**Love Letters** (96). Transfer from off Broadway of the play by A.R. Gurney. Produced by Roger L. Stevens, Thomas Viertel, Steven Baruch and Richard Frankel at the Edison Theater. Opened October 31, 1989. (Closed January 21, 1990)

Andrew Makepeace Ladd III:

| | |
|---|---|
| Oct. 31–Nov. 5 | Jason Robards |
| Nov. 7–12 | John Rubinstein |
| Nov. 14–19 | Richard Thomas |
| Nov. 21–26 | Robert Foxworth |
| Nov. 28–Dec. 3 | Edward Herrmann |
| Dec. 5–10 | Fritz Weaver |
| Dec. 12–17 | David Dukes |
| Dec. 19–24 | Timothy Hutton |
| Dec. 26–31 | John Clark |
| Jan. 2–7 | Robert Vaughn |
| Jan. 9–14 | Treat Williams |
| Jan. 16–21 | Cliff Robertson |

Melissa Gardner:

| | |
|---|---|
| Oct. 31–Nov. 5 | Colleen Dewhurst |
| Nov. 7–12 | Stockard Channing |
| Nov. 14–19 | Swoosie Kurtz |
| Nov. 21–26 | Elizabeth Montgomery |
| Nov. 28–Dec. 3 | Jane Curtin |
| Dec. 5–10 | Nancy Marchand |
| Dec. 12–17 | Kate Nelligan |
| Dec. 19–24 | Elizabeth McGovern |
| Dec. 26–31 | Lynn Redgrave |
| Jan. 2–7 | Polly Bergen |
| Jan. 9–14 | Kate Nelligan |
| Jan. 16–21 | Elaine Stritch |

Directed by John Tillinger; scenic consultant, John Lee Beatty; lighting, Dennis Parichy; casting, Linda Wright; production stage manager, William H. Lang; press, the Joshua Ellis Office, Chris Boneau.

Two-character staged reading with a different cast each week, of letters revealing the relationships of the duo from second grade on through a period of 50 years, presented in two parts. Previously produced in regional theater at the Long Wharf Theater, New Haven; OOB in a series of special performances last season; and in a regular off-Broadway run 8/22/89 for 64 more performances; see its entry in the Plays Produced Off Broadway section of this volume.

A Best Play; see page 151.

**Sid Caesar & Company** (5). Transfer from off Broadway of the revue subtitled *Does Anybody Know What I'm Talking About?* Produced by Ivan Bloch and Harold Thau in association with Larry Spellman at the John Golden Theater. Opened November 1, 1989. (Closed November 5, 1989)

| | |
|---|---|
| Sid Caesar | Linda Hart |
| Lee Delano | Carolyn Michel |
| Erick Devine | Peter Shawn |
| Lubitza Gregus | Laura Turnbull |

Directed by Martin Charnin; musical direction, Elliot Finkel; scenery and lighting, Neil Peter Jampolis; costumes, Karen Roston; sound, Bruce Cameron; orginal songs, Martin Charnin; associate producers, J. Scott Broder, Sonny Bloch, Robert Courson; production stage manager, Frank Hartenstein; press, Solters/Roskin/Friedman, Keith Sherman.

Presented without authorship credits, in two parts, the show included some of the roles and sketches its star made famous on TV. Previously produced off Broadway at the Village Gate 6/22/89 for 72 performances; see its entry in the Plays Produced Off Broadway section of this volume.

MUSICAL NUMBER AND SKETCHES: Sleep, A Boy at His First Dance, A Man Walking Down the Aisle, Zero Hour—Sid Caesar; A Man With His Wife Arguing to the First Movement of Beethoven's Fifth Symphony—Caesar, Laura Turnbull; The Last Angry Bull—Caesar, Company; At the Movies—Caesar, Linda Hart, Lee Delano, Peter Shawn; We Aren't Fooling Anyone—Company; The World Through the Eyes of a Baby, The Penny Candy Gum Machine, The Grieg Piano Concerto—Caesar; The Professor—Caesar, Delano; "Make a New Now, Now!"—Caesar, Company.

**\*Meet Me In St. Louis** (236). Musical based on *The Kensington Stories* by Sally Benson and the M-G-M motion picture *Meet Me in St. Louis*; book by Hugh Wheeler; songs by Hugh Martin and Ralph Blane. Produced by Brickhill-Burke Productions, Christopher Seabrooke and EPI Products at the Gershwin Theater. Opened November 2, 1989.

| | | | |
|---|---|---|---|
| Lon Smith | Michael O'Steen | Agnes Smith | Rachel Graham |
| Randy Travis | Brian Jay | Alonzo Smith | George Hearn |
| Katie | Betty Garrett | Warren Sheffield | Peter Reardon |
| Motorman | Jim Semmelman | Ida Boothby | Naomi Reddin |
| Tootie Smith | Courtney Peldon | Douglas Moore | Gregg Whitney |
| Mrs. Smith | Charlotte Moore | Eve Finley | Shauna Hicks |
| Grandpa Prophater | Milo O'Shea | Dr. Bond | Gordon Stanley |
| Esther Smith | Donna Kane | Lucille Ballard | Karen Culliver |
| Rose Smith | Juliet Lambert | Clinton A. Badger | Craig A. Meyer |
| John Truitt | Jason Workman | | |

Orchestra: Stephen Bates assistant conductor, keyboards; Marilyn Reynolds, Katherine LiVolsi, Sandra Billingslea, Andrew Stein, Melanie Baker violin; Jeffrey Szabo, Garfield Moore cello; Susan Jolles harp; Seymour Red Press, Raymond Beckenstein, Dennis Anderson, Steven Boschi woodwinds; Hollis Burridge, Laurie Frink, Kamau Adilifu trumpet; Santo Russo, Earl McIntyre trombone; Russell Rizner, Albert Richmond, French horn; Andrew Schwartz guitar, banjo; Ronald Raffio bass; John Redsecker drummer; Eric Kivnick percussion; Seymour Red Press music coordinator.

Company: Kevin Backstrom, Dan Buelow, Victoria Lynn Burton, Karen Culliver, Deanna Dys, H. David Gunderman, Shauna Hicks, K. Craig Innes, Brian Jay, Rachel Jones, Nancy Lemenager, Joanne McHugh, Frank Maio, Carol Lee Meadows, Craig A. Meyer, Christopher Lee Michaels, Ron Morgan, Georga L. Osborne, Rachelle Ottley, Christina Pawl, Naomi Reddin, Carol Schuberg, Jim Semmelman, Ken Shepski, Gordon Stanley, Sean Frank Sullivan, Cynthia Thole, Gregg Whitney, Kyle Whyte, Lee Wilson.

Dance Captains: Carol Schuberg, K. Craig Innes.

Understudies: Messrs. Hearn, O'Shea—Gordon Stanley; Miss Moore—Cynthia Thole; Miss Garrett—Georga L. Osborne; Miss Kane—Shauna Hicks; Misses Peldon, Graham—Victoria Lynn Burton; Messrs. Workman, Semmelman—Christopher Lee Michaels; Misses Lambert, Culliver—Rachelle Ottley; Mr. O'Steen—H. David Gunderman; Mr. Reardon—Sean Frank Sullivan; Mr. Whitney—Ken Shepski.

Directed by Louis Burke; choreography, Joan Brickhill; musical direction, Bruce Pomahac; scenery and costumes, Keith Anderson; lighting, Ken Billington; musical supervision, Milton Rosenstock; orchestrations, Michael Gibson; dance arrangements, James Raitt; sound, Alan Stieb, James Brousseau; vocal arrangements, Hugh Martin, Bruce Pomahac; ice choreographer, Michael Tokar; assistant director, Lonnie Chase; associate choreographer, Herman-Jay Miller; associate producers, Loren Krok, P.K. Sloman, L. Everett Chase; production stage manager, Robert Bennett; stage manager, Jay Adler; press, the Joshua Ellis Office, Adrian Bryan-Brown.

Time: From summer 1903 to the spring of 1904 and the opening of the Louisiana Purchase Exposition. Place: In and around the Smith family home, 5135 Kensington Ave., St. Louis.

The *New Yorker* short story and 1944 movie material and story reworked for the stage, with a new book and ten new Martin-Blane songs added to their original film score.

## ACT I

Overture ............................................................................................................................ Orchestra
Scene 1: Street outside the Smith family home—summer 1903
"Meet Me in St. Louis" ....................................................................................................... Ensemble
    (new lyrics by Hugh Martin and Ralph Blane)
Scene 2: Interior of the Smith home
"Meet Me in St. Louis" (reprise) ................................................................................. Grandpa, Tootie
"The Boy Next Door" ................................................................................................................. Esther
"Be Anything But a Girl" ............................................................................... Grandpa, Agnes, Tootie
Scene 3: Lon's Princeton party
"Skip to My Lou" ................................................. Rose, Esther, Lon, Douglas, John, Warren, Company
    (new lyrics by Hugh Martin and Ralph Blane)
"Under the Bamboo Tree" ............................................................................................... Esther, Tootie
"Banjos" ........................................................................................................................ Lon, Company
Scene 4: Preparing for Halloween
"Ghosties and Ghoulies and Things That Go Bump in the Night" ........................... Katie, Agnes, Tootie,
                                                            Neighborhood Kids
Halloween Ballet .................................................................................................................... Company

*MEET ME IN ST. LOUIS*—Juliet Lambert, Betty Garrett and Donna Kane in the Hugh Wheeler-Hugh Martin-Ralph Blane musical

Scene 5: The girls' bedroom and the Smith home
  "Wasn't It Fun?" ................................................................................................Mr. and Mrs. Smith
Scene 6: Esther's dream
  "The Trolley Song" .......................................................................................... Esther, Company
Scene 7: The bedroom again—the next morning

## ACT II

Scene 1: The frozen pond—before Thanksgiving
  "Ice" ..................................................................................Rose, Warren, Douglas, Company
  (Featured Skaters: Rachelle Ottley, Ron Morgan)
  "Raving Beauty" .............................................................................Warren, Douglas, Rose
Scene 2: The Smith home—preparing for Thanksgiving
  "A Touch of the Irish" ..................................................................................Katie, Esther, Rose
  "You Are for Loving" ..............................................................................................John, Esther
Scene 3: Tree-trimming time
  "A Day in New York" .........................................................................................Mr. Smith, Family
Scene 4: Snowy men—Christmas Eve
Scene 5: The ball and portico outside
  "The Ball" ..............................................................................................Grandpa, Company
  "Diamonds in the Starlight" .........................................................................................John, Esther
Scene 6: Back home—later that evening
  "Have Yourself a Merry Little Christmas .................................................................... Esther

Scene 7:  The Louisiana Purchase Exposition—spring 1904
"Paging  Mr.  Sousa"................................................................................. Mr. Smith, Company
Finale .....................................................................................................................Company

**3 Penny Opera** (65).  Revival of the musical with book and lyrics by Bertolt Brecht; music
by Kurt Weill; translated by Michael Feingold.  Produced by Jerome Hellman in association
with Haruki Kadokawa and James M. Nederlander at the Lunt-Fontanne Theater.  Opened
November 5, 1989.  (Closed December 31, 1989)

Ballad Singer..............................Ethyl Eichelberger
Jenny  Diver.............................. Suzzanne Douglas
Jonathan Jeremiah Peacham ...............Alvin Epstein
Filch.......................................Jeff Blumenkrantz
Mrs. Peachum ...........................Georgia Brown
Polly Peachum ....................... Maureen McGovern
Macheath.................................................. Sting
Macheath's Gang:
    Matt of the Mint...........................Josh Mostel
    Crook-Finger Jack.................Mitchell Greenberg
    Sawtooth  Bob..........................David Schechter
    Ed.............................................Philip Carroll
    Walter.......................................Tom Robbins

Jimmy .......................................Alex Santoriello
Tiger Brown..................................Larry Marshall
Whores:
    Dolly..................................... Anne Kerry Ford
    Betty.............................................Jan Horvath
    Vixen..........................................Teresa De Zarn
    Molly .......................................Nancy Ringham
    Suky Tawdry..............................K. T. Sullivan
Old Whore ...............................Fiddle Viracola
Smith .............................................David Pursley
Policemen...........MacIntyre Dixon, Michael Piontek
Lucy ....................................... Kim Criswell

Beggars, Bystanders:  Philip Carroll, MacIntyre Dixon, Michael Piontek, David Schechter, Steven Major
West.

Orchestra:  Robert Fisher associate conductor; Chris Gekker, Carl Albach trumpet; William Blount
clarinet; Michael Powell trombone; William Schimmel accordion; Elizabeth Mann flute; Scott Kuney guitar,
banjo; Ted Nash alto saxophone; Maya Gungi tympani; Myron Lutske cello; Paul Pizzuti percussion; Roger
Rosenberg tenor saxophone; Stephen Hinnenkamp piano; Robert Wolinsky keyboard; John Kulowitsch bass.

Understudies:  Sting—Alex Santoriello; Miss Brown—Fiddle Viracola; Miss McGovern—Nancy
Ringham; Mr. Epstein—David Pursley; Miss Criswell—Teresa De Zarn; Miss Douglas—Jan Horvath; Mr.
Marshall—Steven Major West; Messrs. Mostel, Eichelberger, Pursley, Carroll, Robbins, Santoriello,
Schechter, Dixon, Piontek—Robert Ousley; Misses Ringham, Ford, Horvath, De Zarn, Sullivan—Leslie
Castay.

Directed by John Dexter; musical staging, Peter Gennaro; musical direction, additional orchestrations and
musical continuity, Julius Rudel; scenery and costumes, Jocelyn Herbert; associate scenic design, Duke
Durfee; lighting, Andy Phillips, Brian Nason; sound, Peter Fitzgerald; associate producers, Margo Lion,
Hiroshi Sugawara, Lloyd Phillips, Kiki Miyake, Nancy Ellison; production stage manager, Bob Borod; stage
managers, Joe Cappelli, Arti Gaffin; press, Shirley Herz Associates, Pete Sanders, Glenna Freedman.

Time:  The 19th century. Place: London.

*3 Penny Opera* (also billed as *The Threepenny Opera* in past productions) last appeared in New York in
major revival by New York Shakespeare Festival at the Vivian Beaumont Theater 5/1/76 for 307 performances
(and subsequently brought to the Delacorte in Central Park 6/28/77 for 27 more performances) in a new
translation by Ralph Manheim and John Willett which received a special Best Play revival citation.  The
Macheath making his stage debut in the present production is billed under the stage name "Sting," by which he
was already famous as a singing and recording star.  This revival previously appeared in regional theater
production at the National Theater, Washington, D.C.

## ACT I

Prologue:  Street fair in Soho
Overture .............................................................................................................. Orchestra
    "Ballad of Mack the Knife (Moritat)" ..........................................................Ballad Singer
Scene 1:  Peachum's shop, Wednesday morning
    "Peachum's Morning Hymn" .............................................................................Mr. Peachum
    "Why-Can't-They Song" .........................................................................Mr. and Mrs. Peachum
Scene 2:  A deserted stable, 5 p.m.
    "Wedding Song" ...................................................................................................Gang

"Pirate Jenny" .................................................................................................................. Polly
"Soldiers' Song" ................................................................................................ Macheath, Brown
"Wedding Song" (Reprise) ...................................................................................................Gang
"Love Song" ..................................................................................................Macheath, Polly
Scene 3: Peachum's shop, Thursday morning
"Barbara Song" ................................................................................................................. Polly
First 3 Penny Finale ............................................................Polly, Mr. and Mrs. Peachum

## ACT II

Scene 1: The stable, Thursday afternoon
"Melodrama and Polly's Song" ............................................................................Macheath, Polly
Interlude
"Ballad of the Prisoner of Sex" ..................................................................... Mrs. Peachum
Scene 2: A whorehouse in Tunbridge, later that afternoon
"Pimp's Ballad (Tango)" ..................................................................................... Macheath, Jenny
Scene 3: Old Bailey jail, immediately afterward.
"Ballad of Living in Style" ................................................................................................Macheath
"Jealousy Duet" ..........................................................................................................Lucy, Polly
Second 3 Penny Finale ................................................Macheath, Mrs. Peachum, Chorus

## ACT III

Scene 1: Peachum's shop, late that night
"Ballad of the Prisoner of Sex" (Reprise) ..................................................... Mrs. Peachum
"Song of Futility" ............................................................................................Mr. Peachum
Scene 2: Lucy's room in the Old Bailey
"Lucy's Aria" ...............................................................................................................Lucy
Interlude
"Solomon Song" ..............................................................................................................Jenny
Scene 3: Macheath's cell in the Old Bailey, 6 a.m. Friday
"Call From the Grave" ................................................................................................Macheath
"Epitaph" ......................................................................................................................Macheath
"March to the Gallows" ..........................................................................................Orchestra
Third 3 Penny Finale ..............................................................................Entire Company

**Prince of Central Park** (4). Musical based on the novel by Evan H. Rhodes; music by
Don Sebesky; lyrics by Gloria Nissenson. Produced by Abe Hirschfeld and Jan McArt,
Karen Poindexter executive producer, Belle M. Deitch associate producer, at the Belasco
Theater. Opened November 9, 1989. (Closed November 11, 1989)

Jay-Jay .......................................Richard H. Blake
School Guard; Park Ranger Rupp;
    Waiter ............................................. Sel Vitella
Street Person; Stock Broker; Young
    Richard .......................................John Hoshko
Street Person; Officer Simpson ...........Adrian Bailey
Agnes; Anna Squagliatoria .............. Bonnie Perlman
Officer Washinski; Young Margie .... Ruth Gottschall
Bag Lady; Floor Walker .................Marilyn Hudgins
May Berg; Twitchy .....................Anne-Marie Gerard
Aerobics Instructor ......................Stephen Bourneuf
Margie Miller ...............................Jo Anne Worley
Sally ................................................Chris Callen
Fist .....................................................Sean Grant
Bird Brain .............................................Jason Ma
Feather; Ballet Dancer ...................... Alice Yearsley
Elmo ..............................................Anthony Galde
Carpenter; Maitre d' ............................. Terry Eno

Aerobics Students: Adrian Bailey, Terry Eno, Ruth Gottschall, Anne-Marie Gerard, John Hoshko, Sel
Vitella. Tap Dancers: Adrian Bailey, Stephen Bourneuf, Ruth Gottschall, John Hoshko, Bonnie Perlman.
Mannequins, Tango Dancers: Adrian Bailey, Stephen Bourneuf, Ruth Gottschall, John Hoshko, Jason Ma,
Bonnie Perlman, Alice Yearsley.

Musicians: Joel Silberman conductor, keyboards; Henry Aronson associate conductor, synthesizer; Jim
Young drums; Vince Fay fender bass; Ron Delsini synthesizer, programmer; Ken Sebesky guitar; Tony
Kadleck, Jeff Parke trumpet; Keith O'Quinn trombone; John Purcell, Lawrence Feldman woodwinds.

Standbys: Miss Worley—Jan McArt; Mr. Blake—David Burdick. Understudies: Mr. Galde—Sean Grant; Miss Yearsley—Anne-Marie Gerard; Misses Callen, Hudgins, Perlman—Terry Iten. Swings: Terry Iten, Jody Keith Barrie.

Directed and choreographed by Tony Tanner; musical direction and vocal arrangements, Joel Silberman; scenery and costumes, Michael Bottari, Ronald Case; lighting, Norman Coates; sound, Daryl Bornstein; associate choreographer, Stephen Bourneuf; supervisor orchestrator, Don Sebesky; dance arrangements, Henry Aronson; production stage manager, Steven Ehrenberg; stage manager, Susan Whelan; press, Shirley Herz Associates, Glenna Freedman.

Time: The present. Place: Various locations in and around Central Park.

The adventures of an orphan youth managing to live in a tree house in Central Park. Previously produced in regional theater in Key West and Miami Beach, Fla.

## ACT I

"Here's Where I Belong" ..................................................................................................... Jay-Jay, Ensemble
"All I've Got Is Me" ......................................................................................................................... Jay-Jay
"New Leaf" ........................................................................................................... Margie, Aerobics Club
"Follow the Leader" ......................................................................................... Elmo, Gang, Jay-Jay
Montage: "Here's Where I Belong" ............................................................................... Ensemble
"We Were Dancing" .................................................... Margie, Young Richard, Young Margie
"One of a Kind" ............................................................................................................ Margie, Jay-Jay
"I Fly by Night" ................................................................................................................. Elmo, Gang
"Zap" ..................................................................................................... Margie, Jay-Jay, Ensemble

## ACT II

"Good Evening" ............................................................................................................................ Ensemble
"All I've Got Is Me (Reprise)" .................................................................................. Margie, Jay-Jay
"They Don't Give You Life at Sixteen" ................................................................. Elmo, Gang
"Red" ................................................................................................................... Margie, Ensemble
"I Fly by Night" (Reprise) ....................................................................... Elmo, Gang, Jay-Jay
"The Prince of Central Park" ............................................................................................... Jay-Jay
"One of a Kind" (Reprise) ....................................................................................................... Margie

**\*Grand Hotel** (229). Musical based on Vicki Baum's *Grand Hotel*; book by Luther Davis; songs by Robert Wright and George Forrest; additional music and lyrics by Maury Yeston. Produced by Martin Richards, Mary Lea Johnson, Sam Crothers, Sander Jacobs, Kenneth D. Greenblatt, Paramount Pictures and Jujamcyn Theaters, in association with Patty Grubman and Marvin A. Krauss, at the Martin Beck Theater. Opened November 12, 1989.

| | | | |
|---|---|---|---|
| Col. Dr. Otternschlag | John Wylie | Zinnowitz | Hal Robinson |
| Doorman | Charles Mandracchia | Gen. Dr. Preysing | Timothy Jerome |
| Countess and Gigolo | Yvonne Marceau, | Flaemmchen | Jane Krakowski |
| | Pierre Dulaine | Otto Kringelein | Michael Jeter |
| Mme. Peepee | Kathi Moss | Raffaela | Karen Akers |
| Rohna | Rex D. Hays | Sandor | Mitchell Jason |
| Bellboys: | | Witt | Michel Moinot |
| Georg Strunk | Ken Jennings | Elizaveta Grushinskaya | Liliane Montevecchi |
| Kurt Kronenberg | Keith Crowningshield | Baron Felix Von Gaigern | David Carroll |
| Hanns Bittner | Gerrit de Beer | The Jimmys | David Jackson, Danny Strayhorn |
| Willibald | J. J. Jepson | Scullery Workers: | |
| Erik | Bob Stillman | Ernst Schmidt | Henry Grossman |
| Telephone Operators: | | Franz Kohl | William Ryall |
| Hildegarde Bratts | Jennifer Lee Andrews | Werner Holst | David Elledge |
| Sigfriede Holzheim | Suzanne Henderson | Gunther Gustafsson | Walter Willison |
| Wolffe Bratts | Lynnette Perry | Courtesan | Suzanne Henderson |
| Chauffeur | Ben George | Maid | Jennifer Lee Andrews |

Standbys: Misses Montevecchi, Akers, Moss—Penny Worth; Messrs. Carroll, Jerome, Wylie—Mark Jacoby. Understudies: Mr. Jason—Gerrit de Beer; Messrs. Robinson, Stillman—Michael DeVries; Miss Marceau—Niki Harris; Mr. Moinot—Ken Jennings; Messrs. Jeter, Dulaine—J. J. Jepson; Miss Krakowski—Lynnette Perry; Messrs. Hays, George—William Ryall; Messrs. Jackson, Strayhorn—Glenn Turner. Swings: Michael DeVries, Niki Harris, Glenn Turner.

Directed and choreographed by Tommy Tune; musical and vocal direction, Jack Lee; scenery, Tony Walton; costumes, Santo Loquasto; lighting, Jules Fisher; sound, Otts Munderloh; orchestrations, Peter Matz; music supervision and additional music, Wally Harper; associate director, Bruce Lumpkin; musical coordinator, John Monaco; associate producers, Sandra Greenblatt, Martin R. Kaufman, Kim Poster; stage managers, Bruce Lumpkin, David Wolfe, Robert Kellogg; press, the Jacksina Company, Judy Jacksina, Julianne Waldheim, Laura Leinweber, Brig Berney.

Time: 1928. Place: Grand Hotel, Berlin. The play was presented without intermission.

Lives of glamorous and lowly hotel customers interconnect and give off sparks of drama and romance in this stage version subtitled *The Musical*, as in the novel, the 1932 stage version by W.A. Drake produced on Broadway 11/13/30 for 257 performances and the 1932 motion picture version starring Greta Garbo and John Barrymore, with Lionel Barrymore as Kringelein. A version of the present show was produced in tryout as *At the Grand* in 1958 on the West Coast.

Brent Barrett replaced David Carroll 5/8/90; Rex Smith replaced Brent Barrett 5/29/90.

A Best Play; see page 166.

## SCENES AND MUSICAL NUMBERS

The Presentation of the Comany
"The Grand Parade"** .................................................................................................Company
Scene 1: The Grand Hotel lobby and far below in the scullery
"As It Should Be"* ...........................................................................................................Baron
"Some Have, Some Have Not"* .....................................................................Scullery Workers
"At the Grand Hotel"** ...............................................................................................Kringelein
"Table With a View"* ................................................................................................Kringelein
Scene 2: The Moroccan Coffee Bar
"Maybe My Baby Loves Me" ...........................................................................................Jimmys
Scene 3: A corner of the Grand Ballroom
"Fire and Ice"* ....................................................................................................Grushinskaya
"Twenty-Two Years"** ....................................................................................................Raffaela
"Villa on a Hill" ..............................................................................................................Raffaela
Scene 4: The ladies' powder room
"I Want to Go to Hollywood"** ...............................................................................Flaemmchen
Scene 5: Men's washroom and the hotel bar
"Everybody's Doing It"** .................................................................................................Preysing
"The Crooked Path"* ......................................................................................................Preysing
Scene 6: The Baron's room
"As It Should Be"* (Reprise)................................................................................................Baron
Scene 7: The Yellow Pavilion
"Who Couldn't Dance With You?" ...............................................................................Kringelein
Scene 8: The hotel conference room
"The Boston Merger"* ....................................................................................................Preysing
Scene 9: Backstage at the Opera House
"No Encore" .............................................................................................................Grushinskaya
Scene 10: The financial corner of the hotel lobby
Scene 11: The roof of the Grand Hotel
"Fire and Ice" (Reprise) ......................................................................................................Baron
Scene 12: Grushinskaya's suite
"Love Can't Happen"** ...............................................................................Baron, Grushinskaya
Scene 13: Raffaela's room
"What She Needs"* .........................................................................................................Raffaela
Scene 14: The hotel conference room and just inside the ever-revolving door
Scene 15: Raffaela's room

Scene 16: Grushinskaya's suite
"Bonjour Amour"** ...................................................................................................................Grushinskaya
Scene 17: The hotel bar
"Happy"...........................................................................................................................................Company
"We'll Take a Glass Together"* ......................................................................................................Kringelein
Scene 18:  A cross corridor upstairs in the hotel; the Doctor's room; Preysing's room; Flaemmchen's
           adjoining room; Kringelein's room; the bedchamber of the Countess and the Gigolo.
"I Waltz Alone"* ..................................................................................................................................Doctor
"Roses at the Station"** ...........................................................................................................................Baron
Scene 19:  Grushinskaya's suite; Kringelein's room; Preysing's room
"How Can I Tell Her?"*.........................................................................................................................Raffaela
Scene 20:  The lobby of the Grand Hotel
"As It Should Be"* (Reprise)....................................................................................................Company
"Some Have, Some Have Not"* (Reprise) ...............................................................................Scullery Workers
"The Grand Parade"** (Reprise) .......................................................................................................Company
The Grand Finale
"The Grand Waltz" .............................................................................................................................Company
*Lyrics revised by Maury Yeston
**Music and lyrics by Maury Yeston

**A Few Good Men** (226).  By Aaron Sorkin.  Produced by David Brown, Lewis Allen, Robert Whitehead, Roger L. Stevens, Kathy Levin, Suntory International Corp. and The Shubert Organization at The Music Box.  Opened November 15, 1989.

| | | | |
|---|---|---|---|
| Sentry | Ron Ostrow | Pfc. William T. Santiago | Arnold Molina |
| Lance Cpl. Harold W. Dawson | Victor Love | Lt. Col. Nathan Jessep | Stephen Lang |
| Pfc. Louden Downey | Michael Dolan | Lt. Jonathan James Kendrick | Ted Marcoux |
| Lt. j.g. Sam Weinberg | Mark Nelson | Lt. Jack Ross | Clark Gregg |
| Lt. j.g. Daniel A. Kaffee | Tom Hulce | Cpl. Jeffrey Owen Howard | Geoffrey Nauffts |
| Lt. Cmdr. Joanne Galloway | Megan Gallagher | Capt. Julius Alexander Randolph | Paul Butler |
| Capt. Isaac Whitaker | Edmond Genest | Cmdr. Walter Stone | Fritz Sperberg |
| Capt. Matthew A. Markinson | Robert Hogan | | |

Marines, Sailors, M.P.s, Lawyers, et al:  Stephen Bradbury, Jeffrey Dreisbach, Michael Genet, George Gerdes, Joshua Molina.

Understudies:  Mr. Hulce—Clark Gregg; Messrs. Nelson, Dolan, Nauffts—Arnold Molina; Messrs. Love, Molina—Michael Genet; Messrs. Genest, Hogan, Butler—Stephen Bradbury; Messrs. Lang, Gregg—George Gerdes; Messrs. Marcoux, Sperberg—Jeffrey Dreisbach; Marines, Sailors, M.P.s, Lawyers—Ron Ostrow. Standby:  Miss Gallagher—Annette Helde.

Directed by Don Scardino; scenery, Ben Edwards; costumes, David C. Woolard; lighting, Thomas R. Skelton; sound score and design, John Gromada; produced in association with John F. Kennedy Center for the Performing Arts; production stage manager, Dianne Trulock; stage manager, John Handy; press, David Powers.

Time:  The summer of 1986.  Place:  Various locations in Washington, D.C. and on the United States Naval Base in Guantanamo Bay, Cuba.  The play was presented in two parts.

"A work of fiction inspired by an occurrence which served as a point of departure for the author," Navy lawyers confront the problem of a Marine martinet who exceeds the demands of discipline and authority while guarding the Navy Base's fence line.  Previously produced at the University of Virginia, Charlottesville, and Washington, D.C.

Timothy Busfield replaced Tom Hulce 5/14/90.

**Gypsy** (225).  Revival of the musical suggested by the memoirs of Gypsy Rose Lee; book by Arthur Laurents; music by Jule Styne; lyrics by Stephen Sondheim; original production directed and choreographed by Jerome Robbins.  Produced by Barry and Fran Weissler, Kathy Levin and Barry Brown at the St. James Theater.  Opened November 16, 1989.

THE CIRCLE—Rex Harrison, Glynis Johns and Stewart
Granger in the revival of the comedy by W. Somerset Maugham

| | | | |
|---|---|---|---|
| Uncle Jocko; Kringelein | Tony Hoty | Yonkers | Bruce Moore |
| George; Mr. Goldstone | John Remme | L.A. | Craig Waletzko |
| Clarence | Bobby John Carter | Kansas | Ned Hannah |
| Balloon Girl | Jeana Haege | Flagstaff | Paul Geraci |
| Baby Louise | Kristen Mahon | St Paul | Alec Timerman |
| Baby June | Christen Tassin | Miss Cratchitt; Tessie Tura | Barbara Erwin |
| Rose | Tyne Daly | Agnes | Lori Ann Mahl |
| Pop; Cigar | Ronn Carroll | Pastey; Bougeron-Cochon | Jim Bracchitta |
| Weber; Phil | Mace Barrett | Mazeppa | Jana Robbins |
| Herbie | Jonathan Hadary | Electra | Anna McNeely |
| Louise | Crista Moore | Maid | Ginger Prince |
| June | Tracy Venner | Swings | Julie Graves, Eric H. Kaufman |
| Tulsa | Robert Lambert | | |

Newsboys: Demetri Callas, Bobby John Carter, Danny Cistone, Jason Minor. Hollywood Blondes: Barbara Folts, Teri Furr, Nancy Melius, Michele Pigliavento, Robin Robinson.

Standbys: Misses Robbins, Erwin, McNeely—Ginger Prince; Mr. Hadary—Mace Barrett; Miss Daly—Jana Robbins. Understudies: Mr. Remme—Jim Bracchitta; Messrs. Carroll, Bracchitta—John Remme; Mr. Barrett—Tony Hoty; Mr. Lambert—Alec Timerman; Miss Moore—Michele Pigliavento; Misses Mahl, Venner—Teri Furr; Misses Venner, Moore—Jeana Haege.

Directed by Arthur Laurents; Jerome Robbins's choreography reproduced by Bonnie Walker; musical direction, Eric Stern; scenery, Kenneth Foy; costumes, Theoni V. Aldredge; lighting, Natasha Katz; sound, Peter Fitzgerald; automation and showdeck, Feller Precision; orchestrations, Sid Ramin, Robert Ginzler; dance music arrangements, John Kander; assistant to the director, Richard Sabellico; musical coordinator, John Monaco; produced in association with Tokyo Broadcasting System International, Inc. and Pace Theatrical Group; production stage manager, Craig Jacobs; stage manager, Tom Capps; press, Shirley Herz Associates, Robert Larkin.

Time: From the 1920s to the 1930s. Place: In various cities throughout the U.S.A. The play was presented in two parts.

*Gypsy* was first produced on Broadway 5/21/59 for 702 performances and was revived on Broadway 9/23/74 for 120 performances. The present production was first produced on a tour of the U.S. which began 5/2/89 in Chattanooga.

The list of musical numbers in *Gypsy* appears on page 338 of *The Best Plays of 1958–59.*

Jana Robbins replaced Tyne Daly and Ginger Prince replaced Jana Robbins 2/20/90–2/25/90.

**The Circle** (208). Revival of the play by W. Somerset Maugham. Produced by Elliot Martin, The Shubert Organization and Suntory International Corp. at the Ambassador Theater. Opened November 20, 1989. (Closed May 20, 1990)

| | |
|---|---|
| Arnold Champion-Cheney.............. Robin Chadwick | Clive Champion-Cheney ................ Stewart Granger |
| Mrs. Shenstone............................Patricia Conolly | Butler.............................................Louis Turenne |
| Footman......................................Robertson Dean | Lady Catherine Champion-Cheney........Glynis Johns |
| Elizabeth .......................................Roma Downey | Lord Porteous...................................Rex Harrison |
| Edward Luton ............................... Harley Venton | |

Understudies: Messrs. Harrison, Granger—Louis Turenne; Messrs. Chadwick, Venton—Robertson Dean; Misses Downey, Conolly—Ellen Maguire; Messrs. Turenne, Dean—Hugh A. Rose.

Directed by Brian Murray; scenery, Desmond Heeley; costumes, Jane Greenwood; lighting, John Michael Deegan; production stage manager, Mitchell Erickson; stage manager, Wally Peterson; press, Jeffrey Richards Associates, Irene Gandy.

Place: The drawing room at Aston-Adey, Arnold Champion-Cheney's house in Dorset. The play was presented in three parts.

*The Circle* was first produced on Broadway 9/12/21 and was named a Best Play of its season. It has been revived on Broadway 4/18/38 for 72 performances and off Broadway 3/26/74 for 71 performances and 2/20/86 for 33 performances.

**Artist Descending a Staircase** (37). By Tom Stoppard. Produced by The Staircase Company (Emanuel Azenberg, Roger Berlind, Dick Button, Dennis Grimaldi, Robert Whitehead & Roger L. Stevens, Kathy Levin, Michael Brandman associate producer) at the Helen Hayes Theater. Opened November 30, 1989. (Closed December 31, 1989)

| | |
|---|---|
| Beauchamp.......................................Harold Gould | Young Beauchamp.......................Michael Cumpsty |
| Martello ...................................Paxton Whitehead | Young Martello .....................................Jim Fyfe |
| Donner.........................................John McMartin | Young Donner............................. Michael Winther |
| Sophie ......................................... Stephanie Roth | |

Standbys: Messrs. Gould, Whitehead, McMartin—Edmund Lyndeck; Messrs. Cumpsty, Fyfe, Winther—Brian Cousins; Miss Roth—Marcia Cross.

Directed by Tim Luscombe; scenery, Tony Straiges; costumes, Joseph G. Aulisi; lighting, Tharon Musser; sound, Tom Morse; music and sound effects, Kevin Malpass; production stage manager, Peter Lawrence; stage manager, Don Judge; press, Bill Evans & Associates, Becky Flora, Jim Randolph.

Time: Symmetrically arranged around Scene 6. Scene 1: A summer afternoon, 1972. Scene 2: A few hours earlier. Scene 3: A week earlier. Scene 4: 1922. Scene 5: 1920.

Scene 6: 1914

Scene 7: Continues from the end of Scene 5. Scene 8: Continues from the end of Scene 4. Scene 9: Continues from the end of Scene 3. Scene 10: Continues from the end of Scene 2. Scene 11: Continues from the end of Scene 1.

Moving backward from 1972 to 1914 and forward to 1972 again, a series of episodes about art and artists, with love and murder as ingredients. A foreign play previously produced as a play by the BBC and on the stage in London.

**\*Lincoln Center Theater**. Schedule of two programs. **The Tenth Man** (41). Revival of the play by Paddy Chayefsky. Opened December 10, 1989. (Closed January 14, 1990) **\*Some Americans Abroad** (33). Transfer from off Broadway of the play by Richard

Nelson. Opened May 2, 1990. Produced by Lincoln Center Theater, Gregory Mosher director, Bernard Gersten executive director, at the Vivian Beaumont Theater.

## THE TENTH MAN

| | | | |
|---|---|---|---|
| Hirschman; Cabalist | Joseph Wiseman | Arthur Brooks | Peter Friedman |
| Schlissel | Bob Dishy | Harris | Carl Don |
| Zitorsky | Jack Weston | Elder Kessler | David Berman |
| Sexton | Sidney Armus | Younger Kessler | Kenny Morris |
| Alper | Ron Rifkin | Rabbi | Michael Mantell |
| Foreman | Alan Manson | Policeman | Dan Daily |
| Evelyn Foreman | Phoebe Cates | | |

Standbys: Messrs. Wiseman, Weston—Ben Kapen; Messrs. Dishy, Rifkin, Armus—Stan Lachow; Mr. Friedman—David Berman; Mr. Mantell—Kenny Morris; Miss Cates—Cara Buono; Mr. Manson—Carl Don; Messrs. Berman, Morris, Daily—David Pittu.

Directed by Ulu Grosbard; scenery, Santo Loquasto; costumes, Jane Greenwood; lighting, Dennis Parichy; sound, Daniel Schreier; poster art, James McMullan; production stage manager, Maureen F. Gibson; stage manager, Fredric H. Orner; press, Merle Debuskey, Bruce Campbell.

Time: 1959. Place: An Orthodox synagogue in Mineola, L.I. Act I: Before morning prayers. Act II, Scene 1: The morning prayers. Scene 2: Before the afternoon prayers. Act III: The exorcism.

The last major New York revival of *The Tenth Man* took place on Broadway at City Center 11/8/67 for 23 performances.

## SOME AMERICANS ABROAD

| | | | |
|---|---|---|---|
| Joe Taylor | Colin Stinton | Harriet Baldwin | Jane Hoffman |
| Philip Brown | John Bedford Lloyd | Orson Baldwin | Henderson Forsythe |
| Henry McNeil | Nathan Lane | Joanne Smith | Ann Talman |
| Betty McNeil | Kate Burton | An American | John Rothman |
| Frankie Lewis | Frances Conroy | Donna Silliman | Elisabeth Shue |
| Katie Taylor | Cara Buono | | |

Musicians: Michelle Johnson singer; Joshua Rosenblum musical director, pianist; Michael Goetz bass.

Understudies: Messrs. Stinton, Lloyd, Rothman—Stephen Rowe; Misses Buono, Shue, Talman—Carol Schneider; Mr. Forsythe—Robert Hock; Misses Conroy, Burton—Rebecca Nelson; Miss Hoffman—Jennie Ventriss.

Directed by Roger Michell; scenery and costumes, Alexandra Byrne; lighting, Rick Fisher; original music, Jeremy Sams; poster art, Edward Sorel; production stage manager, Michael F. Ritchie; stage manager, Michael Goetz.

Time: The present. Place: Various locations in England. The play was presented in two parts.

American professors, Anglophiles, on a group theater tour of England. An American play previously produced in London and off Broadway in this production by Lincoln Center Theater 2/11/90–4/22/90 for 81 performances; see its entry in the Plays Produced Off Broadway section of this volume.

**City of Angels** (214). Musical with book by Larry Gelbart; music by Cy Coleman; lyrics by David Zippel. Produced by Nick Vanoff, Roger Berlind, Jujamcyn Theaters, Suntory International Corp. and The Shubert Organization at the Virginia Theater. Opened December 11, 1989.

| PERFORMER | MOVIE CAST | HOLLYWOOD CAST |
|---|---|---|
| Rene Auberjonois | Irwin S. Irving | Buddy Fidler |
| James Cahill | Dr. Mandril | Barber |
| Gregg Edelman | | Stine |
| Shawn Elliott | Munoz | Pancho Vargas |
| Tom Galantich | Orderly; Officer Pasco | Gene |
| Eleanor Glockner | Madame | Hairdresser; Masseuse |
| Randy Graff | Oolie | Donna |

| PERFORMER | MOVIE CAST | HOLLYWOOD CAST |
|---|---|---|
| James Hindman | Orderly; Mahoney | Del DaCosta |
| Dee Hoty | Alaura Kingsley | Carla Haywood |
| Alvin Lum | Yamato | Cinematographer |
| Jacquey Maltby | Bootsie | |
| Kay McClelland | Bobbi | Gabby |
| James Naughton | Stone | |
| Keith Perry | Luther Kingsley | Werner Kriegler |
| Herschel Sparber | Big Six | Studio Cop |
| Susan Terry | Margaret | Stand-In |
| Evan Thompson | Commissioner Gaines | Shoeshine |
| Doug Tompos | Peter Kingsley | Gerald Pierce |
| Scott Waara | Jimmy Powers | Jimmy Powers |
| Raymond Xifo | Sonny | Studio Cop |
| Rachel York | Mallory Kingsley | Avril Raines |

Angel City 4: Peter David, Amy Jane London, Gary Kahn, Jackie Presti.

Orchestra: Gordon Lowry Harrell conductor; Kathy Sommer associate conductor, keyboards; Lee Musiker keyboards; Dave Ratajczak drums; Dave Fink bass; Bob Rose guitar; Charles Descarfino percussion; Byron Stripling, Glenn Drewes, Dave Rogers trumpet; Jim Pugh, Sy Berger, George Flynn trombone; Peter Gordon, French horn; Mike Migliori, Ed Salkin, Bob Steen, Ken Hitchock, John Campo reeds; Belinda Whitney concertmistress; Cenovia Cummins, Carl Kawahara violin; Astrid Schween cello.

Swings: Chrissy Faith, Jan Maxwell, Marcus Neville. Understudies (listed by role): Stone, Jimmy Powers—Tom Galantich; Stein, Buddy, Irwin S. Irving, Munoz, Sonny—James Hindman; Alaura, Carla—Jan Maxwell, Susan Terry; Gabby, Bobbi—Susan Terry; Oolie, Donna, Madame, Masseuse, Hairdresser—Jacquey Maltby; Luther, Werner, Dr. Mandril, Big Six—Evan Thompson; Barber, Peter Kingsley, Gerald Pierce, Orderly, Mahoney, DaCosta, Officer Pasco, Gene, Commissioner Gaines, Angel City 4—Marcus Neville; Margaret, Bootsie, Angel City 4—Chrissy Faith.

Directed by Michael Blakemore; musical numbers staged by Walter Painter; musical direction, Gordon Lowry Harrell; scenery, Robin Wagner; costumes, Florence Klotz; lighting, Paul Gallo; sound, Peter Fitzgerald, Bernard Fox; orchestrations, Billy Byers; vocal arrangements, Cy Coleman, Yaron Gershovsky; fight staging, B. H. Barry; production stage manager, Steven Zweigbaum; stage manager, Brian Meister; press, Bill Evans & Associates, Becky Flora, Jim Randolph.

Time: The late 1940s. Place: Los Angeles.

The cinema adventures of a Philip Marlowe-type private eye (Stone), synchronized with the studio experiences of the author (Stine) who is writing a screen play about him, sometimes ingeniously intermingled.

A Best Play; see page 220.

## ACT I

Prelude: Theme from *City of Angels*.........................................................Angel City 4, Studio Orchestra
Scene 1: L.A. County Hospital
Scene 2: Stone's office, one week earlier
  "Double Talk"...................................................................................................... Stone, Alaura
Scene 3: Writer's cell, Master Pictures Studio
Scene 4: Buddy Fidler's office
  "Double Talk"...................................................................................................Buddy, Stine
Scene 5: Stone's office
Scene 6: Stine's bedroom, the Garden of Allah
  "What You Don't Know About Women"................................................................Gabby, Oolie
Scene 7: Stone's bungalow
  "Ya Gotta Look Out for Yourself".........................................................Jimmy Powers, Angel City 4
Scene 8: Buddy's office
  "The Buddy System"...............................................................................................Buddy, Donna
Scene 9: Stone's bungalow
Scene 10: The Blue Note
  "With Every Breath I Take"............................................................................................Bobbi
Scene 11: Bobbi's dressing room

Scene 12: Writer's cell
Scene 13: The Kingsley Mansion
Scene 14: The solarium
"The Tennis Song"......................................................................................... Stone, Alaura
Scene 15: The Search
"Ev'rybody's Gotta Be Somewhere".................................................. Stone, Angel City 4
Scene 16: Stone's bungalow
"Lost and Found"........................................................................................................Mallory
Scene 17: Donna's bedroom
Scene 18: Stone's bungalow
Scene 19: L.A. County Morgue
Scene 20: Buddy's office
Scene 21: The Morgue
"All Ya Have to Do Is Wait"............................................... Munoz, Yamato, Mahoney, Officer Pasco
"You're Nothing Without Me" ...................................................................................Stine, Stone

## ACT II

Scene 1: A recording studio
"Stay With Me"...........................................................................Jimmy Powers, Angel City 4
Scene 2: A Bel-Air bedroom
Scene 3: L.A. County Jail
Scene 4: Oolie's bedroom
"You Can Always Count on Me"........................................................................... Oolie
Scene 5: Donna's bedroom
"You Can Always Count on Me".............................................................................Donna
Scene 6: A Bel-Air garden
Scene 7: Buddy's study
Scene 8: The Jail
Scene 9: Buddy's study
Scene 10: Alaura's bedroom
Scene 11: Buddy's office
Scene 12: Stine's apartment, New York
"It Needs Work"................................................................................................Gabby
Scene 13: The Red Room
"With Every Breath I Take" (Reprise)........................................................Stone, Bobbi
Scene 14: The Kingsley solarium
Scene 15: Writer's cell
"Funny"...............................................................................................................Stine
Scene 16: A sound stage, Master Pictures Studio
"You're Nothing Without Me" (Reprise) ........................................... Stone, Stine, Gabby

**\*Tru** (191). One-man performance by Robert Morse of a play by Jay Presson Allen; adapted from the words and works of Truman Capote. Produced by Lewis Allen and David Brown with Suntory International Corp. and The Shubert Organization, in association with Landmark Entertainment Corp., at the Booth Theater. Opened December 14, 1989.

Recorded voices: Jan—Jayne Atkinson; Telephone Operator—Jill Choder; Mrs. Ferguson—Sara Schiff; Secretary—Jeanne Tripplehorn.
Directed by Jay Presson Allen; scenery, David Mitchell; costumes, Sarah Edwards; lighting, Ken Billington, Jason Kantrowitz; sound, Otts Munderloh; production stage manager, Ruth Kreshka; stage manager, Jane Grey; press, Bill Evans & Associates, Becky Flora, Jim Randolph.
Time: The week before Christmas, 1975. Place: Truman Capote's New York apartment at 870 United Nations Plaza. The play was presented in two parts.
Robert Morse as a lonely Truman Capote, ostracized by his high society friends after his expose of their foibles and lifestyles in *Answered Prayers*. Previously produced by the New York Stage and Film Company in association with the Powerhouse Theater of Vassar, Poughkeepsie, N.Y.

THE MERCHANT OF VENICE—Two moods of Shylock as portrayed by Dustin Hoffman in the Peter Hall Company revival of the play by William Shakespeare

**The Merchant of Venice** (81). Revival of the play by William Shakespeare. Produced by Duncan C. Weldon and Jerome Minskoff in association with Punch Productions, in the Peter Hall Company production at the Forty-Sixth Street Theater. Opened December 19, 1989. (Closed March 10, 1990)

| | | | |
|---|---|---|---|
| Antonio | Leigh Lawson | Lancelot Gobbo | Peter-Hugo Daly |
| Bassanio | Nathaniel Parker | Old Gobbo | Leo Leyden |
| Lorenzo | Richard Garnett | Portia | Geraldine James |
| Gratiano | Michael Siberry | Nerissa | Julia Swift |
| Salerio | Donald Burton | Balthasar | Neal Ben-Ari |
| Solanio | Gordon Gould | Stefano | John Wojda |
| Leonardo | Ben Browder | Prince of Morocco | Herb Downer |
| Shylock | Dustin Hoffman | Prince of Aragon | Michael Carter |
| Jessica | Francesca Buller | Duke of Venice | Basil Henson |
| Tubal | Leon Lissek | | |

Others: William Beckwith, Neal Ben-Ari, Margery Daley, Dale Dickey, Elisabeth Engan, Denis Holmes, Wilbur Pauley, Margaret Poyner, Gary Rayppy, John Norman Thomas, Isaiah Whitlock Jr., John Wojda, Taylor Young.

Musician: Christina Sunnerstam violin. Singers: Margery Daley, Elisabeth Engan sopranos; Wilbur Pauley bass. Electronic programming: Graeme Pleeth.

Understudies: Messrs. Garnett, Wojda—Ben Browder; Mr. Lawson—Michael Carter; Messrs. Hoffman, Carter—Neal Ben-Ari; Messrs. Leyden, Lissek, Henson—Denis Holmes; Messrs. Burton, Ben-Ari—William Beckwith; Mr. Parker—John Wojda; Messrs. Downer, Browder—Isiah Whitlock Jr.; Messrs. Gould, Siberry—Gary Rayppy; Mr. Daly—John Norman Thomas; Miss James—Taylor Young; Misses Buller, Swift—Dale Dickey; Miss Daley, Engan (as sopranos)—Margaret Poyner; Mr. Pauley (as bass)—John Norman Thomas.

Directed by Peter Hall; design, Chris Dyer; lighting, Neil Peter Jampolis; original lighting, Mark Henderson; costume supervision, Barbara Forbes; associate director, Giles Block; music, Robert Lockhart; sound, Paul Arditti; executive producer, Thelma Holt; production stage manager, Thomas A. Kelly; stage manager, Charles Kindl; press, the Joshua Ellis Office, Adrian Bryan-Brown.

The last major New York revival of *The Merchant of Venice* took place off Broadway by CSC Repertory 12/14/86 for 36 performances. This production in the Oxford Edition, presented in two parts, was previously produced in London.

**Junon and Avos: The Hope** (48). Musical in the Russian language with book and lyrics by Andrey Voznesensky; music by Alexis Ribnikov. Produced by Pierre Cardin at the New York City Center. Opened January 7, 1990. (Closed February 4, 1990)

| | |
|---|---|
| Count Nikolai Rezanov........... Nikolai Karachentsev | Count Alexey Ruminatsev; Gov. of |
| Conchita........................................Yelena Shanina | San Francisco........................Vladimir Shiryayev |
| 1st Conjurer..................................... Yuri Naumkin | Padre Abella...............................Villor Kuznetsov |
| 2d Conjurer...............................Gennady Trofimov | Interpreter ..................................Rady Ovchinnikov |
| Burning Heretic; Fernando Lopez; | Conchita's Messenger ........................ Yury Zelenin |
| Theatrical Narrator.................. Alexander Abdulov | Singing Mask.............................. Alexander Sado |
| Vision of Woman With Infant ...... Ludmilla Porgina | Storyteller.......................................Philip Casnoff |

Naval Officers: Vladimir Belousov, Boris Chunayev, Vladimir Kuznetsov, Rady Ovchinnikov.

Spanish Ladies: Irena Alfiorova, Tatiana Derbeneva, Ludmilla Porgina, Alexandra Zakharova, Tatiana Rudina, Ludmilla Artemieva.

Russian Sailors, Spaniards, Shareholders of the Russian-American Company, Monks, Chimeras, Others: Vladislav Bykov, Victor Rakov, Alexander Sririn, Nikolai Shucharin, Alexander Karnaushkin, Igor Fokin, Andrey Leonov, Yury Zelenin, Andrey Druzhkin, Gennady Kozlov, Sergey Chonishvilli, Oleg Ruduk, Leonid Luvinsky, Leonid Gromov, Denis Karasov.

Choir: Irene Musayelian, Valentina Prokhorova, Zinaida Morozova, Natalia Mishenko sopranos; Irena Kushnarenko, Valeria Zhivova, Lilia Semashko, Yelena Rudnitskaya altos; Vladimir Tursky tenor; Alexey Larin, Vladimir Prokhorov, Sergey Stepanchenko basses.

Rock Group Araks: Sergey Rudnitsky keyboards; Sergey Rizhov bass guitar; Alexander Sado, Nikolai Parfenyuk, Pavel Smeian vocals; Sergey Berezkin guitar, violin, cello; Anatoly Abromov drums; Yakov Levda, Viktor Denisov brass section; Dimitri Kudriavtsev conductor.

Directed by Mark Zakharov; choreography, Vladimir Vassiliev; scenery, Oleg Sheintsiss; costumes, Valentina Komolova; sound, Abe Jacob; English narration, Susan Silver, Albert Todd; technical supervisor, Steve Cochrane; American producer, Lucy Jarvis; produced by special arrangement with Lencom Theater and the Theater Union of the U.S.S.R.; production stage manager, Paul Moore; stage manager Robin Gray; press, Philip Rinaldi.

Russian rock musical with English narration, a Count gets permission from the Czar to open trade with the U.S. in 1806, comes to America and falls in love. A foreign play previously produced in Moscow and Paris.

**Miss Margarida's Way** (11). Revival of the play by Roberto Athayde. Produced by Bernard and Toby Nussbaum at the Helen Hayes Theater. Opened February 15, 1990. (Closed February 25, 1990)

| | |
|---|---|
| Miss Margarida............................. Estelle Parsons | The Rest of Her Students....................The Audience |
| One of Her Students.........................Koji Okamura | |

Directed by Roberto Athayde; costumes, Santo Loquasto; lighting, Jason Sturm; executive producer, Laurel Ann Wilson; stage manager, Lisa Ledwich; press, the Fred Nathan Company, Marc P. Thibodeau.

*Miss Margarida's Way* was originally produced off Broadway (after a workshop production) by New York Shakespeare Festival 7/31/77 for 30 performances before being transferred by them to Broadway 9/27/77 for 98 additional performances.

**The Sound of Music** (54). Revival of the musical suggested by *The Trapp Family Singers* by Maria Augusta Trapp; book by Howard Lindsay & Russel Crouse; music by Richard Rodgers; lyrics by Oscar Hammerstein II. Produced by New York City Opera in association with James M. Nederlander at the New York State Theater. Opened March 8, 1990. (Closed April 22, 1990)

| | | | |
|---|---|---|---|
| Maria Rainer | Debby Boone | Kurt | Ted Huffman |
| Sister Berthe | Jill Bosworth | Brigitta | Kia Graves |
| Sister Margaretta | Michele McBride | Marta | Lauren Gaffney |
| Mother Abbess | Claudia Cummings | Gretl | Mary Mazzello |
| Sister Sophia | Robin Tabachnik | Rolf Gruber | Marc Heller |
| Capt. Georg von Trapp | Laurence Guittard | Elsa Schraeder | Marianne Tatum |
| Franz | David Rae Smith | Ursula | Bridget Ramos |
| Frau Schmidt | Ellen Tovatt | Max Detweiler | Werner Klemperer |
| Capt. von Trapp's Children: | | Herr Zeller | Louis Perry |
| Liesl | Emily Loesser | Baron Elberfeld | William Ledbetter |
| Friedrich | Richard H. Blake | Postulant | Barbara Shirvis |
| Louisa | Kelly Karbacz | Admiral von Schreiber | Glenn Rowen |

New York City Opera Orchestra: John Pintavalle concert master; Alicia Edelberg, Yevgenia Strenger associate concert masters; Martha Marshall assistant concert master; Anne Fryer, Jack Katz, Kate Light, Nancy McAlhany, Junko Ota, Helene Shomer, Sander Strenger, Eric Wyrick, Fred Vogelgesang first violin; Alan Martin (principal), Heidi Carney, Susan Gellert, Yana Goichman, Abram Kapstan, Martha Mott, Jan Mullen, Barbara Randall, Meyer Schumitzky, Helen Strilec second violin; Eufrosina Raileanu (principal), Robert Benjamin, Donald Dal Maso, Laurence Fader, Susan Gingold, Warren Laffredo, Jack Rosenberg viola; Robert Gardner (principal), Gregorio Follari, Alla Goldberg, Esther Gruhn, Charles Moss, Bruce Rogers cello; Lewis Paer (principal), Joseph Bongiorno, Marji Danilow, Harold Schachner bass; John Wion (principal), Janet Arms, Gerardo Levy flute.

Also Janet Arms piccolo; Leonard Arner (principal), Doris Goltzer, Livio Caroli oboe; Doris Goltzer, English horn; Charles Russo (principal), Mitchell Kriegler, Laura Flax clarinet; Mitchell Kriegler bass clarinet; Frank Morelli (principal), Cyrus Segal, Bernadette Zirkuli bassoon; Cyrus Segal contra bassoon; Stewart Rose (principal), Katherine Eisner, Anthony Miranda, Frank Santonicola, Sharon Moe horn; Thomas Lisanbee (principal), Bruce Revesz, Philip Ruecktenwald trumpet; Robert Hauck (principal), James Biddlecombe, David Titcomb trombone; Stephen Johns tuba; Francesca Corsi harp; Leonard Schulman tympani; Howard Van Hyning (principal), Paul Fein percussion. Assistant Conductors: John Beeson, Susan Caldwell, Robert DeCeunynk, Steven Mosteller, Douglas Stanton, Stephen Sulich.

New York City Opera Chorus: Lee Bellaver, Lila Herbert, Paula Hostetter, Paula Liscio, Joyce Lynn, Rita Metzger, Madeleine Mines, Bridget Ramos, Mary Ann Rydzeski, Barbara Shirvis, Kathleen Smith, Sally Williams, Marie Young.

New York City Opera Character Mimes: Eugene Buica, John Csenger, Ernest Foederer, Michael Irwin, John Henry Thomas.

Standbys: Miss Boone—Kathleen Williams; Mr. Guittard—Hal Davis; Miss Cummings—Jill Bosworth; Miss Tatum—Paula Hostetter; Mr. Klemperer—David Rae Smith; Miss Loesser—Kirsten Gamble; Mr. Heller—Andrew Denier; Children—Michelle Aravena, Kirsten Gamble, Elizabeth Hart, Sam Riegel.

Directed by James Hammerstein; musical direction, Richard Parrinello; scenery and lighting, Neil Peter Jampolis; costumes, Suzanne Mess; sound, Abe Jacob; musical staging, Joel Bishoff; orchestrations, Robert Russell Bennett; chorus master, Joseph Colaneri; press, Shirley Herz Associates, Glenna Freedman, Susan Woelzl.

Time: Early in 1938. Place: Austria.

The last major revival of *The Sound of Music* was by New York City Center Light Opera Company 4/26/67 for 23 performances.

The list of scenes and musical numbers in *The Sound of Music* appears on page 303 of *The Best Plays of 1959–60*.

**Oba Oba '90** (45). Musical revue with popular music, folk songs and rhythms of Brazil. Produced by Franco Fontana at the Marquis Theater. Opened March 15, 1990. (Closed April 22, 1990)

| | |
|---|---|
| Monica Acioli | Mara Boeing |
| Velly Bahia | Marcelo Boim |
| Bananal | Mauro Boim |

*OBA OBA '90*—Members of the company in a number from the Brazilian musical

| | |
|---|---|
| Andrea Candida | Maranhao |
| Claudia Capoiera | Wilson Mauro |
| Mario Capoiera | Meia-Noite |
| Aderson Cirne | Maguila Meneses |
| Curima | Mirna Montenegro |
| Robertino Da Cuica | Edilson Nery |
| Marquinho Da Dona Geralda | Carlos Oliviera |
| Cesar De Alabama | Pele |
| Pe De Cao | Julio Peluchi |
| Branca De Neve | Edgar Pretinho |
| Delma De Oliviera | Toco Preto |
| Heron DeAngola | Norberto Queiroz |
| Evelyn Eduardo | Paulo Ramos |
| Edson Escovao | Glaucia Ribeiro |
| Betho Filho | Katia Rio |
| Renny Flores | Pena Rodrigues |
| Formiguinha | Ivon Rosas |
| Gerson Galante | Jorge Rum |
| Eliane Garcia | Edmilson Santos |
| Marta Jacintho | Jaime Santos |
| Carlos Leca | Janete Santos |
| Rui Lima | Sonia Santos |
| Amilton Lino | Vivian M. Soares |
| Elisangela Maia | Val Ventilador |
| Malaguti | |

Musical direction, Wilson Mauro; choreography, Roberto Abrahao; technical direction, Mario Ruffa; lighting consultant, Giancarlo Campora; stage manager, Monica Goncalves; press, Peter Cromarty, Kevin Brockman.

New edition of the Brazilian revue of musical variety entertainment, named for a famous showcase in Rio de Janeiro. The previous version was produced on Broadway 3/29/88 for 46 performances.

ACT I: 1. Liberation from Slavery; 2. Homage to "Chorinho"; 3. Samba de Roda-Lambada. 4. Homage to "Chorinho"; 5. Homage to the Northeast; 6. Brazil Capela; 7. Homage to the Bossanova and the 1970s; 8. Tribute to the Brazilian Bombshell, Carmen Miranda.

ACT II: 1. Macumba; 2. Afro-Brazilian folk songs and dances, Berimbau medley, Capoeira of Angola (dance), Maculele, acrobatic Capoeira; 3. Rhythm beaters; 4. Show of Samba dancers; 5. Grand carnival.

**\*Cat on a Hot Tin Roof** (64). Revival of the play by Tennessee Williams. Produced by Barry and Fran Weissler at the Eugene O'Neill Theater. Opened March 21, 1990.

| | | | |
|---|---|---|---|
| Maggie | Kathleen Turner | Rev. Tooker | Nesbitt Blaisdell |
| Brick | Daniel Hugh Kelly | Dr. Baugh | Jerome Dempsey |
| Mae | Debra Jo Rupp | Trixie | Erin Torpey |
| Big Mama | Polly Holliday | Polly | Suzy Bouffard |
| Sookey | Edwina Lewis | Buster | Seth Jerome Walker |
| Dixie | Amy Gross | Sonny | Billy L. Sullivan |
| Big Daddy | Charles Durning | Brightie | Ron Brice |
| Gooper | Kevin O'Rourke | Lacey | Marcial Howard |

Understudies: Misses Turner, Rupp—Mary Layne; Mr. Durning—Jerome Dempsey; Messrs. Kelly, O'Rourke—Tom Stechschulte; Messrs. Blaisdell, Dempsey—John Newton; Miss Gross—Suzy Bouffard.

Directed by Howard Davies; scenery, William Dudley; costumes, Patricia Zipprodt; lighting, Mark Henderson; sound, T. Richard Fitzgerald; music, Ilona Sekacz; technical supervisor, Arthur Siccardi; associate lighting designer, Beverly Emmons; associate producer, Alecia Parker; produced in association with Jujamcyn Theaters and James and Maureen O'Sullivan Cushing; production stage manager, Patrick Horrigan; stage manager, Betsy Nicholson; press, Shirley Herz Associates, Pete Sanders.

Time: An evening in summer. Place: A bed-sitting room and section of the gallery of a plantation home in the Mississippi Delta. The play was presented in three parts.

The last major New York revival of *Cat on a Hot Tin Roof* took place on Broadway 9/24/74 for 160 performances.

**\*The Grapes of Wrath** (81). Adapted by Frank Galati from the novel by John Steinbeck. Produced by The Shubert Organization, Steppenwolf Theater Company, Suntory International Corp. and Jujamcyn Theaters in the Steppenwolf Theater Company production, Randall Arney artistic director, Stephen B. Eich managing director, at the Cort Theater. Opened March 22, 1990.

| | | | |
|---|---|---|---|
| 1st Narrator; Car Salesman; Man Going Back; Weedpatch Camp Director; Mr. Wainright | Francis Guinan | Ruthie | Zoe Taleporos |
| | | Uncle John | James Noah |
| Jim Casy | Terry Kinney | Winfield | Calvin Lennon Armitage |
| Tom Joad | Gary Sinise | Rose of Sharon | Sally Murphy |
| Muley Graves; Floyd Knowles | Rick Snyder | Connie Rivers | Mark Deakins |
| Willy; Mayor of Hooverville | Ron Crawford | Al | Jim True |
| Car Salesman | Keith Byron-Kirk | Gas Station Attendant | Steve Ramsey |
| Car Salesman; Camp Proprietor | Terrance MacNamara | Gas Station Owner; Contractor; 3d Narrator; Hooper Ranch Guard | Michael Hartman |
| Car Salesman; Hooper Ranch Bookkeeper | Eric Simonson | 2d Narrator; Elizabeth Sandry | Cheryl Lynn Bruce |
| Car Salesman; Deputy Sheriff; 4th Narrator | Skipp Sudduth | Agricultural Officers | Theodore Schulz, P. J. Brown |
| | | Camp Nurse | Nicola Sheara |
| Pa | Robert Breuler | Al's Girl | Jessica Wilder |
| Ma | Lois Smith | Mrs. Wainright | Rondi Reed |
| Granma | Lucina Paquet | Aggie Wainright | Kathryn Erbe |
| Grampa | Nathan Davis | Man in the Barn | Lex Monson |
| Noah | Jeff Perry | His Son | Jeremiah Birkett |

Musicians: Michael Smith guitar; Miriam Sturm fiddle; L. J. Slavin harmonica, saw, jaw harp, banjo; William Schwarz accordion, bass.

Understudies: Messrs. Guinan, Monson, Birkett—Keith Byron-Kirk; Messrs. Kinney, Guinan—Rick Snyder; Mr. Sinise—Jeff Perry; Messrs. Snyder, Perry, Crawford—Theodore Schulz; Mr. Breuler—Michael Hartman; Misses Smith, Sturm—Rondi Reed; Misses Paquet, Bruce, Reed—Nicola Sheara; Messrs. Davis, Hartman, MacNamara—Ron Crawford; Miss Taleporos—Meghan Andrews; Mr. Noah—Terrance MacNamara; Mr. Armitage—Tommy J. Michaels; Misses Murphy, Wilder, Sheara—Kathryn Erbe; Mr. Deakins—Eric Simonson; Messrs. True, Slavin—Steve Ramsey; Mr. Smith—William Schwarz; Messrs. Schwarz, Ramsey—Jeremiah Birkett; Mr. Sudduth—P. J. Brown; Miss Erbe—Jessica Wilder; Messrs. Simonson, Schulz, Brown—Skipp Sudduth.

Directed by Frank Galati; scenery and lighting, Kevin Rigdon; costumes, Erin Quigley; sound, Rob Milburn; original music composed and directed by Michael Smith; production stage manager, Malcolm Ewen; stage managers, Janet Friedman, Robyn Karen Taylor; press, the Fred Nathan Company, Ellen Levene.

Time: 1938. Place: Oklahoma and California. The play was presented in two parts.

Saga of the "Okies," driven from their farms by dust storms and moving to California. Previously produced in this Steppenwolf production in Chicago (9/17/88), La Jolla (5/14/89) and in London (6/22/89).

A Best Play; see page 293.

**\*Lettice & Lovage** (76). By Peter Shaffer. Produced by The Shubert Organization, Robert Fox Ltd. and Roger Berlind at the Ethel Barrymore Theater. Opened March 25, 1990.

| | | | |
|---|---|---|---|
| Lettice Douffet | Maggie Smith | Miss Framer | Bette Henritze |
| Surly Man | Dane Knell | Mr. Bardolph | Paxton Whitehead |
| Lotte Schoen | Margaret Tyzack | Felina, Queen of Sorrows | Herself |

Visitors to Fustian House: Herb Foster, Prudence Wright Holmes, Patricia Kilgarriff, Dane Knell, Barbara Lester, Sybil Lines, Laurine Towler, Tyrone Wilson, Ronald Yamamoto.

Standbys: Miss Smith—Margaret Hall; Miss Tyzack—Barbara Lester; Messrs. Whitehead, Knell—Herb Foster; Miss Henritze—Prudence Wright Holmes.

Directed by Michael Blakemore; scenery, Alan Tagg; costumes, Frank Krenz; Miss Smith's costumes, Anthony Powell; lighting, Ken Billington; production stage manager, Mitchell Erickson; stage manager, John Hand; press, the Fred Nathan Company, William Schelble.

Time: The present. Act I, Scene 1: The grand hall of Fustian House, Wiltshire, England. Scene 2: Miss Schoen's office at the Preservation Trust, London. Act II: Miss Douffet's basement flat, Earls Court, London, ten weeks later. Act III: The same, six months later.

Vivid imagination and lively personality of a tour guide lead her to invent material to make history seem more exciting but get her into trouble with her fact-obsessed boss and other forms of established authority. The background music, for brass instruments, was composed in the reigns of Elizabeth I, James I and William and Mary. A foreign play previously produced in London.

**\*Aspects of Love** (61). Musical with book by Andrew Lloyd Webber, adapted from the novel by David Garnett; music by Andrew Lloyd Webber; lyrics by Don Black and Charles Hart. Produced by The Really Useful Theater Company, Inc. at the Broadhurst Theater. Opened April 8. 1990.

| | | | |
|---|---|---|---|
| Rose Vibert | Ann Crumb | Man on Date | Eric Johnson |
| Alex Dillingham | Michael Ball | His Date | Suzanne Briar |
| George Dillingham | Kevin Colson | Actors: Philip Clayton, John Dewar, Marcus | |
| Giulietta Trapani | Kathleen Rowe McAllen | Lovett, Kurt Johns. Actresses: Elinore | |
| Marcel Richard | Walter Charles | O'Connell, Lisa Vroman, Wysandria Woolsey. | |
| Jenny Dillingham, age 12 | Deanna Du Clos | At the fairground: | |
| Jenny Dillingham, age 14 | Danielle Du Clos | 1st Barker | Eric Johnson |
| Elizabeth | Suzanne Briar | 2d Barker | Kurt Johns |
| Hugo Le Muenier | Don Goodspeed | Alex's Friends | Don Goodspeed, Philip Clayton |
| Jerome | Philip Clayton | Their Girlfriends | Elinore O'Connell, Lisa Vroman |
| At the cafe: | | Alex's Date | Jane Todd Baird |
| Stage Manager | Don Goodspeed | War Veteran | John Dewar |
| Asst. Stage Manager | Jane Todd Baird | His Wife | Suzanne Briar |
| Waiter | Gregory Mitchell | Local Men | Marcus Lovett, Gregory Mitchell |

Local Woman......................Wysandria Woolsey
In Venice:
Gondolier.........................................Kurt Johns
Hotel Cashier ...............................Lisa Vroman
Nun....................................Elinore O'Connell
Doctor............................................John Dewar
Hotelier.......................................Eric Johnson
Pharmacist...........................Wysandria Woolsey
Registrar.......................................Eric Johnson
Assistant Registrar ...........................John Dewar
In Rose's dressing room:
   Rose's Friends:  Jane Todd Baird, Suzanne

Briar, Philip Clayton, John Dewar, Kurt Johns, Eric Johnson, Marcus Lovett, Gregory Mitchell, Elinore O'Connell, Lisa Vroman, Wysandria Woolsey.
At the circus:
Knife Thrower..................................Kurt Johns
His Assistant .......................Wysandria Woolsey
   Clowns:  Gregory Mitchell, Marcus Lovett, Philip Clayton, John Dewar
At the wake:
Young Peasant .........................Gregory Mitchell

Other Roles:  The Ensemble.

*Aspects of Love* Orchestra: Sanford Allen concert master; Dale Stuckenbruck violin; Jenny Hansen viola; Mark Shuman cello; Deb Spohnheimer bass; Grace Paradise harp; Diva Goodfriend-Koven flute, piccolo, alto flute; Blaire Tindall oboe, English horn; Jon Manasse clarinet, bass clarinet; Lawrence Feldman saxophone, clarinet, flute; Russell Rizner, French horn; Paul Sportelli piano, celeste; Nicholas Archer associate conductor, synthesizers; Louis Oddo percussion.

Understudies:  Miss Crumb—Elinore O'Connell, Wysandria Woolsey; Mr. Ball—Don Goodspeed; Mr. Colson—Walter Charles; Miss McAllen—Lisa Vroman, Wysandria Woolsey; Mr. Charles—Eric Johnson; Miss Danielle Du Clos—Jane Todd Baird; Miss Deanna Du Clos—Brooke Sunny Moriber; Mr. Goodspeed—Marcus Lovett.

Swings:  Wiley Kidd, Brad Oscar, Anne Marie Runolfsson.

Directed by Trevor Nunn; choreography, Gillian Lynne; musical direction, Paul Bogaev; scenery and costumes, Maria Bjornson; lighting, Andrew Bridge; sound, Martin Levan; orchestrations, David Cullen, Andrew Lloyd Webber; production stage manager, Perry Cline; stage managers, Elisabeth Farwell, Michael J. Passaro; press, the Fred Nathan Company, Merle Frimark.

Literally, various aspects of love including the romance of a 17-year-old boy with an actress in her mid-20s.  A foreign show previously produced in London.

## ACT I

Prologue:  On the terrace at Pau, 1964
  "Love Changes Everything"..................................................................................................... Alex
France, 1947
  A small theater in Montpellier..................................................................Rose, Marcel, Ensemble
  A cafe in Montpellier
    "Parlez-Vous Français?"................................................................................Rose, Alex, Ensemble
  The railway station...........................................................................................................Alex, Rose
  In a train compartment
    "Seeing Is Believing".........................................................................................................Alex, Rose
  The house at Pau ..............................................................................................................Alex, Rose
  A sculpture exhibition in Paris
    "A Memory of a Happy Moment" ...................................................................George, Giulietta
  In many rooms in the house at Pau .............................................................................Rose, Alex
  On the terrace........................................................................................................ Rose, Alex, George
  Outside the bedroom..........................................................................................................Rose, Alex
  Up in the Pyrenees
    "Chanson d'Enfance"....................................................................................................................Rose
  The house at Pau ................................................................................................................Rose, Alex
  The railway station........................................................................................................Rose, Marcel
Two Years Later
  A fairground in Paris
    "Everybody Loves a Hero" .....................................................................................Barkers, Ensemble
  George's flat in Paris
    "She'd Be Far Better Off With You".....................................Alex, George, Rose, Elizabeth
  Giulietta's studio in Venice
    "Stop. Wait. Please.".............................................................Giulietta, George, Ensemble

A Registry Office.................................................................Rose, George, Registrars, Giulietta, Guests
A military camp in Malaya............................................................................................................. Alex

## ACT II

Thirteen years later
A grand theater in Paris
"Leading Lady" ...............................................................................................Marcel, Ensemble
At the stage door............................................................................................................Rose, Alex
George's house at Pau
"Other Pleasures" ...........................................................................................George, Jenny, Alex, Rose
A cafe in Venice/the house at Pau
"There Is More to Love"................................................................................... Giulietta, Rose
The garden at Pau......................................................................................... George, Rose, Alex
"Mermaid Song" .........................................................................................................Jenny Alex
The countryside around the house.............................................................................................Jenny, Alex
Two years later
The garden at Pau............................................................................................Jenny, Alex, Rose
On the terrace
"The First Man You Remember".......................................................................George, Jenny
Up in the Pyrenees................................................................................................Jenny, Alex
In the vineyard at Pau ....................................................................................................Company
A circus in Paris
"The Journey of a Lifetime" ..............................................................................................Company
Outside the circus
"Falling" ...............................................................................................George, Rose, Alex, Jenny
Jenny's bedroom in Paris.............................................................................................................Alex, Jenny
The vineyards at Pau
"Hand Me the Wine and the Dice".................Giulietta, Ensemble, Rose, Jenny, Alex, Marcel, Hugo
A hayloft................................................................................................................Giulietta, Alex
On the terrace ........................................................................... Alex, Jenny, Rose, Giulietta
"Anything But Lonely" ..........................................................................................................Rose

**\*The Piano Lesson** (52). By August Wilson. Produced by Lloyd Richards, Yale
Repertory Theater, Center Theater Group/Ahmanson Theater, Gordon Davidson and the
Jujamcyn Theaters with Benjamin Mordecai executive producer, in association with Eugene
O'Neill Theater Center, Huntington Theater Company, Goodman Theater and Old Globe
Theater, and in New York in association with Manhattan Theater Club, at the Walter Kerr
Theater. Opened April 16, 1990.

| | | | |
|---|---|---|---|
| Doaker | Carl Gordon | Maretha | Apryl R. Foster |
| Boy Willie | Charles S. Dutton | Avery | Tommy Hollis |
| Lymon | Rocky Carroll | Wining Boy | Lou Myers |
| Berniece | S. Epatha Merkerson | Grace | Lisa Gay Hamilton |

Directed by Lloyd Richards; scenery, E. David Cosier Jr.; costumes, Constanza Romero; lighting,
Christopher Akerlind; musical director and composer; Dwight D. Andrews; sound, G. Thomas Clark; associate
producer, Stephen J. Albert; production stage manager, Karen L. Carpenter; press, Jeffrey Richards Associates,
David LeShay.

Black American family's past and present in conflict, as a Mississippi farmer comes to Pittsburgh (in
1936) to persuade his city-dwelling sister to sell a family heirloom, a piano, so that he can buy farmland back
home. Previously produced in regional theater in New Haven, Boston, Chicago, San Diego, Washington,
D.C. and Los Angeles.

A Best Play; see page 313.

**Truly Blessed** (33). Musical with conception, book, music and lyrics by Queen Esther
Marrow; additional music and lyrics by Reginald Royal. Produced by Howard Hurst, Philip

Rose and Sophie Hurst in association with Frankie Hewitt at the Longacre Theater. Opened April 22, 1990. (Closed May 20, 1990)

Mahalia Jackson...............................................................................................Queen Esther Marrow

Ensemble: Carl Hall, Lynette G. DuPré, Doug Eskew, Gwen Stewart.

Musicians: Aaron Graves conductor; Konrad Adderly bass; Brian Grice drums; Willard Meeks organ, assistant conductor.

Understudies: Miss Marrow—Tina Fabrique, Lynette G. DuPré; Misses DuPré, Stewart—Tina Fabrique.

Directed by Robert Kalfin; choreography, Larry Vickers; scenery and lighting, Fred Kolo; costumes, Andrew B. Marlay; sound, Peter Fitzgerald; musical supervision and orchestrations, Joseph Joubert; executive producers, Philip Rose, Howard Hurst; production stage manager, Kenneth Hanson; stage manager, Janice C. Lane; press, the Joshua Ellis Office, Jackie Green.

Act I, Scene 1: Opening. Scene 2: New Orleans. Scene 3: Going to Chicago. Scene 4: The church. Scene 5: Touring. Scene 6: On the backsteps. Scene 7: Mayor Daley and the rally. Scene 8: Mr. Sigmond Galloway. Scene 9: On top of the world. Act II, Scene 1: Carnegie Hall. Scene 2: The march on Washington. Scene 3: Mahalia in the Berkshires. Scene 4: In the Holy Land. Scene 5: Epilogue and celebration.

Subtitled *A Musical Celebration of Mahalia Jackson*, a presentation of the life and songs of the great gospel singer, with occasional excusions into new blues, pop and jazz numbers. Previously produced at Ford's Theater, Washington, D.C. as *Don't Let This Dream Go*.

MUSICAL NUMBERS, ACT I: "I Found the Answer;" "St. Louis Blues;" "It's Amazing What God Can Do;" Medley, "On the Battlefield for My Lord," "Glory Hallelujah;" "He May Not Come When You Want Him;" "Lord, I'm Determinded;" "Happy Days Are Here Again;" "Precious Lord;" "Jesus Remembers When Others Forget;" "Thank You for the Change in My Life;" "Come on Children, Let's Sing."

ACT II: "Even Me;" "Didn't It Rain;" Spiritual Medley, "Wade in the Water," "Old Ship of Zion," "Battle Hymn of the Republic," "I've Been 'Buked;" "Soon I Will Be Done;" "His Gift to Me;" "Move on Up a Little Higher;" "Rusty Bell;" "Truly Blessed;" "He's Got the Whole World in His Hand."

## *Accomplice (41). By Rupert Holmes. Produced by Alexander H. Cohen & Hildy Parks, Max Cooper and Norman Kurtz at the Richard Rodgers Theater. Opened April 26, 1990.

CAST: Michael McKean, Natalia Nogulich, Jason Alexander, Pamela Brüll.

Standbys: Paul Del Gatto, Samuel Maupin, John Hickok, Mary Kane, Margot Dionne.

Directed by Art Wolff; scenery, David Jenkins; costumes, Alvin Colt; lighting, Martin Aronstein; special effects, Gregory Meeh; incidental music, Rupert Holmes; music performed by Deborah Grunfeld; sound, Peter J. Fitzgerald; production stage manager, Thomas A. Kelly; stage manager, Glen Gardall; press, John Springer, Gary Springer.

Act I, Scene 1: The moorland cottage of Derek and Janet Taylor on an English autumn afternoon in the mid-1970s. Scene 2: The same, early the next evening. Act II, Scene 1: The same, a week later, in the afternoon. Scene 2: A suite at Claridge's Hotel, a week later.

Comedy thriller with a plot of surprises, previously produced in regional theater at the Pasadena Playhouse.

## A Change in the Heir (17). Musical with book by George H. Gorham and Dan Sticco; music by Dan Sticco; lyrics by George H. Gorham. Produced by Stewart F. Lane at the Edison Theater. Opened April 29, 1990. (Closed May 13, 1990)

| | | | |
|---|---|---|---|
| Aunt Julia | Brooks Almy | Lady Enid | Mary Stout |
| Giles | Brian Sutherland | Prince Conrad | Judy Blazer |
| Edwin | J. K. Simmons | Princess Agnes | Jeffrey Herbst |
| Nicholas | David Gunderman | Martha | Jan Neuberger |
| Countess | Connie Day | Lady Elizabeth | Jennifer Smith |

Musicians: Rob Bowman conductor, piano; Lorraine Wolf synthesizer; Dale Thompson bass; Keith Zaharia woodwinds; Thad Wheeler percussion.

Understudies: Miss Almy—Connie Day; Mr. Herbst—David Gunderman; Misses Blazer, Smith, Neuberger, Day—Kathy Morath; Messrs. Simmons, Gunderman, Sutherland—David Serko.

Directed and choreographed by David H. Bell; musical direction and dance arrangements, Rob Bowman; scenery, Michael Anania; costumes, David Murin; lighting, Jeff Davis; orchestrations, Robby Merkin; production stage manager, Terrence J. Witter; stage manager, Cheryl Mintz; press, Shirley Herz Associates, Sam Rudy.

Prologue: Once upon a time, long, long ago, in a castle far, far away. Act I: 20 years later, Friday and Saturday. Act II: Sunday morning.

Vieing for the crown of a mythical kingdom, rival factions bring their children up disguised as members of the sex opposite to the one they are in reality. Previously produced in regional theater at New Tuners, Chicago.

## ACT I

Prologue...............................................................................................................Company
"The Weekend" ................................................Julia, Countess, Martha, Enid, Edwin, Giles
"Here I Am"............................................................................................................ Conrad
"Exactly the Same as It Was" ...........................Enid, Edwin, Giles, Julia, Countess, Martha
"Look at Me" ...............................................................................................Agnes, Conrad
"Take a Look at That"...............................................................................Agnes, Elizabeth
"I Tried and I Tried and I Tried" ................................Edwin, Enid, Agnes, Countess, Conrad
"Can't I?" .............................................................................................................. Conrad
"When" ........................................................................................................Julia, Martha
"A Fairy Tale"...........................................................................................Agnes, Conrad
"An Ordinary Family".............................................................................................Company

*THE CEMETERY CLUB*—Elizabeth Franz, Doris Belack
and Eileen Heckart in a scene from the play by Ivan Menchell

## ACT II

"Happily Ever After, After All".................................................................................................... Agnes
"Shut Up and Dance" ....................................................................................................Nicholas, Elizabeth
"Can't I?" (Reprise) ............................................................................................................... Conrad
"Duet"...............................................................................................................................Agnes, Conrad
"Hold That Crown"................................................................................................................................
"By Myself"..................................................................................................................... Conrad, Company
Finale .........................................................................................................................................Company

**\*Prelude to a Kiss** (36). Transfer from off Broadway of the play by Craig Lucas. Produced by Christopher Gould, Suzanne Golden and Dodger Productions in the Circle Repertory Company production, Tanya Berezin artistic director, Connie L. Alexis managing director, at the Helen Hayes Theater. Opened May 1, 1990.

| | | | |
|---|---|---|---|
| Peter | Timothy Hutton | Dr. Boyle | Larry Bryggman |
| Rita | Mary-Louise Parker | Minister | Craig Bockhorn |
| Taylor | John Dossett | Aunt Dorothy; Leah | Joyce Reehling |
| Tom; Jamaican Waiter | L. Peter Callender | Uncle Fred | Michael Warren Powell |
| Mrs. Boyle | Debra Monk | Old Man | Barnard Hughes |

Party Guests, Barflies, Wedding Guests, Vacationers: Craig Bockhorn, Brian Cousins, Kimberly Dudwitt, Michael Warren Powell.

Understudies: Mr. Hutton—John Dossett; Misses Parker, Reehling—Susan Gabriel; Mr. Dossett—Brian Cousins; Messrs. Callender, Bockhorn—Monte Russell; Miss Monk—Cynthia Darlow; Messrs. Bryggman, Powell, Hughes—Ron Parady, Wyman Pendleton.

Directed by Norman Rene; scenery, Loy Arcenas; costumes, Walter Hicklin; lighting, Debra J. Kletter; sound, Scott Lehrer; associate producer, Lawrence J. Wilker; production stage manager, James Harker; stage manager, M. A. Howard; press, the Joshua Ellis Office, Adrian Bryan-Brown.

A love affair and marriage followed by a strange kiss which seems to have the power to exchange souls between bodies. The play was presented in two parts. Previously produced off Broadway in this production 3/14/90–4/1/90 and 4/12/90–4/19/90 for 33 performances; see its entry in the Plays Produced Off Broadway section of this volume.

A Best Play; see page 269.

**\*The Cemetery Club** (20). By Ivan Menchell. Produced by Howard Hurst, Philip Rose, David Brown and Sophie Hurst at the Brooks Atkinson Theater. Opened May 15, 1990.

| | | | |
|---|---|---|---|
| Ida | Elizabeth Franz | Sam | Lee Wallace |
| Lucille | Eileen Heckart | Mildred | Judith Granite |
| Doris | Doris Belack | | |

Standbys: Misses Heckart, Granite—Lucille Patton; Misses Franz, Belack—Catherine Wolf, Judith Granite; Mr. Wallace—Roger Serbagi.

Directed by Pamela Berlin; scenery, John Lee Beatty; costumes, Lindsay W. Davis; lighting, Natasha Katz; sound, Scott T. Anderson; music, Robert Dennis; executive producers, Philip Rose, Howard Hurst; production stage manager, Barbara-Mae Phillips; stage manager, Charles Kindl; press, the Joshua Ellis Office, Jackie Green.

Place: The living room of Ida's house and a cemetery in Forest Hills, Queens. The play was presented in two parts.

Comedy, three widows meet each month at the graves of their husbands, but then a widower intrudes on their friendship. Previously produced in regional theater at Yale Repertory Theater, New Haven, and the Cleveland Play House.

# PLAYS WHICH CLOSED
# PRIOR TO BROADWAY OPENING

Productions which were organized by New York producers for Broadway presentation but which closed during their production and tryout period are listed below.

**Durante.** Musical based on the life and times of Jimmy Durante; by Frank Peppiatt and John Aylesworth; musical numbers by various authors (see credits below); additional dialogue by Caroline Peppiatt. Produced on tour by the First Durante Tour Company (Nicky Fylan and Mary Murphy), John MacNamara executive producer. Opened August 12, 1989 at the St. Lawrence Center, Toronto. (Closed November 26, 1989 at the Shubert Theater, Los Angeles)

| | |
|---|---|
| Jimmy Durante.................................. Lonny Price | Moe's Girl #2 ..................................... Terrie Turai |
| Coney Tony; Irving Thalberg; | Jeanne............................................Jane Johanson |
| Radio Announcer............................Ralph Small | David.........................................Timothy French |
| Eddie Jackson ..................................Evan Pappas | Major Domo (Courtship Ballet).......Michel LaFleche |
| Moe the Gimp.............................. B. Alan Geddes | Chorus Girl ................................... Melodee Finlay |
| Lou Clayton.....................................Joel Blum | Autograph Seeker............................ Kim Scarcella |
| Moe's Girl #1................................ Risa Waldman | Sound Effects Man...............................David Gibb |

Radio Singers: Susan Gattoni, Michel LaFleche, Lea Parrell, Kim Scarcella, Michael Whitehead.

Ensemble: Michael Arnold, Dale Azzard, Stephen Beamish, Patric A. Creelman, Ira Denmark, Melodee Finlay, Lili Francks, Timothy French, Susan Gattoni, B. Alan Geddes, David Gibb, Jacqueline Haigh, Michel LaFleche, Lea Parrell, Bob Riddell, Kim Scarcella, Kent Sheridan, Bernadette Taylor, Terrie Turai, Risa Waldman, Michael Whitehead.

Swings: Michel Gervais, Darcia Kember. Understudies: Messrs. Small, Geddes—Stephen Beamish. Mr. Pappas—Patric A. Creelman; Mr. Price—Ira Denmark; Miss Johanson—Melodee Finlay; Mr. Blum—David Gibb; Mr. French—Michel LaFleche; Mr. Gibb—Michael Whitehead.

Directed by Ernest O. Flatt; choreography, Toni Kaye; musical direction, Grant Sturiale; scenery, Cameron Porteous; costumes, Christina Poddubiuk; lighting, Sholem Dolgoy; sound, John Hazen; dance and vocal arrangements, David Crane, Grant Sturiale; orchestrations, James E. Dale; special consultant, Mrs. Margie Durante; stage manager, Roman Humeniuk; press, Patt Dale.

Fifty years in the life of the great comedian.

## ACT I

Scene 1: Coney Tony's speakeasy
"Grandpa's Spells" ............................................................................................................Ensemble
    (by Ferd Morton)
Scene 2: An alley
"People Would Laugh"............................................................................................................Jimmy
    (by Lonny Price and Grant Sturiale)
Scene 3: Moe the Gimp's Place
"Who Will Be With You When I'm Far Away" .............................................................Jimmy, Eddie
    (by William H. Farrell and Jimmy Durante)
Scene 4: Club Durant
"What a Day".................................................................... Eddie, Jimmy, Jacqueline, Lea, Susan
    (by Jimmy Durante)
"Put Your Arms Around Me Honey" ...............................................................Jeanne, Bob, David
    (by Alex Von Tilser and Junie McCree)

Scene 5: Central Park
"I'll Do the Strutaway" ..................................................................................Jimmy, Jeanne
    (by Harry Donnelly, Jimmy Durante and Irving Caesar)
Courtship Ballet ...............................................................................Jimmy, Jeanne, Ensemble
    (by David Krane)
Scene 6: Club Durant
"Hello, Hello, Hello" ...............................................................Kim, Melodee, Risa, Terrie
    (by David Krane, Frank Peppiatt and John Aylesworth)
"Jimmy the Well-Dressed Man" ....................................................................Jimmy, Eddie
    (by Jimmy Durante)
"Whispering" .........................................................................................................Lou
    (by Richard Coburn, Vincent Rose and John Schonberger)
"Challenge" ..........................................................................................Lou, Eddie, Jimmy
"I Know Darn Well I Can Do Without Broadway" ....................................Lou, Eddie, Jimmy
    (by Jimmy Durante)
Scene 7: Club Durant
Scene 8: "Don't Lose Your Sense of Humor" ....................................................Jimmy
    (by Jimmy Durante)
Scene 9: The Palace
"You Gotta Start Off Each Day With a Song" .................................................Ensemble
    (by Jimmy Durante)
"I Love Ya, Love Ya, Love Ya" ..................................................Lou, Eddie, Jimmy
    (by Jack Barnett, Jimmy Durante and Jules Buffano)
"Bill Bailey" ..........................................................................................Lou, Eddie, Jimmy

# ACT II

Scene 1: Club Durant
"I Love Ya, Love Ya, Love Ya" ..................................................Lou, Eddie, Jimmy
Scene 2: Club Durant; Durante home in Flushing
"Goodnight, Goodnight" (by Jimmy Durante and Jack Barnett)/"Bill Bailey" ...............Jimmy, Lou, Eddie
Scene 3: Durante home in Flushing
"What Do I Have to Say" .....................................................Jeanne, Lou, Eddie, Jimmy
    (by Jerry Powell)
Scene 4: Club Durant
"Did You Ever Get the Feeling" .................................................................Jimmy
    (by Jimmy Durante)
Scene 5: The hospital
"One Room Home" ................................................................................Jimmy
    (by Jimmy Durante)
Scene 6: Lindy's Restaurant
Scene 7: Hollywood
Scene 8: Screening room, Hollywood
Scene 9: Durante home in Hollywood
Scene 10: Radio station
"Who Will Be With You When I'm Far Away" (Reprise) .......................................Jimmy
"Inka Dinka Doo" ...........................................................................Jimmy, Radio Singers
    (by Jimmy Durante and Ben Ryan)
Scene 11: Mountain View/Durante home in Hollywood
"Don't Lose Your Sense of Humor" (Reprise) ...................................................Jimmy
Scene 12: Television studio
"We're the Men" .................................................... David, Michael, Michel, Tim
"A Razz a Ma Tazz" ...............................................................Jimmy, Ensemble
    (by Irving Taylor and David Coleman)
"September Song" ....................................................................Jimmy, Ensemble
    (by Maxwell Anderson and Kurt Weill)
"Goodnight, Goodnight" ......................................................................Jimmy

**Annie 2: Miss Hannigan's Revenge.** Musical based on Harold Gray's comic strip *Little Orphan Annie*; book by Thomas Meehan; music by Charles Strouse; lyrics by Martin Charnin. Produced in tryout by Lewis Allen, Roger Berlind, Martin Heinfling and Fifth Avenue Productions/Margo Lion Ltd. at the John F. Kennedy Center for the Performing Arts Opera House, Washington, D.C. Opened January 4, 1990. (Closed January 20, 1990)

| | |
|---|---|
| Grace Farrell......................................Lauren Mitchell | Miss Hannigan..............................Dorothy Loudon |
| Felix Frankfurter.............................Laurent Giroux | Rochelle............................................Sarah Knapp |
| Oliver Warbucks.............................Harve Presnell | Drake........................................Terrence P. Currier |
| Ticktin; Arnold................................Michael Duran | Marie..........................................Michelle O'Steen |
| Nussbaum; Ed; Barney Sullivan; | Punjab.........................................Gerry McIntyre |
| Ford Bond........................................ Bill Nolte | The Asp............................................Fiely Matias |
| Deutch; Sgt Clancy; | Babe Ruth .......................................T. J. Meyers |
| H.V. Kaltenborn .........................J. K. Simmons | Lionel McCoy...............................Ronny Graham |
| Annie Warbucks...........................Danielle Findley | Maurice.................................... Scott Robertson |
| Sandy......................................................... Beau | Walter S. Dobbins; Father Pullam; |
| Mrs. Marietta Christmas...................Marian Seldes | Fletcher; Seaman ................Brian Everet Chandler |
| Peabody; Pianist; Jenkins ....................Bobby Clark | 'Monica ..........................................Juliana Marx |
| Eubanks; Hot Dog Vendor ..................Don Percassi | Fungo............................................. Courtney Earl |
| Lupe.......................................Corinne Melançon | Fish Mongers..............Mary-Pat Green, Ellyn Arons |
| Myrna..........................................Karen L. Byers | Franklin D. Roosevelt ..................Raymond Thorne |
| Patsy ..........................................Mary-Pat Green | Lee DeForest..................................Oliver Woodall |
| Slam; Miss Melissa Dabney.............. Karen Murphy | Fiorello H. LaGuardia...................... Michael Cone |
| Detention Guard............................Dorothy Stanley | |

Warbuck's Aides: Jane Bodle, Ellyn Arons, Karen Murphy. Firemen: T. J. Meyers, Michael Cone, Brian Everet Chandler. Warbucks's Staff: Jane Bodle, Michael Duran, Mary-Pat Green, Sarah Knapp, Karen Murphy, Bill Nolte. Beauticians: Karen L. Byers, Bobby Clark, Michael Duran, Sarah Knapp, Corinne Melançon, Karen Murphy, Don Percassi, J.K. Simmons, Oliver Woodall. Apple Sellers: Karen L. Byers, Sarah Knapp, Bobby Clark. Street People: Jane Bodle, Don Percassi, Oliver Woodall.

Orchestra: The Kennedy Center Opera House Orchestra, John Mauceri music director, Jane Golemon concertmaster.

Standby: Miss Loudon—Dorothy Stanley. Understudies: Mr. Presnell—Terrence P. Currier; Mr. Graham—J.K. Simmons; Miss Findley—Courtney Earl; Miss Mitchell—Jane Bodle; Mr. Thorne—Michael Duran; Mr. Robertson—T.J. Meyers; Mr. McIntyre—Brian Everet Chandler; Mr. Matias—Don Percassi; Beau—Moolly; Ensemble Alternates—D. J. Giagni, Barbara Moroz.

Directed by Martin Charnin; choreography, Danny Daniels; musical direction and dance arrangements, Peter Howard; scenery, David Mitchell; costumes, Theoni V. Aldredge; lighting, Ken Billington; sound, Abe Jacob; orchestrations, Michael Starobin; additional orchestrations, Larry Wilcox; executive producers, R. Tyler Gatchell Jr., Peter Neufeld; produced in association with Stephen Graham and the John F. Kennedy Center for the Performing Arts; associate producers, Stuart Thompson, Mutual Benefit Productions; associate choreographer, D.J. Giagni; production stage manager, Bill Buxton; stage manager, Gwendolyn M. Gilliam; press, David Powers.

Sequel to the 1977 musical *Annie* with Miss Hannigan, the former orphanage mistress, seeking revenge for her previous humiliation and incarceration.

## ACT I

Oliver Warbucks's office on the 125th floor of the Warbucks Building, New York City, early March 1934
   "1934"..................................................Warbucks, Grace, Annie, Felix Frankfurter, Accountants, Aides
   "1934" (Reprise)..................................................................................................................Annie
The Women's House of Detention, New York City, the next day
   "You Ain't Seen the Last of Me!"........................................................................ Miss Hannigan
The Warbucks mansion, the tennis court, a week later
   "A Younger Man"..................................................................................................Warbucks
A pier of the East River, later that night
   "How Could I Ever Say No?"........................................................................Miss Hannigan, Lionel

*ANNIE 2: MISS HANNIGAN'S REVENGE*—Danielle Findley (Annie)
and Beau (Sandy) in the sequel to the 1977 Broadway musical hit

The Warbucks mansion on Fifth Avenue, the art gallery, the following morning
  "The Lady of the House" ............................................................................... Grace, Drake, Staff
A beauty parlor in Brooklyn, a few days later, just before 4 a.m.
  "Beautiful"................................................................Maurice, Beauticians, Lionel, Miss Hannigan
  "Beautiful" (Reprise)....................................................................Miss Hannigan, Lionel
The New York Yankees locker room, Yankee Stadium, a week later
  "The Lady of the House" (Reprise) .................................................Grace, Mrs. Christmas, Contestants
  "He Doesn't Know I'm Alive"................................................................Grace, New York Yankees
The Fulton Fish Market, later that afternoon
  "You! You! You!".............................................................................................. Miss Hannigan

## ACT II

Wall Street, two months later, a Tuesday afternoon in June
  "When You Smile" ..................................................................F.D.R., Annie, People on Wall Street
  "Just Let Me Get Away With This One" ................................................................. Miss Hannigan
The Warbucks Mansion, another part of the art gallery, Saturday morning, June 16
  "Coney Island" ........................................................................Warbucks, Grace, Drake
Coney Island, Saturday afternoon, June 16
  "Coney Island" ...............................Warbucks, Grace, Annie, Punjab, The Asp, People at Coney Island
A deserted street near Coney Island, early Saturday evening, June 16
  "All I've Got Is Me"...........................................................................................Annie
Oliver Warbucks's office, the night of Saturday, June 16
  "Cortez" ............................................................................Miss Melissa Dabney
  (music by Joseph Nohl, libretto by Dieter Dorfmunder)
  "A Tenement Lullaby" ................................................................. Miss Hannigan
  "A Younger Man" (Reprise)........................................................................Warbucks
The silver stateroom on the Warbucks yacht, Sunday morning, June 17

"I Could Get Used to This" .............................................................Miss Hannigan, Drake, Stewards
The Warbucks yacht, the main deck, Sunday afternoon, June 17
"When You Smile" (Reprise) ....................................... Warbucks, Grace, Annie, F.D.R., Staff, Guests

**The King and I.** Revival of the musical based on Margaret Landon's book; book and lyrics by Oscar Hammerstein II; music by Richard Rodgers. Produced on tour by Manny Kladitis, Columbia Artists Management, Inc., Concert Productions International and Pace Theatrical Group. Opened at the Civic Theater, Syracuse, N.Y., August 18, 1989. (Closed at the Orpheum Theater, San Francisco, March 3, 1990)

| | | | |
|---|---|---|---|
| Capt. Orton; Sir Edward Ramsay....... | Kenneth Garner | Tuptim........................................... | Suzan Postel |
| Louis Leonowens............................. | Kenny Lund | Lady Thiang.......................... | Irma-Estel La Guerre |
| Anna Leonowens............................. | Liz Robertson | Prince Chulalongkorn ........................ | Jason Brown |
| Interpreter ...................................... | Kaipo Daniels | Princess Ying.......................... | Shana Sueoka-Matos |
| Kralahome ............................... | Michael Kermoyan | Lun Tha ...................................... | Patrick A'Hearn |
| King............................................ | Rudolf Nureyev | | |

Royal Dancers, Wives: Lori Lynn Bauer, Nancy Latuja, Deborah Harada, Jayne Ackley Lynch, Grace Napier, Ryoko Sawaishi, Sandy Sueoka-Matos, Marie Takazawa, Kyoko Takita, Chiaki Toda, Kym Weber, Sylvia Yamada.

Princes: John Babcock, Jeffrey Rosato. Priests, Slaves: Alberto Guzman, Michael Hayward-Jones, Stanley Earl Harrison, Stuart Marland, Kenji Nakao, Sal Mistretta, Harold Yi.

Directed by Arthur Storch; original choreography, Jerome Robbins, reproduced by Patricia Weber; musical direction, Michael D. Biagi; scenery, John Jay Moore; costumes, Stanley Simmons, based on original designs by Irene Sharaff; lighting, Jason Kantrowitz; associate director, Cornell S. Worthington II; musical supervisor, Don Pippin; sound, Gary Stocker; press, Joshua Ellis.

The last major New York revival of *The King and I* took place on Broadway 1/7/85 for 191 performances, with Yul Brynner in his final appeareance in the role he created, the King.

The list of musical numbers in *The King and I* appears on page 361 of the 1950–51 *Best Plays* volume.

**Jake's Women.** By Neil Simon. Produced in tryout by Emanuel Azenberg and the Old Globe Theater at the Old Globe Theater, San Diego. Opened March 8, 1990. (Closed March 15, 1990).

| | | | |
|---|---|---|---|
| Karen............................................ | Candice Azzara | Jake................................................... | Peter Coyote |
| Sheila ............................................ | Talia Balsam | Mollie (at 13)........................ | Sarah Michelle Gellar |
| Mollie (at 21)............................. | Amelia Campbell | Julie .......................................... | Felicity Huffman |
| Maggie.................................... | Stockard Channing | Edith.......................................... | Joyce Van Patten |

Directed by Ron Link; scenery, Tony Straiges; costumes, Joseph G. Aulisi; lighting, Tharon Musser; sound coordinator, Jeff Ladman; stage managers, Douglas Pagliotti, Peter Lawrence; press, Bill Evans & Associates, Jim Randolph.

Place: A duplex apartment in the Soho section of New York. The play was presented in two parts.

The six most important women in the life of a middle aged writer.

# PLAYS PRODUCED OFF BROADWAY

Some distinctions between off-Broadway and Broadway productions at one end of the scale and off-off-Broadway productions at the other were blurred in the New York Theater of the 1970s and 1980s. For the purposes of this *Best Plays* listing, the term "off Broadway" is used to distinguish a professional from a showcase (off-off-Broadway) production and signifies a show which opened for general audiences in a mid-Manhattan theater seating 499 or fewer and 1) employed an Equity cast, 2) planned a regular schedule of 8 performances a week in an open-ended run and 3) offered itself to public comment by critics at designated opening performances.

Occasional exceptions of inclusion (never of exclusion) are made to take in visiting troupes, borderline cases and nonqualifying productions which readers might expect to find in this list because they appear under an off-Broadway heading in other major sources of record.

Figures in parentheses following a play's title give number of performances. These figures do not include previews or extra non-profit performances.

Plays marked with an asterisk (*) were still in a projected run on June 1, 1990. Their number of performances is figured from opening night through May 31, 1990.

Certain programs of off-Broadway companies are exceptions to our rule of counting the number of performances from the date of the press coverage. When the official opening takes place late in the run of a play's regularly-priced public or subscription performances (after previews) we count the first performance of record, not the press date, as opening night—and in each such case in the listing we note the variance and give the press date.

In a listing of a show's numbers—dances, sketches, musical scenes, etc.—the titles of songs are identified wherever possible by their appearance in quotation marks (").

Most entries of off-Broadway productions which ran fewer than 20 performances are somewhat abbreviated, as are entries on running repertory programs repeated from previous years.

# HOLDOVERS FROM PREVIOUS SEASONS

Plays which were running on June 1, 1989 are listed below. More detailed information about them appears in previous *Best Plays* volumes of appropriate date. Important cast changes since opening night are recorded in the Cast Replacements section of this volume.

**\*The Fantasticks** (12,523; longest continuous run of record in the American theater). Musical suggested by the play *Les Romanesques* by Edmond Rostand; book and lyrics by Tom Jones; music by Harvey Schmidt. Opened May 30, 1960.

**Vampire Lesbians of Sodom** and **Sleeping Beauty or Coma** (2,024). Program of two plays by Charles Busch. Opened June 19, 1985. (Closed May 27, 1990)

**\*Nunsense** (1,844). Musical with book, music and lyrics by Dan Goggin. Opened December 12, 1985.

**Driving Miss Daisy** (1,195). By Alfred Uhry. Opened April 15, 1987. (Closed June 3, 1990)

**Steel Magnolias** (1,126). By Robert Harling. Opened June 19, 1987. (Closed February 25, 1990)

**\*Perfect Crime** (1,259). By Warren Manzi. Opened October 16, 1987.

**\*Tamara** (983). By John Krizanc; conceived by Richard Rose and John Krizanc. Opened December 2, 1987. (Recessed January 18, 1988) Reopened February 2, 1988.

**Forbidden Broadway 1988** (later **1989**) (534). Revised version of the revue with concept and parody lyrics by Gerard Alessandrini. Opened September 15, 1988. (Closed December 24, 1989)

**The Cocktail Hour** (351). By A.R. Gurney. Opened October 20, 1988. (Closed August 10, 1989)

**Bunnybear** (260). By Nico Hartos. Opened January 19, 1989. (Closed September 17, 1989)

**The Kathy and Mo Show: Parallel Lives** (466). Two-character play written and performed by Mo Gaffney and Kathy Najimi. Opened January 31, 1989. (Closed April 29, 1990)

**Cantorial** (136). By Ira Levin. Opened February 14, 1989. (Closed June 11, 1989)

**\*Other People's Money** (535). By Jerry Sterner. Opened February 16, 1989.

**Only Kidding!** (300). By Jim Geoghan. Opened April 14, 1989. (Closed December 31, 1989)

**Aristocrats** (186). By Brian Friel. Opened April 25, 1989. (Closed September 24, 1989)

**Yankee Dawg You Die** (33). By Philip Kan Gotanda. Opened May 14, 1989. (Closed June 11, 1989)

**Arms and the Man** (61). Revival of the play by George Bernard Shaw. Opened May 17, 1989. (Closed July 9, 1989)

**S.J. Perelman in Person** (38). One-man performance with Lewis J. Stadlen; written by Bob Shanks; based on the published works of S.J. Perelman. Opened May 17, 1989. (Closed June 18, 1989)

**Laughing Matters** (85). Revue of playlets by and with Linda Wallem and Peter Tolan; with music and lyrics by Peter Tolan. Opened May 18, 1989. (Closed August 6, 1989)

**Showing Off** (172). Cabaret revue with music, lyrics and sketches by Douglas Bernstein and Denis Markell. Opened May 18, 1989. (Closed October 15, 1989)

**Cymbeline** (55). Revival of the play by William Shakespeare. Opened May 31, 1989. (Closed June 25, 1989)

# PLAYS PRODUCED JUNE 1, 1989–MAY 31, 1990

**Circle Repertory Company**. 1988–89 schedule concluded with **Florida Crackers** (30). By William S. Leavengood. Produced by Circle Repertory Company, Tanya Berezin artistic director, Connie L. Alexis managing director, at Circle Repertory. Opened June 1, 1989. (Closed June 25, 1989)

| | | | |
|---|---|---|---|
| Joe | John C. McGinley | Dean | Joel Anderson |
| Russell | Scott Rymer | Strings | Brian Jensen |
| Grant | Michael Piontek | Tracey | Cyndi Coyne |
| Lori | Kim Flowers | | |

Directed by John Bishop; scenery, John Lee Beatty; costumes, Connie Singer; lighting, Dennis Parichy; sound, Chuck London, Stewart Werner; music, Jonathan Brielle; production stage manager, Fred Reinglas; press, Gary Murphy.

Three brothers not unwilling to resort to drug-dealing in the Florida of 1979. The play was presented in two parts.

**Manhattan Theater Club**. 1988–89 schedule concluded with **The Lisbon Traviata** (128). By Terrence McNally. Opened June 6, 1989. (Closed July 2, 1989 after 24 performances) Reopened October 31, 1989 at the Promenade Theater. (Closed January 28, 1990 after 104 additional performances) **The Loman Family Picnic** (16). By Donald Margulies. Opened June 20, 1989. (Closed July 2, 1989) Produced by Manhattan Theater Club, Lynne Meadow artistic director, Barry Grove managing director, *The Lisbon Traviata* at City Center Stage 1, *The Loman Family Picnic* at City Center Stage 2.

### THE LISBON TRAVIATA

| | | | |
|---|---|---|---|
| Stephen | Anthony Heald | Mike | Dan Butler |
| Mendy | Nathan Lane | Paul | John Slattery |

Directed by John Tillinger; scenery, Philipp Jung; costumes, Jane Greenwood; lighting, Ken Billington; sound; Gary and Timmy Harris; fight staging, B.H. Barry; production stage manager, Pamela Singer; stage manager, Craig Palanker; press, Helene Davis, Clay Martin.

Homosexual lovers mingling their emotions with their obsessive love of opera. The play was presented in two parts, with Act II rewritten during the initial run. Previously produced off off Broadway at Theater Off Park.

## THE LOMAN FAMILY PICNIC

| | | | |
|---|---|---|---|
| Doris | Marcia Jean Kurtz | Herbie | Larry Block |
| Mitchell | Michael Miceli | Marsha | Wendy Makkena |
| Stewie | Judd Trichter | | |

Directed by Barnet Kellman; scenery, G.W. Mercier; costumes, Jess Goldstein; lighting, Debra J. Kletter; music, David Shire; musical direction, Mark Goodman; sound, Aural Fixation; choreography, Mary Jane Houdina; production stage manager, Renee Lutz; stage manager, Laura Kravets.

Time: Around 1965. Place: A middle-class high-rise apartment in Coney Island, Brooklyn, N.Y. The play was presented in two parts.

Overstressed family trying to get through the bar mitzvah of a son who finds escape in his imagination, writing a musical version of *Death of a Salesman*.

A Best Play; see page 131.

**Sid Caesar & Company** (72). Musical revue produced by Art D'Lugoff and Larry Spellman at the Village Gate Downstairs. Opened June 22, 1989. (Closed September 10, 1989 and transferred to Broadway; see its entry in the Plays Produced on Broadway section of this volume)

|  |  |
|---|---|
| Sid Caesar | Gerrianne Raphael |
| Lee Delano | Marilyn Sokol |
| Elliot Finkel Orchestra | |

Understudy: Misses Sokol, Raphael—Carolyn Michel.

Stage manager, Neil Haynes; press, Solters/Roskin/Friedman, Keith Sherman, Philip Leshin Communications.

Subtitled "The Legendary Genius of Comedy," the show was presented without authorship, directorial or other creative credits and included some of the roles and sketches its star made famous on TV.

ACT I: Overture—Elliot Finkel Orchestra. Man Walking Down the Aisle, Boy at His First Dance, World Through the Eyes of a Baby—Sid Caesar; Man and Wife Arguing to the First Movement of Beethoven's Fifth Symlphony—Caesar, Gerrianne Raphael; "The Wicked Man"—Raphael; At the Movies—Caesar, Lee Delano, Marilyn Sokol.

ACT II: Entr'acte—Elliot Finkel Orchestra; "*Little Me* Medley"—Sokol, Raphael, Caesar; The Penny Candy Gum Machine—Caesar; Grieg Piano Concerto—Caesar, Elliot Finkel; "Gershwin Medley"—Ian Finkel, xylophone; The Professor—Caesar, Delano; Finale—Caesar, Company.

**Lincoln Center Theater.** 1989–90 schedule concluded with **Ubu** (25). Adapted from Alfred Jarry's play *Ubu Roi* by Larry Sloan and Doug Wright; based on a literal translation by Jacqueline de la Chaume. Produced by Lincoln Center Theater, Gregory Mosher director, Bernard Gersten executive producer, at the Mitzi E. Newhouse Theater. Opened June 25, 1989. (Closed July 23, 1989)

| | | | |
|---|---|---|---|
| Pere Ubu | Oliver Platt | Bougrelas | Barnabas Miller |
| Mere Ubu | Jodie Markell | Boleslas; Michael Federovitch; | |
| Capt. Bordure | Olek Krupa | Russian Soldier | K. Todd Freeman |
| Pile | Ramiro Carrillo | Ladislas; Czar; Bear | Ralph Marrero |
| Cotice | Trip Hamilton | Ubu's Conscience | Christopher Durang |
| King Venceslas; Stanislas Leczinski; | | The Imagemaker; Younger Peasant | Patrick Garner |
| Gen. Lasky | Bill Alton | Nobles; Nicola Rensky | Tom Aulino |
| Queen Rosamund | Kristine Nielsen | | |

Russian Army, Polish Army, Financiers, Magistrates, Penny Pinchers, Disembraining Machine, etc., played by the cast.

Directed by Larry Sloan; original score, Greg Cohen; scenery, Douglas Stein; costumes, Susan Hilferty; lighting, Stephen Strawbridge; sound, Bill Dreisbach; musical direction and orchestration, Greg Cohen; movement director, Tim Carryer; production manager, Jeff Hamlin; production stage manager, Matthew T. Mundinger; stage manager, Sarah Manley; press, Merle Debuskey, Bruce Campbell.

The play was presented without an intermission.

Apart from various stagings off off Broadway, the only previous New York productions of record of Jarry's play (which was first performed in Paris in 1896) were by The Living Theater off Broadway, in English translation, during the 1952–53 season and in the Serbo-Croatian language off Broadway 6/28/68 for 6 performances.

Robert Stanton replaced Christopher Durang 7/4/89.

**New York Shakespeare Festival** Shakespeare Marathon. Schedule of four revivals of plays by William Shakespeare (see note). **Twelfth Night** (25). Opened July 6, 1989. (Closed July 23, 1989) **Titus Andronicus** (26). Opened August 17, 1989. (Closed September 3, 1989). Produced by New York Shakespeare Festival, Joseph Papp producer, in association with New York Telephone and with the cooperation of the City of New York,

*HAMLET*—Dana Ivey as Gertrude and Kevin Kline as Hamlet in the New York Shakespeare Festival Marathon revival

Edward I. Koch mayor, Mary Schmidt Campbell commissioner of cultural affairs, Henry J. Stern commissioner of parks and recreation, at the Delacorte Theater in Central Park.

Also **Macbeth** (24). Opened January 16, 1990. (Closed February 4, 1990) **Hamlet** (32). Opened May 8, 1990. (Closed June 3, 1990) Produced by New York Shakespeare Festival, Joseph Papp producer, at the Public Theater (see note).

ALL PLAYS: Associate producer, Jason Steven Cohen; plays and musicals development, Gail Merrifield; press, Richard Kornberg, Barbara Carroll, Reva Cooper, Carol Fineman, Steven J. Krementz.

## TWELFTH NIGHT

| | |
|---|---|
| Feste.............................................Gregory Hines | Olivia.........................................Michelle Pfeiffer |
| Orsino........................................Stephen Collins | Malvolio.......................................Jeff Goldblum |
| Curio.............................................L. Peter Callender | Antonio ......................................Andre Braugher |
| Valentine...........................................Frank Raiter | Sebastian....................................Graham Winton |
| Viola ..........................Mary Elizabeth Mastrantonio | Servant .......................................... Mary Mara |
| Sea Captain...............................Stephen Mendillo | Priest...........................................James Cahill |
| Sir Toby Belch ................................John Amos | Waiter.................................................Bill Camp |
| Maria.......................................Charlaine Woodard | Harpist.........................................Carol Emanuel |
| Sir Andrew Aguecheek .....................Fisher Stevens | |

Officers: John Hickey, Daniel Berkey, Jake Weber. Illyrians, Sailors, Croupiers: Daniel Berkey, Gigi Bermingham, David Borror, Bill Camp, Lisa Gay Hamilton, John Hickey, Mary Mara, Mari Nelson, Patrick Rameau, Jake Weber, Rainn Wilson.

Understudies: Mr. Hines—L. Peter Callender; Mr. Collins—John Hickey; Mr. Callender—Patrick Rameau; Messrs. Raiter, Mendillo, Cahill—Daniel Berkey; Miss Mastrantonio—Mary Mara; Mr. Amos— Stephen Mendillo; Miss Woodard—Lisa Gay Hamilton; Mr. Stevens—Rainn Wilson; Miss Pfeiffer—Mari Nelson; Mr. Goldblum—Andre Braugher; Mr. Braugher—Jake Weber; Mr. Winton—David Borror; Miss Mara—Gigi Bermingham.

Directed by Harold Guskin; scenery, John Lee Beatty; costumes, Jeanne Button; lighting, Richard Nelson; music, Peter Golub; fights, B.H. Barry; clown/movement consultant, Bob Berky; production stage manager, James Harker; stage manager, Allison Sommers.

Time: Around the turn of the century. Place: Illyria can be found somewhere on the Mediterranean. It is a self-contained resort community, somewhat like Monaco. The play was presented in two parts.

The last major New York revival of *Twelfth Night* was by New York Shakespeare Festival in Central Park 6/20/86 for 26 performances.

## TITUS ANDRONICUS

| | |
|---|---|
| Titus Andronicus.............................. Donald Moffat | Alarbus; Goth 1; Messenger.............Armand Schultz |
| Lucius............................................ David Purdham | Aaron ................................................Keith David |
| Mutius; Publius..............................Steve Pickering | Saturninus...................................Don R. McManus |
| Quintus; Goth 2............................... Deryl Caitlyn | Bassianus; Goth 3...................Robert Curtis-Brown |
| Martius .........................................Rainn Wilson | Marcus Andronicus............................Jon DeVries |
| Lavinia...........................................Pamela Gien | Young Lucius ...................................Bradley Kane |
| Tamora............................................Kate Mulgrew | Aemilius.....................................Joseph M. Costa |
| Chiron .....................................Conan McCarty | Nurse.........................................Tanny McDonald |
| Demetrius.........................................Don Harvey | Clown..........................................Peter Appel |

Senators, Soldiers, Attendants: N. Richard Arif, Daniel Berkey, Bill Camp, Bryan Hicks, Susan Knight, William Langan, James McCauley, Cameron Miller, Erik Onate, Joshua Perl, Guy S. Wagner, William Wheeler.

Understudies: Mr. Moffat—Joseph M. Costa; Mr. Kane—William Wheeler; Mr. DeVries—William Langan; Mr. McManus—Daniel Berkey; Mr. Purdham—Steve Pickering; Miss Mulgrew—Tanny McDonald; Mr. David—Bryan Hicks; Misses McDonald, Gien—Susan Knight; Mr. McCarty—Bill Camp; Mr. Harvey— Guy S. Wagner; Mr. Costa—N. Richard Arif; Messrs. Curtis-Brown, Caitlyn—Cameron Miller; Messrs. Schultz, Pickering—Erik Onate; Mr. Appel—James McCauley; Mr. Wilson—Joshua Perl.

Directed by Michael Maggio; scenery, John Lee Beatty; costumes, Lewis D. Rampino; lighting, Jennifer Tipton; music, Louis Rosen; fights, B.H. Barry; production stage manager, Pat Sosnow; stage manager, Chris Sinclair.

Time and place: Act I, Ancient Rome; Act II, The same, one year later.

The last major New York production of *Titus Andronicus* was by New York Shakespeare Festival in Central Park 8/2/67 for 17 performances.

## MACBETH

| | |
|---|---|
| Witch #1; Gentlewoman........... Mary Louise Wilson | Gentlewoman................................... Laura Sametz |
| Witch #2 ....................................... Jeanne Sakata | Lady Macbeth.............................. Melinda Mullins |
| Witch #3; Messenger ...................... Katherine Hiler | Gentleman; Lord............................ Reg E. Cathey |
| Malcolm.................................... Thomas Gibson | Fleance .................................................. Gabriel Olds |
| Lennox................................Peter Jay Fernandez | Porter; Menteith .......................... Harry S. Murphy |
| Duncan; Doctor.............................. Mark Hammer | Old Man; Messenger; Old Siward........ Joseph Costa |
| Donalbain; Murderer; Messenger ...... Scott Allegrucci | Murderer #1; Seyton........................... Rene Rivera |
| Soldiers...................... Daniel Berkey, Rob LaBelle | Murderer #2; Cathness.............. Christopher McHale |
| Captain; Macduff............. William Converse-Roberts | Servant; Murderer; Young |
| Ross...................................... Daniel von Bargen | Siward .............................. Matt Bradford Sullivan |
| Angus........................................... Stephen Rowe | Lady Macduff ................................. Harriet Harris |
| Macbeth ......................................... Raul Julia | Boy, Son to Macduff ...................... Jesse Bernstein |
| Banquo........................................ Larry Bryggman | |

Directed by Richard Jordan; scenery, John Conklin; costumes, Jeanne Button; lighting, Brian Gale; music composed by Daniel Schreier; fight director, Peter Nels; production stage manager, Michael Chambers; stage manager, Buzz Cohen.

Time: The late Middle Ages. Place: Scotland. Act I, Scene 1: On the heath. Scene 2: The battlefield. Scene 3: Another part of the battlefield; Scene 4: The King's camp. Scene 5: Macbeth's castle at Inverness. Scene 6: In front of the castle. Scene 7: A chamber in the castle. Act II, Scene 1: The court of Macbeth's castle. Scene 2: Outside the castle. Act III, Scene 1: The King's castle at Forres. Scene 2: A chamber in the castle. Scene 3: Outside the King's castle. Scene 4: A banquet hall in the castle.

Act IV, Scene 1: On the heath. Scene 2: The King's castle. Scene 3: Macduff's castle at Fife. Scene 4: England, before the King's palace. Act V, Scene 1: Macbeth's castle at Dunsinane. Scene 2: The country near Dunsinane. Scene 3: Dunsinane, in the castle. Scene 4: Birnam Wood near Dunsinane; Scene 5: Dunsinane, within the castle. Scene 6: Near the castle. Scene 7: The castle gates.

The play was presented in two parts with the intermission following Act III.

The last major New York revival of *Macbeth* took place on Broadway 4/21/88 for 77 performances.

## HAMLET

| | |
|---|---|
| Bernardo; Player (Lucianus).................. Rene Rivera | Polonius .......................................... Josef Sommer |
| Francisco; Player (Prologue); | Ghost of Hamet's Father; Priest.......... Robert Murch |
| Clown.................................... MacIntyre Dixon | Osric .............................................. Leo Burmester |
| Horatio................................. Peter Francis James | Rosencrantz ................................... Philip Goodwin |
| Marcellus; Sailor.............................. Bill Camp | Guildenstern.................................. Reg E. Cathey |
| Claudius............................................. Brian Murray | Player King ................................. Clement Fowler |
| Voltemand; Messenger ...................... Miguel Perez | Player Queen................................. Susan Gabriel |
| Laertes ..................................... Michael Cumpsty | Fortinbras..................................... Don Reilly |
| Hamlet............................................ Kevin Kline | Norwegian Captain............................ Larry Green |
| Gertrude.............................................. Dana Ivey | Messenger ....................................... Erik Knutsen |
| Ophelia ......................................... Diane Venora | |

Guards, Players, Ladies-in-Waiting, Attendants, Lords: Claire Beckman, Bill Camp, Susan Gabriel, Larry Green, Curt Hostetter, Erik Knutsen, Rene Rivera.

Understudy: Player Queen, Lady-in-Waiting, Gertrude—Tanny McDonald.

Directed by Kevin Kline; scenery, Robin Wagner; costumes, Martin Pakledinaz; lighting, Jules Fisher; music, Bob James; fights, B.H. Barry; production stage manager, Maureen F. Gibson; stage manager, Fredric H. Orner.

Place: Elsinore Castle and its environs. The play was presented in two parts.

The last major New York revival of *Hamlet* was by New York Shakespeare Festival at the Public Theater (with Kevin Kline as Hamlet and Liviu Ciulei directing) 3/9/86 for 70 performances.

Note: New York Shakespeare Festival's Shakespeare Marathon will continue through following seasons until all of Shakespeare's plays have been presented. *A Midsummer Night's Dream, Julius Caesar* and *Romeo and Juliet* were presented in the 1987–88 season (see their entries in *The Best Plays of 1987–88*). *Much Ado About Nothing, King John, Coriolanus, Love's Labor's Lost, The Winter's Tale* and *Cymbeline* were presented last season (see their entries in *The Best Plays of 1988–89*)

Note: In Joseph Papp's Public Theater there are many auditoria. *Macbeth* and *Hamlet* played the Anspacher Theater.

### The Lady in Question (143). By Charles Busch. Produced by Kyle Renick and Kenneth Elliott at the Orpheum Theater. Opened July 25, 1989. (Closed December 3, 1989)

| | |
|---|---|
| Gertrude Garnet...............................Charles Busch | Hugo Hoffmann; Lotte von Elser........Andy Halliday |
| Voice of the Announcer......................James Cahill | Baron Wilhelm von Elsner..............Kenneth Elliott |
| Prof. Mittelhoffer; Dr. Maximilian....Mark Hamilton | Kitty, Countess de Borgia...................Julie Halston |
| Heidi Mittelhoffer.........................Theresa Marlowe | Augusta von Elsner; |
| Karel Freiser.....................................Robert Carey | Raina Aldric ..........................Meghan Robinson |
| Prof. Erik Maxwell.........................Arnie Kolodner | |

Directed by Kenneth Elliott; scenery, B.T. Whitehill; costumes, Robert Locke, Jennifer Arnold; lighting, Vivian Leone; production stage manager, Robert Vandergriff; press, Shirley Herz Associates, Sam Rudy.

Comedy, an arrogant female concert pianist confronts the Nazis in Bavaria. The play was presented in two parts. Previously produced off off Broadway at WPA.

### The People Who Could Fly (41). Conceived by Joe Hart. Produced by Eric Krebs in the Warp and Woof Theater Company production at South Street Theater. Opened August 2, 1989. (Closed September 3, 1989)

| | |
|---|---|
| Rich Bianco | Jennifer Krasnansky |
| Heide Brehm | Chris Petit |
| Michael Calderone | Anne Shapiro |
| Caprice Cosgrove | Steve Siegler |
| John Dimaggio | Kristina Swedlund |
| Jacqueline Gregg | Scott Wasser |

Directed by Joe Hart; scenery, Ron Cadry; costumes, Vickie Esposito; lighting, Chris Gorzelnick; stage manager, Jackie Gill; press, Shirley Herz Associates, Miller Wright.

Theater and dance performance presenting tales from India, Majorca, Scotland, Haiti, Japan and the antibellum South.

Note: This production was also presented at Town Hall for 9 performances 12/26/89–12/29/89.

### Love Letters (64). By A.R. Gurney. Produced by Roger L. Stevens, Thomas Viertel, Steven Baruch and Richard Frankel at the Promenade Theater. Opened August 22, 1989. (Closed October 15, 1989 and transferred to Broadway; see its entry in the Plays Produced on Broadway section of this volume)

| Andrew Makepeace Ladd III: | | Melissa Gardner: | |
|---|---|---|---|
| Aug. 22–27...............................John Rubinstein | | Aug. 22–27..........................Stockard Channing |
| Aug. 29–Sept. 3 ...........................George Segal | | Aug. 29–Sept. 3................................Dana Ivey |
| Sept. 5–10...............................Richard Thomas | | Sept. 5–10................................Swoosie Kurtz |
| Sept. 12–17 ...............................Jason Robards | | Sept. 12–17...............................Elaine Stritch |
| Sept. 19–24 ...........................Edward Herrmann | | Sept. 19–24...................................Jane Curtin |
| Sept. 26–Oct. 1 ...........................Josef Sommer | | Sept. 26–Oct. 1.......................Colleen Dewhurst |
| Oct. 3–8.....................................Treat Williams | | Oct. 3–8.....................................Kate Nelligan |
| Oct. 10–15...............................John Rubinstein | | Oct. 10–15 ..............................Joanna Gleason |

Directed by John Tillinger; scenic consultant, John Lee Beatty; lighting, Dennis Parichy; casting, Linda Wright; production stage manager, William H. Lang; press, the Joshua Ellis Office, Chris Boneau.

Two-character staged reading, with a different cast each week, of letters revealing the relationships of the duo from second grade on through a period of 50 years, presented in two parts. Previously produced in regional theater at the Long Wharf Theater, New Haven, and OOB in a series of 42 special performances last season.

A Best Play; see page 151.

**Roundabout Theater Company.** 1988–89 season concluded with **Privates on Parade** (64). Play with music by Peter Nichols; music by Denis King; lyrics by Peter Nichols. Produced by the Roundabout Theater Company, Gene Feist artistic director, Todd Haimes producing director, at the Christian C. Yegen Theater. Opened August 22, 1989. (Closed October 15, 1989)

| | | | |
|---|---|---|---|
| Pvt. Steven Flowers | Jim Fyfe | Sylvia Morgan | Donna Murphy |
| Cpl. Len Bonny | Ross Bickell | Sgt.-Maj. Reg Drummond | Donald Burton |
| Acting Capt. Terri Dennis | Jim Dale | Maj. Giles Flack | Simon Jones |
| Flight-Sgt. Kevin Cartwright | Gregory Jbara | Lee | Tom Matsusaka |
| Lance Cpl. Charles Bishop | John Curry | Cheng | Stephen Lee |
| Leading Aircraftman | | | |
| Eric Young-Love | Edward Hibbert | | |

Musicians: Philip Campanella piano ; Jack Bashkow woodwinds; Jim Pietsch percussion.

Directed by Larry Carpenter; choreography, Daniel Pelzig; musical direction, Philip Campanella; scenery, Loren Sherman; costumes, Lindsay W. Davis; lighting, Marcia Madeira; sound, Robert E. Casey; additional sound, Eric Santaniello; dialect coach, Howard Samuelsohn; production stage manager, Kathy J. Faul; press, the Joshua Ellis Office, Joshua Ellis, Susanne Tighe.

Time: 1948. Place: Singapore and districts of Malaya.

Female impersonator is part of a British special service regiment on entertainment duty in Malaya (musical numbers are part of their show; none is sung in character). A foreign play previously produced in London and at the Long Wharf Theater, New Haven, Conn.

## ACT I

| | |
|---|---|
| "S.A.D.U.S.E.A." | Company |
| "Les Girls" | Steve, Kevin |
| "Danke Schön" | Terri, Charles, Len, Eric, Kevin |
| "Western Approaches Ballet" | Sylvia, Terri, Charles, Kevin |
| "The Little Things We Used to Do" | Terri, Eric, Kevin, Charles, Len, Steve |
| "Black Velvet" | Charles, Kevin, Eric, Len |
| "The Price of Peace" | Company |

## ACT II

| | |
|---|---|
| "Could You Please Inform Us" | Terri |
| "Privates on Parade" | Company |
| "The Latin American Way" | Terri, Kevin, Eric |
| "Sunnyside Lane" | Charles, Len |
| "Sunnyside Lane" (Reprise) | Company |

**\*New York Shakespeare Festival Public Theater.** Schedule of ten programs. **Carnage, a Comedy** (25). By Adam Simon and Tim Robbins; in the Actors' Gang production. Opened September 17, 1989. (Closed October 8, 1989) **Kate's Diary** (23). By Kathleen Tolan. Opened November 29, 1989. (Closed December 17, 1989) **Up Against It** (16). Musical based on a screen play by Joe Orton; adapted by Tom Ross; music and lyrics by Todd Rundgren. Opened December 4, 1989. (Closed December 17, 1989) **Kingfish** (14). By Marlane Meyer. Opened December 21, 1989. (Closed December 31,

*PRIVATES ON PARADE*—Simon Jones and Jim Dale in the Roundabout's production of the Peter Nichols play with Denis King music

1989) **Romance in Hard Times** (6). Musical with book, music and lyrics by William
Finn. Opened December 28, 1989. (Closed December 31, 1989)

Also **A Mom's Life** (48). One-woman play written and performed by Kathryn Grody.
Opened March 13, 1990. (Closed April 22, 1990) **Jonah** (8). Musical adapted by Elizabeth
Swados from Robert Nathan's novel *Jonah and the Whale*; music and lyrics by Elizabeth
Swados; additional texts adapted from the Old Testament. Opened March 20, 1990. (Closed
March 25, 1990) **\*Spunk** (50). Program of three one-act plays adapted by George C.
Wolfe from tales by Zora Neale Hurston; music by Chic Street Man: *Sweat, Story in Harlem
Slang* and *The Gilded Six-Bits*.Opened April 18, 1990. **Ice Cream With Hot Fudge**
(38). Program of two one-act plays by Caryl Churchill: *Ice Cream* and *Hot Fudge*. Opened
May 3, 1990. (Closed June 3, 1990) **\*The B. Beaver Animation** (12). Revival of the
play by Lee Breuer in The Mabou Mines' production, Anthony Vasconcello managing
director. Opened May 20, 1990. Produced by New York Shakespeare Festival, Joseph Papp
producer, at the Public Theater; see note.

ALL PLAYS: Associate producer, Jason Steven Cohen; director of plays and musical development, Gail Merrifield; production manager, Andrew Mihok; press, Richard Kornberg, Barbara Carroll, Reva Cooper, Carol Fineman, Steven J. Krementz.

## CARNAGE, A COMEDY

| | |
|---|---|
| Rev. Dr. Cotton Slocum ....................Lee Arenberg | Ralph ............................................. Brent Hinkley |
| Deacon Tack......................................Ned Bellamy | Dot ............................................... Shannon Holt |
| Opie; A-Company Commando; | Tipper Slocum; TV Anchorwoman; |
| Photographer; Donner Child................Jack Black | Donner Child; Homeless Reject; |
| Pristeena; Dana Donner; Reporter.... Cynthia Ettinger | Sycophant ....................................Lisa Moncure |
| Jerry; Butcher; Sycophant; | Phil the War Vet; A-Company |
| Homeless Reject ...............................Jeff Foster | Commando; Huckleman; God's |
| Chip Donner; Henry Henderson; | Happy Acre Guard....................... Dean Robinson |
| Bob; A-Company Commando; | Clare the Cripple; Magpie; |
| Photographer.....................................Kyle Gass | Pocahontas .......................Cari Dean Whittemore |

Music: "Lost Highway" by Leon Payne; "Battle of Armageddon" by Acuff/McCloud; "Land of God" music by Kyle Gass, lyrics by Tim Robbins; "After the End" music by David Robbins, Kyle Gass and Tim Robbins, lyrics by Tim Robbins. Original music and arrangements performed by Anarchestra.

Gangland Musicians: Kyle Gass, David Robbins, Darryl Tewes.

Understudy: Gabrielle Robbins.

Directed by Tim Robbins; The Actors' Gang—artistic director Tim Robbins, managing director and producer Patti McGuire; musical direction, David Robbins; scenery, Catherine Hardwicke; backdrop artist, Ethan Johnson; costumes, Neil Spisak; lighting, Robert Wierzel; production stage manager, Michel Chenelle.

Time: The present. Act I, Scene 1: The back room, God's Happy Acre. Scene 2: The backwoods of Arkansas. Scene 3: The tract home of Dot and Ralph. Scene 4: The board room, God's Happy Acre. Scene 5: The tract home of Dot and Ralph. Scene 6: God's Happy Acre revival hall. Scene 7: Bob and Pep's filling station. Scene 8: The interstate. Scene 9: Indian Falls National Monument.

Act II, Scene 1: Motel 6. Scene 2: Inner sanctum. Scenes 3, 4 and 5: Somewhere in the desert. Scene 6: Gates of God's Happy Acre. Scene 7: Inside God's Happy Acre. Scene 8: God's Happy Acre revival hall. Scene 9: Outside God's Happy Acre.

The wayward ways and means of modern TV evangelism. Previously produced by Pipeline/Museum of Contemporary Art, Los Angeles.

## KATE'S DIARY

| | |
|---|---|
| Kate...........................................Lizbeth Mackay | Father Hernandez; Walter .................John Griesemer |
| Tim; Frank ..........................Michael Bryan French | Pablo.................................................. Rafael Baez |
| Ellen; Angie; Trish...........................Laura Hughes | |

Directed by David Greenspan; scenery, William Kennon; costumes, Elsa Ward; lighting, David Bergstein; production stage manager, Diane Hartdagen; stage manager, Mark McMahon.

Time: The recent past. Place: New York City, Kate's bedroom and Kate's imagination. The play was presented without intermission.

Woman has written a play of political intrigue and relates its scenes to her life. Previously produced OOB by Playwrights Horizons New Theater Wing 6/7/89 for 13 workshop performances.

## UP AGAINST IT

| | |
|---|---|
| Father Brodie; Old Man ..............Stephen Temperley | Rowena............................................. Mari Nelson |
| Miss Drumgoole...............................Alison Fraser | Bernard Coates.................................. Tom Aulino |
| Ian McTurk....................................Philip Casnoff | Man in the Hole; Lilly Corbett........... Judith Cohen |
| Mayor Terence O'Scullion .....Joel McKinnon Miller | Georgina ...............................Marnie Carmichael |
| Christopher Low................................ Roger Bart | Jack Ramsay.......................................Dan Tubb |
| Connie Boon................................Tony Dibuono | Guard...............................................Scott Carollo |

Ensemble: Brian Arsenault, Scott Carollo, Mindy Cooper, Dorothy R. Earle, Julia C. Hughes, Gary Mendelson, Jim Newman.

Orchestra: Tom Fay piano, conductor; Wendy Bobbitt keyboard, assistant conductor; Wayne Abravanel keyboard; Steve Greenfield woodwinds; Deborah Assael cello; Kenneth Freeman bass; Larry Spivack percussion.

Understudies: Misses Dibuono, Cohen—Marnie Carmichael; Messrs. Tubb, Casnoff—Scott Carollo; Miss Carmichael—Mindy Cooper; Misses Fraser, Nelson—Deborah Graham; Mr. Bart—Jim Newman; Messrs. Temperley, Miller, Aulino—Ron Wisniski; Mr. Carollo—Brian Arsenault; Swings—Joe Langworth, Elizabeth Mozer.

Directed by Kenneth Elliott; choreography, Jennifer Muller; musical direction, Tom Fay; scenery, B.T. Whitehill; costumes, John Glaser; lighting, Vivien Leone; sound, John Kilgore; orchestrations, Doug Katsaros; vocal arrangements, Todd Rundgren; production stage manager, Ron Nash; stage manager, Lisa Buxbaum.

Time: The 1960s. Place: A mythical place not unlike England.

Originally written as a screen play for the Beatles in 1967, rejected and then revised but unproduced, *Up Against It* in its stage version concerns, in satirical vein, male friends who are victimized by women and plot to assassinate the female prime minister.

## ACT I

Scene 1: Near the allegorical Figure of Peace
Scene 2: Father Brodie's study
  "When Worlds Collide"....................................................................Father Brodie, Mayor, Connie
Scene 3: The back of Father Brodie's house
  "Parallel Lines" ..........................................................................................Miss Drumgoole
Scene 4: The outskirts of town
  "Free, Male and Twenty-One"......................................................................McTurk, Low
Scene 5: The forest
  "The Smell of Money"..........................................................................................Coates
Scene 6: Money Box Lodge
  "The Smell of Money" (Waltz)..............................................................................Rowena
Scene 7: Through the forest to the city
  "If I Have To Be Alone"........................................................................................McTurk
  "Up Against It" ..................................................................................Ramsay, Company
Scene 8: A palmist's shop
  "Life Is a Drag" ......................................Ramsay, McTurk, Mayor, Low, Old Man, Men
Scene 9: Outside the Conference Hall
Scene 10: The Conference Hall
  "Lilly's Address"........................................................................................Lilly, Company
Scene 11: Connie's office, the palmist's shop, the town square
  "Love in Disguise"...............................................Rowena, Ramsay, McTurk, Low, Company

## ACT II

Scene 1: The Conference Hall
  "You'll Thank Me in the End".................................................................................Connie
Scene 2: A prison cell
  "Maybe I'm Better Off"............................................................................ McTurk, Ramsay
Scene 3: The ocean
Scene 4: Topside of a yacht
Scene 5: The ocean
Scene 6: Near the beach
  "From Hunger"...........................................................................................................Low
Scene 7: An army camp
  "Entropy"........................................Miss Drumgoole, Ramsay, McTurk, Low, Company
Scene 8: Near the allegorical Figure of Peace
  "Parallel Lines" (Reprise) ...........................................................McTurk, Company
  Finale...............................................................................................................Company

## KINGFISH

| | | | |
|---|---|---|---|
| Wylie | Buck Henry | Wanda | Jacque Lynn Colton |
| Hal | Barry Sherman | Edward; Mack | Tony Abatemarco |
| Finney | Kevin O'Rourke | Kingfish | Arthur Hanket |

Stage directions read by David Schweizer.

Directed by David Schweizer; scenery, Rosario Provenza; costumes, Susan Nininger; lighting, Robert Wierzel; music composed by Steven Moshier; projections, Perry Hoberman; production stage manager, David S. Franklin; stage manager, J. Michael Stein.

A dog, his master and their strange relationships with a thief and others. The play was presented in two parts. Previously produced in regional theater at Los Angeles Theater Center.

## ROMANCE IN HARD TIMES

| | | | |
|---|---|---|---|
| Hennie | Lillias White | The Older | Amanda Naughton |
| Harvey | Lawrence Clayton | The Younger | Stacey Lynn Brass |
| Boris | Cleavant Derricks | Gus | Michael Mandell |
| Zoe | Alix Korey | Eleanor Roosevelt | Peggy Hewett |
| Polly | J.P. Dougherty | The Kid | Victor Trent Cook |

Handcuffed Sisters:

Harmonizing Fools, Radio Announcers, Supreme Court Justices, Prisoners, Celebrities: Rufus Bonds Jr., Victor Trent Cook, Melodee Savage, John Sloman, James Stovall.

Orchestra: Ted Sperling conductor; Tim Weill assistant conductor, keyboards; Robert DeBellis, Aaron Heick, David Weiss woodwinds; Randall T. Andos trombone, tuba; Ronald J. Buttacavoli trumpet; Roger Wendt, French horn; Steven A. Freeman keyboards; Norbert Goldberg drums, percussion; Douglas Romoff acoustic and electric bass; Gregory M. Utzig guitar, banjo.

Understudies: Messrs. Clayton, Mandell—Rufus Bonds Jr.; Misses Naughton, Brass—Linda Gabler; Misses Korey, Hewett—Audrey Lavine; Miss White—Kecia Lewis-Evans; Mr. Cook—W. Ellis Porter; Mr. Derricks—James Stovall; Swings—Linda Gabler, W. Ellis Porter, Harrison White.

Time: The Great Depression. Place: A soup kitchen, New York City.

Characters immersed in the socioeconomic problems of the 1930s look forward to better times a-coming.

### ACT I

| | |
|---|---|
| "Harvey" | Hennie |
| "Standing in Line" | Polly, Handcuffed Sisters, Harmonizing Fools, Gus, Zoe |
| "Out of Here" | Boris |
| "Harvey Promised to Change the World" | Boris, Hennie, Harvey, Harmonizing Fools |
| "The Supreme Court Saved From Fire" | Announcer, Hennie, Justices |

(Radio Announcer—James Stovall; Chief Justice—Rufus Bonds Jr.)

| | |
|---|---|
| "Goodbye" | Polly, Handcuffed Sisters |
| "Charity Quartet" | Handcuffed Sisters, Zoe, Gus |
| "Lovesong" | Hennie, Boris, Harvey |
| "Charity Quartet" (Reprise) | Handcuffed Sisters, Zoe, Gus |
| "Eleanor Roosevelt: A Discussion of Soup" | Eleanor, Zoe, Company |
| "I Never Said I Didn't Love You" | Harvey |
| "You Got Me Grinding My Teeth" | Boris, Hennie, Company |
| "That's Enough For Me" | Hennie |
| "Places I Fainted From Hunger/Time Passes" | Polly, Company |
| "All Fall Down" | Zoe |
| "The Good Times Are Here" | Hennie, Boris, Eleanor, Company |

### ACT II

| | |
|---|---|
| "Feeling Rich" | Zoe, Gus, Polly, Handcuffed Sisters, Harmonizing Fools |
| "Hold My Baby Back" | Hennie |
| "Hennie Soup" | Eleanor, Hennie, Gus, Company |
| "Thinking About You/Out of Here" (Reprise) | Boris, Hennie |
| "I Don't Want to Feel What I Feel" | Hennie |

"The Prosperity Song" ........................................................Eleanor, Gus, Handuffed Sisters, Polly, Zoe
"A Gaggle of Celebrities" ..........................................................................................Hennie, Celebrities
    (Babe Ruth—John Sloman; Shirley Temple—Melodee Savage; Bojangles Robinson—Rufus Bonds Jr.)
"I'll Get You Out of My Life"..................................................................................... Boris, Hennie
"How Could You Do This to Someone Who
    Robbed for You?" (Prison Music) ...............................................Handcuffed Sisters, Gus, Zoe, Polly,
    Eleanor, Prisoners, Hennie, Boris
"Blame It on These Times" ..........................................................................................................Boris
"Standing in Line" (Reprise).............................................................................. Hennie, Company
"You Can't Let Romance Die"..............................................................................................The Kid
"That's Enough for Me Duet" ....................................................................................... Hennie, Boris
Finale ........................................................................................................................................Company

## A MOM'S LIFE

Directed by Timothy Near; scenery, James Youmans; costumes, Holland Vose; lighting, Phil Monat; production stage manager, Chris Sinclair.

Prologue: An overview. Time: The present. Place: New York City. The play was presented without intermission.

A mother, played by Kathryn Grody, acts out a day in her life of raising children in the modern city.

## JONAH

Jonah.............................................................................................................Jake Ehrenreich
Jonettes and All Other Roles:
  Phillis Jonette ...............................................................................................Cathy Porter
  Marguarita Jonette ..............................................................................Ann Marie Milazzo

Musicians: Paul O'Keefe, Michael S. Sottile.
Understudy: Mr. Ehrenreich—Eric Sanders.
Directed by Elizabeth Swados; choreography and musical staging, Bill Castellino; musical direction, Michael S. Sottile; scenery, Michael E. Downs; costumes, Judy Dearing; lighting, Beverly Emmons; whale design, Tobi Kahn; production stage manager, Lisa Buxbaum.

Musical credits: Drum solos played by Jake Ehrenreich; instrumental and vocal arrangements evolved by the company; last song based on Corinthians.

A version of the Biblical story of Jonah, with music, presented without intermission.

## SPUNK

Guitar Man ...................................Chic Street Man
Blues Speak Woman.....................Ann Duquesnay
  The Folks: Danitra Vance, Reggie Montgomery, Kevin Jackson, K. Todd Freeman.
Prologue.................................................Ensemble

*Sweat*
Delia.............................................Danitra Vance
Sykes...................................Reggie Montgomery
Men on Joe's Clark's
  Porch................ Kevin Jackson, K. Todd Freeman

*Story in Harlem Slang*
"Livin' With the Blues".................Chic Street Man
"Hey Baby" ...........Ann Duquesnay, Chic Street Man
"Slang Talk Man" ...........................Kevin Jackson

Jelly.............................................K. Todd Freeman
Sweet Back...........................Reggie Montgomery
Girl ................................................. Danitra Vance

*The Gilded Six-Bits*
"You Bring Out the Boogie
  in Me"..............Chic Street Man, Ann Duquesnay
Players; Slemmons; Joe's Mother;
Ice Cream Parlor Folk;
  Clerk....... Reggie Montgomery, K. Todd Freeman, Ann Duquesnay
Missie May ................................... Danitra Vance
Joe..................................................Kevin Jackson
"Tell Me Mama"..........................Chic Street Man, Ann Duquesnay, Ensemble

Directed by George C. Wolfe; choreography, Hope Clarke; scenery, Loy Arcenas; costumes, Toni-Leslie James; lighting, Don Holder; mask and puppet design, Barbara Pollitt; production stage manager, Jacqui Casto; stage manager, Jenny Peek.

*Story in Harlem Slang* is a linguistic spree of two panhandlers in the Harlem of the 1920s. *Sweat*, about an abused wife, and *The Gilded Six-Bits*, about a betrayed husband, are set in Zora Neale Hurston's home town of Eatonville, Fla. The show was presented in two parts with the intermission following *Story in Harlem Slang*. Previously produced in regional theater at the Mark Taper Forum, Los Angeles.

## ICE CREAM WITH HOT FUDGE

| PERFORMER | "HOT FUDGE" | "ICE CREAM" |
|---|---|---|
| Jane Kaczmarek | June; Grace | Vera |
| Robert Knepper | Matt; Hugh | Phil |
| Julianne Moore | Sonia; Lena | Jaq |
| John Pankow | Colin | Man in Devon; Shrink; Colleague; Fellow Guest; Hitcher; Professor |
| James Rebhorn | Charlie; Jerry | Lance |
| Margaret Whitton | Ruby | Drunk Woman; Hitcher's Mother; South American Woman Passenger |

BOTH PLAYS: Directed by Les Waters; scenery and costumes, Annie Smart; lighting, Stephen Strawbridge; fight staged by B.H. Barry; production stage manager, Karen Armstrong; stage manager, Buzz Cohen.

HOT FUDGE: Time: One evening. Place: Pub, 7 p.m.; winebar, 9 p.m.; club, 11 p.m.; Colin's flat, 1 a.m.

East End girl, trying to impress a boy friend, becomes ensnared in a web of lies and violence. A foreign (British) play in its world premiere in this production.

ICE CREAM: Scenes 1–10; The United Kingdom during a summer in the late 1980s. Scene 11–20: The United States, the following year.

Middle class American couple, romanticizing Britain and seeking for their roots there, find them among the punk set. A foreign play previously produced in London at the Royal Court Theater.

## THE B. BEAVER ANIMATION

B. Beaver ................................................................................................................................. Frederick Neumann

Chorus: Honora Fergusson, Clove Galilee, Ruth Maleczech, Greg Mehrten, David Neumann, Terry O'Reilly.

Musicians: Steve Peabody, Frier McCollister.

Directed by Lee Breuer; original design, Tina Girouard; scenery adapted by Marcia Altieri; costumes adapted by Gabriel Berry; lighting, David Tecson; music, Jimmy Harry, Steve Peabody; stage manager, Jack Doulin.

The first productions of record of *The B. Beaver Animation* were by Mabou Mines at the Paula Cooper Gallery in 1972 and off off Broadway at New York Theater Ensemble and Theater for the New City in the season of 1974–75.

Among its 1989–90 special events, New York Shakespeare Festival Public Theater offered the Moscow Art Theater School's production of *My Big Land*, a 1957 play by Alexander Galich (nee Ginsburg) but banned in the Soviet Union until this year, about a Jewish family living in the Ukraine during the Stalin era and the rise of Hitler, directed by Oleg Tabakov, presented at the Susan Stein Shiva Theater in the Russian language with simultaneous English translation, for 6 performances 8/15/89–8/19/89, with the original Russian cast: Filip Yankovsky, Vladimir Mashkov, Roman Kuznechenko, Alyona Khovanskaya, Irina Apeksemova, Liya Yelshevskaya, Dmitri Stolbstov, Yuri Yekimov, Igor Kozlov, Irina Gordina, Sergei Shentalinsky, Yevgeny Mironov, Nina Muzhikova.

Note: In Joseph Papp's Public Theater there are many auditoria. *Carnage, a Comedy*, *Kate's Diary*, *A Mom's Life*, and *The B. Beaver Animation* played the Susan Stein Shiva Theater; *Up Against It* played LuEsther Hall; *Kingfish, Jonah* and *Spunk* played Martinson Hall; *Romance in Hard Times* and *Ice Cream With Hot Fudge* played the Estelle R. Newman Theater.

**The Man Who Shot Lincoln** (14). By Luigi Creatore. Produced by William De Silva in association with Claridge Productions at the Astor Place Theater. Opened September 21, 1989. (Closed October 1, 1989)

| | | | |
|---|---|---|---|
| Edwin Booth | Sam Tsoutsouvas | The Player | Eric Tull |
| Mary Devlin | Marcia Gay Harden | John Wilkes Booth | Conan McCarty |

Directed by Crandall Diehl; scenery and costumes, Michael Bottari, Ronald Case; lighting, Craig Miller; production stage manager, Renee F. Lutz; press, Peter Cromarty.

The assassination from Edwin Booth's point of view, with the Booth brothers' rivalry a major issue.

**Playwrights Horizons.** Schedule of five programs. **Young Playwrights Festival** (20). Program of four one-act plays: *Painted Rain* by Janet Allard, *Finnegan's Funeral Parlor and Ice Cream Shoppe* by Robert Kerr, *Twice Shy* by Debra Neff and *Peter Breaks Through* by Alejandro Membreno. Presented in the Foundation of the Dramatists Guild production, Nancy Quinn producing director, Sheri M. Goldhirsch managing director. Opened September 21, 1989. (Closed October 8, 1989) **Hyde in Hollywood** (15). By Peter Parnell; co-produced with American Playhouse Theater Productions. Opened November 29, 1989. (Closed December 10, 1989) **When She Danced** (38). By Martin Sherman. Opened February 19, 1990. (Closed March 24, 1990) **Once on This Island** (24). Musical with book and lyrics by Lynn Ahrens; music by Stephen Flaherty; based on the novel *My Love, My Love* by Rosa Guy; presented in association with AT&T: OnStage. Opened May 6, 1990. (Closed May 27, 1990) And *Falsettoland* by William Finn scheduled to open 6/8/90. Produced by Playwrights Horizons, Andre Bishop artistic director, Paul S. Daniels executive director, at Playwrights Horizons (*Hyde in Hollywood* at American Place Theater).

*WHEN SHE DANCED*—Elizabeth Ashley (as Isadora Duncan) with Robert Sean Leonard in a scene from Martin Sherman's play

## YOUNG PLAYWRIGHTS FESTIVAL

*Painted Rain*

Teddy............................................Kimble Joyner
Dustin......................................Christopher Shaw
Barbara..............................................Debra Monk
Directed by Mary B. Robinson; playwright advisor, Morgan Jenness; stage manager, Jeanne Fornadel. Two boys growing up in an orphanage.

*Finnegan's Funeral Parlor*
*And Ice Cream Shoppe*

Kevin......................................David Barry Gray
Arthur....................................James McDonnell
Anvil......................................David Eigenberg
Mona.................................................Debra Monk
Pamela.................................................Jill Tasker
Carol ..............................................Allison Dean
Mrs. Dewey .....................................Mary Testa
Directed by Thomas Babe; playwright advisor, Christopher Durang; stage manager, James

FitzSimmons. An undertaker decides that funerals should be fun.

*Twice Shy*

Jonathan.........................................Ray Cochran
Louise ..........................................Katherine Hiler
Desmond....................................David Lansbury
Steven ....................................Mark W. Conklin
Cookie.............................................Lauren Klein
Directed by Mark Brokaw; playwright advisor, Morgan Jenness; stage manager, James FitzSimmons. Young woman tries to sort out her relationships with family and close friends.

*Peter Breaks Through*

Mona.................................................Mary Testa
Guido ......................................James McDonnell
Peter.................................................Ray Cockran
Directed by Thomas Babe; playwright advisor, Albert Innaurato; stage manager, Jeanne Fornadel. Comedy of urban life leading to a comeuppance.

ALL PLAYS: Scenery, Allen Moyer; costumes, Jess Goldstein; lighting, Karl E. Haas; sound, Janet Kalas; production stage manager, Mimi Apfel; press, Shirley Herz Associates, Sam Rudy.

These four plays by young authors (Janet Allard 15, Robert Kerr 18, Debra Neff 18 and Alejandro Membreno 18 at the time of submission) were selected from hundreds of entries in the Foundation of the Dramatists Guild's 8th annual playwriting contest for young people. The program was presented in two parts with the intermission following *Finnegan's Funeral Parlor.*

Three more contest entries were selected to be presented in a program of staged readings at Playwrights Horizons for 2 performances 10/1 and 10/2/89: *A Night With Doris* by Stephanie Brown, 18, directed by Thomas Babe; *And One Bell Shattered* by Karen Hartman, 18, directed by Lisa Peterson; *Hat* by Gilbert David Feke, 14, directed by R.J. Cutler.

## HYDE IN HOLLYWOOD

Julian Hyde.........................................Robert Joy
Hollywood Confidential................. Keith Szarabajka
Charles Hock.............................Stephen Pearlman
Jake Singer ....................................Peter Frechette
David Hogarth .......................Robert Curtis-Brown
Betty Armstrong .....................................Fran Brill
Lida Todd; Susan..................................Julie Boyd
Reynaldo Romero; Agent................ Derek D. Smith

Bookie; Andrew; Florist..................... Kurt Deutsch
Buddy; Art Director; Sidney
  Sargent .............................. Matthew Locricchio
Harry Slezak; Rex Markum;
  Sugie Sugerman; Senator ............. Herbert Rubens
Ricardo; Ensemble ......................Kenneth L. Marks
Martin; Ensemble ...........................Richard Topol

Reporters, Film Crew, Extras: Thomas Eldon, Thia Gartner, Ed Mahler, Rob Richards.

Directed by Gerald Gutierrez; scenery, Douglas Stein; costumes, Ann Hould-Ward; lighting, Frances Aronson; sound, Scott Lehrer; projection design, Wendall K. Harrington; incidental music, Robert Waldman; production stage manager, Peter B. Mumford; stage manager, Kate Riddle; press, Philip Rinaldi.

Time: 1939 and in the mid-1950s. Place: Hollywood.

Hollywood dreams and aspirations dramatized as nightmares.

## WHEN SHE DANCED

Isadora........................Elizabeth Ashley
Sergei ...........................Jonathan Walker
Jeanne..........................Jacqueline Bertrand
Mary..............................Marcia Lewis

Miss Belzer..............................Marcia Jean Kurtz
Alexandros................................Robert Sean Leonard
Luciano.....................................Robert Dorfman
Christine ......................................Clea Montville

Directed by Tim Luscombe; scenery, Steven Rubin; costumes, Jess Goldstein; lighting, Nancy Schertler; original music and sound design, John Gromada; choreography, Peter Anastos; production stage manager, Roy Harris.

Time: 1923. Place: Paris, a house on the Rue de la Pompe. The play was presented in two parts.

Isadora Duncan's inspired devotion to art in the twilight of her life and career.

## ONCE ON THIS ISLAND

| | | | |
|---|---|---|---|
| Daniel | Jerry Dixon | Armand | Gerry McIntyre |
| Erzulie | Andrea Frierson | Agwe | Milton Craig Nealy |
| Mama Euralie | Sheila Gibbs | Andrea | Nikki Rene |
| Ti Moune | La Chanze | Papa Ge | Eric Riley |
| Asaka | Kecia Lewis-Evans | Tonton Julian | Ellis E. Williams |
| Little Ti Moune | Afi McClendon | | |

Musicians: Stephen Marzullo conductor, keyboards; Tony Conniff bass; Norbert Goldberg percussion; Richard Prior winds; Garth Roberts keyboards.

Understudies: Misses Gibbs, La Chanze, Lewis-Evans, Rene—Fuschia Walker; Miss Frierson—Nikki Rene; Messrs. Dixon, McIntyre, Williams—Keith Tyrone; Messrs. Nealy, Riley—Gerry McIntyre.

Directed and choreographed by Graciela Daniele; musical direction, Stephen Marzullo; scenery, Loy Arcenas; costumes, Judy Dearing; lighting, Allen Lee Hughes; sound, Scott Lehrer; orchestrations, Michael Starobin; production stage manager, Leslie Loeb.

Time: Night, in a storm. Place: An island in the French Antilles. The play was presented without intermission.

Group of people on a Caribbean island pass the time during a storm by telling (and acting out) a fairy tale about gods, "grand hommes" and ordinary folk involved in the adventures of a peasant waif who falls in love with an aristocrat.

A Best Play; see page 344.

## MUSICAL NUMBERS

| | |
|---|---|
| "We Dance" | Storytellers |
| "One Small Girl" | Mama Euralie, Tonton Julian, Little Ti Moune, Storytellers |
| "Waiting for Life" | Ti Moune, Storytellers |
| "And the Gods Heard Her Prayer" | Asaka, Agwe, Papa Ge, Erzulie |
| "Rain" | Agwe, Storytellers |
| "Pray" | Ti Moune, Tonton Julian, Mama Euralie, Guard, Storytellers |
| "Forever Yours" | Ti Moune, Daniel, Papa Ge |
| "The Sad Tale of the Beauxhommes" | Armand, Storytellers |
| "Ti Moune" | Mama Euralie, Tonton Julian, Ti Moune |
| "Mama Will Provide" | Asaka, Storytellers |
| "Waiting for Life" (Reprise) | Ti Moune |
| "Some Say" | Storytellers |
| "The Human Heart" | Erzulie, Storytellers |
| "Pray" (Reprise) | Storytellers |
| "Some Girls" | Daniel |
| "The Ball" | Andrea, Daniel, Ti Moune, Storytellers |
| "Forever Yours" (Reprise) | Papa Ge, Ti Moune, Erzulie, Storytellers |
| "A Part of Us" | Mama Euralie, Little Ti Moune, Tonton Julian, Storytellers |
| "Why We Tell the Story" | Storytellers |

**The Aunts** (15). By Gary Bonasorte. Produced by Ervin Litkei in association with Ethel Gabriel and Larry Lipp at the 47th Street Theater. Opened October 4, 1989. (Closed October 15, 1989)

| | | | |
|---|---|---|---|
| Meg | Bethel Leslie | Pita | Mia Dillon |
| Nan | Ann Wedgeworth | Chuck | Christopher Wynkoop |

Directed by Charles Maryan; scenery, Atkin Pace; costumes, Lana Fritz; lighting, John Gleason; sound, Brian Ronan; dances, Bertram Ross; production stage manager, Bill McComb; press, Shirley Herz, Miller Wright.

Conflicts within a family keeping watch over a dying husband.

**All God's Dangers** (41).   By Theodore Rosengarten, Michael Hadley and Jennifer Hadley; based on *All God's Dangers: The Life of Nate Shaw* by Theodore Rosengarten. Produced by John Cullen and Jennifer Hadley & Michael Hadley at the Lamb's Theater. Opened October 22, 1989. (Closed November 26, 1989)

Nate Shaw ................................................................................................................ Cleavon Little

Directed by William Partlan; scenery and costumes, G.W. Mercier; lighting, Tina Charney; sound, Greg Sutton; associate producer, Rick Azar; production stage manager, Tom Aberger; press, Callaghan and Company, Edward Callaghan, Brigitte Devine, Judy Larkin.

Place: The staging ground of memory; rural Alabama.

One-man play based on real characters and events as told to the historian Theodore Rosegarten by an Alabama cotton farmer, "Nate Shaw" (real name Ned Cobb), who was born in 1885 and lived into the 1970s. Previously produced in regional theater at the Cricket Theater, Minneapolis, and the Alabama Shakespeare Festival, Montgomery.

**\*Circle Repertory Company.** Schedule of five programs. **Beside Herself** (40). By Joe Pintauro. Opened October 17, 1989. (Closed November 19, 1989) **Sunshine** (33). By William Mastrosimone. Opened December 17, 1989. (Closed January 14, 1990) **Imagining Brad** (24). By Peter Hedges. Opened February 6, 1990. (Closed February 25, 1990) **Prelude to a Kiss** (33).   By Craig Lucas.   Opened March 14, 1990. (Suspended April 1, 1990) Reopened April 12, 1990 (Closed April 19, 1990 and transferred to Broadway; see its entry in the Plays Produced on Broadway section of this volume) **\*Each Day Dies With Sleep** (18).   By Jose Rivera; produced in association with Berkeley Repertory Theater (Sharon Ott artistic director, Mitzi Sales managing director) and AT&T: OnStage. Opened May 16, 1990. Produced by Circle Repertory Company, Tanya Berezin artistic director, Connie L. Alexis managing director, at Circle Repertory.

### BESIDE HERSELF

| | | | |
|---|---|---|---|
| Mary | Lois Smith | Violet | Susan Bruce |
| Harry; Bear | Edward Seamon | Augie-Jake | William Hurt |
| Alexandra | Melissa Joan Hart | Skidie | Calista Flockhart |

Directed by John Bishop; scenery, John Lee Beatty; costumes, Ann Emonts; lighting, Dennis Parichy; sound, Chuck London, Stewart Werner; music, Jonathan Brielle; production stage manager, Denise Yaney; press, Gary Murphy.

Time: September-October. Place: A house in the woods on an island. The play was presented in two parts.

Character study of a female poet at various stages of her life.

### SUNSHINE

| | | | |
|---|---|---|---|
| Sunshine | Jennifer Jason Leigh | Nelson | John Dossett |
| Robby | Jordan Mott | Jerry | Bruno Alberti |

Directed by Marshall W. Mason; scenery, David Potts; costumes, Susan Lyall; lighting, Dennis Parichy; sound, Stewart Werner, Chuck London; original music, Peter Kater; production stage manager, Fred Reinglas.

Time: November. Place: The Jersey Shore—Sunshine's booth, Nelson's studio apartment and the booth again. The play was presented without an intermission.

Intensifying relationship between a peep-show stripper and a paramedic.

## IMAGINING BRAD

Valerie .......................................Melissa Joan Hart    Brad's Wife ...........................Erin Cressida Wilson
Dana Sue Kaye ...............................Sharon Ernster

Directed by Joe Mantello; scenery, Loy Arcenas; costumes, Laura Cunningham; lighting, Dennis Parichy; sound, Stewart Werner, Chuck London; production stage manager, Denise Yaney.

Conversation of women dissecting their husbands. The play was presented without an intermission.

## PRELUDE TO A KISS

Peter...............................................Alec Baldwin    Dr. Boyle ...................................Larry Bryggman
Taylor..........................................John Dossett    Minister......................................Craig Bockhorn
Rita.....................................Mary-Louise Parker    Aunt Dorothy; Leah ......................Joyce Reehling
Tom; Jamaican Waiter.................L. Peter Callender    Uncle Fred........................Michael Warren Powell
Mrs. Boyle.....................................Debra Monk    Old Man......................................Barnard Hughes

Party Guests, Barflies, Wedding Guests, Vacationers: Kimberly Dudwitt, Pete Tyler.

Directed by Norman Rene; scenery, Loy Arcenas; costumes, Walter Hicklin; lighting, Debra J. Kletter; sound, Scott Lehrer; production stage manager, M.A. Howard.

A love affair and marriage followed by a strange kiss which seems to have the power to exchange souls between bodies. The play was presented in two parts.

Timothy Hutton replaced Alec Baldwin 4/12/90.

A Best Play; see page 269.

## EACH DAY DIES WITH SLEEP

Johnny.........................................Randy Vasquez    Augie.................................................Alex Colon
Nelly ...............................................Erica Gimpel

Directed by Roberta Levitow; scenery, Tom Kamm; costumes, Tina Cantu Navarro; lighting, Robert Wierzel; New York sound design, Janet Kalas; scenic projection design, Charles Rose; production stage manager, Fred Reinglas.

Young Hispanic woman, one of 21 children of a tyrannous father, escapes to California and a questionable marriage. A selection of the AT&T New Plays for the Nineties Project, previously produced in regional theater at Berkeley, Calif. The play was presented in two parts.

**Manhattan Theater Club.** Schedule of four programs. **The Talented Tenth** (27). By Richard Wesley. Opened October 29, 1989. (Closed November 22, 1989) **The Art of Success** (54). By Nick Dear. Opened December 20, 1989. (Closed February 11, 1990) **Bad Habits** (40). Revival of the program of two one-act plays by Terrence McNally: *Dunelawn* and *Ravenswood*. Opened March 20, 1990. (Closed April 22, 1990) And *Prin* by Andrew Davies scheduled to open 6/6/90. Produced by Manhattan Theater Club (*The Talented Tenth* in association with AT&T: OnStage), Lynne Meadow artistic director, Barry Grove managing director, at City Center Stage I.

## THE TALENTED TENTH

Father; Sam Griggs .........................Graham Brown    Rowena................................La Tanya Richardson
Bernard.......................................Richard Lawson    Irene.................................................Elain Graham
Pam.............................................Marie Thomas    Ron..................................................Rony Clanton
Marvin..........................................Richard Gant    Tanya .....................................Lorraine Toussaint

Directed by M. Neema Barnette; scenery, Charles McClennahan; costumes, Alvin B. Perry; lighting, Anne Militello; sound, James Mtume; production stage manager, Diane Ward; stage manager, Harold Moore; press, Helene Davis, Linda Feinberg, Clay Martin.

Time: The 1980s. The play was presented in two parts.

Civil rights activist has moved upward to the middle class but is still dissatisfied with his status; winner of the 1989 AT&T New Plays for the Nineties Project.

*BESIDE HERSELF*—Calista Flockhart, Lois Smith and Susan Bruce with Melissa Joan Hart (*foreground*) in Joe Pintauro's play at Circle Rep

## THE ART OF SUCCESS

| | | | |
|---|---|---|---|
| Jane Hogarth | Mary-Louise Parker | Mrs. Needham | Patricia Kilgarriff |
| William Hogarth | Tim Curry | Louisa | Suzanne Bertish |
| Harry Fielding | Nicholas Woodeson | Sarah Sprackling | Jayne Atkinson |
| Frank | Patrick Tull | Robert Walpole | Daniel Benzali |
| Oliver | Don R. McManus | Queen Caroline | Jodie Lynne McClintock |

Others: Members of the Company.

Directed by Adrian Noble; scenery and costumes, Ultz; lighting, Beverly Emmons; original music and sound, John Gromada; production stage manager, Ed Fitzgerald; stage manager, Ara Marx.

The troubled life and times of the painter William Hogarth, set in 1730 and presented in two parts. A foreign play previously produced in England by Royal Shakespeare Company in 1986.

## BAD HABITS

| PERFORMER | "DUNELAWN" | "RAVENSWOOD" |
|---|---|---|
| Bill Buell | Francis Tear | Mr. Ponce |
| Robert Clohessy | Roy Pitt | Bruno |
| David Cromwell | Hiram Spane | Dr. Toynbee |
| Nathan Lane | Jason Pepper | Hugh Gumbs |
| Michael Mantell | Harry Scupp | Mr. Blum |
| Ralph Marrero | Otto | Mr. Yamadoro |
| Kate Nelligan | April Pitt | Ruth Benson |
| Faith Prince | Dolly Scupp | Becky Hedges |

Directed by Paul Benedict; scenery, John Lee Beatty; costumes, Jane Greenwood; lighting, Peter Kaczorowski; sound, John Gromada; production stage manager, Tom Aberger; stage manager, Melissa L. Burdick.

*Bad Habits* was first produced off Broadway 2/4/74 for 96 performances, was transferred to Broadway 5/5/74 for 126 additional performances and was named a Best Play of its season.

**\*Closer Than Ever** (252). Musical revue conceived by Steven Scott Smith; music by David Shire; lyrics by Richard Maltby Jr. Produced by Janet Brenner, Michael Gill and Daryl Roth at the Cherry Lane Theater. Opened November 6, 1989.

Brent Barrett                          Richard Muenz
Patrick Scott Brady                    Lynne Wintersteller
Sally Mayes

Understudies: Misses Mayes, Wintersteller—Claudine Cassan-Jellison; Messrs. Barrett, Muenz—Scott Hayward Eck; Mr. Brady—John Spalla.

Directed by Richard Maltby Jr.; co-directed by Steven Scott Smith; musical staging by Marcia Milgrom Dodge; musical direction and additional vocal arrangements, Patrick Scott Brady; scenery, Philipp Jung; costumes, Jess Goldstein; lighting, Natasha Katz; associate producer, Bryan Burch; production stage manager, Brian A. Kaufman; stage manager, Scott Hayward Fox; press, Shirley Herz Associates, Pete Sanders.

Compilation of Maltby-Shire songs about urban life and times written over the past ten years, some new and some cut from previous productions. Previously produced in regional theater at Williamstown, Mass.

Craig Wells replaced Richard Muenz and Jim Walton replaced Brent Barrett 5/90.

MUSICAL NUMBERS, ACT I: "Doors"—Company; "She Loves Me Not"—Brent Barrett, Lynne Wintersteller, Richard Muenz; "You Wanna Be My Friend"—Sally Mayes, Barrett; "Fandango"—Wintersteller, Muenz; "What Am I Doing?"—Barrett; "The Bear, the Tiger, the Hamster and the Mole"—Wintersteller; "If I Sing"—Muenz; "Miss Byrd"—Mayes; "The Sound of Muzak"—Company; "One of the Good Guys"—Barrett; "There's Nothing Like It"—Company; "Life Story"—Wintersteller; "Next Time"—Muenz, Company; "I Wouldn't Go Back"—Company.

ACT II: "The March of Time"—Company; "There"—Mayes, Patrick Scott Brady; "'Cause I'm Happy" (lyrics by David Shire)—Muenz; "Three Friends"—Mayes, Wintersteller, Barrett; "Back on Base" (lyrics by David Shire)—Mayes; "Patterns"—Wintersteller; "Wedding Song"—Barrett, Company; "Another Wedding Song" (lyrics by David Shire)—Muenz, Mayes; "Father of Fathers"—Barrett, Brady, Mayes; "It's Never That Easy/I've Been Here Before"—Wintersteller, Mayes; "Closer Than Ever"—Muenz, Company.

**The Widow's Blind Date** (40). By Israel Horovitz. Produced by David Bulasky, Barbara Darwall and Peter von Mayrhauser at Circle in the Square Downtown. Opened November 7, 1989. (Closed Dec. 10, 1989)

George Ferguson ............................... Tom Bloom    Margy Burke ........................... Christine Estabrook
Archie Crisp ..................................... Paul O'Brien

Directed by Israel Horovitz; scenery, Edward Gianfrancesco; costumes, Janet Irving; lighting, Craig Evans; fight sequences, B.H. Barry; production stage manager, Crystal Huntington; press, Jeffrey Richards Associates, Jillana Devine.

Time: October evening, the present. Place: Bailing-press room, waste paper company, Wakefield, Mass. The play was presented in two parts.

Widow's return visit to her home town and date with two onetime high school classmates cause an explosion of violence. Previously produced at Gloucester, Mass, other regional theaters and in Paris.

**Songs of Paradise** (32). Return engagement of the musical in the Yiddish language based on the Biblical poetry of Itsik Manger; book by Miriam Hoffman and Rena Berkowicz Borow; music by Rosalie Gerut. Produced by Ray Greenwald and Jack Levitt Productions, Inc. in association with Ben Sprecher, in the Joseph Papp Yiddish Theater production, at the Astor Place Theater. Opened November 13, 1989. (Closed December 10, 1989)

| | |
|---|---|
| Adrienne Cooper | David Kenner |
| Rosalie Gerut | Eleanor Reissa |
| Avi Hoffman | |

Understudies: Women's Roles—Betty Silberman; Men's Roles—Richard Silver.

Directed by Avi Hoffman; choreography, Eleanor Reissa; musical direction, Jonny Bowden; scenery, Steven Perry; lighting, Anne Militello; arrangements, Bevan Manson; production stage manager, Jeanne Fornadel; press, Jeffrey Richards.

This production of *Songs of Paradise* was produced by New York Shakespeare Festival 1/23/89 for 136 performances, in Yiddish with English translation and some new material in English added to this production.

The list of roles, scenes and musical numbers in *Songs of Paradise* appears on page 441 of *The Best Plays of 1988–89*.

**Roundabout Theater Company**. Schedule of four programs. **The Tempest** (40). Revival of the play by William Shakespeare. Opened November 14, 1989. (Closed December 17, 1989) **The Doctor's Dilemma** (30). Revival of the play by George Bernard Shaw. Opened January 25, 1990. (Closed February 18, 1990) **The Crucible** (53). Revival of the play by Arthur Miller. Opened March 29, 1990. (Closed May 13, 1990) And *The Price of Fame* scheduled to open 6/13/90. Produced by Roundabout Theater Company, Gene Feist artistic director, Todd Haimes producing director, at the Christian C. Yegen Theater.

### THE TEMPEST

| | | | |
|---|---|---|---|
| Boatswain | Evan O'Meara | Adrian | Erik Knutsen |
| Master of a Ship | Craig Wroe | Miranda | Angela Sherrill |
| Alonso | Jack Ryland | Prospero | Frank Langella |
| Antonio | Rocco Sisto | Ariel | B.D. Wong |
| Sebastian | Gabriel Barre | Caliban | Jay Patterson |
| Gonzalo | Robert Stattel | Trinculo | Michael Countryman |
| Ferdinand | John Wittenbauer | Stephano | Michaeljohn McGann |

Sailors, Spirits, Goddesses: Vincent Dopulos, Ed Hart, Jason MacDonald, Jack Smith, Dave Spaulding, Buddy Stoccardo.

Directed by Jude Kelly; scenery, Franco Colavecchia; costumes, Lindsay W. Davis; lighting, Dennis Parichy; music, Michael Ward; sound, Eric Santaniello; assistant director, Michael Birch; production stage manager, Roy W. Backes; press, the Joshua Ellis Office, Susanne Tighe.

The last major New York revival of *The Tempest* was by New York Shakespeare Festival in Central Park 6/26/81 for 24 performances. The present revival was presented in two parts.

### THE DOCTOR'S DILEMMA

| | | | |
|---|---|---|---|
| Redpenny; Mr. Danby | Adam Redfield | Sir Colenso Ridgeon | Charles Keating |
| Emmy | Avril Gentles | Leo Schutzmacher | Victor Raider-Wexler |

| | |
|---|---|
| Sir Patrick Cullen ...............................George Hall | Jennifer Dubedat .............................Anne Newhall |
| Cutler Walpole .....................................Ian Stuart | Louis Dubedat..............................Graham Winton |
| Sir Ralph Bloomfield Bonington..........Jerome Kilty | Minnie Tinwell ...............................Cate McNider |
| Dr. Blenkinsop .............................Gregg Almquist | Newspaper Man..............................Adam LeFevre |

Directed by Larry Carpenter; scenery, Campbell Baird; costumes, John Falabella; lighting, Jason Kantrowitz; sound, Philip Campanella; production stage manager, Kathy J. Faul.

Act I, Scene 1: The home of Sir Colenso Ridgeon, London, June 15, 1903, forenoon. Scene 2: Terrace at the Star and Garter, Richmond, a few days later. Act II, Scene 1: Dubedat's studio, the next afternoon. Scene 2: The same, some days later. Scene 3: The Bond Street art gallery, four months later.

The last major New York revival of *The Doctor's Dilemma* took place on Broadway 1/11/55 for 58 performances.

## THE CRUCIBLE

| | |
|---|---|
| Rev. Parris................................Noble Shropshire | Giles Corey ....................................Maury Cooper |
| Betty Parris....................................Julia Gibson | Rev. John Hale............................... William Leach |
| Tituba.........................................Hazel J. Medina | Elizabeth Proctor .............................Harriet Harris |
| Abigail Williams ..........................Justine Bateman | Francis Nurse.....................................George Hall |
| Susanna Walcott ...............................Maria Deasy | Ezekiel Cheever................................. Frank Muller |
| Mrs. Ann Putnam ......................Kathleen Chalfant | Marshal Herrick.................................. Scott Cohen |
| Thomas Putnam...............................Joseph Costa | Judge Hathorne ................................ Robert Donley |
| Mercy Lewis ...............................Valorie Hubbard | Deputy Gov. Danforth ........................Neil Vipond |
| Mary Warren ...................................Vicki Lewis | Sarah Good......................................Deedy Lederer |
| John Proctor.....................................Randle Mell | Hopkins...........................................Joe Ambrose |
| Rebecca Nurse ...................................Ruth Nelson | |

Directed by Gerald Freedman; scenery, Christopher H. Barreca; costumes, Jeanne Button; lighting, Mary Jo Dondlinger; sound, Philip Campanella; production stage manager, Kathy J. Faul.

Time: Early spring of the year 1692. Act I, Scene 1: A bedroom in Rev. Samuel Parris's house, Salem Village, Mass. Scene 2: The common room of Proctor's house, eight days later. Act II, Scene 1: The vestry room of the meeting house, two weeks later. Scene 2: The Salem jail, that fall.

The last major New York revival of *The Crucible* was in a Broadway production by Lincoln Center 4/27/72 for 44 performances.

**Lincoln Center Theater.** Schedule of three programs. **Oh, Hell** (32). Program of two one-act plays: *The Devil and Billy Markham* by Shel Silverstein and *Bobby Gould in Hell* by David Mamet. Opened December 3, 1989. (Closed December 31, 1989) **Some Americans Abroad** (81). By Richard Nelson; presented by arrangement with the Royal Shakespeare Theater. Opened February 11, 1990. (Closed April 22, 1990 and transferred to Lincoln Center's Vivian Beaumont Theater; see its entry in the Plays Produced on Broadway section of this volume) And *Six Degrees of Separation* scheduled to open 6/14/90. Produced by Lincoln Center Theater, Gregory Mosher director, Bernard Gersten executive producer, at the Mitzi E. Newhouse Theater.

## OH, HELL

*The Devil and Billy Markham*

   With Dennis Locorriere.

   In a monologue of rhymed jive talk, a musician tells how he lost a foolish bet with the devil.

*Bobby Gould in Hell*

Bobby Gould..................................Treat Williams

| | |
|---|---|
| Interrogator's Assistant ................. Steven Goldstein | |
| Interrogator........................................ W.H. Macy | |
| Glenna......................................Felicity Huffman | |

   The movie-producer character of Mamet's *Speed-the-Plow* pleads his cause in a rather elegant hell on his day of judgement.

BOTH PLAYS: Directed by Gregory Mosher; scenery, John Lee Beatty; costumes, Jane Greenwood; lighting, Kevin Rigdon; sound, Bill Dreisbach; illusionist consultant, George Schindler; production stage manager, Michael F. Ritchie; stage manager, Sarah Manley; press, Merle Debuskey, Bruce Campbell.

## SOME AMERICANS ABROAD

| | |
|---|---|
| Joe Taylor......................................Colin Stinton | Harriet Baldwin...............................Jane Hoffman |
| Philip Brown............................John Bedford Lloyd | Orson Baldwin........................Henderson Forsythe |
| Henry McNeil...................................Bob Balaban | Joanne Smith.................................... Ann Talman |
| Betty McNeil.....................................Kate Burton | An American.................................John Rothman |
| Frankie Lewis..............................Frances Conroy | Donna Silliman............................Elisabeth Shue |
| Katie Taylor.....................................Cara Buono | |

Musicians: Michelle Johnson singer; Joshua Rosenblum musical director, piano; Michael Goetz bass.

Understudies: Messrs. Stinton, Lloyd, Rothman—Stephen Rowe; Misses Buono, Shue, Talman—Carol Schneider; Mr. Forsythe—Robert Hock.

Directed by Roger Michell; scenery and costumes, Alexandra Byrne; lighting, Rick Fisher; original music, Jeremy Sams; poster art, Edward Sorel; production stage manager, Michael F. Ritchie; stage manager, Sarah Manley.

Time: The present. Place: Various locations in England. The play was presented in two parts.

American professors, Anglophiles, on a group theater tour of England. An American play previously produced in London.

**My Children! My Africa!** (28). By Athol Fugard. Produced off off Broadway in a limited engagement by New York Theater Workshop, James C. Nicola artistic director, Nancy Kassak Diekmann managing director, at the Perry Street Theater. Opened December 18, 1989. (Closed January 14, 1990)

| | |
|---|---|
| Mr. M...............................................John Kani | Thami Mbikwana......................Courtney B. Vance |
| Isabel Dyson .....................................Lisa Fugard | |

Directed by Athol Fugard; scenery and costumes, Susan Hilferty; lighting, Dennis Parichy; sound, Mark Bennett; associate director, Susan Hilferty; production stage manager, Mary Michele Miner; press, Gary Murphy.

Time: Autumn of 1984. Place: A small Eastern Cape Karoo town. The play was presented in two parts.

The troubled friendship of a black and a white student brought together by a devoted teacher. A foreign play previously produced by the Market Theater, Johannesburg in June 1989.

A Best Play (in our policy of citing specified special cases of OOB production); see page 193.

**Juan Darién** (80). Return engagement of the play based on the short story by Horacio Quiroga; written by Julie Taymor and Elliot Goldenthal; composed by Elliot Goldenthal. Produced by Music-Theater Group, Lyn Austin producing director, Diane Wondisford managing director, at St. Clements. Opened December 26, 1989. (Closed March 3, 1990)

CAST: Vocal soloists—Thuli Dumakude, Matthew Kimbrough, Lawrence A. Neals Jr./Jamie Blachly; Mother—Ariel Ashwell, Dumakude; Hunter—Kristofer Batho; Mr. Bones—Lenard Petit; Shadows—Stephen Kaplin, Company; Juan (puppet)—Batho, Andrea Kane, Kaplin; Juan (boy)—Neals/Blachly; Schoolteacher—Petit; Schoolchildren—Kimbrough, Nancy Mayans, Irene Wiley; Moth—Mimi Wyche; Drunken Couple—Batho, Kane; Senor Toledo—Batho; Circus Tigers—Dumakude, Mayans, Wiley; Circus Barker—Kimbrough; Old Woman—Ashwell; Green Dwarf—Kane.

Musicians: Richard Cordova conductor, keyboards; Richard Martinez keyboards; Geoffrey Gordon, Valerie Naranjo percussion; Philip Johnson violin; Susan Rawcliffe didjeridu, wind instruments; John C. Thomas trumpet; didjeridu, keyboard; Ray Stewart, tuba.

Understudy: Barbara Pollitt.

Directed by Julie Taymor; puppetry and masks, Julie Taymor; text chosen and arranged by Elliot Goldenthal; musical direction, Richard Cordova; scenery and costumes, G.W. Mercier, Julie Taymor; lighting, Debra Dumas; sound, Bob Bielecki; synthesizer sound design, Richard Martinez; Latin excerpts from the Requiem Mass: *Lullabye* by Elliot Goldenthal, *Trance* by Horacio Quiroga; production manager, Steven Ehrenberg; stage manager, Anne Marie Hobson; press, Peter Cromarty, Kevin Brockman.

*Juan Darién*, winner of the 1989 Richard Rodgers Production Award, was first produced off off Broadway by Music-Theater Group 3/4/88 for 21 performances.

*BURNER'S FROLIC*—Adam Wade and O. L. Duke (*foreground*) and (*background*) Sandra Nutt, William Jay, Graham Brown, Charles Weldon, Ed Wheeler, Cynthia Bond and Iris Little in the Negro Ensemble Company production of Charles Fuller's play, Part IV of his *We* series

**The Negro Ensemble Company.** Schedule of three programs. **We, Part III: Jonquil** (30). By Charles Fuller. Opened January 11, 1990. (Closed February 4, 1990) **We, Part IV: Burner's Frolic** (22). By Charles Fuller. Opened February 25, 1990. (Closed March 18, 1990) **Lifetimes on the Streets** (57). By Gus Edwards. Opened April 8, 1990. (Closed May 27, 1990) Produced by The Negro Ensemble Company, Douglas Turner Ward artistic director and president, Susan Watson Turner general manager, at Theater Four.

### JONQUIL

| | | | |
|---|---|---|---|
| Jonquil | Cynthia Bond | Hannah | Rebecca Nelson |
| Klux #2; Daniel | Samuel L. Jackson | Aunt Bessie | Peggy Alston |
| Klux #3; Isaiah | O.L. Duke | Silas | Graham Brown |
| Sally | Iris Little | George Turner | Ed Wheeler |
| Calvin | Charles Weldon | Bobby Williams | William Jay |
| Cable | Tracy Griswold | Woman; Hallie Bridges | Amanda Jobe |
| Judge Bridges | William Mooney | Colson | Curt Williams |

Black Farmers: Kenshaka Ali, Tiffany McClinn, Leonard Thomas.

Directed by Douglas Turner Ward; scenery, Charles McClennahan; costumes, Judy Dearing; lighting, Sylvester A. Weaver Jr.; production stage manager, Ed De Shae; press, Howard Atlee.

Time: Fall 1866. Place: Neal County, S.C. The play was presented in two parts.

Part III of Charles Fuller's *We* cycle of plays about freed slaves dramatizes a voting-rights quarrel and other conflicts in the Reconstruction era.

## BURNER'S FROLIC

| | | | |
|---|---|---|---|
| Burner | Adam Wade | Jim Paine | Samuel L. Jackson |
| Albert Tunes | Ed Wheeler | Kimble | William Mooney |
| Ralph Buford | Charles Weldon | Aunt Becky | Peggy Alston |
| Rev. Quash | Graham Brown | Reed | Wayne Elbert |
| Tiche | Sandra Nutt | Vaughn | William Jay |
| Miss Charlotte | Cynthia Bond | Tommy | Leonard Thomas |
| Mabel Buford | Iris Little | Jasper | Mitchell Marchand |
| Wade Harris | O.L. Duke | Curtis | Gregory Glenn |

Directed by Douglas Turner Ward; costumes, Judy Dearing; lighting, Sylvester A. Weaver Jr.; sound, Eric King; production stage manager, Ed De Shae.

Time: 1876. Place: Virginia. The play was presented in two parts.

Fourth play in the *We* cycle, upwardly mobile blacks are offered bribes to vote for a white man who promises them economic betterment.

## LIFETIMES ON THE STREETS

CAST, ACT I: Peggy Alston (Mavis, three scenes), Douglas Turner Ward (New Ice Age), Iris Little (Hooker, Marvin Gaye Died for Your Sins), O.L. Duke (Sorry to Disturb You), Charles Weldon (Ain't No Other City Like It), Cynthia Bond (Stop Me if You've Heard This), Graham Brown (A Garden in the City).

ACT II: Leonard Thomas (Collector), Adam Wade (Lifetimes on the Streets), Peggy Alston (Mavis, two scenes), Sandra Nutt (How I Lost Religion), Graham Brown (War Story), Charles Brown (Streetwalker), O.L. Duke (Baglady), Company (Interlude), Douglas Turner Ward (New Ice Age II).

Directed by Douglas Turner Ward; scenery, Lisa L. Watson; costumes, Judy Dearing; lighting, Sandra Ross; sound design, composer, Richard V. Turner; production stage manager, Ed De Shae.

Time: The Present. Place: Harlem.

Series of monologues dealing with various facets of life in today's Harlem, the five *Mavis* scenes combining into a tale of a visitor looking for part of her past but finding a love affair in the present.

**\*Forbidden Broadway 1990** (167). New edition of the musical revue with concept and parody lyrics by Gerard Alessandrini. Produced by Jonathan Scharer at Theater East. Opened January 23, 1990.

Suzanne Blakeslee                         Marilyn Pasekoff
Philip Fortenberry                          Bob Rogerson
Jeff Lyons

Understudies: Misses Blakeslee, Pasekoff—Denice Guanci; Messrs. Lyons, Rogerson—Phillip George.

Directed by Gerard Alessandrini; costumes, Erika Dyson; wigs, Teresa Vuoso, Bobby Pearce; production consultants, Pete Blue, Phillip George; associate producer, Chip Quigley; production stage manager, Jerry James; press, Shirley Herz Associates, Glenna Freedman.

Eighth version of the revue taking off current Broadway attractions. The show was presented in two parts. Music and lyrics for the songs "Forbidden Broadway 90," "Who Do They Know?" and "The Phantom of the Musical" by Gerard Alessandrini.

**American Place Theater.** Schedule of three programs. **Zora Neale Hurston** (32). By Laurence Holder. Opened February 4, 1990. (Closed March 4, 1990) **Neddy** (9). By Jeffrey Hatcher. Opened April 1, 1990. (Closed April 8, 1990) **Ground People** (19). By Leslie Lee. Opened May 6, 1990. (Closed May 20, 1990) Produced by American Place Theater, Wynn Handman director, at American Place Theater.

## ZORA NEALE HURSTON

Zora Neale Hurston.....................................................................................Elizabeth Van Dyke
Herbert Sheen; Langston Hughes; Alain Locke; Richard Wright...........................................Tim Johnson

Offstage flute: Tim Johnson.
Directed by Wynn Handman; scenery, Terry Chandler; lighting, Shirley Prendergast; production stage manager, Lloyd Davis Jr.; press, David Rothenberg.
Timke: Christmas Eve, 1949. Place: A bus station, New York City. The play was presented without intermission.
Theater biography of "The Queen of the Harlem Renaissance," an important literary figure of the 1920s and 1930s, offered as part of American Place's ongoing celebration of ethnic America, *Jubilee.*

## NEDDY

Elizabeth ....................................Kristine Nielsen
Fayle...........................................Colette Kilroy
Raymond...................................Kevin Chamberlin
Allan ...................................John Michael Higgins
David......................................Don R. McManus
Ned.........................................Michael Heintzman

Directed by Amy Saltz; scenery and costumes, G.W. Mercier; lighting, Frances Aronson; sound, Rob Gorton; production stage manager, Richard Hester.
Comedy, a hapless prep school teacher undergoes a sort of rehabilitation by his well-meaning friends.

## GROUND PEOPLE

Berlinda...........................................Bahni Turpin
Singin' Willie Ford .......................Ron Richardson
Holly Day.......................Denise Burse-Mickelbury
Reggie ........................Raymond Anthony Thomas
Viola ...........................................Frances Foster
Bertha ........................................Erma Campbell
Johnny Hopper .................................Kim Sullivan

Musicians: Tajj As-Swaudi guitar; Arthur Harper bass.
Directed by Walter Dallas; scenery, Charles McClennahan; costumes, Beth A. Ribblett; lighting, Shirley Prendergast; sound, David Lawson; movement consultant, Bernard J. Marsh; musical arrangements, Robert LaPierre; music coordinator, Don Meissner; "Louisiana Mama" composed and musical arrangements by Tajj As-Swaudi; production stage manager, Lloyd Davis Jr.
Time: Summer 1920. Place: The Mississippi Delta. The play was presented in two parts.
Sharecroppers trying to stay on the land are compared and contrasted with a troupe of black minstrels.

**Sex, Drugs, Rock & Roll** (103). One-man performance by Eric Bogosian; written by Eric Bogosian. Produced by Frederick Zollo and Robert Cole in association with 126 Second Ave. Corp. and Sine/D'Addario, Ltd. at the Orpheum Theater. Opened February 8, 1990. (Closed May 20, 1990)

Directed by Jo Bonney; scenery, John Arnone; lighting, Jan Kroeze; sound, Jan Nebozenko; produced in association with Ethel Bayer and William Suter; production stage manager, Pat Sosnow; press, Philip Rinaldi.
Another round of performance portraits of troubled individuals in today's troubled world, from the homeless to the rock star, in both dramatic and comic vein.
A Best Play; see page 258.

**Come as You Are** (7). By N. Richard Nash. Produced by Roger Bowen at Actors' Playhouse. Opened February 14, 1990. (Closed February 18, 1990)

Becky McAlister ..........................Susan Pellegrino
John McAlister.............................. Mark Hofmaier
Cora Briggs........................................Jane Welch
Lowell Briggs.......................... Donald Symington

Directed by N. Richard Nash; scenery, James Morgan; costumes, Steven Perry; lighting, Kenneth Posner; incidental music, Steven Aprahamian; production stage manager, Alan Fox; press, Peter Cromarty, Richard Brandt.
Family conflicts and ghostly presences around the dinner table.

**A Spinning Tale** (92). Musical with book and lyrics by C.E. Kemeny and A. Kemeny; music by C.E. Kemeny. Produced by Mariner James Pezza at Playhouse 91. Opened February 20, 1990. (Closed May 11, 1990)

| | | | |
|---|---|---|---|
| The Elf | Marianne Monroe | Henry | Sean Lawless |
| Prince Rupert | Eric Ellisen | Melinda | Karen Bianchini |
| Page; Musette | Ruth Lauricella | Queen Regina | Sherrylee Dickinson |
| Sidney | George Lombardo | Yvette | Sally O'Shea |
| Ralph | David L. Jackins | King Maximilian | Robert Puleo |

Musicians: Pat Lombardo reeds; Jim Marbury trombone; C.E. Kemeny synthesizers.

Directed by Jack Ross and C.E. Kemeny; choreography, Sally O'Shea; scenery, Mariner James Pezza; costumes, Sandora Associates; lighting, Kevin Connaughton; orchestrations, C.E. Kemeny; stage manager, Joyce Remeny; press, Robert Ganshaw.

Musical fantasy loosely based on the fairy tale *Rumpelstiltskin* previously produced on a tour of Connecticut theaters.

## ACT I

Prologue: "A Spinning Tale"/"Fall
  Under the Spell" ............................................................................................................Company
Scene 1: A forest clearing
  "The Last Elf Aria" ................................................................................................................Elf
  "Another Life".................................................................... Melinda, Prince Rupert, Page, Elf
  "Remember the Time" ........................................................Melinda, Ralph, Sidney, Henry
Scene 2: The royal court
  "Hello Stranger!" ................................................... Yvette, Musette, Sidney, Henry, Ralph
  "Straw Into Gold" ................................................................ King Maximilian, Company
Scene 3: The dungeon
Scene 4: The tower
  "Locked and Secluded"..................................................................................................Melinda
  "Spin! Spin! Spin!".................................................................................Elf, Melinda, Sprites
  "Gold! Gold!"/"I Have a Little Secret" ..............King Maximilian, Queen Regina, Melinda, Prince Rupert
  "Together as One" ..................................................................................Melinda, Prince Rupert
  "The Shadow" ..................................................................................................Melinda, Elf

## ACT II

Scene 1: Melinda's chambers
  "What's in a Name?" ............................................... Sidney, Ralph, Henry, Yvette, Musette
  "Precious to Me" ......................................................................................................Melinda
  "Never Met a Man I Didn't Like"......................................Queen Regina, Yvette, Musette
Scene 2: The Queen's boudoir
  "Ah, Sweet Youth!" .............................................................................. King Maximilian
Scene 3: Somewhere in the castle
  "Trust Me Tango" ........................................................................................ Yvette, Sidney
Scene 4: In the forest
  "Another Life" (Reprise)..................................................................................................Elf
Scene 5: The royal court
  Finale
  "You Get What You Give"/"Spin! Spin! Spin!" (Reprise)......................................Company

**Spare Parts** (32). By Elizabeth Page. Presented by Pamela Kantor in association with Douglas L. Feldman and Paul A. Kaplan at Circle in the Square Downtown. Opened March 12, 1990. (Closed April 8, 1990)

| | | | |
|---|---|---|---|
| Henry | Stephen Hamilton | Selma | Margo Skinner |
| Lois | Robin Groves | Perry | Reed Birney |
| Jax | Donna Haley | | |

Directed by Susan Einhorn; scenery, Ursula Belden; costumes, Elsa Ward; lighting, Norman Coates; sound, One Dream; production stage manager, Crystal Huntington; press, Penny M. Landau.

Lesbian couple decide they want a child and choose a man to help them have one.

**Feast of Fools** (26). One-man performance written and performed by Geoff Hoyle. Produced by Raymond L. Gaspard, Charles H. Duggan and Drew Dennett by arrangement with Randall Kline upstairs at the Westside Arts Theater. Opened March 15, 1990. (Closed April 8, 1990)

Directorial consultant, Anthony Taccone; scenery Scott Welsin; lighting, Neil Peter Jampolis; sound, Michael Holten; *Folk Fool* choreographic consultant, Kim Okada; *Folk Fool* score, Keith Terry; stage manager, Michael Sunkel; press, Robert Ganshaw.

Act I: Folk Fool, Court Jester, Feast of Fools, Commedia, Two Waiters. Act II: The Fundraiser, Mr. Sniff, Spare.

A one-man sampling of clowning styles and characterizations, previously produced on tour in the U.S. and Canada.

**St. Mark's Gospel** (23). Revival of the one-man performance by Alec McCowen of the Gospel According to St. Mark. Produced by Arthur Cantor at the Lamb's Theater. Opened March 21, 1990. (Closed April 15, 1990)

Lighting, Lloyd Sobel; press, Arthur Cantor Associates, Deborah Navins.

The complete text of the Gospel committed to memory and recited by Mr. McCowen, presented in two parts. First produced off Braodway 9/7/78 for 16 performances and moved to Broadway 10/24/78 for 18 performances.

**Making Movies** (9). By Aaron Sorkin. Produced by John A. McQuiggan in association with Lucille Lortel, Promenade Partners, Inc. and Pace Theatrical Group, Inc. at the Promenade Theater. Opened March 27, 1990. (Closed April 1, 1990)

| | | | |
|---|---|---|---|
| Jeff | David Marshall Grant | Reuben | Christopher Murney |
| Robert | Michael Countryman | Marty | Sharon Schlarth |
| Craig | Kurt Deutsch | | |

Understudies: Messrs. Murney, Deutsch—Jordan Mott; Messrs. Grant, Countryman—Alan McCullough.

Directed by Don Scardino; scenery, David Potts; costumes, Laura Crow; lighting, Dennis Parichy; sound, Aural Fixation; associate producers, Graconn Ltd., David H. Peipers; production stage manager, Fred Reinglas; press, the Joshua Ellis Office, Adrian Bryan-Brown.

Act I: A sound stage in Astoria, Queens, late June. Act II: A hill overlooking a farm in Schenectady, 15 weeks later.

Comedy, trials and tribulations of writing and filming today's motion pictures.

**King Lear** (5). Revival of the play by William Shakespeare in the Georgian (Russian) language; translated into Georgian by C. Tcharkviani, R. Sturua and L. Popkhadze. Produced by Brooklyn Academy of Music, Harvey Lichtenstein president and executive director, in the Rustaveli Theater Company production, Robert Sturua artistic director, in a limited engagement at the Majestic Theater. Opened April 2, 1990. (Closed April 8, 1990)

| | | | |
|---|---|---|---|
| King Lear | Ramaz Tchkhikvadze | Cornwall | Ivan Ghoghitidze |
| Goneril | Tatuli Dolidze | Kent | Mourman Djinoria |
| Regan | Daredjan Kharshiladze | Fool | Zhanri Lolashvili |
| Cordelia | Marina Kakhiani | Burgundy | Guram Sagharadze |
| Gloucester | Avtandil Makharadze | King of France | Soso Laghidze |
| Edmund | Akaki Khidasheli | Oswald | David Papuashvili |
| Edgar | Ghia Dzneladze | Doctor | Revaz Tchkhaidze |
| Albany | Djemal Ghaghanidze | | |

*ZORA NEALE HURSTON*—Tim Johnson and Elizabeth
Van Dyke (in the title role) of Laurence Holder's biographical
play about "The Queen of the Harlem Renaissance"

Others: Ioseb Abramishvili, Irakli Apakidze, Zaza Baratashvili, Tengiz Ghiorgadze, Kakhaber Tavartkiladze, Pridon Guledani, Tengiz Tavariani, Giorgi Turkiashvili, Mamuka Loria, Guram Mgaloblishvili, Gela
Otarashvili, Tristan Saralidze, David Tchkhikvadze, David Kvirtskhalia.

Directed by Robert Sturua; choreography, Giorgi Aleksidze; composer, Ghia Kancheli; assistant directors,
Revaz Tchkhaidze, Lily Burbutashvili; interpreter, Georgy Alexy-Meshishvili; designer, Mirian Mshvelidze;
lighting, Valeri Arutiunov, David Longurashvili; sound, Bezhan Sherazadishvili; stage manager, Georgy
Lapachi; press, Peter B. Carzasty, Steven Style, Bill Keeler.

This *King Lear* was presented in a three-hour, two-act Russian Georgian version with simultaneous
translation through headsets. The last major New York revival of this play took place off Broadway in CSC
repertory 2/28/82 for 52 performances.

**Mountain** (54). By Douglas Scott. Produced by K & D Productions, Margery Klain and
Robert G. Donnalley Jr. in association with Lucille Lortel at the Lucille Lortel Theater.
Opened April 5, 1990. (Closed May 20, 1990)

William O. Douglas ..................................................................................................Len Cariou
F.D.R.; Gordon Hirabayashi; Jasper Crisbody; Richard Nixon; Amir Ahmadi;
    Louis Brandeis; Others ..............................................................................John C. Vennema
Julia Fisk Douglas; Mildred Riddle Douglas; Mercedes Davidson Douglas;
    Catherine Heffernan Douglas; Others...............................................Heather Summerhayes
        Standby: Miss Summerhayes—Mary Dierson.
        Directed by John Henry Davis; scenery, Philipp Jung; costumes, David C. Woolard; lighting, Dennis Parichy; score and sound, John Gromada; associate producer, Susan Urban Horsey; production stage manager, James Fitzsimmons; press, David Rothenberg Associates, Meg Gordean.
        Act I, Scene 1: January 19, 1980. Scene 2: 1968–1975. Scene 3: 1949–1957. Scene 4: 1922–1945. Scene 5: 1898–1922. Act II, Scene 1: 1910–1922. Scene 2: 1940–1953. Scene 3: 1953–1954. Scene 4: 1954–1975. Scene 5: January 19, 1990.
        The life, career and marriages of Justice Douglas. Previously produced at White Barn Theater, Westport, Conn. and George Street Playhouse, New Brunswick, N.J.

**\*By and for Havel** (51). Transfer from off off Broadway of the program of two one-act revivals: *Audience* by Vaclav Havel and *Catastrophe* by Samuel Beckett. Produced by Eric Krebs in association with the Raft Theater at the John Houseman Studio Theater. Opened April 17, 1990.

| *Audience* | *Catastrophe* |
|---|---|
| Brewmaster ................................ Kevin O'Connor | Protagonist ..................................... Lou Brockway |
| Vanek .......................................... Lou Brockway | Assistant .........................................Evelyn Tuths |
| | Director...................................... Kevin O'Connor |

        Directed by Vasek C. Simek; scenery, E.F. Morrill; costumes, Iris Bazan; lighting and sound, Marc D. Malamud; associate director, Steve Brennan; production stage manager, Elizabeth Greenberg; press, David Rothenberg Associates, Meg Gordean.
        *By and for Havel* was presented as an OOB attraction 3/8/90 and moved up to full off-Broadway status 4/17/90. *Audience* was previously produced by New York Shakespeare Festival 11/20/83 for 95 performances and in Prague in January 1990. *Catastrophe* was previously produced on an off-Broadway program of Beckett one-acts 6/15/83 for 350 performances.

**\*The Rothschilds** (40). Transfer from off off Broadway of the revival of the musical based on *The Rothschilds* by Frederic Morton; book by Sherman Yellen; music by Jerry Bock; lyrics by Sheldon Harnick. Produced by Jeffrey Ash and Susan Quint Gallin in association with Tommy Valando in the American Jewish Theater production, Stanley Brechner artistic director, at Circle in the Square Downtown. Opened April 27, 1990.

| | |
|---|---|
| Prince William of Hesse; Joseph Fouche; | 2d Vendor; 2d Banker; |
|   Herries; Prince Metternich...........Allen Fitzpatrick |   Amshel Rothschild......................... David Cantor |
| Guard; 1st Vendor; Jacob Rothschild...... Nick Corley | 3d Vendor; Beggar; |
| Mayer Rothschild............................. Mike Burstyn |   Kalman Rothschild.......................... Joel Malina |
| 1st Urchin; Young Nathan Rothschild.. Evan Ferrante | Budurus........................................... David Wasson |
| 2d Urchin; Young Solomon | 1st Banker; Mr. Blum; |
|   Rothschild ..................................... Hal Goldberg |   Solomon Rothschild; Sceptic.............. Ray Wills |
| 3d Urchin; Young Jacob | Young Amshel Rothschild.............. Joshua Shanker |
|   Rothschild .................... Etan Ofrane, Josh Ofrane | Mrs. Kaufman; Hannah Cohen ...............Leslie Ellis |
| Gutele Rothschild................. Sue Anne Gershenson | Mrs. Segal................................. Judith Thiergaard |
| | Nathan Rothschild............................ Bob Cuccioli |

        Understudies: Mr. Fitzpatrick—David Wasson; Messrs. Shanker, Ferrante, Goldberg—Josh Ofrane; Misses Gershenson, Ellis, Thiergaard—Lynne Halliday.
        Directed by Lonny Price; choreography, Michael Arnold; musical direction, Grant Sturiale; scenery, Russell Metheny; costumes, Gail Brassard; lighting, Betsy Adams; associate producers, Dana Sherman, Phil Witt; stage manager, Rachel Levin; press, Shirley Herz Associates, Sam Rudy.
        Place: The Frankfort Ghetto, the Hessian and Austrian courts, London and Aix-la-Chapelle.

*The Rothschilds* was originally produced on Broadway 10/19/70 for 507 performances. This is its first major New York revival.

The list of musical numbers in *The Rothschilds* appears on page 291 of *The Best Plays of 1970–71*.

## *Talking Things Over With Chekhov (25). By John Ford Noonan. Produced by Bill Repicci at Actors' Playhouse. Opened May 10, 1990.

Jeremy M. ................................................................................................................John Ford Noonan
Marlene D. ....................................................................................................................Diane Salinger

Directed by Marjorie Mahle; scenery, Ron Kron; costumes, Gene Lauze; lighting, Tracy Dedrickson; associate producers, M.D. Minichiello, Albert Repicci; production stage manager, Joe McGuire; press, Robert Ganshaw.

Time: The present. Place: A park bench in Riverside Park in the West 80s. Act I, Scene 1: Autumn— early October, just after 1 in the afternoon. Scene 2: The following day, just after 1 in the afternoon. Scene 3: The following day, just after 1 in the afternoon. Act II, Scene 1: The following day, 1 in the afternoon. Scene 2: Two weeks and two days later, 20 minutes after 1. Scene 3: A month later, morning, just after dawn.

Comedy-drama, a playwright and actress discuss their emotional and professional relationships and, over time, the reception of his new play in which she has appeared.

## *Further Mo' (18). Musical conceived and written by Vernel Bagneris. Produced by Norzar Productions, Inc. and Michael Frazier at The Village Gate Downstairs. Opened May 17, 1990.

Theater Owner .........................James "Red" Wilcher    Ma Reed........................................Frozine Thomas
Thelma........................................Topsy Chapman    Big Bertha............................Sandra Reaves-Phillips
Papa Du ........................................Vernel Bagneris

New Orleans Blue Serenaders: Joseph Daley, Bill Dillard, Orange Kellin, Emme Kemp, Kenneth Sara.

Understudies: Mr. Bagneris—Ronald Wyche; Mr. Wilcher—Ron Woodall; Miss Reaves-Phillips— Barbara Shorts; Miss Chapman—Wanda Rouzan.

Directed by Vernel Bagneris; choreography, Pepsi Bethel; musical direction, Orange Kellin; scenery, Charles McClennahan; costumes, Joan Clevenger; lighting, John McKernon; sound, Peter Fitzgerald; musical arrangements, Lars Edegran, Orange Kellin; vocal arrangements, Topsy Chapman, Lars Edegran; production stage manager, K.R. Williams; press, the Jacksina Company, Mary Lugo.

Time: 1927. Place: Lyric Theater, New Orleans.

Backstage doings are a small story base for a large collection of New Orleans blues and jazz numbers in a sequel to the author's *One Mo' Time* which was produced off Broadway 10/22/79 for 1,372 performances.

### ACT I

"Shake It and Break It" .......................................................................................................Serenaders
"Messing Around".............................................................................Thelma, Papa Du, Ma Reed
"Sweetie Dear"........................................................................................... Thelma, Papa Du
"Salty Dog" ........................................................................................................................Ma Reed
"One Hour Mama"..........................................................................................................Big Bertha
"Mississippi Mud" ..........................................................................Papa Du, Thelma, Ma Reed
"Wild Women" ..................................................................................................................Ma Reed
"Sweet Man".........................................................................................................................Thelma
"Positively No (Construction Gang)" ................................................. Big Bertha, Papa Du
"Had to Give Up Gym" ................................................................................Ma Reed, Thelma
"Pretty Doll"........................................................................................................................Serenaders
"Trouble in Mind"..............................................................................................................Big Bertha
"Here Comes the Hot Tamale Man"........................................................................Company

## ACT II

"Boogie Woogie" ............................................................................................................Serenaders
"Come On In" ...............................................................................................................Company
"My Man" ........................................................................................................................Thelma
"Don't Advertise Your Man" .....................................................................................Big Bertha
"Baby, Won't You Please Come Home" .........................................Big Bertha, Ma Reed, Thelma
"Funny Feathers" ...........................................................................................................Papa Du
"Clarinet Marmalade" ................................................................................................Serenaders
"West Indies Blues" ........................................................Ma Reed, Big Bertha, Thelma
"Boot-It Boy" ..................................................................................................................Papa Du
"Alabamy Bound"........................................................................Thelma, Ma Reed, Papa Du
"Home Sweet Home"..................................................................Thelma, Big Bertha
"Hot Times in the Old Town Tonight" .........................................................................Company

**\*Forever Plaid** (12). Musical by Stuart Ross. Produced by Gene Wolsk in association with Steven Suskin at Steve McGraw's. Opened May 20, 1990.

Jinx................................................Stan Chandler  Sparky ..............................................Jason Graae
Smudge........................................... David Engel  Francis............................................Guy Stroman

Directed and staged by Stuart Ross; musical continuity, arrangements and direction by James Raitt; scenery, Neil Peter Jampolis; costumes, Debra Stein; lighting, Jane Reisman; assistant director, Larry Raben; production stage manager, John Rainwater; stage manager, Steven Loehle; press, Shirley Herz Associates, Miller Wright.

Quartet of reincarnated singers brings the songs and styles of the 1950s forward with them to celebrate—and lampoon—the entertainment of the decade. An expanded version of the show previously produced last season in Teaneck, N.J. and off off Broadway.

**\*The Grand Guignol** (9). Program of three one-act plays: *Experiment at the Asylum* by Annie G. Hogue and Mitch Hogue, *The Treatment of Dr. Love* by William Squier and *Orgy in the Air-Traffic Control Tower* by Sean Burke and Steve Nelson. Produced by Aboutface and Sean Burke at Playhouse 91. Opened May 24, 1990.

ALL PLAYS: Scenery, Vicki R. Davis; lighting, Ken Davis; costume consultant, Mary Myers; original music, Robert Montgomery; press, Arthur Cantor Associates, Deb Navins. With the Aboutface Theater Company: Robert Alexander, Dina Corsetti, Gary Evans, Leslie R. Hollander, Kelleigh McKenzie, Ellen McQueeney, Gina Menza, Chuck Pooler, J.J. Reap, J. Kelly Salvadore, Nomi Tichman, David D. Yezzi. Three new horror shows in the style of the famous Grand Guignol in Paris, previously produced off off Broadway at the Nat Horne Theater.

EXPERIMENT AT THE ASYLUM: Directed by Richard Galgano. 19th century psychiatrists allow an unstable patient a disastrous interlude of freedom.

THE TREATMENT OF DR. LOVE: Directed by Linda Feinberg and Martin Fluger. A gynecologist is publicly confronted by a patient he harmed.

ORGY IN THE AIR-TRAFFIC CONTROL TOWER: Directed by Michael Hillyer. Three scabs divert themselves with booze, drugs and women while on duty.

# CAST REPLACEMENTS AND TOURING COMPANIES

## *Compiled by Stanley Green*

The following is a list of the more important cast replacements in productions which opened in previous years, but were still playing in New York during a substantial part of the 1989–90 season; or were still on a first-class tour in 1989–90 (casts of first-class touring companies of previous seasons which were no longer playing in 1989–90 appear in previous *Best Plays* volumes of appropriate years).

The name of each major role is listed in *italics* beneath the title of the play in the first column. In the second column directly opposite appears the name of the actor who created the role in the original New York production (whose opening date appears in *italics* at the top of the column). Indented immediately beneath the original actor's name are the names of subsequent New York replacements, together with the date of replacement when available.

The third column gives information about first-class touring companies, including London companies (produced under the auspices of their original New York managements). When there is more than one roadshow company, #1, #2, etc., appear before the name of the performer who created the role in each company (and the city and date of each company's first performance appears in *italics* at the top of the column). Their subsequent replacements are also listed beneath their names, with dates when available. A very long-run entry is sometimes abbreviated in this annual listing, but in recognition of the closing this season of *A Chorus Line*, we have listed all the New York cast changes of record from April 15, 1975 to April 28, 1990.

ANYTHING GOES

|  |  | *#1 London 7/4/89* |
|  | *New York 10/13/87* | *#2 Costa Mesa 9/12/89* |
| *Reno Sweeney* | Patti LuPone | #1 Elaine Paige |
|  | Leslie Uggams 3/21/89 | #2 Mitzi Gaynor |
| *Billy Crocker* | Howard McGillin | #1 Howard McGillin |
|  | Gregg Edelman 5/25/89 |     John Barrowman 10/89 |
|  |  | #2 Scott Stevenson |
| *Moonface Martin* | Bill McCutcheon | #1 Bernard Cribbins |
|  | Gerry Vichi 8/8/89 | #2 Robert Nichols |

432

| | | |
|---|---|---|
| *Elisha Whitney* | Rex Everhart | #1 Harry Towb |
| | | #2 Gordon Connell |
| *Evangeline Harcourt* | Anne Francine | #1 Ursula Smith |
| | | #2 Evelyn Page |
| *Erma* | Linda Hart | #1 Kathryn Evans |
| | Maryellen Scilla 4/89 | #2 Dorothy Kiara |
| | Linda Hart 7/89 | |
| *Lord Evelyn Oakleigh* | Anthony Heald | #1 Martin Turner |
| | Walter Bobbie 4/14/89 | #2 Richard Sabellico |
| *Hope Harcourt* | Kathleen Mahoney-Bennett | #1 Ashleigh Sendin |
| | Nancy Opel 10/4/88 | #2 Donna English |

## CATS

*New York 10/7/82*

| | |
|---|---|
| *Bustapher Jones; Asparagus;*<br>    *Growltiger* | Stephen Hanan |
| | Timothy Jerome |
| | Gregg Edelman |
| | Bill Carmichael |
| | Stephen Hanan |
| | Paul Harman |
| | Dale Hensley |
| *Cassandra* | Rene Ceballos |
| | Christina Kumi Kimball |
| | Nora Brennan |
| | Charlotte d'Amboise |
| | Jessica Northrup |
| | Roberta Stiehm |
| | Julietta Marcelli |
| | Leigh Webster |
| *Coricopat; Mungojerrie* | Rene Clemente |
| | Guillermo Gonzalez |
| | Joe Antony Cavise |
| | Johnny Anzalone |
| | Ray Roderick |
| | Johnny Anzalone |
| *Demeter* | Wendy Edmead |
| | Marlene Danielle |
| | Jane Bodle |
| | Patricia Ruck |
| | Beth Swearingen |
| *Grizabella* | Betty Buckley |
| | Laurie Beechman |
| | Loni Ackerman |
| *Jennyanydots* | Anna McNeely |
| | Marcy DeGonge |
| | Cindy Benson |
| *Mistoffelees* | Timothy Scott |
| | Herman W. Sebek |
| | Jamie Torcellini |
| | Michael Scott Gregory |

Barry K. Bernal
Don Johanson
Kevin Poe
Michael Barriskill
Michael Arnold

*Munkustrap*                    Harry Groener
Claude R. Tessier
Mark Fotopoulos
Rob Marshall
Robert Amirante
Greg Minahan

*Old Deuteronomy*              Ken Page
Kevin Marcum
Clent Bowers
Larry Small

*Plato; Macavity; Rumpus Cat*  Kenneth Ard
Scott Wise
Brian Andrews
Jamie Patterson
Randy Wojcik

*Rum Tum Tugger*               Terrence Mann
Jamie Rocco
Rick Sparks
Steve Yudson
Frank Mastrocola

*Rumpleteazer*                 Christine Langner
Paige Dana
Kristi Lynes

*Skimbleshanks*                Reed Jones
Michael Scott Gregory
Robert Burnett
Reed Jones
Richard Stafford
Eric Scott Kincaid

## A CHORUS LINE

*N.Y. Off Broadway 4/15/75*
*N.Y. Bway 7/25/75*

*Kristine*                     Renee Baughman
Cookie Vazquez 4/26/76
Deborah Geffner 10/76
P.J. Mann 9/78
Deborah Geffner 1/79
Christine Barker 3/79
Kerry Casserly 8/81
Christine Barker 10/81
Kerry Casserly
Flynn McMichaels 6/29/87
Cynthia Fleming

*Sheila*                       Carol Bishop (name changed to Kelly Bishop 3/76)
Kathryn Ann Wright 8/76
Bebe Neuwirth 6/80

Susan Danielle 3/81
Jane Summerhays 9/82
Kelly Bishop
Kathryn Ann Wright 4/84
Susan Danielle 9/84
Cynthia Fleming 11/86
Dana Moore 11/16/87
Susan Danielle 3/27/89

*Val*        Pamela Blair
Barbara Monte-Britton 4/26/76
Karen Jablons 10/76
Mitzi Hamilton 3/1/77
Karen Jablons 12/77
Mitzi Hamilton 3/78
Lois Englund 7/78
Deborah Henry 10/79
Mitzi Hamilton 10/80
Wanda Richert
Delyse Lively-Mekka
Wanda Richert 11/88
Diana Kavilis 2/20/89

*Mike*        Wayne Cilento
Jim Litten 6/77
Jeff Hyslop 1/79
Don Correia 6/79
Buddy Balou' 6/80
Cary Scott Lowenstein 7/81
Scott Wise 7/82
Danny Herman 4/83
Don Correia 7/84
J. Richard Hart 8/84
Danny Herman
Charles McGowan
Mark Bove
Tommy Re 7/30/87
Kelly Patterson 9/14/87
Danny Herman
Michael Gruber 1/16/89

*Larry*        Clive Clerk
Jeff Weinberg 10/76
Adam Grammis 2/77
Paul Charles 12/77
R.J. Peters 3/79
T. Michael Reed 11/79
Michael Day Pitts 3/80
Donn Simione 4/81
J. Richard Hart 7/81
Scott Plank 9/82
Brad Jeffries 11/82
J. Richard Hart 8/83
Jim Litten 7/84
J. Richard Hart
Kevin Neil McCready

*Maggie*        Kay Cole
Lauree Berger 4/26/76

Donna Drake 2/77
Christina Saffran 7/78
Betty Lynd 6/5/79
Marcia Lynn Watkins 8/79
Pam Klinger 9/81
Ann Heinricher 9/84
Pam Klinger
Dorothy Tancredi 12/23/87
Michele Pigliavento 1/16/89
Susan Santoro 4/21/89

*Richie*                    Ronald Dennis
Winston DeWitt Hemsley 4/26/76
Edward Love 6/77
A. William Perkins 12/77
   (name changed to Wellington Perkins 6/78)
Larry G. Bailey 1/79
Carleton T. Jones 3/80
Ralph Glenmore 6/80
Kevin Chinn 1/81
Reggie Phoenix 10/83
Eugene Fleming 9/84
Gordon Owens 3/85
Bruce Anthony Davis 12/86
Gordon Owens 2/20/89

*Judy*                     Patricia Garland
Sandahl Bergman 4/26/76
Murphy Cross 12/77
Victoria Tabaka 11/78
Joanna Zercher 7/79
Angelique Ilo 8/79
Jannet Horsley 9/80
   (name changed to Jannet Moranz 2/81)
Melissa Randel 12/81
Angelique Ilo
Trish Ramish 2/87
Cindi Klinger 11/23/87
Angelique Ilo 4/24/89

*Don*                      Ron Kuhlman
David Thome 4/26/76
Dennis Edenfield 3/80
Michael Weir 8/81
Michael Danek 10/81
Keith Bernardo

*Bebe*                     Nancy Lane
Gillian Scalaci 4/26/76
Rene Ceballos 9/77
Karen Meister 1/78
Rene Ceballos 3/81
Pamela Ann Wilson 1/82
Tracy Shayne
Karen Ziemba 2/29/88
Christine Maglione

*Connie*                   Baayork Lee
Lauren Kayahara 4/26/76

Janet Wong 2/77
Cynthia Carrillo Onrubia 11/79
Lauren Tom 10/80
Lily-Lee Wong 10/81
Sachi Shimizu 11/83
Lauren Tom 4/84
Sachi Shimizu

*Diana*          Priscilla Lopez
Carole Schweid 5/7/76
Rebecca York 8/76
Loida Iglesias 12/76
Chris Bocchino 10/78
Diane Fratantoni 9/79
Chris Bocchino 12/79
Dorothy Tancredi 3/82
Diane Fratantoni 6/82
Kay Cole 8/82
Gay Marshall 11/82
Roxann Caballero 1/83
Loida Santos 3/83
     (previously known as Loida Iglesias)
Gay Marshall
Roxann Caballero
Mercedes Perez 10/86
Denise DiRenzo 2/25/88
Arminae Azarian 2/13/89
Roxann Biggs
     (previously known as Roxann Caballero)

*Zach*          Robert LuPone
Joe Bennett 4/26/76
Eivind Harum 10/76
Robert LuPone 1/31/77
Kurt Johnson 5/77
Anthony Inneo 8/78
Eivind Harum 10/78
Scott Pearson 8/79
Tim Millett 3/81
Steven Boockvor 8/23/82
Eivind Harum 7/83
Robert LuPone 3/19/86
Eivind Harum
Scott Pearson 2/29/88
Randy Clements 9/9/88
Robert LuPone 11/21/88
Eivind Harum

*Mark*          Cameron Mason
Paul Charles 10/76
Timothy Scott 12/77
R.J. Peters 4/78
Timothy Wahrer 3/79
Dennis Daniels 5/80
Gregory Brock 8/80
Danny Herman 5/81
Chris Marshall 4/83
Gib Jones
Andrew Grose 11/86

|              | Matt Zarley 8/8/88 |
|              | Jack Noseworthy 2/21/90 |

*Cassie*        Donna McKechnie
                Ann Reinking 4/26/76
                Donna McKechnie 9/27/76
                Ann Reinking 11/29/76
                Vicki Fredericks 2/9/77
                Pamela Sousa 11/14/77
                Candace Tovar 1/78
                Pamela Sousa 3/78
                Cheryl Clark 12/78
                Deborah Henry 10/80
                Pamela Sousa 11/81
                Cheryl Clark 10/83
                Wanda Richert 6/84
                Angelique Ilo 7/86
                Donna McKechnie 9/1/86
                Laurie Gamache 5/18/87

*Al*            Don Percassi
                Bill Nabel 4/26/76
                John Mineo 2/77
                Ben Lokey 4/77
                Don Percassi 7/77
                Jim Corti 1/79
                Donn Simione 9/79
                James Warren 5/80
                   (name changed to James Young 9/80)
                Jerry Colker 5/81
                Scott Plank 11/82
                Buddy Balou' 3/83
                Mark Bove
                Kevin Neil McCready
                Tommy Re 9/17/87
                Stephen Bourneuf 3/27/89
                Tommy Re

*Greg*          Michael Stuart
                Justin Ross 4/26/76
                Danny Weathers 6/78
                Ron Navarre 9/82
                Michael Day Pitts
                Justin Ross 10/83
                Danny Weathers 8/84
                Bradley Jones
                Ron Navarre 3/23/89
                Doug Friedman

*Bobby*         Thomas J. Walsh
                Christopher Chadman 6/77
                Ron Kurowski 1/78
                Tim Cassidy 11/78
                Ronald Stafford 3/79
                Matt West 9/80
                Ron Kurowski 8/84

*Paul*          Sammy Williams
                George Pesaturo 4/26/76

Rene Clemente 2/78
Tommy Aguilar 5/82
Sammy Williams 10/19/83
Wayne Meledandri 1/85
Drew Geraci 6/10/88

## THE COCKTAIL HOUR

|  | *New York 10/20/88* | *Chicago 11/20/89* |
|---|---|---|
| *Bradley* | Keene Curtis<br>Burt Edwards 7/11/89 | Barry Nelson |
| *Ann* | Nancy Marchand | Elizabeth Wilson |
| *John* | Bruce Davison<br>Richard Backus 4/11/89 | Mark Metcalf |
| *Nina* | Holland Taylor | Jean DeBaer |

## DRIVING MISS DAISY

|  |  | *#1 Chicago 4/23/88*<br>*#2 Birmingham 9/19/89* |
|---|---|---|
|  | *New York 4/15/87* | *#3 Philadelphia 9/21/88* |
| *Daisy Werthan* | Dana Ivey<br>Frances Sternhagen 1/19/88 | #1 Sada Thompson<br>  Ellen Burstyn 8/9/88<br>  Dorothy Loudon 10/26/88<br>  Charlotte Rae 8/8/89<br>#2 Rosemary Prinz<br>#3 Julie Harris |
| *Hoke Coleburn* | Morgan Freeman<br>Earle Hyman 2/23/88<br>Arthur French 11/7/89 | #1 Bill Cobbs<br>  Bruce Young<br>#2 Ted Lange<br>#3 Brock Peters |
| *Boolie Werthan* | Ray Gill<br>Anderson Matthews | #1 Matt DeCaro<br>#2 Fred Sanders<br>#3 Stephen Root |

## THE FANTASTICKS

|  | *New York 5/3/60* |
|---|---|
| *El Gallo* | Jerry Orbach<br>Robert Vincent Smith 8/18/87 |
| *Luisa* | Rita Gardner<br>Sharon Camille 11/7/89<br>Marilyn Whitehead 1/23/90 |
| *Matt* | Kenneth Nelson<br>Matthew Eaton Bennett 4/89<br>Neil Nash 1/23/90 |

Note: As of May 31, 1990, 33 actors had played the role of El Gallo, 28 had played Matt and 33 had played Luisa. Only the most recent cast replacements are listed above under the names of the original cast members. For previous replacements, see previous editions of *The Best Plays*.

## THE HEIDI CHRONICLES

|  | *N.Y. Off-Bway 12/11/88*<br>*N.Y. Bway 3/9/89* |
|---|---|
| *Heidi Holland* | Joan Allen<br>    Christine Lahti 9/5/89<br>    Brooke Adams 1/2/90 |
| *Peter Patrone* | Boyd Gaines<br>    David Pierce 9/5/89<br>    David Lansbury 3/6/90 |
| *Scoop Rosenbaum* | Peter Friedman<br>    Tony Salhoud 9/5/89 |

## INTO THE WOODS

|  | *New York 11/5/87* | *Ft. Lauderdale 11/22/88* |
|---|---|---|
| *Witch* | Bernadette Peters<br>    Phylicia Rashad 4/14/88<br>    Betsy Joslyn 7/5/88<br>    Nancy Dussault 12/13/88<br>    Bernadette Peters 5/23/89<br>    Nancy Dussault 5/27/89<br>    Ellen Foley 8/1/89 | Cleo Laine<br>    Betsy Joslyn 5/89 |
| *Baker's Wife* | Joanna Gleason<br>    Lauren Mitchell 6/28/88<br>    Kay McClelland (alt.) 6/28/88<br>    Mary Gordon Murray 7/19/88<br>    Cynthia Sikes 11/15/88<br>    Joanna Gleason 5/23/89<br>    Kay McClelland 5/27/89 | Mary Gordon Murray<br>    Judy McLane |
| *Baker* | Chip Zien | Ray Gill<br>    Adam Grupper |
| *Narrator* | Tom Aldredge<br>    Dick Cavett 7/19/88<br>    Tom Aldredge 9/13/88 | Rex Robbins<br>    Peter Walker |
| *Mysterious Man* | Tom Aldredge<br>    Edmund Lyndeck 7/19/88<br>    Tom Aldredge 9/13/88 | Rex Robbins<br>    Peter Walker |
| *Wolf; Cinderella's Prince* | Robert Westenberg | Chuck Wagner<br>    James Weatherstone |
| *Jack's Mother* | Barbara Bryne | Charlotte Rae<br>    Nora Mae Lyng 5/89<br>    Frances Ford |
| *Little Red Riding Hood* | Danielle Ferland<br>    LuAnne Ponce 9/20/88 | Tracy Katz |
| *Cinderella* | Kim Crosby | Kathleen Rowe McAllen<br>    Jill Geddes 3/89<br>    Patricia Ben Peterson |
| *Rapunzel* | Pamela Winslow<br>    Marin Mazzie 3/7/89 | Marguerite Lowell<br>    Gay Willis |

| | | |
|---|---|---|
| *Rapunzel's Prince* | Chuck Wagner | Douglas Sills |
| | Dean Butler 3/7/89 | Jonathan Hadley |

## JEROME ROBBINS' BROADWAY

*New York 2/26/89*

*The Setter, etc.*

Jason Alexander
  Terrence Mann 7/25/89
  Tony Roberts 1/15/90

Susann Fletcher
Angelo H. Fraboni
Nancy Hess
Susan Kikuchi
Michael Kubala
Karen Mason
Steve Ochoa
Dorothy Stanley
Nancy Ticotin
Lori Werner
Scott Wise

Note: Apart from the actors who have played The Setter, the above is an alphabetical list of the major performers in *Jerome Robbins' Broadway* as of May 31, 1990. Replacements do not generally succeed specific performers in this production.

## LEND ME A TENOR

*New York 3/2/89*

| | |
|---|---|
| *Max* | Victor Garber |
| | Patrick Quinn 1/16/90 |
| *Tito Merelli* | Ron Holgate |
| *Saunders* | Philip Bosco |
| *Maria Merelli* | Tovah Feldshuh |
| | Chris Callen 1/16/90 |
| *Julia* | Jane Connell |
| *Diana* | Caroline Lagerfelt |
| | Jane Summerhays 8/22/89 |
| *Maggie* | J. Smith-Cameron |
| | Wendy Makkena 1/16/90 |

## LES MISERABLES

| | | |
|---|---|---|
| | | *#1 Boston 12/5/87* |
| | | *#2 Los Angeles 5/21/88* |
| | *New York 3/12/87* | *#3 Tampa 11/28/88* |
| *Jean Valjean* | Colm Wilkinson | #1 Wiliam Solo |
| | Gary Morris 11/30/87 | Craig Schulman 4/88 |
| | Timothy Shew 5/30/88 | #2 William Solo |
| | William Solo 7/3/89 | Jean Bennett |
| | Craig Schulman 1/13/90 | #3 Gary Barker |

| Javert | Terrence Mann | #1 Herndon Lackey |
| | Anthony Crivello 11/30/87 | #2 Jeff McCarthy |
| | Norman Large 1/18/88 | #3 Peter Samuel |
| | Anthony Crivello 3/14/88 | |
| | Norman Large 7/19/88 | |
| | Herndon Lackey 1/17/89 | |
| | Peter Samuel 1/15/90 | |
| Fantine | Randy Graff | #1 Diane Fratantoni |
| | Maureen Moore 7/19/88 | Ann Crumb |
| | Susan Dawn Carson 1/17/89 | Laurie Beechman 1/89 |
| | Laurie Beechman 1/15/90 | #2 Elinore O'Connell |
| | | #3 Hollis Resnik |
| Enjolras | Michael Maguire | #1 John Herrera |
| | Joseph Kolinski | #2 Greg Blanchard |
| | Joe Locarro 1/15/90 | #3 Greg Zerkle |
| | Joseph Kolinsky | |

Craig Schulman as Jean Valjean in *Les Misérables*

| | | |
|---|---|---|
| *Marius* | David Bryant<br>Ray Walker<br>Hugh Panaro | #1 Hugh Panaro<br>#2 Reece Holland<br>#3 Matthew Porretta |
| *Cosette* | Judy Kuhn<br>Tracy Shayne | #1 Tamara Jenkins<br>#2 Karen Fineman<br>#3 Jacqueline Piro |
| *Eponine* | Frances Ruffelle<br>Kelli James 9/15/87<br>Natalie Toro 7/88 | #1 Renee Veneziale<br>#2 Michelle Nicastro<br>#3 Michele Maika |
| *Thenardier* | Leo Burmester<br>Ed Dixon | #1 Tom Robbins<br>Neal Ben Ari 12/5/88<br>#2 Gary Beach<br>#3 Paul Ainsley |
| *Mme. Thenardier* | Jennifer Butt<br>Evalyn Baron 1/15/90 | #1 Victoria Clark<br>#2 Kay Cole<br>#3 Linda Kerns |
| *Gavroche* | Braden Danner<br>Danny Gerard<br>Joey Rigol<br>Alex Dizen | #1 Lantz Landry or<br>Andrew Renshaw<br>#2 Phillip Glasser or<br>Josh C. Williams<br>#3 Andrew Harrison Leeds<br>or Sam Brent Riegel |

## M. BUTTERFLY

| | *New York 3/20/88* | *London 4/20/89* |
|---|---|---|
| *Rene Gallimard* | John Lithgow<br>David Dukes 8/22/88<br>John Rubinstein 2/20/89<br>Tony Randall 8/21/89 | Anthony Hopkins<br>Peter Egan 11/89 |
| *Song Liling* | B.D. Wong<br>A. Mapa 9/25/89 | G.G. Goei<br>R.M. Rees |

## ME AND MY GIRL

| | *New York 8/10/86* |
|---|---|
| *Bill Snibson* | Robert Lindsay<br>Jim Dale 6/16/87<br>James Brennan 1/31/89 |
| *Sally Smith* | Maryann Plunkett<br>Ellen Foley 2/23/88<br>Judy Blazer 7/4/89 |
| *Lady Jacqueline* | Jane Summerhays<br>Dee Hoty 2/23/88<br>Lauren Mitchell 9/26/89 |

## ONLY KIDDING!

| | *New York 4/18/89* |
|---|---|
| *Jackie Dwayne* | Larry Keith |

| *Sheldon Kelinsky* | Howard Spiegel |
| *Tom Kelly* | Andrew Hill Newman |
| *Jerry Goldstein* | Paul Provenza<br>Ralph Macchio 11/24/89 |
| *Sal D'Angelo* | Sam Zap |

## OTHER PEOPLE'S MONEY

| | *New York 2/26/89* | *Baltimore 3/20/90* |
|---|---|---|
| *Lawrence Garfinkel* | Kevin Conway<br>Jon Polito 1/21/90<br>Kevin Conway 4/24/90 | Tony Lo Bianco |
| *Kate Sullivan* | Mercedes Ruehl<br>Janet Zarich 4/18/89<br>Mercedes Ruehl 10/24/89<br>Priscilla Lopez 1/21/90 | Julie Boyd |

## THE PHANTOM OF THE OPERA

| | *New York 1/26/88* | *#1 Los Angeles 5/31/89*<br>*#2 Toronto 9/20/89*<br>*#3 Chicago 5/24/90* |
|---|---|---|
| *The Phantom* | Michael Crawford<br>Timothy Nolen 10/10/88<br>Cris Groenendaal 3/20/89<br>Steve Barton 3/19/90 | #1 Michael Crawford<br>Robert Guillaume 5/1/90<br>#2 Colm Wilkinson<br>#3 Mark Jacoby |
| *Christine Daaé* | Sarah Brightman<br>Patti Cohenour 6/7/88<br>Dale Kristien (alt.) 7/88*<br>Rebecca Luker (alt.) 3/89*<br>Rebecca Luker 6/5/89<br>Katherine Buffaloe (alt.) (6/5/89)* | #1 Dale Kristien<br>Mary D'Arcy (alt.)*<br>#2 Rebecca Caine<br>#3 Karen Culliver<br>Teri Bibb (alt.)* |
| *Carlotta Giudicelli* | Judy Kaye<br>Marilyn Caskey 1/2/89 | #1 Leigh Munro<br>#2 Lyse Guerin<br>#3 Patricia Hurd |
| *Raoul* | Steve Barton<br>Kevin Gray 9/18/90<br>Davis Gaines 3/12/90 | #1 Reece Holland<br>#2 Byron Nease<br>#3 Keith Buterbaugh |

Alternates play the role of Christine Monday and Wednesday evenings.

## RUMORS

| | *New York 11/17/88* | *Washington 10/31/89* |
|---|---|---|
| *Lenny* | Ron Leibman<br>Greg Mulvaney 11/6/89 | Peter Marshall<br>Ron Liebman |
| *Chris* | Christine Baranski<br>Kendis Chappell 7/4/89<br>Catherine Cox 10/9/89 | Kendis Chappell |

| | | |
|---|---|---|
| *Cookie* | Joyce Van Patten<br>Alice Playten 10/9/89 | Heather MacRae<br>Peggy Pope |
| *Claire* | Jessica Walter<br>Veronica Hamel 11/6/89 | Patty McCormick<br>Jessica Walter |
| *Welch* | Charles Brown | L. Kenneth Richardson<br>Charles Brown |
| *Ken* | Mark Nelson<br>Richard Levine | Gibby Brand |
| *Pudney* | Cynthia Darlow<br>Kathleen Marsh 11/7/89 | Nancy Hillner<br>Mary O'Brady |
| *Ernie* | Andre Gregory<br>Dick Latessa 6/5/89<br>Dan Desmond 9/26/89 | Reno Roop<br>Dan Desmond |
| *Cassie* | Lisa Banes<br>Lisa Emery 6/11/89 | Lynnda Ferguson<br>Lisa Emery |
| *Glenn* | Ken Howard<br>Larry Linville 12/26/88<br>Timothy Landfield 8/29/89 | Michael Minor<br>Timothy Landfield |

## SHIRLEY VALENTINE

*New York 2/16/89*

| | |
|---|---|
| *Shirley* | Pauline Collins<br>Patricia Kilgarriff 7/3/89<br>Ellen Burstyn 7/17/89 |

## TAMARA

*New York 12/2/87*

| | |
|---|---|
| *Tamara de Lempicka* | Sara Botsford<br>Christine Dunford 7/88<br>Elke Sommer 11/19/89<br>Anne Swift |

THE SEASON
OFF OFF BROADWAY

# OFF OFF BROADWAY

### By Mel Gussow

There was a sense of renewal as well as innovation off off Broadway this season. Everett Quinton revitalized the Ridiculous Theatrical Company with his revival of Charles Ludlam's *Der Ring Gott Farblonjet* and proved with this Wagnerian spoof that he is a worthy successor to his late mentor. The Mabou Mines celebrated its 20th anniversary with a revival of Lee Breuer's *The B. Beaver Animation*, and other theaters like Pan Asian Repertory and La Mama demonstrated their continuing vitality. At the same time, such newer companies as Naked Angels and Cucaracha were springing up and making an impression on the experimental scene.

As always, OOB allowed for the assertion of an individual vision. That was certainly true with Fred Curchack, who brought his one-man version of *The Tempest* to the Brooklyn Academy of Music's Next Wave Festival. Curchack's *Stuff as Dreams Are Made On*, cited here as an outstanding 1989–90 OOB production, was a wildly fanciful exploration of Shakespeare in which the author-director played all the roles and also created the sets, masks and puppets. This was clearly an act of virtuosity.

*Imperceptible Mutabilities in the Third Kingdom*, also cited as an outstanding production, was more of a collaborative venture between a playwright, Suzan-Lori Parks, a director, Liz Diamond, and a cast headed by Pamala Tyson. In four tantalizing scenes, Miss Parks, the season's most provocative new playwright, depicted crises of black Americans through history (from slavery to the present). The play was presented as part of the Fringe Series at BACA Downtown in Brooklyn.

Brooklyn was an active arena for new work—at The New Theater of Brooklyn (TNT), as well as at BACA and BAM, an alphabet soup of challenging theater. TNT offered an intriguing futuristic comedy, Y York's *Rain. Some Fish. No Elephants*, as well as the U.S. premiere of Tom Stoppard's *Rough Crossing*, a freely elaborative adaptation of Ferenc Molnar's *The Play's the Thing*. A failure at London's National Theater, it was a success at TNT—a shipshape production of a shipboard comedy.

*The Waves*, a third outstanding production cited here, the creation of David Bucknam and Lisa Peterson, performed the remarkable feat of musicalizing Virginia Woolf's dense novel about the interwoven lives of six Bloomsbury friends. Miss Peterson staged the show as part of the New Directors Series at the New York Theater Workshop. This venturesome company also gave a stage to *My Children! My Africa!*, Athol Fugard's hortatory drama about South African eduction (Ed. note: Named a Best Play in this volume's policy of including an occasional outstanding OOB work which has already made its mark on the international stage).

The season's other novel musicals were minuscule. David Ives's mite-size cantata, *Philip Glass Buys a Loaf of Bread*, produced in Manhattan Punch Line's festival of one-acts, zanily mocked the rhythms and repetitions in the title composer's music. Michael John LaChiusa's *Eulogy for Mister Hamm*, a vest-pocket section of a musical trilogy, satirized the craze for setting the most ordinary words to recitative. *Mister Hamm* shared the Ensemble Studio Theater stage (during Marathon 1990) with such diverting comedies as Shel Silverstein's *Hamlet* (a street-talking dude played by Melvin Van Peebles), Bill Bozzone's *The Second Coming*, Frank D. Gilroy's *Match Point* and OyomO's stereotype-smashing *The Stalwarts*.

Early in the season, LaChiusa was responsible for the music for *Buzzsaw Berkeley*, a misguided attempt at merging Busby Berkeley musicals with chainsaw massacre movies. *Buzzsaw* was one of several self-styled "silly" shows at the WPA Theater, having a disappointing season that also included *20 Fingers, 20 Toes*, a dreadful musical about Siamese twins.

Anne Hamburger's En Garde Arts spread its site-specific premise next door to Broadway, taking over a derelict movie house, the Victory, on West 42nd Street and recalling, in *Crowbar*, the Victory's past theatrical splendor. This historical melodrama was written by Mac Wellman and directed by Richard Caliban (with James Sanders acting as archivist). Wellman was also the author of *Terminal Hip*, a non-stop geyser of language, delivered by Stephen Mellor at Performance Space 122, itself a valuable center for performance art.

Caliban, a playwright as well as director, was the author of *Rodents and Radios*, a kaleidoscopic collage about the lives of obsessive young people, including a defecting East European tennis star and a prodigal wife hellbent on broadening her horizons through travel. *Rodents and Radios* was staged at the Cucaracha Theater, a Tribeca company that also offered Jeffrey Klayman's *Indian Dog*, a shaggy comedy about another journeyman explorer.

The Naked Angels presented one of the season's most expansive productions, with 29 actors crowding the stage in *Chelsea Walls*, Nicole Burdette's environmental collage about people passing in the night at New York's Chelsea Hotel. This richly textured tapestry of vignettes was given a visceral production by Ed Sherin. The Home for Contemporary Theater and Art con-

## Mel Gussow Citations: Outstanding OOB Productions

*Right,* Fred Curchack in *Stuff as Dreams Are Made On* at BAM's Next Wave Festival—"a wildly fanciful exploration of Shakespeare, clearly an act of virtuosity"; *below,* the ensemble in *Imperceptible Mutabilities in the Third Kingdom* in BACA's Fringe Series—"the season's most provocative new playwright depicted crises of black Americans through history." Also cited was *The Waves* (not shown) at New York Theater Workshop—"musicalizing Virginia Woolf's dense novel."

tinued its search for new voices, with *II Samuel 11, Etc.*, David Greenspan's modernized approach to David and Bathsheba (starring the talented Mary Shultz). Also at the Home was *New Anatomies*, Timberlake Wertenbaker's reflections about the turn-of-the-century adventuress Isabelle Eberhardt.

The San Francisco Mime Troupe, America's leading political theater, made one of its rare trips to New York with *Seeing Double*, an irreverent comedy about a most stressful situation, the Arab-Israeli conflict. Richard Foreman offered the abstruse but evocative *Lava*, and Ping Chong was represented by *Brightness*, a study in light and shadow.

In *Everything That Rises Must Converge*, which moved from The Kitchen to the American Spoleto Festival in Charleston, John Jesurun continued his elliptical, intriguing investigation of the linkage between stage and video.

There were two widely disparate versions of *King Lear*. In Manhattan, Lee Breuer opened his controversial cross-gendered version, starring Ruth Maleczech in the title role (Lear's daughters became sons and the Fool, played by Greg Mehrten, was an hermaphrodite). Transporting the play into Tennessee Williams country, the production had its striking moments as well as its lapses. Robert Sturua's *King Lear* came from the other Georgia, in the Soviet Union. Presented by BAM, this production of the Rustaveli Theater Company unearthed comedy in the demonic tragedy.

The CSC began its season with a revival of Carey Perloff's production of Harold Pinter's *The Birthday Party* (with Jean Stapleton added to the cast), combined with the New York premiere of *Mountain Language*, a short, sharp play about political repression. Late in the season, the CSC broadly adapted Bulgakov's satiric novel *Heart of a Dog*, followed by Michael Feingold's translation of the melodrama *The Tower of Evil* by Alexandre Dumas.

The season at the Pan Asian Repertory was highlighted by the return of David Henry Hwang's first play, *FOB*, directed by the author. After presenting the local premiere of Doug Lucie's English Drama, *Progress*, The Hudson Guild dimmed its reputation with a misreading of Genet's *The Balcony*.

Another low point was *By and for Havel*, a heavy-handed revival of Vaclav Havel's *Audience* and Samuel Beckett's *Catastrophe*. The one-acts were intended to commemorate Beckett's death and Havel's election as president of Czechoslovakia, two monumental events in the history of playwriting.

With stark precision, Romulus Linney wove together a collage of stories about *Three Poets*, including Anna Akhmatova. The Irish Repertory theater revived Brian Friel's *Philadelphia, Here I Come!*, along with one splendid live performance of Beckett's radio play *All That Fall*, during a special benefit evening honoring the author.

The Women's Project featured two plays of interest—Lavonne Mueller's *Violent Peace* (love-hate in a military family) and Constance Congdon's *Tales of the Lost Formicans* (people from outer space comment on American suburbia). Marsha Norman returned with *Traveler in the Dark*—a cloudy play about a loss of faith—at the York Theater. The York, which in the past has offered fine revivals of Stephen Sondheim musicals, scraped musical (and OOB) bottom with *Frankie*, a woeful modernization of *Frankenstein*, conceived by the indomitable George Abbott. Definably eclectic, OOB remained hospitable to all varieties of theater during 1989–90.

# PLAYS PRODUCED
# OFF OFF BROADWAY

## AND ADDITIONAL PRODUCTIONS

Here is a comprehensive sampling of off-off-Broadway and other experimental or peripheral 1989–90 productions in New York, compiled by Camille Croce. There is no definitive "off-off-Broadway" area or qualification. To try to define or regiment it would be untrue to its fluid, exploratory purpose. The listing below of hundreds of works produced by more than 100 OOB groups and others is as inclusive as reliable sources will allow, however, and takes in all leading Manhattan-based, new-play producing, English-language organizations.

The more active and established producing groups are identified in **bold face type**, in alphabetical order, with artistic policies and the names of the managing directors given whenever these are a matter of record. Each group's 1989–90 schedule is listed with play titles in CAPITAL LETTERS. Often these are works-in-progress with changing scripts, casts and directors, sometimes without an engagement of record (but an opening or early performance date is included when available).

Many of these off-off-Broadway groups have long since outgrown a merely experimental status and are offering programs which are the equal in professionalism and quality (and in some cases the superior) of anything in the New York theater, with special contractual arrangements like the showcase code, letters of agreement (allowing for longer runs and higher admission prices than usual) and, closer to the edge of the commercial theater, a so-called "mini-contract." In the list below, all available data on opening dates, performance numbers and major production and acting credits (almost all of them Equity members) is included in the entries of these special-arrangement offerings.

A large selection of lesser-known groups and other shows that made appearances off off Broadway during the season appears under the "Miscellaneous" heading at the end of this listing.

**Amas Musical Theater.** Dedicated to bringing all people, regardless of race, creed, color or economic background, together through the creative arts. Rosetta LeNoire, founder and artistic director.

PARIS '31 (22). Book by John Fearnley; music and lyrics by Cole Porter. November 2, 1989. Director, John Fearnley; choreography, Robert Longbottom; scenery, Jane Sablow; lighting, Beau Kennedy; costumes, Kathryn Wagner. With Thelma Carpenter, Zellie Daniels, Kevin John Gee, Nancy Groff, Randy Hills, Sebastian Hobart, Michael McAssey, Debbie Petrino, Brian Quinn, Monte Ralstin, Pamela Shaddock, Jeffrey Solis, Betty Winsett, Ellen Zachos.

CAPITOL CAKEWAKE (24). Book by Elmer Kline and Perry Arthur Kroeger; music by Terry Waldo; lyrics by Lou Carter. February 21, 1990. Director, Tom O'Horgan; choreography, Wesley Fata; scenery, Perry Arthur Kroeger; lighting, Howard Thies; costumes, Kathryn Wagner. With Adrian Bailey, Tena Wilson, Jack Waddell, Minnette Coleman, Philip Gilmore, Sharon Hope, Kimberly Jones, Jack Landron, Miron Lockett, Yoko Matsamura, Aaron Mendelson, Leonard Parker, Jeffery Smith, Marc D. Summers.

**American Place Theater.** In addition to the regular off-Broadway season, other special products are presented. Wynn Handman, director, Stephen Lisner, general manager.

*American Humorists' Series*

BOBO'S BIRTHDAY (6). Written and performed by Catherine Butterfield. April 23, 1990.

THE CONSUMING PASSIONS OF LYDIA E. PINKHAM AND REV. SYLVESTER GRAHAM (9). Conceived by Margery Cohen. April 30, 1990. Director, Wynn Handman. With Margery Cohen, Eric Johnson.

**American Theater of Actors.** Dedicated to providing a creative atmosphere for new American playwrights, actors and directors. James Jennings, artistic director.

EYE TO EYE. By Matthew Davis. June 14, 1989. Director, Ted Mornel. With Mike Pierce, Rebecca Tilney, George Barber.

BEST FRIENDS. By John Voulgaris. June 28, 1989. Director, Donald L. Brooks. With Chris Kelly, David Conaway.

SAY GOODBYE TO HOLLYWOOD. By Tony Jerris. July 12, 1989. Director, Jack Mahan. With Colette Nielsen, Nancy Baines, Tony Jerris.

FRANZ AND DORA by Hal Lieberman. July 12, 1989. Director, Shep Pamplin. With John O'Donohue, Gretchen Hopkins, John List, David Sobel, Gregory Sartin.

THE CAST IRON SMILE. By Nancy Bruff Gardner. July 12, 1989. Director, James Jennings. With Sally Graudons, Tom Bruce, Ken Kamlet, Lorraine Marshall, Lou Lagalante, Brian Landy.

SCORPIONS IN THE CRADLE. By Marc Garcia. August 2, 1989. Director, James Jennings. With Elaine Leone, Vincent Zangari, Lynn Pickett, James Sweeney.

THE ACT. By Roberto Monticello. August 23, 1989. Director, Valerie Harris. With Will Buchanan, David Hayden, Robert Sterling, Susan Talbot.

HENRY'S FOLLY. Written and directed by Eliza Miller. August 23, 1989. With Sally Graudons, Tom Bruce, Kerry Mortell, Peg O'Donoghue, Andrea Cione, Frank O'Donnell.

DAKOTA COWBOY. Written and directed by James Jennings. August 23, 1989. With Nancy Kaiser, Kathryn Singer, Jon Shipley, Christopher Jennings.

PICTURES IN GLASS. By Brett Busang. September 7, 1989. Director, Anne Marie Marcazzo. With Helen Whittemore, J.J. Clark, Anne Parker, Beverly Jean Favre.

WOLVES. By Marc Garcia. October 4, 1989. Director, James Jennings. With Alexandra Lancer, Pati Sands, Kerry Martell.

NIGHT OF THE 3 MOONS. By James Crafford. October 18, 1989. With Bob Crafford, Kevin Judson, James Crafford.

ANGEL DUST and ASHES TO ASHES. By James Jennings. October 25, 1989. Director, Shep Pamplin. With Lillo Way, Clark Tufts, Jessica Lynn Jennings, Paul Nielsen, Chris Hoffman.

DAY OF THE DOGSTAR. Written and directed by James Jennings. November 21, 1989. With Patrick Connelly, Marie Dahl, Carrie Hall, Joseph Holmgren.

AWAITING THE LARK. By Joseph McDonald. December 6, 1989. Director, Shep Pamplin. With Patrick Connelly, Chris Hoffman, Janet Kennedy, P.J. O'Connor.

DID SHE FALL, OR WAS SHE PUSHED? Written and directed by Milburn Smith. December 13, 1989. With Joyce Blint, Barbara Thompson, Eric Hoffmaster.

SONG OF THE NOVA. Written and directed by James Jennings. December 20, 1989. With Powell Leonard, Catherine Libbey, Irv Butler.

READERS. By Doug Williams. December 27, 1989. Director, Gail Michelson. With Ken Kamlet, Lorraine Marshall, Joseph Holmgren, Robin Lilly, Joel Vic, Vincent Zangari.

3 A.M. IN A COFFEE SHOP. By Ellen Besserman. December 27, 1989. Director, Phil Setren. With Lynn Pickett, Damien Bosco, Don Sheehan, Amy Freedman.

LIGHT ON THE OCEAN FLOOR. By John Akamine. January 17, 1990. Director, Raymond Nedzel. With Patricia Barker, Marie Trusits, Jackie Underwood, Vincent Zangari, Raymond Nedzel.

NAGASAKI MARU. By John Quinn. February 7, 1990. Director, James Jennings. With Patrick Connelly, Mike Pierce, Powell Leonard, Robert Canaan, Miki Yoshida, Tomoko Nakamaru, Kazuki Takase, Jose Evangelista, Judith Boxley.

SCARSDALE STATION. By Peter Chelnik. February 21, 1990. Director, James Jennings. With James Cesa, Pati Sands, Jerome Brenner.

JACK. By Stuart Edelson. March 14, 1990. Director, James Jennings. With Jon Shipley, Janice Bremac, Joe Zimmerman, Judith Boxley, Mat Sarter.

END OF SUMMER. By Gene Ruffini. March 21, 1990. Director, Mark Corum. With Will Buchanan, Grace Pettijohn, Donna Avery, Mary Ellen Lyon, Matthew Caldwell.

ELDEST SON, OLDEST ENEMY. By Douglas Bergman. April 18, 1990. With Margaret Mackey, Gerry Hambel.

I SAW THE SWEDE. By Nicholas Wenckheim. April 25, 1990. Director, Shep Pamplin. With Joe Zimmerman.

DESOLATION ROW. By Mitch Ganem. May 23, 1990. Director, James Jennings. With Patrick Connelly, Marie Dahl.

GREY-DOG SPEAKS OUT. Written and directed by James Jennings. May 30, 1990. With Richard Dafein.

**Circle Repertory Projects-in-Progress**. Developmental programs for new plays. Tanya Berezin, artistic director, Connie L. Alexis, managing director.

THE GIRL IN PINK. By Peter Hedges. June 5, 1989. Director, Joe Mantello.

WALKING THE DEAD. By Keith Curran. October 16, 1989. Director, June Stein.

OH! DUBROVNIK! Written and directed by Jonathan Bolt. October 30, 1989.

LAST GAS TILL TURNPIKE. By Lanie Robertson. December 18, 1989. Director, B. Rodney Marriott.

INCOMMUNICADO. By Tom Dulack. March 19, 1990. Director, Robert F. Fuhrmann.

THE COLORADO CATECHISM. By Vincent Cardinal. May 9, 1990. Director, Mark Ramont.

*Extended Readings*

CHARLIE'S WEDDING DAY. By Patricia Goldstone. January 15, 1990. Director, Mark Ramont.
READY FOR THE RIVER. By Neal Bell. March 5, 1990. Director, Gitta Honegger.
BEFORE IT HITS HOME. By Cheryl West. May 14, 1990. Director, Tazewell Thompson.
THE MASK. By Bill Elverman. May 21, 1990. Director, John Bishop.

EN GARDE ARTS—Paul Zimet in *Krapp's Last Tape*

**CSC Repertory, Ltd. (Classic Stage Company).** Aims to produce classics with a bold, contemporary sensibility. Carey Perloff, artistic director.

MOUNTAIN LANGUAGE and THE BIRTHDAY PARTY (53). By Harold Pinter. November 8, 1989. Director, Carey Perloff; scenery, Loy Arcenas; lighting, Beverly Emmons; costumes, Gabriel Berry; music for "Mountain Language" by Wayne Horvitz; sound, Daniel Moses Schreier. With Jean Stapleton, Wendy Makkena, Richard Riehle, David Strathairn, Peter Riegert, Miguel Perez, Thomas Delling, Bill Moor.

HEART OF A DOG. By Deloss Brown, from Mikhail Bulgakov's novella. March 15, 1990. Director, Robert Lanchester; scenery, Tom Kamm; lighting, Mary Louise Geiger; costumes, Jane Eliot. With Jace Alexander, Josh Pais, Leslie Geraci, Gwynne Rivers, Bill Raymond, William Newman, Anna Levine Thomson, Anthony Fusco, Mary Beth Kilkelly.

THE TOWER OF EVIL (43). By Alexandre Dumas, translated by Michael Feingold. May 9, 1990. Director, Carey Perloff; scenery, Donald Eastman; lighting, Frances Aronson; costumes, Gabriel Berry; music, Elizabeth Swados. With Kathleen Widdoes, Patrick O'Connell, Thomas Delling, Michael Reilly, Bradley Whitford, Ethan Mintz, Katharine Cohen, Olek Krupa, David Bishins, Armand Schultz, Ellie Hannibal, Mary Beth Kilkelly, Frank Raiter, Gwynne Rivers.

**En Garde Arts.** Dedicated to developing the concept of "site-specific theater" in the streets, parks and buildings of the city. Anne Hamburger, founder and producer.

KRAPP'S LAST TAPE. By Samuel Beckett. November 30, 1989. Director, Alan Mokler; with Paul Zimet. (Co-produced by The Talking Band.)

CROWBAR (57). By Mac Wellman. February 18, 1990. Director, Richard Caliban; scenery, Kyle Chepulis; lighting, Brian Aldous; costumes, Claudia Brown; music, David Van Tieghem. With Yusef Bulos, Steve Coats, Elzbieta Czyzewska, Nora Dunfee, Jan Leslie Harding, Cordelia Richards, Omar Shapli, Ascanio Sharpe, David Van Tieghem, Sara Bladen, Karen Casteel, Anita Durst, Llewellyn Jones, K.C. Ligon, Julia Mengers, Kevin Barry O'Connor, Catherine Porter, Ken Schatz, Liz Sherman.

**Ensemble Studio Theater.** Membership organization of playwrights, actors, directors and designers dedicated to supporting individual theater artists and developing new works for the stage. Over 250 projects each season, ranging from readings to fully-mounted productions. Curt Dempster, artistic director, Peter Shavitz, managing director.

MARATHON '89 (festival of one-act plays). THE ESSENCE OF MARGOVIA by Jenny Lombard, directed by Lisa Peterson; SELF-TORTURE AND STRENUOUS EXERCISE by Harry Kondoleon, directed by Max Mayer; WINK-DAH by William Yellow Robe Jr., directed by Richard Lichte; WOMAN FLOATING OUT A WINDOW by Jacklyn Maddux, directed by Charles Karchmer; PATHOLOGICAL VENUS by Brighde Mullins, directed by Jimmy Bohr; THE OPEN BOAT by Neal Bell, directed by Curt Dempster; OUTSIDE THE RADIO by Kermit Frazier, directed by Oz Scott; BIG FROGS by David Golden, directed by Matthew Penn; WATER MUSIC by Michael Erickson, directed by Beth A. Schachter. May 27–June 18, 1989.

BRIAR PATCH (20). By Deborah Pryor. December 2, 1989. Director, Lisa Peterson; scenery, David Birn; lighting, Greg MacPherson; costumes, Michael Krass; music and sound, Michael Keck. With Elizabeth Berridge, Victor Slezak, Paul McCrane, Connie Ray, William Ragsdale, Nancy Franklin.

*New Works Series*

SEDALIA RUN. By Katherine Long. November 9, 1989. Director, Mary B. Robinson. With Martin Shaker, Jenny O'Hara, Polly Adams, Bill Cwikowski, Cameron Johnson, Kathy Hiler.

HARRY BLACK. By Dakota Powell. March 21, 1990. Director, Christopher Smith.

*New Voices (Staged Readings)*

CAPTAIN. By Paul Weitz. January 30, 1990. Director, Susan Brinkley.
SPIKE HEELS. By Theresa Rebeck. February 1, 1990. Director, Lynn Thompson.
LOST AND FOUND. By Jacqueline Reingold. February 3, 1990.
THE SCRAMBLED LIFE OF CHRISTOPHER COLUMBUS. By Billy Aronson. February 5, 1990. Director, Christopher Smith.

MARATHON 1990 (festival of one-act plays). MATCH POINT by Frank D. Gilroy, directed by Billy Hopkins; TWO WAR SCENES: CROSS PATCH and GOLDBERG STREET by David Mamet, directed by W.H. Macy; THE SECOND COMING by Bill Bozzone, directed by Donato J. D'Albis; CAPTIVE by Paul Weitz, directed by Susan Brinkley; HAMLET by Shel Silverstein, directed by Curt Dempster; THE STALWARTS by OyamO, directed by Jack Gelber; EULOGY FOR MR. HAMM by Michael John LaChiusa, directed by Kirsten Sanderson; THE ECLIPSE by Joyce Carol Oates, directed by Curt Dempster; DEATH AND THE MAIDEN by Susan Kim, directed by Lisa Peterson; STAY AWAY A LITTLE CLOSER by John Ford Noonan, directed by Bill Roudebush; TONIGHT WE LOVE by Romulus Linney, directed by John Stix; MERE MORTALS by David Ives, directed by Jason McConnell Buzas. May 9–June 17, 1990.

**Hudson Guild Theater.** Has presented plays in their New York, American or world premieres; this was announced as their final season. Geoffrey Sherman, producing director, John Daines associate director.

UP 'N' UNDER. By John Godber. June 4, 1989. Director, Geoffrey Sherman; scenery and lighting, Paul Wonsek; costumes, Pamela Scofield. With Ivar Brogger, Ray Collins, John Curless, Fredrick Hahn, Elaine Rinehart.

HOME GAMES (28). By Tom Ziegler. September 21, 1989. Director, Roderick Cook; scenery, Paul Wonsek; lighting, Stuart Drake; costumes, Barbara Forbes. With John Braden, Kymberly Dakin, Michael E. Knight.

PROGRESS (56). By Doug Lucie. November 29, 1989. Director, Geoffrey Sherman; scenery, Paul Wonsek; lighting, Phil Monat; costumes, Pamela Scofield. With Nelson Avidon, Anne Bobby, Ivar Brogger, John Curless, Edmond Lewis, Joe Mantello, Diana Van Fossen, Ray Virta.

DYLAN THOMAS: RETURN JOURNEY (one-man show) (32). Based on the works of Dylan Thomas. February 20, 1990. Director, Anthony Hopkins. With Bob Kingdom. (Co-produced by Arthur Cantor.)

THE BALCONY by Jean Genet, translated by Bernard Frechtman. March 28, 1990. Directed by Geoffrey Sherman. With Freda Foh Shen, Charles E. Gerber, Matt Penn, Valerie Pettiford, Mimi Quillin, John

Henry Redwood, Will Rhys, Angela Sargeant, David Schechter, Albert Sinkys, Lynne Flijian Taylor, Sharon Washington.

**INTAR.** Mission is to identify, develop and present the talents of gifted Hispanic American theater artists and multicultural visual artists. Max Ferra, artistic director, Eva Brune, acting executive director.

> PARTING GESTURES. By Rafael Lima. December 17, 1989. Director, John Ferraro; scenery, Loren Sherman; lighting, Jackie Manassee; costumes, Jennifer Von Mayrhauser. With John Leguizamo, Ilka Tanya Payan.
>
> GOING TO NEW ENGLAND. By Ana Maria Simo. March 4, 1990. Direction, scenery and costumes, Maria Irene Fornes; lighting, Stephen Quandt. With Elizabeth Clemens, Divina Cook, Rene Rivera, Martin Treat.
>
> THE BODY BUILDER'S BOOK OF LOVE. By Fernando Arrabal, translated by Lorenzo Mans. April 11, 1990. Director, Tom O'Horgan; scenery, Christina Weppner; lighting, Debra Dumas; costumes, Deborah Shaw. With Mark Dold, Saul Philip Stein.

**Interart Theater.** Committed to producing innovative work by women theater artists and to introducing New York audiences to a bold range of theater that is non-traditional in form or theme. Margot Lewitin, artistic director.

*Schedule included:*

DRAGON'S NEST (8). Written and directed by Lee Nagrin. May 3, 1990. Scenery, James Meares; lighting, Tony Giovannetti; costumes, Sally Ann Parsons; flying, Foy. With Lee Nagrin, David Brooks, Janet Aisawa, Deborah McLaughlin, Linda Seifert, Michael A. Mehlmann, Joseph Pupello, Diane Grotke. (Co-produced by La Mama ETC.)

**La Mama (a.k.a. LaMama) Experimental Theater Club (ETC).** A busy workshop for experimental theater of all kinds. Ellen Stewart, founder and artistic director.

*Schedule included:*

L'ALTRA ITALIA (one-act plays): SAAVEDRA by Santagata Morgandi; ECCE HOMO written and directed by Marcello Sambati; AUTOBIOGRAPHY OF AN ECLIPSE and MEMORIES OF AN ADULT WOMAN by Daviano Ingravallo; TUTTI NON CI SONO written and directed by Dario D'Ambrosi; MOSCHE VOLANTI by Siro Ferrone, directed by Marcello Bartoli. June 8–25, 1989.

THE JACK BENNY PROGRAM (opera). By John Moran. September 28, 1989. Director, Bob McGrath. With the Ridge Theater.

POSITIVE ME. By Lisa Edelstein. November 9, 1989. Director, Ethan Silverman; choreography, Robert La Fosse; scenery, John de Fazio; lighting, Howard Thies; costumes, Michelle Freedman. With Stephanie Berry, Lisa Edelstein, Thomas Gibson, Margaux Guerard, Robert I., Mark Anthony Wade, Joe Warfield, Mary Lou Wittmer.

BRIGHTNESS. Created by Ping Chong in collaboration with Matthew Yokobosky; text by Louise Smith, after Petronius, Hippocrates and Josephine Baker. November 15, 1989. Scenery and costumes, Howard Thies; lights, Brian Hallas. With Karen Booth, Ping Chong, John Fleming, Dan Froot, Larry Malvern, Louise Smith.

LOTTO—THE SLEEPING AMERICA. By Glenn O'Brien. November 30, 1989. Director, Carlos Almada; scenery and lighting, Carlos and Paulette Almada.

LOCO 7. By and with Frederico Restrepo's Puppets and Drummers. December 7, 1989.

YOU CAN'T THINK OF EVERYTHING. By Alfred de Musset, translated by Michael Feingold. November 28, 1989. Director, Bernd Hagg; scenery and lighting, Christine Tritthart; costumes, Martha Bromelmeier. With Craig Bockhorn, Valorie Hubbard, Ursula Mihelic, Daniel Pardo, Edward Seamon.

CASA. Conceived, directed and performed by Denise Stoklos. January 4, 1990. Lighting, Isla Jay. With Joan Evans, Eli Daruj, Jonathan Slaff, Antonio Herculano, Leticia Monte, Hyunyup Lee, Thais Stoklos Kignel, Piata Stoklos Kignel.

MANA GOES TO THE MOON. By David Rousseve; music by Edwina Lee Tyler. January 4, 1990. Director, Molly Davies.

FREDERICK DOUGLASS NOW. Created and performed by Roger Guenveur Smith. January 25, 1990.

JUICE. Written and directed by Roger Babb; music by Neal Kirkwood. January 31, 1990. With the Otrabanda Company.

INCREASE. Book and lyrics by Brighde Mullins; music by Charles Goldbeck. February 15, 1990. Director, Adrienne Weiss.

LOST IN A FLURRY OF CHERRIES. Written and directed by Tsunetoshi Hirowatari; based on a short story by Ango Sakaguchi. March 14, 1990. Choreography, Takashi Nishida; scenery, Shigeo Okajima; lighting, Sadahiko Tachiki; costumes, Michiko Kitamura; music, Shinichiro Ikebe. With the Tokyo Engeki Ensemble.

AGAINST THE EARTH (opera). By Ed Herbst and Beth Skinner. March 29, 1990. With the Thunder Bay Ensemble.

LA GRANDE JOSEPHINE. By Samantha A. Martin; conceived by Andrea Black. April 19, 1990. Director, John McGrath; choreography, Jakky Bernadette; musical direction, Mario E. Sprouse; scenery, Judy Gailen; costumes, Wendy A. Rolfe. With Andrea Black, Gary Flake, Tom Judson, Cameron Miller, Mamie Moore, Terrance Reily, Faye Smolen.

THE CRY OF THE BODY (mime). Conceived and directed by Benito Gutmacher. May 24, 1990.

*The Club Schedule included:*

DIVA DEN. October 5, 1989. With Marleen Menard, Liz Prince, Joey Arias, Felicia March.

NIGHT OF SHAMANS. October 30, 1989. With Tom Murrin, Blue Man Group, Karen Finley, James Godwin.

THE FESTER AND ROT RAW REVIEW. By Brian Glover. November 13, 1989.

NOBODY'S MISS AMERICA. By and with Lisa Kotin. December 4, 1989.

SPECTRE WOMAN CHRONICLES. January 8, 1990. With Roy Nathanson, Cathy Zimmerman, Theresa Haney, Paul Langland, Meredith Monk, Terry Fox, Hearn Gadbois.

ANNIVERSARY WALTZ. February 15, 1990. With Lois Weaver, Peggy Shaw.

I THINK IT'S GONNA WORK OUT FINE. By Ed Bullins. March 8, 1990. Director, Brian Freeman; choreography, Roger Dillahunty; scenery, Kemit Amenophis; lighting, Stephanie Johnson; costumes, Rene Walker, Pat Stewart; music, Idris Ackamoor, Rhodessa Jones, Peter Fuji and Rock of Ages.

SHOW 'N' TELL (work-in-progress). By Holly Hughes. April 5, 1990.

DILBERT DINGLE-DONG (THE DOOMED), OR A NEST FULL OF NINNIES. By Ethyl Eichelberger; music by Peter Golub. April 19, 1990.

TRIBUTE TO DIANA VREELAND. By John Heys. April 30, 1990.

THE FALL OF THE WALL REVIEW. May 7, 1990. With Hot Peaches.

**Lamb's Theater Company.** Committed to developing and presenting new works in their most creative and delicate beginnings. Carolyn Rossi Copeland, producing director.

GIFTS OF THE MAGI. Book and lyrics by Mark St. Germain, based on the O. Henry story; music and lyrics by Randy Courts. December 7, 1989.

SMOKE ON THE MOUNTAIN. Book by Connie Ray; conceived and directed by Alan Bailey. May 12, 1990. Scenery, Peter Harrison; lighting, Don Ehman; costumes, Pamela Scofield; musical directors, John

Foley, Michael Craver. With Reathel Bean, Kevin Chamberlin, Linda Kerns, Dan Manning, Robert Olsen, Jane Potter, Connie Ray.

**The Mabou Mines.** Theater collaborative whose work is a synthesis of motivational acting, narrative acting and mixed-media performance. Collective artistic leadership.

LEAR. Adapted and directed by Lee Breuer from William Shakespeare's *King Lear*. January 25, 1990. Score, Pauline Oliveros; lighting, Arden Fingerhut, Lenore Doxsee; costumes, Ghretta Hynd; fight staging, B.H. Barry. With Ruth Maleczech, Greg Mehrten, Isabell Monk, Kimberly Scott, Lola Pashalinski, Ellen McElduff, Karen Evans-Kandel, Bill Raymond, Ron Vawter, Black-Eyed Susan, Honora Fergusson, Lute Ramblin', Clove Galilee, Maya O'Reilly, Joanna Adler, Allison Dubin, Frier McCollister, Pedro Rosado.

THE B. BEAVER ANIMATION. Written and directed by Lee Breuer. May 15, 1990. (Co-produced by New York Shakespeare Festival; see its entry in the Plays Produced Off Broadway section of this volume.)

**Manhattan Punch Line.** New York's only theater company devoted to comedy. Steve Kaplan, artistic director.

*Schedule included:*

MERTON OF THE MOVIES, THE BUTTER AND EGG MAN, STAGE DOOR, JUNE MOON. By George S. Kaufman. November 13, 1989 (staged readings).

NEW VAUDEVILLE '89: MASS HYSTERIA with The Normals, Mindfield, Good Clean Fun; THE BEST OF BOSTON; WOMEN IN COMEDY, with Carrissa Channing, Nancy Mura, Alice Eve Cohen; VAUDEVILLE NOUVEAU; ALTERNATIVE VOICES; Retrospective of Songs by Al Carmines, with Al Carmines, Kathrin King Segal; Wallem and Tolan. October 26–November 12, 1989.

SIXTH ANNUAL FESTIVAL OF ONE-ACT COMEDIES: PHILIP GLASS BUYS A LOAF OF BREAD by David Ives, directed by Jason McConnell Buzas; PORTFOLIO by Tom Donaghy, directed by Chris Ashley; THE SHOW MUST GO ON by Laurence Klavan, directed by Stephen Hollis; HOW ARE THINGS IN COSTA DEL FUEGO? by Rick Louis, directed by Steve Kaplan; THE FERTILIZATION OPERA, music and lyrics by Peter Tolan, directed by Jason McConnell Buzas, musical director, Albert Aronheim; GRUNIONS by Barbara Lindsay, directed by Kay Matschulat; BRUNCH AT TRUDY AND PAUL'S by Michael Aschner, directed by Louis Scheeder; FELLOW TRAVELERS by Jeffrey Hatcher, directed by Jonathan Mintz; THE ARTISTIC DIRECTION by Roger Hedden, directed by Greg Johnson. January 20–March 11, 1990. Scenery, David K. Gallo; lighting, Danianne Mizzy; costumes, Sharon Lynch and Julie Doyle. With Michael Aschner, Deryl Caitlyn, Bill Cohen, Kitty Crooks, Randy Danson, Daniel Hagen, Rhonda Hayter, Ryan Hilliard, David Konig, Liz Larsen, Dea Lawrence, Donald Lawrence, Donald Lowe, Theresa McElwee, Robert Montano, Paul O'Brien, Gus Rogerson, Caryn Rosenthal, Nicholas Sadler, Howard Samuelson, Kathrin King Segal, Christopher Wells, Gary Yudman, Peter Basche, Michael Kelly Boone, Robert Burke, Warren Burton, Mark Chmiel, Charles E. Gerber, Robin Groves, Arthur Hanket, Patricia Hodges, Cheryl Hulteen, Chris A. Kelly, Ken Martin, Janine Leigh Robbins, Anita Rogerson, Linda Wallem.

BEYOND BELIEF (33). Written and directed by Fiona Laird. Lighting, Cliff Vic and Fiona Laird; costumes, Julie Speechley. THE CLOUDS by Aristophanes, adapted and directed by Fiona Laird; music, Fiona Laird; lighting, Peter Meineck; costumes, Julie Speechley. Presented in rotating repertory April 11–May 5, 1990 with The London Small Theater Company (Antony James, Fiona Laird, Adrian Schiller, Nicholas Smith, Rachel Spriggs, Jonathan Williams).

**Manhattan Theater Club Downtown/Uptown.** Festival of alternative performances, in addition to its regular off-Broadway season. Lynne Meadow, artistic director, Barry Grove, managing director, Matthew Maguire, festival curator.

CITIES OUT OF PRINT. By Susan Mosakowski. March 27, 1990. Scenery, Tom Dale Keever; lighting, Pat Dignan; costumes, Deborah Scott. With Matthew Maguire, Susan Mosakowski.

MANHATTAN PUNCH LINE—Michael Aschner, Theresa McElwee and Gary Yudman in Tom Donaghy's *Portfolio*

**P.S. 122 FIELD TRIPS.** Programs by Dancenoise, Terry Galloway, Ishmael Houston-Jones, Ruthi Peyser, Guy Yarden. April 3, 1990.

**ORANGE GROVE.** By Sidney Goldfarb. April 10, 1990. Director, Roger Babb; choreography, Rocky Bornstein; music, Blue Gene Tyranny. With The Otrabanda Company.

THIS IS NOT A SOAP BOX written and performed by Richard Elovich and Gregg Bordowitz; TERMINAL HIP by Mac Wellman, with Stephen Mellor; WORLD WITHOUT END written and performed by Holly Hughes, directed by Kate Stafford. April 17, 1990.

RADIANT CITY. Created and performed by Theodora Skipitares; music, Pat Irwin; lyrics, Andrea Balis. April 19, 1990.

FRINGES (plays premiered in BACA Downtown's Fringe Series): GREEKS by Suzan-Lori Parks, directed by Liz Diamond, with Jasper McGruder, Peter Schultz, Kenya Scott, Shona Tucker, Pam Tyson; THE CRAZY PLAYS written and directed by Jeffrey M. Jones, with Zivia Flomenhaft, Gary McCleery, Nicky Paraiso, Liz Schofield, Mary Schultz. April 21, 1990.

**Musical Theater Works.** Developmental workshop where writers of musical theater learn by doing. Anthony J. Stimac, artistic director.

MIDSUMMER NIGHTS (21). Book and lyrics by Brian D. Leys; music by Kevin Kuhn. September 20, 1989. Director, David Saint; choreography, Jonathan Cerullo; scenery, James Noone; lighting, Mark London; costumes, Amanda J. Klein; musical director, Seth Rudetsky. With Judith Moore, George Merritt, Wally Dunn, Kristine Nevins, Eric Kornfeld, Tracey Berg, Harold Perrineau Jr., Traci Lyn Thomas, Peter Marc, Brenda Braxton, Howard Samuelson, Joyce P. King, Jamie Martin, Stacy Morze.

GOOSE! BEYOND THE NURSERY (21). Book by Scott Evans; music by Mark Frawley; lyrics by Scott Evans. January 31, 1990. Director, Peter Gennaro; scenery, Allen Moyer; lighting, Mary Louise Geiger; costumes, Gregg Barnes; musical director, Joe Baker. With Adinah Alexander, Jeff Blumenkrantz, Jennifer Leigh Warren, Mark Lotito, Jan Neuberger, David Schechter.

SUGAR HILL (19). Book by Louis St. Louis and Roberto Fernandez, based on a story by Roberto Fernandez; music by Louis St. Louis; lyrics by Roberto Fernandez, Louis St. Louis and Tony Walsh. April 25, 1990. Director, Carmen de Lavallade; scenery, James Noone; lighting, Ken Smith; costumes, Carrie Robbins; musical director, Pookie Johnson. With Ethel Beatty Barnes, Cheryl Freeman, Tatyana Ali, Jeree Palmer Wade, Edwin Battle, Carol Jean Lewis, James Stovall, Marcella Lowery, Tony Hoylen.

**Music-Theater Group.** Pioneering in the development of new music-theater. Lyn Austin, producing director, Diane Wondisford, associate producing director.

JUAN DARIÉN by Julie Taymor and Elliot Goldenthal; music by Elliot Goldenthal. December 26, 1989 (see its entry in the Plays Produced Off Broadway section of this volume).

PARADISE FOR THE WORRIED (27). Conceived by Kinematic, Tamar Kotoske, Maria Lakis, Mary Richter and Holly Anderson; text and lyrics by Holly Anderson; music by Stanley Silverman, adapted by Jill Jaffe. April 5, 1990. Director, Diane Wondisford; choreography, Kinematic and Eric Barsness; scenery, Victoria Petrovich; lighting, Debra Dumas; costumes, Donna Zakowska; musical director, Jill Jaffe. With Campbell Scott, Eric Barsness, Laura Innes, Mary Richter, Maria Lakis, Tamar Kotoske, Jill Jaffe, Ted Sperling, Alfredo Pedernera.

**New Dramatists.** An organization devoted to playwrights; member writers may use the facilities for anything from private cold readings of their material to public script-in-hand readings. Joel Ruark, managing director.

*Studio and Rehearsed Readings*

ASCENSION DAY. By Michael Henry Brown. October 2, 1989. Director, Liz Diamond. With Denise Kennedy, Jason Green, Regina Taylor, Josh Schanker, Keith David, Miles Watson, Hillary Jones, Robert Jason, Dennis Green, Matt Lamaj, Maria Vail, Ed Baran, Jerry Bradley.

DREAMHOUSE. By Stuart Duckworth. October 4, 1989. Director, Amy Potozkin. With Cassie Barasch, Steve Friedman, Kristin Griffith, Chris McCann, Jackie Mary Roberts.

CASANOVA. By Constance Congdon. October 13, 1989. Director, R J Cutler; with Jennifer Bacon-Blaine, Kathleen Chalfant, Thom Christopher, Stuart Duckworth, Steve Friedman, Alice Haining, Benjamin Lloyd, Brennan Murphy, Rebecca Nelson, Peggy Pope, Jill Tasker, Joseph Warren.

JOY SOLUTION. By Stuart Duckworth. October 16, 1989. Director, Joan McGillis. With Kelly McGillis, Kate Skinner, Richard Riehle, Reginald L. Flowers, Summer Mullin.

GERALD'S GOOD IDEA. By Y York. October 30, 1989. Director, Mark Lutwak. With Lynne Thigpen, Lorey Hayes, Michael Countryman, Julia Glander, Anna Levine, Patrick Garner, Dennis Green, Miles Watson, Jennifer Leigh-Warren, Phil Soltonoff.

STATE OF THE ART. By Stuart Duckworth. November 1, 1989. Director, John Astracan. With Denise Kennedy, Steve Friedman, Mark Hammer, Ed Baran, Pirie MacDonald, Mirron Willis, Maria Spasoff.

IN THE EYE OF THE HURRICANE. By Eduardo Machado. November 9, 1989. Director, Jaime Hammerstein. With Ivonne Coll, Thom Christopher, Christofer De Oni, Bertila Damas, Ching Valdes-Aran, Ted Minos, Ernesto Gonzalez, Al Rodrigo, Steve Guevara.

GENUINE MYTH. By Ben Siegler. November 14, 1989. Director, Jonathan Hogan. With Stephanie Gordon, Ian Rosenberg, Ben Siegler.

THE TOWER. Written and directed by Matthew Maguire. November 21, 1989. With Susan Lambert, Dennis Green, Derrick McQueen, Cheryl Freeman, Jennifer Bacon-Blaine.

CROWBAR. Written and directed by Mac Wellman. December 4, 1989. With John Seitz, Reg E. Cathey, Elzbieta Czyzewska, Jan Leslie Harding, Chris McCann, Mary Schultz, Zach Grenier, Anne O'Sullivan, Julian Clark, Sarah Higgins, Paul Kolsby, Doyle Avant.

INDIAN LOVE CALL. By Paul D'Andrea. January 19, 1990. Director, Alma Becker. With Steve Coats, Charlotte Colavin, Robert Emmet, Pam Matthews, Woody Sempliner.

THE DEADLY AIM OF THE STRAIGHT AND TRUE. By Michael Henry Brown. January 26, 1990. Director, Joel Bishoff. With Wafa Cunningham, Bruce Katzman, Matt Lamaj, Jerry Mayer, Eugene Nesmith, John Terrell, Charles Turner.

SLO-PITCH. By Stuart Duckworth. January 29, 1990. Director, Liz Diamond. With David Mogentale.

MARIE-ANTOINE, OPUS ONE. By Lise Vialliancourt. February 20, 1990. Director, Liz Diamond. With Caroline Aaron, Robert Emmet, Jan Harding, Sophie Maletsky, Becky Borczon, Kate Fugeli, Sarah Bragaw, Jennifer Bacon-Blaine, Becky London.

THREE JOHNSONS AND A MULE. By Ben Siegler. February 26, 1990. With Chris Shaw, Gerry Vichi, Bill Cwikowski, Kathy Rossiter, Amy Ryan, Gary Dean Rubesamen.

NOT FOR PROFIT. By Stuart Duckworth. March 13, 1990. Director, Kara Green. With Larry Block, Judith Kirtley, Jackie Roberts, Howie Muir, Sharon Brady, Lynn Cohen, Cordelia Gonzalez, David Mogentale, Dayne Williams.

THE BENEFITS OF DOUBT. By Joe Sutton. April 9, 1990. Director, Josh Astracan. With Dennis Boutsikaris, Steve Coats, John Seitz, Charles Rucker, Mary Mara, Kristine Nielsen.

THE PLACE TO BE. By Chris Widney. April 9, 1990. Director, Stone Widney. With Tom Crow, Cheryl Hulteen, Alison Martin, Ken Martin.

PAINT. By Sean Eve. April 10, 1990. Director, Scott Stohler. With Jill Tasker, Kyle Shannon, Colette Kilroy, Wyman Pendleton, Zach Grenier, Ed Baran, Jurian Hughes, April Shawhan, Bobo Lewis.

ANGELS STILL FALLING. By Richard Blake. April 23, 1990. Director, John McGrath. With Kent Adams, Hannes McEchron, Sarah Brown, Maria Vail, Margaret Ritchie, Oliver Wadsworth, Murray Rubinstein, Peter Guttmacher.

WIPEOUT. By Nathaniel Nesmith. May 25, 1990.

**New Federal Theater.** Dedicated to presenting new playwrights and plays dealing with the minority and Third World experience. Woodie King Jr., producer.

GOREE (12). By Matsemela Manaka; music by Motsumi Makhene, Matsemela Manaka and Peter Boroko. September 17, 1989. Director, John Kani; choreography, Nomsa Manaka; scenery, Matsemela Manaka; lighting, Sephiwe Khumalo; costumes, Kate Manaka. With Sibangile Khumalo, Nomsa Manaka.

GOD'S TROMBONES! (45). Gospel musical adaptation of James Weldon Johnson's writings. October 4, 1989. Director, Woodie King Jr.; choreography, Dianne McIntyre; scenery, Llewellyn Harrison; lighting, William H. Grant III; costumes, Judy Dearing. With Cliff Frazier, Lex Monson, Rhetta Hughes, Sabrynaah Pope, Theresa Merritt, Trazana Beverley, Debbie Blackwell-Cook, Don Corey Washington.

SURVIVAL (30). Written and performed by Fana Kekana, Selaelo Maredi, Mshengu, Themba Ntinga, Seth Sibanda. January 31, 1990. Director, Jerry Mofokeng; scenery, Craig Kennedy; lighting, Richard Harmon; costumes, Ali Turns.

**New York Shakespeare Festival Public Theater.** Schedule of special projects, in addition to its regular off-Broadway productions. Joseph Papp, producer.

FESTIVAL LATINO IN NEW YORK. Schedule included: AMAZONIA by Larry Herrera, translated by Jack Agueros, directed by Oscar Ciccone, with Pablo Alarcon, Claribel Medina, Cari Gorostiza, Joseph Palmas, Norberto Kerner, Al Rodriguez, Tino Juarez; SUENO DE UNA NOCHE DE VERANO (A Midsummer Night's Dream) by William Shakespeare, adapted by Manuel Rueda, translated by Melia Bensussen, directed by Ramon Pareja, with Angel Mejia, Monina Sola, Oleka Fernandez, Reynaldo Disla, Juan Maria Almonte, Miriam Bello, Pipito Guerra, Kenny Grullon, Elvira Taveras; NO + (No More) written and directed by Raul Osorio, music, Andreas Bodenhoffer, with Rebeca Ghigliotto, Juan Carlos Montagna, Patricio Strahovsky Villagran, Manuel Pena; THE MIRACLE written and directed by Felipe Santander, translated by Amlin Gray in collaboration with Felipe Santander; EL CORONEL NO TIENE

NEW FEDERAL THEATER—Selaelo Maredi, Themba Ntinga, Fana Kekana and Seth Sibanda, co-authors as well as performers, in *Survival*

EL CORONEL NO TIENE QUIEN LE ESCRIBA (No One Writes to the Colonel) adapted and directed by Carlos Gimenez from Gabriel Garcia Marquez's story, translated by Nina Miller, with Jose Tejera, Aura Rivas, Anibal Grunn, Francisco Alfaro, Daniel Lopez, Pedro Pineda, Aitor Gaviria, Eric Wildpret, Jose Borges, Rolando Felizola, Mimi Sills, Norman Santana. PEGGY AND JACKSON book and direction by Michael Alasa, music by David Welch, with Michael Alasa, Ann Marie Milazzo; ADIOS TROPICANA book and lyrics by Chuck Gomez, music and direction by Mark Pennington, Elaine M. Carinci, Francesca MacAaron, Iliana Guibert; FANTASMA book by Edward Gallardo, music by Marc Allen Trujillo, directed by Bill Castellino, with John Aller, Olga Merediz; EL PASO, O PARABOLA DEL CAMINO (El Paso, or Parable of the Path) by La Candelaria, translated by Nina Miller, directed by Santiago Garcia; EL GRAN CRICO EU CRANIANO (The Great U.S. Kranial Circus) written, translated and directed by Myrna Casas, with Josie Perez, Angel Domenech, Elsa Roman. August 1–31, 1989.

CARNAGE, A COMEDY (12). By Adam Simon and Tim Robbins. September 8, 1989. (Transferred to off-Broadway status; see its entry in the Plays Produced Off Broadway section of this volume.)

JACKIE MASON—BRAND NEW (18). January 27, 1990.

JACKIE MASON (12). May 5, 1990.

**New York Theater Workshop.** Dedicated to the production of plays of intelligence and conscience and the development of new plays and emerging stage directors. James C. Nicola, artistic director, Nancy Kassak Diekmann, managing director.

MY CHILDREN! MY AFRICA! (47). Written and directed by Athol Fugard. December 18, 1989 (see its entry in the Plays Produced Off Broadway section of this volume).

A FOREST IN ARDEN (30). Adapted and directed by Christopher Grabowski from William Shakespeare's *As You Like It*. February 7, 1990. Scenery, Tom Kamm; lighting, Pat Dignan; costumes, Claudia Brown; music/sound, Scott Killian. With Fanni Green, Michael James-Reed, Susan Knight, Michael Liani.

THE NATURE OF THINGS (28). Written and performed by David Cale in collaboration with Roy Nathanson, Marc Ribot and E.J. Rodriguez. March 15, 1990. Director, Bill Barnes; lighting, Anne Militello; sound, Richard Kirschner.

THE WAVES (37). Text adapted by David Bucknam and Lisa Peterson from Virginia Woolf's novel; music and additional lyrics by David Bucknam. May 8, 1990. Director, Lisa Peterson; choreography, Marcia Milgrom Dodge; scenery, Randy Benjamin; lighting, Brian MacDevitt; costumes, Michael Krass; musical director, Helen Gregory. With Catherine Cox, Diane Fratantoni, Aloysius Gigi, John Jellison, Sarah Rice, John Sloman.

**The Open Eye: New Stagings.** Goal is to gather a community of outstanding theater artists to collaborate on works for the stage for audiences of all ages and cultural backgrounds. Jean Erdman, founding director, Amie Brockway, artistic director.

THE CONTRAST. By Royall Tyler. December 6, 1989. Director, Russell Treyz. With Marilyn Mays, Debra Whitfield, Chet Carlin, Beverly Lambert, Curt Hostetter, Jim Helsinger, Joseph O'Brien, Jonathan Smedley, Nicola Stimac.

ON THE MOVE (16). By Tony Howarth. March 7, 1990. Director, Kim T. Sharp; scenery, Adrienne J. Brockway; lighting, Donald A. Gingrasso; costumes, Leslie McGovern. With Roger Howarth, Debra Whitfield, Al Mohrmann.

NEW STAGINGS LAB/CHICAGO NEW PLAYS (staged readings): THE UNFINISHED REACH by Robyn Dana Guest, directed by Alyce Mott; COTILLION by David Rush, music by Errol Pearlman, directed by Kim T. Sharp; HANGING BY A PINSTRIPE by Richard Strand, directed by Chris Van Groningen; AN UNCERTAIN HOUR by Nicholas A. Patricca, directed by Amie Brockway; DOLLS by Anne McGravie, directed by Michelle Frenzer-Cornell. April 7–8, 1990.

**Pan Asian Repertory Theater.** Strives to provide opportunities for Asian American artists to perform under the highest professional standards and to create and promote plays by and about Asians and Asian Americans. Tisa Chang, artistic/producing director.

THE SONG OF SHIM CHUNG (24). Conceived and directed by Du-Yee Chang; written by Terrence Cranendonk in collaboration with Du-Yee Chang. November 7, 1989. Scenery, masks and puppets, Atsushi Moriyasu; lighting, Victor En Yu Tan; costumes, James Livingston; music, Du-Yee Chang. With June Angela, William Lucas, Mary Lee, Norris M. Shimabuku, Ernest Abuba, Donald Li, Mia Katigbak, Steve Park, Shigeko, Christen Villamor, Tsuyu Shimizu.

AND THE SOUL SHALL DANCE. By Wakako Yamauchi. March 21, 1990. Directed by Kati Kuroda. With Ron Nakahara, Roxanne Chang, Norris M. Shimabuku, Dawn A. Saito, Yuko Komiyama.

F.O.B. (30). Written and directed by David Henry Hwang. May 15, 1990. Choreography, Jamie H.J. Guan; scenery, Alex Polner; lighting, Victor En Yu Tan; costumes, Eiko Yamaguchi; music, Lucia Hwong. With Stan Egi, Ann M. Tsuji, Dennis Dun.

**Playwrights Horizons New Theater Wing.** Full productions of new works, in addition to the regular off-Broadway productions. Andre Bishop, artistic director, Paul S. Daniels, executive director.

KATE'S DIARY (13). By Kathleen Tolan. June 7, 1989. Director, David Greenspan; scenery, William Kennon; lighting, David Bergstein; costumes, Elsa Ward. With Lizbeth Mackay, Laura Hughes, Michael Brian French, John Griesemer, Rafael Baez.

LUCY'S LAPSES (13). Libretto by Laura Harrington; music by Christopher Drobny. July 19, 1989. Director, David Warren; choreography, John Carrafa; scenery, James Youmans; lighting, Debra Dumas; costumes, David C. Woolard; musical director, Paulette Haupt. With Rita Gardner, Jamie Ross, Lynnette Perry, Robert Duncan McNeill. (Produced in association with the Portland Opera.)

SUBFERTILE (14). By Tom Mardirosian. March 14, 1990. Director, John Ferraro; scenery, Rick Dennis; lighting, Brian MacDevitt; costumes, Abigail Murray. With Richard Council, Kitty Crooks, Susan Knight, Tom Mardirosian, Frederica Meister.

**Puerto Rican Traveling Theater.** Professional company presenting bilingual productions primarily of Puerto Rican and Hispanic playwrights, emphasizing subjects of relevance today. Miriam Colon, founder and producer.

CHINESE CHARADE (23). By Manuel Pereiras; music by Sergio Garcia Marruz and Saul Spangenberg. August 6, 1989. Director, Susana Tubert; choreography, Poli Rogers; scenery, Robert Klingelhoefer; costumes, Maria Ferreira-Contessa; musical director, Sergio Garcia Marruz. With Bonnie Diaz, Cintia Cruz, Jorge Oliver, Eileen Galindo, Jack Landron.

ARIANO. By Richard V. Irizarry, translated by Margarita Lopez Chiclana. January 17, 1990. Directed by Vicente Castro.

I AM A WINNER (42). By Fred Valle. March 14, 1990. Director, Melia Bensussen; scenery, Carl Baldasso; lighting, Bill Simmons; costumes, Mary Marsicano. With Jose Rey, Marta Vidal, Jorge Luis Abreu, Jack Landron, Joseph Jamrog, James Hunt.

SPANISH EYES (42). By Eduardo Ivan Lopez, translated by Graciela Lecube. May 9, 1990. Director, Roger Franklin; scenery, Robert Klingelhoefer; lighting, Bill Simmons; costumes, Mary Marsicano. With Eddie Andino, Jimmy Borbon, Edouard de Soto, Alexandra Reichler, Christofer de Oni.

**Quaigh Theater.** Primarily a playwrights' theater, devoted to the new playwright, the established contemporary playwright and the modern (post-1920) playwright. Will Lieberson, artistic director.

*Summer Reading Series*

UNTITLED evening of one-act plays by David Pownall. July 25, 1989.
GETTING TOGETHER by George Kreek. August 1, 1989.
KID OF MAN by Adam Kraar. August 9, 1989.
THE LAST APPOINTMENT by Dosortsev Vladlen.
SEPARATION by Tom Kempenski. August 22, 1989.
DEADLOCK by Edie Cope and Jim Barnhard. August 30, 1989.

BEFORE DAWN. By Terence Rattigan. August 29, 1989. Directed by Will Lieberson; with Elizabeth Karr, Eddie Lane, Lee Moore, Steven Colantti.

*Lunchtime Series*

A MATTER OF LIFE OR DEATH. By Carol Costa. August 21, 1989. Director, Kricker James. With John Otis, Alexander Manette, Alexandra Self, Sam Goodyear, Donna Davidge, Wilbur Edwin Henry, Mary Connally.

PICNIC BASKETS. By Art Kelly. September 11, 1989. Director, Patricia Wing Tobias. With Cornelia Mills, Tom Verica, Patricia Randell, Peter Gregory Thomson.

THE CONVERSATION OF THE TARANTULA. By Winifred V. Powers. October 23, 1989. Director, Harry Mahnken. With Winkie Powers, Bob Mahnken.

UPSTATE MOURNING. By Carol Holland. November 6, 1989. Director, Kricker James. With Hal Blankenship, Joan Jaffe, Amelia Romano, Rachel Stephens.

INSIDE A. By Bob Mahnken. November 21, 1989. Director, Scott Schneider. With Bruce Siegel, Linda Witzel.

BREAKING IN. By James McCartin. December 4, 1989. Director, James Keeler. With Willi Kirkham, David Charles.

SLUGGER BY MOONLIGHT. By Heide Arbitter. December 18, 1989. Driector, Kricker James. With McKee Anderson, Michael Decker, Scott Weil.

THE RESTAURANT and MAKE US BELIEVE IT. By Dan Greenburg. February 19, 1990. Director, Leigh Lawson. With Elizabeth Karr, Ivan Kronenfeld, Mark Shaw, David Konig, Jon Rubin, John Tucket, Ruth Callahan.

DRAMATHON '89 (one-act plays in marathon): BEULAH BALLENTINE by D. Lee Miller, directed by Stephanie Klapper; HEAR THE ANGELS' VOICES by Joseph Burby, directed by Robert Putnam; THE SON WHO HUNTED TIGERS IN JAKARTA by Ronald Ribman, directed by Joseph Levin; L 305 by Ralph Hunt, directed by Carol Gerber; INSIDE A by Bob Mahnken, directed by Scott Schneider; MAESTRO written and performed by Charles Gerber; BUILT TO LAST, HOLDING THE FAMILY TOGETHER and PLANNING AHEAD by Gary Carsel, directed by Sharon Mazer; STICK FIGURES by Ken Melamed, directed by Bill Zeleni; RED QUARTERS by D. Lee Miller, directed by Jeff Mausseau; THE CONVERSATION by Dale N. Wickleffe, directed by Charles Gemmill; CHRISTMAS ROBBERY written and directed by Louis M. Ponderoso; POWER PLAY by Peter Zablotsky, directed by Edward Saroskelsky; HOME BREW by Larry Cadman, directed by Deirdre Walsh; SOUTH FERRY written and directed by Will MacAdam; HOWARD AND LOIS written and directed by Alan Magill; IN ANSWER by Todd Jaime Stein, directed by Amy Hausman; PLACEBO by Andrew Vachss, directed by Brian Reich; SLUGGER BY MOONLIGHT by Heide Arbitter, directed by Kricker James; UGLY by Gary Carsel, directed by Sharon Mazer; STRESSED OUT by James DeMarse, directed by Alma Becker; LUNCH DATE written and directed by Todd Jaime Stein.

Also, THE THING'S THE PLAY by O. Henry, adapted and directed by Warren Kliewer; WELCOME TO THE MOON by John Patrick Shanley, directed by Carl Zeliger; THE DAMAGING EFFECTS OF LOVE written and directed by Louis M. Ponderoso; ESCAPE IN YOU written and directed by John Bale; BRUTES OUTSIDE THE BLUE ROOM written and directed by John Bale; THE TWELVE DAYS OF CHRISTMAS by Ora McBride Julie, directed by Gary Reed; ELEVATOR by Ora McBride Julie, directed by Gary Reed; THE FROZEN DEAD by Doug Mancheski, directed by Barbara Bregstein; THERE'S NO SUCH THING AS AN UNWANTED MILLIONAIRE by Abigail Quart, directed by Jason Rosenbaum; INNER REFLECTIONS OF AN ISLAND by Elizabeth Sordelet, directed by Rick Sordelet; 100 PERCENT ALL NATURAL by Claire M. Ressenger, directed by Chris Van Groningen; TALES OF THE

CENTRAL PARK WOODS written and directed by Peter Manos; FIVE SLICES OF STEELE by Donald Steele, directed by Charles Gerber; TICKET TO PLAINFIELD by Don Wollner, directed by Sam Schacht; HONEYMOON AT DEALEY PLAZA by Terry Krauser, directed by Todd Olson; WINSLOW BY THE SEA and REMINGTON NOTES written and directed by Bob Van Lindt; DIVISION: THE STRANGE CASE OF DR. JEKYLL & MR. HYDE RETOLD by Tom Szentgyorgyi, directed by Tracy Brigden; STRAGGLERS by Fran Pettinelli, directed by Nicola Sheara, BUMS by Robert Shaffron, adapted by John Behan, directed by Michael Griffith; HALL OF FAME by Joseph Hart, directed by Will Lieberson; ZACHARY by Geoffrey Knox, directed by Deirdre Walsh; A FISH STORY: AN AMERICAN SOAP OPERA by Peter Buchman, directed by Eliza Miller. December 30, 1989–January 1, 1990.

THE BENCH: NEW LISTINGS by Jane Stanton Hitchcock and ON THE BENCH by Carole Schweid (13). May 31, 1990. Director, Jeffrey Wolf; scenery, Chris Pickart; lighting, John Sellars. With Kristin Griffith, Pamela Moller, Robin Moseley, Karen Valentine.

**The Ridiculous Theatrical Company.** The late Charles Ludlam's comedic troupe devoted to productions of his original scripts and new adaptations of the classics. Everett Quinton, artistic director, Steve Asher, managing director.

BIG HOTEL. By Charles Ludlam. September 13, 1989. Director, Everett Quinton; scenery, Mark Beard; lighting, Richard Currie; costumes, Susan Young; music and sound, James S. Badrak, Alan Gregorie, Jan Bell. With Everett Quinton, Bryan Webster, Stephen Pell, Terence Mintern, Gary Mink, Bobby Reed, Sophie Maletsky, James Robert Lamb, Eureka, Christine Weiss, H.M. Koutoukas, Therese McIntyre.

DR. JEKYLL AND MR. HYDE (103). By Georg Osterman. November 10, 1989. Director, Kate Stafford; scenery, Mark Beard; lighting, Richard Currie; costumes, Susan Young; music and sound, James S. Badrak, Alan Gregorie and Jan Bell. With Terence Mintern, Eureka, Everett Quinton, Mary Neufeld, Georg Osterman, Minnette Coleman.

DER RING GOTT FARBLONJET (48). By Charles Ludlam. March 27, 1990. Director, Everett Quinton. With Adam MacAdam, H.M. Koutoukas, Jim Lamb, Sophie Maletsky, Stephen Pell, Bryan Webster, Mary Neufeld, Eureka, Everett Quinton, Ivory, Robert Lanier, Gary Mink, Bobby Reed, Jean-Claude Vasseux, Christine Weiss, Therese McIntyre.

**Second Stage Theater.** Committed to producing plays believed to deserve another look, as well as new works. Robyn Goodman, Carole Rothman, artistic directors.

SHIMMER (one-man show) (34). By and with John O'Keefe. July 10, 1989. Lighting, James Cave.

BABA GOYA. By Steve Tesich. December 5, 1989. Director, Harris Yulin. With Estelle Parsons, Jack Wallace, David Clarke, Patrick Breen, Martha Gehman, Ron Faber, Thom Sesma, Irving Metzman.

SQUARE ONE (56). By Steve Tesich. February 22, 1990. Director, Jerry Zaks; scenery, Tony Walton; lighting, Paul Gallo, costumes, Ann Roth. With Dianne Wiest, Richard Thomas. (Lizbeth Mackay replaced Dianne Wiest.)

WHAT A MAN WEIGHS (48). By Sherry Kramer. May 22, 1990. Director, Carole Rothman; scenery, Andrew Jackness; lighting, Dennis Parichy; costumes, Susan Hilferty. With Christine Estabrook, Harriet Harris, Katherine Hiler, Richard Cox.

**Soho Rep.** Dedicated to a new, non-naturalistic plays. Marlene Swartz, artistic director.

*24 performances each*

AMERICAN BAGPIPES. By Iain Heggie. December 3, 1989. Direction and scenery, Julian Webber; lighting, Donald Holder; costumes, Patricia Adshead. With Amelia White, Darcy Pulliam, Peter McRobbie, Simon Brooking.

LIMBO TALES. By Len Jenkin. January 26, 1990. Director, Thomas Babe; scenery, Stephen Olson; lighting, Greg MacPherson; costumes, Claudia Brown. With Leslie Lyles, Steve Hofvendahl (replaced by Steve Mellor), Scott Renderer; voices of Walter Bobbie, Reg E. Cathey, Crystal Field, Steve Hofvendahl, Jess Lynn, Jodie Markell, Bill Raymond.

**Theater for the New City.** Developmental theater and new American experimental works. George Bartenieff, Crystal Field, artistic directors.

*Schedule included:*

ROOKIE OF THE YEAR (13). Music, Christopher Cherney; lyrics and direction, Crystal Field. August 5, 1989. Scenery, Anthony Angel; costumes, Claire Cundiff, Laurie Graves, Jill Kincade; sound, Paul Garrity; masks, Myrna Duarte; animals, Jo Anne Basinger. With George Bartenieff, Crystal Field, Joseph C. Davies, Michael-David Gordon, George Liker, Mark Marcante, Margaret Miller, Rome Nela, Nan Wilson, Stan Winston.

ANULAH, LET THEM EAT CAKE. By Karen Williams and Mark Bradford. September 7, 1989. Direction and design, Karen Williams and Tom Andrews; music, Mickele Navazio and Tonny Prabowo; film, Peter von Ziegesar; video, Scott Anderson, Peter von Ziegesar. With Chutes and Ladders Theater Company (Arswendi Nasution, Fien Herman, Tom Andrews, Roderick Murray, Maria Sriningsih, Derrick McQueen, Karen Williams, Agus Tono).

ANTIGONA HURTADO ESGUERRA. Written and directed by Nelly Vivas. September 28, 1989.

SOUR SPRINGS. By John Jiler. October 5, 1989. Director, Stefano Loverso.

BODY GAME. By Roger Durling. October 5, 1989. Director, Eduardo Machado.

WATCHMAN. Written and directed by Bina Sharif. October 5, 1989.

MONSTER TIME. By Stephen DiLauro. November 2, 1989.

THIN AIR. Written and directed by Glyn Vincent. November 9, 1989. Scenery, Caroline Gerry; lighting, Jan Bael. With Rebecca Chace, Steven Cook, Rob Donaldson, Cecil Mackinnon, Alan Wynroth.

THE TROJAN WOMEN by Euripides, adapted by Robert Patrick. November 9, 1989.

THREE POETS: KOMACHI, HROSVITHA AND AKHMATOVA. Written and directed by Romulus Linney. November 16, 1989. Scenery and costumes, Anne C. Patterson; lighting, David Finley. With Adrienne Thompson, Kathleen Chalfant, Scott Sowers, John MacKay, Mary Foskett.

THE FOUNDATION. By Antonio Buero Vallejo, translated by Marion Peter Holt. December 21, 1989. Director, James Houghton; scenery, E. David Cosier Jr.; lighting, Amarntha Motte; costumes, Teresa Snider-Stein. With Thomas Nahrwold, Mark Schaller, Joyce O'Connor, John Woodson, Peter G. Morse, Sean O'Sullivan, Scott Sowers, Juff Sugerman, Bill Quinlan, Andrew Fetheroff.

SMOTHERING COALS. By Kay Osborne. December 21, 1989.

STEALTH (solo works). December 21, 1989. Directors, Sandy Mowbray-Clarke, Robert Landau. With Margo Lee Sherman.

BETTER PEOPLE. By Karen Malpede. January 25, 1990.

CARRION SISTERS AND THE VULGAR MOTHER. By Heidi Erica Herr. February 1, 1990.

'TILL THE EAGLE HOLLERS and SCRAP OF PAPER. By James Purdy. February 8, 1990. With Sheila Dabney, Crystal Field.

DOSE CENTER. By Michael Brodsky. February 15, 1990.

COYOLXUAHQUI: WOMAN WITHOUT BORDERS. Written and performed by Vira and Hortensia Colorado. February 16, 1990.

TWO CENTURIES. By Mario Fratti and Penelope Bradford. March 8, 1990. Director, Eve Collyer; scenery, Romy Phillips; lighting, Andrew Douglas; costumes, E.G. Widulski. With Roy Blum, Julie Whitney.

FEATURE FILM. By Bob Morris. March 15, 1990.

LOVE OF THE OPERETTA. By Jiri Schubert. March 29, 1990.

RELATED RETREATS. Written and directed by Eduardo Machado. April 5, 1990. Scenery, Donald Eastman; lighting, Stephen Quandt; costumes, E.G. Widulski. With Lisa Gluckin, Roger Durling, Ching Valdes-Aran, Kimberly Anne Ryan, John Finch, Ana K. Long.

WHITE BOYS CAN'T TAP. By Larry Myers. April 12, 1990.

MUSIC RESCUE SERVICE. By Sidney Goldfarb; music, Ellen Maddow. May 10, 1990. Director, Roger Babb. With The Talking Band.

ON THE ROAD TO WHOLENESS. By J. Lois Diamond. May 10, 1990. Director, Chris Mealey.

FUTURE TENSE. Works by Walter Corwin; music, Arthur Abrams. May 31, 1990. Director, Shep Pamplin.

**Theater Off Park.** Concentrates on producing and developing new plays or musicals and revivals of obscure works by well-known writers, with an emphasis on social consciousness. Albert Harris, artistic director, Joseph Piazza, managing director.

A QUIET END (28+). By Robin Swadow. May 29, 1990. Director, Tony Giordano; scenery, Philipp Jung; lighting, Dennis Parichy; costumes, David Murin. With Lonny Price, Philip Coccioletti, Rob Gomes, Paul Milikin, Jordan Mott.

VINEYARD THEATER—Julie Wilson in *Hannah . . .
1939*, a musical with book, music and lyrics by Bob Merrill

**The Vineyard Theater.** A multi-art chamber theater dedicated to the development of new plays and musicals, music-theater collaborations and innovative revivals. Douglas Aibel, artistic director, Barbara Zinn Krieger, executive director, Jon Nakagawa, managing director.

THE VALUE OF NAMES (39). By Jeffrey Sweet. June 1, 1989. Director, Gloria Muzio; scenery, William Barclay; lighting, Phil Monat; costumes, Jess Goldstein. With John Seitz, Ava Haddad, Stephen Pearlman.

FEAST HERE TONIGHT (musical) (30). Text, Ken Jenkins; music and lyrics, Daniel Jenkins. November 15, 1989. Director, Gloria Muzio; scenery, William Barclay; lighting, Phil Monat; costumes, Jess Goldstein. With Daniel Jenkins, Susan Glaze, Patrick Tovatt, Cass Morgan, Kenny Kosek, Don Brooks, Tom Hanway, Larry Cohen.

THE HOUSE OF HORROR (21). Written, directed and performed by Paul Zaloom. October 11, 1989. Scenery, Joseph John, Paul Zaloom; lighting, Lori A. Dawson; projections, Jan Hartley; slide photography, Paul Sharratt; puppet heads, Paul Zaloom.

MOVING TARGETS (33). By Joe Pintauro. January 18, 1990. Director, Andre Ernotte; scenery, William Barclay; lighting, Phil Monat; costumes, Juliet Polcsa. With Reed Birney, Ned Eisenberg, Ron Faber, Anita Gillette, Mary Mara.

HANNAH ... 1939 (46). Book, music and lyrics, Bob Merrill. May 31, 1990. Director, Douglas Aibel; choreography, Tina Paul; scenery, G.W. Mercier; lighting, Phil Monat; costumes, James Scott; musical director, Stephen Milbank. With Julie Wilson, Mark Ankeny, Leigh Beery, Yusef Bulos, Tony Carlin, Allan Heinberg, Leah Hocking, Paul Klementowicz, Kirk Lombard, Deirdre Lovejoy, Kathleen Mahoney-Bennett, Patti Perkins, Nicolette Salas, Mary Setrakian, Neva Small, Richard Thomsen, Lori Wilner.

**The Women's Project and Productions.** Nurtures, develops and produces plays written and, for the most part, directed by women. Julia Miles, founder and artistic director.

*13 performances each*

MILL FIRE. By Sally Nemeth. October 10, 1989. Director, David Petrarca. Scenery, Linda Buchanan; lighting, Robert Christen; costumes, Laura Cunningham. With Kate Buddeke, Kelly Coffield, Timothy Grimm, B.J. Jones, Jim Krag, Martha Lavey, Paul Mabon, Mary Ann Thebus, Jacqueline Williams.

VIOLENT PEACE. By Lavonne Mueller. February 20, 1990. Director, Bryna Wortman; scenery, James Noone; lighting, Victor En Yu Tan; costumes, Mimi Maxmen. With Dennis Parlato, Jenny Robertson.

TALES OF THE LOST FORMICANS. By Constance Congdon. April 17, 1990. Director, Gordon Edelstein; scenery, James Youmans; lighting, Anne Militello; costumes, Daniele Hollywood; music, Melissa Shiflett. With Michael Countryman, Noel Derecki, Lizbeth Mackay, Deidre O'Connell, Rosemary Prinz, Fred Sanders, Edward Seamon.

**WPA Theater.** Produces new American plays and neglected classics in the realistic idiom. Kyle Renick, artistic director, Edward T. Gianfrancesco, resident designer, Donna Lieberman, managing director.

THE GOOD COACH (28). By Ben Siegler. June 11, 1989. Director, Michael Bloom; scenery, Edward T. Gianfrancesco; lighting, Craig Evans; costumes, Deborah Shaw. With Tom Mardirosian, Richard Council, Mary Kane, Jace Alexander, Sal Barone, Bill Cwikowski, Kathryn Rossetter.

BUZZSAW BERKELEY (28). By Doug Wright; conceived by Christopher Ashley and Doug Wright; music and lyrics, Michael John LaChiusa. August 1, 1989. Director, Christopher Ashley; choreography, Joe Lanteri; scenery, Edward T. Gianfrancesco; lighting, Craig Evans; costumes, Don Newcomb. With Peter Bartlett, Shauna Hicks, Keith Reddin, John Hickok, Ethyl Eichelberger, Becky Gelke, Vicki Lewis.

HEAVEN ON EARTH (28). By Robert Schenkkan. October 24, 1989. Director, Mark Brokaw; scenery, Edward T. Gianfrancesco; lighting, Craig Evans; costumes, Ellen McCartney. With Jay O. Saunders, Helen Stenborg, Bobo Lewis, Steven Rodriguez, Arthur Hanket, Raynor Scheine.

TWENTY FINGERS, TWENTY TOES (31). Book, Michael Dansicker and Bob Nigro; music and lyrics, Michael Dansicker. December 19, 1989. Director, Bob Nigro; choreography, Ken Prescott; scenery, Edward T. Gianfrancesco; lighting, Craig Evans; costumes, Gregg Barnes; musical director, Dick Gallagher. With Jonathan Courie, Ann Brown, Maura Hanlon, Roxie Lucas, Paul Kandel, Ken Prymus.

STARTING MONDAY (34). By Anne Commire. March 20, 1990. Director, Zina Jasper; scenery, Edward T. Gianfrancesco; lighting, Craig Evans; costumes, Mimi Maxmen. With Pamela Wiggins, David Manis, Ellen Greene, Ilo Orleans, Patricia O'Connell, Paddy Croft, Susan Brenner, Pamela Tucker-White.

**York Theater Company.** Specializing in producing new works as well as in reviving great musicals. Janet Hayes Walker, producing director.

FRANKIE (20). Book by George Abbott, based on Mary Shelley's *Frankenstein*; music by Joseph Turrin; lyrics by Gloria Nissenson. October 6, 1989. Directors, George Abbott, Donald Saddler; scenery, James Morgan; lighting, Stuart Duke; costumes, Beba Shamash. With Richard White, Elizabeth Walsh, Ellia English, Gil Rogers, Casper Roos, Mark Zimmerman, Kim Moore, Howard Pinhasik, Ron Wisniski, Colleen Fitzpatrick.

TRAVELER IN THE DARK (16). By Marsha Norman. January 12, 1990. Director, D. Lynn Meyer; scenery, Joe Tilford; lighting, Mary Jo Dondlinger; costumes, Becky Senske. With Dennis Parlato, Lynn Ritchie, Jeffrey Landman, Jim Oyster.

THE GOLDEN APPLE. By John Latouche; music by Jerome Moross. March 23, 1990. Director, Charles Kondek. With Ann Brown, Mimi Wyche, Mary Stout, Cynthia Sophiea, Muriel Costa-Greenspon, Sylvia Rhyne, Gordon Stanley, Tim Warmen, Alan Souza, Glen Pannell, John Kozeluh, Bryan Batt, Tim Salce, Robert R. McCormick, Kelly Patterson, Kip Niven, Mary Phillips, Mary Lee Marson, Gina Todd, Jim Athens, Mitchel Kantor, Brent Winborn.

THE CHERRY ORCHARD. By Anton Chekhov; revised English version by Jean-Claude van Itallie. May 11, 1990. Director, Luke Yankee. With Paul Hecht, Corliss Preston, Michael Nostrand, Cynthia Nixon, Penny Fuller, Louise Roberts, David Canary, Merle Louise, Victor Raider-Wexler, Paul Schoeffler, Phillip Pruneau, Tim Loughrin, Scott Barton, Robert Warren.

# *Miscellaneous*

In the additional listing of 1989–90 off-off-Broadway productions below, the names of the producing groups or theaters appear in CAPITAL LETTERS and the titles of the works in *italics*. This list consists largely of new or reconstituted works and excludes most revivals, especially of classics. It includes a few productions staged by groups which rented space from the more established organizations listed previously.

ACTOR'S OUTLET. *Slay It With Music* (musical) book and lyrics by Michael Colby; music by Paul Katz. October 19, 1989. Directed by Charles Repole; with Susan Bernstein, J.P. Dougherty, Louisa Flaningam, Janet Metz, Virginia Sandifur, Barry Williams. *Deep to Center* by James O'Connor. January 18, 1990. Directed by Ken Lowstetter; with Howie Muir, Metty McKinley, Larry Filiaci, Lawrence Maxwell, John Barilla, Stephanie Silverman. *Black Medea* by Ernest Ferlita, based on Euripides. March 7, 1990. Directed by Ken Lowstetter; with Essene R, Simon Jutras, Kilian Ganly, John Steber, Lola Loui, Marie McKinney, Carolyn Webb, Mari Nobles-DaSilva.

ACTORS PLAYHOUSE. *Arrivederci Papa* by Richard Iorio, Tony Bondi and Sal Piro. June 7, 1989. With Tony Bondi, Philip McDowell, Razor Sharp, Anthony Linzalone, Thom Hansen, Richard Iorio, Vincent Bandille, Lou Valentino, Michael H. Pritchard, Tommy Phillips. *Best Friends* by John Voulgaris. August 10, 1989. Directed by Donald L. Brooks; with David Conaway, Chris A. Kelly.

ALCHEMY THEATER COMPANY. *Runyon on Wry* (one-acts). By Joseph Purdy and Gita Donovan; adapted from the Damon Runyon short stories *A Piece of Pie, The Melancholy Dane* and *Romance in the Roar-*

*ing Forties.* June 21, 1989. Directed by Linda Kay, Sam Howell, Gita Donovan; with Craig Bockhorn, Scott Bryant, Mark W. Conklin, Reid Davis, Vince DePaolo, Gita Donovan, Fern Dorsey, Wally Dunn, Sarah Eckhardt, Adam Grant, Michael Hill, Bill Lopatto.

ALLEY CAT PRODUCTIONS. *Beauty Marks* by Kim Merrill. September 21, 1989. Directed by Peter Askin; with Bernie Barrow, Elizabeth Lawrence.

AMERICAN JEWISH THEATER. *Call Me Ethel!* by Christopher Powich and Rita McKenzie. June 9, 1989. Directed by Christopher Powich; with Rita McKenzie. *The Puppetmaster of Lodz* by Gilles Segal, translated by Sara O'Connor. December 26, 1989. Directed by John Driver; with Ann Hillary, Sam Tsoutsouvas, Jay Rubenstein, Leo Rouvain, Ron Hunter. *The Rothschilds* (musical) book by Sherman Yellen, based on Frederic Morton's biography; music, Jerry Bock; lyrics, Sheldon Harnick. February 25, 1990. (Transferred to off Broadway; see its entry in the Plays Produced Off Broadway section of this volume.) *Made in Heaven!* by Edward Belling. May 7, 1990. Directed by Stanley Brechner; with Jack Aaron, Alexandra Gersten, Anita Keal, Bruce Nozick, Grace Roberts, Herbert Rubens, Stuart Zagnit.

APPLE CORPS THEATER. *The Passion of Narcisse Mondoux* by Gratien Gelinas, translated by Linda Garboriau and Gratien Gelinas. June 14, 1989. Directed by Peter Moss; with Huguette Oligny, Gratien Gelinas. *Adam and the Experts* by Victor Bumbalo. November 14, 1989. Directed by Nicholas Deutsch; with John Finch, Althea Lewis, Joseph Di Rocco, Benjamin Evett, John Seidman. *A Perfect Diamond* by Don Rifkin. May 24, 1990. Directed by Philip D. Giberson; with Michael Cullen, Paul O'Brien, Earl Whitted, Josh Mostel, Dennis Sook, Daryl Edwards, Milton Elliott, Iona Morris.

AVERY FISHER HALL. *Babes in Arms* book by Richard Rodgers and Lorenz Hart; music by Richard Rodgers; lyrics by Lorenz Hart (concert version). June 5, 1989. With Judy Blazer, Donna Kane, Judy Kaye, Gregg Edelman, Jason Graae, Adam Grupper.

BACA DOWNTOWN. *Imperceptible Mutabilities in the Third Kingdom* by Suzan-Lori Parks. September, 1989. Directed by Liz Diamond; with Peter Schmitz, Pamala Tyson, Jasper McGruder, Kenya Scott, Shona Tucker. *White Chocolate for My Father* written and directed by Laurie Carlos. February, 1990.

THE BALLROOM (cabaret). *Carried Away: Jeff Harnar Sings Comden and Green.* October 3, 1989. Michael Moriarty. February, 1990.

BARROW GROUP. *The Weather Outside* by Tom Donaghy. January 11, 1990. Directed by Leonard Foglia; with Seth Barrish, Lee Brock, Marcia DeBonis, Tom Farrell, Martha French, Lance Guest, Nate Harvey, Robert Jimenez, Michael Warren Powell, Raymond Anthony Thomas.

BEACON PROJECT. *Hyde Park* by James Shirley. November 3, 1989. Directed by Michael R. Fife; with Elizabeth Huffman, Stuart Laurence, Robert L. Rowe, Nancy Learmonth, Leah Cartmell. *Gogol* by Roderick O'Reilly. April 4, 1990. Directed by Stuart Laurence; with Anthony John Lizzul, Robert L. Rowe, Marc F. Nohe, Nancy Learmonth.

BEACON THEATER. *Shelly Garrett's Beauty Shop* written and directed by Shelly Garrett. March 5, 1990. With Teal Marchande, Mirage Micheaux, Steven Gamage, Judy Hardy.

BILLIE HOLIDAY THEATER. *Boochie* by Mari Evans and *Every Goodbye Ain't Gone* by Bill Harris. June, 1989. Directed by Mikell Pinkney; with Denise Burse-Mickelbury, Marcus Naylor, Gwendolyn Roberts-Frost. *Faith Journey.* January 9, 1990. Directed by Trazana Beverley; with Natalie Carter, Sonya DeSilva, Carl Hancock-Rux, Marque Mundy, Fred Owens, Trina Parks, Timothy Strong, Stephen J. Whitley, C'Esther L. Wooten, Rowland Wright (Believers Musical Theater production). *Halley's Comet* by and with John Amos. May 23, 1990.

BROOKLYN ACADEMY OF MUSIC. Next Wave Festival works included: *Empty Places* by and with Laurie Anderson; *Stuff as Dreams Are Made On* by and with Fred Curchack, based on Shakespeare's *The Tempest.* October 3–December 3, 1989.

CITY CENTER THEATER STUDIO III. *The Critic: The Fun I've Had* by Ward Morehouse III. November 2, 1989. Directed by Will Lieberson; with Sean O'Sullivan.

CRITERION CENTER (cabaret). *Christopher Durang & Dawne.* September 26, 1989.

CUBICULO. *Dorian Gray* book and lyrics by Joseph Bravaco, music by Robert Cioffi, based on the Oscar Wilde novel. April 5, 1990. Directed by Joseph Bravaco; with Doug Welty, Danette Blitz, Celeste Goch,

Michael Griffo, Ann Leenay, Nick Locilento, Philip McDowell, Stephen Newport, Lillian Piro, Gary Reed, Linda Owen Sager, Chris Tomaine, Marie Vitalo, Margaret Wehrle.

CUCARACHA THEATER. *Indian Dog* by Jeffrey Klayman. September 14, 1989. Directed by Mervyn Willis; with Glen M. Santiago, David Simonds, Elizabeth Thompson, Kathryn Atwood, Damian Young, David Phillips. *Tiny Dimes* written and directed by Peter Mattei. February 23, 1990. With Joey L. Golden, Lauren Hamilton, Hugh Palmer, Elizabeth Thompson, Damian Young, Brennan Murphy. *Rodents and Radios* written and directed by Richard Caliban. April 19, 1990. With Damian Young, Sharon Brady, Mollie O'Mara, Glen M. Santiago, Lauren Hamilton.

DANCE THEATER WORKSHOP. *The Story of Kufur Shamma* by Jackie Lubeck and Francois Abu Salem. July 26, 1989. Directed by Francois Abu Salem; with Nabil El-Hajjar, Amer Khalil, Jackie Lubeck, Edward Muallem, Iman Aoun, Akram Tallawi.

THE DIRECTOR'S COMPANY. *White Collar.* By Peter B. Hedges. April 27, 1990. Directed by Terry Dudley; with Sarah Brogaw, Drew Eliot, Arthur Hanket, Brian Kurlander, Matthew Lewis, Helen March, Sussanne Marley.

EIGHTY-EIGHT'S (cabaret). Cy Coleman. January 6, 1990.

EQUITY LIBRARY THEATER. *Wonderful Town* (musical) book by Joseph Fields and Jerome Chodorov, based on their play, *My Sister Eileen,* from Ruth McKenney's stories; music by Leonard Bernstein; lyrics by Betty Comden and Adolph Green. September 28, 1989. Directed by Adrienne Weiss; with Stacey Logan, Colette Kilroy, Allen Fitzpatrick.

GENE FRANKEL THEATER. *Carreno* (one-woman show) created by Pamela Ross and Gene Frankel. October 12, 1990. Directed by Gene Frankel; with Pamela Ross.

THE GLINES. *The Quintessential Image* by Jane Chambers and *In Her Own Words (A Portrait of Jane)* compiled by John Glines from Jane Chambers's writings. July 14, 1989. Directed by Peg Murray; with Rochelle DuBoff, Ruth Kulerman, Mary Kay Adams, Shelley Conger, Judy Tate.

HECKSCHER THEATER. *Mama, I Want to Sing, Part II* (musical) book and lyrics by Vy Higginsen and Ken Wydro; music by Wesley Naylor. March 25, 1990. Directed by Ken Wydro; with D'Atra Hicks, Norwood, Doris Troy, Kathleen Murphy-Palmer, Charles Stewart, Knoelle Higginsen-Wydro, Vy Higginsen.

HENRY STREET SETTLEMENT. *Spirit Time* by Wilfred Carey, adapted by Lumengo Jay Hooks. July 7, 1989. Directed by Meachie Jones; with Lumengo Jay Hooks, Kathy Smith, Stephen Hooks. *An Evening with Hazelle.* December 1, 1989. Directed by Dudley Findlay Jr.; with Hazelle Goodman.

HOME FOR CONTEMPORARY THEATER. *The Year of the Baby* by Quincy Long. August 11, 1989. Directed by Joumana Rizk; with Quincy Long, Kathleen Dimmick, Viki Boyle, Patrick Kerr, Edward Baran, Verna Hampton. *II Samuel 11, Etc.* written and directed by David Greenspan. October, 1989. With Ron Bagden, Mary Shultz. *New Anatomies* by Timberlake Wertenbaker. February 14, 1990. Directed by Melia Bensussen; with Colette Kilroy, Alison Stair Neet, Kate Fuglei, Ching Valdes-Aran, Regina Taylor.

THE HUMAN THEATER COMPANY. *Owl's Breath* written and directed by Nathaniel Kahn. October, 1989.

IRISH ARTS CENTER. *Away Alone* by Janet Noble. December 4, 1989. Directed by Terence Lamude; with Michael Healy, Anto Nolan, Barry O'Rourke, Don Creedon, Cora Murray, Bronagh Murphy.

IRISH REPERTORY THEATER COMPANY. *A Whistle in the Dark* by Tom Murphy. November 16, 1989. Directed by Charlotte Moore; with Chris A. Kelly, Ciaran O'Reilly, Ron Bottitta, Jean Parker, Denis O'Neill, Maurice Sheehan, W.B. Brydon, Patrick Fitzgerald. *All That Fall* by Samuel Beckett.

JEAN COCTEAU REPERTORY. *The Importance of Being Earnest* by Oscar Wilde. September 8, 1989. Directed by Robert Perillo; with Christopher Oden, Robert Ierardi, Joseph Menino, Carol Dearman, Lyn Wright, Zenon Zelenich, Harris Berlinsky, Angela Vitale. *Travesties* by Tom Stoppard. October 6, 1989. Directed by Robert Hupp; with Harris Berlinsky, Christopher Oden, Joseph Menino, Robert Ierardi, Carol Dearman, Lyn Wright. *Life Is a Dream* by Calderon de la Barca, translated by Roy Campbell. November 16, 1989. Directed by Eve Adamson; with Craig Smith, Harris Berlinsky, Robert Ierardi, Elise Stone, James Sterling, Angela Vitale, Joseph Menino. *A Man's a Man* by Bertolt Brecht, translated by Eric Bentley. January 25, 1990. Directed by Robert Hupp; with Joseph Menino, Craig Smith, Elise Stone, Lyn Wright.

*The Prince of Homburg* by Heinrich von Kleist, translated by Douglas Langworthy. March, 1990. Directed by David Herskovits; with James Sterling, Joseph Menino, Christopher Oden, Angela Vitale, Craig Smith.

JEWISH REPERTORY THEATER. *Double Blessing* by Brenda Shoshanna Lukeman. June 29, 1989. Directed by Edward M. Cohen; with Rosalind Harris, Helen Greenberg, Victor Raider-Wexler, Mark Ethan. *The Witch* based on Abraham Goldfaden's musical; book adapted and lyrics by Amielle Zemach, conceived and directed by Benjamin Zemach; additional music by Max Helfman, Lori McKelvey and Henoch Cohn; additional lyrics by Itzik Manger and Dennis Perman; with Emily Loesser, Anna Bess Lank, Avery Saltzman, Daniel Neiden. *The Return* by Frederic Glover. January 4, 1990. Directed by Michael Bloom; with Dominic Chianese, Joseph Ragno, Annie Korzen, Bruce Nozick, Jennifer Sternberg; *Dividends* by Gary Richards. March 1, 1990. Directed by Tony Giordano; with James Rutigliano, Reizl Bozyk, Fyvush Finkel. *New York 1937* by Jose Yglesias. April 26, 1990. Directed by Charles Maryan; with Antonia Rey, Joseph Palmas, Michael Egan, Ann Dowd.

JUDITH ANDERSON THEATER. *The Pixie Led* by Christopher Harris. July 20, 1989. Directed by Julian Richards; with John Wylie, Amanda Boxer, Steven Crossley. *The Dreams of Clytemnestra* by Dacia Maraini. September 19, 1989. Directed by Greg Johnson. *Carbondale Dreams: Bradley and Beth* (in repertory) by Steven Sater. November, 1989. Directed by Byam Stevens; with Jeff Bender, Deanna Du Clos, Anita Keal, James Lish, James Maxson, Navida Stein, Cheryl Thornton, Robert Trumbull. *Arnold* by Steven Sater. (Joined repertory December 26, 1989). Directed by Byam Stevens; with Richard Thomsen, Anita Keal, James Lish, Bob Ari, Cheryl Thornton, Jeffrey Bender, Navida Stein, Fabiana Furgal.

JUDSON MEMORIAL CHURCH. *The Journey of Snow White* (opera) by Al Carmines. May 10, 1990. Directed by Russell Treyz.

THE KITCHEN. *Everything That Rises Must Converge* by John Jesurun. *We Keep Our Victims Ready* by and with Karen Finley. April, 1990.

SOUTH STREET THEATER—Kathryn Meisle and Katherine Leask in a scene from *Cahoots* by Rick Johnston

LAMB'S THEATER. *All God's Dangers* by Theodore Rosengarten, Michael Hadley and Jennifer Hadley from a book by Theodore Rosengarten. October 22, 1989. Directed by William Partlan, with Cleavon Little.

LINCOLN CENTER. *Serious Fun!* schedule included *The Fall of the House of Usher* (chamber opera) by Philip Glass and Arthur Yorinks, based on Edgar Allan Poe's story, directed by Richard Foreman; *Terrors of Pleasure: The Uncut Version* by and with Spalding Gray; *Objects of Desire*, performances by Stuart Sherman, Dancenoise, Paul Zaloom, Danny Mydlack; *Oral Fixations*, with Reno, Tom Caylor, John O'Keefe, Michael Peppe; *An American Chorus* by and with Eric Bogosian. July 14–August 3, 1989. Lincoln Center Out-of-Doors schedule included *Angels: Visions and Apparitions* by David Borden, directed by Neely Bruce; Clown Theater Day; First Annual All-American Juggle-In. August 1-27, 1989.

LIVING THEATER. *The Tablets* by Armand Schwerner, adapted and directed by Hanon Reznikov. June, 1989. With George McGrath, Alan Arenius, Amber, Elena Jandova, Henry Freeman, Jerry Goralnick, Laura Kolb, Lois Kagan Mingus, Michael St. Clair, Nina Zivancevic, Pat Russell, Sheila Dabney, Thomas Walker, Willie C. Barnes. *I & I* by Else Lasker-Schuler. September, 1989. Directed by Judith Malina; with Alan Arenius, Carlo Altomarem, Elena Jandova, Gary Brackett, Ilion Troya, Initia, Jerry Goralnick, Joanie Fritz, Laura Kolb, Laurence Frommer, Lilian Jenkins, Lois Kagan, Lola Ross, Michael Saint Clair, Philip Brehse, Rain House, Robert Projansky, Sander Van Dam, Sheila Dabney, Thomas Walker, Tim Wright, Victoria Murphy, Willie C. Barnes.

NAT HORNE THEATER. *Canterbury Tales* by Geoffrey Chaucer, adapted by Phil Woodworth. June 23, 1989. Directed by Yvonne Opffer; with Kate Britton, Michael A. Healy, Alexia Kadilis, Benjamin Miller, Alexandra Jones. *Once/Twice* adaptation, music and lyrics by Paul Dick. January, 1990. Directed by Jack Horner.

NEW ARTS THEATER CO. *Apocalyptic Butterflies* by Wendy MacLeod. June 6, 1989. Directed by Marcus Stern; with Colette Kilroy, Greg Germann, Susan Knight, Marylouise Burke, Matthew Lewis. *Beauty Marks* by Kim Merrill. September 21, 1989. Directed by Peter Askin; with Bernie Barrow, Elizabeth Lawrence, Kim Merrill, Colleen Quinn.

NEW THEATER OF BROOKLYN. *Jacques and His Master* by Milan Kundera, translated by Simon Callow. October 26, 1989. Directed by Deborah J. Pope; with Ray Virta, Gregory Salata, Monica Merryman. *Rain. Some Fish. No Elephants.* by Y York. April 26, 1990. Directed by Mark Lutwak; with Angela Pietropinto, Leon Addison Brown, Alice Haining, Julia Glander, Tim Halligan, Arabella Field. *Rough Crossing* by Tom Stoppard, adapted from Ferenc Molnar's *The Play's the Thing*.

NEW YORK GILBERT AND SULLIVAN PLAYERS. *The Gondoliers*. December 21, 1989. Directed by Albert Bergeret; with Todd Murray, Shawn Churchman, Cynthia Reynolds, Katie Geissinger, Joy Hermalyn, Del-Bouree Bach, Keith Jurosko. *The Pirates of Penzance*. January 10, 1990. *Of Thee I Sing* (musical) book by George S. Kaufman and Morrie Ryskind; music by George Gershwin; lyrics by Ira Gershwin. March 29, 1990. Directed by Kristin Garver; with Del-Bouree Bach, Keith Jurosko, Kate Egan, Jayne Lynch, Alan Lane.

OHIO THEATER. Tweed (Theater Works: Emerging Experimental Directions) New Works Festival. Schedule included: *The Blue Piano* by Tom Judson; *Pornsongspiel* by Kevin Malony. May 31, 1990.

PEARL THEATER COMPANY. *A Midsummer Night's Dream* by William Shakespeare. October 7, 1989. Directed by Shepard Sobel; with Frank Geraci, Robin Leslie Brown, Donnah Welby, Joanne Camp, Laura Rathgeb, James Nugent. *The Three Sisters* by Anton Chekhov, translated by Earle Edgerton. November 11, 1989. Directed by Allan Carlsen; with Joanne Camp, Donnah Welby, Robin Leslie Brown, Frank Geraci, Joseph Warren, Michael John McGuinness, Laura Rathgeb. *The School for Wives* by Molière, translated by Earle Edgerton. December 16, 1989. Directed by Joel Bernstein; with James Nugent, Stuart Lerch, Kevin Hogan, Robin Leslie Brown, Miller Lide. *The Importance of Being Earnest* by Oscar Wilde. February 24, 1990. Directed by Anthony Cornish; with Michael John McGuinness, Donnah Welby, Stuart Lerch, Laura Rathgeb, Margaret Hilton.

PERFORMANCE SPACE 122. *Herd of Buffalo* written and directed by Ethyl Eichelberger. June, 1989. With Ethyl Eichelberger, Jonathan Baker, Helen Shumaker, Gerard Little, Katy Dierlam, Joan Moossy. *True Stories* (one-woman show) by and with Penny Arcade (Susana Ventura). August, 1989. *Terminal Hip* written and directed by Mac Wellman. December, 1989. With Stephen Mellor. 5th annual Veselka Festival. Schedule included: *Lost and Found in America: Some of the Stories* by Celeste Miller; *Stretch Marks* by Tim Miller; *Women Preachers* by Peggy Pettit; *Cobra* by John Zorn. May, 1990.

PLAYHOUSE 91. *A Bronx Tale* by and with Chazz Palminteri. October 18, 1989. Directed by Mark W. Travis.

PLAYWRIGHTS PREVIEW PRODUCTIONS. *Homesick* by Danny Cahill. March 1, 1990. Directed by Bruce Lumpkin; with Michael Santoro, Paul Doherty, Marcia De Bonis, Georgia Bennett, David Dawson, Claudia Gold.

PRIMARY STAGES COMPANY. *Hollywood Scheherazade* by Charlie Peters. September 17, 1989. Directed by Gregory Lehane; with Michael Keck, Daniel Ahearn, Herbert Rubens. *Black Market* by Joe Sutton. November 22, 1989. Directed by Scott Rubsam; with Elaine Rinehart, Bruce McCarty, Charlotte Colavin, Christopher McCann. *Bovver Boys* by Willy Holtzman. February 18, 1990. Directed by John Pynchon Holms; with Calista Flockhart, Jack Gwaltney, Holt McCallany, Robert Kerbeck.

PRODUCERS CLUB. *Everybody Knows Your Name* by Ed Cachianes. May 31, 1990. Directed by John Albano; with John Finch, Robert Zukerman.

RAFT THEATER. *Simon Says ...* by Joseph James. June 1, 1989. Directed by Jeff Mousseau. *By and for Havel: Audience* by Vaclav Havel and *Catastrophe* by Samuel Beckett. March 8, 1990. Directed by Vasek Simek; with Kevin O'Connor, Lou Brockway, Evelyn Tuths.

RAINBOW AND STARS (cabaret). Phyllis Newman. August 15, 1989.

RIVERSIDE SHAKESPEARE COMPANY. *Cyrano de Bergerac* by Edmond Rostand, translated by Brian Hooker. June 30, 1989. Directed by Robert Mooney and Timothy W. Oman; with Frank Muller, Susan Pellegrino, Weston Blakesley, Daniel Timothy Johnson, Robert Sedgwick. *Bard-a-thon IV* (staged readings). September 29–October 8, 1989. *Siren Tears* by Veronica Francis, based on Shakespeare's sonnets. November 3, 1989. With Veronica Francis, Jeffrey Green.

RIVERSIDE THEATER. *The Aching Heart of Samuel Kleinerman* by Marion Andre. August 28, 1989. Directed by Donald Hampton; with Michael Colliere, J.D. Daniels, Kristin Norton, J.T. Phillips. *Women of Manhattan* by John Patrick Shanley. October 12, 1989. Directed by John Eisner; with Leslie Block, Jennifer Dorr White, Pamela Wiggins, Kevin Davis, John Heath Stewart. *Out to Lunch* by George Rattner. November 9, 1989. Directed by Sue Lawless; with David Bailey, Richard Bell, Jonathan Bustle, Chet Carlin, Carolyn Casenave, Mark Hofmaier, Patricia Hunter, Liz Otto, Jack Schmidt, Gavin Troster, Rene Tywang. (Co-produced with CHS Productions.) *The Fabulous LaFontaine* by Owen S. Rackleff; music adapted by Dennis Deal from Saint-Saens' "Carnival of the Animals." February 1, 1990. With Maurice Edwards, Colby Thomas. *Riverman* by Sam Dowling. May 21, 1990. Director, Anne DeMare; with Dave Burland, Timothy Lane, Nina F. Minton, Barbara Schofield, Paul Todaro, Frederick Zimmer, Christine Zito. In repertory with *Troubador* book by Bert Dreisel and John Martin, music by Bert Dreisel, lyrics by John Martin. May 22, 1990. Director, John Margulies; with Keith Brian Clark, Sibel Ergener, Daniel T. Johnson, Drew Kelly, Evan Matthews, Christopher Mellon, Paul Romanello, Thomas Tomasovic.

SAGE THEATER COMPANY. *God's Policemen* by Richard Lay. October 13, 1989. Directed by Judy Strawn; with Derek Conte, Dennis Dooley, Bonnie Haagenbuch, Angie Kristic, Victoria Taylor, Lynn Guberman, Helen Abrams, Chris Monte.

SAN FRANCISCO MIME TROUPE. *Seeing Double* by Sinai Peter, Joan Holden, Emily Shihadeh, Jody Hirsh, Henri Picciotto, Nabil al-Hadithy, Isa Nidal Totah, Harvey Varga, Arthur Holden and Nidal Nazzal; music by Bruce Bathol, Randy Craig and Dan Hart; lyrics by Bruce Bathol, Randy Craig and Isa Nidal Totah. November, 1989. Directed by Daniel Chumley. With Keiko Shimosato, Jeri Lynn Cohen, Harry Rothman, Ed Holmes, Michael Sullivan, Rebecca Klingler, Warren Sata, Isa Nidal Totah, Elliot Kavee, Dan Hart.

SOUTH STREET THEATER. *Real Family* by Harvey Huddleston. June 2, 1989. Directed by Richard Lichte. *The People Who Could Fly* written and directed by Joe Hart. August 2, 1989. With Rich Bianco, Heide Brehm, Michael Calderone, Caprice Cosgrove, John Dimaggio, Jacqueline Gregg, Jennifer Krasnansky, Christopher Pettit, Anne Shapiro, Steve Siegler, Kristina Swedlund, Scott Wasser. *Magical Circles* by Carmen Moore. December, 1989. With Skymusic Ensemble. *Cahoots* by Rick Johnston. March 4, 1990. Directed by David Taylor; with Kathryn Meisle, Katherine Leask, Malachy Cleary, James DeMarse, John Hickey.

STEPPIN' OUT REPERTORY. *Twilight Tales II* (two programs of one-acts): Program A, *Heart of the South* directed by Erica Gould, *Don't Touch That Dial* directed by Steven Helgoth, *Girl Talk* directed by Patricia Cucco; with Laurie Sanders-Smith, Maria Jessop, Margaret Weber, David Gill, John Durant, Dominic

Dellaporte, Karen Wimmer, Stacey Polacco, Mitch Rund, Richard Nahem, Mark Dempsey, Greg Kinsey. Program B, *Mirror Image* directed by Patricia Cucco, *The Keeper* directed by Erica Gould, *Time Traveler* directed by Dan McKereghan; with Kim Basset, Erika Cohen, Dennis Dooley, Julian Baron, Richard Rodgers, Mimi Stuart, Pip N. Smits, Dominique Debroux, Kristin Charney, Stephen Haproff, Michelle Defranco, Julie Mermelstein, John Durant, Julie A. Lynch, Scot Pacheco.

STEVE MCGRAW'S (cabaret). *Forever Plaid* (musical revue) by Stuart Ross. November, 1989. With Stan Chandler, Guy Stroman, Gabriel Barre, Jason Graae. (Reopened May 15, 1990.)

THEATER FOR A NEW AUDIENCE. *The Red Sneaks* (musical) written and directed by Elizabeth Swados, based on *The Red Shoes*. June 28, 1989. With Shawn Benjamin, James Sheffield-Dewees, Dedre Guevara, Kenny Lund, Raquel Richard, Valerie Evering, Donald (Shun) Faison, Teresina Sullo. (Reopened May 19, 1990.)

THETA THEATER COMPANY. *Orient Beach* by Donald Kvares. July 7, 1989. Directed by Anthony Spina; with Deborah Alexander, Gisella Bruckner, Michael Philip Del Rio, Paul Dommermuth, Lori Marcusson.

TIME AND SPACE LIMITED. *Little Stumps: The Deal* by Linda Mussman. March, 1990. With Claudia Bruce.

TRG PRODUCTIONS. *The First Time* (musical) book and lyrics by Dan Clancy; music by Lynn Portas. April 11, 1990. Directed by Marvin Kahan; with Jill Corey, Maureen McNamara, Tim Pinckney, Dale Sandish, Michael Shelle, Joan Smyth.

TRIANGLE THEATER COMPANY. *In Pursuit of the Song of Hydrogen* by Tom Dunn. November 25, 1989. Directed by Michael Ramach; with Fred Burrell, Peter Guttmacher, Cynthia Hayden, Woody Sempliner, Abby Dylan. *Ahead of the Hitter* by Anthony Salerno. April 19, 1990. Directed by Lou Jacob; with Thomas Martell Brimm, Tom Fervoy, Noble Lee Lester, Lori Shearer.

UBU REPERTORY. *Abel and Bela* and *Architruc* by Robert Pinget, translated by Barbara Wright and Barbara Bray. September 19, 1989. Directed by Nicholas Kepros; with Robert Burke, Peter Mackenzie, Tom Lacy, Jarlath Conroy. *Your Handsome Captain* by Simone Schwartz-Bart, translated by Jessica Harris and Catherine Temerson. October 29, 1989. Directed by Francoise Kourilsky; with Reg E. Cathey, Sharon McGruder.

VIETNAM VETERANS ENSEMBLE THEATER COMPANY. *The Ambassador* by Slawomir Mrozek, translated by Ralph Manheim and Slawomir Mrozek. October 15, 1989. Directed by Mac Ewing; with David Adamson, Anthony Chisholm, Sharon Ernster, James Gleason, Michael Manetta. *The Strike* by Rod Serling. January 24, 1990. Directed by Thomas Bird; with David Adamson, Anthony Chisholm, Ralph DeMatthews, Russ Ericson, Stephen Lee, Michael Manetta, Brian Markinson, Sean Michael Rice, Ray Robertson, Tucker Smallwood, Matt Tomasino, Jim Tracy.

WESTBETH THEATER. *The Writing on the Wall* by Seth Zvi Rosenfeld. February 12, 1990. Directed by Juda Youngstrom assisted by Roger Mrazek; with Jason Andrews, Tai Bennett, Paul Geier, Michael Imperioli, Amy-Lynn Rosenfeld, Fabio Urena. *Cities Out of Print* written and directed by Susan Mosakowski. March, 1990. With Matthew Maguire, Susan Mosakowski.

WESTBETH THEATER CABARET. *The Cardigans ... Those Swingin' Singin' Guys from Alpha Mu Phi Pi* conceived by Rick Lewis. November 10, 1989. With Brad Carpenter, Steve Fickinger, Brian Hurst, Ray Willis.

THE WOOSTER GROUP. *Frank Dell's Temptation of St. Anthony* (Part 3 of the trilogy *The Road to Immortality*). September 9, 1989. With Ron Vawter, Valerie Charles, Anna Kohler, Payton Smith, Michael Stumm, Jeff Webster, Kate Valk. *Lava* written and directed by Richard Foreman. December 5, 1989. With Neil Bradley, Matthew Courtney, Peter Davis, Kyle DeCamp, Hiedi Tradewell, Richard Foreman. (Co-produced by Ontological-Hysteric Theater.)

WORKING THEATER. Working One-Acts '89: *The Closer* by Will Holtzman, directed by R.J. Cutler; *Floor Above the Roof* by Daniel Therriault, directed by John Pynchon Holms; *Freeze Tag* by Jackie Reingold, directed by Evan Handler; *Sand Mountain Matchmaking* written and directed by Romulus Linney. June 9, 1989. *Special Interests* by Joe Sutton. February 7, 1990. Directed by Mark Lutwak; with Jude Ciccolella, Judith Granite, James DuMont, Lynn Anderson, Robert Arcaro, Lorey Hayes.

# THE SEASON
# AROUND
# THE UNITED STATES

O
O
O

# OUTSTANDING NEW PLAYS CITED BY AMERICAN THEATER CRITICS ASSOCIATION

*and*

# A DIRECTORY OF NEW-PLAY PRODUCTIONS

O
O
O

THE American Theater Critics Association (ATCA) is the organization of 250 leading drama critics in all media in all sections of the United States. One of this group's stated purposes is "To increase public awareness of the theater as a *national* resource" (italics ours). To this end, ATCA has cited three outstanding new plays produced this season around the country, to be represented in our coverage of The Season Around the United States by excerpts from each of their scripts demonstrating literary style and quality. And one of these—2 by Romulus Linney—was designated the first-place play and received the fourth annual ATCA New Play Award of $1,000.

The process for selection of these outstanding plays is as follows: any ATCA member critic may nominate a play if it has been given a production in a professional house. It must be a finished play given a full production (not a reading or an airing as a play-in-progress). Nominated scripts were studied and discussed by an ATCA play-reading committee chaired by T.H. McCulloh of the Los Angeles *Times* and comprising Jeffrey Borak of the *Berkshire Eagle*, Richard Christiansen of the Chicago *Herald*, Ann Holmes of the Houston *Chronicle*, Damien Jaques of the Milwaukee *Journal*, Dan Sullivan of the Los Angeles *Times* and Bernard Weiner of the San Francisco *Chronicle*. The committee members made their choices on the basis of script rather than production, thus placing very much the same emphasis as the editors of this volume in making the New York Best Play selections. There were no eligibility requirements except that a nominee be the first full professional production of a new work outside New York City within this volume's time frame of June 1, 1989 to May 31, 1990. If the timing of nominations and opening prevented some works from being considered this year, they will be eligible for consideration next year if they haven't since moved on to New York production. We offer our sincerest thanks and admiration to the ATCA members and their committee for the valuable insight into the 1989–90 theater season around the United States which their selections provide for this *Best Plays* record, in the form of the following excerpts from outstanding scripts illustrating their style and the nature of their content, with brief introductions provided by T.H. McCulloh (2), Bernard Weiner (*Pick Up Ax*) and Jonathan Abarbanel (*Marvin's Room*).

# Cited by American Theater Critics as Outstanding New Plays of 1989–90

## 2

### A Play in Two Acts

### BY ROMULUS LINNEY

Cast and credits appear on page 520

*2*: Only a playwright of the rich imagination of Romulus Linney could take a subject, a theme, that has been thoroughly covered before dramatically, and give it a new twist, a different theatrical identity. In his play *2*, commissioned by and produced at Actors Theater of Louisville, Linney examines with empathy, humor and great wit—and his usual depth of understanding of the human condition—the character of Hermann Goering during the Nuremberg war crimes trials of 1945–46.

Linney makes no apologies for Goering's reasoning—he allows Goering that privilege—but gives him an opportunity to seek out the self-deception that guided him, in the hearts and minds of all men who set out to change the map of the world. Linney also lets Goering examine Nazi prejudices and compare them with those existing in every country. *2* forces us to study ourselves more deeply.

In a preliminary meeting with his decidedly unfriendly Counsel, Goering is genuinely shocked at some of the Tribunal's accusations, enumerated by his opponent:

GOERING:  Me?  Exterminate Jews?

COUNSEL:  I think they may accuse you of that, yes.

GOERING:  What could be more grotesque or untrue?  I did everything I could for the Jews.  So did my wife.  Actor after actor from her old theater days we got out.  And many others.  Let me tell you—

COUNSEL:  None of that matters.

GOERING:  I WAS SPEAKING TO YOU!

COUNSEL:  And talking nonsense!  You wrote the Nuremberg Laws that stripped them of citizenship.  *You* were what the Jews ran away from!

GOERING (*pause*):  My dear man, I beg your pardon.  Please proceed, as you think best.

COUNSEL:  One.  Crimes Against Peace.  Here you can defend yourself. You simply restored a country to prosperity, under the legal orders of a Chancellor.  Just don't brag about it.

GOERING:  But of course I am going to brag about it.  I am proud of what I did.

COUNSEL:  I wouldn't put it quite like that, if I were you.  You will be asked if you created the Gestapo.

GOERING:  What does that have to do with crimes against peace?

COUNSEL:  Hostages, reprisals, conspiracies, infiltration of other countries, murder.

GOERING:  Every country has a Gestapo.  I established ours, then did more important work.  It ran itself, until Himmler got it in 1934.

COUNSEL:  You will be asked if you created the Air Force.

GOERING:  As Germany's greatest flier who else—

COUNSEL:  Bombing civilians, machine gunning evacuees, and so on. Wanton destruction.

GOERING:  Wanton destruction?  Me?

COUNSEL:  Yes, Defendant, you.

GOERING:  Britain's Dresden?  America's atom bomb?  The Russians?

COUNSEL:  No accusations against Great Britain, Russia or the United States are to be admitted as testimony.

GOERING:  *What?*

COUNSEL:  Two.  War Crimes.

GOERING:  Absolutely not guilty!  Never!

COUNSEL:  Prisoners of war?

GOERING:  Yes, some prisoners were shot, I know it happened, but I did not do it, and no genuine document will say I did!  Now, Himmler, I don't know.

COUNSEL: I thought we weren't shifting blame.

GOERING: To subordinates. Himmler was no subordinate of mine, no matter what it looked like. Listen. When Adolf Hitler gave somebody something to do, he gave somebody else the same thing to do, so they would fight each other for his approval. That is the way he kept control of his staff. So I hated Goebbels, and he hated me, and we both hated Himmler, and everybody hated Bormann, and so on.

COUNSEL: It was really that simple for Hitler to control the leaders of the Reich?

GOERING: He did it in other ways, too. He had a photographic memory. Purely mechanical. He could recall how many ball bearings were packed into a crate twenty years ago in May. Not June, May. He ridiculed everyone that way. Generals, ministers, me, everyone. He knew. You didn't.

COUNSEL: Tell the tribunal that!

GOERING: Never. That's all about Hitler. I will not hide behind him. The truth is, I was his war hero, who stood up to Hindenburg for him. I made him Chancellor. But whenever he looked at me, my heart jumped out of my chest. I was his, get used to it. Any order I signed I am responsible for, no matter what. Period.

COUNSEL: Very well. Plunder?

GOERING: Of course I plundered. I stripped Europe of everything we needed to win the war!

COUNSEL: Paintings? Statues? Altarpieces? Tapestries? To win the war?

GOERING: All right, art collections. Everything was bought. Bills of sale exist for each transaction. I paid a fortune for a collection of art that would bear my name and be left to the German people! Hitler did the same.

COUNSEL: Legitimate purchases?

GOERING: Absolutely. Hitler, lucky for me, bought naked women with snakes around their navels, sleeping monks and perfect children, for God's sakes! I left him all that and found my Cranach *Adam and Eve*! I bought Rubens and my Van Dycks: the best!

COUNSEL: Three. Crimes Against Humanity.

GOERING: None! Never! None! I was hard, yes! I did my duty twice over! But humanity I love!

COUNSEL: You will be asked if you created the concentration camps.

GOERING: Using as models the British enclaves in South Africa and the Indian Reservations of the United States, yes I created concentration camps.

COUNSEL: And if you put Jews in them.

GOERING: Along with others when they threatened us, yes.

COUNSEL: What do you think happened to them there?

GOERING: They worked hard. To death, sometimes, yes, I understand that, and regret it, and always did what I could to stop it.

William Duff-Griffin as Hermann Goering and Percy Metcalf as the
Sergeant in Romulus Linney's *2* at Actors Theater of Louisville

COUNSEL: As the creator of those camps, you can say that was all that
was done in them?

GOERING: In the beginning, some camps presumed to disobey my
directives. I made short work of them, and closed them down.

COUNSEL: Defendant!

GOERING: Later, Himmler and Heydrich, and some major—ah, Eichmann,
who became very competent, took them over.

COUNSEL (*pause*): Defendant. (*Pause. Goering doesn't answer.*) You
asked me if I loved Germany. I said yes. I asked you if you were going to tell
me the truth. You said yes.

GOERING: I *am* telling you the truth!

COUNSEL: You can't be. Everyone knew what terrible things happened in
those camps. First in Germany, then in Poland, and the east. No one said a
word, since we could all be in one the next day.

GOERING: So where did you hear such things? Gossip?

COUNSEL: Yes, gossip, and the radio. It was everywhere. How can I tell
the Tribunal that the second most powerful man in Germany knew nothing
about the camps? You knew!

GOERING:  Before 1934!  After that, I was busy rebuilding the German economy and creating the Air Force.  What Himmler did then was none of my business.

COUNSEL:  You expect me to say that in court?

GOERING:  If you won't, I will.  (*Pause.*)  I only ask you to believe me.

COUNSEL:  I will try.

GOERING:  Thank you.

Goering's unflappable convictions are echoed in touching moments with one of his guards, the black American sergeant who eventually becomes the play's *deus ex machina*.

SERGEANT:  Cranach?

GOERING:  What?

SERGEANT:  Cranach.  The painter.

GOERING:  Yes?  Go ahead, talk.  We are alone.  I give you my word, no one will know what you say to me.

SERGEANT:  You bought his pictures?

GOERING:  I did.

SERGEANT:  Did you buy his *Jesus, Mary and Joseph*?

GOERING:  Which one?

SERGEANT:  I don't know.

GOERING:  There were many.

SERGEANT:  Mary and Joseph were on a road, under some pine trees. Joseph had that worried look an old man'd get with a wife real young, like Mary was.  Baby Jesus was reaching out to a lot of little angels, messing around like any bunch of kids.  One caught a bird and, see, had that bird fluttering by the wings and didn't know how to get it to Jesus.  I liked that.

GOERING:  A *Flight into Egypt*.  I remember.  How did you come across the paintings of Cranach, if you don't mind my asking?

SERGEANT:  I found them in books.

GOERING:  You have good taste.

SERGEANT:  There's something you ought to know.

GOERING:  My dear man, what is it?

SERGEANT:  They're not going to shoot you.

GOERING:  Oh?

SERGEANT:  I was at personnel, and I saw orders cut.  Dated two months ahead but cut.  For a master sergeant, the U.S. Army executioner.  They already know.  They going to hang your ass.

After an officer has called the black sergeant "boy," Goering addresses him.

GOERING: He insulted you, didn't he?

SERGEANT: Yeah.

GOERING: Calling you a boy?

SERGEANT: Way he did it, means nigger.

GOERING: Ah. I see. (*Pause.*) All my fliers respected each other.

SERGEANT: Glad to hear it.

GOERING: I taught them that. Would you like to know how?

SERGEANT: Just leave me alone!

GOERING: Shhhh. My dear sir. Not another word.

SERGEANT: Don't need to tell me about it. (*Pause.*) What did you say to your men?

GOERING: Do you really want to know?

SERGEANT: I wouldn't mind.

GOERING: In the first war there was a caste system, officers looked down on enlisted men. We made everyone equal as a man. I told my fliers this: "You are young and you will pay for it. Go have your fun. I want you to. But when you get into that place, you will be honorable, decent comrades, each respecting the next, so that in battle you will be warriors, destroying all resistance, and if it must be, dying for each other." No man in my command called another man "boy."

SERGEANT: (*Pause.*) How many Cranachs did you have?

GOERING: Fourteen.

SERGEANT: Lord. Think of that.

*2 was commissioned by Actors Theater of Louisville and premiered at its 14th Annual Humana Festival of New American Plays March 8, 1990.*

# PICK UP AX

*A Play in Two Acts*

BY ANTHONY CLARVOE

Cast and credits appear on page 536

*PICK UP AX:* Many of America's most dynamic computer companies were born in garages in Silicon Valley, California, where young men devised their hardware, software and chip programs. Often with backgrounds in rock music and video games, these young inventors suddenly found themselves, in their mid-20s, heading up multi-million dollar companies, forced to play hardball finance in a world of quick-buck greed. Keith and Brian in *Pick Up Ax* are two young men who came up via the garage-entrepeneurial route.

As the satirical comedy opens, Brian, the company's CEO, is trying to deal with the difficulty of getting chip deliveries without having to pay kickbacks. Keith, his buddy and the company's resident software-genius, is having fun coming up with a new computer-wrinkle. It won't be long before the two are joined by Mick, a thug who is acquainted with how a large part of American business really works. But, in the opening scenes, the two young innocents merely are trying to cope.

> *As the house lights go down, we hear Boston's "Foreplay/Long Time." Brian is standing behind the desk, talking on the phone. Keith is fidgeting with a toy from the Museum of Modern Art gift shop.*

491

BRIAN (*on phone*):  —and I'll go to the media. I'll go to your other customers. What with? What with, with my grievances, I'll go to them with this
grief you're giving me. Yes, you, Prescott, with your monopoly-wannabe in
microchips. Emerging businesses, like me, try to stand this fucking country on
its punchdrunk legs again, and you—what? Bottleneck, right, you've got a
bottleneck, so what are you doing, tourniquet around mine. Okay, you do that.
And then call me back. (*Hangs up.*) Bottleneck, right, what you are is a bottle
*rocket*, want to leave the rest of us punks on the ground.

KEITH: Anyway.

BRIAN: You may need to know about this.

KEITH: Tell me when you're sure. Anyway. Augie is running across this
rope bridge, waving the magic broadsword?

BRIAN: I'm with you.

KEITH: Which was really stupid, even for Augie. I set him up good. He's
flailing this snickersnee, of course he slices right through the support ropes on
the bridge. So he's toast.

BRIAN: Oh, sure, there's the bridge troll under that one.

KEITH: Was he surprised.

BRIAN: You run a mean dungeon, Keith.
      *The phone rings. Brian picks it up.*
(*On phone.*) Yes. Put him through. I'm listening, Prescott. All right, when?
We won't be here by then. What relationship? Mnemonico won't sell me any
chips. If you won't take my money, what does our relationship consist of? My
money used to be good for you. Okay, so they have bigger money, you can't
be satisfied with my size of money any more? I want to see you. I want to
talk to you. Not productive, don't tell me productive, what do you produce?
Produce something I can buy, make my product out of, get my ass back in the
food chain. We'll talk.
      *Slams phone, picks it up again, pushes two buttons.*
He's not budging. Set up a press conference. Call the other CEOs getting
squeezed, put them through to me. God, you're right. God. All right, then, we
tell the board of directors—

BRIAN and KEITH: The shitheads!

BRIAN: —but that goddamn flock of albatrosses better flap their wings for
once. Now get me Legal. No, I'll wait.

KEITH: I bet I could get all his credit cards cancelled. You want me to? I
could find him in here—
      *Patting his terminal.*
—have him buy imaginary stuff, send him past his limits?

BRIAN: Keith, maybe you'd better go back to your office.

KEITH: I can't.

BRIAN: Why not?

KEITH: It's full.

BRIAN: Full of what?

KEITH: This and that. I filled it up.

BRIAN: It's a room, not a disk drive. (*Into phone.*) Hi, yeah, he's not budging. What does the Justice Department say? Yeah? Then Justice is a fucking misnomer. Can we get a restraining order? Yes I know what a restraining order is, you're here to tell me. Try that. (*Hangs up.*) Keith, listen.

*Keith quickly puts his head down on the desk, ear to the surface.*

KEITH: Many buffalo, Kemosabe.

BRIAN: Keith—

KEITH: 132,982 buffalo, Kemosabe.

BRIAN: You know I try to keep this shit away from you. But you're going to read it off the networks anyway.

*Keith sits up, surprised.*

We are in real trouble this time.

KEITH: What you mean—(*Brian joins in.*)—we, white man.

BRIAN: Microchips. Demand is exceeding supply. Remember, I explained how that works? Mnemonico will only sell to the big boys. I can't win a bidding war with the big boys. Dude, I think they want to put us little boys out of business, and the chip makers are letting them.

KEITH: I don't get it.

BRIAN: No hardware, no product; no product, no company.

KEITH: But I hate hardware!

BRIAN: I'm calling the competition. Together we can beat the big fish. Everybody's in his own corporation, but we all grew up in the same place.

*He pats the top of the computer monitor.*

Lotta late nights. Now the time is right to go networking in the street.

KEITH: I never should have strayed from pure programming.

BRIAN: The product had to run off a card, there was no way around it.

KEITH: I would die of happiness if I could design software that didn't need any hardware.

BRIAN: They have that already. It's called "thought."

KEITH: Meanwhile I'm tied forever to a cross of silicon. The computers' last tie to the fucking world of matter.

BRIAN: Dude, the world of matter is where we sell things. We've been over this. A transaction has to leave a trace. Something changes hands.

KEITH: It's all these goddamned stand-alones. If everything were networked, I could function!

BRIAN: What happened, you have a revelation, you see a floppy disc wheeling around way up in the middle of the air? Is this the whole world of matter you're writing off?

KEITH: What's it done for us lately? Look at what's left of you.

BRIAN: Keith, listen to me. Without the world of matter, there would be no Rolling Stones.

KEITH: Okay.  You have a point.
    *Tapping at the terminal.*
I have a surprise for you.
    BRIAN: All I'm saying is, reconcile yourself.  Use it to your advantage.
    KEITH: It's an old idea I dug up.  Move two feet to your left.
        *Brian does so.  Grand Funk Railroad's "We're an American Band"*
        *starts up, low.*
    BRIAN: What's going on?
    KEITH: You break the plane, the sensor picks up your body temperature by
infrared.  Digitizes your mood.  You like it?
    BRIAN: Sympathetic Muzak.  Cute.
    KEITH: See, I listen to you.  I try to meet the world halfway.  You want to
go out tonight?  We could get stoned and play miniature golf.
        *Music up.  Blackout.*


Samuel Gregory as Brian Weiss, Jeffrey King as Mick Palomar and John
Bellucci as Keith Rienzi in a scene from Anthony Clarvoe's *Pick Up Ax* in its
world premiere at the Eureka Theater Company, San Francisco

Keith is at a computer in a room whose walls are *"a cold shade of blue"* when Brian enters. Brian comments sarcastically about the color, and Keith changes it with the press of a button.

Brian tells Keith that their directors offer them no help, but Keith is preoccupied with other events of the day before.

KEITH: I was in meetings till late yesterday. This kid made a presentation. *Keith waves a piece of paper covered with calculations. On and off during the following, almost unconsciously, he folds it into an odd-looking paper airplane.*

BRIAN: One of the new kids?

KEITH: One of the new kids. Summer intern.

BRIAN: How was it?

KEITH: We'd given him a little something. He was at the chalkboard. He was talking. He'd gone way above and beyond. And I was following him. I was following what he was saying.

BRIAN: Great, so?

KEITH: I'm not telling this right. He was retracing his line of thought, and I was following. Along. Behind him.

BRIAN: Oh.

KEITH: Right. When have I ever had to follow anybody through the numbers? I'm always blindsiding them and running on ahead.

BRIAN: You were tired. It was late.

KEITH: I came back here. I worked all night.

BRIAN: Like the old days.

KEITH: The old days weren't work, so much. I'd look up, it'd be hours later, like flying across the time zones. And I'd brought back all this stuff on disk.

BRIAN: I've seen you going after ideas.

KEITH: They came to me. You saw me operating my arms, that's all. Last night I was running after it.

BRIAN: Meanwhile the kid went out with his friends, and they bought him a pitcher, and they told him he was going to be the next Keith Rienzi, and a few beers later he believed them, and somebody drove him home, and he looked in the bathroom mirror and said, "I am the next Keith Rienzi." And all this time Keith Rienzi was back here working. The once and future kid.

KEITH: You know, I'm twenty-seven years old. That's fifty-four in nerd years.

*Keith breathes on one wing of his airplane, making it slightly heavier to cause the plane to bank. Keith flies the paper airplane across the room.*

BRIAN: He had the element of surprise this time. That won't happen again.

KEITH: No. I'll be looking over my shoulder. That's always productive.

What I design almost doesn't exist at all. Hardware, now, you're in the world of wires and boards and trays. Bound for the junkyard. With software, cathedrals of logic vanish into the ozone. In a twinkling.

BRIAN: I'd say you're still thinking.

KEITH: I'm remembering thinking. If I were really thinking, I wouldn't say these things.

*Pause.*

BRIAN: Here's what we do. First of all, for God's sake don't tell anyone, our stock will go to hell. We'll pull you out of everything. Global erase. O.K.? R. and D. management, new product oversight, everything. We'll say what I was talking about before: Keith Rienzi has a new product and screw your old memory chips.

KEITH: Can I move in here?

BRIAN: Of course. You have a nightmare, you head for Mom and Dad's room. We'll take you out of yourself and things'll come back to you.

KEITH: That's it, that's how it was. They'd come right out of the dark. I always knew they were out there, the ideas.

*Keith taps a few keys and waits for a program to boot up.*

BRIAN: That's my boy. (*Comes around to read over Keith's shoulder.*) "You are standing near a small stone cottage ... " Keith, you're playing Adventure?

KEITH: Different game, same idea. It's where I used to get away to think.

BRIAN: Threading your way through a nonexistent labyrinth?

KEITH: Some people pace.

BRIAN: Okay, whatever breaks you out of the slump.

*Pause.*

KEITH: What if I don't?

BRIAN: Hey. This place is our life's work. It owes you.

*Pause.*

KEITH: You try it.

BRIAN: I've hated this stupid pastime since high school.

KEITH: You'll get it one of these days. Every time you get killed you start right up again. Come on, it's highly educational.

BRIAN: Educational, if we did business with swords, I'd learn all kinds of useful stuff.

KEITH: Help me, Obi-wan Kenobi. You're my only hope.

BRIAN: I'll play for a while, but we've got a crisis, you go on without me, all right? "You are standing near a small stone cottage in a forest clearing. Suddenly a dwarf carrying a stone ax runs out of the woods. He drops the stone ax, opens the cottage door, runs through and slams the door." O.K. Go through door?

KEITH: You sure you want to do that?

BRIAN: I hate it when you say that! I'm good at Dungeons and Dragons.

KEITH:  You always were better with people than computers.

BRIAN:  I still am. I'm trying everything.

KEITH:  I know, I didn't mean—

BRIAN:  Keith. If anyone asks the question, what do you say?

KEITH:  Brian is trying everything. How's your stomach?

BRIAN:  Don't mention my stomach.

KEITH:  Brian is trying everything.

BRIAN:  I'm on top of the situation.

KEITH:  I'm sure you are.

BRIAN:  If anyone asks.

KEITH:  "You are standing near a small stone cottage in a forest clearing."

BRIAN:  I know where I'm standing! Leave forest clearing, go to Taco Bell? I don't know.

KEITH:  Look at what you have.

BRIAN:  A clearing. A cottage. A door. A disappearing dwarf.

KEITH:  A stone ax.

BRIAN:  Aha. Pick up stone ax.

KEITH:  It doesn't know "pick up." Try "get."

BRIAN:  You see? Complex, exotic, pathetically limited. "Get stone ax. Enter." O.K. "The stone ax says, 'Command me, O Master.'" Now we're happening.

 *Blackout.*

*PICK UP AX premiered at Eureka Theater Company, San Francisco, Jan. 18, 1990, after development in staged readings by Upstart Stage and South Coast Repertory and a workshop production by American Conservatory Theater's Plays in Progress.*

# MARVIN'S ROOM

*A Play in Two Acts*

BY SCOTT McPHERSON

Cast and credits appear on pages 506–507

*MARVIN'S ROOM*: Sisters Bessie and Lee haven't seen each other for 20 years. Bessie, the older, never married, while Lee's broken marriage left her with Hank and Charlie, two emotionally troubled sons now 18 and 11. Bessie has lived in Florida all the while as caretaker for her unseen invalid father (the Marvin of the title) and her affectionate semi-invalid Aunt Ruth. Now in her early 40s, Bessie has been diagnosed with leukemia. Her sister and nephews arrive in Florida to have their bone marrow tested for a possible transplant that could save Bessie's life.

Characteristic of his small body of work to date, McPherson's dark comedy about family dysfunction uses satire, irony, non-sequitur, silence and a dash of gallows humor as its principal tools. The text is spare and the words ordinary to an extreme, and the lives on view are somber, yet from them McPherson has created rich subtext and a deeply caring work that expresses a conservative yearning for extended family renewal. Bessie is the play's fulcrum with sister Lee and nephew Hank in the balance. Through them the play's secondary theme of achieving personal grace is developed.

In Act II, Scene 5, Bessie justifies her life as a care provider for her father and aunt and accepts the inevitability of her death.

*Walt Disney World. The Lost Children's hut. Bessie lies on a small bed. Lee sits in a small chair. Bessie wakes up violently, as if from a nightmare.*

LEE: You're all right.

BESSIE: Hmmmm.

LEE: You're all right.

BESSIE: Where am I?

LEE: You're in the Lost Children's hut.

BESSIE: Where?

RUTH (*appears in the doorway*): Bessie?

LEE: She's O.K., Ruth.

BESSIE: Ruth?

RUTH: Bessie?

BESSIE: I'm fine.

RUTH: Are you all right now?

BESSIE: I just got real tired.

RUTH: You should rest.

BESSIE: I am.

RUTH: You do too much. You always do too much.

BESSIE: I won't do so much any more. I promise.

LEE: She's fine, Ruth.

Laura Esterman as Bessie and Lee Guthrie as Lee in Scott McPherson's *Marvin's Room* at the Goodman Theater, Chicago

BESSIE: We've only paid Marvin's nurse till seven o'clock.

LEE: Don't worry about that.

BESSIE: Is there a phone?

RUTH: I'll call. (*She exits.*)

LEE: Dr. Serat and Dr. Wally are meeting us at the hospital.

BESSIE: Dr. Serat?

LEE: He's back.

BESSIE: I have to go back in the hospital?

LEE: They want to look at you. If you feel good, there's no reason you can't come home.

BESSIE: I feel good.

LEE: What happened?

BESSIE: I fainted.

LEE: From the heat?

BESSIE: There was blood in my mouth.

LEE: Is your mouth still bleeding?

BESSIE: No. Did a doctor look at me?

LEE: No. He just thought you fainted, so he carried you in here to lie down.

BESSIE: Who's "he?"

LEE: The gopher man.

BESSIE: The gopher man?

LEE: Yes.

BESSIE: Carried me to the Lost Children's hut?

LEE: He just thought you fainted. He didn't know you had been bleeding.

BESSIE: I couldn't have bled that much.

LEE: Maybe you were kind of faint from not eating, too. That might be all it is.

BESSIE: I fainted because . . . I was scared.

LEE: You're all right.

BESSIE: I was so scared.

LEE: That's O.K.

BESSIE: What's happening to me?

LEE: Sssh.

BESSIE: I can't sleep any more. I never sleep. I'm afraid to close my eyes. I'll close my eyes and I won't wake up. So I jerk myself awake. I yank myself awake all night long.

LEE: Bessie . . .

BESSIE: I pour myself some coffee.

LEE: It's O.K.

BESSIE: I just want to find a place to hide.

LEE: You're O.K.

BESSIE: I'm trying to be brave.

LEE: Shh. Shh.

BESSIE: But I'm scared. I'm so scared.

> *They hug.*

LEE: Ssh. Ssh. You're O.K. Oh, you're O.K.

> *Comforts her silently.*

What have you got to be scared of? Everything is going to be O.K. You'll see. There's still Hank and Charlie. Are you forgetting that? You're O.K.

BESSIE: Where are they?

LEE: They're sitting out front.

BESSIE: Was Space Mountain fun?

LEE: Uh-huh, it was real fun.

BESSIE: You're lucky to have those boys.

LEE: I know I am.

BESSIE: They're good boys, both of them.

LEE: Yes, they are.

BESSIE: And you know?

LEE: What?

BESSIE: I'm lucky to have Dad and Ruth.

LEE: Mm-hmmm.

BESSIE: I've had such love in my life. I look back, and I've had such love.

LEE: They love you very much.

BESSIE: I don't mean . . . I mean I love them. I am so lucky to have been able to love someone so much. I am so lucky to have loved so much. I am so lucky.

LEE: Yes, you are. You are.

BESSIE: We're fooling ourselves, Lee.

> *Hank appears in the doorway.*

LEE: How?

BESSIE: Hank and Charlie aren't going to match.

LEE: We don't know that.

BESSIE: They're my nephews. They're once removed.

LEE: It could still happen.

BESSIE: I don't want to pretend any longer. We have too many decisions to make before you leave.

HANK: Is that true?

LEE: We don't have to make them right now. (*Notices Hank.*) Hank, would you find me a wheelchair?

HANK: Charlie is.

LEE: Do you feel up to going to the car.

BESSIE: Oh, sure.

> *Bessie sits up. Charlie enters with a wheelchair and stops it next to the tiny chair. Hank picks Bessie up and puts her in the wheelchair. She looks at the tiny chair.*

BESSIE: I don't remember ever being that small.
LEE: Ready?
        *End scene.*

*MARVIN'S ROOM was developed with the assistance of Victory Gardens Theater and premiered at the Goodman Theater, Chicago in its Studio Series in a Chicago Theater Group production Feb. 9, 1990.*

# A DIRECTORY OF NEW-PLAY PRODUCTIONS

## Compiled by Sheridan Sweet

Professional 1989–90 productions of new plays by leading companies around the United States that supplied information on casts and credits at Sheridan Sweet's request, plus a few reported by other reliable sources, are listed below in alphabetical order of the locations of the 80-plus producing organizations. Date given is opening date, included whenever a record was obtainable from the producing management. All League of Resident Theaters (LORT) and other Equity groups were queried for this comprehensive Directory. Those not listed here either did not produce new or newly-revised scripts in 1989–90 or had not responded by press time. Most of the productions listed—but not all—are American or world premieres. Some are new revisions, second looks or scripts produced previously but not previously reported in Best Plays.

## Allentown: Pennsylvania Stage Company

(Producing director, Peter Wrenn-Meleck)

*Staged Reading:*

KURU. By Josh Manheimer. March 23, 1990. Director, Peter Wrenn-Meleck.

| | |
|---|---|
| Dr. Arthur Roman | Steve Asciolla |
| Mary Lou Anderson | Lisa Seacrist |
| Mokina | Deanna Duplechain |

## Atlanta: The Alliance

(Artistic director, Robert J. Farley; managing director, Edith H. Love)

SOUTHERN CROSS. By Jon Klein. September 16, 1989. Director, Robert J. Farley; scenery, Victor Becker; lighting, Jim Sale; costumes, Pamela Scofield.

| | |
|---|---|
| William T. Sherman | Tom Stechschulte |
| Henry Hitchcock | Ken Strong |
| The Captain | William Jay |
| Huey P. Long | Tom Key |
| Ralph Jackson; John Rankins | John Purcell |
| Jim Clark; Sheriff of Money; Major John Cloud; Spears | James Mayberry |
| Colonel Tom Parker | Brian Reddy |
| Oscar Davis; Sam Irby | Jack Mason |
| Hattie | Carol Mitchell Leon |
| Billy Daniel; A Poor Farmer | Afemo Omilami |
| Roy Bryant | Sam Peabody |
| J.W. Milam; Gene Smith | Bruce Evers |
| Mose Wright | William Jay |
| Emmett Till | Jamal Peoples |
| James Foster; Lamar Fike | Larry Larson |
| Nancy Foster | Rosemary Newcott |
| Elvis Presley | Mark Kincaid |
| Mrs. Turner | Elizabeth Omilami |
| Webb; Gilbert; General Davis | Peter Thomasson |
| Body Guards of Huey Long | Bruce Evers, Sam Peabody |

503

Jack Tabb; Edwin M. Stanton........ Stuart Culpepper
Time: 1850 to the present. Place: The Southern United States. One intermission.

GAL BABY. By Sandra Deer. March 3, 1990. Director, Kenny Leon; scenery, Michael Olich; lighting, Ann G. Wrightson; costumes, Susan E. Mickey.
Gal Baby Partain Summers ..............Brenda Bynum

Mr. Le...........................................Mr. Kim Chan
Tommy Summers........................Peter Thomasson
Leonard Partain .............................Jeffrey Watkins
Carlotta Partain...........................Sylvia Cardwell
Grady Hicks.................................... Raphael Nash
Place: The patio of Tommy and Gal Baby's home across the lake from Rose Park Plantation. One intermission.

## Baltimore: Center Stage

(Artistic director, Stan Wojewodsky Jr.)

MISS EVERS' BOYS. By David Feldshuh. November 22, 1989. Director, Irene Lewis; scenery, Douglas Stein; costumes, Catherine Zuber; lighting, Pat Collins; sound, Janet Kalas; choreography, Dianne McIntyre; musical direction, Dwight Andrews.
Caleb Humphries ............................ Delroy Lindo

Hodman Bryan ...............................Damien Leake
Willie Johnson...........................K. Todd Freeman
Ben Washington...........................Allie Woods Jr.
Dr. John Douglass......................... Ethan Phillips
Dr. Eugene Brodus........................David Downing
Eunice Evers.......................................Seret Scott
One intermission.

## Berkeley, Calif.: Berkeley Repertory Theater

(Artistic director, Sharon Ott; managing director, Mitzi Sales)

EACH DAY DIES WITH SLEEP. By Jose Rivera. Director, Roberta Levitow; scenery, Tom Kamm; lighting, Robert Wierzel; costumes, Tina Cantu Navarro.

Augie...............................................Alex Colon
Nellie................................................Erica Gipel
Johnny .........................................Randy Vasquez
One intermission.

## Bethlehem, Pa.: Touchstone Theater

(Associate director, Bridget George)

HOW FAR TO BETHLEHEM. By Bridget George. Director, Jennie Gilrain; scenery, Richard Kendrick; lighting, Vicki Neal; costumes, Polly Kendrick; sound, Ben Emerson.
Edie........................................ Miriam Hamilton
Sofia...................................... Martha De La Cruz
Megan.......................................Sara Zielinska
Ricky............................................... Eric Beatty
Joe ............................................. Mark McKenna

Sofia's Family:
Miguel...................Rene Ursua, Orlando Rosario
Lucy..................... Denise Cruz, Carmen Trinidad
Carlos................................. Emanuel De Jesus,
                            Dino Cadiz, Radoberto Matos
Rosa............................... Rosemarie Rebimbas
Time: 1980s, the week before Christmas. Place: Southside of Bethlehem. One intermission.

## Blue Lake, Calif.: Dell'Arte Players Company

(Artistic directors, Michael Fields, Donald Forest, Joan Schirle)

SLAPSTICK. By Michael Fields, Donald Forest, Joan Schirle and Jael Weisman. October 12, 1989. Director, Jael Weisman; scenery, Alain Schons;

lighting, Michael Foster; costumes, Nancy Jo Smith; original music, Gina Leishman.
Norm; Junior..................................Donald Forrest

Sheila; Missy.....................................Joan Schirle
Roger...........................................Michael Fields

Gloria..........................................Gina Leishman
One intermission.

## Buffalo:  Studio Arena Theater

(Artistic director, David Frank; executive director, Raymond Bonnard)

GALILEO (musical).  Book and lyrics by Keith Levenson and Alexa Junge; music by Jeanine Levenson.  November 28, 1989.  Director, David Frank; scenery, David Jenkins; lighting, Peter Kaczorowski; costumes, Julie Weiss; sound, Rick Menke; musical director, Doug Besterman; orchestrator, Daniel Troob; musical staging, Sam Viverito.
Galileo Galilei.....................................Paul Harman
Young Mara (age 8)...Emily Ball, Natalie Rosenberg
Cardinal Robert Bellarmine..............David Holliday
Cardinal Maffeo Barberini............James J. Stein Jr.
Roberto Mazzoleni............................Scott Elliott
Mara Galilei.............................Natalie Rosenberg

Angela Ornini..............................Joanne Glushak
Duchess, Signora Essio.................Susan Arundale
Luka Vinto; Signor Camerata.......David Clemmons
Student; Citizen of Florence and Rome...Peter Davis
Christina; Signorina Tucci..................Kate Fuglei
Vincenzo Fabrizzi............................Sean Greenan
Benito Zabaldi; Cosimo de Medici;
   Pasqualigo...................................John Hoffman
Landini; Inquisitor...........................Walker Joyce
Signora Battaglia............................Joanna Lange
Princess le Feuvre; Signora
   Innuncio..............................Dominique Plaisant
Signora Fabrizzi.................................Amy Ryder

STUDIO ARENA THEATER—Natalie Rosenberg and Paul Harman in the Keith Levenson-Alexa Junge-Jeanine Levenson musical *Galileo*

Citizens of Florence and Rome ........Carolyn Saxon,
        Wendy Schurr, Katy Clancy
Firenzuola; Father Scheiner; Salvati.... Peter Schmitz
Paulo Celli; Signor Cruzi................Tom Treadwell

Father Tasso......................................Robert Zolli
    Time: 17th century. Place: Italy. One
intermission.

## Cambridge, Mass: Back Alley Theater

(Managing director, Douglas Marney)

THE GIFT. By Rosemary Cummings. December
14, 1989. Director, Jay Skelton; scenery, Bobby
Summerlin; lighting, David Reynolds.
Christine ...........................................Kate Bennis
Anna.............................................Heather Glenn
Mother......................................... Kate Talbot
Father .................................................Nick Harris
Tommy.................................... Danny LaChance
Young Anna.............................. Demeny Pollitt
Stephen................................. Brendon Parry
Patrick .................................................Brad Reed
Jane .................................................Carrie Wykoff
Stranger (man).....................................Nick Harris
Stranger (woman)...............................Adele Hars
Second Woman............................Sarah Fitzgerald
    One intermission.

THE GREAT AMERICAN BICENTENNIAL
ELECTRIC CHAIR SALUTE. By John Crabtree.
February 1, 1990. Director, Eileen Sullivan;
scenery, Eileen Sullivan; lighting, Janine S. Brunell;
costumes, Lucy Bloomfield; sound, Helen Wheelock.
Bob.................................................. Dan McCleary
Terry.......................................Ronald Porembski
Nathan................................................. Nick Harris
Ben................................................Idris Rahim
Fish.................................................Jeff Garlin
Carl ...................................... Richard D. Rosenfeld
Jesus......................................George Saulnier III
Moose................................................John Porell
    Time: Various times, July 2, 1976. Place: Exe-
cution chamber annex used to house overflow of
death-row inmates.

## Chicago: Body Politic Theater

(Artistic director, Pauline Brailsford)

THE GOOD TIMES ARE KILLING ME. By Lynda
Barry; adapted from a novel by Arnold Aprill, Lynda
Barry and Ira Glass. September 24, 1989. Director,
Arnold Aprill; scenery, David Lee Csicsko; cos-
tumes, Catherine Evans; choreography and musical
direction, Steve Reshid, Beatrice Reshid; lighting,
Thomas C. Hase; sound, Lou Mallozzi, Dawn
Mallozzi.
Edna Arkins ...............................Lorell J. Wyatt
Lucy Arkins...............................Jeannie Affelder

Elvin Willis; Earl Stelly;
    Marcus................................Michael A. Shepperd
Bonna Willis ...........................Glenda Starr Kelley
Mom...................................................Jan Pessin
Aunt Margaret........................... Maripat Donovan
Uncle Jim ...........................................Page Hearn
Cousin Ellen ........................... Kathryn Gallagher
Dod; Cousin Steve; Mr. Lozimana......David Cromer
    One intermission.

## Chicago: The Goodman Theater

(Artistic director, Robert Falls; producing director, Roche Schulfer)

MARVIN'S ROOM. By Scott McPherson. Febru-
ary 9, 1990. Director, David Petrarca; scenery, Linda
Buchanan; lighting, Robert Christen; costumes,
Claudia Boddy; sound and original music, Rob
Milburn.
Bessie .........................................Laura Esterman
Dr. Wally ......................................Tim Monsion

Ruth ................................................Jane MacIver
Bob....................................................Peter Rybolt
Lee .................................................Lee Guthrie
Dr. Charlotte; Retirement Home Director...Ora Jones
Hank........................................ Mark Rosenthal
Charlie ...........................................Karl Maschek
Marvin .................................William T. Gallagher

Time: The present. One intermission. (An ATCA selection; see introduction to this section.)

ELLIOT LOVES. By Jules Feiffer. April 14, 1990. Director, Mike Nichols; scenery, Tony Walton; lighting, Paul Gallo; costumes, Ann Roth; sound, Rob Milburn.

| | |
|---|---|
| Elliot | Anthony Heald |
| Joanna | Christine Baranski |
| Vera | La Tanya Richardson |
| Phil | David Pierce |
| Larry | Oliver Platt |
| Bobby | Bruce A. Young |

Time and Place: Chicago in the mid 1980s. One intermission.

*Workshop:*

THE BOOK OF THE NIGHT (musical). Music by Louis Rosen; lyrics by Louis Rosen and Thom Bishop. Director, Robert Falls.

| | |
|---|---|
| Jill's Husband | David Studwell |
| Wishing Man | Keith Byron-Kirk |
| Wishing Woman | Megon McDonough |
| Streetsinger; Juanita | Ora Jones |
| Cop; Gypsy | Alton White |
| Young Widow | Paula Newsome |

| | |
|---|---|
| Desk Clerk | Skipp Sudduth |
| Dealer | Jim Corti |
| Redhead | Robin Kersey |
| Carlos | David Bedella |
| Jack's Wife | Charlotte Maier |
| Jill | Colette Hawley |

*Staged Readings:*

MARILYN AND MARK. By Steve Feiffer. October 1, 1989.
WINTER. By Claudia Allen. October 15, 1989.
YOUNG RICHARD. By Charles Smith. November 19, 1989.
TUMBLEWEED IN COWTOWN. By Will Kern and Jeff Jones. December 3, 1989.
CHESSIE AND THE GRIFF. By Ron Mark. December 17, 1989.
THE LAND KING. By Eugene Baldwin. January 7, 1990.
THE OLD MAN IS SNORING. By Bob Sloan. January 28, 1990.
TZIGANE. By Zan Skolnick. February 25, 1990.
AUGUST SNOW. By Reynolds Price. April 8, 1990.
VOLGA SUNSET ROOM. By Joe Urbanito. June 3, 1990.

## Chicago: The Immediate Theater Company

(Artistic director, Richard Wharton; managing director, Doug Marshall)

RAGGED DICK. By Neal Bell. February 22, 1990. Director, Jeff Ginsberg; scenery, Tim Morrison; lighting, Ron Greene; costumes, Frances Maggio; sound, Jeff Webb.

| | |
|---|---|
| Dick Hunter | Richard Wharton |
| Susan | Peggy Goss |
| Mrs. Lane | Millie McManus |
| Annie | Lynda Foxman |
| Amos | John Montana |

| | |
|---|---|
| Bunner | Brian Shaw |
| Cecil | Kris Martin |
| Clubber | Randy Colburn |
| Tommy | Eric Saiet |
| Norbert | Raphy Green |
| Copy-Boy | William Jones |
| The Man | Michael McNeal |

Time: Summer, 1890. Place: New York City. One intermission.

## Chicago: The New Tuners

(Artistic director, Byron Schaffer Jr.)

CHARLIE'S OASIS MUSEUM & BAR (musical). Book by Jane Boyd; music and lyrics by Gregg Opelka. Director, Ted Hoerl; scenery, Thomas B. Mitchell; lighting, Thomas B. Mitchell; costumes, Shifra Werch; music director, Judy Myers; orchestrator, Timothy Pleiman.

| | |
|---|---|
| Bruce | David Weynand |
| Diane | Mary Mulligan |
| Michael | Matthew McDonald |

| | |
|---|---|
| Marsha | Rhea Anne Cook |
| Alice | Lizanne Wilson |
| Terry | Tom A. Viveiros |
| Cliff; Marvin | Thomas Cooch |
| Shorty; Winston | Allan Chambers |
| Ginger | Mary Hager |
| Harriet | Kelly Ellenwood |

Time: The present. Place: Charlie's Beach Oasis, St. Pete's, Florida. One intermission.

# Chicago: Organic Theater Company

(Artistic director, Richard Fire; executive director, Richard Friedman)

YOU HOLD MY HEART BETWEEN YOUR TEETH. By Blair Thomas. October 20, 1989. Director, Blair Thomas.

DO THE WHITE THING. By Aaron Freeman and Rob Kolson. February 8, 1990. Directors, Bob Curry, Nate Herman.
With Aaron Freeman, Rob Kolson.

*Workshops:*

ON THE EDGE OF THE WORLD. By Brian Griffin.
M. By Bob Meyer and Jack Clark.
AMERICAN ENTERPRISE. By Jeffrey Sweet.

# Chicago: Theater Center

(Production manager, R.J. Coleman)

SUCH IS LIFE. By Dan LaMorte. November 8, 1989. Director, James Barushok; scenery, Robert G. Smith; lighting, Robert G. Smith; costumes, Darice DaMata-Geiger.
Aida ............................................ Nanette Brown
Diane .................................... Anita M. Chiarenza
Gram ................................................ Lara Novey
Sam .................................................... Peter Kell
Pat .................................................. Leslie Haines
Mafalda ................................... Mary Beth Burns
Jack .......................................... Steve Silverstein
John ............................................... Steve Savage
Joey .......................................... Tony Muscarello
Time and Place: The Martino home, Cicero, Illinois, 1991, the time of the Next Great American Depression. One intermission.

*Staged Reading:*

INSIDE GEORGE. By Dan LaMorte. January 22, 1990. Director, Dan LaMorte.

# Chicago: Victory Gardens Theater

(Artistic director, Dennis Zacek)

BEAU JEST. By James Sherman. November 10, 1989. Director, Dennis Zacek; scenery, Stephen Packard; lighting, Larry Schoeneman; costumes, Jessica Hahn; sound, Galen Ramsey.
Sarah Goldman ............................... Linnea Todd
Chris .............................................. Peter Curren
Bob .............................................. Michael Guido
Joel ............................................... Fredric Stone
Miriam .................................... Roslyn Alexander
Abe ............................................... Bernie Landis
Time: An evening in spring and several weeks later. Place: A one-bedroom apartment in the Lincoln Park area of Chicago. One intermission.

PECONG. By Steve Carter. January 19, 1990. Director, Dennis Zacek; scenery, James Dardenne; lighting, Robert Shook; costumes, Claudia Boddy; sound, Galen G. Ramsey; composer, Willy Steele; choreography, T.C. Carlson.
Mediyah ................................... Celeste Williams
Granny Root ...................................... Pat Bowie
Cedric .............................................. Gary Yates
Persis ............................................ Catherine Slade
Faustina ....................................... Wandachristine
Creon Pandit ............................... Ernest Perry Jr.
Sweet Bella ..................................... Diane White
Jason Allcock .............................. Daniel Oreskes
Time: Well in the past. Place: Trankey Island, an "island of the mind" in the Caribbean. One intermission.

DIESEL MOON. By Robert Auletta. February 8, 1990. Director, James Bohnen; scenery, Chuck Drury; lighting, Ellen E. Jones; costumes, Mark-Anthony Summers, Glenn Billings.
Cap ................................................ Joe D. Lauck
Marth .................................... Cheryl A. Carabelli
Harrow Conroy; The Bear ................ Bruce Barsanti
Starr; Princess .......................... Jane Oppenheimer
Tunnel; Caps' Father ..................... W. Earl Brown
Woody; The Deputy ...................... Richard Schrot
Time: 1984-85. Place: A mountainous state in the American West. One intermission.

THE ANGELS OF WARSAW. By Marisha Chamberlain. March 16, 1990. Director, Sandy Shinner; scenery, Jeff Bauer; lighting, Rita Pietraszek; costumes, Claudia Boddy; sound, Tommy Wiggins.

Grzegorz.............................................Will Zahrn
Howie................................................Guy Mount
The Angel.....................................Greg Vinkler
Clare.............................................Kate Goehring
Jerzy.............................................Dennis Zacek
Rozmarek.................................Les Hinderyckx
Time: 20 hours in October, 1984. Place: A train departing from Paris, bound for Warsaw.

SCARRED GROUND. By Thomas Cadwaleder Jones. April 12, 1990. Director, Philip Euling; scenery, Linda L. Lane; lighting, Ann M. Greenstein; costumes, Lynne Palmer; sound, Lemoyne E. Smith.

Alexandra.................................Moon Hi Hanson
Millard .........................................L. Kent Brown
C.G. Cobb.......................................Craig Spidle
Time: The late 1980s. Place: The Vietnam Veterans Memorial in Washington, D.C. One intermission.

## Cincinnati: Ensemble Theater of Cincinnati

(Artistic director, David A. White III; managing director, Brian D. Griffin)

20 YEARS AGO TODAY. By David A. White III. August 10, 1989. Director, David A. White III.
With Julia Forgy, Jeanne Blessing, Nick DeSantis, Ricky Pettigrew.

RECENT DEVELOPMENTS IN SOUTHERN CONNECTICUT. By John Ford Noonan. February 4, 1990. Directors, David Hertzig, Jim Nelson.
With Michael Hankins, Mary Scott Gruditis, Paul Kennedy, Mary Biedler.

## Cincinnati: Cincinnati Playhouse in the Park

(Artistic director, Worth Gardner; managing director, Kathleen Norris)

TREASURE ISLAND. Adapted by Ara Watson from Robert Louis Stevenson. November 28, 1989. Director, Worth Gardner; scenery, Paul Shortt; lighting, Kirk Bookman; costumes, D. Bartlett Blair.

Black Dog; Pirate...............................Raul Aranas
Jim Hawkins.............................Christopher Cull
Villager; Officer; Officer Arrow........Scott Cummins
Pirate; Villager; Sailor.........................Greg Dolph
Blind Pew; Job Anderson.....................Rafael Ferrer
Officer Dance; Ben Gunn.....................Tom Flagg
Villager; Redruth; Sailor; Dan...........Drew Fracher
Villager; Pirate; Ben; Abe Gray.........Matthew Glave
Captain Smollett.............................Paul Hebron
Villager; Pirate; Dick Jones...............Howard Kaye
Villager; Maid; Apple Seller;
   Pirate....................................Martha M. Kelly
Mr. Hawkins; Israel Hands......Leonard Kelly-Young
Villager; Tom Morgan.....................Tony Lawson
Villager; Officer; Sailor....................Andrew Miller
Margaret Hawkins.......................Catherine Moore
Villager; Pirate; Harry; George...........Mark Niebuhr
Billy Bones................................Roger Robinson
Dr. Livesay.....................................Julian Stone
Long John Silver..............................Paul Vincent
Squire Trelawney..............................K.C. Wilson
One intermission.

¿DE DONDE? By Mary Gallagher. January 4, 1990. Director, Sam Blackwell; scenery, Jay Depenbrock; lighting, Kirk Bookman; costumes, Laura Crow.

Felicia; Rosario; Miriam; Refugee...Marie Barrientos
Pete .........................................Bill Cwikowski
INS Guard; Lillian.............................Betty Miller
Willy; Oscar; INS Man; Translator; Bailiff;
   Border Patrol Agent...........................Ted Minos
Juan; Fredo; Carlos; Barca; Nestor;
   Refugee.........................................Steve Monés
Teto; Mauricio; INS Attorney;
   Refugee.........................................Rene Moreno
Narciso; Alirio; Refugee.................Enrique Muñoz
Victor; INS Paralegal; Refugee...............John Ortiz
Menlo; INS Judges; INS Official;
   Border Patrol Agent.......................Robert Reilly
La Extraña...................................Socorro Santiago
Guard; Randy; CIA Agent;
   Border Patrol Agent......................Phil Soltanoff
Lynne; Kathleen............................Katie C. Sparer
Nydia; Luz; Refugee..........................Marta Vidal
Time and Place: The present in the Rio Grande Valley of Texas and spans almost a year. One intermission.

CINCINNATI PLAYHOUSE IN THE PARK—The cast aboard the
*Hispaniola* in Ara Watson's stage adaptation of *Treasure Island*

## Cleveland: *The Cleveland Play House*

(Artistic director, Josephine R. Abady; managing director, Dean R. Gladden)

NEW MUSIC (trilogy). By Reynolds Price. October 15, 1989. Directors, Josephine R. Abady, David Esbjornson; scenery, Dan Conway; lighting, John Hastings; costumes, C.L. Hundley; sound, Jeffrey Montgomerie.

### August Snow
Neal Avery........................................ Kelly Gwin
Taw Avery.......................................Susan Knight
Roma Avery...............................Sonja Lanzener
Porter Farwell...................................John Hickey
Genevieve Slappy...........Kathleen Mahoney-Bennett
   Time and Place: August, 1937, a small town in eastern North Carolina. One intermission.

### Night Dance
Taw Avery..................................... Susan Knight
Neal Avery.........................................Kelly Gwin
Genevieve Slappy
   Watkins .....................Kathleen Mahoney-Bennett
Roma Avery............................... Sonja Lanzener
Porter Farwell....................................John Hickey
Dob Watkins ...............................John Carpenter
Wayne Watkins..............................David Adkins
   Time and Place: September 1945, a small town in eastern North Carolina.

### Better Days
Taw Avery .............................. Barbara eda-Young

Neal Avery.................................... Bill Raymond
Dob Watkins................................John Carpenter
Porter Farwell............................... James Hurdle
Cody Avery....................................David Adkins
Virginia Wilson...................................Jody Gelb
Fontaine Belfont ........................Richard Thomsen
    Time and Place: July 1974, a small town in eastern North Carolina.

MAMA DRAMA. By Leslie Ayvazian, Donna Daley, Christine Farrell, Rita Nachtmann and Ann Sachs; music by the Roches. February 20, 1990. Director, John David Lutz; scenery, Dan Conway; costumes, C.L. Hundley; lighting, John Hastings; sound, Jeffrey Montgomery.
Lee...............................................Leslie Ayvazian
Liz ...................................................Donna Daley
Megan.......................................Christine Farrell

Danny .........................................Rita Nachtmann
Anna............................................... Ann Sachs
    One intermission.

THE MARCH ON RUSSIA. By David Storey. April 17, 1990. Director, Josephine R. Abady; scenery, Marjorie Bradley Kellogg; lighting, Marc B. Weiss; costumes, Linda Fisher; sound, Jeffrey Montgomerie.
Colin ...............................................Sean G. Griffin
Mr. Pasmore...............................John Carpenter
Mrs. Pasmore ................................. Bethel Leslie
Wendy...........................................Carol Locatell
Eileen.......................................Susan Browning
    Time and Place: The present, the Pasmores' 60th wedding anniversary. The Pasmores' retirement bungalow, northern England near the Yorkshire coast. One intermission.

## Cleveland Heights:  Dobama Theater

(Artistic directors, Ron Newell, Joyce Casey)

LAND OF THE FREE and PEN PALS. By Mary Gibson. January 26, 1990. Director, Donald Bianchi; scenery, Ron Newell; lighting, Ron Newell; costumes, Barbara Quill; sound, Bob Wachsberger.

*Pen Pals*
Martha ...............................................Peg Buerkel
Brenda Johnson...........................Lynnette Howard
Tanya......................................Linet Elan Largent

*Land of the Free*
Leslie................................................Mark Hudak
Sarah .........................................Sandra Cox True
    Time: The present. Place: An apartment building in a large city. One intermission.

SOLID GOLD BABY (musical). Book and additional lyrics by Margaret Hunt; music and lyrics by Jan Carol. February 4, 1990. Director, Sarah May; musical direction, Eric Bluffstone.
Laurie...............................................Lisa Paciorek
Barry..............................................Dan McCord
Richard...........................................Mike Cipiti
Carole ...............................................Jeanne Task
Mack.................................... Richard A. Musgrave
Helen .............................Wendy Warren Zangrando
Betty Jean .........................................Amy Walton
    Time: 1983 with flashbacks to the late 1950s and early '60s. The bandstand and dressing room of Fat Wally's nightclub and an alley out back.

## Costa Mesa, Calif.:  South Coast Repertory

(Producing artistic director, David Emmes; artistic director, Martin Benson)

WHEN I WAS A GIRL, I USED TO SCREAM AND SHOUT. By Sharman Macdonald. November 10, 1989. Director, Simon Stokes; scenery, Cliff Faulkner, lighting, Paulie Jenkins; costumes, Shigeru Yaji.
Morag...............................................Dana Ivey
Fiona...................................Elizabeth McGovern
Vari...................................... Katherine Romaine
Ewan ............................................. Bruce Norris
    Time and Place: The East Coast of Scotland over a summer weekend during the 1980s, and in various locations from the past. One intermission.

SEARCH & DESTROY. By Howard Korder. January 12, 1990. Director, David Chambers; scenery, Chris Barreca; lighting, Chris Parry; costumes, Dunya Ramicova; sound, David Budries.
Martin Mirkheim...........................Mark Harelik
Accountant; Dr. Waxling; Carling .....Jarion Monroe
Lauren; Voice of Flight Attendant;
    Voice of Radio Announcer; Jackie........Anni Long
Robert.....................................Anthony Forkush
Kim.............................................Philip Anglim
Businessman; Security Guard; Nunez......Art Koustik
Marie; Terry .................................Dendrie Taylor

Roger; State Trooper................Hubert Baron Kelly
Hotel Clerk; Lee ............................Dom Magwili
Bus Driver ........................................ Bic Trevino
Time: The present. Place: The United States.

HOLY DAYS. By Sally Nemeth. January 26, 1990. Director, Martin Benson; scenery, John Iacovelli; lighting, Tom Ruzika; costumes, Ann Bruice; music and sound, Michael Roth.
Rosie...........................................Jeanne Paulsen
Gant...............................................Richard Doyle
Will...........................................John K. Linton
Molly .......................................Devon Raymond
Time: Easter weekend, 1936. Place: Western Kansas.

ONCE IN ARDEN. By Richard Hellesen. April 20, 1990. Director, Martin Benson; scenery, Deborah Raymond, Dorian Vernacchio; lighting, Tom Ruzika; costumes, Dwight Richard Odel.
I.J. Paderewski...............................Patrick Husted
Karol Bozenta..................................Kay E. Kuter
Helena Modjeska................................Nan Martin
James O'Neill............................Charles Hallahan
J.T. Liddell ...................................Ron Boussom
Stage Assistant...................................Henry Leyva
One intermission.

*California Play Festival Mini-Rep.*
*May 4–June 3, 1990:*

MAN OF THE FLESH. By Octavio Solis. Director, Jose Cruz Gonzalez; scenery, Cliff Faulkner; lighting, Tom Ruzika; costumes, Shigeru Yaji.
Juan Tenorio .....................................Vic Trevino
Don Diego; Mr. Downey.................Jarion Monroe

Romelia; Anne Downey....................Teresa Velarde
Lorena; Heather Downey................Lucy Rodriguez
Martina; Dora Downey ..............Joan Stuart Morris
Concepcion; Flor.............................Rose Portillo
Fracas.........................................Geoffrey Rivas
Luis.................................... Patrick Roman Miller
Time: Takes place every year on November 2. One intermission.

THE RAMP. By Shem Bitterman. Director, Steven D. Albrezzi; scenery, Cliff Faulkner; lighting, Tom Ruzika; costumes, Shigeru Yaji.
Heinrich....................................James R. Winker
Lotte...............................................Pamela Gien
Fredrich ...................................... Norbert Weisser
One intermission.

*Newscripts Readings:*

PICK UP AX. By Anthony Clarvoe. November 9, 1989.
SIGHT UNSEEN. By Donald Margulies. November 13, 1989.
THE RUSSIAN TEACHER. By Alexander Buravsky, adapted by Keith Reddin. January 22, 1990.
THE HABIT OF LYING. By Allan Havis. April 20, 1990.
PIRATES. By Mark Lee. May 14, 1990.

*California Play Festival Readings:*

THE COURSE OF IT. By Neena Beeber. May 11, 1990.
AN OFFICE ROMANCE. By Robert Daseler. May 18, 1990.
EL DORADO. By Milcha Sanchez-Scott. May 19, 1990.

# Denver: The Changing Scene

(Executive producers, Al Brooks, Maxime Munt)

*Summerplay, June 29–July 2, 1989*

MY FATHER, THE PRESIDENT. By Christine MacDonald. July 20, 1989. Director, Hugh Graham.
THE NAMES HAVE BEEN CHANGED TO PROTECT THE INNOCENT. By Christine MacDonald. Director, Hugh Graham.
CONVERSATION WITH THE MOON. By Danny Kerwick. Director, Hugh Graham.
Designers: Lighting, Hugh Graham; sound, Steve Stevens. With Christine MacDonald.

*Summerplay, July 20–30, 1989*

WHEN A DOOR IS NOT A DOOR. By Brian Quinette. Director, Tere Edelen.

Mr. Overture...............................Kent Koprowicz
Mr. Underhand .................................. Glenn Beine
ANOTHER PARK BENCH PLAY. By Sonny Wasinger. Director, Kenneth Grimes.
Man...............................................Jeff Cyronek
Woman................................................Jan Avery
HI MOM. By Wayne Valero. Director, Henry Musmanno.
Mrs. Davis............................Judy Kwasniewski
Johnny ........................... Mickey Maurice Clifton
HAPPY FATHER'S DAY. By J.D. Leithoff. Director, Jim Hunt.
Clay Frazer................................Michael Ingram
Tracy Thompson ..................................Angie Lee

LOVE AND TEARS AND PAIN AND HOPE AND TRIUMPH. By Melinda Brindley. Director, Connie Phillips Denkla.

Elsa Jones................................... Mercedes Magee
Frank Jones.....................................Larry Males
Babette........................................Heidi St. Marie
  Designers: Scenery, Douglas Goodwin; lighting, Peter Nielson; sound, Ron Metzger.

*Summerplay, August 3–13, 1989*

THE ANGELS' HIERARCHIES. By Kevin Shancady Smith. Director, Mary Lee Larison.

Camilia................................. Kimberly Neutzling
Contessa Consuelo Stormundrang ...... Tammy Allen
Lika, Queen of the Amazons ............... Petra Ulrych
SON OF CABIN FEVER. By Jeff Carey. Director, Sonny Wasinger.

Nate............................................... Stacy Carson
Martha ...........................................Juliet Smith
BLUEBLACK. By Douglas R. Goodwin. Director, Dennis C. Beck.

Jane.............................................Karin Johnson
Holly.............................................Therese Allen
IL PESCE (THE FISH). By Phil Cockerille. Director, J.G. McDonald.

Antonia........................................Donna Metallo
Pete............................................Michael Rowan
MONORADO. By Richard Morell. Director, Sara Wright.

Clark .........................................Michael Brooks
Columbine Elizabeth ................Elizabeth Johnson, Kerry Tanner
Chris .......................................... Michael Tatlock
Roy.................................................Bob Leggett
Jehan ........................................ Nancy Solomon
  Designers: Scenery, Douglas Goodwin; costumes, Greta Lindecrantz; lighting, Lisa Scott; sound, David Kopplin.

*Summerplay, August 17–27, 1989*

WATERMELON WAR SONG. By Jerry Ellis
GUNPLAYS. By Brian Quinnette.
THE DEVIL AND JERRY FALWELL. By Katie Morgan
LADIES AND FERNS. By Joan Emmitt.

HONK! By Jay Derrah. November 30, 1989. Director, Doug Goodwin.

Fee ...............................................Jeff Cyronek
Hector ................................................Rich Beall
Gary................................................Callen Harty
Earl................................................Tyrone Clark
Oils ............................................... Doug White
Bill Baron ..................................... Milton Reeve
Andrea............................................ Tere Edelen
Peggy.............................................Juliet Smith
  One intermission.

THE WOMAN, THE MAN AND THE INDIAN. By Rodney Vance. February 22, 1990. Director, Sara Wright; scenery, Joseph M. Cashman; lighting, Joseph M. Cashman; costumes, Wanda Garlinghouse.

Woman.....................................Paula Lindemann
Jack .................................................. Ted Stroud
Girl.............................................Hart De Rose
Man..............................................Roy Lampinen
Old Man .........................................James Mills
Edeth.............................................. Judith Jerome
Indian................................Howard McKinley Jr.
  One intermission.

SAMENESS. By Michael Smith. May 31, 1990.
Rita ...............................................Terri Thaler
Sarah...............................Karen Kermiet Nielson
Anna.............................................Jonelle Pascoe
Man.................................................. Stan Picus

# Denver: Denver Center Theater Company

## (Artistic director, Donovan Marley)

READY FOR THE RIVER. By Neal Bell. April 9, 1990. Director, Gitta Honegger; scenery, Andrew V. Yelusich; lighting, Daniel L. Murray; costumes, Andrew V. Yelusich; sound, Matthew Morgan.

Lorna ........................................... Allison Gregory
Doris .............................................Alice Rorvik
Man in the Ski Mask; Hall .................Ben Bottoms
Ted; Walter ...................................Matthew Mabe
  Time: The present. Place: The Midwest.

MINE ALONE. By Conrad Bishop and Elizabeth Fuller. April 9, 1990. Director, Frank Georgianna; scenery, Carolyn Leslie Ross; lighting, Peter Maradudin; costumes, Patricia Ann Whitelock; sound, Scott R. Bradford.

Ackerman...................................James J. Lawless
Esther...................................... Kay Doubleday
Don ...................................Stephen Lee Anderson
Wendy.........................................Sharon Ullrick
  Time and Place: Early spring to winter, the Midwest. One intermission.

ANIMAL FAIR (musical). Book, music and lyrics by Clark Gesner. April 18, 1990. Director, Steve Stettler; scenery, Richard L. Hay; lighting, Charles MacLeod; costumes, Janet S. Morris; sound, Scott R. Bradford.

With Aron Accurso, P.J. Benjamin, Michael Kelly Boone, Linda Cameron, Louisa Flaningam, Christine Gradl, Michael X. Martin, Thomas-David McDonald. One intermission.

SOUNDBITE. By Gary Leon Hill. April 18, 1990.

Director, Donovan Marley; scenery, Andrew V. Yelusich; lighting, Daniel L. Murray; costumes, Andrew V. Yelusich; sound, Matthew Morgan.

Mummy Digits........................... Leticia Jaramillo
Camomile.......................... Jacqueline Antaramian
Pud.................................................. Jamie Horton
Boot Node; Man with Respirator;
    Dr. Ahshitz; Bio........................ William Brenner
    Time and Place: Midtown office, no window to the outside, so no time. One intermission.

## East Farmingdale, N.Y.: Arena Players Repertory Company of Long Island

(Producer/director, Frederic De Feis)

CARRIE'S CHOICE. By Burton R. Hoffman. Director, Frederic De Feis; scenery, Fred Sprauer; lighting, Al Davis; costumes, Josephine Verdi.

Mrs. Johnson ................................... Jan Anderson
Emily ................................................ Linda Bub
Ralph.................................................. Don Fram
Della.......................................... Barbara S. Herel
Maggie........................... Carolyn Van Bellinghen
Carolyn James............................. Aileen O. Kuss
Jane Grantz ............................... Pamela Laurence
Nettie Lawson ........................... Andrea B. Reiter
George Callahan........................... Joseph Sansone
Orderly........................................... Stephen Sisino
    Place: A room in a nursing-retirement facility on

the outskirts of a town near San Francisco. One intermission.

THE LAST DEAL. By Paul Moses. Director, Fredric De Feis; scenery, Fred Sprauer; lighting, Al Davis; costumes, Josephine Verdi.

Mayor Leo Crossetti ........................... Tony Kruk
Si Rosen.................................... Joseph S. King
Ronald Delgaudio ........................... Arnold Sabino
Rosa Napoli .................................. Sunny Taylor
Clifford Chase............................... Don McMillan
Francis X. Casey........................ Michael Fredricks
Marie Donato................................... Vicki Baum
Jimmy Osrowski............................ Chris Cardona
    Time: The present. Place: The mayor's office in City Hall. One intermission.

## East Haddam, Conn.: Goodspeed Opera House

(Executive producer, Michael P. Price)

*Work-in-Progress:*

A FINE AND PRIVATE PLACE (musical). Book and lyrics by Erik Haagensen; music by Richard Isen. August 3, 1989. Director, Robert Kalfin; scenery, Fred Kolo; lighting, Fred Kolo; musical director, Henry Aronson.

Jonathan Rebeck .............................. Charles Goff
Raven .............................................. Gabriel Barre
Michael Morgan........................... Brian Sutherland
Gertrude Klapper ............................. Evalyn Baron
Laura Durand............................. Maureen Silliman
Campos........................................ Larri Rebbega
    Time: The end of summer. Place: Yorkchester Cemetery, a vernal oasis in the North Bronx. One intermission.

THE REAL LIFE STORY OF JOHNNY DE FACTO (musical). Book, lyrics and music by Douglas Post. November 8, 1989. Director, Andre Ernotte; scenery, William Barclay; lighting, Phil Monat; costumes, Roslyn Brunner; sound, J.W. Hilton Jr.

Leo Sobocinski.................................. Paul Kandel
Johnny de Facto ............................... Jim Morlino
Spaz Bernstein ............................... Scott Dainton
Audrey Janes........................... Heidi Mollenhauer
Beau Pendergast........................... Michael Brian
1st Back-up Singer......................... Edwina Lewis
2d Back-up Singer............................. Steve Beebe
3d Back-up Singer........................... Bertilla Baker
    One intermission.

ARENA PLAYERS REPERTORY COMPANY OF LONG ISLAND—Michael Fredricks, Vicki Baum, Joseph S. King and Arnold Sabino in *The Last Deal* by Paul Moses

## Ft. Worth: Hip Pocket Theater

(Producer, Diane Simons; artistic director, Johnny Simons)

SHAZAM! (musical). By John Simons and Douglas Balentine. July 6, 1989. Musical director, Douglas Balentine; scenery, Brian Fitzmorris; lighting, Paul Chadwick.

| | |
|---|---|
| Captain Marvel | Bob Allen |
| Sivana | John Gibler |
| Black Adam | Adam Collis |
| Shazam | Michael Goggans |
| Freddy Freeman | Conner Kalista |
| Billy Batson | Daniel Sternoff |
| Mary Batson | Jane Mendez |
| Captain Marvel Junior | Mark Heimann |
| Mary Marvel | Tracy Nayer |

Gods and Goddesses: Ronnie Franks, Rick Swain, Zelmer Phillips, Robert Copeland, Dwight Welsh, Jerry Betsill, Ellen Mahoney, Lorca Simons, Holly Nelson Leach, Sharon Fenwalk Chadwick, Ellen Yeakle, Annie Laurie Maxwell. Daughters of Hespyrus: Lake Simons, Ramona Baker, Lauren Ivy.

KURU. By Josh Manheimer. July 27, 1989. Director, Johnny Simons. Scenery, Johnny Simons; lighting, Douglas Balentine; costumes, Diane Simons.

| | |
|---|---|
| Dr. Arthur Roman | Dick Harris |
| Mary Lou Anderson | Dena Brinkley |
| Mokina | Kristy Ramos |

## Gloucester, Mass.: The Gloucester Stage Company

(Artistic director, Israel Horovitz)

THE WIDOW'S BLIND DATE. By Israel Horovitz. July 19, 1989. Director, Israel Horovitz; scenery, David Condino, Michael Renken; lighting, Michael Renken; costumes, Rick Kelly, Janet Irving.

Archie Crisp.....................................Paul O'Brien
George Ferguson................................Tom Bloom
Margy Burke ...............................Dossy Peabody

Time: October afternoon, the present. Place: Baling-press room, waste paper company, Wakefield, Mass. One intermission.

STRONG MAN'S WEAK CHILD. By Israel Horovitz. (Produced at the Los Angeles Theater Company in collaboration with the Gloucester Stage Company). May 17, 1990. Director, Israel Horovitz; scenery, D. Martyn Bookwalter; lighting, D. Martyn Bookwalter; costumes, Ann Bruice; sound, Jon Gottlieb.

Evvie .................................................. Meg Foster
Dede.....................Sheridan Gayr, Sally Levi (alt.)
Auggie .........................................Peter Iacangelo
Franny.......................................... Nick Mancuso
Fast Eddie .........................................Don Yesso

Time: A succession of early mornings, the present. Place: Francis Farina's garage, Gloucester, Mass. No intermission.

## Hartford, Conn.: Hartford Stage Company

(Artistic director, Mark Lamos; managing director, David Hawkanson)

THE ILLUSION. By Tony Kushner; adapted from Pierre Corneille's L'Illusion Comique. January 5, 1990. Director, Mark Lamos; scenery, John Conklin; costumes, Martin Pakledinaz; lighting, Pat Collins.

Pridamant of Avignon.................... Marco St. John
Amanuensis ..................................Jarlath Conroy
Alcandre ................................ Frederick Neumann

Calisto; Clindor; Theogene............J. Grant Albrecht
Melibea; Insabelle; Hippolyta .......... Ashley Gardner
Elicia; Lyse; Clarina ........................Bellina Logan
Pieribo; Adraste; Prince ................Andrew Colteaux
Matamore..................................Philip Goodwin
Musician.............................Robert Edward Smith

One intermission.

## Hollywood, Calif: Theater West

(Managing director, Douglas Marney)

LOVE OF A PIG. By Leslie Caveny. July 7, 1989. Director, Bob McCracken; scenery, Wendy Guidery; lighting, Lawrence Oberman; costumes, Wendy Guidery.

Jenny...........................................Leslie Caveny
Polly ..........................................Andrea Iaderosa

Eddie....................................Joseph P. McCarthy
Joe.............................................. Bob McCracken
Mailman.....................................Kevin McMahon
Crystal .........................................Juleen Murray
Amy ........................................... Vivien Straus
Mr. Michaels........................Paul Anthony Weber

## Houston: AD Players

(Artistic director, Jeannette Clift George)

THE PROMISE COMES AFTER. By Sharla Boyce. June 30, 1989. Director, Sharla Boyce; scenery, Don Hollenbeck Jr.; lighting, Dan Flahive; costumes, Patty Tuel Bailey.

With Lisa Armstrong, Nancy Sherrard, Lee Walker, Marion Arthur Kirby, Don Hollenbeck Jr., Christopher Dunn.

TABS. By Jeannette Clift George. October 5, 1989.

O LITTLE TOWN OF BAGELS, TEACAKES, AND HAMBURGER BUNS. By Jeannette Clift George. Director, Sissy Pulley; scenery, Don Hollenbeck Jr.; lighting, Lee Walker; costumes, Patty Tuel Bailey.

Albert Bartlett........................Marion Arthur Kirby
Pastor ...............................................Dan Flahive
Manager ..........................................Jim Shores
Hepburn ....................................Lisa Armstrong
Rhonda................................. Sherry Joy Rathbun
Inez ............................................... Paulette James
Velma Jean ...............................Patty Tuel Bailey
  Time and Place: The bakery/coffee shop of the depot hotel in Palestine, Tex. It is right after lunch rush on Christmas Eve, 1960. One intermission.

CHRISTMAS WENT THATAWAY! By Sharla Boyce. December 8, 1989. Director, Sharla Boyce; scenery, Don Hollenbeck Jr.; lighting, Dan Flahive; costumes, Patty Tuel Bailey, Lisa Armstrong; sound, Christopher Dunn.
  With Lisa Armstrong, Patty Tuel Bailey, Wayne Ballard, Don Hollenbeck Jr., Sherry Joy Rathbun, Lee Walker.

IF HE SAYS THE WORD. By Carol Anderson.

Spring 1990. Director, Patty Tuel Bailey.
Captain..............................................Eric Moore
Lieutenant.......................................Jim Shores

VIRGULE. By Jeannette Clift George. Spring, 1990. Director, Jim Shores.
Marsha ..................................... Patty Tuel Bailey
Trevlin ................................Sherry Joy Rathbun

RET. By Jeannette Clift George. Spring 1990. Director, Sissy Pulley; scenery, Don Hollenbeck Jr.; lighting, Lee Walker, costumes, Lisa Armstrong.
Clayton ..............................................Larry Balfe
Isabel .......................................Lisa Armstrong
Warren...............................................Lee Walker
Hosea; Joe...........................Marion Arthur Kirby
Eileen; Gomer..................Elizabeth Pentak Averill
Lenore; Margaret ............................ Sharla Boyce
Barbara; Doris..................................Robin Proett
  Time and Place: 1980, Clayton's study. One intermission.

## Jackson, Miss.: New Stage Theater

(Producing artistic director, Jane Reid-Petty)

FULL MOON. By Reynolds Price. April 17, 1990. Director, Jane Reid-Petty; scenery, Richard Crowell; lighting, Richard Crowell; costumes, Patrick McWilliams; sound, Scott Queen.
Kerney Bascomb .......................Maryday Van Over
Kipple Patrick ............................... Nick Dantos
John Bascomb .................................David Lively
Walter Parker.......................................Jay Unger

Sarah Gaskin ...................................Tonea Stewart
Ora Lee Gaskin .................................Lynn Brown
Frank Patrick....................................Jack Stevens
Christine Bascomb......................Francine Thomas
Dorothy Patrick.............................Jaymee Vowell
  Time and Place: Late summer of 1938, in eastern North Carolina. A Saturday night and Sunday.

## Kansas City: Missouri Repertory Theater

(Artistic director, George Keathley)

THE SWEET BY AND BY. By Frank Higgins. June 13, 1989. Director, Ron Schaeffer; scenery, Bruce Hermans; lighting, Shelly Bradshaw; sound, Scott Gregory; musical direction, Allen DeCamp.
Babe Bradley..................................Rebecca Taylor
Libby Bradley.................................... Sara Lahey
Gramma Bradley..............................Nora Denney
Geneva Johnson...........................Barbara Houston
Newton Horton...............................Scott Co.des
Gopher Davenport ....................... William Murphy
Owen Flynn......................Phillip John Schroeder
Preacher............................... William Murphy
  Time: The present. Place: Glen Daniel, W.V., a coal mining town. One intermission.

JEKYLL! By James Costin. July 11, 1989. Direc-

tor, George Keathley; scenery, John Ezell; lighting, Joseph Appelt; costumes, Vincent Scassellati; sound, Tom Mardikes; composer, Allen DeCamp.
Dr. Henry Jekylll/Mr. Edward
  Hyde.......................................... Alan Brasington
Mrs. Pryce ..................................... Nora Denney
Mr. Poole ...................................Edward Conery
Vera.............................................Corliss Preston
Mr. John Utterson ....................Donald Christopher
Sir Danvers Carew............................Edgar Meyer
Mr. Richard Enfield.............................Jay Karnes
Dr. Hastie Lanyon ........................ Richard Bowden
Mrs. Dottie Clark....................Jeannine Hutchings
Inspector Newton..................Richard Alan Nichols
Sergeant Johnson.....................Gary Neal Johnson
Policeman..................................... Michael Wilson

Mrs. Beth Lanyon ..........................Claudia Kaplan
Time: Early 1860s. Place: London. One intermission.

FIVE SCENES FROM LIFE. By Alan Brody. May
10, 1990. Director, George Keathley; scenery, Gary
S. Mosby; lighting, Gary S. Mosby; costumes,
Mary G. Guaraldi; sound, Greg Mackender.
Bobby..........................................Jerome Butler
Nina ..........................................Angela Yannon
Prison Guard ..........................Kenneth M. Boehr
Time: The present. Place: A classroom in a max-
imum security prison somewhere in the Northeast.
One intermission.

Staged Readings:

HEAVEN'S HARD. By Jordan Budde. July 6, 1989.
PURPLE HEARTS. By Brian Kenton. July 27,
1989.
KOOZY'S PIECE. By Frank X. Hogan. August 3,
1989.
SWAMP FOXES. By Laurence Gonzales. August
17, 1989.
FIVE SCENES FROM LIFE. By Alan Brody.
August 31, 1989.
BABYLON GARDENS. By Timothy Mason.
February 15, 1990.
HALLELUJAH IN A HARD TIME. By Frank
Higgins. April 19, 1990.

## La Jolla, Calif.: La Jolla Playhouse

(Artistic director, Des McAnuff)

NEBRASKA. By Keith Reddin. June 25, 1989.
Director, Les Waters; scenery, Loy Arcenas; costumes, David C. Woolard; lighting, Stephen Strawbridge; sound, John Kilgore.
With Robin Bartlett, Susan Berman, Adam Coleman Howard, Barbara Howard, Rob Knepper, John
Cameron Mitchell, James Rebhorn.

One intermission.

DOWN THE ROAD. By Lee Blessing. August 13,
1989. Director, Des McAnuff; scenery, Neil Patel;
costumes, Susan Hilferty; lighting, Peter Maradudin.
With Susan Berman, Jonathan Hogan, James Morrison. No intermission.

## Little Rock: Arkansas Repertory Theater

(Producing artistic director, Cliff Fannin Baker)

BOYS' PLAY. By Jack Heifner. April 4, 1990.
Director, Cliff Fannin Baker; scenery, Mike Nichols;
lighting, Crickette Brendel; costumes, Don Bolinger;
sound, David Polantz.
Tom ..............................Todd William Frampton

Joe..............................................Nathaniel Buck
Time: A moonlit night. Place: A clearing in the
woods by a lake, outside of a small town in Middle
America.

## Los Angeles: East West Players

(Artistic director, Nobu McCarthy; managing director, Michele Garza)

THE CHAIRMAN'S WIFE. By Wakako Yamauchi.
January 17, 1990. Director, Nobu McCarthy;
scenery, Gronk; lighting, Rae Creevey; costumes,
Terence Tam Soon; sound, Nathan Wong, Jonathan
Flood.
Chou En Lai ......................................Yoshio Be
Communist; Shansi.......................Jusak Bernhard
Chiang Ching...................................Karen Huie
Guard...........................................Bill Cho Lee
U.S. Guard; Li Dewen; Tang Na ............Rob Narita
Yu Chi Wei ...................................Kipp Shiotani
Mrs. Li; Zheng Yufeng ........................Bea Soong

Wang Guangmei; Woman Spy........Szu-Ming Wang
One intermission.

PERFORMANCE ANXIETY. By Vernon Takeshita.
April 4, 1990. Director, Alberto Isaac; scenery,
Steven La Ponsie; lighting, Rae Creevey; costumes,
Lydia Tanji.
David ...........................................Timothy Dang
Felice...............................................Ren Hanami
Derek ........................................... Sab Shimono
Twins.....................John Miyasaki, Lisa Tateishi
One intermission.

## Los Angeles: Los Angeles Theater Center

(Artistic director, Bill Bushnell; producing director, Diane White)

DAYTRIPS. By Jo Carson. November, 1989. Director, Steven Kent; scenery, Douglas D. Smith; lighting, Douglas D. Smith; costumes, Donna Barrier; sound, Jon Gottlieb.

Narrator .................................... Victoria Ann-Lewis
Irene; Ree ..................................... Anne Gee Byrd
Rose ..................................... Julianna McCarthy
Pat ......................................... Christine Murdock

STEVIE WANTS TO PLAY THE BLUES (A JAZZ PLAY). By Eduardo Machado; music by Fredric Myrow; lyrics by Eduardo Machado and Fredric Myrow. February 17, 1990. Director, Simon

Callow; scenery, Timian Alsaker; lighting, Douglas D. Smith; costumes, Timian Alsaker; sound, Jon Gottlieb, Mark Friedman; musical director, Fredric Myrow.

Gary Neumiere; Ernest Roach ............. George Buck
Mary Ann .................................... Christie Houser
Ruth Scott ...................................... Paula Kelly
Peter ............................................ Randy Kovitz
Stevie Herman .............................. Amy Madigan
Harry ........................................ Michael Milhoan
Al ............................................... Louie Spears
Time: After World War II. Place: Jazz clubs in the Midwest. One intermission.

## Los Angeles: Mark Taper Forum

(Artistic director, Gordon Davidson)

OUR COUNTRY'S GOOD. By Timberlake Wertenbaker; based on the novel *The Playmaker* by Thomas Keneally. September 13, 1989. Directors, Max Stafford-Clark, Les Waters; scenery and costumes, Peter Hartwell; lighting, Kevin Rigdon; sound, Bryan Bowen, John Gottlieb.

With Tony Amendola, James Walch, John Cameron Mitchell, Michael Morgan, Harris Laskawy, Valerie Mahaffey, Gail Grate, Caitlin Clarke, Mark Moses, Deborah Fallender. One intermission.

THE MYSTERY OF THE ROSE BOUQUET. Adapted by Jeremy Lawrence from Manuel Puig; translated by Allan Baker. November, 1989. Director, Robert Allan Ackerman; scenery and costumes, Kenny Miller; lighting, Arden Fingerhut.

Patient ........................................... Anne Bancroft
Nurse ........................................... Jane Alexander

One intermission.

STAND-UP TRAGEDY. By Bill Cain. May 20, 1990. Director, Ron Link; scenery, Yael Pardess; lighting, Michael Gilliam; costumes, Carol Brolaski; sound, Jon Gottlieb.

Father Ed Larkin ...................... Vaughn Armstrong
Marco Ruiz ................................. Anthony Barrile
Freddy ......................................... Marcus Chong
Tom Griffin ................................... Jack Coleman
Luis ........................................ Marvin Columbus
Bob Kenter ................................... John C. Cooke
Lee Cortez ............................ Michael DeLorenzo
Pierce Brennan ................................. Dan Gerrity
Henry Fernandez ................................. Ray Oriel
Carlos Cruz ............................... Lance Slaughter
Time: 1890s. Place: A small Catholic school for Hispanic boys on New York's Lower East Side. One intermission.

## Louisville: Actors Theater of Louisville

(Producing director, Jon Jory)

*Humana Festival of New American Plays.*
*February 28–April 7, 1990*

THE PINK STUDIO. By Jane Anderson. Director, Steve Schachter; scenery, Paul Owen; lighting, Victor En Yu Tan; costumes, Michael Krass; sound, Mark Hendren.

Claudine ........................................... Beth Dixon
Henri .................................... Peter Michael Goetz

Madame Bidet; Madame Joie ................. Janet Sarno
Pierre .......................................... Joey Argabrite
Cherisse; Nicole ............................. Gail Benedict
Derain ..................................... William McNulty
Lulu; Merique; Lucille ................ Connan Morrissey
Time: The early part of this century. Place: Matisse's paintings. One intermission.

VITAL SIGNS. By Jane Martin. Director, Jon

Jory; scenery, Paul Owen; lighting, Victor En Yu Tan; costumes, Michael Krass; sound, Mark Hendren.

With Kymberly Dakin, V. Craig Heidenreich, Paul Rogers, Pamela Stewart, Randy Danson, Adale O'Brien, Priscilla Shanks, Myra Taylor.

THE SWAN. By Elizabeth Egloff. Director, Evan Yionoulis; scenery, Paul Owen; lighting, Victor En Yu Tan; costumes, Michael Krass; sound, Mark Hendren.

Dora .......................................... Anne O'Sullivan
Bill.......................................... William Youmans
Kevin................................................David Chandler

Time: The present. Place: A house somewhere in Nebraska.

INFINITY'S HOUSE. By Ellen McLaughlin. Director, Jackson Phippin; scenery, Paul Owen; lighting, Victor En Yu Tan; costumes, Michael Krass; sound, Mark Hendren.

Annie.......................................Ellen McLaughlin
Catches Rain................................. Sakina Jaffrey
Carl; Kistiakowsky........................... Greg Porretta
Doolin; Wong; Rabi.................. Christopher Fields
Joe; Gratz; Katz ............................... Scott Sowers
Indian...............................................Bob Burrus
Plug; Cass....................................Josh Liveright
Asa; Jimmy; Edelstein ......................Andrew Polk
Sean; Li; Soldier #1........................Bruce Romans
Silas; Turpin.......................................Steve Wise
Hans Bethe; Na Bok................................Ray Fry
Oppenheimer.........................David A. Kimball
Ba Hong; Matt; Soldier #2; Serber.....Chris Eigeman
Nathan .........................................Joe Burmester
General Groves ................................... Fred Major
Sing; Swaver....................................Jeremy Gold
Fraulein Mittel ............................... Diane Casey

Time and Place: The Humboldt Desert, 1850; Promontory Point, Utah, 1869, The Trinity Site, Alamogordo Desert, 1945. One intermission.

ZARA SPOOK AND OTHER LURES. By Joan Ackemann-Blount. Director, Kyle Donnelly; scenery, Paul Owen; lighting, Victor En Yu Tan; costumes, Michael Krass; sound, Mark Hendren.

Talmadge.....................................David Chandler

Evelyn......................................Anne O'Sullivan
Teale...............................................Ellen Mareneck
Margery......................................Priscilla Shanks
Mel.......................................V. Craig Heidenreich
Ramona...............................................Annette Helde

Time: The present. Place: West Virginia, in Truth or Consequences, New Mexico, and on the road in between. One intermission.

IN DARKEST AMERICA (two plays). By Joyce Carol Oates. Director, Steven Albrezzi; scenery, Paul Owen; lighting, Victor En Yu Tan; costumes, Michael Krass; sound, Mark Hendren.

*Tone Clusters*
Voice .......................................William McNulty
Frank Gulick .........................Peter Michael Goetz
Emily Gulick..................................Adale O'Brien

Time: The present.

*The Eclipse*
Stephanie Washburn........................... Beth Dixon
Muriel Washburn................... Madeleine Sherwood
Aileen Stanley .................................Gail Benedict
Senor Rios....................................... Paul Rogers

Time and Place: An apartment in Philadelphia; the action spans three weeks in the fall in the present.

2. By Romulus Linney. Director, Thomas Allan Bullard; scenery, Paul Owen; lighting, Ralph Dressler, costumes, Lewis D. Rampino; sound, Mark Hendren.

Lieutenant.......................................Scott Sowers
Sergeant.......................................... Percy Metcalf
Commandant ....................................Bob Burrus
Counsel...............................................Ray Fry
Hermann Goering ....................William Duff-Griffin
Psychologist....................................David A. Kimball
Justice Robert Jackson.........................Fred Major
President of the Tribunal.......................Steve Wise
British Prosecutor......................Christopher Fields
Goering's Wife.......................... Ellen McLaughlin
Goering's Daughter..........................Ashley Mueller

Time: May 1945–October 1946. Place: Palace of Justice, Nuremberg, Germany. One intermission. (An ATCA selection; see introduction to this section.)

# Malvern, Pa.: People's Light and Theater Company

(Artistic director, Danny Fruchter)

THE DEVIL AND ALL HIS WORKS. By Ernest Joselovitz. May 18, 1990. Director, Michael Nash; scenery, James F. Pyne Jr.; costumes, P. Chelsea Harriman; lighting, James F. Pyne Jr., Deborah D. Peretz; sound and original music, Adam Wernick.

Arthur Schnitzler...................................Tom Teti

| | |
|---|---|
| Samuel Landau | Paul Meshejian |
| Julia Landau | Elizabeth Soukup |
| Theresa Landau | Rebecca Ellens |
| Marta | Alda Cortese |
| Aaron Margolis | David Ingram |
| Theodor Herzl | Stephen Novelli |

| | |
|---|---|
| Gustav Mahler | Pearce Bunting |
| Karl Lueger | Frank Wood |
| Klaus van Schiff | Peter DeLaurier |
| Eduard Wlassack | Louis Lippa |
| The Device | Joyce Lee, Demetra Tseckares |

One intermission.

## Miami: Coconut Grove Playhouse

(Producing artistic director, Arnold Mittelman)

MIAMI LIGHTS (musical). Book and lyrics by Jacques Levy; music by Stanley Walden. February 5, 1990. Director, Arnold Mittelman; scenery, Kevin Rupnik; lighting, John Ambrosone; costumes, Kevin Rupnik; sound, Gary Harris; musical director, Fernando Rivas; choreographer, Margo Sappington.

| | |
|---|---|
| Felipe | Pedro Roman |
| Miguel | Jack Dadoub |
| Margarita | Yamil Borges |
| Juan | Allen Hidalgo |
| Cristo | Mark Morales |
| Moron | Ronald Hunter |
| Adela | Tracy Lynn Neff |
| Flora | Anne-Marie Gerard |
| Cookie | Sandra Perry |
| Carlotta | Deborah Roshe |
| Priest | Rafael V. Blanco |

Time: 1938. Place: The Florida Keys, midway between Miami and Key West. One intermission.

PAPER MILL PLAYHOUSE—Nora Mae Lyng (*center*) and ensemble in the Hal Hackady-Fred Stark musical *Rhythm Ranch*

# Millburn, N.J.: Paper Mill Playhouse

(Executive producer, Angelo Del Rossi; artistic director, Robert Johanson)

RHYTHM RANCH (musical). Book and lyrics by Hal Hackady; music by Fred Stark. November 1, 1989. Director, Philip William McKinley; choreography, Susan Stroman; scenery, Michael Anania; musical direction, Phil Hall; lighting, Jeff Davis; costumes, Lindsay W. Davis; dance arrangements, Glen Kelly; sound, David R. Peterson.

| | |
|---|---|
| Sam Graybeal | Christopher Durham |
| Babe Blandish | Liz Larsen |
| Conductor; Radio Show Director | Jason Opsahl |
| Cacuts Hatch | Bill Rowley |
| Utah Beaudeen | Billy Padgett |
| Lucy Calhoun | Ruth Williamson |
| Wanda June | Ella Vador |
| Wa Hoo | Chung Kee |
| Ruby Sue | Dorie Herndon |
| Opal Sue | Teri Gibson |
| Pearl | Jessica Sheridan |
| Zeke | Steve Hiltebrand |
| Russ | D.J. Salisbury |
| Beau | Steve Gray |
| Brandy | Nora Mae Lyng |
| Natchez | Jimmy Changa |
| Tulsa del Rio | Bob Cuccioli |
| Velma | Heidi Karol Johnson |
| Little Joey | Buddy Smith |

Time: When it was 1938 forever. Place: Desert Valley, Nev. One intermission.

MIKADO INC. (musical). Book by Jane Waterhouse; lyrics by Albert Evans; musical supervision and adaptation, Glen Kelly. May 16, 1990. Conceived, directed and choreographed by Robert Johanson; musical direction, Tom Helm; scenery, Michael Anania; lighting, Phil Monat; costumes, Lindsay W. Davis; sound, David R. Paterson.

| | |
|---|---|
| Mr. Pish-Tush | Jason Ma |
| Mr. Obuchi; First Brother of the Oxtail | Leslie Feagan |
| Frankie Puccelli | James Rocco |
| Mr. Pooh-Bah | Michael Mulheren |
| Mr. Koko | Philip William McKinley |
| Ms. Nagami; Head Teahouse Maiden | Ako |
| Yum-Yum | Christine Toy |
| Peep-Bo | Mia Korf |
| Pitti-Sing | Ann Harada |
| Mikado Spokesperson | Zoie Lam |
| Katisha | Marsha Bagwell |
| Mikado | Thomas Ikeda |

One intermission.

*Staged Readings:*

BACK HOME (musical). Book by Ron Sproat; lyrics by Frank Evans; music by Christopher Berg. October 2, 1989.

MALICE AFORETHOUGHT. By Erik Jendresen. January 29, 1990.

# Milford, N.H.: American Stage Festival

(Artistic director, Larry Carpenter)

A CHRISTMAS CAROL: A CONTEMPORARY TALE IN FOUR GHOSTS. By Austin Tichenor. December 7, 1989. Director, Richard Rose; scenery, Gary English; lighting, Ken Smith; costumes, Dianne Tyree.

| | |
|---|---|
| Ebenezer Scrooge | Curzon Dobell |
| Robin Cratchit | Christine Stabile |
| Fred; Christmas Future | Austin Tichenor |
| Jacob Marley; Fezziwig | Nicolas Mize |
| Christmas Past | Denise Ryan |
| Young Scrooge | Keith Stevens |
| Belle | Karla Hendrick |
| Fan | Kathryn Forest, Lisa Willis |

| | |
|---|---|
| Christmas Present | Scott Severance |
| Tiny Tim | Kerry Silva, David Forest |
| Peter Cratchit | Rob Nickerson, Nathan Gehan |
| Martha Cratchit | Jessi Philips, Melissa Gentile |

GRACELAND. By Donald Steele. January 23, 1990. Director, Austin Tichenor; scenery, Charles Morgan; lighting, Sid Bennett; costumes, Dianne Tyree.

| | |
|---|---|
| Janelle | Margery Murray |
| Tom | David Bouvier |
| Lana | Gail Harvey |
| Donnie-n-Marie | Connie Howard |

## Milwaukee: Milwaukee Repertory Theater

(Artistic director, John Dillon; managing director, Sara O'Connor)

THE JEREMIAH. By Diane Ney. Director, Mary B. Robinson; scenery, Laura Maurer; lighting, Ann G. Wrightson; costumes, Michael Krass.

| | |
|---|---|
| Thomas Hudson | Alan Mixon |
| Constance Hudson | Jen Jones |
| Mike Hudson | Greg Steres |
| Barbara Hudson | Cynthia Hanson |
| Joe Hudson | James Fletcher |
| Alice Hudson | Carrie Hitchcock |
| Tommy | Brad Moran, John Tenwinkel |
| Jennie | Ruth Eglsaer, Shannon McBee |
| Mr. Ferguson; Congressman | |
| Patton | Richard Halverson |
| Hal Miller | Robert Cornelius |
| Congressional Aide | Anne Durall |
| The Voice | Kenneth Albers |

Time: The present. Place: The Hudson farm, James River County, Va. and various other locations. One intermission.

4 A.M. AMERICA. Conceived and directed by Ping Chong. March 10, 1990. Scenery, Ping Chong, Pat Doty; lighting, Thomas Hase; costumes, Dawna Gregory; sound, Brian Hallas.

| | |
|---|---|
| Father | Jawn Fleming |
| The Clock | Scott Howland |
| Jenny | Jeannie Hutchins |
| Buddy | Larry G. Malvern |
| Emily | Johanna Melamed |
| Francisco | Ric Ocquita |
| Mother | Louise Smith |

## Milwaukee: Theater X

(Executive director, John Sobczak)

THE DESIRE OF THE MOTH FOR THE STAR. By Deborah Clifton, Flora Coker and Wesley Savick. October 22, 1989. Director, Wesley Wavick; scenery, Robert Kushner, John Starmer; lighting, Andrew Meyers; costumes, Ellen M. Kozak.

With Deborah Clifton, Flora Coker, John Kishline, John Starmer, Victor DeLorenzo, Jeruen Janssen, Margaret Fairbanks.

SUCCESS. By John Kishline. May 20, 1990. Director, Mark Anderson; scenery, John Starmer, John Tully; lighting, John Starmer.

With John Kishline, Colin Cabot, Deborah Clifton, Westley Savick.

## Montclair, N.J.: The Whole Theater

(Producing artistic director, Olympia Dukakis)

THE WORLD GOES 'ROUND ... WITH KANDER AND EBB (revue). Music by John Kander; lyrics by Fred Ebb; conceived by Scott Ellis, Susan Stroman and David Thompson. June 6, 1989. Director, Scott Ellis; choreography, Susan Stroman; scenery, Bill Hoffman; costumes, Donna Marie Larsen; lighting, Phil Monat; sound, Gary Stocker; orchestrations, David Krane.

With Brent Barrett, Karen Mason, Paige O'Hara, Jim Walton, Karen Ziemba. One intermission.

## Montgomery, Ala.: Alabama Shakespeare Festival

(Artistic director, Kent Thompson; managing director, Jim Volz)

ALL GOD'S DANGERS: THE LIFE OF NATE SHAW. By Theodore Rosengarten, Jennifer Hadley and Michael Hadley. September 5, 1989. Director, William Partlan; scenery, G.W. Mercier; lighting, Tina Charney; costumes, G.W. Mercier.

| | |
|---|---|
| Nate Shaw | Cleavon Little |

Place: Rural Alabama. One intermission.

## Moylan, Pa.: Hedgerow Theater

(Managing director, David zum Brunnen)

*Mainstage*

UNHOLY TRINITY. By Eric Bentley. March 29, 1990. Directors, Ralph Roseman, Yvonne Vincic; lighting, Dan Patsco; musical director, Brian Hesko.
Galileo.......................................... Steve Masters
Oscar Wilde.................................... Vince Urbani
Jesus Christ ...........................David zum Brunnen

THE SECRET LIFE OF WALTER MITTY. By Tom Teti; adapted from James Thurber. October 12, 1989. Director, Tom Teti.
With Gwen Armstrong, John Barker, Serena Ebhardt, Dale New, George Sheffey, Mark Utermohlen, Susan Wefel, David zum Brunnen.

*Children's Theater Productions:*

UMPY THE PUMPKIN. By Harry H. Hollins. October 21, 1989. Director, Gwen Armstrong.
PUSS IN BOOTS. By Moira Rankin. November 4, 1989. Director, Moira Rankin.
KING'S NEW CLOTHES. By Louis Lippa and Dan Patsco. February 11, 1990. Director, Dan Patsco.
LIMERICKS AND POEMS. By Michael Hagler. March, 1990. Director, Michael Hagler.
THE EMPEROR'S NIGHTINGALE. By Dolores Tanner. May, 1990. Director, David zum Brunnen.

*Staged Readings:*

DRIVERS. By Tony Stafford. April, 1990. Director, Mark Cofta.
THE ONLY YEAR THAT EVER WAS. By James Glossman and Stephen Randoy. May, 1990. Director, James Glossman.

## New Brunswick, N.J.: Crossroads Theater Company

(Producing artistic director, Rick Khan)

SHEILA'S DAY. By Duma Dnlovu. September 14, 1989. Director, Mbongeni Ngema; scenery, Lloyd Harris; lighting, Victor En Yu Tan; costumes, Toni-Leslie James.
With Stephanie Alston, Gina Breedlove, Carla Brothers, Irene Datcher, Thuli Dumakude, Ebony Jo-Ann, Annelen Malebo, Letta Mbulu, Tu Nokwe, Valerie Jerusha Rochon, Gina Torres.
Time: 1975. Place: Soweto, Johannesburg and Perry County, Alabama.

SPUNK (THREE TALES BY ZORA NEALE HURSTON). Adapted by George C. Wolfe. November 2, 1989. Director, George C. Wolfe; scenery, Loy Arcenas; lighting, Don Holder; costumes, Toni-Leslie James.
With Betty K. Bynum, Reggie Montgomery, Kevin Jackson, Danitra Vance, Chic Street Man, Tico Wells.

BLACK EAGLES. By Leslie Lee. February 15, 1990. Director, Rick Khan; scenery, Charles McClennahan; lighting, Shirley Prendergast; costumes, Beth Ribblett; sound, David Lawson; choreographer, Hope Clarke.
Young Clarkie...........................William Christian
Elder Nolan...................................Helmar Cooper
Pia ............................................ Illeana Douglas
Roy ..............................................Milton Elliot
Elder Leon................................Sonny Jim Gaines
Dave ...............................................Larry Green
General Lucas ...............................Michael Greer
Young Cadet..................................Duane Jackson
Rosco............................................Damien Leake
Young Leon ...................................David Rainey
Young Cadet...............................Raymond Reaves
Elder Clarkie............................W. Benson Terry
Buddy .........................Raymond Anthony Thomas
Young Nolan..............................Scott Whitehurst
Time and Place: 1989, Washington, D.C. and Italy, 1944, during World War II. One intermission.

TOD, THE BOY, TOD. By Talvin Wilks. April 19, 1990. Director, Ken Johnson; scenery, Lloyd Harris; lighting, William H. Grant III; costumes, Toni-Leslie James; choreographer, Hope Clarke.
John; The Psychiatrist...........................Jon Avner
Reverend Joe...................Helmar Augustus Cooper
Tod, the Boy, Tod...........................Dennis Green
Committee Executive.......................Michael Greer
Committee Senior ..........................Michael Haney
Committee Junior......................... Spike McClure
Mary Martha........................................ Essene R
Time: The present. Place: In the mind of Tod. One intermission.

# New Brunswick, N.J.: George Street Playhouse

(Producing director, Gregory S. Hurst)

MOUNTAIN. By Douglas Scott. January 3, 1990. Director, John Henry Davis; scenery, Philipp Jung; lighting, Donald Holder; costumes, Barbara Forbes.

William O. Douglas ............................Len Cariou
Woman ............................... Heather Summerhayes
Man..........................................John C. Vennema

Time and Place: The play begins in Walter Reed Hospital, Washington, D.C. on January 19, 1980, the day of Justice Douglas' death, then moves throughout his 81 years of life. One intermission.

JOHNNY PYE AND THE FOOLKILLER (musical). Book and lyrics by Mark St. Germain; music and lyrics by Randy Courts. February 7, 1990. Director, Paul Lazarus; musical direction, Steven M. Alper; scenery, William Barclay; lighting, Donald Holder; costumes, Mary L. Hayes.

Young Johnny................................John Babcock
Bob .................................................Larry Cahn
Suzy Marsh................................Victoria Clark
Johnny Pye.....................................John Hickok
Foolkiller .......................................John Jellison
Wilbur Wilberforce.......................... Tom Robbins
Young Suzy........................ Catherine Satterwhite
Barber ..........................................Ron Lee Savin
Bill.............................................Gordon Stanley
Mrs. Miller...................................Lou Williford

JEKYLL AND HYDE (musical). Book by Leonora Thuna; music by Norman Sachs; lyrics by Mel Mandel. March 14, 1990. Director, Gregory S. Hurst; musical direction, Joel Silberman; choreography, Lynne Taylor-Corbett; scenery, Deborah Jasien; lighting, Donald Holder; costumes, Barbara Forbes.

Lucy Turner ..................................Rebecca Baxter
Dr. Henry Jekyll; Edward Hyde ........... John Cullum

Reverend Luster............................ Terrence Currier
Grace; Billy Bob..........................Marianne Ferrari
Margaret Cavendish...................... Anne Kerry Ford
Sir Danvers Carew; Col. Douglas.........Charles Goff
Catherine; Alicia-Ann...................... Cady Huffman
Richard Enfield...................................James Judy
Elizabeth; Jimmy Joe.....................Nancy Magarill
Poole ..............................................John Rainer
Dr. Hastie Lanyon ............................. Jamie Ross
Gabriel Utterson............................... David Sabin
Madam Goodheart........................ Celia Tackaberry
Inspector Elliot; Capt.
  Beauregard .............................John Vandertholen
Flower Girl; Maid............................Jane Scimeca
Bootblack........................................ Mary Walker

Time and Place: London, 1891.

*Staged Readings:*

VIRAGO. By Laurie Hutzler. December 11, 1989. Director, Wendy Liscow.

TORRENTS OF SPRING. By John Porter. February 15, 1990. Director, Wendy Liscow.

STRANGE SIGHTINGS IN THE SOUTHWEST. By Jacklyn Maddux. February 19, 1990. Director, Wendy Liscow.

SEA CHANGE. By Phyllis Purscell. March 1, 1990. Director, Wendy Liscow.

CASH VALUES. By Leslie Weiner. March 5, 1990. Director, Wendy Liscow.

LES PECHEURS. By Christopher Scherer. March 8, 1990. Director, Wendy Liscow.

PENDRAGON. By Laurie Hutzler. March 18, 1990. Director, Wendy Liscow.

GREETINGS! By Tom Dudzick. May 5, 1990. Director, Wendy Liscow.

# New Haven, Conn.: Long Wharf Theater

(Artistic director, Arvin Brown)

A DANCE LESSON. By David Wiltse. October 27, 1989. Director, Gordon Edelstein; scenery, Hugh Landwehr; lighting, Pat Collins; costumes, David Murin.

Jason ...............................................Eric Conger
Dan Hauser ............................... John Cunningham
Susan Hauser................................. Debra Mooney
Jay Hauser ......................................Josh Charles
Jack Stone .................................Quentin O'Brien
Smitty ............................................Rob Kramer

Time and Place: Cascade, Nebraska, in the mid 1950s. One intermission.

IS HE STILL DEAD? By Donald Freed. May 8, 1990. Director, Charles Nelson Reilly; scenery, Marjorie Bradley Kellogg; lighting, Marc B. Weiss; costumes, Noel Taylor; sound, Brent Evans.

Nora Joyce ........................................Julie Harris
James Joyce................................. Ronny Graham

Time and Place: Saint-Gérand-le-Puy, Vichy, France. A hotel, December 1940, noon. One intermission.

*Workshops:*

ESTABLISHED PRICE.   By Dennis McIntyre.
January 2, 1990. Director, Arvin Brown.
THE GHOSTMAN.   By Wendy Hammond. January
23, 1990. Director, John Tillinger.

A DARING BRIDE.   By Allan Havis. February 13,
1990. Director, Bill Foeller.
THE SUBSTANCE OF FIRE.   By Jon Robin Baitz.
March 6, 1990. Director, David Warren.

## New Haven, Conn.: Yale Repertory Theater

(Artistic director, Lloyd Richards; managing director, Benjamin Mordecai)

TWO TRAINS RUNNING.   By August Wilson.
March 30, 1990. Director, Lloyd Richards; scenery,
Tony Fanning; costumes, Chrisi Karvonides; light-
ing, Geoff Korf; sound, Ann Johnson.
Memphis...............................................Al White
Wolf.....................................Samuel L. Jackson

Risa.....................................................Ella Joyce
Holloway............................... Samuel E. Wright
Sterling .....................................Larry Fishburne
Hambone ....................................Sullivan Walker
West ..........................................Leonard Parker
One intermission.

OMAHA MAGIC THEATER—Members of the cast in Megan Terry's *Headlights*

## Norfolk: Virginia State Theater

(Artistic director, Charles Towers)

THE SECRET GARDEN (musical). Book and lyrics by Marsha Norman; music by Lucy Simon. February 6, 1990. Director, R.J. Cutler; scenery, Heidi Landesman; lighting, Roger Morgan; costumes, Martin Pakledinaz; musical direction, David Loud.

With Victoria Clark, Jedidiah Cohen, Christopher

Davis, Suzanne Dowaliby, Walter Hudson, Bonny Hughes, Michael McCormick, Stacey Moseley, Louis Padilla, Wade Raley, Molly Regan, Sharon Scruggs, Melanie Vaughan, William Youmans, Aaron Boone, Jonathan Frank, Jessica Greene, Joshua Ivey, Mark Molineaux, Greg Moore.

One intermission.

## Omaha: The Omaha Magic Theater

(Artistic director, Jo Ann Schmidman)

LUCY LOVES ME. By Migdalia Cruz. June 9, 1989. Director, Jo Ann Schmidman; scenery, Sora Kim; lighting, Jim Schumacher; sound, Ivy Dow.

Lucy Rodriquez........ Star Graham, Kimberly Wright
Milton Ayala.............Charles Larson, Roger Reeves
Cookie Rodriquez......................... Deborah Leech, Jo Ann Schmidman
Images ................Robert N. Gilmer, Phyllis Kohl, Barbara Loper, Tammi Ziola

One intermission.

FAT (musical). Book, music and lyrics by Terra Daugirda Pressler. June 16, 1989. Director, Jo Ann Schmidman; scenery, Sora Kim; lighting, Jim Schumacher; sound, Ivy Dow.

Cast: Bulimics; Anorexics; Overweights; Skeletals (All Different Shapes and Sizes of Women)—Star Graham, Sunny Johnson, Phyllis Kohl, Deborah Leech, Barbara Loper, Hollie McClay, Jonnie Moneiro, Jo Ann Schmidman, Susan Watts, Kimberly Wright, Tammi Ziola.

One intermission.

ANGEL FACE. By Laura Harrington. June 16, 1989. Director, Jo Ann Schmidman; scenery, Sora

Kim; lighting, Jim Schumacher; sound, Ivy Dow.

Sharkey .................................. William York Hyde
Lil.................................................Hollie McClay
Images—Star Graham, Sunny Johnson, Phyllis Kohl, Deborah Leech, Barbara Loper, Hollie McClay, Jonnie Monteiro, Jo Ann Schmidman, Susan Watts, Kimberly Wright, Tammi Ziola.

One intermission.

HEADLIGHTS. By Megan Terry. September 14, 1989. Director, Jo Ann Schmidman; scenery, Sora Kim, Bill Farmer; lighting, Jim Schumacher, Jo Ann Schmidman; sound, Frank Fong, Luigi Waites; music composition, Frank Fong, Rex Gray, Rick Hiatt.

With Robert N. Gilmer, Star Graham, Rick Hiatt, Sora Kim, Hollie McClay, Roger Reeves, Jo Ann Schmidman.

BODY LEAKS. By Megan Terry, Sora Kim and Jo Ann Schmidman. April 27, 1990. Director, Jo Ann Schmidman; scenery, Sora Kim; lighting, Jo Ann Schmidman; costumes, Kenda Slavin.

With Robert N. Gilmer, Sora Kim, Jo Ann Schmidman, Megan Terry, Susan Watts.

## Palo Alto, Calif.: TheaterWorks

(Artistic director, Robert Kelley)

FRAULEIN DORA. By Carol Lashof. Director, Kathleen Woods; scenery, Keith Snider; lighting, Bruce McLeod; costumes, Allison Connor; sound, Aodh Og O Tuama.

Dora Grunwald................................Sandy Blaine
Sigmund Freud ............................. Frank Widman
Ernst Grunwald..................................Eric Silins
Klara Grunwald............................Louise Carter

Gustav Kraus................................Tom Woosnam
Elisabeth Kraus............................Ashleigh Evans

Time: Dec. 31, 1900, and three years preceding. Place: Vienna, Freud's office, the Grunwald home, the Kraus home and a rented house in the Alps. One intermission.

OUR LADY OF THE DESERT. By Lynn Kaufman. May 11, 1990. Director, Leslie Martinson; scenery, Joe Ragey; lighting, Barry Griffin; costumes, Pamela Ritchey.

Jo McNair....................................Jane Carmichael
Diego Sebastian.............................Miguel Najera
Corazon.....................................Mary Ann Rodgers
Amster Jacobs................................Keith Bentley
Joseph Garber...................................Joe Doscher

*Staged Readings:*

OUT OF CHARACTER. By Bob Fenster. August

18, 1989.
FRAULEIN DORA. By Carol Lashof. August 19, 1989.
OVERLAND (musical). Book and music by Ken Stone, lyrics by Jan Powell. August 26, 1989.
GO DOWN GARVEY (musical). Book, music and lyrics by Danny Duncan. January 29, 1990.
UNCONDITIONAL WAR. By Toni Press. May 29, 1990.

## Philadelphia: Novel Stages

(Artistic director, David Bassuk)

THE EARTH. By David Bassuk, adapted from a novel by Emil Zola; music by Miles Green. November 15, 1989. Director, Dugald MacArthur; scenery, Daniel P. Boylen; costumes, Chryss Hionis; lighting, Rebecca G. Frederick; sound, Robert Biasetti.

Fouan ........................................ Fred Schaffmaster
Buteau.........................................David Urrutia
"The Corporal" ...............................Arturo Castillo
Francoise.....................................Laura Mitchell
Lise..........................................Clista Townsend
"Jesus Christ"....................................Ted Rooney
La Tourille...................................A. Lee Massaro
La Grande ...................................Hazel Weinberg
    Others: Gary Tucker, Deirdre Lewis, Donna Browne, Brian Joyce, Mary Beth Scallen, Neill Hartley, Marcus Zanders, Paul DeSantis, Leigh Smiley, Daniel B. Pierson.
One intermission.

OUT OF THE DEPTHS. By Chaim Potok. April 19, 1990. Director, David Bassuk; scenery, Andrei Efremoff; costumes, Susan Deeley; lighting, Russell Wadbrook; sound, Scott Sanders; music, Jack Kessler.

S. Ansky (young)....................Christopher Stewart

S. Ansky (middle aged).................Alexander Wells
S. Ansky (old) ...........................Fred Schaffmaster
Sonya (young) ...........................Andrea Blumberg
Sonya (older) .............................Clista Townsend
Ansky's Mother .................Hazel Weinberg Bowers
Isaac Chernin.....................................Brian Joyce
Claudine .........................................Barbara Pitts
Theater Director..............................John Cannon
Stanislavsky.................................Marty Sherman
One intermission.

A LOVER'S DISCOURSE (program of 10 playlets). Adapted by Donna Browne, John Erlanger, Brian Joyce, Leigh Smiley, Christopher Stewart, Clista Townsend and David Urrutia from stories by Italo Calvino, Laurie Colwin, Ellen Hunnicutt, Lorrie Moore, Mary Robison, Lynne Sharon Schwartz, Paul Theroux, Luisa Valenzuela, Stephanie Vaughan and Ellen Wilbur. May 21, 1990. Director, Arturo Castillo; scenery, Nanette Hudson-Joyce; costumes, Susan Deeley; lighting, Russell Wadbrook; music, Tony Luisi.
    With Donna Browne, John Erlanger, Charlie Isdell, Litha Johnson, Deirdre Lewis, Leigh Smiley, David Urrutia.

## Philadelphia: Philadelphia Festival Theater for New Plays

(Artistic director, Carol Rocamora)

ANTHONY ROSE. By Jules Feiffer. October 22, 1989. Director, Paul Benedict; scenery, James Wolk; costumes, Vickie Esposito; lighting, Curt Senie; sound, Conny M. Lockwood.

Anthony Rose ..................................Bob Balaban
Chester..............................................Reed Birney
Alec.............................................Anthony Fusco
Nick ............................................Tony Musante
Anita ........................................Socorro Santiago

One intermission.

BELMONT AVENUE SOCIAL CLUB. By Bruce Graham. April 12, 1990. Director, James J. Christy; scenery, James Wolk; costumes, Vickie Esposito; lighting, Curt Senie; sound, Conny M. Lockwood.

Fran Barelli ....................................William Wise
Chickie Barelli.....................................Rik Colitti

Cholly Donahue................................Paul O'Brien
Tommy Krueger.................................James Doerr
One intermission.

THE INUIT. By Bill Bozzone. May 3, 1990. Director, Rob Barron; scenery, Phillip A. Graneto; costumes, Vickie Esposito; lighting, Curt Senie.
Tony..........................................Brian Markinson
Claude.................................... Norris Shimabuku
Bala........................................Charmaine Cruise
Samik...........................................Peter Yoshida
Adamo .........................................Victor Arnold
One intermission.

SINS OF THE FATHER (one-acts). By Chaim Potok. May 24, 1990. Director, Carol Rocamora;

scenery, Phillip A. Graneto; costumes, Vickie Esposito; lighting, Curt Senie; sound, Daniel Osterwell.

*The Gallery*
Asher Lev .......................................Jon Ehrlich
Aryeh Lev..................................David Margulies
Rivkeh Lev .....................................Suzanne Toren
Anna Schaefer............................. Marcia Mahon
Jacob Kahn.......................................Don Auspitz

*The Carnival*
Alex..........................................David Jacobson
Michael ...................................... Rob Kramer
Pitchman ...................................Daniel Richards
Old Man ....................................David Margulies

## Philadelphia:  Play Works

(Artistic director, Christopher Rushton)

DR. CAPULET SPEAKS. By Mort Levy. March 23, 1990. Director, Christopher J. Rushton. With Mort Levy.

TRADITION 1A. By Howard Rice. May 4, 1990. Director, Seth Rozin. With Stephen Hatzai.

LOUIS' LOTTERY. By Joseph Sorrentino. Director, Lionel Ford. With Norma Albritton, John DeSeignora, Robert Hubbard, Phil Hughes, Mike James, Beverly Kelch, Syeed Malik, Jeff Morrison, Bill O'Neill.

*Staged Readings:*

LADY COMMITTING A SIN. By Mort Levy.
HEIR APPARENT. By Jason Crystal.
FORGERIES. By Vivian Green.
ON THE BRINK. By Claudia Perry.
BARBEQUE. By Harriet Levin.
THE BIG KADOSH. By Tom Bissinger.
PRETENDING TO AMERICA. By Tom Gibbons.
DOUBLE SOLITAIRE. By Jim Penzi.

## Philadelphia:  Society Hill Playhouse

(Artistic director, Jay Kogan; managing director, Deen Kogan)

SISTERS IN CRIME. Program of two plays by Susan Turlish. October 6, 1989. Director, Susan Turlish; scenery, Ray Neil; lighting, Robin Miller; musical direction, Freddie Paulin.

*Hog Heaven*
Harry Towers.....................................Jerry Lyden
Policeman...................................... Keith Brooks
Detective ....................................John Opladen

Leigh Endicott ...............................J.J. Van Name
*Stormy Weather*
Casey Cane ....................................Freddie Paulin
Bambi Baker...............................Karen Levinson
Marty Laslo..................................John Opladen
Bill Turner ....................................Dennis Gildea
Waiter ............................................Keith Brooks
Waitress.........................................Jill Friedman

## Philadelphia:  Walnut Street Studio Theater

(Executive director, Bernard Havard)

A MAN WITH CONNECTIONS. By Alexander Gelman. January 3, 1990 (American premiere). Director, Granville Burgess; scenery, Judi Guralnick;

costumes, Robert Pittenridge; lighting and sound, Mark A. Collino; original music, E.A. Alexander.
Andrei Golubev...................................Joe Aufiery

Natasha Colubev ............................ Kathy Lichter
One intermission.

CLEAR AND PRESENT DANGER. By Donald C. Drake. March 27, 1990. Director, David F. Hutchman; scenery, Todd Andrew Rosenthal; lighting, Mark A. Collino; costumes, Audrey Pooler; sound, Mark A. Collino.

Rep 1 ......................................... Richard Alliger
Judy .............................................. Celine Havard
Amy ........................................... Marcia Mahon
Rep 2 ............................................ Deborah Stern
Paul ......................................... Charles Techman
Time: The present. Place: The Dewarts' apartment and the rest of the world. One intermission.

## Philadelphia: Wilma Theater

(Artistic directors, Jiri Zizka, Blanka Zizka)

ALFRED & VICTORIA: A LIFE. By Donald Freed. February 27, 1990. Director, Blanka Zizka; scenery, Andrei Efremoff; costumes, Maxine Hartswick; additional design, Roy Gray; sound and original music, Daniel Osterweil.
Alfred ........................................... Jack Davidson
Victoria ......................................... Bridgit Ryan
No intermission (seven scenes).

SANTIAGO. By Manuel Pereiras Garcia. May 23, 1990. Director, Robert Fuhrmann; scenery, Kevin Joseph Roach; costumes, Maxine Hartswick; lighting, Jerold R. Forsyth; composer, Paul Aston; choreographer, Ranse Howell.
He .................................................... Joe Aufiery
She ............................................ Patricia Mauceri
Interlocutor .............................. Erica McFarguhar
Lover ........................................... Dan Olmstead
Pilar ..................................... Bernadette Pregorac

## Pittsburgh: City Theater Company

(Producing director, Marc Masterson)

*Staged Readings:*

THE GIRL WITH THE HIGH ROUGE. By Vincent Sessa. October 24, 1989. Director, Daniel Wilson. With Jeffrey Howell, John Hall, Bob Tracey, Lori Cardille. Time: A present August, about two hours before sunrise. Place: A sailing craft moored to the end of a pier in a remote seacoast town.
BRICKLAYERS. By Elvira J. DiPaolo. December 5, 1989. Director, Anthony McKay. With Larry John Meyers, John Hall, Mark Brettschneider, Shirley Tannenbaum, Don Wadsworth, Natascia

Diaz. Time: The early 1980s. Place: The neighborhood of South Oakland, Pittsburgh.
CONFESSIONS OF A PLUMBER. By Dennis Kennedy. April 3, 1990. Director, Bob Hofmann. With Richard McMillan, Gillette Elvgren, Larry John Meyers, Lori Cardille, Erica Magnus. Place: The control room of the A.D. Edmonston Pumping Plant on the California Aqueduct, situated off Interstate 5 between Los Angeles and Bakersfield and in Gus's mind.

## Pittsburgh: Pittsburgh Public Theater

(Producing director, William T. Gardner; managing director, Dan Fallon)

ELEANOR (musical). Book by Jonathan Bolt; music by Thomas Tierney; lyrics by John Forster. May 24, 1990. Director, Mel Shapiro; music direction, Keith Lockhart; choreography, Rob Marshall; scenery, Karl Eigsti; lighting, Roger Morgan; costumes, Laura Crow.
With Kelly Aquino, Barbara Broughton, Ted

Brunetti, Catherine Campbell, Anthony Cummings, Linda Gabler, Mary Jay, Tamara Jenkins, Joe Joyce, Ann Kittredge, Michael McCormick, James McCrum, Karyn Quackenbush, Dale Sandish, Allan Stevens, Ty Taylor, William Thunhurst.
Time and Place: A young country in a young time, 1902 to 1924. One intermission.

## Pittsfield, Mass.: Berkshire Public Theater

(Production manager, Ruth Moe)

THE SCARLETT LETTER: A ROMANCE FOR STAGE. Adapted and directed by Frank Bessell. Scenery, Don Mandigo; lighting, Don Mandigo; costumes, Lynda L. Salsbury Emerson; sound, Frank Kennedy.

With Khushi Ponter, Genei Zust, Kim Conley, Colleen Werthmann, Amy Folta, Diedre Bollinger, Nikki Tyson, Matt McKeever, Richard Robbins, David Fisher, Meeghan Holaway, Alex Saunders, Noah Fassell, Jay Whalen, Glenn Barrett, Noel Hanger, Mickey Moss, George Bergen, Bruce T. MacDonald, Christopher Graham, Bob Barger, Lori Tannenbaum, Leah Lotto, David Fisher, Sam Prentice, Brandon Davis.

Time and Place: Prologue: Salem, 1850. Act I, Scene 1: The prison door and marketplace, Boston, 1642, a summer morning in the month of June; Scene 2: A dismal apartment in the prison, several hours later. Act II, Prologue: A small thatched cottage on the outskirts of town, 1645. Scene 1: The Governor's Hall on a summer's day afternoon. Scene 2: Dimmesdale and Chillingworth's lodgings, after a time. Scene 3: The platform of the pillory, a night in early May. Act III, Scene 1: A retired part of the peninsula, an afternoon, not long afterward. Scene 2: A forest walk at brook-side, a chill and somber day. Scene 3: The platform of the pillory, Election Day, late spring, 1649. Epilogue: The Custom House and the thatched cottage, many years later.

## Portland, Me.: Portland Stage Company

(Artistic director, Richard Hamburger; managing director, Caroline F. Turner)

*Work-in-Progress*

A PLAY CALLED NOT AND NOW. Adapted by Cheryl Faver from Gertrude Stein. April 20, 1990.

Director, Cheryl Faver. With Suzy Fay, Colette Kilroy, Brennan Murphy.

## Princeton, N.J.: McCarter Theater Company

(Artistic director, Emily Mann)

TWO GOOD BOYS. By Barry Jay Kaplan. January 19, 1990. Director, Robert Lanchester; costumes, Suzanne Elder; lighting, Stephen J. Howe.
Billie ...........................................Peggy Cowles

Tom...............................................Richard Topol
Annette....................................Stephanie Cannon
Will..............................................Reathel Bean
One intermission.

## Purchase, N.Y.: New Musicals

(Producer, Marty Bell)

KISS OF THE SPIDER WOMAN (musical). Book by Terrence McNally; music by John Kander; lyrics by Fred Ebb; based on the novel by Manuel Puig. Director, Harold Prince; choreography, Susan Stroman; musical direction, Donald Chan; scenery, Thomas Lynch; costumes, Florence Klotz; lighting, Peter A. Kaczorowski; sound, Alan Stieb; orchestrations, Michael Gibson.
Valentin .............................................Kevin Gray
Warden.............................................. Harry Goz
Molina.......................................John Rubinstein

Aurora.........................................Loren Mitchell
Senora Molina ..............................Barbara Andres
Armando.....................................Donn Simione
With Jonathan Brody, Bill Christopher-Myers, Karen Giombetti, Ruth Gottschall, Philip Herandez, Dorie Herndon, David Koch, Rick Manning, Carl Maultsby, Lauren Mufson, Casel Nicholaw, Aurelio Padron, Forest Dino Ray, Lorraine Serabian, John Norman Thomas, Wendy Waring, Matt Zarley, Greg Zerkle.

GEVA THEATER—Cynthia Hayden and Bari Hochwald in a
scene from *Forgiving Typhoid Mary* by Mark St. Germain

## Richmond: *Theater Virginia*

(Executive artistic director, Terry Burgler)

OH, MR. FAULKNER, DO YOU WRITE? By
John Maxwell and Tom Dupree. May 1, 1990. Director, William Partlan; scenery, Jimmy Robertson;
lighting, Terry Cermak; costumes, Martha Wood.

With John Maxwell.
Place: William Faulkner's office at Rowan Oak, Oxford, Miss. One intermission.

SCRATCHY GLASS. By Doug Grissom. May 8, 1990. Director, Terry Burgler; scenery, Chris Harrison; lighting, Terry Cermak; costumes, Lynette Cram.
Darcy Pacetti .....................................Jan Guarino
Art Manucy......................................David Sexton
Linda Pacetti .......................................Erin Draper
Time: The summer of 1964. Place: A clean but run-down diner in Talachee, a small town in north-central Florida.

YEAR OF PILGRIMAGE. By Doug Grissom.

May 15, 1990. Director, Nancy Cates; scenery, Chris Harrison; lighting, Terry Cermak; costumes, Lynette Cram.
Darcy Pacetti .....................................Jan Guarino
Lester Crutchfield ...................Robert Gevrekian III
Ben Monson............................................Ed Sala
Time: The summer of 1964. Place: Inside a diner in Talachee, a small town in north-central Florida.

*Staged Readings:*

OLDEST LIVING CONFEDERATE WIDOW TELLS ALL. By Allan Gurganus. May 8, 1990.
MOTHERWIT. By Katherine Clark and Terry Burgler. May 15, 1990

## Roanoke, Va.: Mill Mountain Theater

(Artistic director, Jere Lee Hodgin)

THE DROPPER. By Ron McLarty. January 16, 1990. Director, Jere Lee Hodgin; scenery, John Sailer; lighting, John Sailer; costumes, Johann Stegmeir; composer, Wayne Joness.
Bobby......................................................John Beard
Shoe Horn .............................................Bob Horen
Jack Polleni ...........................................Cliff Morts
Mo Polleni ........................................Tricia Givens
Young Shoe Horn ...............................Richard Long
Time and Place: The present in New England and in the early part of the century in England.

ZEKE'S VISION. By Hank Bates. January 17, 1990. Director, Mary Best-Bova; scenery, John Sailer; lighting, John Sailer; costumes, Johann Stegmeir.
Mama; Mae Jackson .........................Jolene Carroll
Zeke .................................................Richard Long
Robert Jackson ...............................James Barbour
Leslie Jackson .............................Dawn Westbrook
Levon Jackson..................................Mark Kincaid

Jack Carter ............................................Jeff Berger
Time and Place: The present, the Jacksons' living room on the outskirts of Little Rock.

THE BUG. By Richard Strand. Director, Jere Lee Hodgin; scenery, John Sailer; lighting, John Sailer; costumes, Johann Stegmeir.
Linda Taylor...................................Melody Garrett
Dennis Post.......................................Bob Higgins
Kimberly Miles........................... Sarah Whitcomb
David Rajeski ...............................James Barbour
Time: The present. Place: Administrative offices of Jericho Inc., a large corporation that designs and manufactures factory automation systems.

*Staged Readings:*

HOME DELIVERY. By Ed Falco. January 31, 1990.
BABY FACE. Jo Weinstein. February 7, 1990.

## Rochester, N.Y.: GeVa Theater

(Associate artistic director, Anthony Zerbe; producing artistic director, Howard J. Millman)

*Reflections '90; May 29–July 1, 1990 (in rotation):*

FORGIVING TYPHOID MARY. By Mark St. Germain. Director, Anthony Zerbe.
Mary Mallon...................................Bari Hochwald
Dr. William Mills...........................Mart Hulswit
Dr. Ann Saltzer.............................Cynthia Hayden
Fr. Michael.......................................Josh Brolin

Sarah............................................Rebecca Lamb
Intern ................................................Tim DeWitt
ADULT FICTION. By Brian Richard Mori. Director, Allen R. Belknap.
Earl........................................David S. Howard
Mikie............................................Rick Lawless
Patrons: Rick Christopher, Tim DeWitt,

Diramund McDonnell, Christoher Pitts.

OH, THE INNOCENTS. By Ari Roth. Director, Joe Mantello.

Josh.................................................. Peter Burkenhead
Jeremy ........................................... Michael Liani
Betsy ....................................... Cordelia Richards

Alex.................................. Nicole Orth-Pallavicini
Laurel............................................. Jill Smithgall
Bartender, Waiter ............................... Tim DeWitt
  Designers: Scenery, Marjorie B. Kellogg; costumes, Susan Mickey; lighting, Kirk Bookman; sound, Dan Roach.

## St. Louis: The Repertory Theater of St. Louis

(Artistic director, Steven Woolf)

*Mainstage:*

A HOLIDAY GARLAND OF TALES. By Kim Allen Bozark, Susan May Greenberg, Tim Hendrixson and Sandra Vago. December 20, 1989. Director, Jeffery Matthews; scenery, Kim Wilson; costumes, Norma West.

Bethany........................................... Bethany Barr
Judy.............................................. Judy Dickherber
Larry........................................... Larry Michelson
Robert................................... Robert A. Mitchell

HANSEL AND GRETEL. By Suzie Bradley. March 31, 1990. Director, Jeffery Matthews; scenery, Kim Wilson; costumes, Kim Wilson.

Gretel............................................. Bethany Barr

Witch.......................................... Judy Dickherber
Hansel........................................ Larry Michelson
Father.................................... Robert A. Mitchell

*Lab Project:*

THE LAST SONG OF JOHN PROFFIT. By Tommy Thompson. February 4, 1990. Director, Susan Gregg. With Gordon G. Jones.

THE EDUCATION OF PAUL BUNYAN. By Barbara Field. April 14, 1990. Director, Susan Gregg. With Carl Schurr, Susan Bruce, David Edward Jones, Lianne Kressin, Joneal Joplin, Alan Clarey, Phil Coffield, John Grassilli, Whit Reichert, Chris Reilly.

## Salt Lake City: Pioneer Theater Company

(Artistic director, Charles Morey; managing director, Jack A. Mark)

THE THREE MUSKETEERS. Adapted from Alexandre Dumas by Charles Morey. November 1, 1989. Director, Charles Morey; scenery, Ariel Ballif; lighting, Peter L. Willardson; costumes, David Boushey; original music, James Prigmore; fight director, David Boushey.

  With James Andreassi, Spencer Beckwith, John Camera, Davis Hall, Tara Hugo, Lisa Ivary, Bob Kirsh, Anne Stewart Mark, Richard Mathews, Richard B. Nelson, Patrick Page, Robert Peterson, David Valenza, Christopher Wells.

  Time and Place: Paris, 1844; later, various locations in France, England, and the imagination of Alexandre Dumas in the year 1645. One intermission.

## San Diego: Old Globe Theater

(Artistic director, Jack O'Brien)

BREAKING LEGS. By Tom Dulack. September 6, 1989. Director, Jack O'Brien; scenery, Cliff Faulkner; lighting, John B. Forbes; costumes, Robert Wojewodski; sound, Jeff Ladman.

Terence O'Keefe............................. Greg Mullavey
Lou Graziano.............................. T.J. Castronovo
Angie Graziano..................................... Sue Giosa
Mike Palermo................................. Mike Genovese
Tino De Felice........................... Richard Kneeland
Frankie Salvucci ............................ Eddie Zammit

Time: The present. Place: A restaurant in a New England university town. One intermission.

JAKE'S WOMEN. By Neil Simon. March 8, 1990. Director, Ron Link; scenery, Tony Straiges; lighting, Tharon Musser; costumes, Joseph G. Aulisi; sound, Jeff Ladman.

Karen ........................................... Candice Azzara
Sheila............................................. Talia Balsam
Mollie (at 21) ........................... Amelia Campbell

Maggie....................................Stockard Channing
Jake................................................Peter Coyote
Mollie (at 13).......................Sarah Michelle Gellar
Julie ........................................Felicity Huffman
Edith..........................................Joyce Van Patten
   Place: A duplex apartment in the Soho section of New York. One intermission.

*Latino Play Discovery Series:*

MADE IN BUENOS AIRES. By Nelly Fernandez Tiscornia. June, 1989. Director, Lillian Garrett.

LATINS ANONYMOUS. By Luisa Leschin, Armando Molina, Rick Najera and Diane Rodriguez. September, 1989. Director, Jose Cruz Gonzalez, Miguel Delgado.
DEATH AND THE BLACKSMITH. By Mercedes Rein and Jorge Curi. October, 1989. Director, Craig Noel.
THE WHITE ROSE. By Lillian Garrett-Groag. March 12, 1990. Director, Craig Noel.
METERED PHONE. By Beto Gianola. April 30, 1990. Director, Lillian Garrett-Groag.

## San Diego: San Diego Repertory Theater

(Artistic director, Douglas Jacobs)

THE SCANDALOUS ADVENTURES OF SIR TOBY TROLLOPE. By Ron House and Alan Shearman. July 26, 1989. Director, Stephen Rothman; scenery, Fred Duer and Alan K. Okazaki; costumes, David Kay Mickelsen; lighting, John B. Forbes; sound, Jon Gottlieb.
   With Ron House, Alan Shearman, Anna Mathias, Melinda Peterson, Rodger Bumpass, Ron Vernan, William Dennis Hunt. Two intermissions.

THIN AIR: TALES FROM A REVOLUTION. By Lynne Alvarez. August 10, 1989. Director, Sam Woodhouse; scenery, D. Martyn Bookwalter; costumes, Nancy Jo Smith; lighting, Peter Nordyke.
   With Paul James Kruse, Kat Sawyer-Young, John Hertzler, Davina Dene, Regina Byrd Smith, Jaime Sanchez, Alina Cenal, Mickey Hanley, Shanga Parker, John Diaquino, Damon Bryant, Rodrigo Dorfman.
   One intermission.

ARE YOU LONESOME TONIGHT? By Alan Bleasdale. September 6, 1989 (American premiere). Director, George Ferencz; scenery, Victoria Petrovich; costumes, Sally Lesser; lighting, Brenda Barry; sound and musical direction, Bob Jewett.
   With Rick Sparks, Lillian Byrd, Mindy Hull, J. Michael Ross, Duane Daniels, Drew Tombello, William Dunnam, Tavis Ross, Luther Hanson, Jake Schmidt, Davina Dene, Sam Woodhouse.

ALBANIAN SOFTSHOE. By Mac Wellman. September 20, 1989. Directors, Douglas Jacobs, Michael Roth; scenery, Jill Moon; costumes, Clare Henkel; lighting, Brenda Barry.
   With Darla Cash, Jan Leslie Harding, Tony Simotes, Alex Colon, Bruce McKenzie, Helen Reed Lehman, Larry Ohlson, Douglas Jacobs, Olga Macias, Damon Bryant, Bill Barstad, Peter J. Smith, Lou Romano, Stephanie Paley, Tokeli LeClaire, Patrick Allen, Susan Gelman, Willis Goodlow IV, Adele House.

## San Francisco: American Conservatory Theater

(Artistic director, Edward W. Hastings)

RIGHT MIND (musical). Book by George Coates; music by Marc Ream; lyrics by George Coates. October 7, 1989. Director, George Coates; image process, Charles Rose; musical direction, Michael Grossman; lighting, Larry Neff; sound, Guy Brenner.
Mathematician....................................Ken Ruta
Director........................................Rebecca White
Storyteller; Alice...........................Stephen Hanan
Little Girl Who................................Kate Taylor
Photographer..................................Luis Oropeza
Theatergoer ...........................Michael Scott Ryan

Low Church Official ..........................David Maier
Little Good and Bad Queen .............Marilynn Smith
Insect ..........................................Azizah Hodges
Dancers.........................Lizzie Henry, Eva Popper
Singer ..............................................Noe Venable
   San Jose Taiko Group: P.J. Hirabayashi, Roy Hirabayashi, Jose Alarcon; Gary Tsujimoto, Nancy Ozaki, Toni Yagami, Meri Mitsuyoshi, Keith Morita.
   One intermission.

## San Francisco: Eureka Theater Company

(Artistic director, Suzanne Bennett)

PICK UP AX. By Anthony Clarvoe. January 18, 1990. Director, Susan Marsden; scenery, David Jon Hoffman; costumes, Cassandra Carpenter; lighting, Jack Carpenter.

Keith Rienzi.....................................John Bellucci

Brian Weiss......................................Sam Gregory
Mick Palomar.......................................Jeff King
Time and Place: Silicon Valley, 1980s, many generations in the past. One intermission. (An ATCA selection; see introduction to this section.)

## San Francisco: The Magic Theater

(Artistic director, John Lion; managing director, Harvey Seifter)

*Springfest:*

VAMPIRE DREAMS. By Suzy McKee Charnas. Director, Michael Edwards; scenery, Jeff Rowlings; lighting, Maurice Vercoutere; costumes, Callie Floor.
Kenny......................................Adrian Elfenbaum
Lucille ..................................... Sharon Harrington
Dr. Floria Landauer.................Sandy Kelly Hoffman
Dr. Edward Lewis Weyland.................Earl Kingston
Time: The present. Place: Upper West Side of Manhattan. One intermission.

THE HOUSE OF YES. By Wendy MacLeod. Director, Andrew Doe; scenery, Jeff Rowlings; lighting, Maurice Vercoutere; costumes, Callie Floor.
Marty Pascal .......................................Art Manke
Anthony Pascal................... Kenneth R. Merckx Jr.
Lesly ...............................................Amy Resnick

Mrs. Pascal .....................................Nancy Shelby
Jackie-O.........................................Celia Shuman
Time: Thanksgiving, during a hurricane, some 25 years after JFK's assassination. Place: McLean, Va. One intermission.

DOTTIE & THE BOYS. By Lynne Kaufman. Director, Andrea Gordon; scenery, Jeff Rowlings; lighting, Maurice Vercoutere; costumes, Callie Floor.
Bartender..........................................Wayne Doba
Boss...................................................Ron Kaell
Benchley.........................................James Lewis
Hunk...........................................Brian Lohmann
Dorothy Parker..........................Helen Shumaker
Time: The present, then back to the 1920s, '30s, and '50s. Place: The Algonquin Hotel, New York, and various other locales. One intermission.

## Santa Maria, Calif.: PCPA Theaterfest

(Managing artistic director, Jack Shouse)

CHRISTMAS IS ... A MUSICAL COMEDY. By Brad Carroll and Jeremy Mann. December 7, 1989. Directors, Brad Carroll, Jeremy Mann; scenery, Everett Chase; lighting, David R. White; costumes, Joseph M. Kowalski; sound, Everett Chase.
Karen Barbour.....................................Page Lewis
Jeremy Mann...............................Sandra Singler

Colin Thomson.................................Jay Forman
Time and Place: Act I, Scene 1: 1905, New York. Scene 2: 1917, Cleveland. Scene 3: 1932, Rural Ohio. Scene 4: 1942, a radio station in Chicago. Act II, Scene 1: 1959, a Chicago suburb. Scene 2: 1959 to present, montage. Scene 3: 1989, suburban Southern California.

## Sarasota: Asolo Theater Company

(Artistic director, John Ulmer)

TALKING PICTURES. By Horton Foote. April 20, 1990. Director, John Ulmer; scenery, John Ezell; lighting, Martin Petlock; costumes, Howard Tsvi Kaplan.

Katie Bell Jackson ...........................Meghan Cary
Vesta Jackson .................................Jamie Martin
Myra Tolliver ................................Kathryn Grant
Mr. Jackson...........................Donald Christopher

Willis ...................................Michael James Laird
Mrs. Jackson..........................Barbara Bates Smith
Estaqui................................................Jack Boslet
Pete Anderson...............................Rafael Petlock
Gladys..........................................Carol Hanpeter
Ashenback ........................................Eric Tavares
Gerard Anderson ...............................Jack Conley
  Time: The late 1920s. Place: The Jackson home
in Harrison, Tex. One intermission.

QUARRY. By Ronald Bazarini. May 31, 1990.

Director, Garry Allan Breul; scenery, Keven Lock;
lighting, Martin Petlock; costumes, Howard Tsvi
Kaplan.
Noel..............................................Rob Richards
Oliver.........................................Mark Shannon
Claudette.....................................Jeff Woodman
Manila.....................................Bernadette Wilson
Warren.........................................Chris Hietikko
Hilda...........................................Annie Murray
  Time: March, 1948. Place: The French Quarter
of New Orleans. One intermission.

## Sarasota: Florida Studio Theater

(Artistic director, Richard Hopkins)

INVICTUS. By Laurie H. Hutzler. Director,
Richard Hopkins; scenery, Jeffrey W. Dean; lighting,
Paul D. Romance; costumes, Marcella Beckwith.
Johannus ...........................................Kate Hurd
Nickolas....................................Chris MacCarty
Anastasius ....................................Douglas Jones
Lillith............................... Katharine Bushmann
Beaulac..........................................Roger Kerlew
Apothecary...............................Robert D. Mowry

*New Play Development:*

HOW GERTRUDE STORMED THE PHILOSO-
PHERS' CLUB. By Martin Epstein. November 26,
1989. Director, Doug Jones.
Edgar ......................................... Martin Nicholas
Edward ............................................ Doug Jones
Jason ..............................................Roger Kerlew
Gertrude............................. Donna Bryant-Minard
  Time: The present. Place: The Philosophers'
Club.
A FIERCE ATTACHMENT. By Edward M. Cohen.
November 29, 1989.
Daughter.....................................Carolyn Michel
  Time: The present. Place: The daughter's apart-
ment and in her memory.
PENDRAGON. By Laurie Hutzler. November 29,
1989. Director, Carolyn Michel.

King Arthur......................................Bob Mowry
Morganna............................Patti O'Berg
Lancelot........................................ Todd Covert
Guinivere.......................................Elin Hampton
Garth; Gareth............................... Jeremy Lourde
Mordred ...................................... Dana Helfrich
CHEVALIERE. By David Trainer. December 6,
1989. Director, Henry Fonte.
Chevalier D'Eon...............................Doug Jones
Caron de Beaumarchais ................... B.G. Fitzgerald
  Time: 1775. Place: London. One intermission.
AUTO EROTIX. By Kevin Ottem. December 8,
1989.
Violet...........................................Carolyn Michel
Speed ...................................................Joe Butler
Benny..............................................Steve Spencer
  Time: Act I, Scene 1: An October dusk, the Rea-
gan years; Scene 2: Later that night. Act II, Scene
1: A Saturday evening the following January; Scene
2: Moments later. Place: A parking lot on the
Lower East Side of Manhattan.
HI-HAT HATTIE (musical). By Larry Parr. De-
cember 10, 1989. Director, Carolyn Michel; musical
director, Dan Stetzel.
Miss Hattie McDaniel ...................... Sharon Scott
  Time: Act I: 1895 to 1938. Act II: 1939 to
1952.

## Seattle: Intiman Theater

(Artistic director, Elizabeth Huddle)

FRANKENSTEIN. By R.N. Sandburg; adapted from
the novel by Mary Shelley. October 4, 1989. Director, Andrew J. Traister; original music and sound,
Larry Delinger; scenery, Jeffrey A. Frkonja; costumes, Frances Kenny; lighting, Richard Devin.

Victor Frankenstein......................Stephen Godwin
The Creature.............................David Drummond
Elizabeth..........................................Julia Fletcher
Walden; Father; Professor.............Clayton Corzatte
Mate; Mother; Justine .........................Jane Jones

SEATTLE REPERTORY THEATER—Daniel Sullivan (who also directed) and Loren Dean in Lyle Kessler's *Robbers*

## Seattle: Seattle Repertory Theater

(Artistic director, Daniel Sullivan)

ROBBERS. By Lyle Kessler. December 6, 1989. Director, Daniel Sullivan; scenery, Ralph Funicello; lighting, Paulie Jenkins; costumes, Rose Pederson.

| | |
|---|---|
| Ted | Loren Dean |
| Pop | William Biff McGuire |
| Mr. Feathers | Daniel Sullivan |
| Lucinda | Martha Plimpton |
| Owner | David Margulies |
| Vince | Paul Benvictor |
| Cleo | Lisa Zane |
| Bartender; Others | Don Creery |

Time and Place: Brooklyn, the present. One intermission.

### The Other Season:

MAYDAY. By Conrad Bromberg. April 6, 1990. Director, Daniel Sullivan; scenery, Jeff Frkonja; lighting, Rick Paulsen; costumes, Katherine M. Smurr; sound, Steven M. Klein.

| | |
|---|---|
| Gene | John Procaccino |
| Davis | Alexander Folk |
| Champ | Scott MacDonald |
| Joe | Evan Handler |
| Solly | Daniel Greenfield |

| | |
|---|---|
| Hank | Karen Evans-Kandel |
| Keller | Benjamin Prager |

Time and Place: Los Angeles in the early 1950s. One intermission.

THE END OF THE DAY. By Jon Robin Baitz. April 13, 1990. Director, Michael Engler; scenery, Jeff Frkonja; lighting, Rick Paulsen; costumes, Katherine M. Smurr; sound, Steven M. Klein.

| | |
|---|---|
| Graydon Massey | Daniel Gerroll |
| Jonathan Toffler | Tony Soper |
| Hilton Lasker; Swifty; Lord Kitterson | Kevin Tighe |
| Jeremiah Marton | Mark Chamberlin |
| Helen Lasker-Massey; Lady Hammersmith Urbaine-Supton-Stoat | Katie Forgette |
| Carol Brackett; Joclyn Massey | Meg Mundy |

Place: Act I, San Pedro Clinic. Act II, The Massey residence on Belgrave Square, London, and the San Pedro Clinic.

HOME AND AWAY. By Kevin Kling. April 27, 1989. Director, Kenneth Washington; scenery, Jeff Frkonja; lighting, Richard Moore; costumes, Rose Pederson; sound, Steven M. Klein. With Kevin Kling.

Place: Act I, Home. Act II, Away.

LOVE DIATRIBE. By Harry Kondoleon. May 4, 1990. Director, Douglas Hughes; scenery, Jeff Frkonja; lighting, Richard Moore; costumes, Rose Pederson; sound, Steven M. Klein.

Orin.................................................Peter Crook
Sandy...........................................Katie Forgette

Mrs. Anderson ..................................Peggy Pope
Dennis..........................................John Aylward
Mike......................................Gordon Carpenter
Gerry...........................................Marge Kotlisky
Frieda..................................................Jane Adams
    Time: The present. Place: A suburb of a large city, the "Family Room".

## Stockbridge, Mass.: Berkshire Theater Festival

(Artistic director, Richard Dunlap)

TETE A TETE. By Ralph Burdman. August 16, 1989 (American premiere). Director, Robert Rooney; scenery, Ed Wittstein; costumes, David Murin; lighting, Jeff Davis; sound, Donna Riley.

Jean-Paul Sartre..................................Jose Ferrer
Simone de Beauvoir ..............Constance Cummings
    One intermission.

## Stony Point, N.Y.: Penguin Repertory Company

(Artistic director, Joe Brancato; executive director, Andrew M. Horn)

THE MAN WHO WAS PETER PAN. By Allan Knee. June 2, 1989. Director, Joe Brancato; scenery, Richard Cordtz, Bill Stabile; lighting, Dennis W. Moyes; costumes, Sally Lesser.
    With Geoffrey P. Cantor, Cara Halstead, Norman Howard, Jamie Marsh, Gus Rogerson, Judy Stadt, Geoffrey Tarson.

ONLY THE SKY WAS BLUE! By Joe Brancato, David Rogers and John Simon. February 23, 1990. Director, Joe Brancato; scenery, Chuck Stead; lighting, Dennis W. Moyes; costumes, Michael Sharp; musical director, John Simon; choreography, Barry Finkel.
    With Robert Blaney, Avi Hoffman, Susan Hull, Steve Sterner, Gail Wynters.

## Teaneck, N.J.: The American Stage Company

(Artistic director, Paul Sorvino; executive producer, Theodore Rawlins)

THE LEAST OF THESE. By Martin Halpern. November 15, 1989. Director, Alex Dmitriev; scenery, Ray Recht; lighting, Kenneth Posner; costumes, Barbara Forbes; sound, Richard L. Sirois.

Walter Franklin............................James Pritchett
Mrs. Ellis..................................Joan Matthiessen
Clara Fletcher..........................Martha Thompson
Tom Hobson...............................Matthew Lewis
John Fletcher.................................Jack R. Marks
    Time and Place: February to September, 1911 in various locales in Pittsburgh; the rectory of Franklin's church, a pew in the church, the living room of Fletcher's tenement. One intermission.

LEGAL TENDER. By Mark St. Germain. March

7, 1990. Director, Julianne Boyd; scenery, James Noone; lighting, Kenneth Posner; costumes, C.L. Hundley; sound, Bruce Ellman.

Arthur Wallace...............................Michael Elich
Janice James..................................Liann Pattison
Ivan Krelick.......................................J.R. Horne
    Time and Place: The present. A room at the Captain Hook Motel, located across the highway from Teterboro Airport, New Jersey.

HALLEY'S COMET. By John Amos. April 26, 1990. Director, John Harris Jr.; scenery, Garritt D. Lydecker; lighting, William Yates Jr.; costumes, Phyllis Emery; sound, Ivan Julian.

The Old Man .....................................John Amos

## Tuscon:  Invisible Theater

(Artistic director, Susan Claassen)

*Staged Readings:*

THE CAROUSEL MAN.  By Lois Miller Hibbs.
THE DIVIDING LINE.  Rich Amada.

RAINY DAYS AND FRIDAY NIGHTS.  By Sam Smiley.
UNDERCURRENTS.  By Elaine Romero-Kennedy.

## Washington, D.C.:  Arena Stage

(Producing director, Zelda Fichandler)

CONQUEST OF THE SOUTH POLE.  By Manfred Karge, adapted by Silas Jones and Laurence Maslon. March 16, 1990.  Director, Paul Walker; scenery, David M. Glenn; lighting, Christopher V. Lewton; costumes, Betty Siegel; sound, Eric Annis.

Wolfgang..........................John Leonard Thompson
Belcher....................................Teagle F. Bougere
Schlitz......................................Clayton LeBouef
Moose.............................................David Marks
Belcherella........................................ Margo Hall
Frankie Boy.....................................Chris Bauer
Dee Dee..................................Marissa Copeland
Dude ...............................................M.E. Hart

## Washington, D.C.:  Ford's Theater

(Executive producer, Frankie Hewitt)

DON'T LET THIS DREAM GO (musical).  Book, music and lyrics by Queen Esther Marrow.  Director, Robert Kalfin; scenery, Fred Kolo; lighting, Fred

Kolo; costumes, Andrew B. Marlay.
  With Lynette G. DuPré, Carl Hall, Doug Eskew, Gwen Stewart.

## Waterford, Conn.:  Eugene O'Neill Theater Center

(Artistic director, Lloyd Richards)

*National Playwrights Conference: July 3–July 29, 1989*

READY FOR THE RIVER.  By Neal Bell.  Director, William Partlan.
GULLIVER.  By Lonnie Carter.  Director, Dennis Scott.
DAYLIGHT IN EXILE.  By James D'Entremont. Director, Gitta Honegger.
MAPPING URANIUM.  By Annie Evans.  Director, Amy Salt.
THE CONFESSIONS OF FRANKLIN THOMPSON III.  By Kermit Frazier.  Director, Gitta Honegger.
RATTAN.  By Jeffrey Hatcher.

HAVE YOU SEEN ROAD SMITH?  By Willy Holtzman.
MUD PEOPLE.  By Keith Huff.  Director, Margaret Booker.
THE COTTAGE.  By Yuri Knyazev.
SONGS WITHOUT WORDS.  By Jonathan Levy. Director, William Partlan.
EARTH AND SKY.  By Douglas Post.  Director, Margaret Booker.
HEAVEN ON EARTH.  By Robert Schenkkan.  Director, William Partlan.
RUST AND RUIN.  By William Snowden.  Director, Amy Saltz.

# Woodstock, N.Y.: River Arts Repertory

(Artistic director, Lawrence Sacharow)

LOVE ME OR LEAVE ME. By Michael Cristofer; adapted from the screen play by Isobel Lennart and Daniel Fuchs. Director, Lawrence Sacharow; choreography, Wesley Fata; musical direction, David Arner; costumes, Marianne Powell-Parker; lighting, Frances Aronson.

Ruth Etting..............................Melissa Manchester
Georgie .........................................Michael Perez
Martin Snyder................................Mark Margolis
Frobisher.......................................Ralph Buckley
Johnny Alderman.............................John Slattery
Barney Loomis....................................Jack Marks
One intermission.

FACTS AND
FIGURES

# LONG RUNS ON BROADWAY

The following shows have run 500 or more continuous performances in a single production, usually the first, not including previews or extra non-profit performances, allowing for vacation layoffs and special one-booking engagements, but not including return engagements after a show has gone on tour. In all cases, the numbers were obtained directly from the show's production offices. Where there are title similarities, the production is identified as follows: (p) straight play version, (m) musical version, (r) revival.

THROUGH MAY 31, 1990

(PLAYS MARKED WITH ASTERISK WERE STILL PLAYING JUNE 1, 1990)

| Plays | Number Performances | Plays | Number Performances |
|---|---|---|---|
| A Chorus Line | 6,137 | Evita | 1,567 |
| Oh! Calcutta! (r) | 5,959 | The Voice of the Turtle | 1,557 |
| 42nd Street | 3,486 | Barefoot in the Park | 1,530 |
| Grease | 3,388 | Brighton Beach Memoirs | 1,530 |
| Fiddler on the Roof | 3,242 | Dreamgirls | 1,522 |
| Life With Father | 3,224 | Mame (m) | 1,508 |
| *Cats | 3,193 | Same Time, Next Year | 1,453 |
| Tobacco Road | 3,182 | Arsenic and Old Lace | 1,444 |
| Hello, Dolly! | 2,844 | The Sound of Music | 1,443 |
| My Fair Lady | 2,717 | Me and My Girl | 1,420 |
| Annie | 2,377 | How to Succeed in Business Without Really Trying | 1,417 |
| Man of La Mancha | 2,328 | Hellzapoppin | 1,404 |
| Abie's Irish Rose | 2,327 | The Music Man | 1,375 |
| Oklahoma! | 2,212 | Funny Girl | 1,348 |
| Pippin | 1,944 | Mummenschanz | 1,326 |
| South Pacific | 1,925 | Angel Street | 1,295 |
| The Magic Show | 1,920 | Lightnin' | 1,291 |
| Deathtrap | 1,793 | *Les Misérables | 1,285 |
| Gemini | 1,788 | Promises, Promises | 1,281 |
| Harvey | 1,775 | The King and I | 1,246 |
| Dancin' | 1,774 | Cactus Flower | 1,234 |
| La Cage aux Folles | 1,761 | Sleuth | 1,222 |
| Hair | 1,750 | Torch Song Trilogy | 1,222 |
| The Wiz | 1,672 | 1776 | 1,217 |
| Born Yesterday | 1,642 | Equus | 1,209 |
| The Best Little Whorehouse in Texas | 1,639 | Sugar Babies | 1,208 |
| Ain't Misbehavin' | 1,604 | Guys and Dolls | 1,200 |
| Mary, Mary | 1,572 | | |

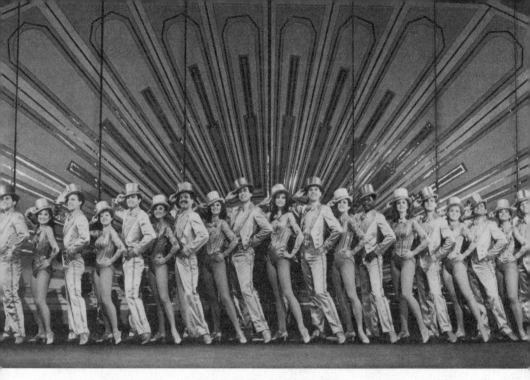

A *CHORUS LINE*, JULY 25, 1975–APRIL 28, 1990—This Michael Bennett–James Kirkwood–Nicholas Dante–Marvin Hamlisch–Edward Kleban musical ended the longest run in Broadway history at 6,137 performances, not counting 101 previous off-Broadway performances at New York Shakespeare Festival

| Plays | Number Performances |
| --- | --- |
| Amadeus | 1,181 |
| Cabaret | 1,165 |
| Mister Roberts | 1,157 |
| Annie Get Your Gun | 1,147 |
| The Seven Year Itch | 1,141 |
| Butterflies Are Free | 1,128 |
| Pins and Needles | 1,108 |
| Plaza Suite | 1,097 |
| They're Playing Our Song | 1,082 |
| Kiss Me, Kate | 1,070 |
| Don't Bother Me, I Can't Cope | 1,065 |
| The Pajama Game | 1,063 |
| Shenandoah | 1,050 |
| The Teahouse of the August Moon | 1,027 |
| Damn Yankees | 1,019 |
| Never Too Late | 1,007 |
| Big River | 1,005 |
| Any Wednesday | 982 |
| *The Phantom of the Opera | 981 |
| A Funny Thing Happened on the Way to the Forum | 964 |

| Plays | Number Performances |
| --- | --- |
| The Odd Couple | 964 |
| Anna Lucasta | 957 |
| Kiss and Tell | 956 |
| Dracula (r) | 925 |
| Bells Are Ringing | 924 |
| The Moon Is Blue | 924 |
| Beatlemania | 920 |
| The Elephant Man | 916 |
| Luv | 901 |
| Chicago (m) | 898 |
| Applause | 896 |
| Can-Can | 892 |
| Carousel | 890 |
| I'm Not Rappaport | 890 |
| Hats Off to Ice | 889 |
| Fanny | 888 |
| Children of a Lesser God | 887 |
| Follow the Girls | 882 |
| Camelot | 873 |
| I Love My Wife | 872 |
| The Bat | 867 |

| Plays | *Number Performances* | Plays | *Number Performances* |
|---|---|---|---|
| My Sister Eileen | 864 | Jesus Christ Superstar | 720 |
| No, No, Nanette (r) | 861 | Carnival | 719 |
| Song of Norway | 860 | The Diary of Anne Frank | 717 |
| Chapter Two | 857 | I Remember Mama | 714 |
| A Streetcar Named Desire | 855 | Tea and Sympathy | 712 |
| Barnum | 854 | Junior Miss | 710 |
| Comedy in Music | 849 | Last of the Red Hot Lovers | 706 |
| Raisin | 847 | Company | 705 |
| You Can't Take It With You | 837 | Seventh Heaven | 704 |
| La Plume de Ma Tante | 835 | Gypsy (m) | 702 |
| Three Men on a Horse | 835 | The Miracle Worker | 700 |
| The Subject Was Roses | 832 | That Championship Season | 700 |
| Inherit the Wind | 806 | Da | 697 |
| Anything Goes (r) | 804 | The King and I (r) | 696 |
| No Time for Sergeants | 796 | Cat on a Hot Tin Roof | 694 |
| Fiorello! | 795 | Li'l Abner | 693 |
| Where's Charley? | 792 | The Children's Hour | 691 |
| The Ladder | 789 | Purlie | 688 |
| Forty Carats | 780 | Dead End | 687 |
| The Prisoner of Second Avenue | 780 | The Lion and the Mouse | 686 |
| M. Butterfly | 777 | White Cargo | 686 |
| Oliver! | 774 | Dear Ruth | 683 |
| The Pirates of Penzance (1980 r) | 772 | East Is West | 680 |
| Woman of the Year | 770 | Come Blow Your Horn | 677 |
| Sophisticated Ladies | 767 | The Most Happy Fella | 676 |
| My One and Only | 767 | The Doughgirls | 671 |
| Bubbling Brown Sugar | 766 | The Impossible Years | 670 |
| Into the Woods | 765 | Irene | 670 |
| State of the Union | 765 | Boy Meets Girl | 669 |
| Starlight Express | 761 | The Tap Dance Kid | 669 |
| The First Year | 760 | Beyond the Fringe | 667 |
| Broadway Bound | 756 | Who's Afraid of Virginia Woolf? | 664 |
| You Know I Can't Hear You When the Water's Running | 755 | Blithe Spirit | 657 |
| Two for the Seesaw | 750 | A Trip to Chinatown | 657 |
| Joseph and the Amazing Technicolor Dreamcoat (r) | 747 | The Women | 657 |
| Death of a Salesman | 742 | Bloomer Girl | 654 |
| For Colored Girls, etc. | 742 | The Fifth Season | 654 |
| Sons o' Fun | 742 | Rain | 648 |
| Candide (mr) | 740 | Witness for the Prosecution | 645 |
| Gentlemen Prefer Blondes | 740 | Call Me Madam | 644 |
| The Man Who Came to Dinner | 739 | Janie | 642 |
| Nine | 739 | The Green Pastures | 640 |
| Call Me Mister | 734 | Auntie Mame (p) | 639 |
| West Side Story | 732 | A Man for All Seasons | 637 |
| High Button Shoes | 727 | The Fourposter | 632 |
| Finian's Rainbow | 725 | The Music Master | 627 |
| Claudia | 722 | Two Gentlemen of Verona (m) | 627 |
| The Gold Diggers | 720 | The Tenth Man | 623 |
| | | Is Zat So? | 618 |
| | | Anniversary Waltz | 615 |

| | *Number* | | | *Number* |
|---|---|---|---|---|
| *Plays* | *Performances* | | *Plays* | *Performances* |
| The Happy Time (p) | 614 | | Sweeney Todd, the Demon Barber | |
| Separate Rooms | 613 | | of Fleet Street | 557 |
| Affairs of State | 610 | | A Majority of One | 556 |
| Oh! Calcutta! | 610 | | The Great White Hope | 556 |
| Star and Garter | 609 | | Toys in the Attic | 556 |
| The Mystery of Edwin Drood | 608 | | Sunrise at Campobello | 556 |
| The Student Prince | 608 | | Jamaica | 555 |
| Sweet Charity | 608 | | Stop the World—I Want to Get Off | 555 |
| Bye Bye Birdie | 607 | | Florodora | 553 |
| Irene (r) | 604 | | Noises Off | 553 |
| Sunday in the Park With George | 604 | | Ziegfeld Follies (1943) | 553 |
| Adonis | 603 | | Dial "M" for Murder | 552 |
| Broadway | 603 | | Good News | 551 |
| Peg o' My Heart | 603 | | Peter Pan (r) | 551 |
| Street Scene (p) | 601 | | Let's Face It | 547 |
| Kiki | 600 | | Milk and Honey | 543 |
| Flower Drum Song | 600 | | Within the Law | 541 |
| A Little Night Music | 600 | | Pal Joey (r) | 540 |
| Agnes of God | 599 | | What Makes Sammy Run? | 540 |
| Don't Drink the Water | 598 | | The Sunshine Boys | 538 |
| Wish You Were Here | 598 | | What a Life | 538 |
| Sarafina | 597 | | Crimes of the Heart | 535 |
| A Society Circus | 596 | | The Unsinkable Molly Brown | 532 |
| Absurd Person Singular | 592 | | Rumors | 531 |
| A Day in Hollywood/A Night in | | | The Red Mill (r) | 531 |
| the Ukraine | 588 | | A Raisin in the Sun | 530 |
| The Me Nobody Knows | 586 | | Godspell | 527 |
| The Two Mrs. Carrolls | 585 | | *Jerome Robbins' Broadway | 527 |
| Kismet (m) | 583 | | Fences | 526 |
| Detective Story | 581 | | The Solid Gold Cadillac | 526 |
| Brigadoon | 581 | | Biloxi Blues | 524 |
| No Strings | 580 | | Irma La Douce | 524 |
| Brother Rat | 577 | | The Boomerang | 522 |
| Blossom Time | 576 | | Follies | 521 |
| Pump Boys and Dinettes | 573 | | Rosalinda | 521 |
| Show Boat | 572 | | The Best Man | 520 |
| The Show-Off | 571 | | Chauve-Souris | 520 |
| Sally | 570 | | Blackbirds of 1928 | 518 |
| Golden Boy (m) | 568 | | The Gin Game | 517 |
| One Touch of Venus | 567 | | Sunny | 517 |
| The Real Thing | 566 | | Victoria Regina | 517 |
| *Black and Blue | 564 | | *The Heidi Chronicles | 514 |
| Happy Birthday | 564 | | Fifth of July | 511 |
| Look Homeward, Angel | 564 | | Half a Sixpence | 511 |
| Morning's at Seven (r) | 564 | | The Vagabond King | 511 |
| The Glass Menagerie | 561 | | The New Moon | 509 |
| I Do! I Do! | 560 | | The World of Suzie Wong | 508 |
| Wonderful Town | 559 | | The Rothschilds | 507 |
| Rose Marie | 557 | | On Your Toes (r) | 505 |
| Strictly Dishonorable | 557 | | Sugar | 505 |

| Plays | Number Performances | Plays | Number Performances |
|-------|---------------------|-------|---------------------|
| Shuffle Along | 504 | Personal Appearance | 501 |
| Up in Central Park | 504 | Bird in Hand | 500 |
| Carmen Jones | 503 | Room Service | 500 |
| The Member of the Wedding | 501 | Sailor, Beware! | 500 |
| Panama Hattie | 501 | Tomorrow the World | 500 |

# LONG RUNS OFF BROADWAY

| Plays | Number Performances | Plays | Number Performances |
|-------|---------------------|-------|---------------------|
| *The Fantasticks | 12,523 | True West | 762 |
| The Threepenny Opera | 2,611 | Isn't It Romantic | 733 |
| Forbidden Broadway 1982-87 | 2,332 | Dime a Dozen | 728 |
| Little Shop of Horrors | 2,209 | The Pocket Watch | 725 |
| Godspell | 2,124 | The Connection | 722 |
| Vampire Lesbians of Sodom | 2,024 | The Passion of Dracula | 714 |
| Jacques Brel | 1,847 | Adaptation & Next | 707 |
| *Nunsense | 1,844 | Oh! Calcutta! | 704 |
| Vanities | 1,785 | Scuba Duba | 692 |
| You're a Good Man Charlie Brown | 1,597 | The Foreigner | 686 |
| The Blacks | 1,408 | The Knack | 685 |
| One Mo' Time | 1,372 | The Club | 674 |
| Let My People Come | 1,327 | The Balcony | 672 |
| *Perfect Crime | 1,259 | Penn & Teller | 666 |
| Driving Miss Daisy | 1,195 | America Hurrah | 634 |
| The Hot l Baltimore | 1,166 | Oil City Symphony | 626 |
| I'm Getting My Act Together and Taking It on the Road | 1,165 | Hogan's Goat | 607 |
| Little Mary Sunshine | 1,143 | Beehive | 600 |
| Steel Magnolias | 1,126 | The Trojan Women | 600 |
| El Grande de Coca-Cola | 1,114 | The Dining Room | 583 |
| One Flew Over the Cuckoo's Nest (r) | 1,025 | Krapp's Last Tape & The Zoo Story | 582 |
| The Boys in the Band | 1,000 | The Dumbwaiter & The Collection | 578 |
| Fool for Love | 1,000 | Dames at Sea | 575 |
| *Tamara | 983 | The Crucible (r) | 571 |
| Cloud 9 | 971 | The Iceman Cometh (r) | 565 |
| Sister Mary Ignatius Explains It All for You & The Actor's Nightmare | 947 | The Hostage (r) | 545 |
| Your Own Thing | 933 | What's a Nice Country Like You Doing in a State Like This? | 543 |
| Curley McDimple | 931 | *Other People's Money | 535 |
| Leave It to Jane (r) | 928 | Forbidden Broadway 1988–89 | 534 |
| The Mad Show | 871 | Frankie and Johnny in the Clair de Lune | 533 |
| Scrambled Feet | 831 | Six Characters in Search of an Author (r) | 529 |
| The Effect of Gamma Rays on Man-in-the-Moon Marigolds | 819 | The Dirtiest Show in Town | 509 |
| A View From the Bridge (r) | 780 | Happy Ending & Day of Absence | 504 |
| The Boy Friend (r) | 763 | Greater Tuna | 501 |
|  |  | A Shayna Maidel | 501 |
|  |  | The Boys From Syracuse (r) | 500 |

# NEW YORK DRAMA CRITICS AWARDS, 1935–36 TO 1989–90

Listed below are the New York Drama Critics Circle Awards from 1935–36 through 1989–90 classified as follows: (1) Best American Play, (2) Best Foreign Play, (3) Best Musical, (4) Best, regardless of category (this category was established by new voting rules in 1962–63 and did not exist prior to that year).

1935–36—(1) Winterset

1936–37—(1) High Tor

1937–38—(1) Of Mice and Men, (2) Shadow and Substance

1938–39—(1) No award, (2) The White Steed

1939–40—(1) The Time of Your Life

1940–41—(1) Watch on the Rhine, (2) The Corn Is Green

1941–42—(1) No award, (2) Blithe Spirit

1942–43—(1) The Patriots

1943–44—(2) Jacobowsky and the Colonel

1944–45—(1) The Glass Menagerie

1945–46—(3) Carousel

1946–47—(1) All My Sons, (2) No Exit, (3) Brigadoon

1947–48—(1) A Streetcar Named Desire, (2) The Winslow Boy

1948–49—(1) Death of a Salesman, (2) The Madwoman of Chaillot, (3) South Pacific

1949–50—(1) The Member of the Wedding, (2) The Cocktail Party, (3) The Consul

1950–51—(1) Darkness at Noon, (2) The Lady's Not for Burning, (3) Guys and Dolls

1951–52—(1) I Am a Camera, (2) Venus Observed, (3) Pal Joey (Special citation to Don Juan in Hell)

1952–53—(1) Picnic, (2) The Love of Four Colonels, (3) Wonderful Town

1953–54—(1) Teahouse of the August Moon, (2) Ondine, (3) The Golden Apple

1954–55—(1) Cat on a Hot Tin Roof, (2) Witness for the Prosecution, (3) The Saint of Bleecker Street

1955–56—(1) The Diary of Anne Frank, (2) Tiger at the Gates, (3) My Fair Lady

1956–57—(1) Long Day's Journey Into Night, (2) The Waltz of the Toreadors, (3) The Most Happy Fella

1957–58—(1) Look Homeward, Angel, (2) Look Back in Anger, (3) The Music Man

1958–59—(1) A Raisin in the Sun, (2) The Visit, (3) La Plume de Ma Tante

1959–60—(1) Toys in the Attic, (2) Five Finger Exercise, (3) Fiorello!

1960–61—(1) All the Way Home, (2) A Taste of Honey, (3) Carnival

1961–62—(1) The Night of the Iguana, (2) A Man for All Seasons, (3) How to Succeed in Business Without Really Trying

1962–63—(4) Who's Afraid of Virginia Woolf? (Special citation to Beyond the Fringe)

1963–64—(4) Luther, (3) Hello, Dolly! (Special citation to The Trojan Women)

1964–65—(4) The Subject Was Roses, (3) Fiddler on the Roof

1965–66—(4) The Persecution and Assassination of Marat as Performed by the Inmates of the Asylum of Charenton Under the Direction of the Marquis de Sade, (3) Man of La Mancha

1966–67—(4) The Homecoming, (3) Cabaret

1967–68—(4) Rosencrantz and Guildenstern Are Dead, (3) Your Own Thing

1968–69—(4) The Great White Hope, (3) 1776

1969–70—(4) Borstal Boy, (1) The Effect of Gamma Rays on Man-in-the-Moon Marigolds, (3) Company

1970–71—(4) Home, (1) The House of Blue Leaves, (3) Follies

1971–72—(4) That Championship Season, (2) The Screens, (3) Two Gentlemen of Verona (Special citations to Sticks and Bones and Old Times)

1972–73—(4) The Changing Room, (1) The Hot l Baltimore, (3) A Little Night Music

1973–74—(4) The Contractor, (1) Short Eyes, (3) Candide
1974–75—(4) Equus, (1) The Taking of Miss Janie, (3) A Chorus Line
1975–76—(4) Travesties, (1) Streamers, (3) Pacific Overtures
1976–77—(4) Otherwise Engaged, (1) American Buffalo, (3) Annie
1977–78—(4) Da, (3) Ain't Misbehavin'
1978–79—(4) The Elephant Man, (3) Sweeney Todd, the Demon Barber of Fleet Street
1979–80—(4) Talley's Folly, (2) Betrayal, (3) Evita (Special Citation to Peter Brook's Le Centre International de Créations Théâtrales for its repertory)
1980–81—(4) A Lesson From Aloes, (1) Crimes of the Heart (Special citations to Lena Horne: The Lady and Her Music and the New York Shakespeare Festival production of The Pirates of Penzance)
1981–82—(4) The Life & Adventures of Nicholas Nickleby, (1) A Soldier's Play

1982–83—(4) Brighton Beach Memoirs, (2) Plenty, (3) Little Shop of Horrors (special citation to Young Playwrights Festival)
1983–84—(4) The Real Thing, (1) Glengarry Glen Ross, (3) Sunday in the Park With George (Special citation to Samuel Beckett for the body of his work)
1984–85—(4) Ma Rainey's Black Bottom
1985–86—(4) A Lie of the Mind, (2) Benefactors (Special citation to The Search for Signs of Intelligent Life in the Universe)
1986–87—(4) Fences, (2) Les Liaisons Dangereuses, (3) Les Misérables
1987–88—(4) Joe Turner's Come and Gone, (2) The Road to Mecca, (3) Into the Woods
1988–89—(4) The Heidi Chronicles, (2) Aristocrats (Special citation to Bill Irwin for Largely New York)
1989–90—(4) The Piano Lesson, (2) Privates on Parade, (3) City of Angels

# NEW YORK DRAMA CRITICS CIRCLE VOTING, 1989–90

The New York Drama Critics Circle voted August Wilson's *The Piano Lesson* the best play of the season on the second ballot after the first ballot failed to produce a majority. On the second ballot of weighted choices considering only those plays which received first-ballot votes under the Circle's rules (3 points for a first choice, 2 for second, 1 for third, winner's point total required to be at least three times the number of members voting, divided by 2, plus 1—i.e. 25 this year) *The Piano Lesson* won handily with 30 points from the 16 voting members (see summary of the balloting below), against *The Grapes of Wrath* (21), *Prelude to a Kiss* (21) and *Some Americans Abroad* (17). Three members of the Circle were represented at the meeting by proxies which were valid only on the first ballot of first choices and were recorded as follows: William Henry III (*Time*), *The Piano Lesson*; Julius Novick (New York *Observer*), *Some Americans Abroad*; Douglas Watt (*Daily News*), *The Grapes of Wrath*. Jack Kroll (*Newsweek*) was absent and not voting. Two other members, Mel Gussow (the Circle's president) and Frank Rich (*Times*), were non-voting, per their paper's policy of barring all its critics from voting in outside consensual procedures.

An American play having been named best regardless of category, the Circle then proceeded to name Peter Nichols's *Privates on Parade* the best foreign play of the year by a first-ballot majority of 9 votes (Clive Barnes, John Beaufort, William Henry III, Howard Kissel, Mimi Kramer, Julius Novick, Edith Oliver, John Simon, Edwin Wilson) against 4 for *The Secret Rapture*

(Michael Kuchwara, Jacques le Sourd, William Raidy, Jan Stuart) and 1 each for *Zoya's Apartment* (Michael Feingold), *The Art of Success* (Richard Hummler) and *Lettice & Lovage* (Don Nelsen), with Douglas Watt and Linda Winer abstaining.

The critics also needed only one ballot to declare *City of Angels*—book by Larry Gelbart, music by Cy Coleman, lyrics by David Zippel—the season's best musical by a majority of 10 votes (Feingold, Henry, Hummler, Kramer, le Sourd, Oliver, Raidy, Simon, Watt, Wilson) against 1 each for *Aspects of Love* (Barnes), *Once on This Island* (Kuchwara) and *Grand Hotel* (Novick), with Beaufort, Kissel, Nelsen, Stuart and Winer abstaining.

## SECOND BALLOT FOR BEST PLAY

| Critic | 1st Choice (3 pts.) | 2d Choice (2 pts.) | 3d Choice (1 pt.) |
|---|---|---|---|
| Clive Barnes<br>*Post* | The Piano Lesson | Prelude to a Kiss | The Grapes of Wrath |
| John Beaufort<br>*Monitor* | The Piano Lesson | Some Americans Abroad | The Grapes of Wrath |
| Michael Feingold<br>*Village Voice* | Prelude to a Kiss | The Piano Lesson | The Grapes of Wrath |
| Richard Hummler<br>*Variety* | The Piano Lesson | Prelude to a Kiss | The Grapes of Wrath |
| Howard Kissel<br>*Daily News* | Some Americans Abroad | The Grapes of Wrath | The Piano Lesson |
| Mimi Kramer<br>*The New Yorker* | Some Americans Abroad | The Grapes of Wrath | Prelude to a Kiss |
| Michael Kuchwara<br>Associated Press | The Piano Lesson | Prelude to a Kiss | The Grapes of Wrath |
| Jacques le Sourd<br>Gannett Newspapers | Prelude to a Kiss | The Grapes of Wrath | Some Americans Abroad |
| Don Nelsen<br>*Daily News* | The Grapes of Wrath | The Piano Lesson | Some Americans Abroad |
| Edith Oliver<br>*The New Yorker* | The Piano Lesson | Prelude to a Kiss | The Grapes of Wrath |
| William Raidy<br>Newhouse Newspapers | The Piano Lesson | The Grapes of Wrath | Some Americans Abroad |
| John Simon<br>*New York* | The Grapes of Wrath | Some Americans Abroad | The Piano Lesson |
| Jan Stuart<br>*Seven Days* | Prelude to a Kiss | Some Americans Abroad | The Piano Lesson |
| Edwin Wilson<br>*Wall Street Journal* | The Piano Lesson | The Grapes of Wrath | Some Americans Abroad |
| Linda Winer<br>*Newsday* | Prelude to a Kiss | The Piano Lesson | Some Americans Abroad |

## CHOICES OF SOME OTHER CRITICS

| Critic | Best Play | Best Musical |
|---|---|---|
| John A. Gambling<br>WOR | A Few Good Men | Gypsy |
| Alvin Klein<br>New York *Times* Regional, WNYC | The Piano Lesson | City of Angels |
| Jeffrey Lyons<br>WPIX-TV/WCBS Radio | The Piano Lesson | City of Angels |
| Liz Smith<br>*Tribune-News* Syndicate | The Grapes of Wrath | City of Angels |
| Leida Snow<br>1010 WINS Radio | Some Americans Abroad | City of Angels |
| Allan Wallach<br>*Newsday* | The Grapes of Wrath | City of Angels |

# PULITZER PRIZE WINNERS, 1916–17 TO 1989–90

1916–17—No award
1917–18—Why Marry?, by Jesse Lynch Williams
1918–19—No award
1919–20—Beyond the Horizon, by Eugene O'Neill
1920–21—Miss Lulu Bett, by Zona Gale
1921–22—Anna Christie, by Eugene O'Neill
1922–23—Icebound, by Owen Davis
1923–24—Hell-Bent fer Heaven, by Hatcher Hughes
1924–25—They Knew What They Wanted, by
    Sidney Howard
1925–26—Craig's Wife, by George Kelly
1926–27—In Abraham's Bosom, by Paul Green
1927–28—Strange Interlude, by Eugene O'Neill
1928–29—Street Scene, by Elmer Rice
1929–30—The Green Pastures, by Marc Connelly
1930–31—Alison's House, by Susan Glaspell
1931–32—Of Thee I Sing, by George S. Kaufman,
    Morrie Ryskind, Ira and George Gershwin
1932–33—Both Your Houses, by Maxwell Anderson
1933–34—Men in White, by Sidney Kingsley
1934–35—The Old Maid, by Zoë Akins
1935–36—Idiot's Delight, by Robert E. Sherwood
1936–37—You Can't Take It With You, by Moss
    Hart and George S. Kaufman
1937–38—Our Town, by Thornton Wilder
1938–39—Abe Lincoln in Illinois, by Robert E.
    Sherwood
1939–40—The Time of Your Life, by William
    Saroyan
1940–41—There Shall Be No Night, by Robert E.
    Sherwood
1941–42—No award
1942–43—The Skin of Our Teeth, by Thornton
    Wilder
1943–44—No award

1944–45—Harvey, by Mary Chase
1945–46—State of the Union, by Howard Lindsay
    and Russel Crouse
1946–47—No award
1947–48—A Streetcar Named Desire, by Tennessee
    Williams
1948–49—Death of a Salesman, by Arthur Miller
1949–50—South Pacific, by Richard Rodgers, Oscar
    Hammerstein II and Joshua Logan
1950–51—No award
1951–52—The Shrike, by Joseph Kramm
1952–53—Picnic, by William Inge
1953–54—The Teahouse of the August Moon, by
    John Patrick
1954–55—Cat on a Hot Tin Roof, by Tennessee
    Williams
1955–56—The Diary of Anne Frank, by Frances
    Goodrich and Albert Hackett
1956–57—Long Day's Journey Into Night, by
    Eugene O'Neill
1957–58—Look Homeward, Angel, by Ketti Frings
1958–59—J.B., by Archibald MacLeish
1959–60—Fiorello!, by Jerome Weidman, George
    Abbott, Sheldon Harnick and Jerry Bock
1960–61—All the Way Home, by Tad Mosel
1961–62—How to Succeed in Business Without
    Really Trying, by Abe Burrows, Willie
    Gilbert, Jack Weinstock and Frank
    Loesser
1962–63—No award
1963–64—No award
1964–65—The Subject Was Roses, by Frank D.
    Gilroy
1965–66—No award
1966–67—A Delicate Balance, by Edward Albee

1967–68—No award
1968–69—The Great White Hope, by Howard Sackler
1969–70—No Place To Be Somebody, by Charles Gordone
1970–71—The Effect of Gamma Rays on Man-in-the-Moon Marigolds, by Paul Zindel
1971–72—No award
1972–73—That Championship Season, by Jason Miller
1973–74—No award
1974–75—Seascape, by Edward Albee
1975–76—A Chorus Line, by Michael Bennett, James Kirkwood, Nicholas Dante, Marvin Hamlisch and Edward Kleban
1976–77—The Shadow Box, by Michael Cristofer

1977–78—The Gin Game, by D.L. Coburn
1978–79—Buried Child, by Sam Shepard
1979–80—Talley's Folly, by Lanford Wilson
1980–81—Crimes of the Heat, by Beth Henley
1981–82—A Soldier's Play, by Charles Fuller
1982–83—'night, Mother, by Marsha Norman
1983–84—Glengarry Glen Ross, by David Mamet
1984–85—Sunday in the Park With George, by James Lapine and Stephen Sondheim
1985–86—No award
1986–87—Fences, by August Wilson
1987–88—Driving Miss Daisy, by Alfred Uhry
1988–89—The Heidi Chronicles, by Wendy Wasserstein
1989–90—The Piano Lesson, by August Wilson

# THE TONY AWARDS, 1989–90

The American Theater Wing's Antoinette Perry (Tony) Awards are presented annually in recognition of distinguished artistic achievement in the Broadway theater. The League of American Theaters and Producers and the American Theater Wing present the Tony Awards, founded by the Wing in 1947. Productions opening in eligible Broadway theaters during the eligibility season of the current year—May 4, 1989 to May 2, 1990—are considered for Tony nominations.

The Tony Awards Administration Committee appoints the Tony Awards Nominating Committee which makes the actual nominations. The 1989–90 Nominating Committee consisted of Schuyler Chapin, former dean of the Columbia University School of the Arts; Jean Dalrymple, producer; Leonard Fleischer, charitable contributions manager and arts advocate; Sheldon Harnick, lyricist; Leonard Harris, writer-critic; Mary Henderson, theater historian and author; Rosetta LeNoire, actress and founder/artistic director of AMAS Musical Theater; R.Z. Manna, corporate advertising and events-marketing director for AT&T; Robert Marx, writer/arts administrator; Eve Merriam, playwright; Carole Rothman, director and co-artistic director of the Second Stage; and Jeffrey Sweet, playwright-critic and associate editor of Best Plays.

The Tony Awards are voted from the list of nominees by the members of the governing boards of the four theater artists' organizations: Actors' Equity Association, the Dramatists Guild, the Society of Stage Directors and Choreographers and the United Scenic Artists, plus the members of the first and second-night theater press, the board of directors of the American Theater Wing and the membership of the League of American Theaters and Producers. Because of fluctuation within these boards, the size of the Tony electorate varies from year to year. In the 1989–90 season, there were 661 qualified Tony voters.

The list of 1989–90 nominees follows, with winners in each category appearing in **bold face type.**

BEST PLAY (award goes to both author and producer). *Lettice & Lovage* by Peter Shaffer, produced by The Shubert Organization, Robert Fox, Ltd., Roger Berlind; *Prelude to a Kiss* by Craig Lucas, produced by Christopher Gould, Suzanne Golden, Dodger Productions; *The Grapes of Wrath* adapted by **Frank Galati,** produced by **The Shubert Organization, Steppenwolf Theater Company, Suntory International Corp., Jujamcyn Theaters;** *The Piano Lesson* by August Wilson, produced by Lloyd Richards, Yale Repertory Theater, Center Theater Group/Ahmanson Theater, Gordon Davidson, Jujamcyn Theaters, Benjamin Mordecai, Eugene O'Neill Theater Company, Huntington Theater Company, Goodman Theater, Old Globe Theater.

BEST MUSICAL (award goes to the producer). *Aspects of Love* produced by The Really Useful Theater Company, Inc.; *City of Angels* produced by **Nick Vanoff, Roger Berlind, Jujamcyn Theaters, Suntory International Corp., The Shubert Organization;** *Grand Hotel* produced by Martin Richards,

*TRU*—Robert Morse in his Tony Award-winning portrayal of Truman Capote in Jay Presson Allen's play

Mary Lea Johnson, Sam Crothers, Sander Jacobs, Kenneth D. Greenblatt, Paramount Pictures, Jujamcyn Theaters, Patty Grubman, Marvin A. Krauss; *Meet Me In St. Louis* produced by Brickhill-Burke Productions, Christopher Seabrooke, EPI Products.

BEST BOOK OF A MUSICAL. *Aspects of Love* by Andrew Lloyd Webber; *City of Angels* by **Larry Gelbart**; *Grand Hotel* by Luther Davis; *Meet Me in St. Louis* by Hugh Wheeler.

BEST ORIGINAL SCORE (Music & Lyrics) WRITTEN FOR THE THEATER. *Aspects of Love*, music by Andrew Lloyd Webber, lyrics by Don Black and Charles Hart; *City of Angels*, music by **Cy Coleman**, lyrics by **David Zippel**; *Grand Hotel*, music and lyrics by Robert Wright and George Forrest, additional music and lyrics by Maury Yeston; *Meet Me in St. Louis*, music and lyrics by Hugh Martin and Ralph Blane.

BEST LEADING ACTOR IN A PLAY. Charles S. Dutton in *The Piano Lesson*, Dustin Hoffman in *The Merchant of Venice*, Tom Hulce in *A Few Good Men*, **Robert Morse** in *Tru*.

BEST LEADING ACTRESS IN A PLAY. Geraldine James in *The Merchant of Venice*, Mary-Louise Parker in *Prelude to a Kiss*, **Maggie Smith** in *Lettice & Lovage*, Kathleen Turner in *Cat on a Hot Tin Roof*.

BEST LEADING ACTOR IN A MUSICAL. David Carroll in *Grand Hotel*, Gregg Edelman in *City of Angels*, Bob Gunton in *Sweeney Todd*, **James Naughton** in *City of Angels*.

BEST LEADING ACTRESS IN A MUSICAL. Georgia Brown in *3 Penny Opera*, **Tyne Daly** in *Gypsy*, Beth Fowler in *Sweeney Todd*, Liliane Montevecchi in *Grand Hotel*.

BEST FEATURED ACTOR IN A PLAY. Rocky Carroll in *The Piano Lesson*, **Charles Durning** in *Cat on a Hot Tin Roof*, Terry Kinney in *The Grapes of Wrath*, Gary Sinise in *The Grapes of Wrath*.

BEST FEATURED ACTRESS IN A PLAY. Polly Holliday in *Cat on a Hot Tin Roof*, S. Epatha Merkerson in *The Piano Lesson*, Lois Smith in *The Grapes of Wrath*, **Margaret Tyzack** in *Lettice & Lovage*.

BEST FEATURED ACTOR IN A MUSICAL. Rene Auberjonois in *City of Angels*, Kevin Colson in *Aspects of Love*, Jonathan Hadary in *Gypsy*, **Michael Jeter** in *Grand Hotel*.

BEST FEATURED ACTRESS IN A MUSICAL. **Randy Graff** in *City of Angels*, Jane Krakowski in *Grand Hotel*, Kathleen Rowe McAllen in *Aspects of Love*, Crista Moore in *Gypsy*.

BEST DIRECTION OF A PLAY.    Michael Blakemore for *Lettice & Lovage*, **Frank Galati** for *The Grapes of Wrath*, Peter Hall for *The Merchant of Venice*, Lloyd Richards for *The Piano Lesson*.

BEST DIRECTION OF A MUSICAL. Michael Blakemore for *City of Angels*, Trevor Nunn for *Aspects of Love*, Susan H. Schulman for *Sweeney Todd*, **Tommy Tune** for *Grand Hotel*.

BEST SCENIC DESIGN. Alexandra Byrne for *Some Americans Abroad*, Kevin Rigdon for *The Grapes of Wrath*, **Robin Wagner** for *City of Angels*, Tony Walton for *Grand Hotel*.

BEST COSTUME DESIGN. Theoni V. Aldredge for *Gypsy*, Florence Klotz for *City of Angels*, **Santo Loquasto** for *Grand Hotel*, Erin Quigley for *The Grapes of Wrath*.

BEST LIGHTING DESIGN. **Jules Fisher** for *Grand Hotel*, Paul Gallo for *City of Angels*, Paul Pyant and Neil Peter Jampolis for *Orpheus Descending*, Kevin Rigdon for *The Grapes of Wrath*.

BEST CHOREOGRAPHY. Joan Brickhill for *Meet Me in St. Louis*, Graciela Daniele and Tina Paul for *Dangerous Games*, **Tommy Tune** for *Grand Hotel*.

BEST REVIVAL OF A PLAY OR MUSICAL (award goes to the producer). *Gypsy* produced by **Barry and Fran Weissler, Kathy Levin, Barry Brown**; *Sweeney Todd* produced by Circle in the Square, Theodore Mann and Paul Libin; *The Circle* produced by Elliot Martin, The Shubert Organization, Suntory International Corp.; *The Merchant of Venice* produced by Duncan C. Weldon, Jerome Minskoff, Punch Productions, Peter Hall.

TONY HONOR: **Alfred Drake** for excellence in the theater.

SPECIAL TONY AWARD. **The Seattle Repertory Theater**.

# TONY AWARD WINNERS, 1947–1990

Listed below are the Antoinette Perry (Tony) Award winners in the categories of Best Play and Best Musical from the time these awards were established until the present.

1947—No play or musical award
1948—Mister Roberts; no musical award
1949—Death of a Salesman; Kiss Me, Kate
1950—The Cocktail Party; South Pacific
1951—The Rose Tattoo; Guys and Dolls
1952—The Fourposter; The King and I
1953—The Crucible; Wonderful Town
1954—The Teahouse of the August Moon; Kismet
1955—The Desperate Hours; The Pajama Game
1956—The Diary of Anne Frank; Damn Yankees
1957—Long Day's Journey Into Night; My Fair
    Lady
1958—Sunrise at Campobello; The Music Man
1959—J.B.; Redhead
1960—The Miracle Worker; Fiorello! and The
    Sound of Music (tie)
1961—Becket; Bye Bye Birdie
1962—A Man for All Seasons; How to Succeed in
    Business Without Really Trying
1963—Who's Afraid of Virginia Woolf?; A Funny
    Thing Happened on the Way to the Forum
1964—Luther; Hello, Dolly!
1965—The Subject Was Roses; Fiddler on the Roof
1966—The Persecution and Assassination of Marat
    as Performed by the Inmates of the Asylum
    of Charenton Under the Direction of the
    Marquis de Sade; Man of La Mancha
1967—The Homecoming; Cabaret
1968—Rosencrantz and Guildenstern Are Dead;
    Hallelujah, Baby!

1969—The Great White Hope; 1776
1970—Borstal Boy; Applause
1971—Sleuth; Company
1972—Sticks and Bones; Two Gentlemen of Verona
1973—That Championship Season; A Little Night
    Music
1974—The River Niger; Raisin
1975—Equus; The Wiz
1976—Travesties; A Chorus Line
1977—The Shadow Box; Annie
1978—Da; Ain't Misbehavin'
1979—The Elephant Man; Sweeney Todd, the
    Demon Barber of Fleet Street
1980—Children of a Lesser God; Evita
1981—Amadeus; 42nd Street
1982—The Life & Adventures of Nicholas
    Nickleby; Nine
1983—Torch Song Trilogy; Cats
1984—The Real Thing; La Cage aux Folles
1985—Biloxi Blues; Big River
1986—I'm Not Rappaport; The Mystery of Edwin
    Drood
1987—Fences; Les Misérables
1988—M. Butterfly; The Phantom of the Opera
1989—The Heidi Chronicles; Jerome Robbins'
    Broadway
1990—The Grapes of Wrath; City of Angels

# THE OBIE AWARDS 1989–90

The *Village Voice* Off-Broadway (Obie) Awards are given each year for excellence in various categories of off-Broadway (and frequently off-off-Broadway) shows, with close distinctions between these two areas ignored. The 35th annual Obies for the 1989–90 season, listed below, were chosen by a panel of judges chaired by Ross Wetzsteon and comprising *Village Voice* critics Michael Feingold, Erika Munk and Alisa Solomon and guest judges Rene Buch and Margo Jefferson.

BEST NEW AMERICAN PLAYS. *Prelude to a Kiss* by Craig Lucas; *Imperceptible Mutabilities in the Third Kingdom* by Suzan-Lori Parks; *Bad Penny, Crowbar* and *Terminal Hip* by Mac Wellman.

SUSTAINED ACHIEVEMENT. Act Up (money awarded to the fight against AIDS).

PERFORMANCE. Alec Baldwin in *Prelude to a Kiss;* Elzbieta Czyzewska in *Crowbar;* Karen Evans-Kandel, Ruth Maleczech, Greg Mehrten and Isabell Monk in *Lear;* Marcia Jean Kurtz in *The Loman Family Picnic* and *When She Danced;* Stephen Mellor in *Terminal Hip;* Jean Stapleton in *Mountain Language* and *The Birthday Party;* Pamala Tyson in *Imperceptible Mutabilities in the Third Kingdom;* Courtney B. Vance in *My Children! My Africa!;* Danitra Vance in *Spunk;* Lillias White in *Romance in Hard Times;* Mary Shultz for sustained excellence.

DIRECTION. Liz Diamond for *Imperceptible Mutabilities in the Third Kingdom;* Norman Rene for *Prelude to a Kiss;* Jim Simpson for *Bad Penny;* George C. Wolfe for *Spunk.*

DESIGN. Daniel Moses Schreier for sustained excellence of sound design; George Tsypin for sustained excellence of set design.

SPECIAL CITATIONS. Eric Bogosian for *Sex, Drugs, Rock & Roll;* Dan Hurlin for *A Cool Million;* Joseph Papp for his courageous stand against censorship; San Francisco Mime Troupe for *Seeing Double.*

# ADDITIONAL PRIZES AND AWARDS, 1989–90

The following is a list of major prizes and awards for achievement in the theater this season. In all cases the names and/or titles of the winners appear in **bold face type.**

5th ANNUAL ATCA NEW-PLAY AWARD. For an outstanding new play in cross-country theater, voted by a committee of the American Theater Critics Association. **2** by Romulus Linney.

1989 ELIZABETH HULL-KATE WARRINER AWARD. To the playwright whose work dealt with controversial subjects involving the fields of political, religious or social mores of the time, selected by the Dramatists Guild Council. **Terrence McNally** for *The Lisbon Traviata.*

9th ANNUAL WILLIAM INGE AWARD. For lifetime achievement in the American Theater. **Betty Comden** and **Adolph Green.**

AMERICAN THEATER WING DESIGN AWARDS. For designs originating in the U.S., voted by a committee comprising Tish Dace, Henry Hewes, Edward F. Kook, Julius Novick and Patricia McKay. Scene design, **Kevin Rigdon** for *The Grapes of Wrath.* Costume design, **Santo Loquasto** for *Grand Hotel.* Lighting design, **Jules Fisher** for *Grand Hotel.* Noteworthy unusual effects, **Fred Curchack** for scenery, lighting, costumes, puppets and masks for *Stuff as Dreams Are Made On;* **Judith Martin** for her work with the Paper Bag Players.

OUTER CRITICS CIRCLE AWARDS. For outstanding achievement in the 1989–90 New York theater season, voted by critics of out-of-town and foreign periodicals. Broadway play, *The Grapes of Wrath.* Performance by an actor, **Robert Morse** in *Tru.* Performance by an actress, **Maggie Smith** in *Lettice & Lovage.* Off-Broadway production (play), *Prelude to a Kiss.* Broadway musical, *City of Angels.* Actor in a musical, **Michael Jeter** in *Grand Hotel.* Actress in a musical, **Tyne Daly** in *Gypsy.* Director, **Michael Blakemore** for *City of Angels* and *Lettice & Lovage.* Design, **Robin Wagner** scenery, **Florence Klotz** costumes and **Paul Gallo** lighting for *City of Angels.* Revival of a play, *Cat on a Hot Tin Roof.* Revival of a musical, *Gypsy.* Debut of an actor, **Rocky Carroll** in *The Piano Lesson.* Debut of an actress, **Megan Gallagher** in *A Few Good Men.* John Gassner Playwright Award, **Aaron Sorkin** for *A Few Good Men.* Off-Broadway production (musical), *Closer Than Ever.* Music in an off-Broadway musical, **David Shire** for *Closer Than Ever.* Lyrics in an off-Broadway musical, **Richard Maltby Jr.** for *Closer Than Ever.* Special awards, **Bill Irwin** for *Largely New York,* **Larry Gelbart** for his contributions to comedy in *Mastergate* and *City of Angels,* **En Garde Arts** for their production of *Crowbar.*

35th ANNUAL DRAMA DESK AWARDS. For outstanding achievement, voted by an association of New York drama reporters, editors and critics. New play, *The Piano Lesson* by August Wilson. Musical, *City of Angels*. Director of a play, **Frank Galati** for *The Grapes of Wrath*. Director of a musical, **Tommy Tune** for *Grand Hotel*. Actor in a play, **Nathan Lane** in *The Lisbon Traviata*. Actor in a musical, **James Naughton** in *City of Angels*. Actress in a play, **Geraldine James** in *The Merchant of Venice*. Actress in a musical, **Tyne Daly** in *Gypsy*. Featured actor in a play, **Charles Durning** in *Cat on a Hot Tin Roof*. Featured actor in a musical, **Michael Jeter** in *Grand Hotel*. Featured actress in a play, **Frances Conroy** in *The Secret Rapture*. Featured actress in a musical, **Randy Graff** in *City of Angels*. Music, **Cy Coleman** for *City of Angels*. Lyrics, **David Zippel** for *City of Angels*. Orchestration, **Billy Byers** for *City of Angels*. Book, **Larry Gelbart** for *City of Angels*. Chreography, **Tommy Tune** for *Grand Hotel*. Revival, *Gypsy*. Scene design, **Robin Wagner** for *City of Angels*. Lighting design, **Jules Fisher** for *Grand Hotel*. Costume design, **Santo Loquasto** for *Grand Hotel*. One-person performance, **Robert Morse** in *Tru*.

Special awards: **Fund for New American Plays; Jule Styne; Kevin Haney** for makeup in shows such as *Tru*.

1990 THEATER WORLD AWARDS. For outstanding new talent in Broadway and off-Broadway productions during the 1989–90 season, selected by a committee comprising Clive Barnes, Douglas Watt and John Willis. **Denise Burse-Mickelbury** and **Erma Campbell** of *Ground People*, **Rocky Carroll** and **Tommy Hollis** of *The Piano Lesson*, **Megan Gallagher** of *A Few Good Men*, **Robert Lambert** and **Crista Moore** of *Gypsy*, **Kathleen Rowe McAllen** of *Aspects of Love*, **Michael McKean** of *Accomplice*, **Mary-Louise Parker** of *Prelude to a Kiss*, **Daniel von Bargen** of *Mastergate*, **Jason Workman** of *Meet Me in St. Louis*.

Special awards. **Stewart Granger** of *The Circle* and **Kathleen Turner** of *Cat on a Hot Tin Roof* for their Broadway debuts.

46th ANNUAL CLARENCE DERWENT AWARDS. For the most promising male and female actors on the metropolitan scene during the 1989–90 season, sponsored by Actors' Equity Association and selected by a committee comprising Clive Barnes, Colleen Dewhurst, William A. Henry III, Walter Kerr, Edith Oliver, Peter Stone, Douglas Watt and Robert Whitehead. **Mary-Louise Parker** of *Prelude to a Kiss* and **Michael Jeter** of *Grand Hotel*.

1990 ALAN SCHNEIDER AWARD. For a director who has exhibited exceptional talent through work in a specific community or region, selected by a panel comprising Tanya Berezin, Arvin Brown and Zelda Fichandler. **Roberta Levitow.**

GEORGE S. KAUFMAN AWARD. For lifetime achievement in the theater, sponsored by the Pittsburgh Public Theater. **Colleen Dewhurst.**

11th ANNUAL GEORGE OPPENHEIMER/ NEWSDAY/NEW YORK NEWSDAY AWARD. For the best new American playwright whose work is produced in New York City or on Long Island. **Jon Robin Baitz** for *The Film Society*.

1989 JUJAMCYN THEATERS AWARDS. Honoring outstanding contribution to the development of creative talent for the theater. **The Foundation of the Dramatists Guild** for its Young Playwrights Festival.

1990 COMMON WEALTH AWARD. For excellence of achievement and high potential for future contributions to the dramatic arts. **Jerome Robbins.**

1st ANNUAL JOE A. CALLAWAY AWARD. For excellence in direction or choreography in New York City, sponsored by the Society of Stage Directors and Choreographers. **Gloria Muzio** for her direction of *Other People's Money*.

12th ANNUAL KENNEDY CENTER HONORS. For distinguished achievement by individuals who have made significant contributions to American culture through the arts. **Harry Belafonte, Claudette Colbert, Mary Martin, Alexandra Danilova, William Schuman.**

6th ANNUAL NEW YORK DANCE AND PERFORMANCE (BESSIE) AWARDS. For choreographers and performance artists who presented new work in New York during the 1988—89 season, selected by a committee of 24 persons active in those fields. Choreographer/creator awards: **Ralf Ralf (Jonathan** and **Barnaby Stone** and **Lars Goran Persson)** for *The Summit*; **Dancenoise (Anne Iobst** and **Lucy Sexton)** for *All the Rage*; **Molissa Fenley** for *State of Darkness*; **Guillermo Gomez-Pena** for *Border Brujo*; **Bill T. Jones** for *D-Man in the Waters*; **Linda Mancini** for her concert at HOME for Contemporary Theater and Art; **Dianne McIntyre** for *In Living Color*; **John O'Keefe** for *Shimmer*; **John Malpede** and **Kevin Williams** for work with the Los Angeles Poverty Dept. Performer awards: **Arthur Aviles, Christopher Batenhorst, Susan Blankensop, Laurie Carlos, Diane Madden; Harry Whittaker Shepard** for sustained achievement. Visual design awards: **Dave Feldman** for lighting *Michael Moschen in Motion*; **Mark Lancaster** for scenery and lighting in *Five Stone Wind*; **David Moodey** for lighting *State of Darkness*; **Howard Thies** for cumulative achievement; **Annette Zindel** for costumes in *Changing Faces* and

*Fear of Standing Upright*. Composer awards: **Jacob Burckhardt** for a body of outstanding sound design; **Miecszyslaw Litwinski** for *Safe Tradition*.

Special awards: **Ellie Covan** for Dixon Place, a space for artists to develop their work; **Lori E. Seid** for making a humane art of stage management.

THEATER HALL OF FAME. Annual election by members of the profession of nominees selected by vote of the members of the American Theater Critics Association. **Jerry Bock, Sheldon Harnick, Jerome Lawrence, Robert E. Lee, Al Hirschfeld, Joseph Papp, Lloyd Richards, Mildred Natwick, Charles Laughton, Jean Dalrymple, Lucille Lortel, Theoni V. Aldredge.**

8th ANNUAL ELLIOT NORTON AWARD. To an individual who has made a distinguished contribution to the theater in Boston during the preceding year. **Robert Morse** for *Tru*.

6th ANNUAL HELEN HAYES AWARDS. In recognition of excellence in the Washington, D.C. theater. Resident shows: Production of a play, *Heathen Valley* by Romulus Linney at Round House Theater; production of a musical, *Lucky Stiff* by Lynn Ahrens and Stephen Flaherty at the Olney Theater; Charles MacArthur Award for best new play, *Briar Patch* by Deborah Pryor; lead actress in a play, **Kelly McGillis** in *Twelfth Night*; lead actor in a play, **David Marks** in *Briar Patch*; supporting actress in a play, **Kaia Calhoun** in *Heathen Valley*; supporting actor in a play, **Philip Goodwin** in *Twelfth Night*; lead actress in a musical, **Adriane Lenox** in *On the Town*; lead actor in a musical, **Evan Pappas** in *Lucky Stiff*; direction, **Michael Kahn** for *Twelfth Night*; scenery, **James Kronzer** for *Return of Herbert Bracewell*; costumes, **Jane Schloss Phelan** for *Heathen Valley*; lighting, **Allen Lee Hughes** for *A Midsummer Night's Dream*; sound, **Neil McFadden** for *Heathen Valley*.

Non-resident shows: Production of a play, *The Road to Mecca* by Athol Fugard at Kennedy Center; lead actress, **Nan Martin** in *The Road to Mecca*; lead actor, **Charles S. Dutton** in *The Piano Lesson*; supporting performer, **Stephen Lang** in *A Few Good Men*; direction, **Athol Fugard** for *The Road to Mecca*.

Washington *Post* Award for distinguished community service, **Michael Kahn** as artistic director of the Folger Theater and **Abel Lopez** as artistic director of the Gala Hispanic Theater. KPMG Peat Marwick Award for service to the Washington theater community, **Marcus Cohn** and **David Lloyd Kreeger.**

21st ANNUAL LOS ANGELES DRAMA CRITICS CIRCLE AWARDS. For distinguished achievement in Los Angeles Theater during 1989. Production, *Cloud Nine* produced by **West Coast Ensemble** in association with **Singular Productions**, *Stand-Up Tragedy* produced by **Gordon Davidson** and **Stephen J. Albert** for the **Mark Taper Forum.** Writing, **Bill Bain** for *Stand-Up Tragedy*, **Larry Shue** for *Wenceslas Square*, **Alfred Uhry** for *Driving Miss Daisy*. Direction, **Allison R. Liddi** for *Cloud Nine*, **Ron Link** for *Stand-Up Tragedy*. Lead performance, **Raymond J. Barry** in *Once in Doubt*, **Roscoe Lee Browne** in *Joe Turner's Come and Gone*, **Michael Crawford** in *The Phantom of the Opera*, **Tyne Daly** in *Gypsy*, **Michael DeLorenzo** in *Stand-Up Tragedy*, **Julie Harris** in *Driving Miss Daisy*, **John Lithgow** in *Who's Afraid of Virginia Woolf?*, **Joe Spano** in *American Buffalo*. Featured performance, **Raymond Cruz** in *Buck*, **I.M. Hobson** in *You Never Can Tell*, **Nancy Lenehan** in *Wenceslas Square*. Ensemble performance, **Russell Alexander, Christy Barrett, John Cardone, Alden Millikan, Andy Philpot, Beth Taylor, Kim Taylor** and **Forrest Witt** in *Cloud Nine*. Special award, the **Los Angeles company** of *Tony 'n' Tina's Wedding*. Original music, **Stephen Sondheim** for *Into the Woods*. Choreography, **Shabba-Doo** for *Stand-Up Tragedy*. Musical direction, **Eric Stern** for *Gypsy*. Scene design, **Maria Bjornson** for *The Phantom of the Opera*, **Michael Devine** for *The Road to Mecca*, **Cliff Faulkner** for *You Never Can Tell*. Costume design, **Maria Bjornson** for *The Phantom of the Opera*, **Ann Hould-Ward** for *Into the Woods*. Lighting design, **Andrew Bridge** for *The Phantom of the Opera*, **Peter Maradudin** for *You Never Can Tell*. Sound design, **Jon Gottlieb** for *Minamata*. Margaret Harford Award, **The Back Alley Theater.**

# 1989–90 PUBLICATION
# OF RECENTLY-PRODUCED PLAYS

*Another Time.* Ronald Harwood. Amber Lane Press (also paperback).
*Art of Success, The/In the Ruins.* Nick Dear. Methuen (also paperback).
*Artist Descending a Staircase.* Tom Stoppard. Faber & Faber (paperback).
*Aspects of Love* (libretto). Don Black and Charles Hart. Viking Studio Books.
*Baby With the Bathwater and Laughing Wild.* Christopher Durang. Grove Press (also paperback).
*Bat Masterson's Last Regular Job.* Bill Ballantyne. Playwrights Canada (paperback).
*Boys' Life and Other Plays.* Howard Korder (paperback).
*Cocktail Hour, The, and Two Other Plays.* A.R. Gurney. Plume/New American Library (paperback).
*Eastern Standard.* Richard Greenberg. Grove Press (paperback).
*1841.* Michael Gow. Currency Press, Australia (paperback).
*Elliot Loves.* Jules Feiffer. Grove Press (paperback).
*Gospel at Colonus, The.* Lee Breuer. Theater Communications Group (paperback).
*In a Pig's Valise.* Eric Overmyer. Broadway Play Publishers (paperback).
*Into the Woods: Libretto.* Stephen Sondheim. Theater Communications Group (also paperback).
*Just Say No.* Larry Kramer. St. Martins Press.
*Lend Me a Tenor.* Ken Ludwig. Samuel French (paperback).
*Lettice & Lovage.* Peter Shaffer. Harper & Row (paperback).
*Madhouse in Goa, A.* Martin Sherman. Amber Lane Press (paperback).
*Making History.* Brian Friel. Faber & Faber (paperback).
*Night Hank Williams Died, The.* Larry L. King. Southern Methodist University Press (also paperback).
*1000 Airplanes on the Roof: A Science Fiction Music-Drama.* Philip Glass and David Henry Hwang. Gibbs-Smith (paperback).
*Phantasie.* Sybille Pearson. Broadway Play Publishing (paperback).
*Promise, The.* Jose Rivera. Broadway Play Publishing (paperback).
*Rain. Some Fish. No Elephants.* Y York. Broadway Play Publishing (paperback).
*Secret Rapture, The.* David Hare. Grove Press (paperback).
*Shirley Valentine.* Willy Russell. Samuel French (paperback).
*Some Americans Abroad.* Richard Nelson. Faber & Faber (paperback).
*Veterans Day.* Donald Freed. Amber Lane Press (paperback).

# A SELECTED LIST OF OTHER PLAYS
# PUBLISHED IN 1989-90

*Antigone.* Bertolt Brecht. Applause (paperback).
*Best Short Plays—1989, The.* Ramon Delgado, editor. Applause (paperback).
*Between Worlds: Contemporary Asian-American Plays.* Misha Berson, editor. Theater
  Communications Group (paperback).
*Black Heroes: 7 Plays.* Errol Hill, editor. Applause (paperback).
*British Women Writers.* Dale Spender and Janet Todd, editors. Peter Bedrock Books
  (paperback).
*Churchill: Shorts.* Caryl Churchill. Nick Hern Books (paperback).
*Coast of Illyria, The.* Dorothy Parker and Ross Evans. University of Iowa Press (also
  paperback).
*Complete Plays of Charles Ludlam, The.* Harper & Row (also paperback).
*Dr. Faustus: Swan Theater Program.* Christopher Marlowe. Methuen (paperback).
*Dramacontemporary: Scandinavia.* Per Brask, editor. PAJ Publications (paperback).
*Elecktra.* Sophocles. Princeton.
*Elizabethan Drama.* John Gassner and William Green, editors. Applause (paperback).
*Exiles.* James Joyce. Grafton Books (paperback).
*Father, The,* Strindberg; and *Hedda Gabler,* Ibsen. John Osborne, adaptor. Faber & Faber
  (paperback).
*Female Wits, The: Women Playwrights of the Restoration.* Fidelis Morgan. Virago Press
  (paperback).
*Five Italian Renaissance Comedies.* Bruce Penman, editor. Penguin (paperback).
*FOB and Other Plays.* David Henry Hwang. New American Library (paperback).
*Fuente Ovejuna/Lost in a Mirror.* Lope de Vega. Absolute Press (paperback).
*Gay Plays: An International Anthology.* Catherine Temerson and Francoise Kourilsky,
  editors. Ubu Repertory Theater Publications (paperback).
*Golden Years/The Man Who Had All the Luck, The.* Arthur Miller. Methuen.
*Great Highway, The.* August Strindberg. Absolute Press (paperback).
*Hero Trilogy, The.* Mark Medoff. Gibbs-Smith (paperback).
*Irish Drama 1900-1980.* Colin D. Owens and Joan N. Radner, editors. Catholic University
  of America (paperback).
*Lady Othello and Other Plays.* Arnold Wesker. Penguin (paperback).
*Long Day's Journey Into Night: Revised Edition.* Eugene O'Neill. Yale (paperback).
*Man, Beast and Virtue.* Luigi Pirandello. Absolute Press (paperback).
*Modern Persian Drama: An Anthology.* Giselle Kapuscinski, translator. University Press of
  America (paperback).
*Mother in Law.* Terence. Aris & Phillips (paperback).
*No Exit and Three Other Plays.* Jean-Paul Sartre. Vintage/Random House (paperback).
*Once Five Years Pass and Other Dramatic Works.* Federico Garcia Lorca. Station Hill Press.
*Plays* (six volumes). Henrik Ibsen. Methuen (paperback).
*Popular Performance Plays of Canada, Volumes 1 and 2.* Marian M. Wilson, editor. Simon
  & Pierre.
*Reckless/Blue Window.* Craig Lucas. Theater Communications Group (paperback).

*Scenarios of the Commedia dell'Arte*. Henry F. Salerno, editor and translator. Limelight (paperback).

*Selected Plays of Ben Jonson: Volumes 1 and 2*. Cambridge (paperback).

*Shorts*. David Edgar. Nick Hern Books (paperback).

*Sir John Vanbrugh: Four Comedies*. Penguin (paperback).

*Three Modern Indian Plays*. Editors of Oxford University Press (paperback).

*Wielopole/Wielopole: An Exercise in Theater*. Tadeusz Kantor. Marion Boyars (paperback).

*Women's Work*. Julia Miles, editor. Applause (paperback).

# NECROLOGY

## MAY 1989–MAY 1990

### PERFORMERS

Adams, Eleanor (92)—June 1, 1989
Albrecht, Leo (98)—August 9, 1989
Alexander, Richard (86)—August 9, 1989
Allen, Clifford Lewis 3rd (45)—October 13, 1989
Allison, Fran (81)—June 12, 1989
Altavista, Juan Carlos (60)—July 20, 1989
Andrews, Nancy (68)—July 29, 1989
Anthony, Gordon (86)—Summer 1989
Appleby, Mel (23)—January 18, 1990
Arthur, Lee (49)—June 7, 1989
Attle, John C. (48)—August 29, 1989
Backus, Jim (76)—July 3, 1989
Bailes, Johnnie Jacob (71)—December 16, 1989
Bailey, Carl (35)—March 6, 1990
Balfour, Katharine (69)—April 3, 1990
Banks, Johnny Sr. (55)—November 28, 1989
Bankston, Arnold (34)—March 28, 1990
Barbo, Sal (64)—November 25, 1989
Bari, Lynn (70s)—November 20, 1989
Barry, J.J. (58)—January 26, 1990
Barton, Larry (80)—April 10, 1990
Bass, Maudelle (81)—June 11, 1989
Basten, Charles A. (68)—August 19, 1989
Baum, Robert S. (62)—August 23, 1989
Baum, Kurt (81)—December 27, 1989
Bavier, Frances (86)—December 6, 1989
Bayless, Eugene (69)—September 30, 1989
Belcher, Elbert R. (61)—January 6, 1990
Bellamy, Madge (90s)—January 24, 1990
Bennett, Peter (72)—Winter 1989

Berger, Karl (60)—February 4, 1990
Berneau, Christopher (49)—June 14, 1989
Berto, Juliet (42)—January 10, 1990
Bilbrooke, Lydia (101)—January 4, 1990
Blake, Amanda (60)—August 16, 1989
Blanc, Mel (81)—July 10, 1989
Bledsoe, Elsa Andresen (92)—January 2, 1990
Bloom, George (95)—May 8, 1989
Bond, Raleigh (54)—August 10, 1989
Bouise, Jean (60)—July 6, 1989
Brandon, Henry (77)—February 15, 1990
Brauer, Harold G. (82)—March 19, 1990
Breen, Anne Rita Carey (71)—July 12, 1989
Breen, Robert (80)—March 31, 1990
Brooks, Mary Rogers (76)—December 13, 1989
Brotherson, Eric (78)—October 21, 1989
Bruce, Jean (86)—November 25, 1989
Brummer, Martin (28)—July 19, 1989
Bryant, John (72)—July 13, 1989
Burns, Stephan (35)—February 22, 1990
Calloway, Northern J. (41)—January 9, 1990
Capucine (Germaine Lefebvre) (57)—March 17, 1990
Carey, Mary Jane (66)—January 11, 1990
Carmine, Michael (30)—October 14, 1989
Casson, Ann (74)—May 2, 1990
Case, Lee (68)—February 9, 1990
Cass, Henry (86)—Spring 1989
Chang, Yankee (82)—December 24, 1989
Chapman, Graham (48)—October 4, 1989
Charleson, Ian (40)—Winter 1990
Childs, Peter (50)—November 1, 1989
Ching, William (75)—July 1, 1989

Christie, Audrey Florence (79)—December 20, 1989

Clark, Jerry (45)—August 27, 1989

Clement, Marc R. (39)—February 17, 1990

Coburn, Brian (53)—Winter, 1990

Cookson, Peter (76)—January 6, 1990

Corbin, Albert H. (63)—July 27, 1989

Cunliffe, C. Thomas (60)—May 31, 1989

Dale, Sunny (78)—July 10, 1989

D'Andrie, Sonia (98)—January 3, 1990

Daniel, Henry K. (59)—June 1, 1989

Dansereau, Muriel Tannehill (96)—May 13, 1989

Dapporto, Carlo (78)—October 1, 1989

Davis, Bette (81)—October 6, 1989

Davis, Bowlin (49)—August 4, 1989

Davis, Lee (81)—December 2, 1989

Davis, Pepper (66)—April 6, 1990

Davis, Sammy Jr. (64)—May 16, 1990

de Haven, Evelyn (83)—January 10, 1990

De Santis, Joseph V. (80)—August 30, 1989

Deane, Palmer (56)—April 23, 1990

DeGaetani, Jan (56)—September 15, 1989

Dermota, Anton (79)—June 22, 1989

Dexter, John (54)—March 23, 1990

Di Tillio, Frank (82)—March 14, 1990

Dickson, Eleanor Shaler (89)—December 22, 1989

Dignam, Mark (80)—September 20, 1989

Dolf, John (29)—May 2, 1990

Drake, Fabia (86)—February 28, 1990

Drane, Gary (46)—August 3, 1989

Dunn, Patricia (60)—May 3, 1990

Dunn, Peter (68)—April 14, 1990

Eames, John Matthew (64)—June 13, 1989

Eddy, Helen Jerome (92)—January 27, 1990

Eglevsky, Leda Anchutina (73)—December 15, 1989

Elliott, Leonard (84)—December 31, 1989

Engel, Walter (78)—January 27, 1990

Enriquez, Rene (58)—March 23, 1990

Fabrizi, Aldo (85)—April 2, 1990

Farrell, Charles (89)—May 6, 1990

Farrell, Timothy (66)—May 9, 1989

Fehlman, Lester (84)—August 5, 1989

Fiorito, Tony (55)—October 6, 1989

Fletcher, Jack (68)—February 15, 1990

Fleullen, Joel (82)—February 2, 1990

Franchi, Sergio (64)—May 1, 1990

French, Norma (47)—June 26, 1989

French, Victor (54)—June 15, 1989

Gambarelli, Maria (89)—February 4, 1990

Garbo, Greta (84)—April 15, 1990

Garde, Betty (84)—December 25, 1989

Gardner, Ava (67)—January 25, 1990

Garfin, Rose Lischner (84)—April 2, 1990

Gee, Jean Marie (87)—April 18, 1990

Gentry, Britt Nilsson (46)—July 27, 1989

George, Ann (85)—Summer 1989

Gerard, Denny—Winter 1990

Gerringer, Robert (63)—November 8, 1989

Goddard, Paulette (78)—April 23, 1990

Gorman, Lynne (69)—November 1, 1989

Goulding, Ray (68)—March 24, 1990

Gravline, Alder J. (85)—April 2, 1990

Gray, Pauline (100)—March 20, 1990

Guard, Pamela (57)—November 21, 1989

Gugler, Anne (87)—March 22, 1990

Guilford, Nanette (86)—March 17, 1990

Gunter, Cornell (53)—February 24, 1990

Haig, Jack (76)—July 4, 1989

Hale, Alan Jr. (71)—January 2, 1990

Hamer, Rusty (42)—January 18, 1990

Hardy Ian Dudley (79)—January 25, 1990

Harper, Charles T. (40)—July 4, 1989

Harris, Robin (36)—March 18, 1990

Hawk, Bob—July 4, 1989

Haymer, Johnny (69)—November 18, 1989

Henson, Jim (53)—May 16, 1990

Herbert, Pitt (74)—June 23, 1989

Hernandez, Sercio (28)—June 16, 1989

Hesler, G. Christian (33)—June 11, 1989

Hill, Ken (49)—January 3, 1990

Holt, Ben (34)—May 6, 1990

Houle, Daniel (41)—December 2, 1989

Howes, Ann Haley (86)—December 5, 1989

Hubbard, Shirley Anne (62)—August 25, 1989

Ibbs, Ronald (54)—April 14, 1990

Ireland, Jill (54)—May 19, 1990

Ismond, Edward (44)—January 25, 1990

Jackson, Gordon (66)—January 15, 1990
Jackson, Ray (58)—October 25, 1989
James, Jessica (60)—May 7, 1990
Jarvis, Scott (48)—February 26, 1990
Johnson, Mason (67)—September 30, 1989
Joseph, Bernice Hamsler (88)—August 9, 1989
Karr, James (32)—November 11, 1989
Kaufman, Hazel (83)—December 28, 1989
Kaye, Georgie (70's)—September 9, 1989
Kaye-Martin, Edward (50)—August 13, 1989
Kennedy, Arthur (75)—January 5, 1990
Kermack, Paul (57)—March 17, 1990
Kessler, Charles (93)—January 21, 1990
Khmara, Ilia (93)—August 5, 1989
Kowalski, Bob (37)—May 15, 1990
Kreel, Kenneth (48)—December 3, 1989
Lang, Howard (78)—December 12, 1989
LaRue, Bart (57)—January 3, 1990
LaSpada, Vincent (73)—January 20, 1990
Leberman, Joseph (85)—April 24, 1990
Lee, Billy (60)—November 17, 1989
Lee, Brian (36)—July 25, 1989
Levine, Adelyne (67)—March 5, 1990
Lewis, Ed (103)—September 29, 1989
Lewis, Eleanor J. (81)—November 11, 1989
Lias, Bernard (44)—May 9, 1990
Lockwood, Alexander (88)—January 25, 1990
Loring, Ruth (62)—July 24, 1989
Lucas, Gail (37)—January 7, 1990
Luce, Claire (88)—August 31, 1989
Luce, Kathleen LeBaron (92)—January 23, 1990
Lynch, Ken (79)—February 13, 1990
Lyman-Farquhar, Christine (82)—June 25, 1989
Maguire, Kathleen (64)—August 9, 1989
Mahoney, Jock (70)—December 14, 1989
Malamood, Herman (57)—September 23, 1989
Mangano, Silvana (59)—December 16, 1989
Manteo, Miguel (80)—September 13, 1989
Marquard, Yvonne Peattie (73)—January 10, 1990

Masters, Johnny (79)—January 7, 1990
McAnally, Ray (63)—June 15, 1989
McCrindle, Alex (78)—April 20, 1990
McGee, David (43)—February 2, 1990
McGregor, George R.J. (82)—October 31, 1989
McHaynes, Johnnie L. (42)—May 25, 1989
Merivale, John (72)—February 6, 1990
Merrill, Gary (74)—March 5, 1990
Migel, Helene Marcella (74)—February 22, 1990
Milanov, Zinka (83)—May 30, 1989
Miller, Millicent (81)—May 29, 1990
Millington, Rodney (84)—September 19, 1989
Milton, Billy (84)—November 23, 1989
Molese, Michele (60)—July 5, 1989
Moor, Edward (62)—February 19, 1990
Morrison, Ernie (76)—July 24, 1989
Moss, Arnold (80)—December 15, 1989
Mower, Margaret (93)—September 1, 1989
Mueller, Cookie (40)—November 10, 1989
Neely, Arthur (93)—February 26, 1990
Nilsen, Margit (83)—September 13, 1989
Nixon, Franke (83)—January 14, 1990
Noel-Noel (Lucien Noel) (92)—October 5, 1989
O'Brien, Sean (59)—March 29, 1990
Oliver, Susan (53)—May 10, 1990
Olivier, Laurence (82)—July 11, 1989
Olivo, Bob (50s)—April 27, 1989
Osborne, Kerrie (39)—December 18, 1990
Panette, Jackie (70)—June 7, 1989
Pass, Lenny H. (37)—August 18, 1989
Payne, John (77)—December 6, 1989
Pelligrino, Francis M. (76)—August 30, 1989
Perotti, Helen (84)—October 6, 1989
Perrin, Vic (73)—July 4, 1989
Plummer, Josephine (76)—January 9, 1990
Polley, Diane (54)—January 10, 1990
Pollitt, Clyde (76)—November 10, 1989
Pomerantz, David (76)—February 1, 1990
Pompeii, James S. (51)—November 20, 1989

Post, William Jr. (88)—September 26, 1989

Potter, Coral S. (49)—January 25, 1990

Pringle, Aileen (94)—December 16, 1989

Quayle, Anthony (76)—October 20, 1989

Raitzin, Misha (59)—May 9, 1990

Rand, Kathryn (76)—August 5, 1989

Rappaport, David (38)—May 2, 1990

Ray, Johnnie (63)—February 24, 1990

Reid, Vivian (95)—July 20, 1989

Rhodes, Erik (84)—February 17, 1990

Rice, Mary Alice (78)—October 9, 1989

Robb, Eleanore Sullivan—September 20, 1989

Robb, Lawrence (65)—January 8, 1990

Robinson, Carol (49)—January 17, 1990

Rodensky, Shmuel (85)—July 19, 1989

Rolfing, Tom (40)—April 24, 1990

Rome, Ruth (27)—April 7, 1990

Royle, Derek (61)—January 23, 1990

Sachs, Susan (50)—October 20, 1989

Sadler, Barry (49)—October 29, 1989

Salmi, Albert (62)—April 23, 1990

Sato, Isao (40)—March 9, 1990

Sayer, Philip (42)—September 19, 1989

Schaeffer, Rebecca (21)—July 19, 1989

Schumacher, Billy (38)—March 26, 1990

Schumm, Hans (93)—February 2, 1990

Seales, Frank (37)—May 21, 1990

Shelley, Dave (53)—June 27, 1989

Shenar, Paul (53)—October 11, 1989

Sherman, Connie (72)—December 3, 1989

Shirley, Bill (68)—August 27, 1989

Sloane, Doreen (56)—April 8, 1990

Southern, Danny (68)—December 28, 1989

Stanwyck, Barbara (82)—January 20, 1990

Steinfeld, Eddie (75)—February 9, 1990

Stevens, Napua (71)—January 2, 1990

Sumner, Geoffrey (80)—Fall 1989

Sundin, Michael (28)—July 24, 1989

Swan, Betty (85)—November 3, 1989

Swigart, Ruth Robison Bailey (84)—September 20, 1989

Sydnor, Earl L. (81)—July 9, 1989

Tafoya, Alfonso (60)—September 22, 1989

Talvela, Martti (54)—July 22, 1989

Tayback, Vic (60)—May 25, 1990

Templeton, John F. Sr. (79)—September 10, 1989

Terris, Norma (87)—November 15, 1989

Terry-Thomas (Thomas Terry Hoar Stevens) (78)—January 8, 1990

Thomas, Frank M. (100)—November 25, 1990

Thomas, Madoline (90)—December 30, 1989

Thompson, Joel (32)—January 6, 1990

Thor, Dan (34)—September 2, 1989

Thorpe-Bates, Peggy (75)—December 26, 1989

Traylor, William (60)—September 23, 1989

Treen, Mary (82)—July 20, 1989

Trenker, Luis (97)—April 13, 1990

Trinder, Tommy (80)—July 10, 1989

Unger, Bertil (69)—April 22, 1990

Vale, Freddie (64)—December 15, 1989

Van Cleef, Lee (64)—December 16, 1989

Vidalin, Robert (86)—December 3, 1989

Vinton, Doris (81)—September 9, 1989

Wall, Max (82)—May 22, 1990

Wallace, Jean (61)—February 14, 1990

Wallace, Mary Lewis (92)—August 21, 1989

Waller, John (60)—November 4, 1989

Walsh, Leland Jr. (41)—April 14, 1990

Watkins, June (73)—May 26, 1989

Weaver, Carl Earl (36)—July 13, 1989

Webster, Nell (63)—January 11, 1990

Wells, Billy (90)—December 18, 1989

Westbrook, John (66)—June 16, 1989

Westbury, Marjorie (84)—December 16, 1989

White, Harry (91)—January 30, 1990

Wick, Bobby (59)—October 17, 1989

Wilde, Cornel (74)—October 15, 1989

Williams, Barbara (56)—December 2, 1989

Williams, Hope (92)—May 3, 1990

Williams, Lavinia (73)—July 19, 1989

Willis, Marion III (75)—March 30, 1990

Winckler, Robert (62)—December 28, 1989

Winters, Roland (84)—October 22, 1989

Witkin, Miriam (97)—April 22, 1990

Wong, Iris (68)—September 2, 1989
Woods, Elaine—August 24, 1989
Woods, Edward—October 8, 1989
Worth, Harry (71)—July 20, 1989
Wright, Ben (74)—July 2, 1989
Wright, William A. (46)—December 29, 1989
Wurschmidt, Sigrid (37)—March 24, 1990
Yudenich, Alexi (46)—January 25, 1990
Zacchini, Eddie—December 7, 1989
Zettel, Rose Mary—August 16, 1989

## COMPOSERS AND LYRICISTS

Alexander, Jeff (79)—December 23, 1989
Bacon, Ernst (91)—March 16, 1990
Berkeley, Lennox (86)—December 26, 1989
Berlin, Irving (101)—September 22, 1989
Boone, Philip S. (71)—August 4, 1989
Butts, R. Dale (79)—Winter 1990
Capo, Bobby (68)—December 18, 1989
Dawson, William L. (90)—May 2, 1990
Fain, Sammy (87)—December 6, 1989
Fieger, Addy Oppenheimer (58)—
    September 22, 1989
Hakins, Dick (87)—February 22, 1990
King, Larry Peyton (58)—April 12, 1990
Lerner, Sammy (86)—December 13, 1989
Miller, Frank Jr. (64)—July 13, 1989
Milner, Arthur Sylvan (65)—June 11, 1989
Murray, Lyn (79)—May 20, 1989
Saunders, Jimmy (73)—January 20, 1990
Shannon, Del (50)—February 9, 1990
Stanton, Frank (76)—November, 1989
Thomson, Virgil (92)—September 30, 1989
Timm, Doug (29)—July 21, 1989
Tomei, Margaret (81)—August 23, 1989
Ussachevsky, Vladimir (78)—November 4, 1989
van Heusen, Jimmy (Edward Chester
    Babcock) (77)—February 6, 1990
van Steeden, Peter II (85)—January 3, 1990
Walker, Don (81)—September 12, 1989

Weingarden, Louis (45)—June 8, 1989
Witkin, Beatrice (73)—February 7, 1990
Zwar, Charles (78)—December 2, 1989

## CONDUCTORS

Allen, Ross (36)—June 13, 1989
Alvarez, Al (60)—November 8, 1989
Barclay, Robert (59)—January 4, 1990
Barton, Ben (89)—December 8, 1989
Bradley, Will (78)—July 15, 1989
Braman, Walter (68)—December 3, 1989
Brico, Antonia (87)—August 3, 1989
Buckley, Emerson (73)—November 18, 1989
Cavallaro, Carmen (76)—October 12, 1989
Cincione, Ray (76)—November 12, 1989
Cohen, Bernard I. (59)—October 27, 1989
Eddy, Chuck (67)—February 3, 1990
Gilbert, N. Scott (37)—October 12, 1989
Goldstein, Lee (37)—January 12, 1990
Goodall, Reginald (84)—May 5, 1990
Goshae, Hazel E. La Rochesse (84)—
    February 19, 1990
Jennings, Donald (58)—October 2, 1989
Katz, Paul (81)—August 31, 1989
Kent, William Brad (72)—July 12, 1989
Lawrence, Ashley (55)—May 7, 1990
Lewis, Mel (60)—February 2, 1990
Miesch, Joseph J. (93)—March 3, 1990
Moir, James (87)—December 10, 1990
Mossey, Guy E.—November 4, 1989
Munro, Bonnie (91)—July 3, 1989
Naskiewicz, John L. (42)—November 15, 1989
Nolan, Larry (53)—March 14, 1990
Ragsdale, Harvey (59)—March 4, 1990
Simpkins, George P. (72)—October 10, 1989
Simpson, Roger (56)—September 26, 1989
Stewart, Ian (80)—July 30, 1989
Stivender, David (56)—February 9, 1990
Tucker, Tommy (86)—June 11, 1989
von Karajan, Herbert (81)—July 16, 1989
Wallace, Al (84)—December 22, 1989
Wilson, Pete (86)—August 3, 1989

Wolf, Charles H. (70)—June 9, 1989
Woodbury, Al (79)—May 26, 1989
Wright, Rayburn (67)—March 21, 1990

## CRITICS

Colby, Julius (91)—February 16, 1990
Davis, Clifford (72)—November 24, 1989
Echelson, Robert H. (77)—November 14, 1989
Galkin, Elliott (69)—May 24, 1990
Harriss, R.P. (87)—September 26, 1989
Hayes, Richard P. (60)—January 9, 1990
Iams, Jack (79)—January 27, 1990
Killen, Tom (33)—August 12, 1989
Krim, Seymour (68)—August 30, 1989
Lutz, Fred (52)—November 12, 1989
Mann, William (65)—September 5, 1989
Marcello, Alfred (85)—April 14, 1990
McBride, Raymond E. (77)—October 15, 1989
Shain, Percy (84)—October 16, 1989
Soupault, Philippe (92)—March 12, 1990
Swisher, Viola Hegyi (86)—April 16, 1990
Taylor, Clarke (46)—January 5, 1990
Trewin, John C. (81)—February 16, 1990

## MUSICIANS

Annino, Elvira (80)—September 30, 1989
Anthony, Fred F. (75)—April 4, 1990
Applebaum, Kurt (84)—January 29, 1990
Audino, John (62)—November 15, 1989
Auld, Georgie (70)—January 11, 1990
Bailey, Lyle (79)—September 5, 1989
Bajek, Gilbert E. (78)—August 19, 1989
Baker, Donald H. (86)—June 24, 1989
Balchowsky, Eddie (73)—November 29, 1989
Baldwin, Lois F. (90)—November 12, 1989
Balogh, Erno (92)—June 2, 1989
Barron, Bill (62)—September 21, 1989
Bates, Norman C. (58)—November 5, 1989

Bonzek, Frank P. (83)—January 9, 1990
Boszormenyi-Nagy, Bela (77)—January 6, 1990
Breuer, Harry (87)—June 22, 1989
Burton, Morgan J. (54)—February 15, 1990
Butterfield, Mark B. (29)—September 29, 1989
Buxton, Jimmy (65)—June 28, 1989
Carn, John B. III (41)—August 16, 1989
Carter, Alice Collins (60)—November 20, 1989
Chapman, Keith (44)—June 29, 1989
Chassman, Joachim (88)—January 21, 1990
Cipollina, John (45)—May 29, 1989
Claiborne, Robert (70)—February 3, 1990
Clayton, Freddie (62)—Fall 1989
Cline, Joseph B. (91)—July 1, 1989
Colavolpe, Nicholas B. (53)—February 2, 1990
Coleman, Neal (82)—Summer 1989
Collins, Allen (37)—January 23, 1990
Cooley-Coehrs, Alma (81)—October 15, 1989
Coppola, Lou (65)—May 1, 1990
Cottler, Irv (71)—August 8, 1989
Crossman, Joe (84)—Fall 1989
Crossman-Hecht, Eva (59)—October 16, 1989
Davis, Andrew (94)—January 9, 1990
Davison, Wild Bill (83)—November 14, 1989
Deschevaux-Dumesnil, Suzanne (89)—July 17, 1989
DeVorzon, Evelyn (88)—September 26, 1989
Diane, Nancy (46)—January 12, 1990
Ditto, Fred—August 17, 1989
Doktor, Paul (70)—June 21, 1989
DuBrow, George (72)—January 10, 1990
Durham, Charles Jr. (63)—August 23, 1989
Emerson, Elsie Mae (86)—January 28, 1990
Evans, Lester (60)—October 17, 1989
Gluskin, Ludwig (90)—October 13, 1989
Gold, Arthur (72)—January 3, 1990
Gordon, Dexter (67)—April 25, 1990

Gregory, Charles (89)—March 26, 1990
Greitzer, Sol (63)—August 31, 1989
Griffin, Thomas S. (62)—May 22, 1989
Guerin, Raymond R. (74)—February 17, 1990
Hafid, Ali (54)—September 22, 1989
Hall, Henry (91)—October 28, 1989
Hammond, Bunch (59)—December 13, 1989
Harper, Frances M. (73)—November 20, 1989
Harrington, Johnny (75)—September 18, 1989
Harris, Robert (74)—April 17, 1990
Hibbs, Harry (47)—December 21, 1989
Hoffman, Ben Jr. (75)—December 2, 1989
Horowitz, Vladimir (85)—November 3, 1989
Howie, Viola (95)—February 6, 1990
Hussman, Terry C. (37)—January 26, 1990
Ingber, Louis (85)—August 21, 1989
Iverson, Clarence (85)—January 10, 1990
James, Lucille (70)—August 4, 1989
Jones, Dr. Gordon (74)—February 7, 1990
Joseph, Pleasant (81)—October 2, 1989
Kaufman, Sam Jack (88)—February 7, 1990
Kayton, Elizabeth Adams (89)—February 11, 1990
Kennedy, David L. (63)—June 1, 1989
LaReau, Kathleen A.—January 8, 1990
Lazlo, Stanley J. (83)—February 27, 1990
Leibowitz, Edward J. (82)—February 12, 1990
Leonard, Mildred Louise (88)—November 12, 1989
Linderme, Charles (71)—March 1, 1990
Little, Billy (45)—September 23, 1989
Manna, Silvano (67)—February 4, 1990
Mario, Bob (78)—July 24, 1989
Marion, John P.M. (87)—October 10, 1989
Marsh, Harry Thomas (52)—October 5, 1989
Martin, Rose D. (99)—April 17, 1990
McClean, Bates D. (69)—August 15, 1989
McConnell, Alan (73)—June 1, 1989

McGee, Dennis (96)—October 3, 1989
McKinley, Cal (67)—September 11, 1989
Mitchell, Walter J. (70)—January 10, 1990
Mitchell, William D. (89)—January 23, 1990
Momblow, Donald L. (68)—October 7, 1989
Moore, Eddie (51)—May 21, 1990
Morgan, Mary (102)—October 10, 1989
Morgan, Stanley (67)—November 21, 1989
Murphy, Chee Chee (76)—November 16, 1989
Nelson, Louis (87)—April 5, 1990
Nemenoff, Genia (84)—September 17, 1989
Newborn, Phineas (57)—May 26, 1989
Nix, Herbert A. Jr. (47)—July 4, 1989
Noga, John J. (73)—September 15, 1989
Nuzzo, Frank M. (94)—January 5, 1990
Oden, Clarence (54)—October 12, 1989
Ogdon, John (52)—August 1, 1989
Orio, Christopher (22)—February 8, 1990
Palanchian, John (56)—December 2, 1989
Perry, Charles F. (87)—March 18, 1990
Pickhardt, Elizabeth Marshall (76)—December 1, 1989
Post, Carl (79)—September 20, 1989
Prioli, Frank (81)—August 7, 1989
Remler, Emily (32)—May 4, 1990
Renzulli, Franco (54)—March 26, 1990
Ross, Scott (38)—June 13, 1989
Rostvold, Bjarne (54)—July 12, 1989
Roth, Manuel (83)—February 21, 1990
Roth, Muriel (82)—February 9, 1990
Rubin, Sol (67)—March 5, 1990
Sabicas (78)—April 14, 1990
Sears, Al (80)—July 21, 1989
Sektberg, Willard (87)—July 28, 1989
Sellen, Leslie C. (85)—August 5, 1989
Sharpe, Clarence (53)—January 28, 1990
Sheldon, Ann (64)—April 13, 1990
Sherwood, Rosamond (90)—January 28, 1990
Shirley, Jimmy (76)—December 3, 1989
Shkolnik, Sheldon (52)—March 24, 1990
Simpson, Bob (66)—October 18, 1989
Sternberge, Kurt (91)—December 31, 1989

Suranovich, George (45)—February 15, 1990
Thompson, Tauno T. (76)—June 23, 1989
Trampletti, Arturo (86)—February 18, 1990
Trapani, Frank (52)—June 26, 1989
Turner, Kenneth P. (67)—October 7, 1989
Van Urk, Marion (83)—January 5, 1990
Waits, Frederick Dawud (49)—November 18, 1989
Walt, Sherman (66)—October 26, 1989
Watters, Lu (77)—November 5, 1989
Weigl, George L. (88)—January 27, 1990
Wiegert, Rene (59)—June 26, 1989
Willis, Elizabeth Firestone (67)—October 18, 1989
Willis, Jack Jr. (69)—October 1, 1989
Wolff, Konrad (82)—October 23, 1989
Wyllie, Douglas (56)—Winter 1990
Young, Daniel (76)—June 24, 1989
Young, Karl E. (85)—November 25, 1989
Young, Louis I. (66)—July 16, 1989
Zaveski, Edward (76)—November 12, 1989
Zielinski, John C. (79)—March 25, 1990

## PRODUCERS, DIRECTORS, CHOREOGRAPHERS

Abrams, Morris R. (79)—September 18, 1989
Adler, Philip (84)—January 26, 1990
Aikens, Charles (59)—July 22, 1989
Ailey, Alvin (58)—December 1, 1989
Antonio, Juan (45)—May 24, 1990
Beruh, Joseph (65)—October 30, 1989
Besser, Ernestine (89)—July 1, 1989
Canady, James L. III (44)—August 12, 1989
Casstevens, William Evan (54)—May 22, 1989
Ciro, Steve (46)—June 14, 1989
Cisney, Marcella (76)—December 8, 1989
Crandall, Victoria (81)—March 26, 1990
Davis, John (39)—September 24, 1989
de Vega, José Jr. (56)—April 8, 1990
Duncan, Jeff (59)—May 26, 1989

Dunscombe, Jane—February 25, 1990
Earle, Kevin Davie (51)—November 23, 1989
Ferguson, Tony (58)—January 8, 1990
Fishburn, James (57)—October 20, 1989
Fisz, S. Benjamin (67)—November 17, 1989
Gavers, Mattlyn (75)—August 19, 1989
Glenn, Peter (69)—March 5, 1990
Goelet, Robert Jr. (68)—June 28, 1989
Goossen, Lawrence (46)—October 9, 1989
Gordon, Ashley (29)—September 16, 1989
Gordon, Marvin (59)—August 31, 1989
Gordon, Milton A. (82)—January 31, 1990
Green, Nancy (72)—December 16, 1989
Hackett, Harold L. (86)—January 23, 1990
Halicki, Toby (48)—August 20, 1989
Handley, Alan (77)—January 5, 1990
Harren, William J. (34)—October 4, 1989
Hines, John Jr. (62)—September 1989
Hole, William J. Jr. (71)—February 11, 1990
Honeycutt, Ann (87)—September 26, 1989
Hostettler, Andy (41)—December 25, 1989
Jani, Robert F. (54)—August 6, 1989
Jones, Reed (35)—June 19, 1989
Katzka, Gabriel (58)—February 19, 1990
Lefebre, Jose (54)—May 1990
Leonidoff, Leon (95)—July 29, 1989
Levine, Joseph I. (63)—October 17, 1989
Long, Peter (66)—August 11, 1989
MacDonald, John Bristol (53)—June 15, 1989
Maffeo, Neil T. (55)—May 1, 1990
Moss, Leland (41)—January 24, 1990
Nicholson, Arch (48)—February 23, 1990
Norman, Jerry (55)—September 13, 1989
Noyes, Thomas Ewing (67)—October 28, 1989
Powell, Michael (84)—February 19, 1990
Reynolds, Lee (65)—June 2, 1989
Richards, Mary Lee Johnson (63)—May 3, 1990
Ross, Frank (85)—February 19, 1990
Salce, Luciano (67)—December 17, 1989
Salmaggi, Felix W. (77)—March 17, 1990

Schaffner, Franklin J. (60)—July 2, 1989
Shawn, Michael (45)—April 28, 1990
Simon, Cyril (68)—July 17, 1989
Spindler, John (48)—Fall 1989
Steinmann, Herbert (87)—March 29, 1990
Tager, Max (90)—January 2, 1990
Taylor, Jason (44)—March 17, 1990
Vandergriff, Robert (55)—October 25, 1989
Vitez, Antoine (59)—April 30, 1990
Wengerd, Tim (44)—September 12, 1989
Werner, Eleanor R. (67)—May 20,1 989
Wester, Carl W. (89)—December 28, 1989
Wisberg, Aubrey (78)—March 14, 1990
Zuckerman, Ira (53)—April 22, 1990

## PLAYWRIGHTS

Appel, Don (73)—May 4, 1990
Ariel, Harry (74)—July 6, 1989
Barrett, James Lee (60)—October 15, 1989
Barzman, Ben (79)—December 15, 1989
Beckett, Samuel (83)—December 22, 1989
Behan, Dominic (60)—August 3, 1989
Bialk, Elisa (81)—February 28, 1990
Bowne, Alan (44)—November 24, 1989
Bright, John (61)—September 14, 1989
Colin, Sid (74)—December 12, 1989
Cucci, Francis X. (54)—July 1, 1989
Dennis, Nigel (77)—July 19, 1989
Derwent, Lavinia (83)—November 25, 1989
Doan, Richard K. (78)—May 31, 1989
d'Usseau, Arnaud (73)—January 29, 1990
Friedberg, Gertrude T. (81)—September 17, 1989
Gass, Marc J. (38)—November 25, 1989
Gethers, Steven (67)—December 4, 1989
Gilliam, Roscoe (34)—October 27, 1989
Goodwin, Nancy (76)—July 23, 1989
Haines, William Wister (81)—November 18, 1989
Haislmaier, Jerry (33)—June 14, 1989
Holloway, Jean (60s)—October 18, 1989
Huffaker, Clair (63)—April 2, 1990
Jaray, Hans (83)—January 6, 1990
Lee, Maryat (66)—September 18, 1989
MacColl, Ewan (74)—October 22, 1989

Marshall, Andrew III (52)—August 10, 1989
Mazzucco, Robert (62)—November 6, 1989
McIntyre, Dennis (47)—February 1, 1990
Moore, Sam (85)—October 13, 1989
Paice, Eric (62)—July 6, 1989
Paterson, Alex B. (82)—Winter 1990
Phillips, Arthur (81)—Spring 1990
Planer, Lillian (86)—April 20, 1990
Rive, Richard (59)—June 5, 1989
Rivkin, Allen (86)—February 17, 1990
Rozakis, Gregory (46)—August 24, 1989
Ruthven, Nancy (62)—August 20, 1989
Salacrou, Armand (90)—November 23, 1989
Selden, George (60)—December 5, 1989
Seller, Ghomas (76)—October 28, 1989
Sherwood, Bill (37)—February 10, 1990
Shyre, Paul (63)—November 19, 1989
Smith, Jack (57)—September 18, 1989
Spewack, Bella (91)—April 27, 1990
Tobin, Jean Holloway (72)—November 11, 1989
Tugend, Harry (91)—September 11, 1989
Tute, Warren (75)—November 26, 1989
Warren, Robert Penn (84)—September 15, 1989
Whyte, Ron (47)—September 13, 1989
Wolfson, Victor (81)—May 23, 1990
Zavattini, Cesare (87)—October 13, 1989

## OTHERS

Ambro, Harold (76)—February 1, 1990
*Fantasia* animator
Atkinson, Oriana (94)—July 31, 1989
Widow of Brooks Atkinson
Bass, Elsa Adler (94)—June 27, 1989
Lake Placid music colony
Beach, Donn (81)—June 7, 1989
Restaurateur
Beinicke, Joy Dewey (59)—November 15, 1989
Dance teacher
Blum, William (88)—January 11, 1990
Publicist

Callanan, Brian John (32)—May 26, 1989
American Theater Prods.
Canchola, Jim Jr. (40)—April 11, 1990
Agent
Carli, Alphonsus J. (89)—September 15,
1989
Philadelphia theaters
Cohen, Bernice (64)—February 5, 1990
ASCAP
Connelly, Kay—May 16, 1989
Dramatists Guild receptionist
Crosby, Lindsay (51)—December 11,
1989
Bing's son
Daniels, Joseph Arthur (85)—May 5, 1989
Booking agent
Davis, Hal (73)—May 13, 1990
Publicist
Drake, Galen (83)—June 30, 1989
Radio commentator
Drinkwater, Terry (53)—May 31, 1989
Journalist
Ekstrom, P.M. (81)—November 14, 1989
Ballet historian
Elterman, Samuel (70)—March 13, 1989
Wardrobe supervisor
Finkelstein, Herman (87)—May 20, 1990
ASCAP
Fitzgerald, Gerald (57)—May 22, 1990
*Opera Magazine*
Foster, Richard (59)—November 13, 1989
Vocal coach
Gardner, Hy (80)—July 17, 1989
Columnist
Goldman, Milton (75)—October 4, 1989
Talent agent
Gosa, Jim (58)—December 18, 1989
Jazz expert
Harmon, Tom (70)—March 15, 1990
Sportscaster
Helgeson, Douglas (84)—September 11,
1989
Company manager
Hong, Mae Sien (75)—May 4, 1990
Publicist
Howard, Robin (65)—June 11, 1989
London Contemporary Dance Theater
Hyams, Barry (78)—September 1, 1989
Publicist

Jones, Angeline J. (64)—February 16,
1990
Atlanta theater
Jordan, Jim (67)—October 12, 1989
Graphic artist
Kearsley, Barry Andrew (42)—October 7,
1989
Stage manager
Kelly, Margaret Majer (91)—January 6,
1990
Mother of Princess Grace
Kohn, Bernard A. (84)—December 20,
1989
Music publisher
Kurtis, Fred (89)—June 4, 1989
Carnegie Hall
Landerson, Louis (40)—March 7, 1990
Theater lawyer
Lasker, Jay H. (65)—June 11, 1989
Music industry pioneer
Leonard, Mary Anne—October 26, 1989
Journalist
Levine, Jules (79)—October 31, 1989
Publicist
Lopatin, David S. (30)—August 4, 1989
Publicist
Malone, Dudley Field (59)—January 1,
1990
Agent
McCarthy, Mary (77)—October 25, 1989
Novelist
McEntee, James C. (65)—September 6,
1989
Stage manager
McFadden, Frank (75)—February 8, 1990
Publicist
Meltzer, Allan (77)—June 17, 1989
Publicist
Miele, Louis—August 6, 1989
Journalist
Monaster, Nathan (78)—May 19, 1990
Writers Guild of America
Morris, William Jr. (90)—November 3,
1989
William Morris Agency
Mullins, Greg (41)—December 21, 1989
Agent
Newhouse, Mitzi E. (87)—June 29, 1989
Philanthropist

Newman, Martin H. (76)—January 8, 1990
Variety Club of New York
Oshins, Bertram A. (65)—February 11, 1990
Agent
Palmieri, Edmund L. (82)—June 15, 1989
Federal Court judge
Phelps, Robert (66)—August 2, 1989
Translator
Pretz, Lavinia C. (87)—August 3, 1989
Atlanta Opera
Priore, Bonnie (54)—September 25, 1989
Makeup artist
Reese, Jesse C. Jr. (60)—January 17, 1990
Director, Town Hall
Ricciardelli, James P. (39)—December 17, 1989
Annenberg Center, Philadelphia
Rogers, Kipp Alan (32)—May 26, 1990
Lawyer
Roos, Gilla—September 18, 1989
Talent agent
Rose, Wesley (72)—April 26, 1990
Country Music Hall of Fame
Rosenbloom, Milton M. (82)—October 1, 1989
Copyright lawyer
Rule, Elton (72)—May 5, 1990
ABC-TV
Salkow, Irving—September 23, 1989
Talent agent
Schakne, Robert (63)—August 31, 1989
Journslist
Schattner, Mayer (78)—January 31, 1989
Theater party executive
Scherker, Michael (32)—February 19, 1990
Dance Theater of Harlem
Scobey, Raphael (72)—August 4, 1989
Lawyer
Sell, Stephen (47)—May 26, 1989
Philadelphia Orchestra

Senz, Ira (85)—August 15, 1989
Wigmaker
Sherman, Ellen Neuwald (74)—January 2, 1990
Agent
Shwartz, Martin (67)—April 29, 1990
Publicist
Siederman, Maurice (82)—July 18, 1989
Scene painter
Siloti, Kyriena (94)—July 21, 1989
Piano teacher
Simenon, Georges (86)—September 4, 1989
Belgian novelist
Stone, Irving (86)—August 26, 1989
Novelist
Stone, Kurt (77)—June 15, 1989
Musicologist
Striesfield, Herb (43)—April 17, 1990
Publicist
Sunshine, Morton (74)—April 9, 1990
Tony Awards
Tobin, Margaret Batts (91)—August 3, 1989
Metropolitan Opera
Tropper, Joel M. (46)—February 22, 1990
Stage manager
Villasenor, Edgar Ricardo (57)—April 14, 1990
Publisher
Waggoner, Keith (42)—December 23, 1989
Jujamcyn Theaters
Webber, Mildred (86)—May 1, 1990
Talent scout
Weicher, Denise Sharon (39)—September 29, 1989
Hayes Registry
Weinhold, Kurt (88)—April 27, 1990
Columbia Artists Management
White, Nelson C. (89)—November 21, 1989
Father of George C. White

# THE BEST PLAYS, 1894–1989

Listed in alphabetical order below are all those works selected as Best Plays in previous volumes of the *Best Plays* series. Opposite each title is given the volume in which the play appears, its opening date and its total number of performances. Two separate opening-date and performance-number entries signify two separate engagements off Broadway and on Broadway when the original production was transferred from one area to the other, usually in an off-to-on direction. Those plays marked with an asterisk (*) were still playing on June 1, 1990 and their number of performances was figured through May 31, 1990. Adaptors and translators are indicated by (ad) and (tr), the symbols (b), (m) and (l) stand for the author of the book, music and lyrics in the case of musicals and (c) signifies the credit for the show's conception.

NOTE: A season-by-season listing, rather than an alphabetical one, of the 500 Best Plays in the first 50 volumes, starting with the yearbook for the season of 1919–1920, appears in *The Best Plays of 1968–69*.

| PLAY | VOLUME | OPENED | PERFS |
|---|---|---|---|
| ABE LINCOLN IN ILLINOIS—Robert E. Sherwood | 38–39 | Oct. 15, 1938 | 472 |
| ABRAHAM LINCOLN—John Drinkwater | 19–20 | Dec. 15, 1919 | 193 |
| ACCENT ON YOUTH—Samson Raphaelson | 34–35 | Dec. 25, 1934 | 229 |
| ADAM AND EVA—Guy Bolton, George Middleton | 19–20 | Sept. 13, 1919 | 312 |
| ADAPTATION—Elaine May; and NEXT—Terrence McNally | 68–69 | Feb. 10, 1969 | 707 |
| AFFAIRS OF STATE—Louis Verneuil | 50–51 | Sept. 25, 1950 | 610 |
| AFTER THE FALL—Arthur Miller | 63–64 | Jan. 23, 1964 | 208 |
| AFTER THE RAIN—John Bowen | 67–68 | Oct. 9, 1967 | 64 |
| AGNES OF GOD—John Pielmeier | 81–82 | Mar. 30, 1982 | 486 |
| AH, WILDERNESS!—Eugene O'Neill | 33–34 | Oct. 2, 1933 | 289 |
| AIN'T SUPPOSED TO DIE A NATURAL DEATH—(b, m, l) Melvin Van Peebles | 71–72 | Oct. 7, 1971 | 325 |
| ALIEN CORN—Sidney Howard | 32–33 | Feb. 20, 1933 | 98 |
| ALISON'S HOUSE—Susan Glaspell | 30–31 | Dec. 1, 1930 | 41 |
| ALL MY SONS—Arthur Miller | 46–47 | Jan. 29, 1947 | 328 |
| ALL OVER TOWN—Murray Schisgal | 74–75 | Dec. 12, 1974 | 233 |
| ALL THE WAY HOME—Tad Mosel, based on James Agee's novel *A Death in the Family* | 60–61 | Nov. 30, 1960 | 333 |
| ALLEGRO—(b, l) Oscar Hammerstein II, (m) Richard Rodgers | 47–48 | Oct. 10, 1947 | 315 |
| AMADEUS—Peter Shaffer | 80–81 | Dec. 17, 1980 | 1,181 |
| AMBUSH—Arthur Richman | 21–22 | Oct. 10, 1921 | 98 |

| PLAY | VOLUME | OPENED | PERFS |
|------|--------|--------|-------|

AMERICA HURRAH—Jean-Claude van Itallie ..................... 66–67 . .Nov.  6, 1966 ... 634
AMERICAN BUFFALO—David Mamet ........................... 76–77 . .Feb. 16, 1977 ... 135
AMERICAN WAY, THE—George S. Kaufman, Moss Hart ..... 38–39 . .Jan. 21, 1939 ... 164
AMPHITRYON 38–Jean Giraudoux, (ad) S.N. Behrman ........ 37–38 . .Nov.  1, 1937 ... 153
AND A NIGHTINGALE SANG—C.P. Taylor ....................... 83–84 . .Nov. 27, 1983 ... 177
ANDERSONVILLE TRIAL, THE—Saul Levitt ..................... 59–60 . .Dec. 29, 1959 ... 179
ANDORRA—Max Frisch, (ad) George Tabori .................... 62–63 . .Feb.  9, 1963 ...... 9
ANGEL STREET—Patrick Hamilton ............................... 41–42 . .Dec.  5, 1941 . 1,295
ANGELS FALL—Lanford Wilson ................................. 82–83 . .Oct. 17, 1982 ...... 65
ANIMAL KINGDOM, THE—Philip Barry ........................ 31–32 . .Jan. 12, 1932 ... 183
ANNA CHRISTIE—Eugene O'Neill ................................ 21–22 . .Nov.  2, 1921 ... 177
ANNA LUCASTA—Philip Yordan .................................. 44–45 . .Aug. 30, 1944 ... 957
ANNE OF THE THOUSAND DAYS—Maxwell Anderson ......... 48–49 . .Dec.  8, 1948 ... 286
ANNIE—(b) Thomas Meehan, (m) Charles Strouse,
  (l) Martin Charnin, based on Harold Gray's
  comic strip "Little Orphan Annie" ............................. 76–77 . .Apr. 21, 1977 . 2,377
ANOTHER LANGUAGE—Rose Franken ........................... 31–32 . .Apr. 25, 1932 ... 344
ANOTHER PART OF THE FOREST—Lillian Hellman ............. 46–47 . .Nov. 20, 1946 ... 182
ANTIGONE—Jean Anouilh, (ad) Lewis Galantiere ............... 45–46 . .Feb. 18, 1946 ..... 64
APPLAUSE—(b) Betty Comden and Adolph Green, (m)
  Charles Strouse, (l) Lee Adams, based on the film
  *All About Eve* and the original story by Marry Orr .......... 69–70 . .Mar. 30, 1970 ... 896
APPLE TREE, THE—(b, l) Sheldon Harnick, (b, m) Jerry
  Bock, add'l (b) Jerome Coopersmith, based on stories
  by Mark Twain, Frank R. Stockton and Jules Feiffer ....... 66–67 . .Oct. 18, 1966 ... 463
ARISTOCRATS—Brian Friel ....................................... 88–89 . .Apr. 25, 1989 ... 186
ARSENIC AND OLD LACE—Joseph Kesselring .................. 40–41 . .Jan. 10, 1941 . 1,444
AS HUSBANDS GO—Rachel Crothers ............................ 30–31 . .Mar.  5, 1931 ... 148
AS IS—William M. Hoffman ...................................... 84–85 . .Mar. 10, 1985 ..... 49
                                                                84–85 . .May  1, 1985 ... 285
ASHES–David Rudkin ............................................. 76–77 . .Jan. 25, 1977 ... 167
AUNT DAN AND LEMON—Wallace Shawn ...................... 85–86 . .Oct.  1, 1985 ... 191
AUTUMN GARDEN, THE—Lillian Hellman ...................... 50–51 . .Mar.  7, 1951 ... 101
AWAKE AND SING—Clifford Odets .............................. 34–35 . .Feb. 19, 1935 ... 209

BAD MAN, THE—Porter Emerson Browne ....................... 20–21 . .Aug. 30, 1920 ... 350
BAD HABITS—Terrence McNally ................................. 73–74 . .Feb.  4, 1974 ... 273
BAD SEED—Maxwell Anderson, based on
  William March's novel ........................................ 54–55 . .Dec.  8, 1954 ... 332
BARBARA FRIETCHIE—Clyde Fitch .............................. 99–09 . .Oct. 23, 1899 ..... 83
BAREFOOT IN ATHENS—Maxwell Anderson ................... 51–52 . .Oct. 31, 1951 ..... 30
BAREFOOT IN THE PARK—Neil Simon .......................... 63–64 . .Oct. 23, 1963 . 1,530
BARRETTS OF WIMPOLE STREET, THE—Rudolf Besier ....... 30–31 . .Feb.  9, 1931 ... 370
BECKET—Jean Anouilh, (tr) Lucienne Hill ...................... 60–61 . .Oct.  5, 1960 ... 193
BEDROOM FARCE—Alan Ayckbourn ............................ 78–79 . .Mar. 29, 1979 ... 278
BEGGAR ON HORSEBACK—George S. Kaufman,
  Marc Connelly ................................................. 23–24 . .Feb. 12, 1924 ... 224
BEHOLD THE BRIDEGROOM—George Kelly .................... 27–28 . .Dec. 26, 1927 ..... 88

| PLAY | VOLUME | OPENED | PERFS |
|------|--------|--------|-------|
| BELL, BOOK AND CANDLE—John van Druten | 50–51 | Nov. 14, 1950 | 233 |
| BELL FOR ADANO, A—Paul Osborn, based on John Hersey's novel | 44–45 | Dec. 6, 1944 | 304 |
| BENEFACTORS—Michael Frayn | 85–86 | Dec. 22, 1985 | 217 |
| BENT—Martin Sherman | 79–80 | Dec. 2, 1979 | 240 |
| BERKELEY SQUARE—John L. Balderston | 29–30 | Nov. 4, 1929 | 229 |
| BERNARDINE—Mary Chase | 52–53 | Oct. 16, 1952 | 157 |
| BEST LITTLE WHOREHOUSE IN TEXAS, THE—(b) Larry L. King, Peter Masterson, (m, l) Carol Hall | 77–78 | Apr. 17, 1978 | 64 |
| | 78–79 | June 19, 1978 | 1,639 |
| BEST MAN, THE—Gore Vidal | 59–60 | Mar. 31, 1960 | 520 |
| BETRAYAL—Harold Pinter | 79–80 | Jan. 5, 1980 | 170 |
| BEYOND THE HORIZON—Eugene O'Neill | 19–20 | Feb. 2, 1920 | 160 |
| BIG FISH, LITTLE FISH—Hugh Wheeler | 60–61 | Mar. 15, 1961 | 101 |
| BILL OF DIVORCEMENT, A—Clemence Dane | 21–22 | Oct. 10, 1921 | 173 |
| BILLY BUDD—Louis O. Coxe, Robert Chapman, based on Herman Melville's novel | 50–51 | Feb. 10, 1951 | 105 |
| BILOXI BLUES—Neil Simon | 84–85 | Mar. 28, 1985 | 524 |
| BIOGRAPHY—S.N. Behrman | 32–33 | Dec. 12, 1932 | 267 |
| BLACK COMEDY—Peter Shaffer | 66–67 | Feb. 12, 1967 | 337 |
| BLITHE SPIRIT—Noel Coward | 41–42 | Nov. 5, 1941 | 657 |
| BOESMAN AND LENA—Athol Fugard | 70–71 | June 22, 1970 | 205 |
| BORN IN THE R.S.A.—Barney Simon in collaboration with the cast | 86–87 | Oct. 1, 1986 | 8 |
| BORN YESTERDAY—Garson Kanin | 45–46 | Feb. 4, 1946 | 1,642 |
| BOTH YOUR HOUSES—Maxwell Anderson | 32–33 | Mar. 6, 1933 | 72 |
| BOY MEETS GIRL—Bella and Samuel Spewack | 35–36 | Nov. 27, 1935 | 669 |
| BOY FRIEND, THE—(b, l, m) Sandy Wilson | 54–55 | Sept. 30, 1954 | 485 |
| BOYS IN THE BAND, THE—Mart Crowley | 67–68 | Apr. 15, 1968 | 1,000 |
| BRIDE OF THE LAMB, THE—William Hurlbut | 25–26 | Mar. 30, 1926 | 109 |
| BRIEF MOMENT—S.N. Behrman | 31–32 | Nov. 9, 1931 | 129 |
| BRIGADOON—(b, l) Alan Jay Lerner, (m) Frederick Loewe | 46–47 | Mar. 13, 1947 | 581 |
| BROADWAY—Philip Dunning, George Abbott | 26–27 | Sept. 16, 1926 | 603 |
| BROADWAY BOUND—Neil Simon | 86–87 | Dec. 4, 1986 | 756 |
| BURLESQUE—George Manker Watters, Arthur Hopkins | 27–28 | Sept. 1, 1927 | 372 |
| BUS STOP—William Inge | 54–55 | Mar. 2, 1955 | 478 |
| BUTLEY—Simon Gray | 72–73 | Oct. 31, 1972 | 135 |
| BUTTER AND EGG MAN, THE—George S. Kaufman | 25–26 | Sept. 23, 1925 | 243 |
| BUTTERFLIES ARE FREE—Leonard Gershe | 69–70 | Oct. 21, 1969 | 1,128 |
| | | | |
| CABARET—(b) Joe Masteroff, (m) John Kander, (l) Fred Ebb, based on John van Druten's play *I Am a Camera* and stories by Christopher Isherwood | 66–67 | Nov. 20, 1966 | 1,165 |
| CACTUS FLOWER—Abe Burrows, based on a play by Pierre Barillet and Jean-Pierre Gredy | 65–66 | Dec. 8, 1965 | 1,234 |
| CAGE AUX FOLLES, LA—(see *La Cage aux Folles*) | | | |
| CAINE MUTINY COURT-MARTIAL, THE—Herman Wouk, based on his novel | 53–54 | Jan. 20, 1954 | 415 |

| PLAY | VOLUME | OPENED | PERFS |
|------|--------|--------|-------|
| CALIFORNIA SUITE—Neil Simon | 76–77 | July 2, 1977 | 445 |
| CALIGULA—Albert Camus, (ad) Justin O'Brien | 59–60 | Feb. 16, 1960 | 38 |
| CALL IT A DAY—Dodie Smith | 35–36 | Jan. 28, 1936 | 194 |
| CANDIDE—(b) Lillian Hellman, based on Voltaire's satire (l) Richard Wilbur, John Latouche, Dorothy Parker, (m) Leonard Bernstein | 56–57 | Dec. 1, 1956 | 73 |
| CANDLE IN THE WIND—Maxwell Anderson | 41–42 | Oct. 22, 1941 | 95 |
| CARETAKER, THE—Harold Pinter | 61–62 | Oct. 4, 1961 | 165 |
| CASE OF REBELLIOUS SUSAN, THE—Henry Arthur Jones | 94–99 | Dec. 29, 1894 | 80 |
| CAT ON A HOT TIN ROOF—Tennessee Williams | 54–55 | Mar. 24, 1955 | 694 |
| *CATS—(m) Andrew Lloyd Webber, based on T.S. Eliot's *Old Possum's Book of Practical Cats* (add'l l) Trevor Nunn, Richard Stilgoe | 82–83 | Oct. 7, 1982 | 3,193 |
| CELEBRATION—(b, l) Tom Jones, (m) Harvey Schmidt | 68–69 | Jan. 22, 1969 | 109 |
| CHALK GARDEN, THE—Enid Bagnold | 55–56 | Oct. 26, 1955 | 182 |
| CHANGELINGS, THE—Lee Wilson Dodd | 23–24 | Sept. 17, 1923 | 128 |
| CHANGING ROOM, THE—David Storey | 72–73 | Mar. 6, 1973 | 192 |
| CHAPTER TWO—Neil Simon | 77–78 | Dec. 4, 1977 | 857 |
| CHICAGO—Maurine Dallas Watkins | 26–27 | Dec. 30, 1926 | 172 |
| CHICAGO—(b) Fred Ebb, Bob Fosse, (m) John Kander, (l) Fred Ebb, based on the play by Maurine Dallas Watkins | 75–76 | June 3, 1975 | 898 |
| CHICKEN FEED—Guy Bolton | 23–24 | Sept. 24, 1923 | 144 |
| CHILDREN OF A LESSER GOD—Mark Medoff | 79–80 | Mar. 30, 1980 | 887 |
| CHILDREN'S HOUR, THE—Lillian Hellman | 34–35 | Nov. 20, 1934 | 691 |
| CHILD'S PLAY—Robert Marasco | 69–70 | Feb. 17, 1970 | 342 |
| CHIPS WITH EVERYTHING—Arnold Wesker | 63–64 | Oct. 1, 1963 | 149 |
| CHORUS LINE, A—(c) Michael Bennett, (b) James Kirkwood, Nicholas Dante, (m) Marvin Hamlisch, (l) Edward Kleban | 74–75 | Apr. 15, 1975 | 101 |
| | 75–76 | July 25, 1975 | 6,137 |
| CHRISTOPHER BLAKE—Moss Hart | 46–47 | Nov. 30, 1946 | 114 |
| CIRCLE, THE—W. Somerset Maugham | 21–22 | Sept. 12, 1921 | 175 |
| CLARENCE—Booth Tarkington | 19–20 | Sept. 20, 1919 | 306 |
| CLAUDIA—Rose Franken | 40–41 | Feb. 12, 1941 | 722 |
| CLEARING IN THE WOODS, A—Arthur Laurents | 56–57 | Jan. 10, 1957 | 36 |
| CLIMATE OF EDEN, THE—Moss Hart, based on Edgar Mittleholzer's novel *Shadows Move Among Them* | 52–53 | Nov. 13, 1952 | 20 |
| CLIMBERS, THE—Clyde Fitch | 99–09 | Jan. 21, 1901 | 163 |
| CLOUD 9—Caryl Churchill | 80–81 | May 18, 1981 | 971 |
| CLUTTERBUCK—Benn W. Levy | 49–50 | Dec. 3, 1949 | 218 |
| COCKTAIL HOUR, THE—A.R. Gurney | 88–89 | Aug. 10, 1989 | 351 |
| COCKTAIL PARTY, THE—T.S. Eliot | 49–50 | Jan. 21, 1950 | 409 |
| COLD WIND AND THE WARM, THE—S.N. Behrman | 58–59 | Dec. 8, 1958 | 120 |
| COLLECTION, THE—Harold Pinter | 62–63 | Nov. 26, 1962 | 578 |
| COME BACK, LITTLE SHEBA—William Inge | 49–50 | Feb. 15, 1950 | 191 |
| COMEDIANS—Trevor Griffiths | 76–77 | Nov. 28, 1976 | 145 |
| COMMAND DECISION—William Wister Haines | 47–48 | Oct. 1, 1947 | 408 |

| PLAY | VOLUME | OPENED | PERFS |
|------|--------|--------|-------|
| COMPANY—(b) George Furth, (m, l) Stephen Sondhein | 69–70 | Apr. 26, 1970 | 705 |
| COMPLAISANT LOVER, THE—Graham Greene | 61–62 | Nov. 1, 1961 | 101 |
| CONDUCT UNBECOMING—Barry England | 70–71 | Oct. 12, 1970 | 144 |
| CONFIDENTIAL CLERK, THE—T.S. Eliot | 53–54 | Feb. 11, 1954 | 117 |
| CONNECTION, THE—Jack Gelber (picked as a supplement to the Best Plays) | 60–61 | Feb. 22, 1961 | 722 |
| CONSTANT WIFE, THE—W. Somerset Maugham | 26–27 | Nov. 20, 1926 | 295 |
| CONTRACTOR, THE—David Storey | 73–74 | Oct. 17, 1973 | 72 |
| COQUETTE—George Abbott, Ann Preston Bridgers | 27–28 | Nov. 8, 1927 | 366 |
| CORN IS GREEN, THE—Emlyn Williams | 40–41 | Nov. 26, 1940 | 477 |
| COUNTRY GIRL, THE—Clifford Odets | 50–51 | Nov. 10, 1950 | 235 |
| COUNTY CHAIRMAN, THE—George Ade | 99–09 | Nov. 24, 1903 | 222 |
| CRADLE SONG, THE—Gregorio & Maria Martinez Sierra, (tr) John Garrett Underhill | 26–27 | Jan. 24, 1927 | 57 |
| CRAIG'S WIFE—George Kelly | 25–26 | Oct. 12, 1925 | 360 |
| CREATION OF THE WORLD AND OTHER BUSINESS, THE—Arthur Miller | 72–73 | Nov. 30, 1972 | 20 |
| CREEPS—David E. Freeman | 73–74 | Dec. 4, 1973 | 15 |
| CRIMES OF THE HEART—Beth Henley | 80–81 | Dec. 9, 1980 | 35 |
|  | 81–82 | Nov. 4, 1981 | 535 |
| CRIMINAL CODE, THE—Martin Flavin | 29–30 | Oct. 2, 1929 | 173 |
| CRUCIBLE, THE—Arthur Miller | 52–53 | Jan. 22, 1953 | 197 |
| CYNARA—H.M. Harwood, R.F. Gore-Browne | 31–32 | Nov. 2, 1931 | 210 |
| D A—Hugh Leonard | 77–78 | May 1, 1978 | 697 |
| DAISY MAYME—George Kelly | 26–27 | Oct. 25, 1926 | 112 |
| DAMASK CHEEK, THE—John van Druten, Lloyd Morris | 42–43 | Oct. 22, 1942 | 93 |
| DANCE AND THE RAILROAD, THE—David Henry Hwang | 81–82 | July 16, 1981 | 181 |
| DANCING MOTHERS—Edgar Selwyn, Edmund Goulding | 24–25 | Aug. 11, 1924 | 312 |
| DARK AT THE TOP OF THE STAIRS, THE—William Inge | 57–58 | Dec. 5, 1957 | 468 |
| DARK IS LIGHT ENOUGH, THE—Christopher Fry | 54–55 | Feb. 23, 1955 | 69 |
| DARKNESS AT NOON—Sidney Kingsley, based on Arthur Koestler's novel | 50–51 | Jan. 13, 1951 | 186 |
| DARLING OF THE GODS, THE—David Belasco, John Luther Long | 99–09 | Dec. 3, 1902 | 182 |
| DAUGHTERS OF ATREUS—Robert Turney | 36–37 | Oct. 14, 1936 | 13 |
| DAY IN THE DEATH OF JOE EGG, A—Peter Nichols | 67–68 | Feb. 1, 1968 | 154 |
| DEAD END—Sidney Kingsley | 35–36 | Oct. 28, 1935 | 687 |
| DEADLY GAME, THE—James Yaffe, based on Friedrich Duerrenmatt's novel | 59–60 | Feb. 2, 1960 | 39 |
| DEAR RUTH—Norman Krasna | 44–45 | Dec. 13, 1944 | 683 |
| DEATH OF A SALESMAN—Arthur Miller | 48–49 | Feb. 10, 1949 | 742 |
| DEATH TAKES A HOLIDAY—Alberto Casella, (ad) Walter Ferris | 29–30 | Dec. 26, 1929 | 180 |
| DEATHTRAP—Ira Levin | 77–78 | Feb. 26, 1978 | 1,793 |
| DEBURAU—Sacha Guitry, (ad) Harley Granville Barker | 20–21 | Dec. 23, 1920 | 189 |
| DECISION—Edward Chodorov | 43–44 | Feb. 2, 1944 | 160 |
| DECLASSEE—Zoë Akins | 19–20 | Oct. 6, 1919 | 257 |

| PLAY | VOLUME | OPENED | PERFS |
|------|--------|--------|-------|
| DEEP ARE THE ROOTS—Arnaud d'Usseau, James Gow | 45–46 | Sept. 26, 1945 | 477 |
| DELICATE BALANCE, A—Edward Albee | 66–67 | Sept. 22, 1966 | 132 |
| DEPUTY, THE—Rolf Hochhuth, (ad) Jerome Rothenberg | 63–64 | Feb. 26, 1964 | 109 |
| DESIGN FOR LIVING—Noel Coward | 32–33 | Jan. 24, 1933 | 135 |
| DESIRE UNDER THE ELMS—Eugene O'Neill | 24–25 | Nov. 11, 1924 | 208 |
| DESPERATE HOURS, THE—Joseph Hayes, based on his novel | 54–55 | Feb. 10, 1955 | 212 |
| DETECTIVE STORY—Sidney Kingsley | 48–49 | Mar. 23, 1949 | 581 |
| DEVIL PASSES, THE—Benn W. Levy | 31–32 | Jan. 4, 1932 | 96 |
| DEVIL'S ADVOCATE, THE—Dore Schary, based on Morris L. West's novel | 60–61 | Mar. 9, 1961 | 116 |
| DIAL "M" FOR MURDER—Frederick Knott | 52–53 | Oct. 29, 1952 | 552 |
| DIARY OF ANNE FRANK, THE—Frances Goodrich, Albert Hackett, based on Anne Frank's *The Diary of a Young Girl* | 55–56 | Oct. 5, 1955 | 717 |
| DINING ROOM, THE—A.R. Gurney | 81–82 | Feb. 24, 1982 | 583 |
| DINNER AT EIGHT—George S. Kaufman, Edna Ferber | 32–33 | Oct. 22, 1932 | 232 |
| DISENCHANTED, THE—Budd Schulberg, Harvey Breit, based on Mr. Schulberg's novel | 58–59 | Dec. 3, 1958 | 189 |
| DISRAELI—Louis N. Parker | 09–19 | Sept. 18, 1911 | 280 |
| DISTAFF SIDE, THE—John van Druten | 34–35 | Sept. 25, 1934 | 177 |
| DODSWORTH—Sidney Howard, based on Sinclair Lewis's novel | 33–34 | Feb. 24, 1934 | 315 |
| DOUBLES—David Wiltse | 84–85 | May 8, 1985 | 277 |
| DOUGHGIRLS, THE—Joseph Fields | 42–43 | Dec. 30, 1942 | 671 |
| DOVER ROAD, THE—A.A. Milne | 21–22 | Dec. 23, 1921 | 324 |
| DREAM GIRL—Elmer Rice | 45–46 | Dec. 14, 1945 | 348 |
| DRESSER, THE—Ronald Harwood | 81–82 | Nov. 9, 1981 | 200 |
| DRINKING IN AMERICA—Eric Bogosian | 85–86 | Jan. 19, 1986 | 94 |
| DRIVING MISS DAISY—Alfred Uhry | 86–87 | Apr. 15, 1987 | 1,195 |
| DUEL OF ANGELS—Jean Giraudoux's *Pour Lucrèce*, (ad) Christopher Fry | 59–60 | Apr. 19, 1960 | 51 |
| DULCY—George S. Kaufman, Marc Connelly | 21–22 | Aug. 13, 1921 | 246 |
| DYBBUK, THE—S. Ansky, (ad) Henry G. Alsberg | 25–26 | Dec. 15, 1925 | 120 |
| DYLAN—Sidney Michaels | 63–64 | Jan. 18, 1964 | 153 |
| | | | |
| EASIEST WAY, THE—Eugene Walter | 09–19 | Jan. 19, 1909 | 157 |
| EASTERN STANDARD—Richard Greenberg | 88–89 | Oct. 27, 1988 | 46 |
| | 88–89 | Mar. 25, 1989 | 92 |
| EASTWARD IN EDEN—Dorothy Garner | 47–48 | Nov. 18, 1947 | 15 |
| EDWARD, MY SON—Robert Morley, Noel Langley | 48–49 | Sept. 30, 1948 | 260 |
| EFFECT OF GAMMA RAYS ON MAN-IN-THE-MOON MARIGOLDS, THE—Paul Zindel | 69–70 | Apr. 7, 1970 | 819 |
| EGG, THE—Felicien Marceau, (ad) Robert Schlitt | 61–62 | Jan. 8, 1962 | 8 |
| ELEPHANT MAN, THE—Bernard Pomerance | 78–79 | Jan. 14, 1979 | 73 |
| | 78–79 | Apr. 19, 1979 | 916 |
| ELIZABETH THE QUEEN—Maxwell Anderson | 30–31 | Nov. 3, 1930 | 147 |
| EMERALD CITY—David Williamson | 88–89 | Nov. 30, 1988 | 17 |

| PLAY | VOLUME | OPENED | PERFS |
|------|--------|--------|-------|
| EMPEROR JONES, THE—Eugene O'Neill | 20–21 | Nov. 1, 1920 | 204 |
| EMPEROR'S CLOTHES, THE—George Tabori | 52–53 | Feb. 9, 1953 | 16 |
| ENCHANTED, THE—Maurice Valency, based on Jean Giraudoux's play *Intermezzo* | 49–50 | Jan. 18, 1950 | 45 |
| END OF SUMMER—S.N. Behrman | 35–36 | Feb. 17, 1936 | 153 |
| ENEMY, THE—Channing Pollock | 25–26 | Oct. 20, 1925 | 203 |
| ENOUGH, FOOTFALLS and ROCKABY—Samuel Beckett | 83–84 | Feb. 16, 1984 | 78 |
| ENTER MADAME—Gilda Varesi, Dolly Byrne | 20–21 | Aug. 16, 1920 | 350 |
| ENTERTAINER, THE—John Osborne | 57–58 | Feb. 12, 1958 | 97 |
| EPITAPH FOR GEORGE DILLON—John Osborne, Anthony Creighton | 58–59 | Nov. 4, 1958 | 23 |
| EQUUS—Peter Shaffer | 74–75 | Oct. 24, 1974 | 1,209 |
| ESCAPE—John Galsworthy | 27–28 | Oct. 26, 1927 | 173 |
| ETHAN FROME—Owen and Donald Davis, based on Edith Wharton's novel | 35–36 | Jan. 21, 1936 | 120 |
| EVE OF ST. MARK, THE—Maxwell Anderson | 42–43 | Oct. 7, 1942 | 307 |
| EXCURSION—Victor Wolfson | 36–37 | Apr. 9, 1937 | 116 |
| EXECUTION OF JUSTICE—Emily Mann | 85–86 | Mar. 13, 1986 | 12 |
| EXTREMITIES—William Mastrosimone | 82–83 | Dec. 22, 1982 | 325 |
| FALL GUY, THE—James Gleason, George Abbott | 24–25 | Mar. 10, 1925 | 176 |
| FAMILY BUSINESS—Dick Goldberg | 77–78 | Apr. 12, 1978 | 438 |
| FAMILY PORTRAIT—Lenore Coffee, William Joyce Cowen | 38–39 | May 8, 1939 | 111 |
| FAMOUS MRS. FAIR, THE—James Forbes | 19–20 | Dec. 22, 1919 | 344 |
| FAR COUNTRY, A—Henry Denker | 60–61 | Apr. 4, 1961 | 271 |
| FARMER TAKES A WIFE, THE—Frank B. Elser, Marc Connelly, based on Walter D. Edmonds's novel *Rome Haul* | 34–35 | Oct. 30, 1934 | 104 |
| FATAL WEAKNESS, THE—George Kelly | 46–47 | Nov. 19, 1946 | 119 |
| FENCES—August Wilson | 86–87 | Mar. 26, 1987 | 526 |
| FIDDLER ON THE ROOF—(b) Joseph Stein, (l) Sheldon Harnick, (m) Jerry Bock, based on Sholom Aleichem's stories | 64–65 | Sept. 22, 1964 | 3,242 |
| 5TH OF JULY, THE—Lanford Wilson (also called *Fifth of July*) | 77–78 | Apr. 27, 1978 | 159 |
| FIND YOUR WAY HOME—John Hopkins | 73–74 | Jan. 2, 1974 | 135 |
| FINISHING TOUCHES—Jean Kerr | 72–73 | Feb. 8, 1973 | 164 |
| FIORELLO!—(b) Jerome Weidman, George Abbott, (l) Sheldon Harnick, (m) Jerry Bock | 59–60 | Nov. 23, 1959 | 795 |
| FIREBRAND, THE—Edwin Justus Mayer | 24–25 | Oct. 15, 1924 | 269 |
| FIRST LADY—Katherine Dayton, George S. Kaufman | 35–36 | Nov. 26, 1935 | 246 |
| FIRST MONDAY IN OCTOBER—Jerome Lawrence, Robert E. Lee | 78–79 | Oct. 3, 1978 | 79 |
| FIRST MRS. FRASER, THE—St. John Ervine | 29–30 | Dec. 28, 1929 | 352 |
| FIRST YEAR, THE—Frank Craven | 20–21 | Oct. 20, 1920 | 760 |
| FIVE FINGER EXERCISE—Peter Shaffer | 59–60 | Dec. 2, 1959 | 337 |
| FIVE-STAR FINAL—Louis Weitzenkorn | 30–31 | Dec. 30, 1930 | 175 |
| FLIGHT TO THE WEST—Elmer Rice | 40–41 | Dec. 30, 1940 | 136 |

| PLAY | VOLUME | OPENED | PERFS |
|------|--------|--------|-------|

FLOATING LIGHT BULB, THE—Woody Allen....................80–81..Apr. 27, 1981 .....65
FLOWERING PEACH, THE—Clifford Odets......................54–55..Dec. 28, 1954 ... 135
FOLLIES—(b) James Goldman, (m, l) Stephen Sondheim......70–71..Apr. 4, 1971 ... 521
FOOL, THE—Channing Pollock....................................22–23..Oct. 23, 1922 ... 373
FOOL FOR LOVE—Sam Shepard..................................83–84..May 26, 1983 . 1,000
FOOLISH NOTION—Philip Barry..................................44–45..Mar. 3, 1945 ... 104
FOREIGNER, THE—Larry Shue ...................................84–85..Nov. 1, 1984 ... 686
FORTY CARATS—Pierre Barillet and Jean-Pierre Gredy,
    (ad) Jay Allen..................................................68–69..Dec. 26, 1968 ... 780
FOXFIRE—Susan Cooper, Hume Cronyn, (m) Jonathan
    Holtzman; based on materials from the *Foxfire* books......82–83..Nov. 11, 1982 ... 213
42ND STREET—(b) Michael Stewart, Mark Bramble,
    (m, l) Harry Warren, Al Dubin, (add'l l) Johnny Mercer,
    Mort Dixon, based on the novel by Bradford Ropes.........80–81..Aug. 25, 1980 . 3,486
FOURPOSTER, THE—Jan de Hartog..............................51–52..Oct. 24, 1951 ... 632
FRONT PAGE, THE—Ben Hecht, Charles MacArthur...........28–29..Aug. 14, 1928 ... 276

GENERATION—William Goodhart.................................65–66..Oct. 6, 1965 ... 299
GEORGE WASHINGTON SLEPT HERE—George S. Kaufman,
    Moss Hart......................................................40–41..Oct. 18, 1940 ... 173
GETTING OUT—Marsha Norman .................................78–79..Oct. 19, 1978 ... 259
GIDEON—Paddy Chayefsky........................................61–62..Nov. 9, 1961 ... 236
GIGI—Anita Loos, based on Colette's novel ....................51–52..Nov. 24, 1951 ... 219
GIMME SHELTER—Barrie Keefe (*Gem, Gotcha*
    and *Getaway*) ...............................................78–79..Dec. 10, 1978 .....17
GIN GAME, THE—D.L. Coburn ...................................77–78..Oct. 6, 1977 ... 517
GINGERBREAD LADY, THE—Neil Simon........................70-71..Dec. 13, 1970 ... 193
GIRL ON THE VIA FLAMINIA, THE—Alfred Hayes,
    based on his novel...........................................53–54..Feb. 9, 1954 ... 111
GLASS MENAGERIE, THE—Tennessee Williams ................44–45..Mar. 31, 1945 ... 561
GLENGARRY GLEN ROSS—David Mamet.......................83–84..Mar. 25, 1984 ... 378
GOBLIN MARKET—(ad) Peggy Harmon and Polly Pen
    from the poem by Christina Rosetti, (m)
    Polly Pen (special citation)..................................85–86..Apr. 13, 1986 .....89
GOLDEN APPLE, THE—(b, l), John Latouche,
    (m) Jerome Moross ...........................................53–54..Apr. 20, 1954 ... 125
GOLDEN BOY—Clifford Odets....................................37–38..Nov. 4, 1937 ... 250
GOOD—C.P. Taylor................................................82–83..Oct. 13, 1982 ... 125
GOOD DOCTOR, THE—Neil Simon; adapted from
    and suggested by stories by Anton Chekhov ................73–74..Nov. 27, 1973 ... 208
GOOD GRACIOUS ANNABELLE—Clare Kummer.................09–19..Oct. 31, 1916 ... 111
GOODBYE, MY FANCY—Fay Kanin .............................48–49..Nov. 17, 1948 ... 446
GOOSE HANGS HIGH, THE—Lewis Beach.......................23–24..Jan. 29, 1924 ... 183
GRAND HOTEL—Vicki Baum, (ad) W.A. Drake ...............30–31..Nov. 13, 1930 ... 459
GREAT DIVIDE, THE—William Vaughn Moody .................99–09..Oct. 3, 1906 ... 238
GREAT GOD BROWN, THE—Eugene O'Neill....................25–26..Jan. 23, 1926 ... 271
GREAT WHITE HOPE, THE—Howard Sackler...................68–69..Oct. 3, 1968 ... 556

| PLAY | VOLUME | OPENED | PERFS |
|---|---|---|---|
| GREEN BAY TREE, THE—Mordaunt Shairp | 33–34 | Oct. 20, 1933 | 166 |
| GREEN GODDESS, THE—William Archer | 20–21 | Jan. 18, 1921 | 440 |
| GREEN GROW THE LILACS—Lynn Riggs | 30–31 | Jan. 26, 1931 | 64 |
| GREEN HAT, THE—Michael Arlen | 25–26 | Sept. 15, 1925 | 231 |
| GREEN JULIA—Paul Ableman | 72–73 | Nov. 16, 1972 | 147 |
| GREEN PASTURES, THE—Marc Connelly, based on Roark Bradford's *Ol Man Adam and His Chillun* | 29–30 | Feb. 26, 1930 | 640 |
| GUS AND AL—Albert Innaurato | 88–89 | Feb. 27, 1989 | 25 |
| GUYS AND DOLLS—(b) Jo Swerling, Abe Burrows, based on a story and characters by Damon Runyon, (l, m) Frank Loesser | 50–51 | Nov. 24, 1950 | 1,200 |
| GYPSY—Maxwell Anderson | 28–29 | Jan. 14, 1929 | 64 |
| HADRIAN VII—Peter Luke, based on works by Fr. Rolfe | 68–69 | Jan. 8, 1969 | 359 |
| HAMP—John Wilson; based on an episode from a novel by J.L. Hodson | 66–67 | Mar. 9, 1967 | 101 |
| HAPPY TIME, THE—Samuel Taylor, based on Robert Fontaine's book | 49–50 | Jan. 24, 1950 | 614 |
| HARRIET—Florence Ryerson, Colin Clements | 42–43 | Mar. 3, 1943 | 377 |
| HARVEY—Mary Chase | 44–45 | Nov. 1, 1944 | 1,775 |
| HASTY HEART, THE—John Patrick | 44–45 | Jan. 3, 1945 | 207 |
| HE WHO GETS SLAPPED—Leonid Andreyev, (ad) Gregory Zilboorg | 21–22 | Jan. 9, 1922 | 308 |
| HEART OF MARYLAND, THE—David Belasco | 94–99 | Oct. 22, 1895 | 240 |
| *THE HEIDI CHRONICLES—Wendy Wasserstein | 88–89 | Dec. 11, 1988 | 81 |
|  | 88–89 | Mar. 9, 1989 | 514 |
| HEIRESS, THE—Ruth and Augustus Goetz, suggested by Henry James's novel *Washington Square* | 47–48 | Sept. 29, 1947 | 410 |
| HELL-BENT FER HEAVEN—Hatcher Hughes | 23–24 | Jan. 4, 1924 | 122 |
| HELLO, DOLLY!—(b) Michael Stewart, (m, l) Jerry Herman, based on Thornton Wilder's *The Matchmaker* | 63–64 | Jan. 16, 1964 | 2,844 |
| HER MASTER'S VOICE—Clare Kummer | 33–34 | Oct. 23, 1933 | 224 |
| HERE COME THE CLOWNS—Philip Barry | 38–39 | Dec. 7, 1938 | 88 |
| HERO, THE—Gilbert Emery | 21–22 | Sept. 5, 1921 | 80 |
| HIGH TOR—Maxwell Anderson | 36–37 | Jan. 9, 1937 | 171 |
| HOGAN'S GOAT—William Alfred | 65–66 | Nov. 11, 1965 | 607 |
| HOLIDAY—Philip Barry | 28–29 | Nov. 26, 1928 | 229 |
| HOME—David Storey | 70–71 | Nov. 17, 1970 | 110 |
| HOME—Samm-Art Williams | 79–80 | Dec. 14, 1979 | 82 |
|  | 79–80 | May 7, 1980 | 279 |
| HOMECOMING, THE—Harold Pinter | 66–67 | Jan. 5, 1967 | 324 |
| HOME OF THE BRAVE—Arthur Laurents | 45–46 | Dec. 27, 1945 | 69 |
| HOPE FOR A HARVEST—Sophie Treadwell | 41–42 | Nov. 26, 1941 | 38 |
| HOSTAGE, THE—Brendan Behan | 60–61 | Sept. 20, 1960 | 127 |
| HOT L BALTIMORE, THE—Lanford Wilson | 72–73 | Mar. 22, 1973 | 1,166 |
| HOUSE OF BLUE LEAVES, THE—John Guare | 70–71 | Feb. 10, 1971 | 337 |
| HOUSE OF CONNELLY, THE—Paul Green | 31–32 | Sept. 28, 1931 | 91 |

PLAY                                                              VOLUME    OPENED        PERFS

HOW TO SUCCEED IN BUSINESS WITHOUT REALLY TRYING—
  (b) Abe Burrows, Jack Weinstock, Willie Gilbert, based
  on Shepherd Mead's novel, (l, m) Frank Loesser............61–62..Oct.   14, 1961 . 1,417
HURLYBURLY—David Rabe......................................84–85..June  21, 1984 .....45
                                                            84–85..Aug.   7, 1984 ... 343

I AM A CAMERA—John van Druten, based on Christopher
  Isherwood's Berlin stories......................................51–52..Nov. 28, 1951 ... 214
I KNOW MY LOVE—S.N. Behrman, based on
  Marcel Achard's Auprès de Ma Blonde ......................49–50..Nov.  2, 1949 ... 246
I NEVER SANG FOR MY FATHER—Robert Anderson...........67–68..Jan.  25, 1968 ... 124
I OUGHT TO BE IN PICTURES—Neil Simon....................79–80..Apr.   3, 1980 ... 324
I REMEMBER MAMA—John van Druten, based on
  Kathryn Forbes's book Mama's Bank Account.............44–45..Oct.  19, 1944 ... 714
ICEBOUND—Owen Davis ............................................22–23..Feb.  10, 1923 ... 171
ICEMAN COMETH, THE—Eugene O'Neill .......................46–47..Oct.   9, 1946 ... 136
IDIOT'S DELIGHT—Robert E. Sherwood .........................35–36..Mar.  24, 1936 ... 300
IF I WERE KING—Justin Huntly McCarthy .....................99–09..Oct.  14, 1901 .....56
I'M NOT RAPPAPORT—Herb Gardner..........................85–86..June   6, 1985 ... 101
                                                            85–86..Nov.  18, 1985 ... 890
IMMORALIST, THE—Ruth and Augustus Goetz, based on
  André Gide's novel ..............................................53–54..Feb.   8, 1954 .....96
IN ABRAHAM'S BOSOM—Paul Green...........................26–27..Dec.  30, 1926 ... 116
IN THE MATTER OF J. ROBERT OPPENHEIMER—Heinar
  Kipphardt, (tr) Ruth Speirs .....................................68–69..Mar.   6, 1969 .....64
IN THE SUMMER HOUSE—Jane Bowles........................53–54..Dec.  29, 1953 .....55
IN TIME TO COME—Howard Koch, John Huston...............41–42..Dec.  28, 1941 .....40
INADMISSIBLE EVIDENCE—John Osborne ......................65–66..Nov. 30, 1965 ... 166
INCIDENT AT VICHY—Arthur Miller............................64–65..Dec.   3, 1964 .....99
INDIANS—Arthur L. Kopit.......................................69–70..Oct.  13, 1969 .....96
INHERIT THE WIND—Jerome Lawrence, Robert E. Lee ........54–55..Apr.  21, 1955 ... 806
INNOCENTS, THE—William Archibald, based on
  Henry James's The Turn of the Screw......................49–50..Feb.   1, 1950 ... 141
INNOCENT VOYAGE, THE—Paul Osborn, based on
  Richard Hughes's novel A High Wind in Jamaica..........43–44..Nov. 15, 1943 .....40
INSPECTOR CALLS, AN—J.B. Priestley.........................47–48..Oct.  21, 1947 .....95
INTO THE WOODS—(b) James Lapine, (m, l)
  Stephen Sondheim .............................................87–88..Nov.  5, 1987 ... 765
ISLAND, THE—Athol Fugard, John Kani, Winston Ntshona ..74–75..Nov. 24, 1974 .....52
"IT'S A BIRD IT'S A PLANE IT'S SUPERMAN"—(b) David
  Newman and Robert Benton, (l) Lee Adams, (m) Charles
  Strouse, based on the comic strip "Superman"...............65–66..Mar. 29, 1966 ... 129
IT'S ONLY A PLAY—Terrence McNally.........................85–86..Jan.  12, 1986 .....17

J.B.—Archibald MacLeish.......................................58–59..Dec.  11, 1958 ... 364
JACOBOWSKY AND THE COLONEL—S.N. Behrman, based on
  Franz Werfel's play .............................................43–44..Mar.  14, 1944 ... 417

| PLAY | VOLUME | OPENED | PERFS |
|---|---|---|---|

JANE—S.N. Behrman, suggested by W. Somerset
Maugham's story.................................................51–52..Feb.   1, 1952 ... 100
JANE CLEGG—St. John Ervine ....................................19–20..Feb.  23, 1920 ... 158
JASON—Samson Raphaelson ......................................41–42..Jan.  21, 1942 ... 125
*JEROME ROBBINS' BROADWAY—(c) Jerome Robbins
(special citation) ......................................88–89..Feb.  26, 1989 ... 527
JESSE AND THE BANDIT QUEEN—David Freeman ..............75–76..Oct.  17, 1975 ... 155
JEST, THE—Sem Benelli, (ad) Edward Sheldon.................19–20..Sept. 19, 1919 ... 197
JOAN OF LORRAINE—Maxwell Anderson ........................46–47..Nov. 18, 1946 ... 199
JOE EGG (see *A Day in the Death of Joe Egg*)
JOE TURNER'S COME AND GONE—August Wilson.............87–88..Mar. 27, 1988 ... 105
JOHN FERGUSON—St. John Ervine .............................09–19..May  13, 1919 ... 177
JOHN LOVES MARY—Norman Krasna...........................46–47..Feb.   4, 1947 ... 423
JOHNNY JOHNSON—(b, l) Paul Green, (m) Kurt Weill.........36–37..Nov. 19, 1936 .....68
JOURNEY'S END—R.C. Sherriff................................28–29..Mar. 22, 1929 ... 485
JUMPERS—Tom Stoppard.........................................73–74..Apr. 22, 1974 .....48
JUNE MOON—Ring W. Lardner, George S. Kaufman..........29–30..Oct.   9, 1929 ... 273
JUNIOR MISS—Jerome Chodorov, Joseph Fields ...............41–42..Nov. 18, 1941 ... 710

K2–Patrick  Meyers..................................................82–83..Mar. 30, 1983 .....85
KATAKI—Shimon Wincelberg ...................................58–59..Apr.   9, 1959 .....20
KEY LARGO—Maxwell Anderson....................................39–40..Nov. 27, 1939 ... 105
KILLING OF SISTER GEORGE, THE—Frank Marcus ............66–67..Oct.   5, 1966 ... 205
KINGDOM OF GOD, THE—G. Martinez Sierra, (ad) Helen
and Harley Granville Barker....................................28–29..Dec.  20, 1928 .....92
KISS AND TELL—F. Hugh Herbert..............................42–43..Mar. 17, 1943 ... 956
KISS THE BOYS GOODBYE—Clare Boothe.......................38–39..Sept. 28, 1938 ... 286
KNOCK KNOCK—Jules Feiffer..................................75–76..Jan.  18, 1976 .....41
                                                             75–76..Feb. 24, 1976 ... 152
KVETCH—Steven Berkoff........................................86–87..Feb. 18, 1987 .....31

LA CAGE AUX FOLLES—(b) Harvey Fierstein, (m, l) Jerry
Herman, based on the play by Jean Poiret ....................83–84..Aug. 21, 1983 . 1,761
LA TRAGÉDIE DE CARMEN—(ad) Peter Brook, Jean-Claude
Carrière, Marius Constant from Georges Bizet's
opera *Carmen* (special citation)..............................83–84..Nov. 17, 1983 ... 187
LADY FROM DUBUQUE, THE—Edward Albee ...................79–80..Jan.  31, 1980 .....12
LADY IN THE DARK—(b) Moss Hart, (l) Ira Gershwin,
(m) Kurt Weill....................................................40–41..Jan.  23, 1941 ... 162
LARGO DESOLATO—Vaclav Havel, (tr) Marie Winn............85–86..Mar. 26, 1986 .....40
LARK, THE—Jean Anouilh, (ad) Lillian Hellman................55–56..Nov. 17, 1955 ... 229
LAST MEETING OF THE KNIGHTS OF THE WHITE
MAGNOLIA, THE—Preston Jones............................76–77..Sept. 22, 1976 .....22
LAST MILE, THE—John Wexley................................29–30..Feb. 13, 1930 ... 289
LAST OF THE RED HOT LOVERS—Neil Simon .................69–70..Dec. 28, 1969 ... 706
LATE CHRISTOPHER BEAN, THE—(ad) Sidney Howard
from the French of René Fauchois............................32–33..Oct.  31, 1932 ... 224

| PLAY | VOLUME | OPENED | PERFS |
|------|--------|--------|-------|

LATE GEORGE APLEY, THE—John P. Marquand, George S.
  Kaufman, based on Mr. Marquand's novel...................44–45..Nov. 23, 1944 ... 385
LEAH KLESCHNA—C.M.S. McLellan ...........................99–09..Dec. 12, 1904 ... 131
LEFT BANK, THE—Elmer Rice....................................31–32..Oct.  5, 1931 ... 242
LEND ME A TENOR—Ken Ludwig ..............................88–89..Mar.  2, 1989 ... 481
LES LIAISONS DANGEREUSES—Christopher Hampton,
  based on Choderlos de Laclos's novel ........................86–87..Apr. 30, 1987 ... 148
*LES MISÉRABLES—(b) Alain Boublil, Claude-Michel
  Schönberg, (m) Claude-Michel Schönberg, (l) Herbert
  Kretzmer, add'l. material James Fenton, based on
  Victor Hugo's novel .............................................86–87..Mar. 12, 1987 . 1,285
LESSON FROM ALOES, A—Athol Fugard........................80–81..Nov. 17, 1980 .....96
LET US BE GAY—Rachel Crothers..............................28–29..Feb. 19, 1929 ... 353
LETTERS TO LUCERNE—Fritz Rotter, Allen Vincent............41–42..Dec. 23, 1941 .....23
LIFE, A—Hugh Leonard.........................................80–81..Nov.  2, 1980 .....72
LIFE & ADVENTURES OF NICHOLAS NICKLEBY,
  THE—(ad) David Edgar, from Charles Dickens's novel ....81–82..Oct.  4, 1981 .....49
LIFE IN THE THEATER, A—David Mamet........................77–78..Oct. 20, 1977 ... 288
LIFE WITH FATHER—Howard Lindsay, Russel Crouse,
  based on Clarence Day's book................................39–40..Nov.  8, 1939 . 3.224
LIFE WITH MOTHER—Howard Lindsay, Russel Crouse,
  based on Clarence Day's book ...............................48–49..Oct. 20, 1948 ... 265
LIGHT UP THE SKY—Moss Hart.................................48–49..Nov. 18, 1948 ... 216
LILIOM—Ferenc Molnar, (ad) Benjamin Glazer.................20–21..Apr. 20, 1921 ... 300
LION IN WINTER, THE—James Goldman.........................65–66..Mar.  3, 1966 .....92
LITTLE ACCIDENT—Floyd Dell, Thomas Mitchell...............28–29..Oct.  9, 1928 ... 303
LITTLE FOXES, THE—Lillian Hellman...........................38–39..Feb. 15, 1939 ... 410
LITTLE MINISTER, THE—James M. Barrie.......................94–99..Sept. 27, 1897 ... 300
LITTLE NIGHT MUSIC, A—(b) Hugh Wheeler, (m, l)
  Stephen Sondheim, suggested by Ingmar Bergman's
  film *Smiles of a Summer Night*...............................72–73..Feb. 25, 1973 ... 600
LIVING ROOM, THE—Graham Greene...........................54–55..Nov. 17, 1954 .....22
LIVING TOGETHER—Alan Ayckbourn...........................75–76..Dec.  7, 1975 .....76
LONG DAY'S JOURNEY INTO NIGHT—Eugene O'Neill.........56–57..Nov.  7, 1956 ... 390
LOOK BACK IN ANGER—John Osborne .........................57–58..Oct.  1, 1957 ... 407
LOOK HOMEWARD, ANGEL—Ketti Frings, based on
  Thomas Wolfe's novel.......................................57–58..Nov. 28, 1957 ... 564
LOOSE ENDS—Michael Weller ...................................79–80..June  6, 1979 ... 284
LOST HORIZONS—Harry Segall, revised by John Hayden.....34–35..Oct. 15, 1934 .....56
LOST IN THE STARS—(b, l) Maxwell Anderson, based on
  Alan Paton's novel *Cry, the Beloved Country*,
  (m) Kurt Weill................................................49–50..Oct. 30, 1949 ... 273
LOVE OF FOUR COLONELS, THE—Peter Ustinov.................52–53..Jan. 15, 1953 ... 141
LOVERS—Brian Friel............................................68–69..July 25, 1968 ... 148
LOYALTIES—John Galsworthy ...................................22–23..Sept. 27, 1922 ... 220
LUNCH HOUR—Jean Kerr.........................................80–81..Nov. 12, 1980 ... 262

PLAY                                                    VOLUME   OPENED    PERFS

LUTE SONG—(b) Sidney Howard, Will Irwin from the
  Chinese classic *Pi-Pa-Ki*, (l) Bernard Hanighen,
  (m) Raymond Scott ............................................45–46..Feb.   6, 1946 ... 385
LUTHER—John Osborne..............................................63–64..Sept. 25, 1963 ... 211
LUV—Murray Schisgal................................................64–65..Nov. 11, 1964 ... 901
M. BUTTERFLY—David Henry Hwang...........................87–88..Mar. 20, 1988 ... 777
MA RAINEY'S BLACK BOTTOM—August Wilson...............84–85..Oct. 11, 1984 ... 275
MACHINAL—Sophie Treadwell .....................................28–29..Sept.  7, 1928 .....91
MADWOMAN OF CHAILLOT, THE—Jean Giraudoux, (ad)
  Maurice Valency.................................................48–49..Dec. 27, 1948 ... 368
MAGIC AND THE LOSS, THE—Julian Funt .......................53–54..Apr.   9, 1954 .....27
MAGNIFICENT YANKEE, THE—Emmet Lavery .................45–46..Jan. 22, 1946 ... 160
MAHABHARATA, THE—Jean-Claude Carrière,
  (ad) Peter Brook....................................................87–88..Oct. 13, 1987 .....25
MALE ANIMAL, THE—James Thurber, Elliott Nugent..........39–40..Jan.   9, 1940 ... 243
MAMMA'S AFFAIR—Rachel Barton Butler.......................19–20..Jan. 29, 1920 .....98
MAN FOR ALL SEASONS, A—Robert Bolt ......................61–62..Nov. 22, 1961 ... 637
MAN FROM HOME, THE—Booth Tarkington,
  Harry  Leon  Wilson..............................................99–09..Aug. 17, 1908 ... 406
MAN IN THE GLASS BOOTH, THE—Robert Shaw...............68–69..Sept. 26, 1968 ... 268
MAN OF LA MANCHA—(b) Dale Wasserman, suggested by
  the life and works of Miguel de Cervantes y Saavedra,
  (l) Joe Darion, (m) Mitch Leigh ...............................65–66..Nov. 22, 1965 .2,328
MAN WHO CAME TO DINNER, THE—George S. Kaufman,
  Moss Hart........................................................39–40..Oct. 16, 1939 ... 739
MARAT/SADE (see *The Persecution and Assassination of Marat*, etc.)
MARGIN FOR ERROR—Clare Boothe.............................39–40..Nov.  3, 1939 ... 264
MARRIAGE OF BETTE AND BOO, THE—Christopher Durang..84–85..May 16, 1985 .....86
MARY, MARY—Jean Kerr............................................60–61..Mar.  8, 1961 .1,572
MARY OF SCOTLAND—Maxwell Anderson ......................33–34..Nov. 27, 1933 ... 248
MARY ROSE—James M. Barrie....................................20–21..Dec. 20, 1921 ... 127
MARY THE 3RD—Rachel Crothers...............................22–23..Feb.  5, 1923 ... 162
MASS APPEAL—Bill C. Davis .....................................79–80..Apr. 22, 1980 ... 104
                                                        80–81..Nov. 12, 1981 ... 214
MASTER HAROLD ... AND THE BOYS—Athol Fugard ..........81–82..May   4, 1982 ... 344
MATCHMAKER, THE—Thornton Wilder, based on Johann
  Nestroy's *Einen Jux Will Er Sich Machen*, based on
  John Oxenford's *A Day Well Spent*...........................55–56..Dec.  5, 1955 ... 486
ME AND MOLLY—Gertrude Berg..................................47–48..Feb. 26, 1948 ... 156
MEMBER OF THE WEDDING, THE—Carson McCullers,
  adapted from her novel .........................................49–50..Jan.  5, 1950 ... 501
MEN IN WHITE—Sidney Kingsley..................................33–34..Sept. 26, 1933 ... 351
MERRILY WE ROLL ALONG—George S. Kaufman,
  Moss Hart........................................................34–35..Sept. 29, 1934 ... 155
MERTON OF THE MOVIES—George S. Kaufman, Marc
  Connelly, based on Harry Leon Wilson's novel .............22–23..Nov. 13, 1922 ... 381

| PLAY | VOLUME | OPENED | PERFS |
|------|--------|--------|-------|
| MICHAEL AND MARY—A.A. Milne | 29–30 | Dec. 13, 1929 | 246 |
| MILK TRAIN DOESN'T STOP HERE ANYMORE, THE—Tennessee Williams | 62–63 | Jan. 16, 1963 | 69 |
| MINICK—George S. Kaufman, Edna Ferber | 24–25 | Sept. 24, 1924 | 141 |
| MISÉRABLES, LES—(see *Les Misérables*) | | | |
| MISS FIRECRACKER CONTEST, THE—Beth Henley | 83–84 | May 1, 1984 | 131 |
| MISTER ROBERTS—Thomas Heggen, Joshua Logan, based on Thomas Heggen's novel | 47–48 | Feb. 18, 1948 | 1,157 |
| MOON FOR THE MISBEGOTTEN, A—Eugene O'Neill | 56–57 | May 2, 1957 | 68 |
| MOON IS DOWN, THE—John Steinbeck | 41–42 | Apr. 7, 1942 | 71 |
| MOONCHILDREN—Michael Weller | 71–72 | Feb. 21, 1972 | 16 |
| MORNING'S AT SEVEN—Paul Osborn | 39–40 | Nov. 30, 1939 | 44 |
| MOTHER COURAGE AND HER CHILDREN—Bertolt Brecht, (ad) Eric Bentley | 62–63 | Mar. 28, 1963 | 52 |
| MOURNING BECOMES ELECTRA—Eugene O'Neill | 31–32 | Oct. 26, 1931 | 150 |
| MR. AND MRS. NORTH—Owen Davis, based on Frances and Richard Lockridge's stories | 40–41 | Jan. 12, 1941 | 163 |
| MRS. BUMSTEAD-LEIGH—Harry James Smith | 09–19 | Apr. 3, 1911 | 64 |
| MRS. MCTHING—Mary Chase | 51–52 | Feb. 20, 1952 | 350 |
| MRS. PARTRIDGE PRESENTS—Mary Kennedy, Ruth Hawthorne | 24–25 | Jan. 5, 1925 | 144 |
| MY FAIR LADY—(b, l) Alan Jay Lerner, based on George Bernard Shaw's *Pygmalion*, (m) Frederick Loewe | 55–56 | Mar. 15, 1956 | 2,717 |
| MY ONE AND ONLY—(b) Peter Stone, Timothy S. Mayer, (m) George Gershwin from *Funny Face* and other shows, (l) Ira Gershwin | 82–83 | May 1, 1983 | 767 |
| MY SISTER EILEEN—Joseph Fields, Jerome Chodorov, based on Ruth McKenney's stories | 40–41 | Dec. 26, 1940 | 864 |
| MY 3 ANGELS—Samuel and Bella Spewack, based on Albert Huston's play *La Cuisine des Anges* | 52–53 | Mar. 11, 1953 | 344 |
| MYSTERY OF EDWIN DROOD, THE—(b, m, l) Rupert Holmes (also called *Drood*) | 85–86 | Aug. 4, 1985 | 25 |
| | 85–86 | Dec. 12, 1985 | 608 |
| | | | |
| NATIONAL HEALTH, THE—Peter Nichols | 74–75 | Oct. 10, 1974 | 53 |
| NATIVE SON—Paul Green, Richard Wright, based on Mr. Wright's novel | 40–41 | Mar. 24, 1941 | 114 |
| NEST, THE—(ad) Grace George, from Paul Geraldy's *Les Noces d'Argent* | 21–22 | Jan. 28, 1922 | 152 |
| NEVIS MOUNTAIN DEW—Steve Carter | 78–79 | Dec. 7, 1978 | 61 |
| NEXT—(see *Adaptation*) | | | |
| NEXT TIME I'LL SING TO YOU—James Saunders | 63–64 | Nov. 27, 1963 | 23 |
| NICE PEOPLE—Rachel Crothers | 20–21 | Mar. 2, 1921 | 247 |
| NICHOLAS NICKLEBY (see *The Life & Adventures of Nicholas Nickleby*) | | | |
| NIGHT OF THE IGUANA, THE—Tennessee Williams | 61–62 | Dec. 28, 1961 | 316 |
| 'NIGHT, MOTHER—Marsha Norman | 82–83 | Mar. 31, 1983 | 380 |
| | 83–84 | Apr. 18, 1984 | 54 |

| PLAY | VOLUME | OPENED | PERFS |
|------|--------|--------|-------|
| NINE—(b) Arthur L. Kopit, (m, l) Maury Yeston, (ad) Mario Fratti, from the Italian | 81–82 | May 9, 1982 | 739 |
| NO MORE LADIES—A.E. Thomas | 33–34 | Jan. 23, 1934 | 162 |
| NO PLACE TO BE SOMEBODY—Charles Gordone | 68–69 | May 4, 1969 | 250 |
| NO TIME FOR COMEDY—S.N. Berhman | 38–39 | Apr. 17, 1939 | 185 |
| NO TIME FOR SERGEANTS—Ira Levin, based on Mac Hyman's novel | 55–56 | Oct. 20, 1955 | 796 |
| NOEL COWARD IN TWO KEYS—Noel Coward (*Come Into the Garden Maud* and *A Song at Twilight*) | 73–74 | Feb. 28, 1974 | 140 |
| NOISES OFF—Michael Frayn | 83–84 | Dec. 11, 1983 | 553 |
| NORMAN CONQUESTS, THE—(see *Living Together, Round and Round the Garden* and *Table Manners*) | | | |
| NUTS—Tom Topor | 79–80 | Apr. 28, 1980 | 96 |
| | | | |
| O MISTRESS MINE—Terence Rattigan | 45–46 | Jan. 23, 19146 | 452 |
| ODD COUPLE, THE—Neil Simon | 64–65 | Mar. 10, 1965 | 964 |
| OF MICE AND MEN—John Steinbeck | 37–38 | Nov. 23, 1937 | 207 |
| OF THEE I SING—(b) George S. Kaufman, Morrie Ryskind, (l) Ira Gershwin, (m) George Gershwin | 31–32 | Dec. 26, 1931 | 441 |
| OH DAD, POOR DAD, MAMA'S HUNG YOU IN THE CLOSET AND I'M FEELIN' SO SAD—Arthur L. Kopit | 61–62 | Feb. 26, 1962 | 454 |
| OHIO IMPROMPTU, CATASTROPHE AND WHAT WHERE— Samuel Beckett | 83–84 | June 15, 1983 | 350 |
| OKLAHOMA!—(b, l) Oscar Hammerstein II, based on Lynn Riggs's play *Green Grow the Lilacs*, (m) Richard Rodgers | 42–43 | Mar. 31, 1943 | 2,212 |
| OLD MAID, THE—Zoë Akins, based on Edith Wharton's novel | 34–35 | Jan. 7, 1935 | 305 |
| OLD SOAK, THE—Don Marquis | 22–23 | Aug. 22, 1922 | 423 |
| OLD TIMES—Harold Pinter | 71–72 | Nov. 16, 1971 | 119 |
| OLDEST LIVING GRADUATE, THE—Preston Jones | 76–77 | Sept. 23, 1976 | 20 |
| ON BORROWED TIME—Paul Osborn, based on Lawrence Edward Watkins's novel | 37–38 | Feb. 3, 1938 | 321 |
| ON GOLDEN POND—Ernest Thompson | 78–79 | Sept. 13, 1978 | 30 |
| | 78–79 | Feb. 28, 1979 | 126 |
| ON TRIAL—Elmer Rice | 09–19 | Aug. 19, 1914 | 365 |
| ONCE IN A LIFETIME—Moss Hart, George S. Kaufman | 30–31 | Sept. 24, 1930 | 406 |
| ONE SUNDAY AFTERNOON—James Hagan | 32–33 | Feb. 15, 1933 | 322 |
| ORPHEUS DESCENDING—Tennessee Williams | 56–57 | Mar. 1, 1957 | 68 |
| *OTHER PEOPLE'S MONEY—Jerry Sterner | 88–89 | Feb. 16, 1989 | 535 |
| OTHERWISE ENGAGED—Simon Gray | 76–77 | Feb. 2, 1977 | 309 |
| OUTRAGEOUS FORTUNE—Rose Franken | 43–44 | Nov. 3, 1943 | 77 |
| OUR TOWN—Thornton Wilder | 37–38 | Feb. 4, 1938 | 336 |
| OUTWARD BOUND—Sutton Vane | 23–24 | Jan. 7, 1924 | 144 |
| OVER 21—Ruth Gordon | 43–44 | Jan. 3, 1944 | 221 |
| OVERTURE—William Bolitho | 30–31 | Dec. 5, 1930 | 41 |
| | | | |
| P.S. 193—David Rayfiel | 62–63 | Oct. 30, 1962 | 48 |

PLAY                                                        VOLUME    OPENED     PERFS

PACIFIC OVERTURES—(b) John Weidman, (m, l)
  Stephen Sondheim, additional material by Hugh Wheeler ..75–76..Jan.  11, 1976 ... 193
PACK OF LIES—Hugh Whitemore.................................84–85..Feb.  11, 1985 ... 120
PAINTING CHURCHES—Tina Howe ..............................83–84..Nov. 22, 1983 ... 206
PARIS BOUND—Philip Barry.....................................27–28..Dec.  27, 1927 ... 234
PASSION OF JOSEPH D., THE—Paddy Chayefsky ..............63–64..Feb.  11, 1964 .....15
PATRIOTS, THE—Sidney Kingsley...............................42–43..Jan.  29, 1943 ... 173
PERFECT PARTY, THE—A.R.  Gurney...........................85–86..Apr.   2, 1986 ... 238
PERIOD OF ADJUSTMENT—Tennessee Williams.................60–61..Nov. 10, 1960 ... 132
PERSECUTION AND ASSASSINATION OF MARAT AS
  PERFORMEDBY THE INMATES OF THE ASYLUM OF
  CHARENTON UNDER THE DIRECTION OF THE
  MARQUIS DE SADE, THE—Peter Weiss, English version
  by Geoffrey Skelton, verse (ad) Adrian Mitchell.............65–66..Dec.  27, 1965 ... 144
PETRIFIED FOREST, THE—Robert E. Sherwood.................34–35..Jan.   7, 1935 ... 197
*PHANTOM OF THE OPERA, THE—(b) Richard Stilgoe,
  Andrew Lloyd Webber, (m) Andrew Lloyd Webber,
  (l) Charles Hart, (add'l l) Richard Stilgoe, adapted from
  the novel by Gaston Leroux (special citation)................87–88..Jan.  26, 1988 ... 981
PHILADELPHIA, HERE I COME!—Brian Friel....................65–66..Feb.  16, 1966 ... 326
PHILADELPHIA STORY, THE—Philip Barry......................38–39..Mar.  28, 1939 ... 417
PHILANTHROPIST, THE—Christopher Hampton.................70–71..Mar.  15, 1971 .....72
PHYSICISTS, THE—Friedrich Duerrenmatt,
  (ad) James  Kirkup...........................................64–65..Oct.  13, 1964 .....55
PICK UP GIRL—Elsa  Shelley..................................43–44..May   3, 1944 ... 198
PICNIC—William Inge.................................................52–53..Feb.  19, 1953 ... 477
PLENTY—David Hare ................................................82–83..Oct.  21, 1982 .....45
                                                           82–83..Jan.   6, 1983 .....92
PLOUGH AND THE STARS, THE—Sean O'Casey ................27–28..Nov. 28, 1927 .....32
POINT OF NO RETURN—Paul Osborn, based on
  John P. Marquand's novel.......................................51–52..Dec.  13, 1951 ... 364
PONDER HEART, THE—Joseph Fields, Jerome Chodorov,
  based on Eudora Welty's story ..................................55–56..Feb.  16, 1956 ... 149
POOR BITOS—Jean Anouilh, (tr) Lucienne Hill.................64–65..Nov. 14, 1964 .....17
PORGY—Dorothy and DuBose Heyward ........................27–28..Oct.  10, 1927 ... 367
POTTING SHED, THE—Graham Greene.........................56–57..Jan.  29, 1957 ... 143
PRAYER FOR MY DAUGHTER, A—Thomas Babe ................77–78..Dec.  27, 1977 ... 127
PRICE, THE—Arthur Miller.......................................67–68..Feb.   7, 1968 ... 429
PRIDE AND PREJUDICE—Helen Jerome, based on
  Jane Austen's novel.............................................35–36..Nov.  5, 1935 ... 219
PRISONER OF SECOND AVENUE, THE—Neil Simon............71–72..Nov. 11, 1971 ... 780
PROLOGUE TO GLORY—E.P. Conkle...........................37–38..Mar.  17, 1938 .....70

QUARTERMAINE'S TERMS—Simon Gray.......................82–83..Feb.  24, 1983 ... 375

R.U.R.—Karel  Capek.............................................22–23..Oct.   9, 1922 ... 184
RACKET, THE—Bartlett  Cormack...............................27–28..Nov. 22, 1927 ... 119

| PLAY | VOLUME | OPENED | PERFS |
|---|---|---|---|

RAIN—John Colton, Clemence Randolph, based on the
story by W. Somerset Maugham ...............................22–23..Nov. 7, 1922 ... 648
RAISIN IN THE SUN, A—Lorraine Hansberry ....................58–59..Mar. 11, 1959 ... 530
RATTLE OF A SIMPLE MAN—Charles Dyer ......................62–63..Apr. 17, 1963 .....94
REAL THING, THE—Tom Stoppard................................83–84..Jan. 5, 1984 ... 566
REBEL WOMEN—Thomas Babe................................75–76..May 6, 1976 .....40
REAL ESTATE—Louise Page .......................................87–88..Dec. 1, 1987 .....55
REBOUND—Donald Ogden Stewart................................29–30..Feb. 3, 1930 ... 114
REHEARSAL, THE—Jean Anouilh, (ad) Pamela Hansford
Johnson, Kitty Black .............................................63–64..Sept. 23, 1963 ... 110
REMAINS TO BE SEEN—Howard Lindsay, Russel Crouse ....51–52..Oct. 3, 1951 ... 199
REQUIEM FOR A NUN—Ruth Ford, William Faulkner,
adapted from William Faulkner's novel .......................58–59..Jan. 30, 1959 .....43
REUNION IN VIENNA—Robert E. Sherwood .....................31–32..Nov. 16, 1931 ... 264
RHINOCEROS—Eugene Ionesco, (tr) Derek Prouse .............60–61..Jan. 9, 1961 ... 240
RITZ, THE—Terrence McNally......................................74–75..Jan. 20, 1975 ... 400
RIVER NIGER, THE—Joseph A. Walker..........................72–73..Dec. 5, 1972 ... 120
72–73..Mar. 27, 1973 ... 280
ROAD—Jim Cartwright...............................................88–89..July 28, 1988 .....62
ROAD TO MECCA, THE—Athol Fugard...........................87–88..Apr. 12, 1988 ... 172
ROAD TO ROME, THE—Robert E. Sherwood....................26–27..Jan. 31, 1927 ... 392
ROCKABY—(see Enough, Footfalls and Rockaby)
ROCKET TO THE MOON—Clifford Odets .........................38–39..Nov. 24, 1938 ... 131
ROMANCE—Edward Sheldon .....................................09–19..Feb. 10, 1913 ... 160
ROPE DANCERS, THE—Morton Wishengrad....................57–58..Nov. 20, 1957 ... 189
ROSE TATTOO, THE—Tennessee Williams.......................50–51..Feb. 3, 1951 ... 306
ROSENCRANTZ AND GUILDENSTERN ARE
DEAD—Tom Stoppard.........................................67–68..Oct. 16, 1967 ... 420
ROUND AND ROUND THE GARDEN—Alan Ayckbourn .........75–76..Dec. 7, 1975 .....76
ROYAL FAMILY, THE—George S. Kaufman, Edna Ferber ....27–28..Dec. 28, 1927 ... 345
ROYAL HUNT OF THE SUN, THE—Peter Shaffer................65–66..Oct. 26, 1965 ... 261
RUGGED PATH, THE—Robert E. Sherwood .....................45–46..Nov. 10, 1945 .....81
RUNNER STUMBLES, THE—Milan Stitt...........................75–76..May 18, 1976191

ST. HELENA—R.C. Sheriff, Jeanne de Casalis..................36–37..Oct. 6, 1936 .....63
SAME TIME, NEXT YEAR—Bernard Slade .......................74–75..Mar. 13, 1975 . 1,453
SATURDAY'S CHILDREN—Maxwell Anderson ..................26–27..Jan. 26, 1927 ... 310
SCREENS, THE—Jean Genet, (tr) Minos Volanakis.............71–72..Nov. 30, 1971 .....28
SCUBA DUBA—Bruce Jay Friedman..............................67–68..Oct. 10, 1967 ... 692
SEA HORSE, THE—Edward J. Moore (James Irwin) ...........73–74..Apr. 15, 1974 ... 128
SEARCHING WIND, THE—Lillian Hellman ......................43–44..Apr. 12, 1944 ... 318
SEASCAPE—Edward Albee..........................................74–75..Jan. 26, 1975 .....65
SEASON IN THE SUN—Wolcott Gibbs............................50–51..Sept. 28, 1950 ... 367
SEASON'S GREETINGS—Alan Ayckbourn.......................85–86..July 11, 1985 .....20
SECOND THRESHOLD—Philip Barry..............................50–51..Jan. 2, 1951 ... 126
SECRET SERVICE—William Gillette...............................94–99..Oct. 5, 1896 ... 176
SEPARATE TABLES—Terence Rattigan...........................56–57..Oct. 25, 1956 ... 332

| PLAY | VOLUME | OPENED | PERFS |
|------|--------|--------|-------|

SERENADING LOUIE—Lanford Wilson............................75–76..May   2, 1976 .....33

SERPENT, THE—Jean-Claude van Itallie.........................69–70..May 29, 19703

SEVEN KEYS TO BALDPATE—(ad) George M. Cohan,
 from the novel by Earl Derr Biggers...........................09–19..Sept. 22, 1913 ... 320

1776—(b) Peter Stone, (m, l) Sherman Edwards,
 based on a conception of Sherman Edwards..................68–69..Mar. 16, 1969 . 1,217

SHADOW AND SUBSTANCE—Paul Vincent Carroll..............37–38..Jan.  26, 1938 ... 274

SHADOW BOX, THE—Michael Cristofer.........................76–77..Mar. 31, 1977 ... 315

SHADOW OF HEROES—(see *Stone and Star*)

SHE LOVES ME—(b) Joe Masteroff, based on
 Miklos Laszlo's play *Parfumerie*,
 (l) Sheldon Harnick, (m) Jerry Bock .........................62–63..Apr. 23, 1963 ... 301

SHINING HOUR, THE—Keith Winter ..............................33–34..Feb. 13, 1934 ... 121

SHIRLEY VALENTINE—Willy Russell .............................88–89..Feb. 16, 1989 ... 324

SHORT EYES—Miguel Piñero .....................................73–74..Feb. 28, 1974 .....54

                                                           73–74..May 23, 1974 ... 102

SHOW-OFF, THE—George Kelly .................................23–24..Feb.  5, 1924 ... 571

SHRIKE, THE—Joseph Kramm....................................51–52..Jan. 15, 1952 ... 161

SILVER CORD, THE—Sidney Howard ...........................26–27..Dec. 20, 1926 ... 112

SILVER WHISTLE, THE—Robert E. McEnroe....................48–49..Nov. 24, 1948 ... 219

SIX CYLINDER LOVE—William Anthony McGuire..............21–22..Aug. 25, 1921 ... 430

6 RMS RIV VU—Bob Randall .....................................72–73..Oct. 17, 1972 ... 247

SKIN GAME, THE—John Galsworthy.............................20–21..Oct. 20, 1920 ... 176

SKIN OF OUR TEETH, THE—Thornton Wilder ..................42–43..Nov. 18, 1942 ... 359

SKIPPER NEXT TO GOD—Jan de Hartog .........................47–48..Jan.  4, 1948 .....93

SKYLARK—Samson Raphaelson.................................39–40..Oct. 11, 1939 ... 256

SLEUTH—Anthony Shaffer .......................................70–71..Nov. 12, 1970 . 1,222

SLOW DANCE ON THE KILLING GROUND—William Hanley...64–65..Nov. 30, 1964 .....88

SLY FOX—Larry Gelbart, based on *Volpone* by Ben Jonson . . 76–77..Dec. 14, 1976 ... 495

SMALL CRAFT WARNINGS—Tennessee Williams...............71–72..Apr.  2, 1972 ... 192

SOLDIER'S PLAY, A—Charles Fuller .............................81–82..Nov. 20, 1981 ... 468

SOLDIER'S WIFE—Rose Franken.................................44–45..Oct.  4, 1944 ... 253

SPEED-THE-PLOW—David Mamet...............................87–88..May  3, 1988 ... 278

SPLIT SECOND—Dennis McIntyre................................84–85..June  7, 1984 ... 147

SQUAW MAN, THE—Edwin Milton Royle.......................99–09..Oct. 23, 1905 ... 222

STAGE DOOR—George S. Kaufman, Edna Ferber..............36–37..Oct. 22, 1936 ... 169

STAIRCASE—Charles Dyer ......................................67–68..Jan. 10, 1968 .....61

STAR-WAGON, THE—Maxwell Anderson......................37–38..Sept. 29, 1937 ... 223

STATE OF THE UNION—Howard Lindsay, Russel Crouse.....45–46..Nov. 14, 1945 ... 765

STEAMBATH—Bruce Jay Friedman.............................70–71..June 30, 1970 ... 128

STEEL MAGNOLIAS—Robert Harling ...........................87–88..June 19, 1987 . 1,126

STICKS AND BONES—David Rabe...............................71–72..Nov.  7, 1971 ... 121

                                                           71–72..Mar.  1, 1972 ... 245

STONE AND STAR—Robert Ardrey (also called
 *Shadow of Heroes*)...............................................61–62..Dec.  5, 1961 .....20

STOP THE WORLD—I WANT TO GET OFF—(b, l, m)
 Leslie Bricusse, Anthony Newley .............................62–63..Oct.  3, 1962 ... 555

STORM OPERATION—Maxwell Anderson.......................43–44..Jan. 11, 1944 .....23

| PLAY | VOLUME | OPENED | PERFS |
|---|---|---|---|

STORY OF MARY SURRATT, THE—John Patrick................46–47..Feb.   8, 1947 .....11
STRANGE INTERLUDE—Eugene O'Neill..........................27–28..Jan.  30, 1928 ... 426
STREAMERS—David Rabe.......................................75–76..Apr.  21, 1976 ... 478
STREET SCENE—Elmer Rice........................................28–29..Jan.  10, 1929 ... 601
STREETCAR NAMED DESIRE, A—Tennessee Williams.........47–48..Dec.   3, 1947 ... 855
STRICTLY DISHONORABLE—Preston Sturges....................29–30..Sept. 18, 1929 ... 557
SUBJECT WAS ROSES, THE—Frank D. Gilroy..................64–65..May  25, 1964 ... 832
SUGAR BABIES—(ad) Ralph G. Allen from traditional
   material (special citation) .......................................79–80..Oct.   8, 1979 . 1,208
SUMMER OF THE 17TH DOLL—Ray Lawler.....................57–58..Jan.  22, 1958 .....29
SUNDAY IN THE PARK WITH GEORGE—(b) James Lapine,
   (m, l) Stephen Sondheim........................................83–84..May   2, 1984 ... 604
SUNRISE AT CAMPOBELLO—Dore Schary ......................57–58..Jan.  30, 1958 ... 556
SUNSHINE BOYS, THE—Neil Simon ............................72–73..Dec.  20, 1972 ... 538
SUN-UP—Lula Vollmer ..........................................22–23..May  25, 1923 ... 356
SUSAN AND GOD—Rachel Crothers..............................37–38..Oct.   7, 1937 ... 288
SWAN, THE—Ferenc Molnar, (tr) Melville Baker...............23–24..Oct.  23, 1923 ... 255
SWEENEY TODD, THE DEMON BARBER OF FLEET STREET—
   (b) Hugh Wheeler, (m, l) Stephen Sondheim, based on
   a version of *Sweeney Todd* by Christopher Bond...........78–79..Mar.   1, 1979 ... 557
SWEET BIRD OF YOUTH—Tennessee Williams.................58–59..Mar.  10, 1959 ... 375

TABLE MANNERS—Alan Ayckbourn...............................75–76..Dec.   7, 1976 .....76
TABLE SETTINGS—James Lapine...............................79–80..Jan.  14, 1980 ... 264
TAKE A GIANT STEP—Louis Peterson..........................53–54..Sept. 24, 1953 .....76
TAKING OF MISS JANIE, THE—Ed Bullins ......................74–75..May   4, 1975 .....42
TALLEY'S FOLLEY—Lanford Wilson .............................78–79..May   1, 1979 .....44
   79–80..Feb.  20, 1980 ... 277
TARNISH—Gilbert Emery.............................................23–24..Oct.   1, 1923 ... 248
TASTE OF HONEY, A—Shelagh Delaney .........................60–61..Oct.   4, 1960 ... 376
TCHIN-TCHIN—Sidney Michaels, based on
   François Billetdoux's play ......................................62–63..Oct.  25, 1962 ... 222
TEA AND SYMPATHY—Robert Anderson........................53–54..Sept. 30, 1953 ... 712
TEAHOUSE OF THE AUGUST MOON, THE—John Patrick,
   based on Vern Sneider's novel ...............................53–54..Oct.  15, 1953 . 1,027
TENTH MAN, THE—Paddy Chayafsky............................59–60..Nov.   5, 1959 ... 623
THAT CHAMPIONSHIP SEASON—Jason Miller..................71–72..May   2, 1972 ... 144
   72–73..Sept. 14, 1972 ... 700
THERE SHALL BE NO NIGHT—Robert E. Sherwood ...........39–40..Apr.  29, 1940 ... 181
THEY KNEW WHAT THEY WANTED—Sidney Howard.........24–25..Nov.  24, 1924 ... 414
THEY SHALL NOT DIE—John Wexley ...........................33–34..Feb.  21, 1934 .....62
THOUSAND CLOWNS, A—Herb Gardner ........................61–62..Apr.   5, 1962 ... 428
THREE POSTCARDS—(b) Craig Lucas, (m, l)
   Craig Carnelia....................................................86–87..May  14, 1987 .....22
THREEPENNY OPERA—(b, l) Bertolt Brecht, (m)
   Kurt Weill, (tr) Ralph Manheim, John Willett ...............75–76..Mar.   1, 1976 ... 307
THURBER CARNIVAL, A—James Thurber........................59–60..Feb.  26, 1960 ... 127
TIGER AT THE GATES—Jean Giraudoux's *La Guerre de*

| PLAY | VOLUME | OPENED | PERFS |
|---|---|---|---|
| *Troie n' aura pas lieu*, (tr) Christopher Fry | 55–56 | Oct. 3, 1955 | 217 |
| TIME OF THE CUCKOO, THE—Arthur Laurents | 52–53 | Oct. 15, 1952 | 263 |
| TIME OF YOUR LIFE, THE—William Saroyan | 39–40 | Oct. 25, 1939 | 185 |
| TIME REMEMBERED—Jean Anouilh's *Léocadia*, (ad) Patricia Moyes | 57–58 | Nov. 12, 1957 | 248 |
| TINY ALICE—Edward Albee | 64–65 | Dec. 29, 1964 | 167 |
| TOILET, THE—LeRoi Jones | 64–65 | Dec. 16, 1964 | 151 |
| TOMORROW AND TOMORROW—Philip Barry | 30–31 | Jan. 13, 1931 | 206 |
| TOMORROW THE WORLD—James Gow, Arnaud d'Usseau | 42–43 | Apr. 14, 1943 | 500 |
| TORCH SONG TRILOGY—Harvey Fierstein (*The International Stud, Fugue in a Nursery, Widows and Children First*) | 81–82 | Jan. 15, 1982 | 117 |
| | 82–83 | June 10, 1983 | 1,222 |
| TOUCH OF THE POET, A—Eugene O'Neill | 58–59 | Oct. 2, 1958 | 284 |
| TOVARICH—Jacques Deval, (tr) Robert E. Sherwood | 36–37 | Oct. 15, 1936 | 356 |
| TOYS IN THE ATTIC—Lillian Hellman | 59–60 | Feb. 25, 1960 | 556 |
| TRACERS—John DiFusco (c); Vincent Caristi, Richard Chaves, John DiFusco, Eric E. Emerson, Rick Gallavan, Merlin Marston, Harry Stephens with Sheldon Lettich | 84–85 | Jan. 21, 1985 | 186 |
| TRAGÉDIE DE CARMEN, LA—(see *La Tragédie de Carmen*) | | | |
| TRANSLATIONS—Brian Friel | 80–81 | Apr. 7, 1981 | 48 |
| TRAVESTIES—Tom Stoppard | 75–76 | Oct. 30, 1975 | 155 |
| TRELAWNY OF THE WELLS—Arthur Wing Pinero | 94–99 | Nov. 22, 1898 | 131 |
| TRIAL OF THE CATONSVILLE NINE, THE—Daniel Berrigan, Saul Levitt | 70–71 | Feb. 7, 1971 | 159 |
| TRIBUTE—Bernard Slade | 77–78 | June 1, 1978 | 212 |
| TWO BLIND MICE—Samuel Spewack | 48–49 | Mar. 2, 1949 | 157 |
| UNCHASTENED WOMAN, THE—Louis Kaufman Anspacher | 09–19 | Oct. 9, 1915 | 193 |
| UNCLE HARRY—Thomas Job | 41–42 | May 20, 1942 | 430 |
| UNDER MILK WOOD—Dylan Thomas | 57–58 | Oct. 15, 1957 | 39 |
| VALLEY FORGE—Maxwell Anderson | 34–35 | Dec. 10, 1934 | 58 |
| VENUS OBSERVED—Christopher Fry | 51–52 | Feb. 13, 1952 | 86 |
| VERY SPECIAL BABY, A—Robert Alan Aurthur | 56–57 | Nov. 14, 1956 | 5 |
| VICTORIA REGINA—Laurence Housman | 35–36 | Dec. 26, 1935 | 517 |
| VIEW FROM THE BRIDGE, A—Arthur Miller | 55–56 | Sept. 29, 1955 | 149 |
| VISIT, THE—Friedrich Duerrenmatt, (ad) Maurice Valency | 57–58 | May 5, 1958 | 189 |
| VISIT TO A SMALL PLANET—Gore Vidal | 56–57 | Feb. 7, 1957 | 388 |
| VIVAT! VIVAT REGINA!—Robert Bolt | 71–72 | Jan. 20, 1972 | 116 |
| VOICE OF THE TURTLE, THE—John van Druten | 43–44 | Dec. 8, 1943 | 1,557 |
| WAGER, THE—Mark Medoff | 74–75 | Oct. 21, 1974 | 104 |
| WAITING FOR GODOT—Samuel Beckett | 55–56 | Apr. 19, 1956 | 59 |
| WALK IN THE WOODS, A—Lee Blessing | 87–88 | Feb. 28, 1988 | 136 |
| WALTZ OF THE TOREADORS, THE—Jean Anouilh, (tr) Lucienne Hill | 56–57 | Jan. 17, 1957 | 132 |
| WATCH ON THE RHINE—Lillian Hellman | 40–41 | Apr. 1, 1941 | 378 |

PLAY                                                                    VOLUME    OPENED      PERFS

WE, THE PEOPLE—Elmer Rice.....................................32–33..Jan. 21, 1933.....49
WEDDING BELLS—Salisbury Field...............................19–20..Nov. 12, 1919...168
WEDNESDAY'S CHILD—Leopold Atlas..........................33–34..Jan. 16, 1934.....56
WENCESLAS SQUARE—Larry Shue..............................87–88..Mar. 2, 1988.....55
WHAT A LIFE—Clifford Goldsmith ..............................37–38..Apr. 13, 1938...538
WHAT PRICE GLORY?—Maxwell Anderson,
    Laurence Stallings...............................................24–25..Sept. 3, 1924...433
WHAT THE BUTLER SAW—Joe Orton ............................69–70..May 4, 1970...224
WHEN YOU COMIN' BACK, RED RYDER?—Mark Medoff.....73–74..Dec. 6, 1974...302
WHERE HAS TOMMY FLOWERS GONE?—Terrence McNally . 71–72..Oct. 7, 1972.....78
WHITE HOUSE MURDER CASE, THE—Jules Feiffer ...........69–70..Feb. 18, 1970...119
WHITE STEED, THE—Paul Vincent Carroll.......................38–39..Jan. 10, 1939...136
WHO'S AFRAID OF VIRGINIA WOOLF?—Edward Albee........62–63..Oct. 13, 1962...664
WHOSE LIFE IS IT ANYWAY?—Brian Clark.....................78–79..Apr. 17, 1979...223
WHY MARRY?—Jesse Lynch Williams...........................09–19..Dec. 25, 1917...120
WHY NOT?—Jesse Lynch Williams ..............................22–23..Dec. 25, 1922...120
WIDOW CLAIRE, THE—Horton Foote...........................87–87..Dec. 17, 1986...150
WILD BIRDS—Dan Totheroh ......................................24–25..Apr. 9, 1925.....44
WILD HONEY—Michael Frayn, from an
    untitled play by Anton Chekhov...............................86–87..Dec. 18, 1986.....28
WINGED VICTORY—Moss Hart, (m) David Rose ...............43–44..Nov. 20, 1943...212
WINGS—Arthur L. Kopit ...........................................78–79..June 21, 1978.....15
                                                                      78–79..Jan. 28, 1979...113
WINGS OVER EUROPE—Robert Nichols, Maurice Browne ....28–29..Dec. 10, 1928.....90
WINSLOW BOY, THE—Terence Rattigan.........................47–48..Oct. 29, 1947...215
WINTERSET—Maxwell Anderson...................................35–36..Sept. 25, 1935...195
WINTER SOLDIERS—Daniel Lewis James.......................42–43..Nov. 29, 1942.....25
WISDOM TOOTH, THE—Marc Connelly .........................25–26..Feb. 15, 1926...160
WISTERIA TREES, THE—Joshua Logan, based on Anton
    Chekhov's The Cherry Orchard................................49–50..Mar. 29, 1950...165
WITCHING HOUR, THE—Augustus Thomas .....................99–09..Nov. 18, 1907...212
WITNESS FOR THE PROSECUTION—Agatha Christie............54–55..Dec. 16, 1954...645
WOMEN, THE—Clare Boothe .....................................36–37..Dec. 26, 1936...657
WONDERFUL TOWN—(b) Joseph Fields, Jerome Chodorov,
    based on their play My Sister Eileen and Ruth
    McKenney's stories, (l) Betty Comden, Adolph Green,
    (m) Leonard Bernstein..........................................52–53..Feb. 25, 1953...559
WORLD WE MAKE, THE—Sidney Kingsley, based on
    Millen Brand's novel The Outward Room....................39–40..Nov. 20, 1939.....80

YEARS AGO—Ruth Gordon .......................................46–47..Dec. 3, 1946...206
YES, MY DARLING DAUGHTER—Mark Reed....................36–37..Feb. 9, 1937...405
YOU AND I—Philip Barry..........................................22–23..Feb. 19, 1923...178
YOU CAN'T TAKE IT WITH YOU—Moss Hart,
    George S. Kaufman.............................................36–37..Dec. 14, 1936...837
YOU KNOW I CAN'T HEAR YOU WHEN THE WATER'S
    RUNNING—Robert Anderson...................................66–67..Mar. 13, 1967...755
YOUNG WOODLEY—John van Druten............................25–26..Nov. 2, 1925...260

PLAY                                            VOLUME  OPENED      PERFS

YOUNGEST, THE—Philip Barry.....................................24–25..Dec. 22, 1924 ... 104
YOUR OWN THING—(b) Donald Driver, (m, l) Hal Hester
    and Danny Apolinar, suggested by William Shapespeare's
    *Twelfth Night*......................................................67–68..Jan. 13, 1968 ... 933
YOU'RE A GOOD MAN CHARLIE BROWN—(b, m, l)
    Clark Gesner, based on the comic strip "Peanuts" by
    Charles M. Schulz................................................66–67..Mar. 7, 1967 . 1,597

ZOOMAN AND THE SIGN—Charles Fuller.........................80–81..Dec. 7, 1980 .....33

INDEX

# INDEX

Play titles appear in bold face. *Bold face italic* page numbers refer to those pages where complete cast and credit listings for New York productions may be found.

Aaron, Caroline, 464
Aaron, Jack, 474
Abady, Josephine R., 510, 511
Abarbanel, Jonathan, 484
Abatemarco, Tony, 410
Abbott, George, 453, 473
Abdulov, Alexander, 383
**Abel and Bela**, *479*
Aberger, Tom, 416, 419
Aboutface Theater Company, 431
Abrahao, Roberto, 385
Abramishvili, Ioseb, 428
Abrams, Arthur, 471
Abrams, Helen, 478
Abravanel, Wayne, 409
Abreu, Jorge Luis, 467
Abromov, Anatoly, 383
Abuba, Ernest, 364, 467
**Accomplice**, 4, 8, 30, *390*, 559
Accurso, Aron, 514
**Aching Heart of Samuel Kleinerman, The**, *478*
Acioli, Monica, 384
Ackamoor, Idris, 460
Ackemann-Blount, Joan, 520
Ackerman, Barbara, 362
Ackerman, Loni, 433
Ackerman, Robert Allan, 519
Act Up, 558
**Act, The**, *455*
Actors Playhouse, 473
Actors Theater of Louisville, 490, 519
Actors' Equity Association, 554, 559
Actors' Gang, The, 408
Actor's Outlet, 473
Acuff/McCloud, 408
AD Players, 516
**Adam and the Experts**, *474*
Adams, Betsy, 429

Adams, Brooke, 440
Adams, Jane, 539
Adams, Kent, 464
Adams, Mary Kay, 475
Adams, Polly, 458
Adamson, David, 479
Adamson, Eve, 475
Adderly, Konrad, 390
Adilifu, Kamau, 370
**Adios Tropicana**, *466*
Adkins, David, 510, 511
Adler, Jay, 370
Adler, Joanna, 461
Adshead, Patricia, 469
**Adult Fiction**, *533*
Affelder, Jeannie, 506
**Against the Earth**, *460*
Aguilar, Tommy, 439
**Ahead of the Hitter**, *479*
Ahearn, Daniel, 478
A'Hearn, Patrick, 397
Ahrens, Lynn, 41, 42, 43 413, 560
Aibel, Douglas, 472
Ainsley, Paul, 443
Aisawa, Janet, 459
Akamine, John, 456
Akerlind, Christopher, 389
Akers, Karen, 36, 374
Akhmatova, Anna, 452
Ako, 522
al-Hadithy, Nabil, 478
Alabama Shakespeare Festival, 416, 523
Alan Schneider Award, 559
Alarcon, Jose, 535
Alasa, Michael, 466
Albach, Carl, 372
**Albanian Softshoe**, *535*
Albano, John, 478
Albers, Kenneth, 523
Albert, Stephen J., 389, 560
Alberti, Bruno, 416

Albrecht, J. Grant, 516
Albrezzi, Steven D., 512, 520
Albritton, Norma, 529
Alchemy Theater Company, 473
Alchourron, Rodolfo, 365, 366
Aldous, Brian, 457
Aldredge, Theoni V., 377, 395, 556
Aldredge, Tom, 440
Aleksidze, Giorgi, 428
Alessan, Henry, 362
Alessandrini, Gerard, 399, 424
Alexander, Adinah, 463
Alexander, Deborah, 479
Alexander, E.A., 529
Alexander, Jace, 457, 472
Alexander, Jane, 519
Alexander, Jason, 390, 441
Alexander, Robert, 431
Alexander, Roslyn, 508
Alexander, Russell, 560
Alexis, Connie L., 392, 400, 416, 456
Alexy-Meshishvili, Georgy, 428
Alfaro, Francisco, 466
Alfiorova, Irena, 383
**Alfred & Victoria: A Life**, *530*
Ali, Kenshaka, 423
Ali, Tatyana, 463
**All God's Dangers: The Life of Nate Shaw**, 11, 27, 416, *416, 477, 523*
**All That Fall**, 452, *475*
**All the Rage**, 559
Allard, Janet, 413, 414
Allegrucci, Scott, 404
Allen, Bob, 515
Allen, Claudia, 507
Allen, Jay Presson, 6, 27, 28, 381

599

Allen, Joan, 440
Allen, John Edward, 367
Allen, Lewis, 376, 381, 395
Allen, Patrick, 535
Allen, Sanford, 388
Allen, Tammy, 513
Allen, Therese, 513
Aller, John, 466
Alley Cat Productions, 474
Alliance, The, 503
Alliger, Richard, 530
Allison, Patti, 364
Almada, Carlos and Paulette, 459
Almonte, Juan Maria, 465
Almquist, Gregg, 421
Almy, Brooks, 390
Alper, Steven M., 525
Alsaker, Timian, 519
Alston, Peggy, 30, 423, 424
Alston, Stephanie, 524
**Alternative Voices, *461***
Altieri, Marcia, 412
Altomarem, Carlo, 477
Alton, Bill, 401
Alvarez, Lynne, 535
Amada, Rich, 540
**Amadeus,** 26
Amami, Yuki, 367
Amaro, Richard, 365
Amas Musical Theater, 454, 554
**Amazonia, *465***
**Ambassador, The, *479***
Amber, 477
Ambrose, Joe, 421
Ambrosone, John, 521
Amendola, Tony, 519
Amenophis, Kemit, 460
**American Bagpipes, *469***
**American Buffalo,** 560
American Conservatory Theater, 497, 535
**American Enterprise, *508***
American Jewish Theater, 429, 474
American Music Theater Festival, 366
American Place Theater, 11, 424, 455
American Playhouse Theater Productions, 413
American Repertory Theater, 365
American Spoleto Festival, 452

American Stage Company, The, 539
American Stage Festival, 522
American Theater Critics Association, viii, 520, 536, 558, 560
American Theater of Actors, 455
American Theater Wing Design Awards, 558
American Theater Wing's Antoinette Perry (Tony) Awards, 554
Amirante, Robert, 434
Amos, John, 52, 403, 474, 539
**An American Chorus, *477***
**An Evening With Hazelle, *475***
**An Office Romance, *512***
**An Uncertain Hour, *466***
Anania, Michael, 391, 522
Anarchestra, 408
Anastos, Peter, 415
**And One Bell Shattered, *414***
**And the Soul Shall Dance, *467***
Andersen, Hans Christian, 41
Anderson, Carol, 517
Anderson, Dennis, 370
Anderson, Elman, 367
Anderson, Holly, 463
Anderson, Jan, 514
Anderson, Jane, 519
Anderson, Joel, 400
Anderson, Keith, 370
Anderson, Kevin, 46, 364
Anderson, Laurie, 474
Anderson, Lynn, 479
Anderson, Mark, 523
Anderson, Maxwell, 394
Anderson, McKee, 468
Anderson, Scott, 392, 470
Anderson, Stephen Lee, 513
Andino, Eddie, 467
Andos, Randall T., 410
Andre, Marion, 478
Andreassi, James, 534
Andres, Barbara, 531
Andrews, Bert, viii
Andrews, Brian, 434
Andrews, Dwight D., 389
Andrews, Dwight, 504
Andrews, Jason, 479
Andrews, Jennifer Lee, 374
Andrews, Meghan, 387
Andrews, Tom, 470

Andros, Andrea, 367
**Angel Dust, *455***
**Angel Face, *527***
Angel, Anthony, 470
Angela, June, 467
**Angels of Warsaw, The, *509***
**Angels Still Falling, *464***
**Angels' Hierarchies, The, *513***
**Angels: Visions and Apparitions, *477***
Anglim, Philip, 511
**Animal Fair, *514***
Ankeny, Mark, 472
**Annie,** 395
**Annie 2: Miss Hannigan's Revenge,** 55, *395*
Annis, Eric, 540
**Anniversary Waltz, *460***
**Another Park Bench Play, *512***
*Answered Prayers,* 27, 381
Antaramian, Jacqueline, 514
**Anthony Rose, *528***
**Antigona Hurtado Esguerra, *470***
**Anulah, Let Them Eat Cake, *470***
**Anything Goes,** 14, 432, 360
Anzalone, Johnny, 433
Aodh Og O Tuama, 527
Aoun, Iman, 475
Apakidze, Irakli, 428
Apeksemova, Irina, 412
Apfel, Mimi, 368, 414
**Apocalyptic Butterflies, *477***
Appel, Peter, 403
Appelt, Joseph, 517
Apple Corps Theater, 474
**Apple Tree, The,** 5
Aprahamian, Steven, 425
Aprill, Arnold, 506
Aquino, Kelly, 530
Aranas, Raul, 509
Aravena, Michelle, 384
Arbiter, Heide, 468
Arcaro, Robert, 479
Arcenas, Loy, 392, 411, 415, 417, 457, 518, 524
Archer, Nicholas, 388
**Architruc, *479***
Ard, Kenneth, 365, 434
Arditti, Paul, 364, 383
**Are You Lonesome Tonight?, *535***

Arena Players Repertory
  Company of Long Island,
  514
Arena Stage, 540
Arenberg, Lee, 408
Arenius, Alan, 477
Argabrite, Joey, 519
Ari, Bob, 476
Ari, Neal Ben, 443
**Ariano**, *467*
Arias, Joey, 460
Arif, N. Richard, 403
**Aristocrats**, 400
Aristophanes, 461
Arkansas Repertory Theater,
  518
Arlt, Lewis, 364
Armitage, Calvin Lennon, 386
**Arms and the Man**, 400
Arms, Janet, 384
Armstrong, Gwen, 524
Armstrong, Karen, 368, 412
Armstrong, Lisa, 516, 517
Armstrong, Vaughn, 519
Armus, Sidney, 379
Arner, David, 541
Arner, Leonard, 384
Arney, Randall, 386
**Arnold**, *476*
Arnold, Jennifer, 405
Arnold, Michael, 393, 429, 434
Arnold, Victor, 529
Arnone, John, 425
Aronheim, Albert, 461
Arons, Ellyn, 395
Aronson, Billy, 458
Aronson, Frances, 414, 425,
  457, 541
Aronson, Henry, 367, 373,
  374, 514
Aronstein, Martin, 390
Arrabal, Fernando, 459
Arrabal, Miguel, 365
**Arrivederci Papa**, *473*
Arsenault, Brian, 408, 409
**Art of Success, The**, 6, 11,
  17, 31, *417*, *418*, 552
Artemieva, Ludmilla, 383
Arthur Cantor Associates, 427,
  431
**Artist Descending a**
  **Staircase**, 4, 6, 10, *378*
**Artistic Direction, The**, *461*
Arundale, Susan, 505
Arutiunov, Valeri, 428
Arzberger, Kenneth, 367

**As You Like It**, 466
As-Swaudi, Tajj, 425
**Ascension Day**, *463*
Aschner, Michael, 461
Asciolla, Steve, 503
Ash, Jeffrey, 429
Asher, Steve, 469
**Ashes to Ashes**, *455*
Ashford, Robert, 367
Ashley, Chris, 461
Ashley, Christopher, 472
Ashley, Elizabeth, 12, 414
Ashwell, Ariel, 422
Askin, Peter, 474, 477
Askler, David, 367
Asolo Theater Company, 536
**Aspects of Love**, 4, 6, 34, 35,
  44, *387*, 552, 555, 556,
  559
Assael, Deborah, 409
Aston, Paul, 530
Astracan, John, 464
Astracan, Josh, 464
Asuka, Yu, 367
**At the Grand**, 375
AT&T New Plays for the
  Nineties Project, 417
AT&T, 554
AT&T: OnStage, ix, 413, 416,
  417
ATCA New-Play Award, 558
ATCA, viii, 520, 536, 558,
  560
Athayde, Roberto, 383
Athens, Jim, 473
Atkinson, Jayne, 381, 418
Atlee, Howard, 424
Atwood, Kathryn, 475
Auberjonois, Rene, 33, 379,
  556
**Audience**, *429*, 452, *478*
Aufiery, Joe, 529, 530
**August Snow**, *507*, *510*
Auletta, Robert, 508
Aulino, Tom, 401, 408
Aulisi, Joseph G., 378, 397,
  534
**Aunts, The**, 11, *415*
Aural Fixation, 401, 427
Auspitz, Don, 529
Austin, Lyn, 422, 463
**Auto Erotix**, *537*
**Autobiography of an Eclipse**,
  *459*
Avant, Doyle, 464
Averill, Elizabeth Pentak, 517

Avery Fisher Hall, 474
Avery, Donna, 456
Avery, Jan, 512
Avidon, Nelson, 458
Aviles, Arthur, 559
Avner, Jon, 524
**Awaiting the Lark**, *456*
**Away Alone**, *475*
Aylesworth, John, 393, 394
Aylward, John, 539
Ayvazian, Leslie, 511
Azar, Rick, 416
Azarian, Arminae, 437
Azenberg, Emanuel, 378, 397
Azzara, Candice, 397, 534
Azzard, Dale, 393

**B. Beaver Animation, The**,
  11, *407*, *412*, 449, *461*
**Baba Goya**, *469*
Babb, Roger, 460, 462
Babcock, John, 397, 525
Babe, Thomas, 414, 469
**Babes in Arms**, *474*
**Baby Face**, *533*
**Baby**, 37
**Babylon Gardens**, *518*
BACA Downtown Fringe
  Series, 449, 463, 474
Bach, Del-Bouree, 477
Back Alley Theater, The, 506,
  560
**Back Home**, *522*
Backes, Roy W., 420
Backstrom, Kevin, 370
Backus, Richard, 439
Bacon-Blaine, Jennifer, 463,
  464
**Bad Habits**, 6, 11, 49, *417*,
  *419*
**Bad Penny**, 558
Badrak, James S., 469
Bael, Jan, 470
Baez, Rafael, 408, 467
Bagden, Ron, 475
Bagneris, Vernel, 6, 42, 430
Bagwell, Marsha, 522
Bahia, Velly, 384
Bahler, Tom, 368
Bailey, Adrian, 373, 455
Bailey, Alan, 460
Bailey, David, 478
Bailey, Larry G., 436
Bailey, Patty Tuel, 516, 517
Bain, Bill, 560
Baines, Nancy, 455

Baird, Campbell, 421
Baird, Jane Todd, 387, 388
Baitz, Jon Robin, 526, 538, 559
Baker, Allan, 519
Baker, Bertilla, 514
Baker, Cliff Fannin, 518
Baker, Joe, 463
Baker, Jonathan, 477
Baker, Josephine, 459
Baker, Melanie, 370
Baker, Ramona, 515
Balaban, Bob, 422, 528
**Balcony, The**, 452, *458*
Baldassare, Jim, 362
Baldasso, Carl, 467
Baldwin, Alec, 25, 417, 558
Baldwin, Eugene, 507
Bale, John, 468
Balentine, Douglas, 515
Balfe, Larry, 517
Balis, Andrea, 463
Ball, Emily, 505
Ball, Michael, 387
Ballard, Wayne, 517
Ballif, Ariel, 534
Ballroom, The, 474
Balou', Buddy, 435, 438
Balsam, Talia, 397, 534
BAM, 427, 452, 474
Bananal, 384
Bancroft, Anne, 519
**Band Wagon, The**, 33
Bandille, Vincent, 473
Banes, Lisa, 445
Bankhead, Tallulah, 48
Baran, Edward, 463, 464, 475
Baranski, Christine, 444, 507
Barasch, Cassie, 463
Baratashvili, Zaza, 428
**Barbeque**, *529*
Barber, George, 455
Barber, Jean, 367
Barbour, James, 533
Barclay, William, 472, 514, 525
**Bard-a-thon IV**, *478*
Barger, Bob, 531
Barilla, John, 473
Barishnikov, Mikhail, 3
Barker, Christine, 434
Barker, Gary, 441
Barker, John, 524
Barker, Patricia, 456
Barnes, Bill, 466
Barnes, Clive, 551, 552, 559

Barnes, Ethel Beatty, 463
Barnes, Gregg, 463, 473
Barnes, Willie C., 477
Barnett, Jack, 394
Barnette, M. Neema, 417
Barnhard, Jim, 468
Baron, Evalyn, 443, 514
Baron, Julian, 479
Barone, Sal, 472
Barr, Bethany, 534
Barre, Gabriel, 420, 479, 514
Barreca, Christopher H., 421, 511
Barrett, Brent, 37, 419, 523
Barrett, Christy, 560
Barrett, Glenn, 531
Barrett, James Lee, 362
Barrett, Mace, 377
Barrie, Jody Keith, 374
Barrientos, Marie, 509
Barrier, Donna, 519
Barrile, Anthony, 519
Barrish, Seth, 474
Barriskill, Michael, 434
Barron, David, 363
Barron, Rob, 529
Barrow Group, 474
Barrow, Bernie, 474, 477
Barrowman, John, 432
**Barry Manilow at the Gershwin**, 361
Barry, B. H., 366, 380, 401, 403, 404, 412, 420, 461
Barry, Brenda, 535
Barry, Lynda, 506
Barry, Raymond J., 560
Barsanti, Bruce, 508
Barsness, Eric, 463
Barstad, Bill, 535
Bart, Roger, 408
Bartenieff, George, 470
Bartlett, George, 367
Bartlett, John, 367
Bartlett, Peter, 472
Bartlett, Robin, 518
Bartoli, Marcello, 459
Barton, Scott, 473
Barton, Steve, 444
Baruch, Steven, 369, 405
Barushok, James, 508
Basche, Peter, 461
Bashkow, Jack, 406
Basinger, Jo Anne, 470
Bass, Jorge Alfano, 365
Basset, Kim, 479
Bassuk, David, 528

Bateman, Justine, 48, 421
Batenhorst, Christopher, 559
Bates, Hank, 533
Bates, Stephen, 370
Batho, Kristofer, 422
Bathol, Bruce, 478
Batt, Bryan, 473
**Battle of Angels**, 364
Battle, Edwin, 463
Bauer, Chris, 540
Bauer, Gilbert, 367
Bauer, Jeff, 509
Bauer, Lori Lynn, 397
Baughman, Renee, 434
Baum, Vicki, 35, 374, 514
Baxter, Rebecca, 525
Bayer, Ethel, 425
Bazan, Iris, 429
Bazarini, Ronald, 537
Be, Yoshio, 518
Beach, Gary, 443
Beacon Project, 474
Beacon Theater, 474
Beall, Rich, 513
Beamish, Stephen, 393
Bean, Reathel, 461, 531
Beard, John, 533
Beard, Mark, 469
Bearden, Jim, 362
Beatty, Carol, 367
Beatty, Eric, 504
Beatty, John Lee, 369, 392, 400, 403, 404, 406, 416, 419, 421
Beatty, Norman, 367
**Beau Jest**, *508*
Beau, 395
Beaufort, John, 551, 552
**Beauty Marks**, *474, 477*
Beck, Dennis C., 513
Beckenstein, Raymond, 370
Becker, Alma, 464, 468
Becker, Victor, 503
Beckett, Samuel, 429, 452, 457, 475, 478
Beckman, Claire, 404
Beckwith, Marcella, 537
Beckwith, Spencer, 534
Beckwith, William, 382
Bedella, David, 507
Beebe, Steve, 514
Beeber, Neena, 512
Beechman, Laurie, 442, 433
Beery, Leigh, 472
Beeson, John, 384
**Before Dawn**, *468*

**Before It Hits Home**, *456*
Behan, John, 469
Beine, Glenn, 512
Belack, Doris, 30, 392
Belafonte, Harry, 3, 559
Belden, Ursula, 427
Believers Musical Theater, 474
Belknap, Allen R., 533
Bell, David H., 391
Bell, Jan, 469
Bell, Marty, 59, 60, 531
Bell, Neal, 456, 458, 507, 513, 540
Bell, Richard, 478
Bellamy, Ned, 408
Bellaver, Lee, 384
Belle, Dottie, 367
Belling, Edward, 474
Bello, Miriam, 465
Bellow, Saul, 3
Bellucci, John, 536
**Belmont Avenue Social Club**, *528*
Belousov, Vladimir, 383
Ben-Ari, Neal, 382
**Bench: New Listings, The**, *469*
Bender, Jeffrey, 476
Benedict, Gail, 519, 520
Benedict, Paul, 6, 419, 528
**Benefactors**, 17
**Benefits of Doubt, The**, *464*
Benjamin, P.J., 514
Benjamin, Randy, 466
Benjamin, Robert, 384
Benjamin, Shawn, 479
Bennett, Georgia, 478
Bennett, Jean, 441
Bennett, Joe, 437
Bennett, Mark, 422
Bennett, Matthew Eaton, 439
Bennett, Michael, 56, 359
Bennett, Robert Russell, 384
Bennett, Robert, 370
Bennett, Sid, 522
Bennett, Suzanne, 536
Bennett, Tai, 479
Bennion, Chris, viii
Bennis, Kate, 506
Benson, Cindy, 433
Benson, Martin, 511, 512
Bensussen, Melia, 465, 467, 475
Bentley, Eric, 475, 524
Bentley, Keith, 528
Benton, Robert, 359

Benvictor, Paul, 538
Benzali, Daniel, 18, 418
Berezin, Tanya, 392, 400, 416, 456, 559
Berezkin, Sergey, 383
Berg, Christopher, 522
Berg, Tracey, 463
Bergen, George, 531
Bergen, Polly, 369
Berger, Jeff, 533
Berger, Lauree, 435
Berger, Sy, 380
Bergeret, Albert, 477
Bergman, Douglas, 456
Bergman, Sandahl, 436
Bergstein, David, 408, 467
Berkeley Repertory Theater, 416, 504
Berkey, Daniel, 403, 404
Berkoff, Steven, 360
Berkshire Public Theater, 531
Berkshire Theater Festival, 539
Berky, Bob, 403
Berlin, Pamela, 392
Berlind, Roger, 378, 379, 395, 555
Berlinsky, Harris, 475
Berman, David, 379
Berman, Susan, 518
Bermingham, Gigi, 403
Bernadette, Jakky, 460
Bernal, Barry K., 434
Bernardo, Keith, 436
Berney, Brig, 375
Bernhard, Jusak, 518
Bernkoff, Mark, 362
Bernstein, Douglas, 400
Bernstein, Jesse, 404
Bernstein, Joel, 477
Bernstein, Leonard, 475
Bernstein, Susan, 473
Berridge, Elizabeth, 458
Berry, Gabriel, 412, 457
Berry, Stephanie, 459
Bertagnolli, Elena, 367
Bertish, Suzanne, 18, 418
Bertrand, Jacqueline, 414
**Beside Herself**, 11, 24, *416*
Bessell, Frank, 531
Besserman, Ellen, 456
**Best Friends**, *455, 473*
**Best of Boston, The**, *461*
Best-Bova, Mary, 533
Besterman, Doug, 505
Bethel, Pepsi, 43, 430
**Betrayal**, 10

Betsill, Jerry, 515
**Better Days,** *510*
**Better People**, *470*
**Beulah Ballentine**, *468*
Beverley, Trazana, 464, 474
**Beyond Belief**, *461*
Biagi, Michael D., 397
Biancardi, Gina, 367
Bianchi, Donald, 511
Bianchini, Karen, 426
Bianco, Rich, 405, 478
Biasetti, Robert, 528
Bibb, Teri, 444
Bicât, Nick, 368
Bickell, Ross, 406
Biddlecombe, James, 384
Biedler, Mary, 509
Bielecki, Bob, 422
**Big Frogs**, *458*
**Big Hotel**, *469*
**Big Kadosh, The**, *529*
Biggs, Roxann, 437
Bill Evans & Associates, 378, 380, 381, 397
Billie Holiday Theater, 474
Billings, Glenn, 508
Billingslea, Sandra, 370
Billington, Ken, 367, 368, 370, 381, 387, 395, 401
Birch, Michael, 420
Bird, Thomas, 479
Birkenhead, Susan, 59
Birkett, Jeremiah, 386, 387
Birn, David, 458
Birney, Reed, 30, 426, 472, 528
**Birthday Party, The**, 452, *457*, 558
Bishins, David, 457
Bishoff, Joel, 384, 464
Bishop, Andre, 413, 467
Bishop, Carol, 434
Bishop, Conrad, 513
Bishop, John, 400, 416, 456
Bishop, Kelly, 434, 435
Bishop, Thom, 507
Bissinger, Tom, 529
Bitterman, Shem, 512
Bjornson, Maria, 6, 34, 35, 388, 560
**Black and Blue**, 360
**Black Eagles**, *524*
**Black Market**, *478*
**Black Medea**, *473*
Black, Andrea, 460
Black, Don, 34, 35, 387, 556

Black, Jack, 408
Black-Eyed Susan, 461
Blackwell, Sam, 509
Blackwell-Cook, Debbie, 464
Bladen, Sara, 457
Blaine, Sandy, 527
Blair, D. Bartlett, 509
Blair, Pamela, 435
Blaisdell, Nesbitt, 386
Blake, Ann-Marie, 367
Blake, Richard, 41, 373, 384, 464
Blake, Robin, 362
Blakemore, Michael, 5, 6, 27, 33, 380, 387, 556, 558
Blakeslee, Suzanne, 424
Blakesley, Weston, 478
Blanchard, Greg, 442
Blanco, Rafael V., 521
Blane, Ralph, 34, 369, 556
Blaney, Robert, 539
Blankenship, Hal, 468
Blankensop, Susan, 559
Blaser, Cathy B., 365
Blazer, Judy, 390, 443, 474
Bleasdale, Alan, 535
Blessing, Jeanne, 509
Blessing, Lee, 518
Blint, Joyce, 456
Blitz, Danette, 474
Blitzstein, Marc, 49
Bloch, Ivan, 369
Bloch, Sonny, 369
Block, Giles, 383
Block, Larry, 16, 401, 464
Block, Leslie, 478
Bloom, Michael, 472, 476
Bloom, Tom, 419, 516
Bloomfield, Lucy, 506
Blount, William, 372
Blue Gene Tyranny, 462
Blue Man Group, 460
**Blue Piano, The, *477***
Blue, Pete, 424
**Blueblack, *513***
Bluffstone, Eric, 511
Blum, Joel, 393
Blum, Roy, 470
Blumberg, Andrea, 528
Blumenkrantz, Jeff, 372, 463
Bobbie, Walter, 433, 469
Bobbitt, Wendy, 409
**Bobby Gould in Hell, 6, 29, *421***
Bobby, Anne, 458
**Bobo's Birthday, *455***

Bocchino, Chris, 437
Bock, Jerry, 49, 429, 474, 560
Bockhorn, Craig, 392, 417, 459, 473
Boddy, Claudia, 506, 508, 509
Bodenhoffer, Andreas, 465
Bodle, Jane, 395, 433
**Body Builder's Book of Love, The, *459***
**Body Game, *470***
**Body Leaks, *527***
Body Politic Theater, 506
Boehr, Kenneth M., 518
Boeing, Mara, 384
Bogaev, Paul, 388
Bogosian, Eric, 5, 28, 29, 30, 55, 425, 477, 558
Bohnen, James, 508
Bohr, Jimmy, 458
Boim, Marcelo, 384
Boim, Mauro, 384
Bolinger, Don, 518
Bollinger, Diedre, 531
Bolt, Jonathan, 456, 530
Bolton, Guy, 360
Bonasorte, Gary, 415
Bond, Christopher, 362
Bond, Cynthia, 423, 424
Bondi, Tony, 473
Bonds, Rufus Jr., 410, 411
Boneau, Chris, 362, 369, 406
Bonfiglio, Robert, 362
Bongiorno, Joseph, 384
Bonnard, Raymond, 505
Bonney, Jo, 425
**Boochie, *474***
Boockvor, Steven, 437
**Book of the Night, The, *507***
Booker, Margaret, 540
Bookman, Kirk, 509, 534
Bookwalter, D. Martyn, 516, 535
Boone, Aaron, 527
Boone, Debby, 52, 384
Boone, Michael Kelly, 461, 514
Booth, Karen, 459
Borak, Jeffrey, 483
Borbon, Jimmy, 467
Borczon, Becky, 464
Borden, David, 477
Border Brujo, 559
Bordowitz, Gregg, 463
Borges, Jose, 466
Borges, Yamil, 521
**Born Yesterday, 360**

Bornstein, Daryl, 374
Bornstein, Rocky, 462
Borod, Bob, 372
Boroko, Peter, 464
Boron, Susan, 367
Borow, Rena Berkowicz, 420
Borror, David, 403
Boschi, Steven, 370
Bosco, Damien, 456
Bosco, Philip, 441
Boslet, Jack, 537
Bosworth, Jill, 384
Botsford, Sara, 445
Bottari, Michael, 374, 413
Bottitta, Ron, 475
Bottoms, Ben, 513
Boublil, Alain, 360
Bouffard, Suzy, 386
Bougere, Teagle F., 540
Bourneuf, Stèphen, 373, 374, 438
Boushey, David, 534
Boussom, Ron, 512
Boutsikaris, Dennis, 464
Bouvier, David, 522
Bova, John, 362
Bove, Mark, 435, 438
**Bovver Boys, *478***
Bowden, Jonny, 420
Bowden, Richard, 517
Bowen, Bryan, 519
Bowen, Roger, 425
Bowerman, Joseph, 367
Bowers, Clent, 434
Bowers, Hazel Weinberg, 528
Bowie, Pat, 508
Bowman, Rob, 390, 391
Boxer, Amanda, 476
Boxley, Judith, 456
Boyce, Sharla, 516, 517
Boyd, Jane, 507
Boyd, Julianne, 539
Boyd, Julie, 414, 444
Boyle, Viki, 475
Boylen, Daniel P., 528
**Boys' Play, *518***
Bozark, Kim Allen, 534
Bozyk, Reizl, 476
Bozzone, Bill, 450, 458, 529
Bracchitta, Jim, 377
Brackett, Gary, 477
Bradbury, Stephen, 376
Braden, John, 458
Bradford, Mark, 470
Bradford, Penelope, 470
Bradford, Scott R., 513, 514

Bradley, Jerry, 463
Bradley, Neil, 479
Bradley, Suzie, 534
Bradshaw, Shelly, 517
Brady, Patrick Scott, 419
Brady, Sharon, 464, 475
Braff, Katy, 367
Bragaw, Sarah, 464
Brailsford, Pauline, 506
Branam, Julie, 367
Brancato, Joe, 539
Brand, Gibby, 445
Brandman, Michael, 378
Brando, Marlon, 45
Brandt, Richard, 425
Brasington, Alan, 517
Brass, Stacey Lynn, 410
Brassard, Gail, 429
Braugher, Andre, 403
Bravaco, Joseph, 474
Braxton, Brenda, 463
Bray, Barbara, 479
Brazil, Tom, viii
**Breaking In, *468***
**Breaking Legs, *534***
Brechner, Stanley, 429, 474
Brecht, Bertolt, 49, 372, 475
Breedlove, Gina, 524
Breen, Patrick, 469
Bregstein, Barbara, 468
Brehm, Heide, 405, 478
Brehse, Philip, 477
Bremac, Janice, 456
Brendel, Crickette, 518
Brennan, James, 443
Brennan, Nora, 433
Brennan, Steve, 429
Brenner, Guy, 535
Brenner, Janet, 419
Brenner, Jerome, 456
Brenner, Susan, 473
Brenner, William, 514
Brettschneider, Mark, 530
Breuer, Lee, 407, 412 449, 452, 461
Breul, Garry Allan, 537
Breuler, Robert, 386
Brian, Michael, 514
**Briar Patch, *458*, 560**
Briar, Suzanne, 387, 388
Brice, Ron, 386
Brickhill, Joan, 370, 556
Brickhill-Burke Productions, 369, 556
**Bricklayers, *530***

Bridge, Andrew, 6, 44, 388, 560
Brielle, Jonathan, 400, 416
Brigden, Tracy, 469
Brightman, Sarah, 444
**Brightness, 452, *459***
Brill, Fran, 15, 414
Brimm, Thomas Martell, 479
Brindley, Melinda, 513
Brinkley, Dena, 515
Brinkley, Susan, 458
Brito, Adrian, 365
Britton, Kate, 477
Brock, Gregory, 437
Brock, Lee, 474
Brockman, Kevin, 385, 422
Brockway, Adrienne J., 466
Brockway, Amie, 466
Brockway, Lou, 429, 478
Broder, J. Scott, 369
Brodsky, Michael, 470
Brody, Alan, 518
Brody, Jonathan, 531
Brogaw, Sarah, 475
Brogger, Ivar, 458
Brokaw, Mark, 414, 472
Brolaski, Carol, 519
Brolin, Josh, 533
Bromberg, Conrad, 538
Bromelmeier, Martha, 459
Bronskill, Reginald, 362
**Bronx Tale, A, 27, *478***
Brooking, Simon, 469
Brooklyn Academy of Music (BAM), 427, 452, 474
Brooklyn Academy of Music's Next Wave Festival, 449
Brooks, Al, 512
Brooks, David, 459
Brooks, Don, 472
Brooks, Donald L., 455, 473
Brooks, Keith, 529
Brooks, Michael, 513
Brothers, Carla, 524
Broughton, Barbara, 530
Brousseau, James, 370
Browder, Ben, 382
Brown, Ann, 473
Brown, Arvin, 48, 525, 526, 559
Brown, Barry, 376, 556
Brown, Blair, 17, 368
Brown, Charles, 424, 445
Brown, Claudia, 457, 466, 469
Brown, David, 376, 381, 392
Brown, Deloss, 457

Brown, Georgia, 49, 372, 556
Brown, Graham, 417, 423, 424
Brown, Jason, 397
Brown, L. Kent, 509
Brown, Leon Addison, 477
Brown, Lynn, 517
Brown, Michael Henry, 463, 464
Brown, Nanette, 508
Brown, P. J., 386, 387
Brown, Robin Leslie, 477
Brown, Roscoe, 53
Brown, Sarah, 464
Brown, Stephanie, 414
Brown, W. Earl, 508
Browne, Donna, 528
Browne, Roscoe Lee, 560
Browning, Susan, 511
Bruce, Cheryl Lynn, 386
Bruce, Claudia, 479
Bruce, Neely, 477
Bruce, Susan, 416, 534
Bruce, Tom, 455
Bruckner, Gisella, 479
Bruice, Ann, 512, 516
**Brunch at Trudy and Paul, *461***
Brune, Eva, 459
Brunell, Janine S., 506
Brunetti, Ted, 530
Brunner, Roslyn, 514
Brustein, Robert, 56
**Brutes Outside the Blue Room, *468***
Brüll, Pamela, 390
Bryan-Brown, Adrian, 364, 370, 383, 392, 427
Bryan-Brown, Marc, viii
Bryant, Damon, 535
Bryant, David, 443
Bryant, Scott, 474
Bryant-Minard, Donna, 537
Brydon, W.B., 475
Bryggman, Larry, 61, 392, 404, 417
Bryne, Barbara, 440
Brynner, Yul, 397
Bub, Linda, 514
Buch, Rene, 557
Buchanan, Linda, 472, 506
Buchanan, Will, 455, 456
Buchman, Peter, 469
**Buck, 560**
Buck, George, 519
Buck, Nathaniel, 518
Buckley, Betty, 433

Buckley, Ralph, 541
Bucknam, David, 450, 466
Budde, Jordan, 518
Buddeke, Kate, 472
Budries, David, 511
Buell, Bill, 419
Buelow, Dan, 370
Buerkel, Peg, 511
Buero-Vallejo, Antonio, 470
Buffaloe, Katherine, 444
Buffano, Jules, 394
**Bug, The**, *533*
Buica, Eugene, 384
**Built to Last**, *468*
Bulasky, David, 419
Bulgakov, Mikhail, 30, 362,
    452, 457
Bullard, Thomas Allan, 520
Buller, Francesca, 382
Bullins, Ed, 460
Bulos, Yusef, 457, 472
Bumbalo, Victor, 474
Bumpass, Rodger, 535
**Bums**, *469*
**Bunnybear**, 399
Bunting, Pearce, 521
Buono, Cara, 379, 422
Buravsky, Alexander, 512
Burbutashvili, Lily, 428
Burby, Joseph, 468
Burch, Bryan, 419
Burckhardt, Jacob, 560
Burdette, Nicole, 450
Burdick, David, 374
Burdick, Melissa L., 419
Burdman, Ralph, 539
Burgess, Granville, 529
Burgler, Terry, 532, 533
Burke, Louis, 370
Burke, Marylouise, 477
Burke, Robert, 461, 479
Burke, Sean, 431
Burkenhead, Peter, 534
Burland, Dave, 478
Burmester, Joe, 520
Burmester, Leo, 404, 443
**Burner's Frolic**, 11, 20, *424*
Burnett, Robert, 434
Burns, Mary Beth, 508
Burrell, Fred, 479
Burridge, Hollis, 370
Burrus, Bob, 520
Burse-Mickelbury, Denise, 425,
    474, 559
Burstyn, Ellen, 3, 439, 445
Burstyn, Mike, 49, 429

Burton, Donald, 382, 406
Burton, Kate, 379, 422
Burton, Victoria Lynn, 370
Burton, Warren, 461
Busang, Brett, 455
Busch, Charles, 13, 399, 405
Busfield, Timothy, 376
Bushmann, Katharine, 537
Bushnell, Bill, 519
Bustle, Jonathan, 478
Buterbaugh, Keith, 444
Butler, Dan, 400
Butler, Dean, 441
Butler, Irv, 456
Butler, Jerome, 518
Butler, Joe, 537
Butler, Paul, 376
Butt, Billy, 368
Butt, Jennifer, 443
Buttacavoli, Ronald J., 410
**Butter and Egg Man, The**,
    *461*
Butterfield, Catherine, 455
Button, Dick, 378
Button, Jeanne, 403, 404, 421
Buxbaum, Lisa, 409, 411
Buxton, Bill, 395
Buzas, Jason McConnell, 458,
    461
**Buzzsaw Berkeley**, 450, *472*
**By and for Havel**, 11, *429*,
    452, *478*
Byers, Billy, 33, 44, 380, 559
Byers, Karen L., 395
Bykov, Vladislav, 383
Bynum, Betty K., 524
Bynum, Brenda, 504
Byrd, Lillian, 535
Byrne, Alexandra, 379, 422,
    556
Byron-Kirk, Keith, 386, 387,
    507

Caballero, Roxann, 437
**Cabaret**, 5
Cabot, Colin, 523
Cachianes, Ed, 478
Cadiz, Dino, 504
Cadman, Larry, 468
Cadry, Ron, 405
Caesar, Irving, 394
Caesar, Sid, 43, 369, 401
Cahill, Danny, 478
Cahill, James, 379, 403, 405
Cahn, Larry, 525
**Cahoots**, *478*

Cain, Bill, 519
Cain, William, 365
Caine, Rebecca, 444
Caitlyn, Deryl, 403, 461
Calderone, Michael, 405, 478
Caldwell, Matthew, 456
Caldwell, Susan, 384
Cale, David, 466
Calhoun, Kaia, 560
Caliban, Richard, 450, 457,
    475
**Call Me Ethel!**, *474*
Callaghan, Edward, 416
Callahan, Ruth, 468
Callas, Demetri, 377
Callen, Chris, 373, 441
Callender, L. Peter, 392, 403,
    417
Callow, Simon, 477, 519
Calvino, Italo, 528
Camera, John, 534
Cameron, Bruce, 369
Cameron, Linda, 514
Camille, Sharon, 439
Camp, Bill, 403, 404
Camp, Joanne, 477
Campanella, Philip, 406, 421
Campbell, Amelia, 397, 534
Campbell, Bruce, 365, 379,
    402, 421
Campbell, Catherine, 530
Campbell, Erma, 425, 559
Campbell, Mary Schmidt, 403
Campbell, Roy, 475
Campo, John, 380
Campora, Giancarlo, 385
Canaan, Robert, 456
Canary, David, 473
Candida, Andrea, 385
Cannon, John, 528
Cannon, Stephanie, 531
**Canterbury Tales**, *477*
Cantor, Arthur, 427, 431, 458
Cantor, David, 429
Cantor, Geoffrey P., 539
Cantor, Lester, 362
**Cantorial**, 399
Canvin, Rue E., viii
**Capitol Cakewake**, *455*
Capoiera, Claudia, 385
Capoiera, Mario, 385
Capote, Truman, 8, 27, 28, 381
Cappelli, Joe, 372
Capps, Tom, 377
**Captain**, *458*
**Captive**, *458*

Carabelli, Cheryl A., 508
**Carbondale Dreams: Bradley and Beth**, *476*
**Cardigans ... Those Swingin' Singin' Guys from Alpha Mu Phi Pi, The**, *479*
Cardille, Lori, 530
Cardin, Pierre, 383
Cardinal, Vincent, 456
Cardona, Chris, 514
Cardone, John, 560
Cardwell, Sylvia, 504
Carey, Jeff, 513
Carey, Robert, 405
Carey, Wilfred, 475
Carinci, Elaine M., 466
Cariou, Len, 29, 51, 429, 525
Carlin, Chet, 466, 478
Carlin, Tony, 472
Carlos, Laurie, 474, 559
Carlsen, Allan, 477
Carlson, T.C., 508
Carmichael, Bill, 433
Carmichael, Jane, 528
Carmichael, Marnie, 408, 409
Carmines, Al, 1, 461, 476
**Carnage, a Comedy**, 6, 11, 15, *406*, *408*, *412*, *466*
Carney, Heidi, 384
**Carnival, The**, *529*
Carol, Jan, 511
Caroli, Livio, 384
Carollo, Scott, 408, 409
**Carousel Man, The**, *540*
Carousel, 43
Carpenter, Brad, 479
Carpenter, Cassandra, 536
Carpenter, Gordon, 539
Carpenter, Jack, 536
Carpenter, John, 510, 511
Carpenter, Karen L., 389
Carpenter, Larry, 12, 406, 421, 522
Carpenter, Thelma, 455
Carrafa, John, 467
**Carreno**, *475*
Carricart, Robertson, 364
**Carrie's Choice**, *514*
**Carried Away: Jeff Harnar Sings Comden and Green**, *474*
Carrillo, Ramiro, 401
**Carrion Sisters and the Vulgar Mother**, *470*
Carroll, Barbara, 368, 403, 408
Carroll, Brad, 536

Carroll, David, 36, 374, 556
Carroll, Jolene, 533
Carroll, Philip, 372
Carroll, Rocky, 21, 389, 556, 558, 559
Carroll, Ronn, 377
Carry, Lou, 367
Carryer, Tim, 402
Carsel, Gary, 468
Carson, Jo, 519
Carson, Stacy, 513
Carson, Susan Dawn, 442
Carter, Bobby John, 377
Carter, Lonnie, 540
Carter, Lou, 455
Carter, Louise, 527
Carter, Michael, 382
Carter, Mrs. Leslie, 48
Carter, Natalie, 474
Carter, Sarah, 367
Carter, Steve, 508
Cartmell, Leah, 474
Cary, Meghan, 536
Carzasty, Peter B., 428
**Casa**, *460*
**Casanova**, *463*
Casas, Myrna, 466
Case, Ronald, 374, 413
Casenave, Carolyn, 478
Casey, Diane, 520
Casey, Joyce, 511
Casey, Robert E., 406
**Cash Values**, *525*
Cash, Darla, 535
Cashman, Joseph M., 513
Caskey, Marilyn, 444
Casnoff, Philip, 41, 383, 408
Cassan-Jellison, Claudine, 419
Casserly, Kerry, 434
Cassidy, Tim, 438
**Cast Iron Smile, The**, *455*
Castay, Leslie, 372
Casteel, Karen, 457
Castellino, Bill, 411, 466
Castillo, Arturo, 528
Casto, Jacqui, 411
Castro, Vicente, 467
Castronovo, T.J., 534
**Cat on a Hot Tin Roof**, 4, 6, 30, 31, 46, 47, 55, 56, 61, *386*, 556, 558, 559
**Catastrophe**, *429*, 452, *478*
**Catch-22**, 15
Cates, Nancy, 533
Cates, Phoebe, 379

Cathey, Reg E., 404, 464, 469, 479
**Cats**, 34, 359, 433
Cava, Frank, 365
Cavanagh, Thomas, 362
Cavargna, Janice, 367
Cave, James, 469
Caveny, Leslie, 516
Cavett, Dick, 440
Cavise, Joe Antony, 433
Caylor, Tom, 477
Ceballos, Rene, 365, 433, 436
Cecil, Pamela, 367
**Cemetery Club, The**, 4, 30, *392*
Cenal, Alina, 535
Center Stage, 504
Center Theater Group/Ahmanson Theater, 389, 555
Cermak, Terry, 532, 533
Ceroni, Phyllis Frew, 367
Cerullo, Jonathan, 463
Cesa, James, 456
Cesarano, Anthony, 367
Chace, Rebecca, 470
Chadman, Christopher, 438
Chadwick, Paul, 515
Chadwick, Robin, 48, 378
Chadwick, Sharon Fenwalk, 515
**Chairman's Wife, The**, *518*
Chalfant, Kathleen, 421, 463, 470
Chamberlain, Marisha, 509
Chamberlin, Kevin, 425, 461
Chamberlin, Mark, 538
Chambers, Allan, 507
Chambers, David, 511
Chambers, Ernie, 361
Chambers, Jane, 475
Chambers, Michael, 404
Chan, Donald, 531
Chan, Mr. Kim, 504
Chandler, Brian Evaret, 395
Chandler, David, 520
Chandler, Stan, 431, 479
Chandler, Terry, 425
Chang, Du-Yee, 467
Chang, Roxanne, 467
Chang, Tisa, 467
Changa, Jimmy, 522
**Change in the Heir, A**, 4, 41, *390*
**Changing Faces**, 559
Changing Scene, The, 512

Chanin, Elizabeth, 367
Channing, Carrissa, 461
Channing, Stockard, 9, 369, 397, 405, 535
Chant, Holley, 364
Chapin, Schuyler, 554
Chapman, Topsy, 42, 43, 430
Chappell, Kendis, 444
Charles MacArthur Award, 560
Charles, David, 468
Charles, Josh, 525
Charles, Paul, 435, 437
Charles, Valerie, 479
Charles, Walter, 387, 388
**Charlie's Oasis Museum & Bar**, *507*
**Charlie's Wedding Day**, *456*
Charnas, Suzy McKee, 536
Charney, Kristin, 479
Charney, Tina, 416, 523
Charnin, Martin, 369, 395
Chase, Everett, 370, 536
Chase, Lonnie, 370
Chase, Stephanie, 367
Chaucer, Geoffrey, 477
Chayefsky, Paddy, 48, 378
Chekhov, Anton, 473, 477
Chelnik, Peter, 456
**Chelsea Walls**, 450
Chenelle, Michel, 408
Chepulis, Kyle, viii, 457
Cherney, Christopher, 470
**Cherry Orchard, The,** *473*
**Chess**, 41
**Chessie and the Griff,** *507*
**Chevaliere**, *537*
Chianese, Dominic, 476
Chiarenza, Anita M., 508
Chic Street Man, 411, 524
Chicago Theater Center, 508
Chicago Theater Group, 502
Chiclana, Margarita Lopez, 467
Chicoine, Susan, 367
**Chinese Charade,** *467*
Chinn, Kevin, 436
Chisholm, Anthony, 479
Chitty, Alison, 364
Chmiel, Mark, 461
Choder, Jill, 381
Chodorov, Jerome, 475
Chong, Marcus, 519
Chong, Ping, 452, 459, 523
Chonishvilli, Sergey, 383
**Chorus Line, A,** 56, 359, 432, 434
Christen, Robert, 472, 506

Christian, William, 524
Christiansen, Richard, 483
**Christmas Carol: A Contemporary Tale in Four Ghosts, A,** *522*
**Christmas Is ... A Musical Comedy,** *536*
**Christmas Robbery,** *468*
**Christmas Spectacular**, 4, *366, 367*
**Christmas Went Thataway!,** *517*
Christopher, Donald, 517, 536
Christopher, Rick, 533
Christopher, Thom, 463, 464
Christopher-Myers, Bill, 531
Christy, James J., 528
CHS Productions, 478
Chumley, Daniel, 478
Chunayev, Boris, 383
Church, Joseph, 367
Churchill, Caryl, 18, 59, 407
Churchman, Shawn, 477
Chutes and Ladders Theater Company, 470
Ciccolella, Jude, 479
Cilento, Wayne, 368, 435
Cincinnati Playhouse in the Park, 509
Cioffi, Robert, 474
Cione, Andrea, 455
Cipiti, Mike, 511
Cippola, John M., 367
Circle in the Square Theater, 30, 49, 51, 362, 556
Circle Repertory Company, 5, 11, 24, 25, 392, 400, 416
Circle Repertory Projects-in-Progress, 456
Circle, The, ix, 4, 48, 56, *378*, 556, 559
Cirne, Aderson, 385
Cistone, Danny, 377
**Cities Out of Print,** *461, 479*
Cittadino, Connie House, 367
City Center Theater Studio III, 474
**City of Angels,** ix, 4, 5, 6, 8, 32, 33, 34, 43, 44, 55, 56, 62, 220-257, *379*, 551, 552, 553, 555, 556, 557, 558, 559
City Theater Company, 530
Ciulei, Liviu, 53, 405
Claassen, Susan, 540
Clancy, Dan, 479

Clancy, Katy, 506
Clanton, Rony, 417
Clarence Derwent Awards, 559
Clarey, Alan, 534
Claridge Productions, 412
Clark, Bobby, 395
Clark, Cheryl, 438
Clark, G. Thomas, 389
Clark, J.J., 455
Clark, Jack, 508
Clark, John, 369
Clark, Julian, 464
Clark, Katherine, 533
Clark, Keith Brian, 478
Clark, Tyrone, 513
Clark, Victoria, 443, 525, 527
Clarke, Caitlin, 519
Clarke, David, 469
Clarke, Hope, 411, 524
Clarvoe, Anthony, 491, 512, 536
Classic Stage Company (see CSC)
Clayton, Lawrence, 410
Clayton, Philip, 387, 388
**Clear and Present Danger,** *530*
Cleary, Malachy, 478
Clemens, Elizabeth, 459
Clemente, Rene, 433, 439
Clements, Randy, 437
Clemmons, David, 505
Clerk, Clive, 435
Cleveland Play House, The, 510, 392
Clevenger, Joan, 430
Clifton, Deborah, 523
Clifton, Mickey Maurice, 512
Cline, Perry, 363, 388
Clohessy, Robert, 419
**Closer Than Ever,** 6, 11, 37, 40, 43, *419*, 558
**Closer, The,** *479*
Cloud Nine, 560
**Clouds, The,** *461*
Clown Theater Day, 477
Coates, George, 535
Coates, Norman, 374, 427
Coats, Steve, 457, 464
Cobb, Ned, 27, 416
Cobbs, Bill, 439
**Cobra,** *477*
Coburn, Richard, 394
Coccioletti, Philip, 471
Cochran, Ray, 414
Cochrane, Steve, 383

Cockerille, Phil, 513
**Cocktail Hour, The,** 399
Coconut Grove Playhouse, 521
Coffield, Kelly, 472
Coffield, Phil, 534
Cofta, Mark, 524
Cohen, Alexander H., 390
Cohen, Alice Eve, 461
Cohen, Bill, 461
Cohen, Buzz, 368, 404, 412
Cohen, Edward M., 476, 537
Cohen, Erika, 479
Cohen, Greg, 402
Cohen, Jason Steven, 368, 403, 408
Cohen, Jedidiah, 527
Cohen, Jeri Lynn, 478
Cohen, Judith, 408
Cohen, Katharine, 457
Cohen, Larry, 472
Cohen, Lynn, 364, 464
Cohen, Margery, 455
Cohen, Scott, 421
Cohenour, Patti, 444
Cohn, Henoch, 476
Cohn, Marcus, 560
Coker, Flora, 523
Colaneri, Joseph, 384
Colantti, Steven, 468
Colavecchia, Franco, 420
Colavin, Charlotte, 464, 478
Colbert, Claudette, 559
Colburn, Randy, 507
Colby, Michael, 473
Cole, Kay, 435, 437, 443
Cole, Robert, 425
Coleman, Cy, 33, 34, 43, 379, 380, 475, 552, 556, 559
Coleman, David, 394
Coleman, Jack, 519
Coleman, Minnette, 455, 469
Coleman, R.J., 508
Colitti, Rik, 528
Colker, Jerry, 438
Coll, Ivonne, 464
Colliere, Michael, 478
Collino, Mark A., 529, 530
Collins, Eileen M., 367
Collins, Pat, 504, 516, 525
Collins, Pauline, 445
Collins, Ray, 458
Collins, Stephen, 52, 403
Collis, Adam, 515
Collyer, Eve, 470
Colon, Alex, 417, 535
Colon, Miriam, 467

**Colorado Catechism, The,** 456
Colorado, Vira and Hortensia, 470
Colson, Kevin, 387, 556
Colt, Alvin, 390
Colteaux, Andrew, 516
Colton, Jacque Lynn, 410
Columbia Artists Management, Inc., 397
Columbus, Marvin, 519
Colwin, Laurie, 528
Comden, Betty, 475, 558
**Come as You Are,** 11, *425*
Commire, Anne, 473
Common Wealth Award, 559
Conaway, David, 455, 473
Concert Productions International, 397
Condino, David, 516
Cone, Michael, 395
Conery, Edward, 517
**Confessions of a Plumber,** *530*
**Confessions of Franklin Thompson III, The,** *540*
Congdon, Constance, 452, 463, 472
Conger, Eric, 525
Conger, Shelley, 475
Conklin, John, 404, 516
Conklin, Mark W., 414, 474
Conley, Jack, 537
Conley, Kim, 531
Connally, Mary, 468
Connaughton, Kevin, 426
Connell, Gordon, 433
Connell, Jane, 441
Connelly, Patrick, 456
Conniff, Tony, 415
Connolly, David, 362
Connor, Allison, 527
Conolly, Patricia, 378
**Conquest of the South Pole,** *540*
Conroy, Frances, 17, 19, 368, 379, 422, 559
Conroy, Jarlath, 479, 516
**Consuming Passions of Lydia E. Pinkham and Rev. Sylvester Graham, The,** *455*
Conte, Derek, 478
Contemporary Theater and Art, 559
**Contrast, The,** *466*

**Conversation, The,** *468*
**Conversation of the Tarantula, The,** *468*
**Conversation with the Moon,** *512*
Converse-Roberts, William, 404
Conway, Dan, 510, 511
Conway, Kevin, 444
Cooch, Thomas, 507
Cook, Divina, 459
Cook, Rhea Anne, 507
Cook, Roderick, 458
Cook, Steven, 470
Cook, Victor Trent, 410
Cooke, Andrew, 363
Cooke, John C., 519
**Cool Million, A,** 558
Cooper, Adrienne, 420
Cooper, Helmar Augustus, 524
Cooper, Maury, 421
Cooper, Max, 390
Cooper, Mindy, 408, 409
Cooper, Reva, 368, 403, 408
Cope, Edie, 468
Copeland, Carolyn Rossi, 460
Copeland, Marissa, 540
Copeland, Robert, 515
Cordes, Scott, 517
Cordova, Richard, 422
Cordtz, Richard, 539
Corey, Jill, 479
**Coriolanus,** 405
Corley, Nick, 429
Corne, Lesley, 362
Corneille, Pierre, 516
Cornelius, Robert, 523
Cornish, Anthony, 477
Correia, Don, 435
Corsetti, Dina, 431
Corsi, Francesca, 384
Cortese, Alda, 521
Corti, Jim, 438, 507
Corum, Mark, 456
Corwin, Walter, 471
Corzatte, Clayton, 537
Cosgrove, Caprice, 405, 478
Cosier, E. David Jr., 389
Costa, Carol, 468
Costa, Joseph M., 403
Costa, Joseph, 404, 421
Costa, Richard, 367
Costa-Greenspon, Muriel, 473
Costin, James, 517
**Cottage, The,** *540*
Council, Richard, 467, 472

Countryman, Michael, 420, 427, 464, 472
Courie, Jonathan, 473
Course of It, The, *512*
Courson, Robert, 369
Court, Paula, viii
Courtney, Matthew, 479
Courts, Randy, 460, 525
Cousins, Brian, 378, 392
Covan, Ellie, 560
Covert, Todd, 537
Cowles, Peggy, 531
Cox, Catherine, 444, 466
Cox, Richard, 469
Coyne, Cyndi, 400
Coyne, Randy, 367
**Coyolxuahqui: Woman Without Borders**, *470*
Coyote, Peter, 397, 535
Crabtree, John, 506
Crafford, Bob, 455
Crafford, James, 455
Craig, Randy, 478
Cram, Lynette, 533
Crandall, Dean, 367
Crane, David, 393
Cranendonk, Terrence, 467
Craver, Michael, 461
Crawford, Constance, 364
Crawford, Kevin, 364
Crawford, Michael, 444, 560
Crawford, Ron, 386, 387
**Crazy Plays, The**, *463*
Creatore, Luigi, 412
Creedon, Don, 475
Creelman, Patric A., 393
Creery, Don, 538
Creevey, Rae, 518
Cribbins, Bernard, 432
Cricket Theater, 416
Crigler, Lynn, 362
Cristofer, Michael, 541
Criswell, Kim, 49, 372
Criterion Center, 474
**Critic: The Fun I've Had, The**, *474*
Crivello, Anthony, 442
Croce, Camille, viii, 454
Croft, Paddy, 473
Cromarty, Peter, 385, 413, 422, 425
Cromer, David, 506
Cromwell, David, 419
Cromwell, Keith, 367
Crook, Peter, 539
Crooks, Kitty, 461, 467

Crosby, Kim, 440
**Cross Patch**, *458*
Cross, Marcia, 378
Cross, Murphy, 436
Crossley, Steven, 476
Crossroads Theater Company, 524
Crothers, Sam, 374, 556
Crouse, Russel, 52, 360, 383
Crouse, Timothy, 360
Crow, Laura, 427, 509, 530
Crow, Tom, 464
**Crowbar**, 450, *457*, *464*, 558
Crowell, Richard, 517
Crowningshield, Keith, 374
**Crucible, The**, 11, 48, *420*, *421*
Cruise, Charmaine, 529
Crumb, Ann, 387, 442
Cruz, Cintia, 467
Cruz, Denise, 504
Cruz, Migdalia, 527
Cruz, Raymond, 560
**Cry of the Body, The**, *460*
Crystal, Jason, 529
CSC Repertory, Ltd. (Classic Stage Company), 383, 452, 457
Csenger, John, 384
Csicsko, David Lee, 506
Cubiculo, 474
Cucaracha Theater, 450, 475
Cucaracha, 449
Cuccioli, Bob, 429, 522
Cucco, Patricia, 478, 479
Cuervo, Alma, 368
Cull, Christopher, 509
Cullen, David, 388
Cullen, John, 416
Cullen, Michael, 474
Culliver, Karen, 370, 444
Cullum, John, 52, 362, 525
Culpepper, Stuart, 504
Cummings, Anthony, 530
Cummings, Claudia, 384
Cummings, Constance, 539
Cummings, Rosemary, 506
Cummins, Cenovia, 380
Cummins, Scott, 509
Cumpsty, Michael, 378, 404
Cundiff, Claire, 470
Cunningham, John, 525
Cunningham, Laura, 417, 472
Cunningham, Peter, viii
Cunningham, Wafa, 464
Curchack, Fred, 449, 474, 558

Curi, Jorge, 535
Curima, 385
Curless, John, 458
Curran, Keith, 456
Curren, Peter, 508
Currie, Richard, 469
Currier, Terrence P., 395, 525
Curry, Bob, 508
Curry, John, 406
Curry, Tim, 18, 418
Curtin, Jane, 369, 405
Curtis, Keene, 439
Curtis-Brown, Robert, 403, 414
Curtis-Michael, John, 367
Cushing, Maureen O'Sullivan and James, 386
Cutler, R.J., 414, 463, 479, 527
Cwikowski, Bill, 458, 464, 472, 509
**Cymbeline**, 400, 405
**Cyrano de Bergerac**, *478*
Cyronek, Jeff, 512, 513
Czyzewska, Elzbieta, 457, 464, 558

D'Albis, Donato J., 458
d'Amboise, Charlotte, 433
D'Ambrosi, Dario, 459
D'Ambrosio, Franc, 363
D'Andrea, Paul, 464
D'Arcy, Mary, 444
D'Entremont, James, 540
D'Lugoff, Art, 401
**D-Man in the Waters**, 559
Da Cuica, Robertino, 385
Da Dona Geralda, Marquinho, 385
Dabney, Sheila, 477
Dace, Tish, 558
Dadoub, Jack, 521
Dafein, Richard, 456
Dahl, Marie, 456
Daily, Dan, 379
Daines, John, 458
Dainton, Scott, 514
Dakin, Kymberly, 458, 520
**Dakota Cowboy**, *455*
Dal Maso, Donald, 384
Dale, James E., 393
Dale, Jim, 12, 406, 443
Dale, Patt, 393
Daley, Donna, 511
Daley, Joseph, 430
Daley, Margery, 382
Dalia Studios, viii

Dallas, Walter, 425
Dalrymple, Jean, 554, 560
Daly, Joseph, 365
Daly, Peter-Hugo, 382
Daly, Tyne, 44, 51, 62, 377, 378, 556, 558, 559, 560
**Damaging Effects of Love, The,** *468*
Damas, Bertila, 464
DaMata-Geiger, Darice, 508
Dana, Paige, 434
**Dance Lesson, A,** *525*
Dance Theater Workshop, 475
Dancenoise, 462, 477, 559
Danek, Michael, 436
Dang, Timothy, 518
**Dangerous Games,** 4, 40, 41, *365, 366,* 556
Daniele, Graciela, 40, 41, 365, 366, 415, 556
Danielle, Marlene, 433
Danielle, Susan, 435
Daniels, Danny, 395
Daniels, Dennis, 437
Daniels, Duane, 535
Daniels, J.D., 478
Daniels, Kaipo, 397
Daniels, Paul S., 413, 467
Daniels, Zellie, 455
Danilova, Alexandra, 559
Danilow, Marji, 384
Danner, Braden, 443
Dansicker, Michael, 473, 473
Danson, Randy, 461, 520
Dante, Nicholas, 359
Dantos, Nick, 517
Dardenne, James, 508
**Daring Bride, A,** *526*
Darlow, Cynthia, 392, 445
Daruj, Eli, 460
Darwall, Barbara, 419
Daseler, Robert, 512
Datcher, Irene, 524
David Rothenberg Associates, 429
David, Keith, 403, 463
David, Peter, 380
Davidge, Donna, 468
Davidson, Gordon, 389, 519, 555, 560
Davidson, Jack, 530
Davies, Andrew, 417
Davies, Fred, 367
Davies, Howard, 6, 47, 57, 386
Davies, Joseph C., 470
Davies, Molly, 460

Davis, Al, 514
Davis, Brandon, 531
Davis, Bruce Anthony, 436
Davis, Christopher, 527
Davis, Fiona, 364
Davis, Hal, 384
Davis, Helene, 401, 417
Davis, Jeff, 391, 522, 539
Davis, John Henry, 429, 525
Davis, Keith, 367
Davis, Ken, 431
Davis, Kevin, 478
Davis, Lindsay W., 392, 406, 420, 522
Davis, Lloyd Jr., 425
Davis, Luther, 36, 43, 374, 556
Davis, Matthew, 455
Davis, Nathan, 386
Davis, Peter, 479, 505
Davis, Reid, 474
Davis, Vicki R., 431
Davison, Bruce, 439
Dawne, 474
Dawson, David, 478
Dawson, Lori A., 472
**Day of the Dogstar,** *456*
Day, Connie, 390, 391
**Daylight in Exile,** *540*
**Daytrips,** *519*
De Alabama, Cesar, 385
De Bonis, Marcia, 478
De Cao, Pe, 385
De Feis, Frederic, 514
De Jesus, Emanuel, 504
De La Cruz, Martha, 504
De Neve, Branca, 385
De Oliviera, Delma, 385
De Oni, Christofer, 464, 467
De Rose, Hart, 513
De Shae, Ed, 424
De Silva, William, 412
De Zarn, Teresa, 372
de Beer, Gerrit, 374, 375
de Fazio, John, 459
de la Barca, Calderon, 475
de la Chaume, Jacqueline, 401
de Lavallade, Carmen, 463
de Musset, Alfred, 459
de Soto, Edouard, 467
Deacon, Linda, 367
**Deadlock,** *468*
**Deadly Aim of the Straight and True, The,** *464*
Deakins, Mark, 386
Deal, Dennis, 478
Dean, Allison, 414

Dean, Jeffrey W., 537
Dean, Loren, 538
Dean, Robertson, 378
DeAngola, Heron, 385
Dear, Nick, 17, 417
Dearing, Judy, 411, 415, 424, 464
Dearman, Carol, 475
Deasy, Maria, 421
**Death and the Blacksmith,** *535*
**Death and the Maiden,** *458*
**Death of a Salesman,** 15, 53, *401*
DeBaer, Jean, 439
DeBellis, Robert, 410
DeBonis, Marcia, 474
Debroux, Dominique, 479
Debuskey, Merle, 363, 365, 379, 402, 421
DeCamp, Allen, 517
DeCamp, Kyle, 479
DeCaro, Matt, 439
DeCastro, Travis, 368
DeCeunynk, Robert, 384
DeCiutiis, Mario, 367
Decker, Michael, 468
Dedrickson, Tracy, 430
Deegan, John Michael, 378
Deeley, Susan, 528
**Deep to Center,** *473*
Deer, Sandra, 504
Defranco, Michelle, 479
DeGonge, Marcy, 433
Deitch, Belle M., 373
Del Gatto, Paul, 390
Del Rio, Philip, 479
Del Rossi, Angelo, 522
Delano, Lee, 369, 401
DeLaurier, Peter, 521
Deleo, Carmine, 367
Delgado, Miguel, 535
Delinger, Larry, 537
Dell'Arte Players Company, 504
Dellaporte, Dominic, 479
Delling, Thomas, 457
DeLorenzo, Michael, 519, 560
DeLorenzo, Victor, 523
Delsener, Ron, 361
Delsini, Ron, 373
DeMare, Anne, 478
DeMarse, James, 468, 478
DeMatthews, Ralph, 479
DeMattis, Ray, 364
Dempsey, Jerome, 47, 386

Dempsey, Mark, 479
Dempster, Curt, 458
Dene, Davina, 535
Denier, Andrew, 384
Denisov, Viktor, 383
Denkla, Connie Phillips, 513
Denmark, Ira, 393
Dennett, Drew, 427
Denney, Nora, 517
Dennis, Rick, 467
Dennis, Robert, 359, 392
Dennis, Ronald, 436
Denver Center Theater
    Company, 513
Denys, Gary, viii
DePaolo, Vince, 474
Depenbrock, Jay, 509
**Der Ring Gott Farblonjet,**
    449, *469*
Derbeneva, Tatiana, 383
Derecki, Noel, 472
DeRose, Teresa, 367
Derrah, Jay, 513
Derricks, Cleavant, 410
Derwent Awards, 559
DeSantis, Nick, 509
DeSantis, Paul, 528
Descarfino, Charles, 380
DeSeignora, John, 529
DeSilva, Sonya, 474
Desmond, Dan, 445
**Desolation Row,** *456*
Deutsch, Kurt, 414, 427
Deutsch, Nicholas, 474
**Devil and All His Works,**
    **The,** *520*
**Devil and Billy Markham,**
    **The,** 29, *421*
**Devil and Jerry Falwell, The,**
    *513*
Devin, Richard, 537
Devine, Brigitte, 416
Devine, Erick, 369
Devine, Jillana, 420
Devine, Michael, 560
DeVries, Jon, 403
DeVries, Michael, 375
Dewar, John, 387, 388
Dewhurst, Colleen, 53, 369,
    405, 559
DeWitt, Tim, 533, 534
Dewitt, Marylee, 367
Dexter, John, 6, 49, 372
Di Rocco, Joseph, 474
Diamond, Dennis, 365
Diamond, J. Lois, 471

Diamond, Liz, 449, 463, 464,
    474, 558
Diaquino, John, 535
Diaz, Bonnie, 467
Diaz, Natascia, 530
Dibuono, Tony, 408
Dick, Paul, 477
Dickens, Charles, 20
Dickey, Dale, 382
Dickherber, Judy, 534
Dickinson, Sherrylee, 426
**Did She Fall, or Was She**
    **Pushed?,** *456*
Diehl, Crandall, 413
Diekmann, Nancy Kassak, 422,
    466
Dierlam, Katy, 477
Dierson, Mary, 429
**Diesel Moon,** *508*
Dietrich, John, 367
Dignan, Pat, 461, 466
DiLauro, Stephen, 470
**Dilbert Dingle-Dong (The**
    **Doomed), or a Nest Full**
    **of Ninnies,** *460*
Dillahunty, Roger, 460
Dillard, Bill, 430
Dillon, John, 523
Dillon, Mia, 415
Dimaggio, John, 405, 478
Dimmick, Kathleen, 475
Dionne, Margot, 390
DiPaolo, Elvira J., 530
Director's Company, The, 475
DiRenzo, Denise, 437
Dishy, Bob, 379
Disla, Reynaldo, 465
**Diva Den,** *460*
**Dividends,** *476*
**Dividing Line, The,** *540*
**Division: The Strange Case**
    **of Dr. Jekyll and Mr.**
    **Hyde Retold,** *469*
Dixon Place, 560
Dixon, Beth, 519, 520
Dixon, Ed, 443
Dixon, Jerry, 415
Dixon, MacIntyre, 372, 404
Dizen, Alex, 443
Djinoria, Mourman, 427
Dmitriev, Alex, 539
Dnlovu, Duma, 524
**Do the White Thing,** *508*
Doba, Wayne, 536
Dobama Theater, 511
Dobell, Curzon, 522

**Doctor's Dilemma, The,** 11,
    *420, 421*
Dodd, Jonathan, vii
Dodds, William, 364
Dodge, Marcia Milgrom, 419,
    466
Dodger Productions, 392, 555
Doe, Andrew, 536
Doerr, James, 529
**Does Anybody Know What**
    **I'm Talking About?,** *369*
Doherty, Paul, 478
Dolan, Michael, 376
Dold, Mark, 459
Dolgoy, Sholem, 393
Dolidze, Tatuli, 427
**Dolls,** *466*
Dolph, Greg, 509
Domenech, Angel, 466
Domingo, Placido, 3
Dominic, Zoe, viii
Dommermuth, Paul, 479
**Don't Let This Dream Go,**
    390, *540*
**Don't Touch That Dial,** *478*
Don, Carl, 379
Donaghy, Tom, 461, 474
Donaldson, Rob, 470
Dondlinger, Mary Jo, 363, 364,
    421, 473
Donley, Robert, 421
Donnalley, Robert G. Jr., 428
Donnelly, Candice, 365
Donnelly, Harry, 394
Donnelly, Kyle, 520
Donovan, Gita, 473, 474
Donovan, Maripat, 506
Dooley, Dennis, 478, 479
Dopulos, Vincent, 420
Dorfman, Robert, 414
Dorfman, Rodrigo, 535
Dorfmunder, Dieter, 396
**Dorian Gray,** *474*
Doris, Susanne, 367
Dorsey, Don, 368
Dorsey, Fern, 474
Doscher, Joe, 528
**Dose Center,** *470*
Dossett, John, 365, 392, 416,
    417
**Dottie & The Boys,** *536*
Doty, Cynthia, 364
Doty, Pat, 523
**Double Blessing,** *476*
**Double Solitaire,** *529*
Doubleday, Kay, 513

Dougherty, J.P., 410, 473
Douglas, Andrew, 470
Douglas, Illeana, 524
Douglas, Justice William O., 29
Douglas, Suzzanne, 372
Doulin, Jack, 412
Dow, Ivy, 527
Dowaliby, Suzanne, 527
Dowd, Ann, 476
Dowling, Sam, 478
**Down the Road,** *518*
Downer, Herb, 382
Downey, Roma, 48, 378
Downing, David, 504
Downs, Michael E., 411
Doxsee, Lenore, 461
Doyle, Julie, 461
Doyle, Richard, 512
**Dr. Capulet Speaks,** *529*
**Dr. Jekyll and Mr. Hyde,** *469*
**Dragon's Nest,** *459*
Drake, Alfred, 556
Drake, Donald C., 530
Drake, Donna, 436
Drake, Stuart, 458
Drama Desk Awards, 558
Dramathon '89, 468
Dramatists Guild, 14, 56, 61, 554, 558
Draper, Erin, 533
**Dreamhouse,** *463*
**Dreams of Clytemnestra, The,** *476*
Dreisbach, Bill, 402, 421
Dreisbach, Jeffrey, 376
Dreisel, Bert, 478
Dressler, Ralph, 520
Drew, John, 48
Drewes, Glenn, 380
**Drinking in America,** 29
Driver, John, 474
**Drivers,** *524*
**Driving Miss Daisy,** 399, 439, 560
Drobny, Christopher, 467
**Dropper, The,** *533*
Drummond, David, 537
Drury, Chuck, 508
Druzhkin, Andrey, 383
Du Clos, Danielle, 387
Du Clos, Deanna, 387, 476
Duarte, Myrna, 470
Dubin, Allison, 461
DuBoff, Rochelle, 475
Duckworth, Stuart, 463, 464

Dudley, Terry, 475
Dudley, William, 386
Dudwitt, Kimberly, 392
Dudzick, Tom, 525
Duer, Fred, 535
Duff-Griffin, William, 520
Duggan, Charles H., 427
Dukakis, Olympia, 53, 523
Duke, O.L., 423, 424
Duke, Stuart, 473
Dukes, David, 369, 443
Dulack, Tom, 456, 534
Dulaine, Pierre, 36, 374
Dumakude, Thuli, 422, 524
Dumas, Alexandre, 452, 457, 534
Dumas, Debra, 422, 459, 463, 467
DuMont, James, 479
Dun, Dennis, 467
Duncan, Danny, 528
Duncan-Gibbs, Mamie, 365
**Dunelawn,** *417*, *419*
Dunfee, Nora, 457
Dunford, Christine, 445
Dunlap, Richard, 539
Dunn, Christopher, 516, 517
Dunn, Tom, 479
Dunn, Wally, 463, 474
Dunnam, William, 535
Duplechain, Deanna, 503
Dupree, Tom, 532
DuPré, Lynette G., 42, 390, 540
Duquesnay, Ann, 411
Durall, Anne, 523
Duran, Michael, 395
Durang, Christopher, 401, 402, 414, 474
Durant, John, 478, 479
**Durante,** *393*
Durante, Jimmy, 393, 394
Durante, Mrs. Margie, 393
Durfee, Duke, 372
Durham, Christopher, 522
Durling, Roger, 470
Durning, Charles, 6, 47, 61, 386, 556, 559
Durst, Anita, 457
Dussault, Nancy, 440
Dutton, Charles S., 21, 389, 556, 560
Dwyer, Frank, 362
Dwyer, Joyce, 367
Dyer, Chris, 383

**Dylan Thomas: Return Journey,** *458*
Dylan, Abby, 479
Dys, Deanna, 370
Dyson, Erika, 424
Dzneladze, Ghia, 427

**Each Day Dies With Sleep,** 11, 25, *416*, *417*, *504*
Earl, Courtney, 395
Earle, Dorothy R., 408
**Earth and Sky,** *540*
**Earth, The,** *528*
East West Players, 518
**Easter Extravaganza,** 4, *366*, *368*
Eastman, Donald, 457, 470
Ebb, Fred, 59, 523, 531
Eberhardt, Isabelle, 452
Ebhardt, Serena, 524
Ebright, Lisa, viii
**Ecce Homo,** *459*
Eck, Scott Hayward, 419
Eckhardt, Sarah, 474
**Eclipse, The,** *458*, *520*
eda-Young, Barbara, 510
Edegran, Lars, 43, 430
Edelberg, Alicia, 384
Edelen, Tere, 513
Edelman, Gregg, 34, 379, 432, 433, 474, 556
Edelson, Stuart, 456
Edelstein, Gordon, 472, 525
Edelstein, Lisa, 459
Edenfield, Dennis, 436
Edgar, David, 20
Edgerton, Earle, 477
Edmead, Wendy, 433
Eduardo, Evelyn, 385
**Education of Paul Bunyan, The,** *534*
Edwards, Ben, 376
Edwards, Burt, 439
Edwards, Daryl, 474
Edwards, Gus, 30, 423
Edwards, Maurice, 478
Edwards, Michael, 536
Edwards, Sarah, 381
Edwards, Stephen, 364
Efremoff, Andrei, 528, 530
Egan, Kate, 477
Egan, Michael, 476
Egan, Peter, 443
Egi, Stan, 467
Egloff, Elizabeth, 520
Eglsaer, Ruth, 523

Ehman, Don, 460
Ehrenberg, Steven, 374, 422
Ehrenreich, Jake, 411
Ehrlich, Jon, 529
Eich, Stephen B., 386
Eichelberger, Ethyl, 372, 460, 472, 477
Eigeman, Chris, 520
Eigenberg, David, 414
Eighty-Eight's, 475
Eigsti, Karl, 530
Einhorn, Susan, 427
Eisenberg, Ned, 472
Eisenhauer, Peggy, 366
Eisner, John, 478
Eisner, Katherine, 384
El Coronel No Tiene Quien le Escriba (No One Writes to the Colonel), 466
El Dorado, 512
El Gran Crico eu Craniano (The Great U.S. Kranial Circus), 466
El Paso, o Parabola del Camino (El Paso, or Parable of the Path), 466
El-Hajjar, Nabil, 475
Elbert, Wayne, 424
Elder, Suzanne, 531
Eldest Son, Oldest Enemy, 456
Eldon, Thomas, 414
Eleanor, 530
Elevator, 468
Elfenbaum, Adrian, 536
Elich, Michael, 539
Eliot, Drew, 475
Eliot, Jane, 457
Eliot, T. S., 359
Elizabeth Hull-Kate Warriner Award, 61, 558
Elledge, David, 374
Ellens, Rebecca, 521
Ellenwood, Kelly, 507
Elliot Finkel Orchestra, 401
Elliot Norton Award, 560
Elliot, Milton, 524
Elliott, Kenneth, 405, 409
Elliott, Milton, 474
Elliott, Scott, 505
Elliott, Shawn, 379
Ellis, Jerry, 513
Ellis, Joshua, 362, 364, 369, 370, 383, 390, 392, 397, 406, 420, 427

Ellis, Leslie, 429
Ellis, Scott, 523
Ellisen, Eric, 426
Ellison, Nancy, 372
Ellison, William, 362
Ellman, Bruce, 539
Elovich, Richard, 463
Elverman, Bill, 456
Elvgren, Gillette, 530
Emanuel, Carol, 403
Emerson, Ben, 504
Emerson, Lynda L. Salsbury, 531
Emery, Kenneth, 367
Emery, Lisa, 445
Emery, Phyllis, 539
Emmes, David, 511
Emmet, Robert, 464
Emmitt, Joan, 513
Emmons, Beverly, 386, 411, 419, 457
Emonts, Ann, 416
Emperor's Nightingale, The, 524
Empty Places, 474
En Garde Arts, 450, 457, 558
En Yu Tan, Victor, 520, 524
End of Summer, 456
End of the Day, The, 538
Engan, Elisabeth, 382
Engel, David, 431
Engler, Michael, 15, 365, 538
English, Donna, 433
English, Ellia, 473
English, Gary, 522
Englund, Lois, 435
Eno, Terry, 373
Ensemble Studio Theater, 450, 457
Ensemble Theater of Cincinnati, 509
EPI Products, 369, 556
Epstein, Alvin, 372
Epstein, Martin, 537
Equity Library Theater, 475
Erbe, Kathryn, 386, 387
Erdman, Jean, 466
Ergener, Sibel, 478
Erickson, Michael, 458
Erickson, Mitchell, 378, 387
Ericson, Russ, 479
Erlanger, John, 528
Ernotte, Andre, 472, 514
Ernster, Sharon, 417, 479
Erté, 368
Erwin, Barbara, 377

Esaki, Katsuko, 367
Esbjornson, David, 510
Escape in You, 468
Escovao, Edson, 385
Eskew, Doug, 42, 390, 540
Esposito, Vickie, 405, 528, 529
Essence of Margovia, The, 458
Established Price, 526
Estabrook, Christine, 419, 469
Esterman, Laura, 506
Estey, SuEllen, 363
Ethan, Mark, 476
Ettinger, Cynthia, 408
Eugene O'Neill Theater Center, 389, 540, 555
Euling, Philip, 509
Eulogy for Mister Hamm, 450, 458
Eureka Theater Company, 497, 536
Eureka, 469
Euripides, 470, 473
Evangelista, Jose, 456
Evans, Albert, 522
Evans, Annie, 540
Evans, Ashleigh, 527
Evans, Brent, 525
Evans, Catherine, 506
Evans, Craig, 420, 472, 473
Evans, Frank, 522
Evans, Gary, 431
Evans, Joan, 460
Evans, Kathryn, 433
Evans, Mari, 474
Evans, Scott, 463
Evans-Kandel, Karen, 461, 538, 558
Eve, Sean, 464
Everhart, Rex, 433
Evering, Valerie, 479
Evers, Bruce, 503
Every Goodbye Ain't Gone, 474
Everybody Knows Your Name, 478
Everything That Rises Must Converge, 452, 476
Evett, Benjamin, 474
Ewen, Malcolm, 387
Ewing, Mac, 479
Experiment at the Asylum, 431
Eye to Eye, 455
Ezell, John, 517, 536

**F.O.B.**, *467*
Faber, Ron, 469, 472
Fabrique, Tina, 390
**Fabulous LaFontaine, The,**
*478*
Fader, Laurence, 384
Fairbanks, Margaret, 523
Faison, Donald (Shun), 479
**Faith Journey,** *474*
Faith, Chrissy, 380
Faith, Percy, 368
Falabella, John, 421
Falco, Ed, 533
**Fall of the House of Usher,**
The, *477*
**Fall of the Wall Review, The,**
*460*
Fallender, Deborah, 519
Fallon, Dan, 530
Falls, Robert, 506, 507
**Falsettoland**, 413
Fanning, Tony, 526
**Fanny Hackabout Jones,** 59
**Fantasma,** *466*
**Fantasticks, The,** 399
Farley, Robert J., 503
Farmer, Bill, 527
Farr, Christiane, 367
Farrell, Christine, 511
Farrell, Tom, 474
Farrell, William H., 393
Farwell, Elisabeth, 388
Fassell, Noah, 531
**Fat,** *527*
Fata, Wesley, 455, 541
Faul, Kathy J., 406, 421
Faulkner, Cliff, 511, 512, 534,
560
Faver, Cheryl, 531
Favre, Beverly Jean, 455
Fay, Suzy, 531
Fay, Tom, 409
Fay, Vince, 373
Feagan, Leslie, 522
**Fear of Standing Upright,**
560
Fearnley, John, 455
**Feast Here Tonight,** *472*
**Feast of Fools,** 11, *427*
**Feature Film,** *470*
Feiffer, Jules, 359, 507, 528
Feiffer, Steve, 507
Feigin, Andy, 368
Fein, Paul, 384
Feinberg, Linda, 417, 431

Feingold, Michael, 49, 372,
452, 457, 459, 552, 557
Feist, Gene, 406, 420
Feke, Gilbert David, 414
Feldman, Dave, 559
Feldman, Douglas L., 426
Feldman, Jack, 361
Feldman, Lawrence, 373, 388
Feldshuh, David, 504
Feldshuh, Tovah, 441
Felizola, Rolando, 466
Feller Precision, 377
**Fellow Travelers,** *461*
**Fences,** 21, 22, 62
Fenley, Molissa, 559
Fenster, Bob, 528
Fenton, James, 360
Ferencz, George, 535
Ferguson, Lynnda, 445
Ferguson, Mark, 362
Fergusson, Honora, 412, 461
Ferland, Danielle, 440
Ferlita, Ernest, 473
Fernandez, Oleka, 465
Fernandez, Peter Jay, 404
Fernandez, Roberto, 463
Ferra, Max, 459
Ferrante, Evan, 429
Ferrari, Marianne, 525
Ferraro, John, 459, 467
Ferreira-Contessa, Maria, 467
Ferrer, Jose, 539
Ferrer, Rafael, 509
Ferrone, Siro, 459
**Fertilization Opera, The,** *461*
Fervoy, Tom, 479
Fessler, Chris, viii
**Fester and Rot Raw Review,**
The, *460*
Festival Latino in New York,
465
Fetheroff, Andrew, 470
**Few Good Men, A,** ix, 4, 6,
23, 55, *376*, 553, 556, 558,
559, 560
Fichandler, Zelda, 540, 559
Fickinger, Steve, 479
Field, Arabella, 477
Field, Barbara, 534
Field, Crystal, 469, 470
Fields, Christopher, 520
Fields, Joseph, 475
Fields, Michael, 504, 505
**Fierce Attachment, A,** *537*
Fife, Michael R., 474

Fifth Avenue
Productions/Margo Lion
Ltd., 395
Filho, Betho, 385
Filiaci, Larry, 473
**Film Society, The,** 559
Finch, John, 470, 474, 478
Findlay, Dudley Jr., 475
Findley, Danielle, 395
**Fine and Private Place, A,**
*514*
Fineman, Carol, 368, 403, 408
Fineman, Karen, 443
Fingerhut, Arden, 461, 519
Fink, Dave, 380
Finkel, Barry, 539
Finkel, Elliot, 369
Finkel, Fyvush, 476
Finkel, Ian, 401
Finlay, Melodee, 393
Finley, David, 470
Finley, Karen, 460, 476
Finn, William, 40, 365, 407,
413
**Finnegan's Funeral Parlor**
**and Ice Cream Shoppe,**
*413, 414*
Fire, Richard, 508
First Annual All-American
Juggle-In, 477
First Durante Tour Company,
393
**First Time, The,** *479*
**Fish Story: An American**
**Soap Opera, A,** *469*
Fishburne, Larry, 526
Fisher, David, 531
Fisher, Jules, 8, 35, 44, 365,
375, 404, 556, 558, 559
Fisher, Linda, 511
Fisher, Rick, 379, 422
Fisher, Robert, 372
Fitzgerald, B.G., 537
Fitzgerald, Ed, 419
Fitzgerald, Patrick, 475
Fitzgerald, Peter J., 390
Fitzgerald, Peter, 372, 377,
380, 390, 430
Fitzgerald, Sarah, 506
Fitzgerald, T. Richard, 386
Fitzmorris, Brian, 515
Fitzpatrick, Allen, 429, 475
Fitzpatrick, Colleen, 473
FitzSimmons, James, 414, 429
**Five Scenes From Life,** *518*
**Five Slices of Steele,** *469*

Five Stone Wind, 559
Flack, Roberta, 3
Flagg, Tom, 509
Flaherty, Stephen, 41, 42, 413, 560
Flahive, Dan, 516, 517
Flake, Gary, 460
Flaningam, Louisa, 473, 514
Flatt, Ernest O., 393
Flax, Laura, 384
Fleckenstein, Paul, 367
Fleischer, Leonard, 554
Fleming, Cynthia, 434, 435
Fleming, Eugene, 436
Fleming, Jawn, 523
Fleming, John, 459
Fletcher, James, 523
Fletcher, Julia, 537
Fletcher, Susann, 441
Flockhart, Calista, 416, 478
Flomenhaft, Zivia, 463
Flood, Jonathan, 518
Floor Above the Roof, 479
Floor, Callie, 536
Flora, Becky, 378, 380, 381
Flores, Renny, 385
Florida Crackers, 11, 24, 400
Florida Studio Theater, 537
Flowers, Kim, 400
Flowers, Reginald L., 464
Fluger, Martin, 431
Flynn, George, 380
FOB, 452
Foederer, Ernest, 384
Foeller, Bill, 526
Foglia, Leonard, 474
Fokin, Igor, 383
Foley, Ellen, 440, 443
Foley, John, 461
Folger Theater, 560
Folk Fool, 427
Folk, Alexander, 538
Follari, Gregorio, 384
Folta, Amy, 531
Folts, Barbara, 377
Fondacaro, Phil, 367
Fong, Frank, 527
Fontana, Franco, 384
Fonte, Henry, 537
Foose, Thomas T., viii, 48, 53
Foote, Horton, 536
Forbes, Barbara, 383, 458, 525, 539
Forbes, John B., 534, 535
Forbidden Broadway 1988, 399

Forbidden Broadway 1990, 11, 424
Ford's Theater, 540
Ford, Anne Kerry, 372, 525
Ford, Frances, 440
Ford, Lionel, 529
Ford, Paul, 362
Foreman, Richard, 452, 477, 479
Forest in Arden, A, 466
Forest, David, 522
Forest, Donald, 504
Forest, Kathryn, 522
Forever Plaid, 6, 11, 42, 43, 431, 479
Forgeries, 529
Forgette, Katie, 538, 539
Forgiving Typhoid Mary, 533
Forgy, Julia, 509
Forkush, Anthony, 511
Forman, Jay, 536
Forman, Milos, 3
Formiguinha, 385
Fornadel, Jeanne, 414, 420
Fornes, Maria Irene, 459
Forrest, Donald, 504
Forrest, George, 36, 374, 556
Forster, John, 530
Forsyth, Jerold R., 530
Forsythe, Henderson, 19, 61, 379, 422
Fortenberry, Philip, 424
Foskett, Mary, 470
Foss, Lukas, 3
Foster, Apryl R., 389
Foster, Frances, 425
Foster, Herb, 387
Foster, Jeff, 408
Foster, Jodie, 25
Foster, Meg, 516
Foster, Michael, 504
Fotopoulos, Mark, 434
Foundation of the Dramatists Guild, The, 413, 414, 559
Foundation, The, 470
Fowler, Beth, 51, 363, 556
Fowler, Clement, 404
Fox, Alan, 425
Fox, Bernard, 380
Fox, Robert, 555
Fox, Scott Hayward, 419
Fox, Terry, 460
Fox, Tony, 368
Foxman, Lynda, 507
Foxworth, Robert, 369

Foy, 459
Foy, Kenneth, 377
Fraboni, Angelo H., 441
Fracher, Drew, 509
Fram, Don, 514
Frampton, Todd William, 518
Francine, Anne, 433
Francis, Veronica, 478
Francks, Lili, 393
Frank Dell's Temptation of St. Anthony, 479
Frank, David, 505
Frank, Jonathan, 527
Frankel, Gene, 475
Frankel, Richard, 369, 405
Frankenstein, 453, 537
Frankie and Johnny in the Clair de Lune, 61
Frankie, 453, 473
Franklin, David S., 410
Franklin, Nancy, 458
Franklin, Roger, 467
Franks, Ronnie, 515
Franz and Dora, 455
Franz, Elizabeth, 30, 392
Fraser, Alison, 41, 408
Fratantoni, Diane, 437, 442, 446
Fratti, Mario, 470
Fraulein Dora, 527, 528
Frawley, Mark, 463
Frayn, Michael, 17
Frazier, Cliff, 464
Frazier, Kermit, 458, 540
Frazier, Michael, 430
Freaky Friday, 25
Frechette, Peter, 414
Frechtman, Bernard, 458
Fred Nathan Company, 383, 387, 388
Frederick Douglass Now, 460
Frederick, Rebecca G., 528
Fredericks, Vicki, 438
Frederico Restrepo's Puppets and Drummers, 459
Fredricks, Michael, 514
Freed, Donald, 525, 530
Freedman, Amy, 456
Freedman, Gerald, 48, 53, 421
Freedman, Glenna, 372, 374, 384, 424
Freedman, Michelle, 459
Freedman, Robert M., 367
Freeman, Aaron, 508
Freeman, Brian, 460
Freeman, Cheryl, 463, 464

Freeman, Henry, 477
Freeman, K. Todd, 401, 411, 504
Freeman, Kenneth, 409
Freeman, LeRoi, 367
Freeman, Morgan, 439
Freeman, Steven A., 410
**Freeze Tag**, *479*
Frei, Nick, 364
Freimanis, Nancy, 367
French, Arthur, 439
French, Martha, 474
French, Michael Bryan, 408, 467
French, Timothy, 393
Frenzer-Cornell, Michelle, 466
Friedman, Doug, 438
Friedman, Janet, 387
Friedman, Jill, 529
Friedman, Mark, 519
Friedman, Peter, 379, 440
Friedman, Richard, 508
Friedman, Steve, 463, 464
Friel, Brian, 400, 452
Frierson, Andrea, 415
Frimark, Merle, 388
Fringe Series, 449
**Fringes**, *463*
Frink, Laurie, 370
Fritz, Joanie, 477
Fritz, Lana, 416
Frkonja, Jeff, 537, 538, 539
Frommer, Laurence, 477
Froot, Dan, 459
**Frozen Dead, The**, *468*
Fruchter, Danny, 520
Fry, Ray, 520
Fry, Stephen, 360
Fryer, Anne, 384
Fuchs, Daniel, 541
Fugard, Athol, vii, 5, 22, 23, 30, 422, 450, 466, 560
Fugard, Lisa, 422
Fugeli, Kate, 464
**Fugitive Kind, The**, 45
Fuglei, Kate, 475, 505
Fuhrmann, Robert, 456, 530
Fuji, Peter, 460
**Full Moon**, *517*
Fuller, Charles, 20, 423, 424
Fuller, Elizabeth, 513
Fuller, Penny, 473
Fund for New American Plays, 559
Funicello, Ralph, 538

**Funny Thing Happened on the Way to the Forum, A**, 33
Furber, Douglas, 360
Furgal, Fabiana, 476
Furr, Teri, 377
**Further Mo'**, 6, 11, 42, *430*
Fusco, Anthony, 457, 528
**Future Tense**, *471*
Fyfe, Jim, 12, 378, 406
Fylan, Nicky, 393

Gabler, Linda, 410, 530
Gabriel, Ethel, 415
Gabriel, Susan, 392, 404
Gadbois, Hearn, 460
Gaffin, Arti, 372
Gaffney, Lauren, 384
Gaffney, Mo, 399
Gailen, Judy, 460
Gaines, Boyd, 440
Gaines, Davis, 444
Gaines, Sonny Jim, 524
**Gal Baby**, *504*
Gala Hispanic Theater, 560
Galante, Gerson, 385
Galantich, Tom, 379, 380
Galati, Frank, 5, 6, 19, 387, 555, 556, 559
Galde, Anthony, 373
Gale, Brian, 404
Galgano, Richard, 431
Galich, Alexander, 412
Galilee, Clove, 412, 461
**Galileo**, *505*
Galindo, Eileen, 467
Gallagher, Colleen, 364
Gallagher, Dick, 473
Gallagher, Kathryn, 506
Gallagher, Mary, 509
Gallagher, Megan, 23, 376, 558, 559
Gallagher, William T., 506
Gallardo, Edward, 466
**Gallery, The**, *529*
Gallin, Susan Quint, 429
Gallo, David K., 461
Gallo, Paul, 33, 380, 469, 507, 556, 558
Galloway, Terry, 462
Gamache, Laurie, 438
Gamage, Steven, 474
Gamble, Kirsten, 384
Gambling, John A., 553
Gandy, Irene, 378
Ganem, Mitch, 456

Ganly, Kilian, 473
Ganshaw, Robert, 426, 427, 430
Gant, Richard, 417
Garber, Victor, 441
Garboriau, Linda, 474
Garcia, Eliane, 385
Garcia, Manuel Pereiras, 530
Garcia, Marc, 455
Garcia, Santiago, 466
Gardall, Glen, 390
Gardner, Ashley, 516
Gardner, Melissa, 10
Gardner, Nancy Bruff, 455
Gardner, Rita, 439, 467
Gardner, Robert, 384
Gardner, William T., 530
Gardner, Worth, 509
Garland, Judy, 34
Garland, Patricia, 436
Garlin, Jeff, 506
Garlinghouse, Wanda, 513
Garner, Kenneth, 397
Garner, Patrick, 401, 464
Garnett, David, 387
Garnett, Richard, 382
Garrett, Betty, 34, 370
Garrett, Lillian, 535
Garrett, Melody, 533
Garrett, Shelly, 474
Garrett-Groag, Lillian, 535
Garrity, Paul, 470
Garside, Bradford P., 367
Gartner, Thia, 414
Garver, Kristin, 477
Garza, Michele, 518
Gaspard, Raymond L., 427
Gass, Kyle, 408
Gatchell, R. Tyler Jr., 395
Gattoni, Susan, 393
Gaviria, Aitor, 466
Gay, Noel, 360
Gaynor, Mitzi, 432
Gayr, Sheridan, 516
Gear, Amy, 367
Geddes, B. Alan, 393
Geddes, Jill, 440
Gee, Kevin John, 455
Geffner, Deborah, 434
Gehan, Nathan, 522
Gehman, Martha, 469
Geier, Paul, 479
Geiger, Mary Louise, 457, 463
Geissinger, Katie, 477
Gekker, Chris, 372
Gelb, Jody, 511

Gelbart, Larry, 15, 33, 364, 379, 552, 556, 558, 559
Gelber, Jack, 458
Geld, Gary, 362
Gelfand-Piper, viii
Gelinas, Gratien, 474
Gelke, Becky, 472
Gellar, Sarah Michelle, 397, 535
Gellert, Susan, 384
Gelman, Alexander, 529
Gelman, Susan, 535
Gemmill, Charles, 468
Gene Frankel Theater, 475
Genest, Edmond, 376
Genet, Jean, 452, 458
Genet, Michael, 376
Geneviere, Deborah, 367
Gennaro, Peter, 372, 463
Genovese, Mike, 534
Gentile, Melissa, 522
Gentles, Avril, 420
**Genuine Myth, 464**
Geoghan, Jim, 399
Geoly, Guy, 362
George Oppenheimer/ Newsday/New York Newsday Award 559
George S. Kaufman Award, 559
George Street Playhouse, 429, 525
George, Ben, 374
George, Bridget, 504
George, Grace, 48
George, Jeannette Clift, 516, 517
George, Phillip, 424
Georgianna, Frank, 513
Geraci, Drew, 439
Geraci, Frank, 477
Geraci, Leslie, 457
Geraci, Paul, 377
**Gerald's Good Idea, 464**
Gerard, Anne-Marie, 373, 374, 521
Gerard, Danny, 443
Gerber, Carol, 468
Gerber, Charles, 458, 461, 468, 469
Gerdes, George, 376
Germann, Greg, 477
Gerrity, Dan, 519
Gerroll, Daniel, 538
Gerry, Caroline, 470
Gershenson, Sue Anne, 429
Gershovsky, Yaron, 380

Gershwin, George, 477
Gershwin, Ira, 477
Gersten, Alexandra, 474
Gersten, Bernard, 379, 401, 421
Gerut, Rosalie, 420
Gervais, Michel, 393
Gesner, Clark, 514
**Getting Together, 468**
GeVa Theater, 533
Gevrekian, Robert III, 533
Geyer, Charles, 365
Ghaghanidze, Djemal, 427
Ghigliotto, Rebeca, 465
Ghiorgadze, Tengiz, 428
Ghoghitidze, Ivan, 427
**Ghostman, The, 526**
Ghosts, 46
Giagni, D. J., 395
Gianfrancesco, Edward T., 420, 472, 473
Gianola, Beto, 535
Gibb, David, 393
Gibbons, Tom, 529
Gibbs, Sheila, 415
Giberson, Philip D., 474
Gibler, John, 515
Gibson, Julia, 421
Gibson, Mary, 511
Gibson, Maureen F., 379, 404
Gibson, Michael, 367, 368, 370, 531
Gibson, Teri, 522
Gibson, Thomas, 404, 459
Gien, Pamela, 403, 512
**Gift, The, 506**
**Gifts of the Magi, 460**
Gigi, Aloysius, 466
Gilbert, Tony, 363
Gildea, Dennis, 529
**Gilded Six-Bits, The, 407, 411**
Gilden, Michael J., 367
Gill, David, 478
Gill, Jackie, 405
Gill, Michael, 419
Gill, Ray, 439, 440
Gillespie, Dizzy, 3
Gillette, Anita, 472
Gilliam, Gwendolyn M., 395
Gilliam, Michael, 519
Gilmer, Robert N., 527
Gilmore, Philip, 455
Gilrain, Jennie, 504
Gilroy, Frank D., 450, 458
Gimenez, Carlos, 466
Gimpel, Erica, 417

Gingold, Susan, 384
Gingrasso, Donald A., 466
Ginsberg, Jeff, 507
Ginzler, Robert, 377
Giombetti, Karen, 531
Giordano, Tony, 471, 476
Giosa, Sue, 534
Giovannetti, Tony, 459
**Girl in Pink, The, 456**
**Girl Talk, 478**
**Girl With the High Rouge, The, 530**
Girouard, Tina, 412
Giroux, Laurent, 395
Givens, Tricia, 533
Gladden, Dean R., 510
Glander, Julia, 464, 477
Glaser, John, 409
Glass, Ira, 506
Glass, Philip, 477
Glasser, Phillip, 443
Glave, Matthew, 509
Glaze, Susan, 472
Gleason, James, 479
Gleason, Joanna, 405, 440
Gleason, John, 416
Gleboya, Tatiana, 364
Glenmore, Ralph, 436
Glenn, David M., 540
Glenn, Gregory, 424
Glenn, Heather, 506
Glines, The, 475
Glines, John, 475
Glockner, Eleanor, 379
**Glory of Easter, 368**
Glossman, James, 524
Gloucester Stage Company, The, 516
Glover, Brian, 460
Glover, Frederic, 476
Gluckin, Lisa, 470
Glushak, Joanne, 505
**Go Down Garvey, 528**
Gobernik, Gregory, 364
Goch, Celeste, 474
**God's Policemen, 478**
**God's Trombones!, 464**
Godber, John, 458
Godwin, James, 460
Godwin, Stephen, 537
Goehring, Kate, 509
Goei, G.G., 443
Goetz, Michael, 379, 422
Goetz, Peter Michael, 519, 520
Goff, Charles, 514, 525
Goggans, Michael, 515

Goggin, Dan, 399
Gogol, *474*
Goichman, Yana, 384
**Going to New England**, *459*
Gold, Claudia, 478
Gold, Jeremy, 520
Goldbeck, Charles, 460
**Goldberg Street**, *458*
Goldberg, Alla, 384
Goldberg, Hal, 429
Goldberg, Norbert, 410, 415
Goldblum, Jeff, 52, 403
**Golden Apple, The**, *473*
Golden, David, 458
Golden, Joey L., 475
Golden, Suzanne, 392, 555
Goldenthal, Elliot, 422, 463
Goldfaden, Abraham, 476
Goldfarb, Sidney, 462, 471
Goldhirsch, Sheri M., 413
Goldstein, Jess, 401, 414, 415,
    419, 472
Goldstein, Steven, 29, 421
Goldstone, Patricia, 456
Golemon, Jane, 395
Goltzer, Doris, 384
Golub, Peter, 403, 460
Gomes, Rob, 471
Gomez, Chuck, 466
Gomez-Pena, Guillermo, 559
Goncalves, Monica, 385
**Gondoliers, The**, *477*
Gonzales, Laurence, 518
Gonzalez, Cordelia, 464
Gonzalez, Ernesto, 464
Gonzalez, Guillermo, 433
Gonzalez, Jose Cruz, 512, 535
Good Clean Fun, 461
**Good Coach, The**, *472*
**Good Times Are Killing Me,
    The**, *506*
Goodfriend-Koven, Diva, 388
Goodlow, Willis IV, 535
Goodman Theater, The, 389,
    502, 506, 555
Goodman, Hazelle, 475
Goodman, Mark, 401
Goodman, Robyn, 469
Goodspeed Opera House, 514
Goodspeed, Don, 387, 388
Goodstein, Gerry, viii
Goodwin, Douglas R., 513
Goodwin, Philip, 404, 516,
    560
Goodyear, Sam, 468

**Goose! Beyond the Nursery,
    463**
Goralnick, Jerry, 477
Gordean, Meg, 429
Gordina, Irina, 412
Gordon, Andrea, 536
Gordon, Carl, 21, 31, 61, 389
Gordon, Geoffrey, 422
Gordon, Michael-David, 470
Gordon, Peter, 380
Gordon, Stephanie, 464
**Goree**, *464*
Gorham, George H., 41, 390
Gorton, Rob, 425
Gorzelnick, Chris, 405
Goss, Peggy, 507
Gotanda, Philip Kan, 400
Gottfried, Martin, 59
Gottlieb, Jon, 516, 519, 535,
    560
Gottschall, Ruth, 373, 531
Gould, Christopher, 392, 555
Gould, Erica, 478, 479
Gould, Gordon, 382
Gould, Harold, 10, 378
Gow, Brian, 362
Goz, Harry, 531
Graae, Jason, 431, 474, 479
Grabowski, Christopher, 466
**Graceland**, *522*
Graconn Ltd., 427
Gradl, Christine, 514
Graff, Randy, 33, 379, 442,
    556, 559
Graham, Bruce, 528
Graham, Christopher, 531
Graham, Deborah, 409
Graham, Elain, 417
Graham, Hugh, 512
Graham, Rachel, 370
Graham, Ronny, 395, 525
Graham, Star, 527
Graham, Stephen, 395
Grammis, Adam, 435
**Grand Guignol, The**, 11, *431*
**Grand Hotel**, 4, 5, 6, 8, 35,
    36, 43, 44, 56, 62, 166-
    192, *374*, 552, 555, 556,
    558, 559
Graneto, Phillip A., 529
Granger, Phil, 362
Granger, Stewart, 48, 378, 559
Granite, Judith, 392, 479
Grant, Adam, 474
Grant, David Marshall, 427
Grant, Kathryn, 536

Grant, Sean, 373, 374
Grant, William H. III, 464, 524
**Grapes of Wrath, The**, ix, 4,
    5, 6, 8, 19, 31, 55, 62,
    293-312, *386*, 551, 552,
    553, 555, 556, 557, 558,
    559
Grassilli, John, 534
Grate, Gail, 519
Graudons, Sally, 455
Graves, Aaron, 390
Graves, Julie, 377
Graves, Kia, 384
Graves, Laurie, 470
Gray, Amlin, 465
Gray, David Barry, 414
Gray, Harold, 395
Gray, Kevin, 444, 531
Gray, Paula, 366
Gray, Prudence, 367
Gray, Rex, 527
Gray, Robin, 383
Gray, Roy, 530
Gray, Spalding, 477
Gray, Steve, 522
**Great American
    Bicentennial Electric
    Chair Salute, The**, *506*
**Greeks**, *463*
Green, Adolph, 475, 558
Green, Dennis, 463, 464, 524
Green, Fanni, 466
Green, Jackie, 362, 390, 392
Green, Jason, 463
Green, Jeffrey, 478
Green, Kara, 464
Green, Larry, 404, 524
Green, Mary-Pat, 395
Green, Miles, 528
Green, Raphy, 507
Green, Stanley, viii, 432
Green, Vivian, 529
Greenan, Sean, 505
Greenberg, Dan, 359
Greenberg, Elizabeth, 429
Greenberg, Helen, 476
Greenberg, May, 534
Greenberg, Mitchell, 372
Greenblatt, Kenneth D., 374,
    556
Greenblatt, Sandra, 375
Greenburg, Dan, 468
Greene, Ellen, 473
Greene, Jessica, 527
Greene, Ron, 507
Greenfield, Daniel, 538

Greenfield, Steve, 409
Greenspan, David, 408, 452, 467, 475
Greenstein, Ann M., 509
Greenwald, Ray, 420
Greenwood, Jane, 368, 378, 379, 401, 419, 421
Greer, Michael, 524
**Greetings!**, *525*
Gregg, Clark, 376
Gregg, Jacqueline, 405, 478
Gregg, Susan, 534
Gregorie, Alan, 469
Gregory, Allison, 513
Gregory, Andre, 445
Gregory, Dawna, 523
Gregory, Helen, 466
Gregory, Michael Scott, 433, 434
Gregory, Sam, 536
Gregory, Scott, 517
Gregus, Lubitza, 369
Gregus, Peter, 367
Grenier, Zach, 365, 464
Grey, Jane, 381
**Grey-Dog Speaks Out**, *456*
Grice, Brian, 390
Griesemer, John, 408, 467
Griffin, Barry, 528
Griffin, Brian, 508, 509
Griffin, Jennifer, 362
Griffin, Sean G., 511
Griffith, Kristin, 463, 469
Griffith, Michael, 469
Griffo, Michael, 475
Grimaldi, Dennis, 378
Grimes, Kenneth, 512
Grimes, Tammy, 46, 364
Grimm, Timothy, 472
Grissom, Doug, 533
Griswold, Tracy, 423
Grody, Kathryn, 27, 407
Groenendaal, Cris, 444
Groener, Harry, 434
Groff, Nancy, 455
Gromada, John, 376, 415, 419, 429
Gromov, Leonid, 383
Gronk, 518
Grosbard, Ulu, 48, 379
Grose, Andrew, 437
Gross, Amy, 386
Grossman, Henry, 374
Grossman, Larry, 368
Grossman, Michael, 535
Grotke, Diane, 459

**Ground People**, 11, 30, *424, 425*, 559
Grove, Barry, 400, 417, 461
Groves, Robin, 30, 426, 461
Gruber, Michael, 435
Grubman, Patty, 374, 556
Gruditis, Mary Scott, 509
Gruhn, Esther, 384
Grullon, Kenny, 465
Grunfeld, Deborah, 390
**Grunions**, *461*
Grunn, Anibal, 466
Grupper, Adam, 440, 474
Guan, Jamie H.J., 467
Guanci, Denice, 424
Guaraldi, Mary G., 518
Guarino, Jan, 533
Guberman, Lynn, 478
Guerard, Margaux, 459
Guerin, Lyse, 444
Guernsey, Otis L. Jr., ix, 8
Guerra, Pipito, 465
Guest, Lance, 474
Guest, Robyn Dana, 466
Guevara, Dedre, 479
Guevara, Steve, 464
Guibert, Iliana, 466
Guidery, Wendy, 516
Guido, Michael, 508
Guillaume, Robert, 444
Guinan, Francis, 386
Guittard, Laurence, 52, 384
Guledani, Pridon, 428
**Gulliver**, *540*
Gunderman, David, 370, 390, 391
Gungi, Maya, 367, 372
Gunn, Moses, 53
**Gunplays**, *513*
Gunton, Bob, 44, 51, 363, 556
Guralnick, Judi, 529
Gurganus, Allan, 533
Gurney, A.R., 5, 6, 9, 369, 399, 405
Guskin, Harold, 403
Gussow, Mel, viii, 59, 449, 551
Guthrie, Lee, 506
Gutierrez, Gerald, 414
Gutmacher, Benito, 460
Guttmacher, Peter, 464, 479
Guy, Rosa, 413
Guzman, Alberto, 397
Gwaltney, Jack, 478
Gwin, Kelly, 510

**Gypsy**, 4, 6, 44, 51, 56, 62, *376, 378*, 553, 556, 558, 559, 560

Haagenbuch, Bonnie, 478
Haagensen, Erik, 514
Haas, Karl E., 414
**Habit of Lying, The**, *512*
Hackady, Hal, 368, 522
Hadary, Jonathan, 44, 51, 377, 556
Haddad, Ava, 472
Hadley, Jennifer, 27, 416, 477, 523
Hadley, Jonathan, 441
Hadley, Michael, 27, 416, 477, 523
Haege, Jeana, 377
Hagen, Daniel, 461
Hager, Mary, 507
Hagg, Bernd, 459
Hahn, Fredrick, 458
Hahn, Jessica, 508
Haigh, Jacqueline, 393
Haimes, Todd, 406, 420
Haines, Leslie, 508
Haining, Alice, 463, 477
Haley, Donna, 426
**Hall of Fame**, *469*
Hall, Adrian, 6
Hall, Carl, 42, 390, 540
Hall, Carrie, 456
Hall, Charles Edward, 367
Hall, Davis, 534
Hall, George, 421
Hall, John, 530
Hall, Margaret, 387
Hall, Margo, 540
Hall, Peter, 6, 31, 45, 47, 53, 54, 364, 382, 383, 556
Hall, Phil, 522
Hallahan, Charles, 512
Hallas, Brian, 459, 523
**Hallelujah in a Hard Time**, *518*
**Halley's Comet**, *474, 539*
Halliday, Andy, 405
Halliday, Lynne, 429
Halligan, Tim, 477
Halpern, Martin, 539
Halpern, Mortimer, 362
Halpern, Pam Kelleher, 367
Halstead, Cara, 539
Halston, Julie, 405
Halverson, Richard, 523
Hambel, Gerry, 456

Hamburger, Anne, 450, 457
Hamburger, Richard, 531
Hamel, Veronica, 445
Hamer, Nigel, 362
Hamilton, Lauren, 475
Hamilton, Lisa Gay, 389, 403
Hamilton, Mark, 405
Hamilton, Miriam, 504
Hamilton, Mitzi, 435
Hamilton, Stephen, 426
Hamilton, Trip, 401
**Hamlet**, 11, 31, 53, *403*, *404*, *405*, 450, *458*
Hamlin, Jeff, 402
Hamlisch, Marvin, 359
Hammer, Mark, 404, 464
Hammerstein, Jaime, 464
Hammerstein, James, 52, 384
Hammerstein, Oscar II, 52, 383, 397
Hammond, Wendy, 526
Hampton, Donald, 478
Hampton, Elin, 537
Hampton, Verna, 475
Hanami, Ren, 518
Hanan, Stephen, 433, 535
Hanayagi, Yoshijiro, 367
Hancock-Rux, Carl, 474
Hand, John, 387
Handler, Evan, 479, 538
Handman, Wynn, 424, 425, 455
Handy, John, 376
Haney, Kevin, 28, 559
Haney, Michael, 524
Haney, Theresa, 460
Hanger, Noel, 531
**Hanging by a Pinstripe**, *466*
Hanket, Arthur, 410, 461, 472, 475
Hankins, Michael, 509
Hanley, Mickey, 535
Hanlon, Maura, 473
**Hannah ... 1939**, *472*
Hannah, Ned, 377
Hannibal, Ellie, 457
Hanpeter, Carol, 537
**Hansel and Gretel**, *534*
Hansen, Jenny, 388
Hansen, Thom, 473
Hanson, Cynthia, 523
Hanson, Kenneth, 390
Hanson, Luther, 535
Hanson, Moon Hi, 509
Hanway, Tom, 472
**Happy Father's Day**, *512*

Haproff, Stephen, 479
Harada, Ann, 522
Harada, Deborah, 397
Harden, Marcia Gay, 413
Harding, Jan Leslie, 457, 464, 535
Harding, Jan, 464
Hardwicke, Catherine, 408
Hardy, Judy, 474
Hare, David, 6, 17, 57, 58, 59, 368
Hare, William, 364
Harelik, Mark, 511
Harker, James, 392, 403
Harling, Robert, 399
Harman, Paul, 433, 505
Harmon, Richard, 465
Harnick, Sheldon, 49, 429, 474, 554, 560
Harper, Arthur, 425
Harper, Don, 367
Harper, Wally, 44, 375
Harrell, Gordon Lowry, 368, 380
Harriman, P. Chelsea, 520
Harrington, Laura, 467, 527
Harrington, Sharon, 536
Harrington, Wendall K., 414
Harris, Arthur, 367
Harris, Barbara, 25
Harris, Bill, 474
Harris, Christopher, 476
Harris, Dick, 515
Harris, Gary and Timmy, 401
Harris, Gary, 521
Harris, Harriet, 48, 404, 421, 469
Harris, Jessica, 479
Harris, John Jr., 539
Harris, Julie, 439, 525, 560
Harris, Leonard, 554
Harris, Lloyd, 524
Harris, Nick, 506
Harris, Niki, 375
Harris, Rosalind, 476
Harris, Roy, 415
Harris, Valerie, 455
Harrison, Barbara, 367
Harrison, Chris, 533
Harrison, Llewellyn, 464
Harrison, Peter, 460
Harrison, Rex, 6, 48, 378
Harrison, Stanley Earl, 397
Harrod, Michael, 368
**Harry Black**, *458*
Harry, Jimmy, 412

Hars, Adele, 506
Hart, Charles, 34, 35, 360, 387, 556
Hart, Dan, 478
Hart, Ed, 420
Hart, Elizabeth, 384
Hart, J. Richard, 435
Hart, Joe, 405, 478
Hart, Joseph, 469
Hart, Linda, 43, 369, 433
Hart, Lorenz, 474
Hart, M.E., 540
Hart, Melissa Joan, 416, 417
Hartdagen, Diane, 408
Hartenstein, Frank, 369
Hartford Stage Company, 516
Hartley, Jan, 472
Hartley, Neill, 528
Hartman, Karen, 414
Hartman, Michael, 386, 387
Hartos, Nico, 399
Hartswick, Maxine, 530
Hartwell, Peter, 519
Harty, Callen, 513
Harum, Eivind, 437
Harvey, Don, 403
Harvey, Gail, 522
Harvey, Nate, 474
Hase, Thomas, 506, 523
Hashimoto, Kazuakira, 367
Hastings, Edward W., 535
Hastings, John, 510, 511
**Hat**, *414*
Hatcher, Jeffrey, 424, 461, 540
Hatzai, Stephen, 529
Hauck, Robert, 384
Haupt, Irene, viii
Haupt, Paulette, 467
Hausman, Amy, 468
Havard, Bernard, 529
Havard, Celine, 530
**Have You Seen Road Smith?**, *540*
Havel, Vaclav, 3, 429, 452, 478
Havis, Allan, 512, 526
Hawkanson, David, 516
Hawley, Colette, 507
Hay, Richard L., 514
Hayama, Kiyomi, 367
Hayden, Cynthia, 479, 533
Hayden, David, 455
Hayes, Helen, 48
Hayes, Jack, 367
Hayes, Lorey, 464, 479
Hayes, Mary L., 525

Haynes, John, viii
Haynes, Neil, 401
Hays, Rex D., 374
Hayter, Rhonda, 461
Hayward-Jones, Michael, 397
Hazen, John, 393
**Headlights**, *527*
Heald, Anthony, 14, 400, 433, 507
Healy, Michael, 475, 477
**Hear the Angel's Voices**, *468*
Hearn, George, 34, 51, 370
Hearn, Page, 506
**Heart of a Dog**, 452, *457*
**Heart of the South**, *478*
Heart, Susan, 367
**Heathen Valley**, 560
**Heaven on Earth**, *472, 540*
**Heaven's Hard**, *518*
Hebron, Paul, 509
Hecht, Paul, 473
Heckart, Eileen, 30, 392
Heckscher Theater, 475
Hedden, Roger, 461
Hedgerow Theater, 524
Hedges, Peter, 24, 416, 456, 475
Heeley, Desmond, 378
Heggie, Iain, 469
Heick, Aaron, 410
Heidenreich, V. Craig, 520
**Heidi Chronicles, The**, 4, 360
Heifner, Jack, 518
Heimann, Mark, 515
Heinberg, Allan, 472
Heinfling, Martin, 395
Heinricher, Ann, 436
Heintzman, Michael, 425
**Heir Apparent**, *529*
Helde, Annette, 376, 520
Helen Hayes Awards, 560
Helfman, Max, 476
Helfrich, Dana, 537
Helgoth, Steven, 478
Heller, Joseph, 15
Heller, Marc, 384
Hellesen, Richard, 512
Hellman, Jerome, 372
Helm, Tom, 522
Helms, Jesse, 60
Helsinger, Jim, 466
Hemsley, Winston DeWitt, 436
Henderson, Mark, 383, 386
Henderson, Mary, 554
Henderson, Suzanne, 374

Hendren, Mark, 519, 520
Hendrick, Karla, 522
Hendrixson, Tim, 534
Henkel, Clare, 535
Henkel, Edward, 367
Henritze, Bette, 27, 364, 387
Henry Street Settlement, 475
**Henry's Folly**, *455*
Henry, Buck, 29, 410
Henry, Deborah, 435, 438
Henry, Lizzie, 535
Henry, O., 460, 468
Henry, Wilbur Edwin, 468
Henry, William A. III, 551, 559
Hensley, Dale, 433
Henson, Basil, 382
Herandez, Philip, 531
Herbert, Jocelyn, 372
Herbert, Lila, 384
Herbst, Ed, 460
Herbst, Jeffrey, 390
Herculano, Antonio, 460
**Herd of Buffalo**, *477*
Herel, Barbara S., 514
Hermalyn, Joy, 477
Herman, Danny, 435, 437
Herman, Fien, 470
Herman, Nate, 508
Hermans, Bruce, 517
Herndon, Dorie, 522, 531
Herr, Heidi Erica, 470
Herrera, John, 442
Herrmann, Edward, 9, 369, 405
Herskovits, David, 476
Hertzler, John, 535
Herz, Shirley, 366, 372, 374, 377, 384, 386, 391, 405, 414, 416, 419, 424, 429, 431
Hesko, Brian, 524
Hess, Nancy, 441
Hester, Richard, 425
Hewes, Henry, viii, 558
Hewett, Peggy, 410
Hewitt, Frankie, 390, 540
Heys, John, 460
**Hi Mom**, *512*
**Hi-Hat Hattie**, *537*
Hiatt, Rick, 527
Hibbert, Edward, 406
Hibbs, Lois Miller, 540
Hibiki, Mito, 367
Hickerson, Vickie, 367
Hickey, John, 403, 478, 510
Hicklin, Walter, 392, 417

Hickok, John, 390
Hickok, John, 472, 525
Hicks, Bryan, 403
Hicks, D'Atra, 475
Hicks, Shauna, 370, 472
Hidalgo, Allen, 521
Hietikko, Chris, 537
Higgins, Bob, 533
Higgins, Frank, 517, 518
Higgins, John Michael, 425
Higgins, Sarah, 464
Higginsen, Vy, 475
Higginsen-Wydro, Knoelle, 475
Hiler, Katherine, 404, 414, 469
Hiler, Kathy, 458
Hilferty, Susan, 402, 422, 469, 518
Hill, Gary Leon, 514
Hill, Michael, 474
Hillary, Ann, 474
Hilliard, Ryan, 461
Hillner, Nancy, 445
Hills, Randy, 455
Hillyer, Michael, 431
Hiltebrand, Steve, 522
Hilton, J.W. Jr., 514
Hilton, Margaret, 477
Hinderyckx, Les, 509
Hindman, James, 380
Hines, Gregory, 52, 403
Hinkley, Brent, 408
Hinnenkamp, Stephen, 372
Hionis, Chryss, 528
Hip Pocket Theater, 515
Hippocrates, 459
Hirabayashi, P.J., 535
Hirabayashi, Roy, 535
Hirowatari, Tsunetoshi, 460
Hirschfeld, Abe, 373
Hirschfeld, Al, viii, 560
Hirsh, Jody, 478
Hitchcock, Carrie, 523
Hitchcock, Jane Stanton, 469
Hitchock, Ken, 380
Hobart, Sebastian, 455
Hoberman, Perry, 410
Hobson, Anne Marie, 422
Hobson, I.M., 560
Hochwald, Bari, 533
Hock, Robert, 379, 422
Hocking, Leah, 472
Hodges, Azizah, 535
Hodges, Patricia, 461
Hodgin, Jere Lee, 533
Hoerl, Ted, 507
Hoffman, Avi, 420, 539

Hoffman, Bill, 523
Hoffman, Burton R., 514
Hoffman, Chris, 455, 456
Hoffman, David Jon, 536
Hoffman, Dustin, 6, 53, 54, 382, 556
Hoffman, Jane, 19, 379, 422
Hoffman, John, 505
Hoffman, Miriam, 420
Hoffman, Sandy Kelly, 536
Hoffmaster, Eric, 456
Hofmaier, Mark, 425, 478
Hofmann, Bob, 530
Hofvendahl, Steve, 365, 469
Hog Heaven, *529*
Hogan, Frank X., 518
Hogan, Jonathan, 464, 518
Hogan, Kevin, 477
Hogan, Robert, 376
Hogue, Annie G., 431
Hogue, Mitch, 431
Hogue, Warren, 60
Holaway, Meeghan, 531
Holden, Arthur, 478
Holden, Joan, 478
Holder, Don, 411, 524
Holder, Donald, 469, 525
Holder, Laurence, 424
Holding the Family Together, *468*
Holgate, Ron, 441
Holiday Garland of Tales, A, *534*
Holland, Carol, 468
Holland, Reece, 443, 444
Hollander, Jack, 53
Hollander, Leslie R., 431
Hollenbeck, Don Jr., 516, 517
Holliday, David, 505
Holliday, Polly, 31, 47, 386, 556
Hollins, Harry H., 524
Hollis, Stephen, 461
Hollis, Tommy, 389, 559
Hollywood Scheherazade, *478*
Hollywood, Daniele, 472
Holmes, Ann, 483
Holmes, Denis, 382
Holmes, Ed, 478
Holmes, Martha, viii
Holmes, Prudence Wright, 387
Holmes, Rupert, 30, 390
Holmes, Violet, 367
Holmgren, Joseph, 456

Holms, John Pynchon, 478, 479
Holt, Marion Peter, 470
Holt, Shannon, 408
Holt, Thelma, 383
Holten, Michael, 427
Holtzman, Merrill, 365
Holtzman, Will, 479
Holtzman, Willy, 478, 540
Holy Days, *512*
Home and Away, *538*
Home Brew, *468*
Home Delivery, *533*
Home Games, *458*
Home for Contemporary Theater and Art, 450, 475
Home, 559
Homesick, *478*
Homewood, Charles, 362
Honegger, Gitta, 456, 513, 540
Honeymoon at Dealey Plaza, *469*
Honk!, *513*
Hooker, Brian, 478
Hooks, Lumengo Jay, 475
Hooks, Stephen, 475
Hope, Sharon, 455
Hopkins, Andrea, 367
Hopkins, Anthony, 443, 458
Hopkins, Billy, 458
Hopkins, Gretchen, 455
Hopkins, Richard, 537
Horen, Bob, 533
Horn, Andrew M., 539
Horne, J.R., 539
Horne, Marilyn, 368
Horner, Jack, 477
Horovitz, Israel, 6, 24, 419, 420, 516
Horrigan, Patrick, 386
Horsey, Susan Urban, 429
Horsley, Jannet, 436
Horton, Jamie, 514
Horvath, Jan, 372
Horvitz, Wayne, 457
Hoshko, John, 373
Hostetter, Curt, 404, 466
Hostetter, Paula, 384
Hot Fudge, 18, *407, 412*
Hot Peaches, 460
Hoty, Dee, 33, 380, 443
Hoty, Tony, 377
Houdina, Mary Jane, 401
Houghton, James, 470
Hould-Ward, Ann, 414, 560
Hounsell, Ginny, 367

House of Horror, The, *472*
House of Yes, The, *536*
House, Adele, 535
House, Rain, 477
House, Ron, 535
Houser, Christie, 519
Houston, Barbara, 517
Houston-Jones, Ishmael, 462
How Are Things in Costa del Fuego?, *461*
How Far to Bethelem, *504*
How Gertrude Stormed the Philosophers' Club, *537*
How to Succeed in Business Without Really Trying, 28
Howard and Lois, *468*
Howard, Adam Coleman, 518
Howard, Barbara, 518
Howard, Connie, 522
Howard, David S., 533
Howard, Ken, 445
Howard, Lynnette, 511
Howard, M. A., 392, 417
Howard, Marcial, 386
Howard, Norman, 539
Howard, Peter, 395
Howarth, Roger, 466
Howarth, Tony, 466
Howe, Stephen J., 531
Howell, Jeffrey, 530
Howell, Ranse, 530
Howell, Sam, 473
Howland, Scott, 523
Hoyle, Geoff, 427
Hoylen, Tony, 463
Hsiang, Bob, viii
Hubbard, Robert, 529
Hubbard, Valorie, 421, 459
Hudak, Mark, 511
Huddle, Elizabeth, 537
Huddleston, Harvey, 478
Hudgins, Marilyn, 373
Hudson Guild Theater, 452, 458
Hudson, Walter, 527
Hudson-Joyce, Nanette, 528
Huff, Keith, 540
Huffman, Cady, 525
Huffman, Elizabeth, 474
Huffman, Felicity, 29, 397, 421, 535
Huffman, Ted, 384
Hughes, Allen Lee, 415, 560
Hughes, Barnard, 25, 392, 417
Hughes, Bonny, 527
Hughes, Douglas, 539

Hughes, Holly, 460, 463
Hughes, Julia C., 408
Hughes, Jurian, 464
Hughes, Laura, 408, 467
Hughes, Phil, 529
Hughes, Rhetta, 464
Hugo, Tara, 534
Hugo, Victor, 360
Huie, Karen, 518
Hulce, Tom, 6, 23, 376, 556
Hull, Mindy, 535
Hull, Susan, 539
Hull-Warriner Award, 61, 558
Hulswit, Mart, 533
Hulteen, Cheryl, 461, 464
Human Theater Company, The, 475
Humana Festival of New American Plays, 490, 519
Humeniuk, Roman, 393
Hummell, Mark, 368
Hummler, Richard, 59, 552
Hundley, C.L., 510, 511, 539
Hunnicutt, Ellen, 528
Hunt, James, 467, 512
Hunt, Margaret, 511
Hunt, Ralph, 468
Hunt, Trey, 363
Hunt, William Dennis, 535
Hunter, Patricia, 478
Hunter, Ronald, 474, 521
Huntington Theater Company, 389, 555
Huntington, Crystal, 420, 427
Huntley, Paul, 28
Hupp, Robert, 475
Hurd, Kate, 537
Hurd, Patricia, 444
Hurd-Sharlein, Adrienne, 365
Hurdle, James, 511
Hurlin, Dan, 558
Hurst, Brian, 479
Hurst, Gregory S., 525
Hurst, Howard, 362, 389, 390, 392
Hurst, Sophie, 362, 390, 392
Hurston, Zora Neale, 6, 19, 407
Hurt, Mary Beth, 17, 368
Hurt, William, 6, 24, 416
Husted, Patrick, 512
Hutchings, Jeannine, 517
Hutchins, Jeannie, 523
Hutchman, David F., 530
Hutton, Timothy, 6, 25, 369, 392, 417
Hutzler, Laurie, 525, 537

Hwang, David Henry, 360, 452, 467
Hwong, Lucia, 467
**Hyde in Hollywood**, 11, 14, *413, 414*
**Hyde Park,** *474*
Hyde, William York, 527
Hyman, Earle, 439
Hynd, Ghretta, 461
Hyslop, Jeff, 435

**I & I,** *477*
**I Am a Winner,** *467*
**I Saw the Swede,** *456*
**I Think It's Gonna Work Out Fine,** *460*
I., Robert, 459
Iacangelo, Peter, 516
Iacovelli, John, 512
Iaderosa, Andrea, 516
**Ice Cream With Hot Fudge,** 6, 11, 18, *407, 412*
**Ice Cream,** 18, *407, 412*
Ierardi, Robert, 475
**If He Says the Word,** *517*
Iglesias, Loida, 437
Ikebe, Shinichiro, 460
Ikeda, Thomas, 522
**Il Pesce (The Fish),** *513*
**Illusion, The,** *516*
Ilo, Angelique, 436, 438
**Imagining Brad**, 11, 24, *416, 417*
Imai, Naoji, 367
Immediate Theater Company, The, 507
**Imperceptible Mutabilities in the Third Kingdom,** 449, *474, 558*
Imperioli, Michael, 479
**Importance of Being Earnest, The,** *475, 477*
**In Answer,** *468*
**In Darkest America,** *520*
**In the Eye of the Hurricane,** *464*
**In Her Own Words (A Portrait of Jane),** *475*
**In Living Color,** 559
**In Pursuit of the Song of Hydrogen,** *479*
**Incommunicado,** *456*
**Increase,** *460*
**Indian Love Call,** *464*
**Indian Dog,** 450, *475*
**Infinity's House,** *520*

Ingram, David, 521
Ingram, Michael, 512
Ingravallo, Daviano, 459
Ingster, Peter, 362
Initia, 477
Innaurato, Albert, 414
Inneo, Anthony, 437
**Inner Reflections of an Island,** *468*
Innes, K. Craig, 370
Innes, Laura, 463
*Innocents Abroad, The*, 18
**Inside A.,** *468*
**Inside George,** *508*
INTAR, 459
Interart Theater, 459
Intiman Theater, 537
**Into the Woods,** 360, 362, 440, 560
**Inuit, The,** *529*
**Invictus,** *537*
Invisible Theater, 540
Iobst, Anne, 559
Iorio, Richard, 473
Irie, Kaoru, 367
Irish Arts Center, 475
Irish Repertory Theater Company, 452, 475
Irizarry, Richard V., 467
Irving, Janet, 420, 516
Irwin, Bill, 361, 558
Irwin, Michael, 384
Irwin, Pat, 463
**Is He Still Dead?,** *525*
Isaac, Alberto, 518
Isdell, Charlie, 528
Isen, Richard, 514
Ishida, Masaya, 367
Ishihama, Hideo, 367
Iten, Terry, 374
Ivary, Lisa, 534
Ives, David, 450, 458, 461
Ivey, Dana, 404, 405, 439, 511
Ivey, Joshua, 527
Ivory, 469
Ivy, Lauren, 515

J, Steven, 408
Jablons, Karen, 435
Jacintho, Marta, 385
**Jack Benny Program, The,** *459*
Jack Levitt Productions, Inc., 420
**Jack,** *456*

**Jackie Mason—Brand New,**
  *466*
Jackins, David L., 426
Jackness, Andrew, 469
Jacksina Company, 375, 430
Jacksina, Judy, 375
Jackson, David, 36, 374
Jackson, Duane, 524
Jackson, Kevin, 411, 524
Jackson, Mahalia, 42
Jackson, Samuel L., 423, 424,
  526
Jacob, Abe, 383, 384, 395
Jacob, Lou, 479
Jacobs, Craig, 377
Jacobs, Douglas, 535
Jacobs, Sander, 374, 556
Jacobson, David, 529
Jacoby, Mark, 375, 444
**Jacques and His Master,** *477*
Jaffe, Jill, 463
Jaffe, Joan, 468
Jaffrey, Sakina, 520
**Jake's Women,** 55, *397*, *534*
James, Antony, 461
James, Bob, 404
James, Geraldine, 54, 382, 556,
  559
James, Harold Dean, 365
James, Jerry, 424
James, Joseph, 478
James, Kelli, 443
James, Kricker, 468
James, Mike, 529
James, Paulette, 517
James, Peter Francis, 404
James, Stephanie, 367
James, Toni-Leslie, 31, 411,
  524
James-Reed, Michael, 466
Jampolis, Neil Peter, 364, 369,
  383, 384, 427, 431, 556
Jamrog, Joseph, 467
Jandova, Elena, 477
Jani, Robert F., 366, 367
Janssen, Jeruen, 523
Jaques, Damien, 484
Jaramillo, Leticia, 514
Jarry, Alfred, 48, 401
Jarvis, Lucy, 383
Jasien, Deborah, 525
Jason, Mitchell, 374
Jason, Robert, 463
Jasper, Zina, 473
Jay, Brian, 370
Jay, Isla, 460

Jay, Mary, 530
Jay, William, 423, 424, 503
Jbara, Gregory, 406
Jean Cocteau Repertory, 475
Jefferson, Margo, 557
Jeffrey Richards Associates,
  367, 378, 389, 420
Jeffries, Brad, 435
**Jekyll and Hyde,** *525*
**Jekyll!,** *517*
Jellison, John, 466, 525
Jendresen, Erik, 522
Jenkin, Len, 469
Jenkins, Daniel, 472
Jenkins, David, 8, 390, 505
Jenkins, Ken, 472
Jenkins, Lilian, 477
Jenkins, Paulie, 511, 538
Jenkins, Tamara, 443, 530
Jenness, Morgan, 414
Jennings, Christopher, 455
Jennings, James, 455, 456
Jennings, Jessica Lynn, 455
Jennings, Ken, 374, 375
Jensen, Brian, 400
Jepson, J. J., 374, 375
**Jeremiah, The,** *523*
**Jerome Robbins' Broadway,**
  55, 360, 441
Jerome, Judith, 513
Jerome, Timothy, 36, 374, 433
Jerris, Tony, 455
Jerry, Philip, 365
Jessop, Maria, 478
Jesurun, John, 452, 476
Jeter, Michael, 6, 36, 44, 62,
  374, 556, 558, 559
Jewett, Bob, 535
Jewish Repertory Theater, 476
Jiler, John, 470
Jimenez, Robert, 474
Jo-Ann, Ebony, 524
Jobe, Amanda, 423
Joe A. Callaway Award, 559
**Joe Turner's Come and**
  **Gone,** 21, 560
Johansen, Mark, 367
Johanson, Don, 434
Johanson, Jane, 393
Johanson, Robert, 522
John F. Kennedy Center for the
  Performing Arts, 55, 376,
  395
John Gassner Playwright
  Award, 558
John, Joseph, 472

**Johnny Pye and the**
  **Foolkiller,** *525*
Johns, Glynis, 48, 378
Johns, Kurt, 387, 388
Johns, Stephen, 384
Johnson, Ann, 526
Johnson, Cameron, 458
Johnson, Daniel Timothy, 478
Johnson, Elizabeth, 513
Johnson, Eric, 387, 388, 455
Johnson, Ethan, 408
Johnson, Gary Neal, 517
Johnson, Greg, 461, 476
Johnson, Heidi Karol, 522
Johnson, James Weldon, 464
Johnson, Karin, 513
Johnson, Ken, 524
Johnson, Kurt, 437
Johnson, Litha, 528
Johnson, Mary Lea, 374, 556
Johnson, Michelle, 379, 422
Johnson, Philip, 422
Johnson, Pookie, 463
Johnson, Stephanie, 460
Johnson, Sunny, 527
Johnson, Tim, 425
Johnston, Rick, 478
Jolles, Susan, 362, 370
*Jonah and the Whale,* 407
**Jonah,** 11, 41, *407*, *412*
Jones, Alexandra, 477
Jones, B.J., 472
Jones, Bill T., 559
Jones, Bradley, 438
Jones, Carleton T., 436
Jones, David Edward, 534
Jones, Douglas, 537
Jones, Ellen E., 508
Jones, Gib, 437
Jones, Gordon G., 534
Jones, Hillary, 463
Jones, Jane, 537
Jones, Jeff, 507
Jones, Jeffrey M., 463
Jones, Jen, 523
Jones, Jennifer, 367
Jones, Kimberly, 455
Jones, Llewellyn, 457
Jones, Meachie, 475
Jones, Ora, 506, 507
Jones, Rachel, 370
Jones, Reed, 434
Jones, Rhodessa, 460
Jones, Silas, 540
Jones, Simon, 12, 406
Jones, Thomas Cadwaleder, 509

Jones, Tom, 399
Jones, William, 507
Joness, Wayne, 533
Jong, Erica, 59
**Jonquil**, 11, 20, *423*
Joplin, Joneal, 534
Jordan, Richard, 52, 404
Jory, Jon, 519, 520
Joselovitz, Ernest, 520
Joseph Papp Yiddish Theater, 420
Joshua Ellis Office, 362, 364, 369, 370, 383, 390, 392, 406, 420, 427
Joslyn, Betsy, 440
Joubert, Joseph, 390
**Journey of Snow White, The**, *476*
**Joy Solution**, *464*
Joy, Robert, 14, 414
Joyce, Brian, 528
Joyce, Ella, 526
Joyce, Joe, 530
Joyce, Walker, 505
Joyner, Kimble, 414
**Juan Darién**, 11, *422, 463*
*Jubilee*, 425
Judd, Rebecca, 363
Judge, Don, 378
Judith Anderson Theater, 476
Judson Memorial Church, 476
Judson, Kevin, 455
Judson, Tom, 460, 477
Judy, James, 525
**Juice**, *460*
Jujamcyn Theaters Awards, 559
Jujamcyn Theaters, 374, 379, 386, 389, 555, 556
Julia, Raul, 52, 404
Julian, Ivan, 539
Julie, Ora McBride, 468
**Julius Caesar**, 405
**June Moon**, *461*
Jung, Philipp, 365, 401, 419, 429, 471, 525
Junge, Alexa, 505
**Junon and Avos: The Hope**, 4, *383*
Jurosko, Keith, 477
Jutras, Simon, 473

K & D Productions, 428
Kaczmarek, Jane, 18, 412
Kaczorowski, Peter, 419, 505, 531
Kadilis, Alexia, 477

Kadleck, Tony, 373
Kadokawa, Haruki, 372
Kaell, Ron, 536
Kafka, Franz, 360
Kagan, Lois, 477
Kahan, Marvin, 479
Kahn, Gary, 380
Kahn, Michael, 560
Kahn, Nathaniel, 475
Kahn, Tobi, 411
Kaiser, Nancy, 455
Kakhiani, Marina, 427
Kalas, Janet, 414, 417, 504
Kalfin, Robert Mark, 366
Kalfin, Robert, 390, 514, 540
Kalista, Conner, 515
Kamlet, Ken, 455, 456
Kamm, Tom, 417, 457, 466, 504
Kancheli, Ghia, 428
Kandel, Lenore, 359
Kandel, Paul, 473, 514
Kander, John, 59, 377, 523, 531
Kane, Andrea, 422
Kane, Bradley, 403
Kane, Donna, 34, 370, 474
Kane, Mary, 390, 472
Kani, John, 23, 422, 464
Kanin, Garson, 360
Kantor, Mary, 365
Kantor, Mitchel, 473
Kantor, Pamela, 426
Kantrowitz, Jason, 368, 381, 397, 421
Kapen, Ben, 379
Kaplan, Barry Jay, 531
Kaplan, Claudia, 518
Kaplan, Howard Tsvi, 536, 537
Kaplan, Paul A., 426
Kaplan, Steve, 461
Kaplin, Stephen, 422
Kapstan, Abram, 384
Karachentsev, Nikolai, 383
Karasov, Denis, 383
Karbacz, Kelly, 384
Karchmer, Charles, 458
Karge, Manfred, 540
Karnaushkin, Alexander, 383
Karnes, Jay, 517
Karr, Elizabeth, 468
Karvonides, Chrisi, 526
Kass, Jon, 365
**Kate's Diary**, 11, 30, *406, 408, 412, 467*
Kater, Peter, 416

**Kathy and Mo Show: Parallel Lives, The**, 399
Katigbak, Mia, 467
Katsaros, Doug, 409
Katz, Jack, 384
Katz, Natasha, 377, 392, 419
Katz, Paul, 473
Katz, Tracy, 440
Katzman, Bruce, 464
Kaufman, Brian A., 362, 419
Kaufman, Eric H., 377
Kaufman, George S., 461, 477
Kaufman, Lynne, 527, 536
Kaufman, Martin R., 375
Kavee, Elliot, 478
Kavilis, Diana, 435
Kawahara, Carl, 380
Kay, Linda, 473
Kayahara, Lauren, 436
Kaye, Howard, 367, 509
Kaye, Judy, 444, 474
Kaye, Toni, 393
Kazan, Elia, 46
Keal, Anita, 474, 476
Keathley, George, 517, 518
Keating, Barry, 361
Keating, Charles, 420
Keck, Michael, 458, 478
Kee, Chung, 522
Keegan, Ted, 363
Keeler, Bill, 428
Keeler, James, 468
**Keeper, The**, *479*
Keever, Tom Dale, 461
Keith, Larry, 443
Kekana, Fana, 465
Kelch, Beverly, 529
Kell, Peter, 508
Kelleher, Joan Peer, 367
Kelley, Glenda Starr, 506
Kelley, Robert, 527
Kellin, Orange, 43, 430
Kellman, Barnet, 16, 401
Kellogg, Marjorie Bradley, 511, 525, 534
Kellogg, Robert, 375
Kelly, Art, 468
Kelly, Chris, 455, 461, 473, 475
Kelly, Daniel Hugh, 46, 386
Kelly, Drew, 478
Kelly, Glen, 522
Kelly, Hubert Baron, 512
Kelly, Jude, 420
Kelly, Martha M., 509
Kelly, Paula, 519

Kelly, Rick, 516
Kelly, Thomas A., 383, 390
Kelly-Young, Leonard, 509
Kember, Darcia, 393
Kemeny, A., 426
Kemeny, C.E., 426
Kemp, Emme, 430
Kempenski, Tom, 468
Kendrick, Polly, 504
Kendrick, Richard, 504
Keneally, Thomas, 519
Kennedy Center Honors, 559
Kennedy Center, 55, 376, 395
Kennedy, Beau, 455
Kennedy, Craig, 465
Kennedy, Denise, 463, 464
Kennedy, Dennis, 530
Kennedy, Frank, 531
Kennedy, Janet, 456
Kennedy, Paul, 509
Kenner, David, 420
Kennon, William, 408, 467
Kenny, Frances, 537
**Kensington Stories, The,**
369
Kent, Roberta, 361
Kent, Steven, 519
Kenton, Brian, 518
Kepros, Nicholas, 479
Kerbeck, Robert, 478
Kerlew, Roger, 537
Kermoyan, Michael, 397
Kern, Will, 507
Kerns, Linda, 443, 461
Kerr, Patrick, 475
Kerr, Robert, 413, 414
Kerr, Walter, 559
Kersey, Robin, 507
Kerwick, Danny, 512
Kessler, Jack, 528
Kessler, Lyle, 538
Key, Tom, 503
Khalil, Amer, 475
Khan, Rick, 524
Kharshiladze, Daredjan, 427
Khidasheli, Akaki, 427
Khovanskaya, Alyona, 412
Khumalo, Sephiwe, 464
Khumalo, Sibangile, 464
Kiara, Dorothy, 433
**Kid of Man,** *468*
Kidd, Wiley, 388
Kignel, Piata Stoklos, 460
Kignel, Thais Stoklos, 460
Kikuchi, Susan, 441

Kilgarriff, Patricia, 387, 418,
445
Kilgore, John, 409, 518
Kilkelly, Mary Beth, 457
Killian, Scott, 466
Kilroy, Colette, 425, 464, 475,
477, 531
Kilty, Jerome, 365, 421
Kim, Sora, 527
Kim, Susan, 458
Kimball, Christina Kumi, 433
Kimball, David A., 520
Kimbrough, Matthew, 422
Kincade, Jill, 470
Kincaid, Eric Scott, 434
Kincaid, Mark, 503, 533
Kindl, Charles, 383, 392
Kinematic, 463
**King and I, The,** *397*
**King John,** 405
**King Lear,** 11, *427*, 452, 461
**King's New Clothes,** *524*
King, Denis, 406
King, Eric, 424
King, Jeff, 536
King, Joseph S., 514
King, Joyce P., 463
King, Woodie Jr., 464
Kingdom, Bob, 458
**Kingfish,** 11, 30, *406*, *410*,
*412*
Kingsley, Gretchen, 363
Kingston, Earl, 536
Kinney, Terry, 19, 31, 386,
556
Kinsey, Greg, 479
Kirby, Marion Arthur, 516, 517
Kirkham, Willi, 468
Kirkwood, James, 56, 359
Kirkwood, Neal, 460
Kirschner, Richard, 466
Kirsh, Bob, 534
Kirtley, Judith, 464
Kishline, John, 523
**Kiss of the Spider Woman,**
59, 60, *531*
Kissel, Howard, 551, 552
Kitamura, Michiko, 460
Kitchen, The, 452, 476
Kittredge, Ann, 530
Kivnick, Eric, 370
Kladitis, Manny, 397
Klain, Margery, 428
Klapper, Stephanie, 468
Klavan, Laurence, 461
Klayman, Jeffrey, 450, 475

Kleban, Edward, 56, 359
Klein, Alvin, 553
Klein, Amanda J., 463
Klein, Jon, 503
Klein, Lauren, 414
Klein, Steven M., 538, 539
Klementowicz, Paul, 472
Klemperer, Werner, 52, 384
Kletter, Debra J., 392, 401, 417
Kliewer, Warren, 468
Kline, Elmer, 455
Kline, Kevin, 6, 53, 404, 405
Kline, Randall, 427
Kling, Kevin, 538
Klingelhoefer, Robert, 467
Klinger, Cindi, 436
Klinger, Pam, 436
Klingler, Rebecca, 478
Klotz, Florence, 33, 380, 531,
556, 558
Klugman, Jack, 51
Knapp, Dee Dee, 367
Knapp, Sarah, 395
Knee, Allan, 539
Kneeland, Richard, 534
Knell, Dane, 387
Knepper, Robert, 18, 412, 518
**Knife, The,** 43
Knight, Michael E., 458
Knight, Susan, 403, 466, 467,
477, 510
Knight, Wayne, 365
Knox, Geoffrey, 469
Knutsen, Erik, 404, 420
Knyazev, Yuri, 540
Kobayashi, Kohei, 366
Koch, David, 367, 531
Koch, Edward I., 403
Kodama, Ai, 367
Kogan, Deen, 529
Kogan, Jay, 529
Kohl, Phyllis, 527
Kohler, Anna, 479
Kolb, Laura, 477
Kolins, Howard, 368
Kolinski, Joseph, 442
Kolo, Fred, 390, 514, 540
Kolodner, Arnie, 405
Kolsby, Paul, 464
Kolson, Rob, 508
Komiyama, Yuko, 467
Komolova, Valentina, 383
Kondek, Charles, 473
Kondoleon, Harry, 458, 539
Konig, David, 461, 468
Kook, Edward F., 558

**Koozy's Piece,** *518*
Kopache, Thomas, 364
Kopplin, David, 513
Koprowicz, Kent, 512
Korder, Howard, 511
Korey, Alix, 410
Korf, Geoff, 526
Korf, Mia, 522
Kornberg, Richard, 368, 403, 408
Kornfeld, Eric, 463
Korzen, Annie, 476
Kosek, Kenny, 472
Kotin, Lisa, 460
Kotlisky, Marge, 539
Kotoske, Tamar, 463
Kourilsky, Francoise, 479
Koustik, Art, 511
Koutoukas, H.M., 469
Kovitz, Randy, 519
Kowal, James, 365, 366
Kowalewski, Joseph, 367
Kowalski, Joseph M., 536
Kozak, Ellen M., 523
Kozeluh, John, 473
Kozlov, Gennady, 383
Kozlov, Igor, 412
KPMG Peat Marwick Award, 560
Kraar, Adam, 468
Krag, Jim, 472
Krakowski, Jane, 6, 36, 44, 374, 556
Kramer, Mimi, 551, 552
Kramer, Rob, 525, 529
Kramer, Sherry, 469
Krane, David, 50, 363, 394, 523
**Krapp's Last Tape,** *457*
Krasnansky, Jennifer, 405, 478
Krass, Michael, 458, 466, 519, 520, 523
Krauser, Terry, 469
Krauss, Marvin A., 374, 556
Kravets, Laura, 401
Krebs, Eric, 405, 429
Kreeger, David Lloyd, 560
Kreek, George, 468
Krementz, Steven J., 403
Krenz, Frank, 387
Kreshka, Ruth, 381
Kressin, Lianne, 534
Kretzmer, Herbert, 360
Krieger, Barbara Zinn, 472
Kriegler, Mitchell, 384
Kringelein, Otto, 44

Kristic, Angie, 478
Kristien, Dale, 444
Krizanc, John, 399
Kroeger, Perry Arthur, 455
Kroeze, Jan, 425
Krogstad, Bob, 367, 368
Krok, Loren, 370
Kroll, Jack, 58, 59, 551
Kron, Ron, 430
Kronenfeld, Ivan, 468
Kronzer, James, 560
Kruk, Tony, 514
Krupa, Olek, 401, 457
Kruschke, Gerhard, 362
Kruse, Paul James, 535
Kubala, Michael, 441
Kuchwara, Michael, viii, 552
Kudriavtsev, Dimitri, 383
Kuhlman, Ron, 436
Kuhn, Judy, 443
Kuhn, Kevin, 463
Kulerman, Ruth, 475
Kulowitsch, John, 372
Kundera, Milan, 477
Kuney, Scott, 372
Kunstler, Julius H., 367
Kurlander, Brian, 475
Kuroda, Kati, 467
Kurowski, Ron, 438
Kurtz, Marcia Jean, 6, 12, 16, 31, 401, 414, 558
Kurtz, Norman, 390
Kurtz, Swoosie, 9, 369, 405
**Kuru,** *503, 515*
Kushnarenko, Irena, 383
Kushner, Robert, 523
Kushner, Tony, 516
Kuss, Aileen O., 514
Kuter, Kay E., 512
Kuznechenko, Roman, 412
Kuznetsov, Villor, 383
Kuznetsov, Vladimir, 383
Kvares, Donald, 479
Kvirtskhalia, David, 428
Kwasniewski, Judy, 512

**L 305,** *468*
La Candelaria, 466
La Chanze, 6, 42, 44, 415
La Fosse, Robert, 459
**La Grande Josephine,** *460*
La Guerre, Irma-Estel, 397
La Jolla Playhouse, 366, 518
La Mama (a.k.a. LaMama) Experimental Theater Club (ETC), 449, 459

La Ponsie, Steven, 518
LaBelle, Rob, 404
LaChance, Danny, 506
LaChiusa, Michael John, 450, 458, 472
Lachow, Stan, 379
Lackey, Herndon, 442
Lacy, Terry, 367
Lacy, Tom, 479
**Ladies and Ferns,** *513*
Ladman, Jeff, 397, 534
**Lady Committing a Sin,** *529*
**Lady in Question, The,** 11, 13, *405*
Laffredo, Warren, 384
LaFleche, Michel, 393
Lagalante, Lou, 455
Lagerfelt, Caroline, 441
Laghidze, Soso, 427
Lahey, Sara, 517
Lahti, Christine, 440
Laine, Cleo, 440
Laird, Fiona, 461
Laird, Marvin, 368
Laird, Michael James, 537
Lakis, Maria, 463
**L'Altra Italia,** *459*
Lam, Zoie, 522
Lamaj, Matt, 463, 464
Lamb, James Robert, 469
Lamb, Rebecca, 533
Lambert, Beverly, 466
Lambert, Juliet, 370
Lambert, Robert, 377, 559
Lambert, Susan, 464
Lamb's Theater Company, 460, 477
LaMorte, Dan, 508
Lamos, Mark, 516
Lampinen, Roy, 513
Lamude, Terence, 475
Lancaster, Mark, 559
Lancer, Alexandra, 455
Lanchester, Robert, 457, 531
**Land King, The,** *507*
**Land of the Free,** *511*
Landau, Penny M., 427
Landau, Robert, 470
Landesman, Heidi, 527
Landfield, Timothy, 445
Landis, Bernie, 508
Landman, Jeffrey, 473
Landmark Entertainment Corp., 381
Landon, Margaret, 397
Landron, Jack, 455, 467

Landry, Lantz, 443
Landry, Lauri, 364
Landwehr, Hugh, 525
Landy, Brian, 455
Lane, Alan, 477
Lane, Eddie, 468
Lane, Janice C., 390
Lane, Linda L., 509
Lane, Nancy, 436
Lane, Nathan, 14, 30, 49, 379, 400, 419, 559
Lane, Stewart F., 390
Lane, Timothy, 478
Lang, Phillip J., 367
Lang, Stephen, 24, 376, 560
Lang, William H., 369, 406
Langan, William, 403
Lange, Joanna, 505
Lange, Ted, 439
Langella, Frank, 52, 420
Langland, Paul, 460
Langner, Christine, 434
Langworth, Joe, 409
Langworthy, Douglas, 476
Lanier, Robert, 469
Lank, Anna Bess, 476
Lansbury, Angela, 51, 52
Lansbury, David, 414, 440
Lanteri, Joe, 472
Lantz, Janet, 362
Lanzener, Sonja, 510
Lapachi, Georgy, 428
LaPierre, Robert, 425
Lapine, James, 360
Large, Norman, 442
**Largely New York**, 361, 558
Largent, Linet Elan, 511
**Largo Desolato**, 3
Larin, Alexey, 383
Larison, Mary Lee, 513
Larkin, Judy, 416
Larkin, Robert W., 366, 377
Larsen, Donna Marie, 523
Larsen, Liz, 461, 522
Larson, Charles, 527
Larson, Larry, 503
Lashof, Carol, 527, 528
Laskawy, Harris, 519
Lasker-Schuler, Else, 477
**Last Appointment, The**, *468*
**Last Deal, The**, *514*
**Last Gas Till Turnpike**, *456*
**Last Song of John Proffit, The**, *534*
Latessa, Dick, 445
Latham, Bradley, 367

Latham, Stacy, 367
**Latins Anonymous**, *535*
Latouche, John, 473
Latuja, Nancy, 397
Lauck, Joe D., 508
**Laughing Matters**, 400
Laughton, Charles, 560
Laurence, Pamela, 514
Laurence, Stuart, 474
Laurenson, Diana, 365
Laurents, Arthur, 6, 52, 376, 377
Lauricella, Ruth, 426
Lauze, Gene, 430
**Lava**, 452, *479*
Lavey, Martha, 472
Lavine, Audrey, 410
Lawless, James J., 513
Lawless, Rick, 533
Lawless, Sean, 426
Lawless, Sue, 478
Lawrence, Burke, 362
Lawrence, Dea, 461
Lawrence, Donald, 461
Lawrence, Elizabeth, 474, 477
Lawrence, Jeremy, 519, 560
Lawrence, Peter, 378, 397
Lawson, David, 425, 524
Lawson, Leigh, 54, 382, 468
Lawson, Richard, 417
Lawson, Tony, 509
Lay, Richard, 478
Layne, Mary, 386
Lazarus, Paul, 525
le Sourd, Jacques, 552
Leach, Holly Nelson, 515
Leach, Nicole, 365
Leach, William, 421
League of American Theaters and Producers, 55, 554
League of Resident Theaters (LORT), 57, 503
Leake, Damien, 504, 524
**Lear**, *461*, 558
Learmonth, Nancy, 474
Leask, Katherine, 478
**Least of These, The**, *539*
Leavengood, William S., 24, 400
LeBouef, Clayton, 540
Lebowsky, Stan, 368
Leca, Carlos, 385
LeClaire, Tokeli, 535
Lecube, Graciela, 467
Ledbetter, William, 384
Lederer, Deedy, 421

Ledwich, Lisa, 383
Lee, Angie, 512
Lee, Baayork, 436
Lee, Bill Cho, 518
Lee, Chandra, 364
Lee, Eugene, 50
Lee, Gypsy Rose, 376
Lee, Hyunyup, 460
Lee, Jack, 375
Lee, Joyce, 521
Lee, Leslie, 30, 424, 524
Lee, Mark, 512
Lee, Mary, 467
Lee, Robert E., 560
Lee, Spike, 3
Lee, Stephen, 406, 479
Leech, Deborah, 527
Leeds, Andrew Harrison, 443
Leenay, Ann, 475
LeFevre, Adam, 421
**Legal Tender**, *539*
Leggett, Bob, 513
Leguizamo, John, 459
Lehane, Gregory, 478
Lehman, Helen Reed, 535
Lehrer, Scott, 392, 414, 415, 417
Leibman, Ron, 444
Leigh, Jennifer Jason, 24, 416
Leigh-Warren, Jennifer, 464
Leinweber, Laura, 375
Leishman, Gina, 504, 505
Leithoff, J.D., 512
Lemac, Linda, 367
Lemenager, Nancy, 370
Lencom Theater, 383
**Lend Me a Tenor**, 360, 441
Lenehan, Nancy, 560
Lengson, Jose, 367, 368
Lennart, Isobel, 541
Lennon, John, 359
LeNoire, Rosetta, 454, 554
Lenox, Adriane, 560
Leon, Carol Mitchell, 503
Leon, Kenny, 504
Leonard, Powell, 456
Leonard, Robert Sean, 414
Leone, Elaine, 455
Leone, Vivian, 405, 409
Leonidoff, Leon, 368
Leonov, Andrey, 383
Lerch, Stuart, 477
Leroux, Gaston, 360
**Les Pecheurs**, *525*
**Les Misérables**, 59, 360, 441
**Les Romanesques**, 399

629

Leschin, Luisa, 535
LeShay, David, 389
Leslie, Bethel, 415, 511
Lesser, Sally, 535, 539
Lester, Barbara, 387
Lester, Noble Lee, 479
**Lettice & Lovage,** 4, 6, 8,
25, 30, 55, 56, 61, *387,*
552, 555, 556, 558
Levan, Martin, 388
Levda, Yakov, 383
Levene, Ellen, 387
Levenson, Jeanine, 505
Levenson, Keith, 505
Levi, Nannette, 367
Levi, Sally, 516
Levin, Harriet, 529
Levin, Ira, 30, 399
Levin, Joseph, 468
Levin, Kathy, 376, 378, 556
Levin, Rachel, 429
Levine, Anna, 464
Levine, Richard, 445
Levinson, Karen, 529
Levitow, Roberta, 417, 504,
559
Levy, Frank, 367
Levy, Gerardo, 384
Levy, Jacques, 359, 521
Levy, Jonathan, 540
Levy, Mort, 529
Lewis, Althea, 474
Lewis, Bobo, 464, 472
Lewis, Carol Jean, 463
Lewis, Deirdre, 528
Lewis, Edmond, 458
Lewis, Edwina, 386, 514
Lewis, Irene, 504
Lewis, James, 536
Lewis, Jim, 365
Lewis, Marcia, 364, 414
Lewis, Matthew, 475, 477, 539
Lewis, Page, 536
Lewis, Rick, 479
Lewis, Vicki, 48, 421, 472
Lewis-Evans, Kecia, 410, 415
Lewitin, Margot, 459
Lewton, Christopher V., 540
Leyden, Leo, 382
Leys, Brian D., 463
Leyva, Henry, 512
Li, Donald, 467
Liani, Michael, 466, 534
Libbey, Catherine, 456
Libin, Paul, 362, 556
Lichte, Richard, 458, 478

Lichtefeld, Michael, 363
Lichtenstein, Harvey, 427
Lichter, Kathy, 530
Liddi, Allison R., 560
Lide, Miller, 477
Lieb, Dick, 368
Lieberman, Donna, 472
Lieberman, Hal, 455
Lieberson, Will, 467, 468, 469,
474
**Life Is a Dream,** *475*
**Lifetimes on the Streets,** 11,
30, *423, 424*
**Lights on the Ocean Floor,**
*456*
Light, Kate, 384
Ligon, K.C., 457
Liker, George, 470
**L'Illusion Comique,** *516*
Lilly, Robin, 456
Lima, Rafael, 459
Lima, Rui, 385
**Limbo Tales,** *469*
**Limericks and Poems,** *524*
Lincoln Center Theater, 11, 48,
378, 379, 401, 421, 477
Lindecrantz, Greta, 513
Lindemann, Paula, 513
Linden, Amelia, 362
Lindo, Delroy, 504
Lindsay, Barbara, 461
Lindsay, Howard, 52, 360, 383
Lindsay, Robert, 443
Lines, Sybil, 387
Link, Ron, 397, 519, 534, 560
Linney, Romulus, 452, 458,
470, 479, 483, 485, 520,
558, 560
Lino, Amilton, 385
Linton, John K., 512
Linville, Larry, 445
Linzalone, Anthony, 473
Lion, John, 536
Lion, Margo, 372
Lipp, Larry, 415
Lippa, Louis, 521, 524
Lisanbee, Thomas, 384
Lisanby, Charles, 367
**Lisbon Traviata, The,** 6, 11,
13, 14, 30, 55, 61, *400,*
558, 559
Liscio, Paula, 384
Liscow, Wendy, 525
Lish, James, 476
Lisner, Stephen, 455
Liss, Richard, 362

Lissek, Leon, 382
List, John, 455
Lithgow, John, 443, 560
Litkei, Ervin, 415
Litten, Jim, 435
**Little Me,** 401
*Little Mermaid, The,* 41
**Little Night Music, A,** 34
*Little Orphan Annie,* 395
**Little Stumps: The Deal,** *479*
Little, Cleavon, 27, 416, 477
Little, Gerard, 477
Little, Iris, 423, 424
Little, Judy, 367
Litwinski, Mieczyslaw, 560
Lively, David, 517
Lively-Mekka, Delyse, 435
Liveright, Josh, 520
Living Theater, The, 402, 477
Livingston, James, 467
Livingston, Sonya, 367
LiVolsi, Katherine, 370
Lizzul, Anthony John, 474
Lloyd, Benjamin, 463
Lloyd, John Bedford, 379, 422
Lo Bianco, Tony, 444
Locarro, Joe, 442
Locatell, Carol, 511
Locilento, Nick, 475
Lock, Keven, 537
Locke, Robert, 405
Lockett, Miron, 455
Lockhart, Keith, 530
Lockhart, Robert, 383
Lockwood, Conny M., 528
**Loco 7,** *459*
Locorriere, Dennis, 29
Locricchio, Matthew, 414
Loeb, Leslie, 415
Loehle, Steven, 431
Loesser, Emily, 384, 476
Logan, Bellina, 516
Logan, Stacey, 475
Logen, Carol, 363
Lohmann, Brian, 536
Lokey, Ben, 438
Lolashvili, Zhanri, 427
**Loman Family Picnic, The,**
5, 6, 8, 11, 15, 131-150,
*400, 401,* 558
Lombard, Jenny, 458
Lombard, Kirk, 472
Lombardo, George, 426
Lombardo, Pat, 426
London Small Theater
Company, The, 461

London, Amy Jane, 380
London, Becky, 464
London, Chuck, 400, 416, 417
London, Mark, 463
Long, Ana K., 470
Long, Anni, 511
Long, Katherine, 458
Long, Quincy, 475
Long, Richard, 533
Long Wharf Theater, 5, 48, 369, 406, 525
Longbottom, Robert, 455
Longo, Robert, 362
Longurashvili, David, 428
Lopatto, Bill, 474
Loper, Barbara, 527
Lopez, Abel, 560
Lopez, Daniel, 466
Lopez, Eduardo Ivan, 467
Lopez, Priscilla, 437, 444
Loquasto, Santo, viii, 8, 44, 368, 375, 379, 383, 556, 558, 559
Loria, Mamuka, 428
LORT, 57, 503
Lortel, Lucille, 427, 428, 560
Los Angeles Drama Critics Circle Awards, 560
Los Angeles Poverty Dept, 559
Los Angeles Theater Center, 410, 519
Los Angeles Theater Company, 516
**Lost and Found, *458***
**Lost in a Flurry of Cherries, *460***
**Lost and Found in America: Some of the Stories, *477***
Lotito, Mark, 463
Lotto, Leah, 531
**Lotto—The Sleeping America, *459***
Loud, David, 527
Loudon, Dorothy, 395, 439
Loughrin, Tim, 473
Loui, Lola, 473
**Louis' Lottery, *529***
Louis, Rick, 461
Louise, Merle, 473
Lourde, Jeremy, 537
**Love and Tears and Pain and Hope and Triumph, *513***
**Love Diatribe, *539***
**Love Letters**, 4, 5, 6, 8, 9, 10, 11, 30, 55, 56, 61, 151-165, *369*, *405*

**Love Me or Leave Me, *541***
**Love of a Pig, *516***
**Love of the Operetta, *470***
**Love's Labor's Lost**, 405
Love, Edith H., 503
Love, Edward, 436
Love, Victor, 376
Lovejoy, Deirdre, 472
**Lover's Discourse, A, *528***
Loverso, Stefano, 470
Lovett, Marcus, 387, 388
Lowe, Donald, 461
Lowell, Marguerite, 440
Lowenstein, Cary Scott, 435
Lowery, Marcella, 463
Lowstetter, Ken, 473
Lubeck, Jackie, 475
Lucas, Craig, 5, 6, 25, 392, 416, 555, 558
Lucas, Roxie, 473
Lucas, William, 467
Lucie, Doug, 452, 458
**Lucky Stiff**, 41, 560
**Lucy Loves Me, *527***
**Lucy's Lapses, *467***
Ludlam, Charles, 449, 469
Ludwig, Ken, 360
Lugo, Mary, 430
Luisi, Tony, 528
Lukeman, Brenda Shoshanna, 476
Luker, Rebecca, 444
*Lullabye*, 422
Lum, Alvin, 380
Lumet, Sidney, 45
Lumpkin, Bruce, 375, 478
**Lunch Date, *468***
Lund, Kenny, 397, 479
Lundell, Kert, 362
LuPone, Patti, 432
LuPone, Robert, 364, 437
Luscombe, Tim, 6, 10, 12, 378, 415
Lutske, Myron, 372
Lutwak, Mark, 464, 477, 479
Lutz, John David, 511
Lutz, Renee, 401, 413
Luvinsky, Leonid, 383
Lyall, Susan, 416
Lydecker, Garritt D., 539
Lyden, Jerry, 529
Lyles, Leslie, 469
Lynch, Jayne, 397, 477
Lynch, Julie A., 479
Lynch, Sharon, 461
Lynch, Thomas, 531

Lynd, Betty, 436
Lyndeck, Edmund, 378, 440
Lynes, Kristi, 434
Lyng, Nora Mae, 440, 522
Lynn, Jess, 469
Lynn, Joyce, 384
Lynne, Gillian, 388
Lyon, Mary Ellen, 456
Lyons, Jeffrey, 424, 553

**M., *508***
**M. Butterfly**, 360, 443
**Ma Rainey's Black Bottom**, 21
Ma, Jason, 373, 522
Mabe, Matthew, 513
Mabon, Paul, 472
Mabou Mines, The, 407, 412, 449, 461
MacAaron, Francesca, 466
MacAdam, Adam, 469
MacAdam, Will, 468
MacArthur Award, 560
MacArthur, Dugald, 528
**Macbeth**, 11, 52, *403*, *404*, *405*
MacCarty, Chris, 537
Macchio, Ralph, 444
MacDevitt, Brian, 466, 467
MacDonald, Bruce T., 531
MacDonald, Christine, 512
MacDonald, Jason, 420
MacDonald, Pirie, 464
MacDonald, Scott, 538
Macdonald, Sharman, 511
Machado, Eduardo, 464, 470, 519
Macias, Olga, 535
MacIver, Jane, 506
Mack, Benjamin, 367
MacKay, John, 470
Mackay, Lizbeth, 30, 408, 467, 472, 469
Mackender, Greg, 518
Mackenzie, Peter, 479
Mackey, Margaret, 456
Mackinnon, Cecil, 470
Mackintosh, Cameron, 5, 59
MacLeod, Charles, 514
MacLeod, Wendy, 477, 536
MacNamara, John, 393
MacNamara, Terrance, 386, 387
MacPherson, Greg, 458, 469
MacRae, Heather, 445
Macy, W.H., 29, 421, 458
Madden, Diane, 559

Madden, Donald, 52
Maddow, Ellen, 471
Maddux, Jacklyn, 458, 525
**Made in Buenos Aires**, *535*
**Made in Heaven!**, *474*
Madeira, Marcia, 406
Madigan, Amy, 519
**Maestro**, *468*
Magarill, Nancy, 525
Magee, Mercedes, 513
Maggio, Frances, 507
Maggio, Michael, 52, 404
Magic Theater, The, 536
**Magical Circles**, *478*
Magill, Alan, 468
Maglione, Christine, 436
Magnani, Anna, 45
Magnus, Erica, 530
Maguire, Ellen, 378
Maguire, Matthew, 461, 464, 479
Maguire, Michael, 442
Magwili, Dom, 512
Mahaffey, Valerie, 519
Mahan, Jack, 455
Maher, William Michael, 366
Mahl, Lori Ann, 377
Mahle, Marjorie, 430
Mahler, Ed, 414
Mahnken, Bob, 468
Mahnken, Harry, 468
Mahon, Kristen, 377
Mahon, Marcia, 529, 530
Mahoney, Ellen, 515
Mahoney-Bennett, Kathleen, 433, 472, 510
Maia, Elisangela, 385
Maidhoff, Robert, 367
Maier, Charlotte, 507
Maier, David, 535
Maier, Jeanne, 367
Maika, Michele, 443
Maio, Frank, 370
Major, Fred, 520
**Make Us Believe It**, *468*
Makharadze, Avtandil, 427
Makhene, Motsumi, 464
**Making Movies**, 11, 24, *427*
Makkena, Wendy, 401, 441, 457
Malaguti, 385
Malamud, Marc D., 429
Malebo, Annelen, 524
Maleczech, Ruth, 412, 452, 461, 558
Males, Larry, 513

Maletsky, Sophie, 464, 469
**Malice Aforethought**, *522*
Malik, Syeed, 529
Malina, Arnold, 376
Malina, Joel, 429
Malina, Joshua, 376
Malina, Judith, 477
Mallard, David E., 363
Mallardi, Michelle, 367
Mallozzi, Dawn, 506
Mallozzi, Lou, 506
Malony, Kevin, 477
Malpass, Kevin, 378
Malpede, John, 559
Malpede, Karen, 470
Maltby, Jacquey, 380
Maltby, Richard Jr., 6, 37, 40, 43, 419, 558
Malvern, Larry, 459, 523
**Mama Drama**, *511*
**Mama, I Want to Sing, Part II**, *475*
Mamet, David, 6, 29, 421, 458
**Man of the Flesh**, *512*
**Man Who Was Peter Pan, The**, *539*
**Man With Connections, A**, *529*
**Man Who Shot Lincoln, The**, 11, *412*
**Man's a Man, A**, *475*
**Mana Goes to the Moon**, *460*
Manaka, Kate, 464
Manaka, Matsemela, 464
Manaka, Nomsa, 464
Manasse, Jon, 388
Manassee, Jackie, 459
Mancheski, Doug, 468
Manchester, Melissa, 541
Mancini, Linda, 559
Mancuso, Nick, 516
Mancuso, Sam, 362
Mandel, Mel, 525
Mandell, Michael, 410
Mandigo, Don, 531
Mandracchia, Charles, 374
**Mandy Patinkin in Concert: Dress Casual**, 4, 43, *361*, *362*
Manetta, Michael, 479
Manette, Alexander, 468
Manger, Itsik, 420, 476
Manhattan Punch Line, 450, 461

Manhattan Theater Club (MTC), 5, 11, 14, 49, 389, 400, 417, 461
Manheim, Ralph, 372, 479
Manheimer, Josh, 503, 515
Manilow, Barry, 361
Manis, David, 473
Manke, Art, 536
Manley, Sandra, 368
Manley, Sarah, 402, 421, 422
Mann, Elizabeth, 372
Mann, Emily, 531
Mann, Jeremy, 536
Mann, P.J., 434
Mann, Terrence, 434, 441, 442
Mann, Theodore, 362, 556
Manna, R.Z., 554
Manning, Dan, 461
Manning, Rick, 531
Manos, Peter, 469
Mans, Lorenzo, 459
Manson, Alan, 379
Manson, Bevan, 420
Mantell, Michael, 379, 419
Mantello, Joe, 417, 456, 458, 534
Manzi, Warren, 399
Mapa, A., 443
**Mapping Uranium**, *540*
Mapplethorpe, Robert, 60
Mara, Mary, 403, 464, 472
Maradudin, Peter, 513, 518, 560
Maraini, Dacia, 476
Maranhao, 385
Marathon 1989, 1990, 458
Marbury, Jim, 426
Marc, Peter, 463
Marcante, Mark, 470
Marcazzo, Anne Marie, 455
Marceau, Yvonne, 36, 374
Marcelli, Julietta, 433
**March on Russia, The**, *511*
March, Felicia, 460
March, Helen, 475
Marchand, Mitchell, 424
Marchand, Nancy, 369, 439
Marchande, Teal, 474
Marcoux, Ted, 376
Marcum, Kevin, 434
Marcus, Joan, viii
Marcusson, Lori, 479
Marder, Samuel, 367
Mardikes, Tom, 517
Mardirosian, Tom, 467, 472
Maredi, Selaelo, 465

Mareneck, Ellen, 520
Margaret Harford Award, 560
Margo Lion Ltd., 395
Margolis, Mark, 541
Margulies, David, 529, 538
Margulies, Donald, 5, 15, 16, 400, 512
Margulies, John, 478
**Marie-Antoine, Opus One,** *464*
**Marilyn and Mark,** *507*
Mark Taper Forum, 412, 519, 560
Mark, Anne Stewart, 534
Mark, Jack A., 534
Mark, Ron, 507
Markell, Denis, 400
Markell, Jodie, 401, 469
Market Theater, 5, 422
Markinson, Brian, 479, 529
Marks, David, 540, 560
Marks, Jack, 539, 541
Marks, Kenneth L., 414
Marland, Stuart, 397
Marlay, Andrew B., 390, 540
Marley, Donovan, 513, 514
Marley, Sussanne, 475
Marlowe, Theresa, 405
Marney, Douglas, 506, 516
Marowitz, Charles, 59
Marquez, Gabriel Garcia, 466
Marrero, Ralph, 401, 419
Marriott, B. Rodney, 456
Marrow, Queen Esther, 42, 389, 390, 540
Marruz, Sergio Garcia, 467
Marsden, Susan, 536
Marsh, Bernard J., 425
Marsh, Jamie, 539
Marsh, Kathleen, 445
Marshak, Bob, viii
Marshall, Chris, 437
Marshall, Doug, 507
Marshall, Gay, 437
Marshall, Larry, 372
Marshall, Lorraine, 455, 456
Marshall, Martha, 384
Marshall, Peter, 444
Marshall, Rob, 434, 530
Marsicano, Mary, 467
Marson, Mary Lee, 473
Martell, Kerry, 455
Martin, Alan, 384
Martin, Alison, 464
Martin, Christopher, 362
Martin, Clay, 401, 417

Martin, Elliot, 378, 556
Martin, Hugh, 34, 369, 370, 556
Martin, Jamie, 463, 536
Martin, Jane, 519
Martin, John, 478
Martin, Judith, 558
Martin, Ken, 461, 464
Martin, Kris, 507
Martin, Mary, 52, 559
Martin, Michael X., 514
Martin, Nan, 512, 560
Martin, Samantha A., 460
Martinez, Richard, 422, 422
Martinson, Leslie, 528
Maruhashi, Setsuko, 367
**Marvin's Room,** 484, 498-502, *506*
Marx, Ara, 419
Marx, Juliana, 395
Marx, Robert, 554
Maryan, Charles, 416, 476
Marzullo, Stephen, 363, 415
Maschek, Karl, 506
Masekela, Hugh, 360
Mashkov, Vladimir, 412
**Mask, The,** *456*
Maslon, Laurence, 540
Mason, Cameron, 437
Mason, Jack, 503
Mason, Karen, 441, 523
Mason, Marshall W., 6, 416
Mason, Nan, 368
Mason, Timothy, 518
**Mass Hysteria,** *461*
Massaro, A. Lee, 528
**Mastergate,** 4, 15, *364*, 558, 559
Masters, Steve, 524
Masterson, Marc, 530
Mastrantonio, Mary Elizabeth, 6, 52, 403
Mastrocola, Frank, 434
Mastrosimone, William, 6, 24, 416
**Match Point,** 450, *458*
Mathews, Richard, 534
Mathias, Anna, 535
Matias, Fiely, 395
Matos, Radoberto, 504
Matsamura, Yoko, 455
Matschulat, Kay, 461
Matsusaka, Tom, 406
Mattei, Peter, 475
**Matter of Life or Death, A,** *468*

Matthews, Anderson, 439
Matthews, Evan, 478
Matthews, Jeffery, 534
Matthews, Pam, 464
Matthiessen, Joan, 539
Matz, Peter, 375
Mauceri, John, 395
Mauceri, Patricia, 530
Maugham, W. Somerset, 48, 378
Maultsby, Carl, 531
Maupin, Samuel, 390
Maurer, Laura, 523
Mauro, Wilson, 385
Mausseau, Jeff, 468
Maxmen, Mimi, 472, 473
Maxson, James, 476
Maxwell, Annie Laurie, 515
Maxwell, Jan, 380
Maxwell, John, 532, 533
Maxwell, Lawrence, 473
May, Sarah, 511
Mayans, Nancy, 422
Mayberry, James, 503
**Mayday,** *538*
Mayer, Jerry, 464
Mayer, Max, 458
Mayes, Sally, 37, 419
Mays, Marilyn, 466
Mazer, Sharon, 468
Mazzello, Mary, 384
Mazzie, Marin, 440
Mbulu, Letta, 524
McAlhany, Nancy, 384
McAllen, Kathleen Rowe, 387, 440, 556, 559
McAnuff, Des, 518
McArt, Jan, 373, 374
McAssey, Michael, 455
McBee, Shannon, 523
McBride, Michele, 384
McCallany, Holt, 478
McCann, Chris, 463, 464, 478
McCann, Elizabeth Ireland, 364
McCarter Theater Company, 531
McCarthy, Jeff, 442
McCarthy, Joseph P., 516
McCarthy, Nobu, 518
McCartin, James, 468
McCartney, Ellen, 472
McCarty, Bruce, 478
McCarty, Conan, 403, 413
McCarty, Michael, 363
McCauley, James, 403
McClay, Hollie, 527

McCleary, Dan, 506
McCleery, Gary, 463
McClelland, Kay, 33, 380, 440
McClendon, Afi, 415
McClennahan, Charles, 417, 424, 425, 430, 524
McClinn, Tiffany, 423
McClintock, Jodie Lynne, 418
McClure, Spike, 524
McCollister, Frier, 412, 461
McComb, Bill, 416
McCord, Dan, 511
McCormick, Michael, 527, 530
McCormick, Patty, 445
McCormick, Robert R., 473
McCowen, Alec, 427
McCracken, Bob, 516
McCrane, Paul, 458
McCready, Kevin Neil, 435, 438
McCree, Junie, 393
McCrum, James, 530
McCulloh, T.H., viii, 483, 484
McCullough, Alan, 427
McCutcheon, Bill, 432
McDermott, Tom, 365
McDonald, J.G., 513
McDonald, Joseph, 456
McDonald, Matthew, 507
McDonald, Tanny, 403, 404
McDonald, Thomas-David, 514
McDonnell, Diramund, 534
McDonnell, James, 414
McDonough, Ann, 365
McDonough, Marty, 367
McDonough, Megon, 507
McDowell, Philip, 473, 475
McEchron, Hannes, 464
McElduff, Ellen, 461
McElwee, Theresa, 461
McFadden, Neil, 560
McFarguhar, Erica, 530
McGann, Michaeljohn, 420
McGillin, Howard, 432
McGillis, Joan, 464
McGillis, Kelly, 464, 560
McGinley, John C., 400
McGovern, Elizabeth, 369, 511
McGovern, Leslie, 466
McGovern, Maureen, 372
McGowan, Charles, 435
McGrath, Bob, 459
McGrath, George, 477
McGrath, John, 460, 464
McGravie, Anne, 466
McGreevey, Anne, 363

McGruder, Jasper, 463, 474
McGruder, Sharon, 479
McGuinness, Michael John, 477
McGuire, Joe, 430
McGuire, Patti, 408
McGuire, William Biff, 538
McHale, Christopher, 404
McHugh, Joanne, 370
McIntosh, Joan, 364
McIntyre, Dennis, 526
McIntyre, Dianne, 464, 504, 559
McIntyre, Earl, 370
McIntyre, Gerry, 395, 415
McIntyre, Stephen, 362
McIntyre, Therese, 469
McKay, Anthony, 530
McKay, Patricia, 558
McKay, Roy, 362
McKean, Michael, 390, 559
McKechnie, Donna, 438
McKeever, Matt, 531
McKelvey, Lori, 476
McKenna, Mark, 504
McKenney, Ruth, 475
McKenzie, Bruce, 535
McKenzie, Kelleigh, 431
McKenzie, Rita, 474
McKereghan, Dan, 479
McKernon, John, 430
McKinley, Howard Jr., 513
McKinley, Metty, 473
McKinley, Philip William, 522
McKinney, Marie, 473
McLane, Judy, 440
McLarty, Ron, 533
McLaughlin, Deborah, 459
McLaughlin, Ellen, 520
McLeod, Bruce, 527
McMahon, Kevin, 516
McMahon, Mark, 408
McManus, Don R., 403, 418, 425
McManus, Millie, 507
McMartin, John, 10, 378
McMichaels, Flynn, 434
McMillan, Don, 514
McMillan, Richard, 530
McMullan, James, 379
McNally, Terrence, 6, 13, 14, 49, 55, 59, 61, 400, 417, 531, 558
McNamara, Mary, 367
McNamara, Maureen, 479
McNamara, Pat, 364

McNeal, Michael, 507
McNeely, Anna, 377, 433
McNeill, Robert Duncan, 467
McNider, Cate, 421
McNulty, William, 519, 520
McPherson, Scott, 498, 506
McQueen, Derrick, 464, 470
McQueeney, Ellen, 431
McQuiggan, John A., 427
McRobbie, Peter, 469
McWilliams, Patrick, 517
McWilliams, Richard, 364
**Me and My Girl**, 360, 443
Meadow, Lynne, 400, 417, 461
Meadows, Carol Lee, 370
Mealey, Chris, 471
Meares, James, 459
Medina, Hazel J., 421
Meeh, Gregory, 390
Meehan, Thomas, 395
Meeks, Willard, 390
**Meet Me in St. Louis**, 4, 34, *369*, 556, 559
Mehlmann, Michael A., 459
Mehrten, Greg, 412, 452, 461, 558
Meia-Noite, 385
Meineck, Peter, 461
Meisle, Kathryn, 478
Meissner, Don, 425
Meister, Brian, 380
Meister, Frederica, 467
Meister, Karen, 436
Mejia, Angel, 465
Melamed, Johanna, 523
Melamed, Ken, 468
Melançon, Corinne, 395
Meledandri, Wayne, 439
Melfi, Leonard, 359
Melius, Nancy, 377
Mell, Randle, 48, 421
Mello, Lori, 367
Mellon, Christopher, 478
Mellor, Stephen, 450, 463, 469, 477, 558
Membreno, Alejandro, 413, 414
Memola, Laraine, 367
**Memories of an Adult Woman**, *459*
Menard, Marleen, 460
Menchell, Ivan, 30, 392
Mendelson, Aaron, 455
Mendelson, Gary, 408
Mendez, Jane, 515
Mendillo, Stephen, 364, 403
Meneses, Maguila, 385

Mengers, Julia, 457
Menino, Joseph, 475, 476
Menke, Rick, 505
Menza, Gina, 431
**Merchant of Venice, The**, 4,
  6, 30, 31, 53, 54, 56, *382*,
  *383*, 556, 559
Mercier, G.W., 401, 416, 422,
  425, 472, 523
Merckx, Kenneth R. Jr., 536
**Mere Mortals**, *458*
Merediz, Olga, 466
Merkerson, S. Epatha, 21, 31,
  389, 556
Merkin, Robby, 391
Merman, Ethel, 51, 52
Mermelstein, Julie, 479
Merriam, Eve, 554
Merrifield, Gail, 403, 408
Merrill, Bob, 472
Merrill, Kim, 474, 477
Merritt, George, 463
Merritt, Theresa, 464
Merryman, Monica, 477
**Merton of the Movies**, *461*
Meshejian, Paul, 521
Mess, Suzanne, 384
Metallo, Donna, 513
**Metamorphosis**, 56, 360
Metcalf, Mark, 439
Metcalf, Percy, 520
**Metered Phone**, *535*
Metheny, Russell, 49, 51, 429
Metz, Janet, 473
Metzger, Rita, 384
Metzger, Ron, 513
Metzman, Irving, 469
Meyer, Bob, 508
Meyer, Craig A., 370
Meyer, D. Lynn, 473
Meyer, Edgar, 517
Meyer, Marlane, 30, 406
Meyers, Andrew, 523
Meyers, Larry John, 530
Meyers, T. J., 395
Mgaloblishvili, Guram, 428
**Miami Lights**, *521*
Miceli, Michael, 401
**Michael Moschen in
  Motion**, 559
Michaels, Christopher Lee, 370
Michaels, Tommy J., 387
Micheaux, Mirage, 474
Michel, Carolyn, 369, 401, 537
Michell, Roger, 6, 18, 379,
  422

Michelson, Gail, 456
Michelson, Larry, 534
Mickelsen, David Kay, 535
Mickey, Susan, 504, 534
**Midsummer Nights**, *463*
**Midsummer Night's Dream,
  A**, 405, *477*, 560
Migliori, Mike, 380
Mihelic, Ursula, 459
Mihok, Andrew, 408
**Mikado Inc.**, *522*
Milazzo, Ann Marie, 411, 466
Milbank, Stephen, 472
Milburn, Rob, 387, 506, 507
Miles, Julia, 472
Milhoan, Michael, 519
Milikin, Paul, 471
Militello, Anne, 417, 420, 466,
  472
**Mill Fire**, *472*
Mill Mountain Theater, 533
Miller, Andrew, 509
Miller, Arthur, 3, 15, 16, 48,
  420
Miller, Barnabas, 401
Miller, Benjamin, 477
Miller, Betty, 509
Miller, Cameron, 403, 460
Miller, Celeste, 477
Miller, Craig, 413
Miller, D. Lee, 468
Miller, Eliza, 455, 469
Miller, Herman-Jay, 370
Miller, Joel McKinnon, 408
Miller, Kenny, 519
Miller, Margaret, 470
Miller, Nina, 466
Miller, Patrick Roman, 512
Miller, Robin, 529
Miller, Tim, 477
Millett, Tim, 437
Millikan, Alden, 560
Millman, Howard J., 533
Mills, Cornelia, 468
Mills, Dana, 364
Mills, James, 513
Milwaukee Repertory Theater,
  523
Minahan, Greg, 434
**Minamata**, 560
Minami, Roger, 367
Mindfield, 461
**Mine Alone**, *513*
Mineo, John, 40, 365, 438
Miner, Mary Michele, 422
Mines, Madeleine, 384

Mingus, Lois Kagan, 477
Minichiello, M.D., 430
Mink, Gary, 469
Minor, Jason, 377
Minor, Michael, 445
Minos, Ted, 464, 509
Minskoff, Jerome, 364, 382,
  556
Mintern, Terence, 469
Minton, Nina F., 478
Mintz, Cheryl, 391
Mintz, Ethan, 457
Mintz, Jonathan, 461
Mirabella, Joan, 367
**Miracle, The**, *465*
Miranda, Anthony, 384
Mironov, Yevgeny, 412
**Mirror Image**, *479*
Mishenko, Natalia, 383
**Miss Evers' Boys**, *504*
**Miss Margarida's Way**, 4,
  55, *383*
Missouri Repertory Theater,
  517
Mistretta, Sal, 397
Mitchell, David, 8, 381, 395
Mitchell, Gregory, 40, 365,
  387, 388
Mitchell, John Cameron, 518,
  519
Mitchell, Laura, 528
Mitchell, Lauren, 395, 440,
  443
Mitchell, Loren, 531
Mitchell, Robert A., 534
Mitchell, Thomas B., 507
Mitsuyoshi, Meri, 535
Mittelman, Arnold, 521
Mixon, Alan, 523
Miyake, Kiki, 372
Miyasaki, John, 518
Mize, Nicolas, 522
Mizzy, Danianne, 461
Moe, Ruth, 531
Moe, Sharon, 384
Moffat, Donald, 403
Mofokeng, Jerry, 465
Mogentale, David, 464
Mohrmann, Al, 466
Moinot, Michel, 374
Mokler, Alan, 457
Molière, 477
Molina, Armando, 535
Molina, Arnold, 376
Molineaux, Mark, 527
Mollenhauer, Heidi, 514

Moller, Pamela, 469
Molnar, Ferenc, 449, 477
**Mom's Life, A**, 11, 27, *407, 411, 412*
Monaco, John, 366, 375, 377
Monat, Phil, 411, 458, 472, 514, 522, 523
Moncure, Lisa, 408
Moneiro, Jonnie, 527
Monés, Steve, 509
Monk, Debra, 392, 414, 417
Monk, Isabell, 461, 558
Monk, Meredith, 460
**Monorado**, *513*
Monroe, Jarion, 511, 512
Monroe, Marianne, 426
Monsion, Tim, 506
Monson, Lex, 386, 464
**Monster Time**, *470*
Montagna, Juan Carlos, 465
Montana, John, 507
Montano, Robert, 461
Monte, Chris, 478
Monte, Leticia, 460
Monte-Britton, Barbara, 435
Monteiro, Jonnie, 527
Montenegro, Mirna, 385
Montevecchi, Liliane, 36, 374, 556
Montgomerie, Jeffrey, 510, 511
Montgomery, Elizabeth, 369
Montgomery, Jeffrey, 511
Montgomery, Reggie, 411, 524
Montgomery, Robert, 431
Monticello, Roberto, 455
Montville, Clea, 414
Moodey, David, 559
Moolly, 395
Moon, Jill, 535
Mooney, Debra, 525
Mooney, Robert, 478
Mooney, William, 423, 424
Moor, Bill, 457
Moore, Bruce, 377
Moore, Carmen, 478
Moore, Catherine, 509
Moore, Charlotte, 34, 370, 475
Moore, Crista, 51, 377, 556, 559
Moore, Dana, 365, 435
Moore, Eric, 517
Moore, Garfield, 370
Moore, Greg, 527
Moore, Harold, 417
Moore, John Jay, 397
Moore, Judith, 463

Moore, Julianne, 18, 412
Moore, Kim, 473
Moore, Lee, 468
Moore, Lorrie, 528
Moore, Mamie, 460
Moore, Maureen, 442
Moore, Paul, 383
Moore, Richard, 538, 539
Moore, Steven Edward, 367
Moore, Tracey, 362
Moossy, Joan, 477
Morales, Mark, 521
Moran, Brad, 523
Moran, John, 459
Moranz, Jannet, 436
Morath, Kathy, 391
Mordecai, Benjamin, 389, 526, 555
Morehouse, Ward III, 474
Morell, Martin, 362
Morell, Richard, 513
Morelli, Frank, 384
Moreno, Rene, 509
Morey, Charles, 534
Morgan, Cass, 472
Morgan, Charles, 522
Morgan, James, 51, 363, 364, 425, 473
Morgan, Katie, 513
Morgan, Matthew, 513, 514
Morgan, Michael, 519
Morgan, Roger, 527, 530
Morgan, Ron, 370
Morgandi, Santagata, 459
Mori, Brian Richard, 533
Moriarty, Michael, 474
Moriber, Brooke Sunny, 388
Morinelli, Patricia M., 366
Morita, Keith, 535
Moriyasu, Atsushi, 467
Morlino, Jim, 514
Mornel, Ted, 455
Moross, Jerome, 473
Moroz, Barbara, 395
Morozov, Boris A., 30, 364
Morozova, Zinaida, 383
Morrill, E.F., 429
Morris, Bob, 470
Morris, Gary, 441
Morris, Iona, 474
Morris, Janet S., 514
Morris, Joan Stuart, 512
Morris, Kenny, 379
Morrison, James, 518
Morrison, Jeff, 529
Morrison, Tim, 507

Morrissey, Connan, 519
Morse, Peter G., 470
Morse, Robert, 28, 30, 62, 381, 556, 558, 559, 560
Morse, Tom, 378
Mortell, Kerry, 455
Morton, Ferd, 393
Morton, Frederic, 429, 474
Morts, Cliff, 533
Morze, Stacy, 463
Mosakowski, Susan, 461, 479
Mosby, Gary S., 518
**Mosche Volanti**, *459*
Moscow Art Theater School, 412
Moseley, Robin, 469
Moseley, Stacey, 527
Moses, Mark, 519
Moses, Paul, 514
Mosher, Gregory, 6, 29, 379, 401, 421
Moshier, Steven, 410
Moss, Charles, 384
Moss, Kathi, 374
Moss, Mickey, 531
Moss, Peter, 474
Mostel, Josh, 372, 474
Mosteller, Steven, 384
**Motherwit**, *533*
Mott, Alyce, 466
Mott, Jordan, 416, 427, 471
Mott, Martha, 384
Motte, Amarntha, 470
Mount, Guy, 509
**Mountain Language**, 452, *457*, 558
**Mountain**, 11, 29, *428*, *525*
Mousseau, Jeff, 478
**Moving Targets**, *472*
Mowbray-Clarke, Sandy, 470
Mowry, Bob, 537
Mowry, Robert D., 537
Moyer, Allen, 414, 463
Moyes, Dennis W., 539
Mozer, Elizabeth, 365, 409
Mrazek, Roger, 479
Mrozek, Slawomir, 479
Mshengu, 465
Mshvelidze, Mirian, 428
Mtume, James, 417
Muallem, Edward, 475
**Much Ado About Nothing**, 405
**Mud People**, *540*
Mueller, Ashley, 520
Mueller, Lavonne, 452, 472

Muenz, Richard, 37, 419
Mufson, Lauren, 531
Muir, Howie, 464, 473
Mulgrew, Kate, 53, 403
Mulheren, Michael, 522
Mullavey, Greg, 534
Mullen, Jan, 384
Muller, Frank, 421, 478
Muller, Jennifer, 409
Mulligan, Mary, 507
Mullin, Summer, 464
Mullins, Brighde, 458, 460
Mullins, Melinda, 365, 404
Mulloy, Paul, 362
Mulvaney, Greg, 444
Mumford, Peter B., 414
Munderloh, Otts, 366, 375, 381
Mundinger, Matthew T., 402
Mundy, Marque, 474
Mundy, Meg, 538
Munk, Erika, 557
Munro, Leigh, 444
Munt, Maxime, 512
Muñoz, Enrique, 509
Mura, Nancy, 461
Murch, Robert, 404
Murin, David, 391, 471, 525, 539
Murney, Christopher, 427
Murphy, Brennan, 463, 475, 531
Murphy, Bronagh, 475
Murphy, Donna, 12, 406
Murphy, Gary, 400, 416, 422
Murphy, Harry S., 404
Murphy, Karen, 395
Murphy, Mary, 393
Murphy, Sally, 386
Murphy, Tom, 475
Murphy, Victoria, 477
Murphy, William, 517
Murphy-Palmer, Kathleen, 475
Murray, Abigail, 467
Murray, Annie, 537
Murray, Brian, 378, 404
Murray, Cora, 475
Murray, Daniel L., 513, 514
Murray, Juleen, 516
Murray, Margery, 522
Murray, Mary Gordon, 440
Murray, Peg, 475
Murray, Roderick, 470
Murray, Todd, 477
Murrin, Tom, 460
Musante, Tony, 528
Musayelian, Irene, 383

Muscarello, Tony, 508
Musgrave, Richard A., 511
**Music Rescue Service**, *471*
Music-Theater Group, 422, 463
**Musical Celebration of
    Mahalia Jackson, A**, *390*
Musical Theater Works, 463
Musiker, Lee, 380
Musmanno, Henry, 512
Musser, Tharon, 378, 397, 534
Mussman, Linda, 479
Mutual Benefit Productions, 395
Muzhikova, Nina, 412
Muzio, Gloria, 472, 559
**My Father, The President**, *512*
**My Big Land**, *412*
**My Children! My Africa!**, 5, 8, 11, 22, 30, 193-219, *242*, 450, *466*, 558
**My Favorite Year**, 59
*My Love, My Love*, 413
**My One and Only**, 36
**My Sister Eileen**, 475
Mydlack, Danny, 477
Myers, Alex, 367
Myers, Judy, 507
Myers, Larry, 471
Myers, Lou, 21, 389
Myers, Mary, 431
Myrow, Fredric, 519
**Mystery of the Rose
    Bouquet, The**, *519*

Nabel, Bill, 363, 438
Nachtmann, Rita, 511
**Nagasaki Maru**, *456*
Nagrin, Lee, 459
Nahem, Richard, 479
Nahrwold, Thomas, 470
Najera, Miguel, 528
Najera, Rick, 535
Najimi, Kathy, 399
Nakagawa, Jon, 472
Nakagawa, Kikue, 367
Nakahara, Ron, 467
Nakamaru, Tomoko, 456
Nakao, Kenji, 397
Naked Angels, 449, 450
**Names Have Been Changed
    To Protect the Innocent,
    The**, *512*
Napier, Grace, 397
Naranjo, Valerie, 422
Narita, Rob, 518

Nash, David J., 366
Nash, Michael, 520
Nash, N. Richard, 425
Nash, Neil, 439
Nash, Raphael, 504
Nash, Ron, 409
Nash, Ted, 372
Nason, Brian, 372
Nason, Susanna, 367
Nasution, Arswendi, 470
Nat Horne Theater, 477
Natel, Jean-Marc, 360
Nathan, Fred, 383, 387, 388
Nathan, Robert, 41, 407
Nathanson, Roy, 460, 466
National Endowment for the
    Arts (NEA), 60, 61, 62
National Playwrights
    Conference, 540
National Theater, 372
**Nature of Things, The**, *466*
Natwick, Mildred, 560
Nauffts, Geoffrey, 376
Naughton, Amanda, 410
Naughton, James, 33, 44, 380, 556, 559
Naumkin, Yuri, 383
Navarre, Ron, 438
Navarro, Tina Cantu, 417, 504
Navazio, Mickele, 470
Navins, Deborah, 427, 431
Nayer, Tracy, 515
Naylor, Marcus, 474
Naylor, Wesley, 475
Nazzal, Nidal, 478
NEA, 60, 61, 62
Neal, Vicki, 504
Neals, Lawrence A. Jr., 422
Nealy, Milton Craig, 415
Near, Timothy, 411
Nease, Byron, 444
Nebozenko, Jan, 425
**Nebraska**, *518*
**Neddy**, 11, *424*, *425*
Nederlander, James M., 364, 365, 372, 384
Nedzel, Raymond, 456
Neet, Alison Stair, 475
Neff, Debra, 413, 414
Neff, Larry, 535
Neff, Tracy Lynn, 521
Negro Ensemble Company,
    The, 11, 30, 423
Neiden, Daniel, 476
Neil, Ray, 529
Nela, Rome, 470

Nelligan, Kate, 9, 30, 49, 62, 369, 405, 419
Nels, Peter, 404
Nelsen, Don, 552
Nelson, Barry, 439
Nelson, Jim, 509
Nelson, Kenneth, 439
Nelson, Mari, 403, 408
Nelson, Mark, 23, 376, 445
Nelson, Rebecca, 379, 423, 463
Nelson, Richard, 6, 18, 19, 362, 368, 379, 403, 421, 534
Nelson, Ruth, 421
Nelson, Steve, 431
Nemeth, Sally, 472, 512
Nery, Edilson, 385
Nesmith, Eugene, 464
Nesmith, Nathaniel, 464
Neuberger, Jan, 390, 463
Neufeld, Mary, 469
Neufeld, Peter, 395
Neumann, David, 412
Neumann, Frederick, 412, 516
Neutzling, Kimberly, 513
Neuwirth, Bebe, 434
Neville, Marcus, 380
Nevins, Kristine, 463
New Anatomies, 452, 475
New Arts Theater Co., 477
New Directors Series, 450
New Dramatists, 463
New Federal Theater, 464
New Music, 510
New Musicals, 59, 60, 531
New Stage Theater, 517
New Theater of Brooklyn, The, 449, 477
New Tuners, 391, 507
New Vaudeville '89, 461
New York 1937, 476
New York City Center Light Opera Company, 384
New York City Opera, 52, 383
New York Dance and Performance (Bessie) Awards, 559
New York Drama Critics Awards, 550
New York Drama Critics Circle, 62, 551
New York Gilbert and Sullivan Players 477
New York Shakespeare Festival Public Theater, 11, 15, 52, 61, 368, 372, 383, 402,

403, 404, 405, 406, 407, 412, 420, 429, 461, 465
New York Shakespeare Festival Shakespeare Marathon, 11, 402, 405
New York Stage and Film Company, 381
New York Telephone, 402
New York Theater Ensemble, 412
New York Theater Workshop, 22, 422, 450, 466
New, Dale, 524
Newcomb, Don, 472
Newcott, Rosemary, 503
Newell, Ron, 511
Newhall, Anne, 421
Newman, Andrew Hill, 444
Newman, David, 359
Newman, Jim, 408, 409
Newman, Paul, 3, 46
Newman, Phyllis, 478
Newman, Ralph, viii
Newman, William, 457
Newport, Stephen, 475
Newsome, Paula, 507
Newton, John, 386
Newton, Lynn, 367
Next Wave Festival, 474
Ney, Diane, 523
Ngema, Mbongeni, 360, 524
Nicastro, Michelle, 443
Nicholas Nickleby, 20
Nicholas, Martin, 537
Nicholaw, Casel, 531
Nichols, Mike, 507, 518
Nichols, Peter, 6, 12, 62, 406, 551
Nichols, Richard Alan, 517
Nichols, Robert, 432
Nicholson, Betsy, 386
Nickerson, Rob, 522
Nicola, James C., 422, 466
Niebuhr, Mark, 509
Nielsen, Colette, 455
Nielsen, Kristine, 401, 425, 464
Nielsen, Paul, 455
Nielson, Karen Kermiet, 513
Nielson, Peter, 513
Niewood, Gerard J., 367
Night of Shamans, 460
Night of the 3 Moons, 455
Night Dance, 510
Night With Doris, A, 414
Nigro, Bob, 473

Nikiforovna, Marya, 364
Nine, 36
Nininger, Susan, 410
Nishida, Takashi, 460
Nissenson, Gloria, 41, 373, 473
Niven, Kip, 473
Nixon, Cynthia, 473
NO + (No More), 465
Noah, James, 386
Noble, Adrian, 18, 419
Noble, Janet, 475
Nobles-DaSilva, Mari, 473
Nobody's Miss America, 460
Noel, Craig, 535
Nogulich, Natalia, 30, 390
Nohe, Marc F., 474
Nohl, Joseph, 396
Nokwe, Tu, 524
Nolan, Anto, 475
Nolen, Timothy, 444
Nolte, Bill, 395
Noonan, John Ford, 430, 458, 509
Noone, James, 463, 472, 539
Nordyke, Peter, 535
Normals, The, 461
Norman, Marsha, 59, 452, 473, 527
Norris, Bruce, 511
Norris, Kathleen, 509
Northrup, Jessica, 433
Norton, Kristin, 478
Norwood, 475
Norzar Productions, Inc., 430
Noseworthy, Jack, 438
Nostrand, Michael, 473
Not for Profit, 464
Novel Stages, 528
Novelli, Stephen, 521
Novey, Lara, 508
Novick, Julius, 551, 552, 558
Noviello, Rosemary, 367
Nozick, Bruce, 474, 476
Ntinga, Themba, 465
Nugent, James, 477
Nunn, Trevor, 6, 20, 359, 388, 556
Nunsense, 399
Nureyev, Rudolf, 397
Nussbaum, Bernard and Toby, 383
Nutt, Sandra, 424

O Little Town of Bagels, Teacakes, and Hamburger Buns, 516

O'Berg, Patti, 537
O'Brady, Mary, 445
O'Brien, Adale, 520
O'Brien, Glenn, 459
O'Brien, Jack, 534
O'Brien, Joseph, 466
O'Brien, Paul, 419, 461, 474,
    516, 529
O'Brien, Quentin, 525
O'Connell, Deidre, 472
O'Connell, Elinore, 387, 388,
    442
O'Connell, Patricia, 473
O'Connell, Patrick, 457
O'Connor, James, 473
O'Connor, Joyce, 368, 470
O'Connor, Kevin, 429, 457,
    478
O'Connor, P.J., 456
O'Connor, Sara, 474, 523
O'Donnell, Frank, 455
O'Donoghue, Peg, 455
O'Donohue, John, 455
O'Hara, Jenny, 458
O'Hara, Paige, 523
O'Horgan, Tom, 455, 459
O'Keefe, John, 469, 477, 559
O'Mara, Mollie, 475
O'Meara, Evan, 420
O'Neill, Bill, 529
O'Neill, Denis, 475
O'Neill Theater Center, 389,
    540, 555
O'Quinn, Keith, 373
O'Reilly, Ciaran, 475
O'Reilly, Maya, 461
O'Reilly, Roderick, 474
O'Reilly, Terry, 412
O'Rourke, Barry, 475
O'Rourke, Kevin, 47, 386, 410
O'Shea, Milo, 34, 370
O'Shea, Sally, 426
O'Steen, Michael, 370, 395
O'Sullivan, Anne, 464, 520
O'Sullivan, Sean, 470, 474
Oates, Joyce Carol, 458, 520
Oatts, Richard, 367
**Oba Oba '90**, 4, *384*
Oberman, Lawrence, 516
Obie Awards, The, 557
**Objects of Desire**, *477*
Ochoa, Steve, 441
Ocquita, Ric, 523
Oddo, Louis, 388
Odel, Dwight Richard, 512
Oden, Christopher, 475, 476

**Of Mice and Men**, 5
**Of Thee I Sing**, *477*
Ofrane, Etan, 429
Ofrane, Josh, 429
**Oh! Dubrovnik!**, *456*
**Oh! Calcutta!**, 56, 359
**Oh, Mr. Faulkner, Do You
    Write?**, *532*
**Oh, Hell**, 6, 11, 29, *421*
Ohara, Hirotoshi, 367
Ohio Theater, 477
Ohlson, Larry, 535
Okada, Kim, 427
Okajima, Shigeo, 460
Okamura, Koji, 383
Okazaki, Alan K., 535
Okrent, Mike, 360
Olcott, Thomas B., 367
**Old Man Is Snoring, The**,
    *507*
Old Globe Theater, 389, 397,
    534, 555
*Old Possum's Book of Practical
    Cats*, 359
Oldakowski, Thomas J., 367
**Oldest Living Confederate
    Widow Tells All**, *533*
Olds, Gabriel, 404
Olich, Michael, 504
Oligny, Huguette, 474
Oliver, Edith, 551, 552, 559
Oliver, Jorge, 467
Oliveros, Pauline, 461
Olivier, Laurence, 47
Oliviera, Carlos, 385
Olmstead, Dan, 530
Olney Theater, 560
Olsen, Robert, 461
Olson, Stephen, 469
Olson, Todd, 469
Omaha Magic Theater, The,
    527
Oman, Timothy W., 478
Omilami, Afemo, 503
Omilami, Elizabeth, 503
**On the Bench**, *469*
**On the Brink**, *529*
**On the Edge of the World**,
    *508*
**On the Move**, *466*
**On the Road to Wholeness**,
    *471*
**On the Town**, 560
Onate, Erik, 403
**Once in Arden**, *512*
**Once in Doubt**, 560

**Once on This Island**, viii, ix,
    5, 6, 8, 11, 41, 42, 43, 44,
    344-355, *413*, *415*, 552
**Once Upon a Mattress**, 41
**Once/Twice**, *477*
One Dream, 427
**One Mo' Time**, 42, 430
126 Second Avenue Corp., 425
**Only the Sky Was Blue!**, *539*
**Only Year That Ever Was,
    The**, *524*
**Only Kidding!**, 399, 443
Onorato, Joseph A., 368
Onrubia, Cynthia Carrillo, 437
Ontological-Hysteric Theater,
    479
Opel, Nancy, 433
Opelka, Gregg, 507
**Open Boat, The**, *458*
Open Eye: New Stagings, The,
    466
Opffer, Yvonne, 477
Opladen, John, 529
Oppenheimer Award, 559
Oppenheimer, Jane, 508
Opsahl, Jason, 522
**Oral Fixations**, *477*
**Orange Grove**, *462*
Orbach, Jerry, 439
Oreskes, Daniel, 508
**Orfeo**, 40, *366*
Organic Theater Company, 508
**Orgy in the Air-Traffic
    Control Tower**, *431*
Oriel, Ray, 519
**Orient Beach**, *479*
Orleans, Ilo, 473
Orner, Fredric H., 379, 404
Oropeza, Luis, 535
**Orpheus Descending**, 4, 6,
    45, 53, *364*, 556
Orth-Pallavicini, Nicole, 534
Ortiz, John, 509
Orton, Joe, 41, 49, 406
Osborne, Kay, 470
Osborne, Georga L., 370
Oscar, Brad, 388
Osorio, Raul, 465
Osser, Glenn, 368
Osterman, Georg, 469
Osterweil, Daniel, 530, 529
Ostrow, Ron, 376
Ota, Junko, 384
Otarashvili, Gela, 428
**Other People's Money**, 399,
    444, 559

Otis, John, 468
Otrabanda Company, 460, 462
Ott, Sharon, 416, 504
Ottem, Kevin, 537
Ottley, Rachelle, 370
Otto, Liz, 478
Our Country's Good, *519*
Our Lady of the Desert, *527*
Oura, Mizuki, 367
Ousley, Robert, 372
Out of Character, *528*
Out of the Depths, *528*
Out to Lunch, *478*
Outer Critics Circle Awards, 558
Outside the Radio, *458*
Ovchinnikov, Rady, 383
Ovenden, Holly, 367
Overland, *528*
Owen, Paul, 519, 520
Owens, Fred, 474
Owens, Gordon, 436
Owl's Breath, *475*
OyomO, 450, 458
Oyster, Jim, 473
Ozaki, Nancy, 535

P.S. 122 Field Trips, *462*
Pace Theatrical Group, 377, 397, 427
Pace, Atkin, 416
Pacheco, Scot, 479
Paciorek, Lisa, 511
Packard, Stephen, 508
Padgett, Billy, 522
Padilla, Louis, 527
Padron, Aurelio, 531
Paer, Lewis, 384
Page, Elizabeth, 30, 426
Page, Evelyn, 433
Page, Geraldine, 48
Page, Ken, 434
Page, Patrick, 534
Pagliotti, Douglas, 397
Paige, Elaine, 432
Paint, *464*
Painted Rain, *413*, *414*
Painter, Walter, 380
Pais, Josh, 457
Pakledinaz, Martin, 404, 516, 527
Pal Joey, 43
Palanker, Craig, 401
Paley, Stephanie, 535
Palmas, Joseph, 476
Palmer, Hugh, 475

Palmer, Lynne, 509
Palmieri, Joe, 364
Palminteri, Chazz, 27, 478
Pamplin, Shep, 455, 456, 471
Pan Asian Repertory Theater, 449, 452, 467
Panaro, Hugh, 443
Pankow, John, 18, 412
Pannell, Glen, 473
Paper Bag Players, 558
Paper Mill Playhouse, 522
Papp, Joseph, 3, 40, 53, 61, 368, 402, 403, 407, 465, 558, 560
Pappas, Evan, 393, 560
Papuashvili, David, 427
Paquet, Lucina, 386
Paracat, Carol, 367
Paradise for the Worried, *463*
Parady, Ron, 392
Paraiso, Nicky, 463
Paramount Pictures, 374, 556
Pardess, Yael, 519
Pardo, Daniel, 459
Pareja, Ramon, 465
Parfenyuk, Nikolai, 383
Parichy, Dennis, 369, 379, 400, 406, 416, 417, 420, 422, 427, 429, 469, 471
Paris '31, *455*
Park, Steve, 467
Parke, Jeff, 373
Parker, Alecia, 386
Parker, Anne, 455
Parker, Jean, 475
Parker, Leonard, 455, 526
Parker, Mary-Louise, 6, 25, 61, 392, 417, 418, 556, 559
Parker, Nathaniel, 382
Parker, Shanga, 535
Parks, Hildy, 390
Parks, Suzan-Lori, 449, 463, 474, 558
Parks, Trina, 474
Parlato, Dennis, 472, 473
Parnell, Peter, 14, 413
Parr, Larry, 537
Parrell, Lea, 393
Parrinello, Richard, 384
Parry, Brendon, 506
Parry, Chris, 511
Parsons, Estelle, 383, 469
Parsons, Sally Ann, 459
Parting Gestures, *459*

Partlan, William, 416, 477, 523, 532, 540
Pasadena Playhouse, 390
Pascoe, Jonelle, 513
Pasekoff, Marilyn, 424
Pashalinski, Lola, 461
Pasqualino, Pam Stacey, 367
Passaro, Michael J., 388
Passion of Narcisse Mondoux, The, *474*
Patel, Neil, 518
Paterson, David R., 522
Pathological Venus, *458*
Patinkin, Mandy, 43, 56, 361
Patricca, Nicholas A., 466
Patrick, Robert, 470
Patsco, Dan, 524
Patterson, Anne C., 470
Patterson, Jamie, 434
Patterson, Jay, 420
Patterson, Kelly, 435, 473
Pattison, Liann, 539
Patton, Lucille, 392
Paul, Talia, 364
Paul, Tina, 40, 365, 366, 472, 556
Paula Cooper Gallery, 412
Pauley, Wilbur, 382
Paulin, Freddie, 529
Paulsen, Jeanne, 512
Paulsen, Rick, 538
Pawl, Christina, 370
Payan, Ilka Tanya, 459
Payne, Leon, 408
PCPA Theaterfest, 536
Peabody, Dossy, 516
Peabody, Sam, 503
Peabody, Steve, 412
Pearce, Bobby, 424
Pearl Theater Company, 477
Pearlman, Errol, 466
Pearlman, Stephen, 15, 414, 472
Pearsall, Kerri, 367
Pearson, Scott, 437
Pecong, *508*
Pedernera, Alfredo, 463
Pederson, Rose, 538, 539
Peek, Jenny, 411
Peggy and Jackson, *466*
Peipers, David H., 427
Peldon, Courtney, 370
Pele, 385
Pell, Stephen, 469
Pellegrino, Susan, 425, 478
Peluchi, Julio, 385

Pelzig, Daniel, 406
**Pen Pals**, *511*
Pena, Manuel, 465
Pendleton, Wyman, 392, 464
**Pendragon**, *525*, *537*
Penguin Repertory Company, 539
Penn, Matthew, 458
Pennington, Mark, 466
Pennsylvania Stage Company, 503
Penny Arcade, 477
Penzi, Jim, 529
**People Who Could Fly, The**, 11, *405*, *478*
People's Light and Theater Company, 520
Peoples, Jamal, 503
Peppe, Michael, 477
Peppiatt, Caroline, 393
Peppiatt, Frank, 393, 394
Percassi, Don, 395, 438
Pereiras, Manuel, 467
Perelman, S.J., 400
Peretz, Deborah D., 520
Perez, Josie, 466
Perez, Luis, 365, 366
Perez, Mercedes, 437
Perez, Michael, 541
Perez, Miguel, 404, 457
**Perfect Crime**, 399
**Perfect Diamond, A**, *474*
**Performance Anxiety**, *518*
Performance Space 122, 450, 477
Perillo, Robert, 475
Perkins, A. William, 436
Perkins, Patti, 472
Perkins, Wellington, 436
Perl, Joshua, 403
Perlman, Bonnie, 373
Perloff, Carey, 452, 457
Perman, Dennis, 476
Perrineau, Harold Jr., 463
Perry, Alvin B., 417
Perry, Claudia, 529
Perry, Ernest Jr., 508
Perry, Jeff, 19, 386, 387
Perry, Keith, 380
Perry, Louis, 384
Perry, Lynnette, 374, 375, 467
Perry, Ryan, 367
Perry, Sandra, 521
Perry, Steven, 420, 425
Persson, Lars Goran, 559
Pesaturo, George, 438

Pessin, Jan, 506
**Peter Breaks Through**, *413*, *414*
Peter Hall Company, 364, 382
Peter, Sinai, 478
Peters, Bernadette, 440
Peters, Brock, 439
Peters, Charlie, 478
Peters, R.J., 435, 437
Peterson, David R., 522
Peterson, Lisa, 414, 450, 458, 466
Peterson, Melinda, 535
Peterson, Patricia Ben, 440
Peterson, Robert, 534
Peterson, Wally, 378
Petit, Chris, 405
Petit, Lenard, 422
Petlock, Martin, 536, 537
Petlock, Rafael, 537
Petrarca, David, 472, 506
Petrino, Debbie, 455
Petronius, 459
Petrovich, Victoria, 463, 535
Pettiford, Valerie, 458
Pettigrew, Ricky, 509
Pettijohn, Grace, 456
Pettinelli, Fran, 469
Pettit, Christopher, 478
Pettit, Peggy, 477
Peyser, Ruthi, 462
Pezza, Mariner James, 426
Pfeiffer, Michelle, 6, 52, 403
**Phantom of the Opera, The**, 34, 360, 560
Phelan, Jane Schloss, 560
Philadelphia Festival Theater for New Plays, 528
**Philadelphia, Here I Come!**, 452
**Philip Glass Buys a Loaf of Bread**, 450, *461*
Philip Leshin Communications, 401
Philips, Jessi, 522
Phillips, Andy, 372
Phillips, Barbara-Mae, 392
Phillips, David, 475
Phillips, Ethan, 504
Phillips, J.T., 478
Phillips, Lloyd, 372
Phillips, Mary, 363, 473
Phillips, Romy, 470
Phillips, Tommy, 473
Phillips, Zelmer, 515
Philpot, Andy, 560

Phippin, Jackson, 520
Phoenix, Reggie, 436
**Piano Lesson, The**, 4, 5, 6, 8, 21, 30, 31, 56, 61, 62, 313-343, *389*, 551, 552, 553, 554, 555, 556, 558, 559, 560
Piazzolla, Astor, 40, 365
Picciotto, Henri, 478
**Pick Up Ax**, 484, 491-497, *512*, *536*
Pickart, Chris, 469
Pickering, Steven, 403
Pickett, Lynn, 455, 456
**Picnic Baskets**, *468*
**Pictures in Glass**, *455*
Picus, Stan, 513
Pierce, David, 440, 507
Pierce, Mike, 455, 456
Pierson, Daniel B., 528
Pietraszek, Rita, 509
Pietropinto, Angela, 477
Pietsch, Jim, 406
Pigliavento, Michele, 377, 436
Pinchot, Bronson, 364
Pinckney, Tim, 479
Pineda, Pedro, 466
Pinget, Robert, 479
Pinhasik, Howard, 473
**Pink Studio, The**, *519*
Pinkney, Mikell, 474
Pintauro, Joe, 24, 416, 472
Pintavalle, John, 384
Pinter, Harold, 10, 452, 457
Pioneer Theater Company, 534
Piontek, Michael, 372, 400
Pipeline/Museum of Contemporary Art, 408
Pippin, Don, 368, 397
Pirandello, 30
**Pirates of Penzance, The**, *477*
**Pirates**, *512*
Piro, Jacqueline, 443
Piro, Lillian, 475
Piro, Sal, 473
Pittenridge, Robert, 529
Pitts, Barbara, 528
Pitts, Christoher, 534
Pitts, Michael Day, 435, 438
Pittsburgh Public Theater, 530, 559
Pittu, David, 379
**Pixie Led, The**, *476*
Pizzuti, Paul, 372
**Place to Be, The**, *464*

**Placebo**, *468*
Plaisant, Dominique, 505
Plank, Scott, 435, 438
**Planning Ahead**, *468*
Platt, Oliver, 401, 507
**Play Called Not and Now, A,**
    *531*
Play Works, 529
**Play's the Thing, The**, 449,
    *477*
Playhouse 91, 478
**Playmaker, The**, *519*
Playten, Alice, 445
Playwrights Preview
    Productions, 478
Playwrights Horizons New
    Theater Wing, 408, 467
Playwrights Horizons, ix, 5,
    11, 413
Pleeth, Graeme, 382
Pleiman, Timothy, 507
**Plenty**, 17
Plimpton, Martha, 538
Plunkett, Maryann, 443
Poddubiuk, Christina, 393
Poe, Edgar Allan, 477
Poe, Kevin, 434
Poindexter, Karen, 373
Poindexter, Porter, 362
Polacco, Stacey, 479
Polantz, David, 518
Polcsa, Juliet, 472
Polito, Jon, 444
Polk, Andrew, 520
Pollack, Maureen Stevens, 367
Pollitt, Barbara, 411, 422
Pollitt, Demeny, 506
Polner, Alex, 467
Pomahac, Bruce, 370
Ponce, LuAnne, 440
Ponderoso, Louis M., 468
Ponter, Khushi, 531
Pooler, Audrey, 530
Pooler, Chuck, 431
Pope, Deborah J., 477
Pope, Peggy, 445, 463, 539
Pope, Sabrynaah, 464
Popkhadze, L., 427
Popper, Eva, 535
Porell, John, 506
Porembski, Ronald, 506
Porgina, Ludmilla, 383
**Pornsongspiel**, *477*
Porretta, Greg, 520
Porretta, Matthew, 443
Portas, Lynn, 479

Porteous, Cameron, 393
Porter, Catherine, 411, 457
Porter, Cole, 360, 455
Porter, John, 525
Porter, W. Ellis, 410
**Portfolio**, *461*
Portillo, Rose, 512
Portland Opera, 467
Portland Stage Company, 531
**Positive Me**, *459*
Posner, Kenneth, 425, 539
Post, Douglas, 514, 540
Postel, Suzan, 397
Poster, Kim, 375
Potok, Chaim, 528, 529
Potozkin, Amy, 463
Potter, Dennis, 32
Potter, Jane, 461
Potts, David, 416, 427
Powell, Anthony, 27, 387
Powell, Dakota, 458
Powell, Jan, 528
Powell, Jerry, 394
Powell, Michael Warren, 372,
    392, 417, 474
Powell-Parker, Marianne, 541
**Power Play**, *468*
Powerhouse Theater of Vassar,
    381
Powers, David, 376, 395
Powers, Winifred V., 468
Powers, Winkie, 468
Powich, Christopher, 474
Pownall, David, 468
Poyner, Margaret, 382
Prabowo, Tonny, 470
Prager, Benjamin, 538
Pregorac, Bernadette, 530
**Prelude to a Kiss**, 4, 5, 6, 8,
    11, 25, 61, 269-292, *392*,
    *416*, *417*, 551, 552, 555,
    556, 558, 559
Prendergast, Shirley, 425, 524
Prentice, Sam, 531
Prescott, Ken, 473
Presky, Gerri, 367
Presnell, Harve, 395
Press, Seymour Red, 370
Press, Toni, 528
Pressler, Terra Daugirda, 527
Presti, Jackie, 380
Preston, Corliss, 473, 517
**Pretending to America**, *529*
Pretinho, Edgar, 385
Preto, Toco, 385
**Price of Fame, The**, *420*

Price, Lonny, 49, 393, 429,
    471
Price, Michael P., 514
Price, Reynolds, 507, 510, 517
Prigmore, James, 534
Primary Stages Company, 478
**Prin**, *417*
**Prince of Central Park**, 4, 41,
    *373*
**Prince of Homburg, The**, *476*
**Prince**, 20
Prince, Faith, 49, 419
Prince, Ginger, 377, 378
Prince, Harold, 50, 51, 59, 363,
    531
Prince, Liz, 460
Prinz, Rosemary, 439, 472
Prior, Richard, 415
Pritchard, Michael H., 473
Pritchett, James, 539
**Privates on Parade**, 6, 11, 12,
    62, *406*, 551
Procaccino, John, 538
Producers Club, 478
Proett, Robin, 517
**Progress**, 452, *458*
Projansky, Robert, 477
Prokhorov, Vladimir, 383
Prokhorova, Valentina, 383
Promenade Partners, Inc., 427
**Promise Comes After, The,**
    *516*
Provenza, Paul, 444
Provenza, Rosario, 410
Pruneau, Phillip, 473
Prymus, Ken, 473
Pryor, Deborah, 458, 560
Puerto Rican Traveling Theater,
    467
Pugh, Jim, 380
Puig, Manuel, 519, 531
Puleo, Robert, 426
Pulitzer Prize Winners, 553
Pulley, Sissy, 516, 517
Pulliam, Darcy, 469
Punch Productions, 382, 556
Pupello, Joseph, 459
**Puppetmaster of Lodz, The,**
    *474*
Purcell, John, 373, 503
Purdham, David, 403
Purdy, Joseph, 473
**Purple Hearts**, *518*
Purscell, Phyllis, 525
Pursley, David, 372
**Puss in Boots**, *524*

Putnam, Robert, 468
Pyant, Paul, 364, 556
Pyne, James F. Jr., 520

Quackenbush, Karyn, 530
Quaigh Theater, 467
Quandt, Stephen, 459, 470
Quarry, *537*
Quart, Abigail, 468
Queen, Scott, 517
Queiroz, Norberto, 385
Quiet End, A, *471*
Quigley, Chip, 424
Quigley, Erin, 387, 556
Quill, Barbara, 511
Quillin, Mimi, 458
Quinette, Brian, 512
Quinlan, Bill, 470
Quinn, Brian, 455
Quinn, Colleen, 477
Quinn, John, 456
Quinn, Nancy, 413
Quinn, Patrick, 441
Quinnette, Brian, 513
Quintessential Image, The, *475*
Quinton, Everett, 449, 469
Quiroga, Horacio, 422

R, Essene, 473, 524
Raben, Larry, 431
Rackleff, Owen S., 478
Radiant City, *463*
Radio City Music Hall Productions, 366
Rae, Charlotte, 439, 440
Raffio, Richard, 367
Raffio, Ronald, 370
Raft Theater, 429, 478
Ragey, Joe, 528
Ragged Dick, *507*
Ragno, Joseph, 476
Ragsdale, William, 458
Rahim, Idris, 506
Raider-Wexler, Victor, 420, 473, 476
Raidy, William, 552
Raileanu, Eufrosina, 384
Rain. Some Fish. No Elephants, 449, *477*
Rainbow and Stars, 478
Rainer, John, 525
Rainey, David, 524
Rainwater, John, 431
Rainy Days and Friday Nights, *540*

Raiter, Frank, 403, 457
Raitt, James, 43, 370, 431
Rakov, Victor, 383
Raley, Wade, 527
Ralf, Ralf, 559
Ralstin, Monte, 455
Ramach, Michael, 479
Rambeau, Careayre, 364
Ramblin', Lute, 461
Rameau, Patrick, 403
Ramicova, Dunya, 511
Ramin, Sid, 377
Ramish, Trish, 436
Ramont, Mark, 456
Ramos, Bridget, 384
Ramos, Kristy, 515
Ramos, Paulo, 385
Ramp, The, *512*
Rampino, Lewis D., 404, 520
Ramsey, Galen G., 508
Ramsey, Steve, 386, 387
Randall, Barbara, 384
Randall, Tony, 443
Randel, Melissa, 436
Randell, Patricia, 468
Randolph, Jim, 378, 380, 381, 397
Randoy, Stephen, 524
Rankin, Moira, 524
Raphael, Gerrianne, 401
Rashad, Phylicia, 440
Ratajczak, Dave, 380
Rathbun, Sherry Joy, 517
Rathgeb, Laura, 477
Rattan, *540*
Rattigan, Terence, 468
Rattner, George, 478
Ravenswood, *417*, *419*
Rawcliffe, Susan, 422
Rawlins, Theodore, 539
Ray, Connie, 458, 460, 461
Ray, Forest Dino, 531
Raymond, Bill, 457, 461, 469, 511
Raymond, Deborah, 512
Raymond, Devon, 512
Rayppy, Gary, 382
Re, Tommy, 435, 438
Readers, *456*
Ready for the River, *456*, *513*, *540*
Real Life Story of Johnny de Facto, The, *514*
Real Family, *478*

Really Useful Theater Company, Inc., The, 387, 555
Ream, Marc, 535
Reap, J.J., 431
Reardon, Peter, 370
Reaves, Raymond, 524
Reaves-Phillips, Sandra, 42, 430
Rebbega, Larri, 514
Rebeck, Theresa, 458
Rebhorn, James, 18, 412, 518
Rebimbas, Rosemarie, 504
Recent Developments in Southern Connecticut, *509*
Recht, Ray, 539
Red Quarters, *468*
Red Shoes, The, *479*
Red Sneaks, The, *479*
Reddin, Keith, 472, 512, 518
Reddin, Naomi, 370
Reddy, Brian, 503
Redfield, Adam, 420
Redgrave, Lynn, 369
Redgrave, Vanessa, 6, 45, 364
Redsecker, John, 370
Redwood, John Henry, 459
Redwood, Manning, 364
Reed, Bobby, 469
Reed, Brad, 506
Reed, Gary, 468, 475
Reed, Rondi, 386, 387
Reed, T. Michael, 435
Reehling, Joyce, 392, 417
Rees, R.M., 443
Reeve, Milton, 513
Reeves, Roger, 527
Regan, Molly, 527
Reich, Brian, 468
Reichert, Whit, 534
Reichler, Alexandra, 467
Reid-Petty, Jane, 517
Reilly, Charles Nelson, 525
Reilly, Chris, 534
Reilly, Don, 404
Reilly, Michael, 457
Reilly, Robert, 509
Reily, Terrance, 460
Rein, Mercedes, 535
Reinglas, Fred, 400, 416, 417, 427
Reingold, Jacqueline, 458, 479
Reinking, Ann, 438
Reisman, Jane, 431
Reissa, Eleanor, 420

Reiter, Andrea B., 514
Related Retreats, *470*
Remeny, Joyce, 426
Remington Notes, *469*
Remme, John, 377
Renderer, Scott, 469
Rene, Nikki, 415
Rene, Norman, 6, 25, 392,
    417, 558
Renick, Kyle, 405, 472
Renken, Michael, 516
Reno, 477
Renshaw, Andrew, 443
Repertory Theater of St. Louis,
    The, 534
Repicci, Albert, 430
Repicci, Bill, 430
Repole, Charles, 473
Repp, Laureen, 367
Reshid, Beatrice, 506
Reshid, Steve, 506
Resnick, Amy, 536
Resnik, Hollis, 442
Ressenger, Claire M., 468
Restaurant, The, *468*
Ret, *517*
Return of Herbert Bracewell,
    560
Return, The, *476*
Revesz, Bruce, 384
Rey, Antonia, 476
Rey, Jose, 467
Reynolds, Cynthia, 477
Reynolds, David, 506
Reynolds, Marilyn, 370
Reznikov, Hanon, 477
Rhodes, Evan H., 41, 373
Rhyne, Sylvia, 363, 473
Rhys, Will, 459
Rhythm Ranch, *522*
Ribblett, Beth A., 425, 524
Ribeiro, Glaucia, 385
Ribman, Ronald, 468
Ribnikov, Alexis, 383
Ribot, Marc, 466
Rice, Howard, 529
Rice, Sarah, 466
Rice, Sean Michael, 479
Rich, Frank, 57, 58, 59, 60,
    551
Richard Rodgers Production
    Award, 422
Richard, Raquel, 479
Richards, Cordelia, 457, 534
Richards, Daniel, 529
Richards, Gary, 476

Richards, Jeffrey, 367, 378,
    389, 420
Richards, Julian, 476
Richards, Lloyd, 6, 21, 389,
    526, 540, 555, 556, 560
Richards, Martin, 374, 555
Richards, Rob, 414, 537
Richardson, L. Kenneth, 445
Richardson, La Tanya, 417, 507
Richardson, Ron, 30, 425
Richert, Wanda, 435, 438
Richmond, Albert, 370
Richmond, Doyle, 364
Richter, Mary, 463
Riddell, Bob, 393
Riddle, Kate, 414
Ridge Theater, 459
Ridiculous Theatrical
    Company, 449, 469
Riegel, Sam, 384, 443
Riegert, Peter, 457
Riehle, Richard, 457, 464
Rifkin, Don, 474
Rifkin, Ron, 379
Rigdon, Kevin, 8, 19, 31, 387,
    421, 519, 556, 558
Right Mind, *535*
Rigol, Joey, 443
Riley, Donna, 539
Riley, Eric, 415
Riley, Linda, 367
Rinaldi, Philip, 383, 414, 425
Rinehart, Elaine, 458, 478
Ringham, Nancy, 372
Rio, Katia, 385
Ritchey, Pamela, 528
Ritchie, Lynn, 473
Ritchie, Margaret, 464
Ritchie, Michael F., 379, 421,
    422
Rivas, Aura, 466
Rivas, Fernando, 521
Rivas, Geoffrey, 512
River Arts Repertory, 541
Rivera, Jose, 25, 416, 504
Rivera, Rene, 404, 459
Riverman, *478*
Rivers, Gwynne, 457
Riverside Shakespeare
    Company, 478
Riverside Theater, 478
Rizhov, Sergey, 383
Rizk, Joumana, 475
Rizner, Russell, 370, 388
Roach, Dan, 534
Roach, Kevin Joseph, 530

Road to Immortality, The,
    *479*
Road to Mecca, The, 560
Robards, Jason, 6, 9, 369, 405
Robbers, *538*
Robbins, Carrie, 463
Robbins, David, 408
Robbins, Gabrielle, 408
Robbins, Jana, 377, 378
Robbins, Janine Leigh, 461
Robbins, Jerome, 36, 360, 376,
    397, 377, 559
Robbins, Rex, 440
Robbins, Richard, 531
Robbins, Tim, 6, 15, 406, 408,
    466
Robbins, Tom, 372, 443, 525
Roberts, Garth, 415
Roberts, Grace, 474
Roberts, Jackie, 463, 464
Roberts, Louise, 473
Roberts, Tony, 441
Roberts-Frost, Gwendolyn, 474
Robertson, Cliff, 369
Robertson, Jenny, 472
Robertson, Jimmy, 532
Robertson, Lanie, 456
Robertson, Liz, 397
Robertson, Pat, 60
Robertson, Ray, 479
Robertson, Scott, 395
Robinson, Dean, 408
Robinson, Hal, 374
Robinson, Mary B., 414, 458,
    523
Robinson, Meghan, 405
Robinson, Robin, 377
Robinson, Roger, 509
Robison, Mary, 528
Rocamora, Carol, 528, 529
Rocco, James, 522, 434
Roches, 511
Rochon, Valerie Jerusha, 524
Rock of Ages, 460
Rodents and Radios, 450,
    *475*
Roderick, Ray, 433
Rodgers, Mary Ann, 528
Rodgers, Mary, 25
Rodgers, Richard, 52, 383, 397,
    474, 479
Rodrigo, Al, 464
Rodrigues, Pena, 385
Rodriguez, Diane, 535
Rodriguez, E.J., 466
Rodriguez, Lucy, 512

Rodriguez, Steven, 472
Roe, Jim, 362
Rogers, Bruce, 384
Rogers, David, 380, 539
Rogers, Gil, 473
Rogers, Paul, 520
Rogers, Poli, 467
Rogerson, Anita, 461
Rogerson, Bob, 424
Rogerson, Gus, 461, 539
Rolfe, Frederick, 53
Rolfe, Wendy A., 460
Romaine, Katherine, 511
Roman, Elsa, 466
Roman, Pedro, 521
**Romance in Hard Times**, 11, 40, 41, *407*, *410*, *412*, 558
Romance, Paul D., 537
Romanello, Paul, 478
Romano, Amelia, 468
Romano, Lou, 535
Romans, Bruce, 520
**Romeo and Juliet**, 405
Romero, Constanza, 389
Romero-Kennedy, Elaine, 540
Romoff, Douglas, 410
Ronan, Brian, 416
**Rookie of the Year**, *470*
Rooney, Robert, 539
Rooney, Ted, 528
Roop, Reno, 445
Roos, Casper, 362, 473
Root, Stephen, 439
Rorvik, Alice, 513
Rosado, Pedro, 461
Rosario, Orlando, 504
Rosas, Ivon, 385
Rosato, Jeffrey, 397
Rose, Bob, 380
Rose, Charles, 417, 535
Rose, Hugh A., 378
Rose, L. Arthur, 360
Rose, Philip, 362, 390, 392
Rose, Richard, 399, 522
Rose, Stewart, 384
Rose, Vincent, 394
Rosegarten, Theodore, 416
Rosegg, Carol, viii
Roseman, Ralph, 524
Rosen, Louis, 404, 507
Rosenbaum, Jason, 468
Rosenberg, Ian, 464
Rosenberg, Jack, 384
Rosenberg, Jan, 363
Rosenberg, Natalie, 505
Rosenberg, Roger, 372

Rosenblum, Joshua, 379, 422
Rosenfeld, Amy-Lynn, 479
Rosenfeld, Richard D., 506
Rosenfeld, Seth Zvi, 479
Rosengarten, Theodore, 27, 416, 477, 523
Rosenstock, Milton, 370
Rosenthal, Caryn, 461
Rosenthal, Mark, 506
Rosenthal, Todd Andrew, 530
Roshe, Deborah, 521
Ross, Bertram, 416
Ross, Carolyn Leslie, 513
Ross, J. Michael, 535
Ross, Jack, 426
Ross, Jamie, 467, 525
Ross, Justin, 438
Ross, Lola, 477
Ross, Pamela, 475
Ross, Sandra, 424
Ross, Stephen, 362
Ross, Stuart, 6, 43, 361, 431, 479
Ross, Tavis, 535
Ross, Tom, 406
Rossetter, Kathryn, 472
Rossiter, Kathy, 464
Rostand, Edmond, 399, 478
Roston, Karen, 369
Roth, Ann, 469, 507
Roth, Ari, 534
Roth, Daryl, 419
Roth, Michael, 512, 535
Roth, Stephanie, 378
Rothenberg, David, 425, 429
Rothman, Carole, 469, 554
Rothman, Harry, 478
Rothman, John, 379, 422
Rothman, Stephen, 535
**Rothschilds, The**, 11, The, 49, 51, *429*, *430*, *474*
Roudebush, Bill, 458
**Rough Crossing**, 449, *477*
Round House Theater, 560
Roundabout Theater Company, 11, 12, 48, 406, 420
Rousseve, David, 460
Rouvain, Leo, 474
Rouzan, Wanda, 430
Roven, Glen, 365
Rowan, Michael, 513
Rowe, Florence, 364
Rowe, Robert L., 474
Rowe, Stephen, 379, 404, 422
Rowen, Glenn, 384
Rowley, Bill, 522

Rowlings, Jeff, 536
**Royal Hunt of the Sun, The**, 26
Royal Shakespeare Company, 419
Royal Shakespeare Theater, 421
Royal, Reginald, 389
Rozin, Seth, 529
Ruark, Joel, 463
Rubens, Herbert, 414, 474, 478
Rubenstein, Jay, 474
Rubesamen, Gary Dean, 464
Rubin, Arthur, 365
Rubin, Jon, 468
Rubin, Steven, 415
Rubinstein, John, 9, 369, 405, 443, 531
Rubinstein, Murray, 464
Rubsam, Scott, 478
Ruck, Patricia, 433
Rucker, Charles, 464
Rudel, Julius, 372
Rudetsky, Seth, 463
Rudina, Tatiana, 383
Rudnitskaya, Yelena, 383
Rudnitsky, Sergey, 383
Ruduk, Oleg, 383
Rudy, Sam, 391, 405, 414, 429
Ruecktenwald, Philip, 384
Rueda, Manuel, 465
Ruehl, Mercedes, 444
Ruffa, Mario, 385
Ruffelle, Frances, 443
Ruffini, Gene, 456
Rum, Jorge, 385
**Rumors**, 360, 444
*Rumpelstiltskin*, 426
Rund, Mitch, 479
Rundgren, Todd, 41, 406, 409
Runolfsson, Anne Marie, 388
**Runyon on Wry**, *473*
Runyon, Damon, 473
Rupert, Mary Six, 367
Rupnik, Kevin, 521
Rupp, Debra Jo, 47, 386
Rush, David, 466
Rushton, Christopher J., 529
Russell, Monte, 392
Russell, Pat, 477
Russell, Willy, 360
**Russian Teacher, The**, *512*
Russo, Charles, 384
Russo, Santo, 370
**Rust and Ruin**, *540*
Rustaveli Theater Company, 427, 452

Ruta, Ken, 535
Rutigliano, James, 476
Ruzika, Tom, 512
Ryall, William, 374, 375
Ryan, Amy, 464
Ryan, Ben, 394
Ryan, Bridgit, 530
Ryan, Denise, 522
Ryan, Kimberly Anne, 470
Ryan, Michael Scott, 535
Rybolt, Peter, 506
Ryder, Amy, 505
Rydzeski, Mary Ann, 384
Ryland, Jack, 420
Rymer, Scott, 400
Ryskind, Morrie, 477

S.J. Perelman in Person, 400
Saavedra, 459
Sabellico, Richard, 377, 433
Sabin, David, 525
Sabino, Arnold, 514
Sablow, Jane, 455
Sacharow, Lawrence, 541
Sachs, Ann, 511
Sachs, Norman, 525
Saddler, Donald, 473
Sadler, Nicholas, 461
Sado, Alexander, 383
Safe Tradition, 560
Saffran, Christina, 436
Sage Theater Company, 478
Sager, Linda Owen, 475
Sagharadze, Guram, 427
Sahl, Mort, 15
Saiet, Eric, 507
Sailer, John, 533
Saint Clair, Michael, 477
Saint, David, 463
Saint-Saens, 478
Saito, Dawn A., 467
Saka, Haruhiko, 366
Sakaguchi, Ango, 460
Sakata, Jeanne, 404
Sala, Ed, 533
Salas, Nicolette, 472
Salata, Gregory, 477
Salce, Tim, 473
Sale, Jim, 503
Salem, Francois Abu, 475
Salerno, Anthony, 479
Sales, Mitzi, 416, 504
Salhoud, Tony, 440
Salinger, Diane, 430
Salisbury, D.J., 522
Salkin, Ed, 380

Sally, 20
Salmon, Scott, 368
Salt, Amy, 540
Saltz, Amy, 425, 540
Saltzman, Avery, 476
Salvadore, J. Kelly, 431
Salzberg, Marc, 365
Sambati, Marcello, 459
Sameness, 513
Sametz, Laura, 404
Sams, Jeremy, 379, 422
Samuel, Peter, 442
Samuelsohn, Howard, 406
Samuelson, Howard, 461, 463
San Diego Repertory Theater, 535
San Francisco Mime Troupe, 452, 478, 558
San Jose Taiko Group, 535
Sanchez, Jaime, 535
Sanchez-Scott, Milcha, 512
Sand Mountain Matchmaking, 479
Sandburg, R.N., 537
Sanders, Amy, 367
Sanders, Fred, 439, 472
Sanders, James, 450
Sanders, Pete, 372, 386, 419
Sanders, Scott, 528
Sanders-Smith, Laurie, 478
Sanderson, Kirsten, 458
Sandifur, Virginia, 473
Sandish, Dale, 479, 530
Sandora Associates, 426
Sands, Pati, 455, 456
Sansone, Joseph, 514
Santana, Norman, 466
Santander, Felipe, 465
Santaniello, Eric, 406, 420
Santiago, 530
Santiago, Glen M., 475
Santiago, Socorro, 509, 528
Santonicola, Frank, 384
Santoriello, Alex, 372
Santoro, Michael, 478
Santoro, Susan, 436
Santos, Edmilson, 385
Santos, Fernando, 362
Santos, Jaime, 385
Santos, Janete, 385
Santos, Loida, 437
Santos, Sonia, 385
Sappington, Margo, 521
Sara, Kenneth, 430
Sarafina!, 360
Saralidze, Tristan, 428

Sargeant, Angela, 459
Sarno, Janet, 519
Saroskelsky, Edward, 468
Sarter, Mat, 456
Sartin, Gregory, 455
Sata, Warren, 478
Sater, Steven, 476
Satterwhite, Catherine, 525
Saulnier, George III, 506
Saunders, Alex, 531
Saunders, Donald, 362
Saunders, Jay O., 472
Saunders, Nicholas, 362
Savage, Melodee, 410, 411
Savage, Steve, 508
Savick, Westley, 523
Savin, Ron Lee, 525
Sawaishi, Ryoko, 397
Sawyer-Young, Kat, 535
Saxon, Carolyn, 506
Say Goodbye to Hollywood, 455
Say, Darling, 28
Scalaci, Gillian, 436
Scallen, Mary Beth, 528
Scandalous Adventures of Sir Toby Trollope, The, 535
Scarcella, Kim, 393
Scardino, Don, 23, 24, 376, 427
Scarlett Letter: A Romance for the Stage, The, 531
Scarred Ground, 509
Scarsdale Station, 456
Scassellati, Vincent, 517
Schachner, Harold, 384
Schacht, Sam, 469
Schachter, Beth A., 458
Schachter, Steve, 519
Schaeffer, Ron, 517
Schaffer, Byron Jr., 507
Schaffmaster, Fred, 528
Schaller, Mark, 470
Schanker, Josh, 463
Scharer, Jonathan, 424
Schatz, Ken, 457
Schechter, David, 372, 459, 463
Scheeder, Louis, 461
Scheine, Raynor, 472
Schelble, William, viii, 387
Schenkkan, Robert, 472, 540
Scherer, Christopher, 525
Schertler, Nancy, 415
Schickele, Peter, 359

Schiff, Sara, 381
Schiller, Adrian, 461
Schimmel, William, 372
Schindler, George, 421
Schirle, Joan, 504, 505
Schlarth, Sharon, 427
Schmidman, Jo Ann, 527
Schmidt, Harvey, 399
Schmidt, Jack, 478
Schmidt, Jake, 535
Schmitz, Peter, 474, 506
Schneider Award, 559
Schneider, Carol, 379, 422
Schneider, Scott, 468
Schnupp, John, 367
Schoeffler, Paul, 473
Schoeneman, Larry, 508
Schofield, Barbara, 478
Schofield, Liz, 463
Schonberger, John, 394
Schons, Alain, 504
**School for Wives, The**, *477*
Schönberg, Claude-Michel, 360
Schreier, Daniel, 379, 404,
    457, 558
Schroeder, Phillip John, 517
Schrot, Richard, 508
Schuberg, Carol, 370
Schubert, Jiri, 470
Schulfer, Roche, 506
Schulman, Craig, 441
Schulman, Leonard, 384
Schulman, Susan H., 51, 363,
    556
Schultz, Armand, 368, 403,
    457
Schultz, Mary, 463, 464
Schultz, Peter, 463
Schulz, Theodore, 386, 387
Schumacher, Jim, 527
Schuman, William, 559
Schumitzky, Meyer, 384
Schurkamp, Richard, 364
Schurr, Carl, 534
Schurr, Wendy, 506
Schwartz, Andrew, 370
Schwartz, Lynne Sharon, 528
Schwartz-Bart, Simone, 479
Schwarz, William, 386, 387
Schween, Astrid, 380
Schweid, Carole, 437, 469
Schweizer, David, 410
Schwerner, Armand, 477
Scilla, Maryellen, 433
Scimeca, Jane, 525

Scofield, Pamela, 458, 460,
    503
**Scorpions in the Cradle**, *455*
Scott, Camilla, 362
Scott, Campbell, 463
Scott, Deborah, 461
Scott, Dennis, 540
Scott, Douglas, 29, 428, 525
Scott, James, 472
Scott, Kenya, 463, 474
Scott, Kimberly, 461
Scott, Lisa, 513
Scott, Oz, 458
Scott, Seret, 504
Scott, Sharon, 537
Scott, Timothy, 433, 437
**Scrambled Life of**
    **Christopher Columbus,**
    **The,** *458*
**Scrap of Paper,** *470*
**Scratchy Glass,** *533*
Scruggs, Sharon, 527
**Sea Change,** *525*
Seabrooke, Christopher, 369,
    556
Seacrist, Lisa, 503
Seamon, Edward, 416, 459, 472
**Search & Destroy,** *511*
Seattle Repertory Theater, 538,
    556
Sebek, Herman W., 433
Sebesky, Don, 41, 373, 374
Sebesky, Ken, 373
**Second Coming, The**, 450,
    *458*
Second Stage Theater, 469, 554
**Secret Garden, The,** *527*
**Secret Life of Walter Mitty,**
    **The,** *524*
**Secret Rapture, The,** 4, 6, 17,
    57, 58, *368*, 551, 559
**Sedalia Run,** *458*
Sedgwick, Robert, 478
**Seeing Double**, 452, *478*, 558
Segal, Cyrus, 384
Segal, George, 405
Segal, Gilles, 474
Segal, Kathrin King, 461
Seid, Lori E., 560
Seidman, John, 474
Seidman, Scott, 367
Seifert, Linda, 459
Seifter, Harvey, 536
Seitz, John, 464, 472
Sekacz, Ilona, 386
Sekiya, Toshiaki, 367

Selbert, Marianne, 367
Seldes, Marian, 395
Self, Alexandra, 468
**Self-Torture and Strenuous**
    **Exercise,** *458*
Sellars, John, 469
Selman, Jim, 362
Semashko, Lilia, 383
Semmelman, Jim, 370
Sempliner, Woody, 464, 479
Sendin, Ashleigh, 433
Senie, Curt, 528, 529
Senske, Becky, 473
**Separation,** *468*
Serabian, Lorraine, 531
Serbagi, Roger, 392
**Serious Fun!,** *477*
Serko, David, 391
Serling, Rod, 479
Serrano, Andres, 60
Sesma, Thom, 469
Sessa, Vincent, 530
Setrakian, Mary, 472
Setren, Phil, 456
Severance, Scott, 522
**Sex, Drugs, Rock & Roll,** 5,
    8, 11, 28, 30, 55, 258-268,
    *425*, 558
Sexton, David, 533
Sexton, Lucy, 559
Shabba-Doo, 560
Shaddock, Pamela, 455
Shaffer, Malinda, 365
Shaffer, Peter, 6, 25, 27, 387,
    555
Shaffron, Robert, 469
Shaker, Martin, 458
Shakespeare, William, 382,
    400, 420, 402, 427, 449,
    461, 465, 466, 474, 477,
    478
Shamash, Beba, 363, 473
Shanina, Yelena, 383
Shanker, Joshua, 429
Shanks, Bob, 400
Shanks, Priscilla, 365, 520
Shanley, John Patrick, 468,
    478
Shannon, Kyle, 464
Shannon, Mark, 537
Shapiro, Anne, 405, 478
Shapiro, Mel, 530
Shapli, Omar, 457
Sharaff, Irene, 397
Sharif, Bina, 470
Sharp, Kim T., 466

Sharp, Michael, 539
Sharp, Razor, 473
Sharpe, Ascanio, 457
Sharratt, Paul, 472
Shavitz, Peter, 458
Shaw, Brian, 507
Shaw, Christopher, 414, 464
Shaw, Deborah, 459, 472
Shaw, George Bernard, 400, 420
Shaw, Mark, 468
Shaw, Peggy, 460
Shaw, Steven, 364
Shawhan, April, 464
Shawn, Peter, 369
Shayne, Tracy, 436, 443
**Shazam!**, *515*
Sheara, Nicola, 386, 387, 469
Shearer, Lori, 479
Shearman, Alan, 535
Sheehan, Don, 456
Sheehan, Jereme, 367
Sheehan, Maurice, 475
Sheffey, George, 524
Sheffield-Dewees, James, 479
**Sheila's Day**, *524*
Sheintsiss, Oleg, 383
Shelby, Nancy, 536
Shelle, Michael, 479
Shelley, Mary, 473, 537
**Shelly Garrett's Beauty Shop**, *474*
Shelton, Sloane, 46, 364
Shen, Freda Foh, 458
**Shenandoah**, 4, 52, *362*
Shentalinsky, Sergei, 412
Shepard, Harry Whittaker, 559
Shepard, Sam, 359
Shepperd, Michael A., 506
Shepski, Ken, 370
Sherazadishvili, Bezhan, 428
Sheridan, Jessica, 522
Sheridan, Kent, 393
**Sherlock's Last Case**, 59
Sherman, Barry, 410
Sherman, Dana, 429
Sherman, Geoffrey, 458
Sherman, James, 508
Sherman, Keith, 369, 401
Sherman, Liz, 457
Sherman, Loren, 406, 459
Sherman, Margo Lee, 470
Sherman, Martin, 10, 12, 413
Sherman, Marty, 528
Sherman, Stuart, 477
Sherrard, Nancy, 516

Sherrill, Angela, 420
Sherwood, Madeleine, 520
Shevelove, Burt, 33
Shevett, Anita and Steve, viii
Shew, Timothy, 441
Shiflett, Melissa, 472
Shigeko, 467
Shihadeh, Emily, 478
Shima, Yuka, 367
Shimabuku, Norris M., 467, 529
Shimizu, Sachi, 437
Shimizu, Tsuyu, 467
**Shimmer**, *469*, 559
Shimono, Sab, 518
Shimosato, Keiko, 478
Shinner, Sandy, 509
Shion, Yu, 367
Shiotani, Kipp, 518
Shipley, Jon, 455, 456
Shire, David, 37, 43, 401, 419, 558
Shirley Herz Associates, 366, 372, 374, 377, 384, 386, 391, 405, 414, 419, 424, 429, 431
**Shirley Valentine**, 360, 445
Shirley, James, 474
Shirvis, Barbara, 384
Shiryayev, Vladimir, 383
Shnek, Zachary, 367
Shomer, Helene, 384
Shook, Robert, 508
Shores, Jim, 517
Shorts, Barbara, 430
Shortt, Paul, 509
Shouse, Jack, 536
**Show 'n' Tell**, *460*
**Show Must Go On, The**, *461*
**Showing Off**, 400
Shropshire, Noble, 421
Shubert Organization, The, 368, 376, 378, 379, 381, 386, 555, 556
Shucharin, Nikolai, 383
Shue, Elisabeth, 422, 379
Shue, Larry, 560
Shultz, Mary, 452, 475, 558
Shumaker, Helen, 477, 536
Shuman, Celia, 536
Shuman, Mark, 388
Sibanda, Seth, 465
Siberry, Michael, 382
Sicangeo, Eduardo, 368
Siccardi, Arthur, 386

**Sid Caesar & Company**, 4, 11, 43, *369*, *401*
Siegel, Betty, 540
Siegel, Bruce, 468
Siegel, Joshua, 367
Siegel, Marvin, 60
Siegler, Ben, 464, 472
Siegler, Steven, 405, 478
**Sight Unseen**, *512*
Sikes, Cynthia, 440
Silber, David, 364
Silberman, Betty, 420
Silberman, Joel, 373, 374, 525
Silins, Eric, 527
Silliman, Maureen, 514
Sills, Douglas, 441
Sills, Mimi, 466
Sills, Paul, 19
Silva, Kerry, 522
Silver, Richard, 420
Silver, Ron, 3, 61
Silver, Susan, 383
Silverman, Ethan, 459
Silverman, Stanley, 463
Silverman, Stephanie, 473
Silverstein, Shel, 29, 421, 450, 458
Silverstein, Steve, 508
Simek, Vasek, 429, 478
Simione, Donn, 435, 438, 531
Simmons, Bill, 467
Simmons, J. K., 390, 395
Simmons, Stanley, 397
Simms, Stephen, 362
Simo, Ana Maria, 459
**Simon Says ...**, *478*
Simon, Adam, 15, 406, 466
Simon, John, 539, 551, 552
Simon, Lucy, 527
Simon, Neil, 55, 360, 397, 534
Simon, Paul, 3
Simonds, David, 475
Simons, Diane, 515
Simons, John, 515
Simons, Lake, 515
Simons, Lorca, 515
Simonson, Eric, 386, 387
Simotes, Tony, 535
Simpson, Jim, 558
Simpson, Marty, 367
Sinclair, Chris, 404, 411
Sine/D'Addario, Ltd., 425
Singer, Connie, 400
Singer, Kathryn, 455
Singer, Pamela, 401
Singler, Sandra, 536

Singular Productions, 560
Sinise, Gary, 19, 386, 556
Sinkys, Albert, 459
Sins of the Father, *529*
Siren Tears, *478*
Sirois, Richard L., 539
Sisino, Stephen, 514
Sisters in Crime, *529*
Sisto, Rocco, 420
Six Degrees of Separation, 421
Sizwi Banzi Is Dead, 23
Skelton, Jay, 506
Skelton, Thomas R., 376
Skinner, Beth, 460
Skinner, Kate, 464
Skinner, Margo, 426
Skipitares, Theodora, 463
Skolnick, Zan, 507
Skymusic Ensemble, 478
Slade, Catherine, 508
Slaff, Jonathan, 460
Slapstick, *504*
Slattery, John, 400, 541
Slaughter, Lance, 519
Slavin, Kenda, 527
Slavin, L. J., 386
Slay It With Music, *473*
Sleeping Beauty or Coma, *399*
Slezak, Victor, 458
Slo-Pitch, *464*
Sloan, Bob, 507
Sloan, Larry, 48, 401, 402
Sloman, John, 410, 411, 466
Sloman, P.K., 370
Slugger by Moonlight, *468*
Small, Larry, 434
Small, Neva, 472
Small, Peg, 364
Small, Ralph, 393
Smallwood, Tucker, 479
Smart, Annie, 412
Smedley, Jonathan, 466
Smeian, Pavel, 383
Smiley, Leigh, 528
Smiley, Sam, 540
Smith, Barbara Bates, 537
Smith, Buddy, 522
Smith, Charles, 507
Smith, Christopher, 458
Smith, Craig, 475, 476
Smith, David Rae, 384
Smith, Derek D., 414
Smith, Don, 368
Smith, Douglas D., 519

Smith, Jack, 420
Smith, Jeffery, 455
Smith, Jennifer, 390
Smith, Juliet, 513
Smith, Kathleen, 384
Smith, Kathy, 475
Smith, Ken, 463, 522
Smith, Kevin Shancady, 513
Smith, Lemoyne E., 509
Smith, Liz, 553
Smith, Lois, 19, 24, 386, 416, 556
Smith, Louise, 459, 523
Smith, Maggie, 6, 25, 30, 387, 556, 558
Smith, Marilynn, 535
Smith, Michael, 386, 387, 513
Smith, Milburn, 456
Smith, Nancy Jo, 504, 535
Smith, Nicholas, 461
Smith, Payton, 479
Smith, Peter J., 535
Smith, Regina Byrd, 535
Smith, Robert Edward, 516
Smith, Robert G., 508
Smith, Robert Vincent, 439
Smith, Roger Guenveur, 460
Smith, Steven Scott, 419
Smith, Ursula, 433
Smith-Cameron, J., 441
Smithgall, Jill, 534
Smits, Pip N., 479
Smoke on the Mountain, *460*
Smolen, Faye, 460
Smothering Coals, *470*
Smurr, Katherine M., 538
Smyth, Joan, 479
Snider, Keith, 527
Snider-Stein, Teresa, 470
Snow, Leida, 553
Snowden, William, 540
Snyder, Rick, 386, 387
Soares, Vivian M., 385
Sobczak, John, 523
Sobel, David, 455
Sobel, Lloyd, 427
Sobel, Shepard, 477
Society Hill Playhouse, 529
Society of Stage Directors and Choreographers, 57, 554, 559
Soho Rep, 469
Sokol, Marilyn, 401
Sola, Monina, 465
Solid Gold Baby, *511*
Solis, Jeffrey, 455

Solis, Octavio, 512
Solo, Wiliam, 441
Solomon, Alisa, 557
Solomon, Nancy, 513
Soltanoff, Phil, 509
Solters/Roskin/Friedman, 369, 401
Soltonoff, Phil, 464
Some Americans Abroad, 4, 6, 11, 18, 61, *378*, *379*, *421*, *422*, 551, 552, 553, 556
Sommer, Elke, 445
Sommer, Josef, 31, 53, 404, 405
Sommer, Kathy, 380
Sommers, Allison, 403
Son of Cabin Fever, *513*
Son Who Hunted Tigers in Jakarta, The, *468*
Sondheim, Stephen, 34, 52, 50, 59, 360, 362, 376, 453, 560
Song of Shim Chung, The, *467*
Song of the Nova, *456*
Songs Without Words, *540*
Songs of Paradise, 11, *420*
Sook, Dennis, 474
Soon, Terence Tam, 518
Soong, Bea, 518
Soper, Tony, 538
Sophiea, Cynthia, 473
Sordelet, Elizabeth, 468
Sordelet, Rick, 468
Sorel, Edward, 379, 422
Sorkin, Aaron, 6, 23, 24, 376, 427, 558
Sorrentino, Joseph, 529
Sorvino, Paul, 539
Sosnow, Pat, 365, 404, 425
Sottile, Michael S., 411
Soukup, Elizabeth, 521
Sound of Music, The, 4, 52, *383*, *384*
Soundbite, *514*
Sour Springs, *470*
Sousa, Pamela, 438
South Ferry, *468*
South Street Theater, 478
South Coast Repertory, 5, 497, 511
Southern Cross, *503*
Souza, Alan, 473
Sowers, Scott, 470, 520
Spalla, John, 419

Spangenberg, Saul, 467
**Spanish Eyes**, *467*
Spano, Joe, 560
Spano, Terry, 367
Sparber, Herschel, 380
**Spare Parts**, 11, 30, *426*
Sparer, Katie C., 509
Sparks, Rick, 434, 535
Spasoff, Maria, 464
Spaulding, Dave, 420
Spears, Louie, 519
**Special Interests**, *479*
**Spectre Woman Chronicles,**
*460*
Speechley, Julie, 461
**Speed-the-Plow**, 29, 421
Spellman, Larry, 369, 401
Spencer, Frank, 367
Spencer, Steve, 537
Sperberg, Fritz, 376
Sperling, Ted, 410, 463
Spidle, Craig, 509
Spiegel, Howard, 444
**Spike Heels**, *458*
Spina, Anthony, 479
**Spinning Tale**, A, 11, *426*
**Spirit Time**, *475*
Spisak, Neil, 408
Spivack, Larry, 409
Spohnheimer, Deb, 388
Spoleto Festival, 366
Sportelli, Paul, 388
Sprauer, Fred, 514
Sprecher, Ben, 420
Spriggs, Rachel, 461
Springer, Gary, 390
Springer, John, 390
Sproat, Ron, 522
Sprouse, Mario E., 460
**Spunk**, 6, 11, 31, *407, 411,*
*412, 524,* 558
**Square One**, *469*
Squier, William, 431
Sriningsih, Maria, 470
Sririn, Alexander, 383
St. Clair, Michael, 477
St. Germain, Mark, 460, 525,
533, 539
St. John, Marco, 516
St. Louis, Louis, 463
St. Marie, Heidi, 513
**St. Mark's Gospel**, 11, *427*
Stabile, Bill, 539
Stabile, Christine, 522
Stadlen, Lewis J., 400
Stadt, Judy, 539

Stafford, Kate, 463, 469
Stafford, Richard, 434
Stafford, Ronald, 438
Stafford, Tony, 524
Stafford-Clark, Max, 519
**Stage Door**, *461*
Staircase Company, The, 378
**Stalwarts, The**, 450, *458*
**Stand-Up Tragedy**, *519*, 560
Stanley, Dorothy, 395, 441
Stanley, Gordon, 370, 473, 525
Stanton, Douglas, 384
Stanton, Robert, 402
Stapleton, Jean, 452, 457, 558
Stark, Fred, 522
Starmer, John, 523
**Starmites**, 361
Starobin, Michael, 44, 395,
415
**Starting Monday**, *473*
**State of the Art**, *464*
**State of Darkness**, 559
Stattel, Robert, 364, 420
**Stay Away a Little Closer,**
*458*
Stead, Chuck, 539
**Stealth**, *470*
Steber, John, 473
Stechschulte, Tom, 386, 503
**Steel Magnolias**, 399
Steele, Donald, 469, 522
Steele, Willy, 508
Steen, Robert, 362, 380
Stegmeir, Johann, 533
Stein, Andrew, 370
Stein, Debra, 431
Stein, Douglas, 402, 414, 504
Stein, Gertrude, 531
Stein, J. Michael, 410
Stein, James J. Jr., 505
Stein, June, 456
Stein, Navida, 476
Stein, Saul Philip, 459
Stein, Todd Jaime, 468
Steinbeck, John, 5, 19
Stenborg, Helen, 472
Stepanchenko, Sergey, 383
Stephens, Rachel, 468
Steppenwolf Theater Company,
5, 19, 386, 555
Steppin' Out Repertory, 478
Steres, Greg, 523
Sterling, James, 475, 476
Sterling, Robert, 455
Stern, Deborah, 530
Stern, Eric, 377, 560

Stern, Henry J., 403
Stern, Leo, 363
Stern, Marcus, 477
Sternberg, Jennifer, 476
Sterner, Jerry, 399
Sterner, Steve, 539
Sternhagen, Frances, 439
Sternoff, Daniel, 515
Stettler, Steve, 514
Stetzel, Dan, 537
Steve McGraw's, 479
Stevens, Allan, 530
Stevens, Byam, 476
Stevens, Fisher, 403
Stevens, Jack, 517
Stevens, Katrina, 365
Stevens, Keith, 522
Stevens, Roger L., 369, 376,
378, 405
Stevens, Steve, 512
Stevenson, Robert Louis, 509
Stevenson, Scott, 432
**Stevie Wants to Play the**
**Blues (A Jazz Play)**, *519*
Stewart, Charles, 475
Stewart, Christopher, 528
Stewart, Ellen, 459
Stewart, Gwen, 42, 390, 540
Stewart, John Heath, 478
Stewart, Pamela, 520
Stewart, Pat, 460
Stewart, Ray, 422
Stewart, Tonea, 517
Sticco, Dan, 41, 390
**Stick Figures**, *468*
Stieb, Alan, 370, 531
Stiehm, Roberta, 433
Stilgoe, Richard, 359, 360
Stillman, Bob, 374
Stimac, Anthony J., 463
Stimac, Nicola, 466
Sting, 49, 372
Stinton, Colin, 19, 379, 422
Stix, John, 458
Stoccardo, Buddy, 420
Stocker, Gary, 397, 523
Stohler, Scott, 464
Stokes, Simon, 511
Stoklos, Denise, 460
Stolbstov, Dmitri, 412
Stone, Elise, 475
Stone, Fredric, 508
Stone, Jonathan and Barnaby,
559
Stone, Julian, 509
Stone, Ken, 528

Stone, Peter, 36, 57, 559
Stoppard, Tom, 10, 378, 449, 475, 477
Storch, Arthur, 397
Storey, David, 511
**Stormy Weather,** *529*
Story in Harlem Slang, 407, *411, 412*
Story of Kufur Shamma, The, *475*
Stout, Mary, 390, 473
Stovall, James, 410, 463
**Stragglers,** *469*
Straiges, Tony, 366, 378, 397, 534
Strand, Richard, 466, 533
**Strange Sightings in the Southwest,** *525*
Strathairn, David, 457
Straus, Vivien, 516
Strawbridge, Stephen, 365, 402, 412, 518
Strawn, Judy, 478
Strayhorn, Danny, 36, 374
Streater, Susan, 367
**Streetcar Named Desire, A,** 5
Strenger, Sander, 384
Strenger, Yevgenia, 384
**Stressed Out,** *468*
**Stretch Marks,** *477*
**Strike, The,** *479*
Strilec, Helen, 384
Stripling, Byron, 380
Stritch, Elaine, 9, 369, 405
Stroman, Guy, 431, 479
Stroman, Susan, 522, 523, 531
**Strong Man's Weak Child,** *516*
Strong, Ken, 503
Strong, Timothy, 474
Stroud, Ted, 513
Strouse, Charles, 395
Stuart, Ian, 421
Stuart, Jan, 552
Stuart, Michael, 438
Stuart, Mimi, 479
Stuckenbruck, Dale, 388
Studio Arena Theater, 505
Studios, Dalia, viii
Studwell, David, 507
**Stuff as Dreams Are Made On,** 449, *474*, 558
Stumm, Michael, 479
Sturiale, Grant, 393, 429
Sturm, Jason, 383

Sturm, Miriam, 386
Sturua, Robert, 427, 428, 452
Style, Steven, 428
Styne, Jule, 52, 376, 559
**Subfertile,** *467*
**Substance of Fire, The,** *526*
**Success,** *523*
**Such Is Life,** *508*
Sudduth, Skipp, 386, 387, 507
**Sueno de Una Noche de Verano (A Midsummer Night's Dream),** *465*
Sueoka-Matos, Shana, 397
**Sugar Hill,** *463*
**Sugar,** 28
Sugawara, Hiroshi, 372
Sugerman, Juff, 470
Sulich, Stephen, 384
Sullivan, Billy L., 386
Sullivan, Brad, 364
Sullivan, Dan, 484
Sullivan, Daniel, 538
Sullivan, Eileen, 506
Sullivan, K. T., 372
Sullivan, Kim, 425
Sullivan, Lynn, 367
Sullivan, Matt Bradford, 404
Sullivan, Michael, 478
Sullivan, Sean Frank, 370
Sullo, Teresina, 479
Sumbatsivily, Josef, 364
Summerhayes, Heather, 29, 429, 525
Summerhays, Jane, 435, 441, 443
Summerlin, Bobby, 506
Summers, Marc D., 455
Summers, Mark-Anthony, 508
**Summit, The,** 559
Sunkel, Michael, 427
Sunnerstam, Christina, 382
**Sunshine,** 6, 11, 24, *416*
Suntory International Corp., ix, 376, 378, 379, 381, 386, 555, 556
**Survival,** *465*
Suskin, Steven, 431
Sussman, Bruce, 361
Suter, William, 425
Sutherland, Brian, 390, 514
Sutton, Greg, 416
Sutton, Joe, 464, 478, 479
Swados, Elizabeth, 41, 407, 411, 457, 479
Swadow, Robin, 471
Swain, Rick, 515

**Swamp Foxes,** *518*
**Swan, The,** *520*
Swartz, Marlene, 469
Swearingen, Beth, 433
**Sweat,** 407, *411*
Swedlund, Kristina, 405, 478
**Sweeney Todd, the Demon Barber of Fleet Street,** 4, 36, 44, 50, 51, *362, 363,* 363, 556
Sweeney, James, 455
**Sweet By and By, The,** *517*
**Sweet Charity,** 33
Sweet, Jeffrey, vii, 3, 472, 508, 554
Sweet, Sheridan, viii, 503
Swerdlove, Dorothy, viii
Swift, Anne, 445
Swift, Julia, 382
Swope, Martha, viii
Symington, Donald, 425
Szabo, Jeffrey, 370
Szarabajka, Keith, 15, 414
Szentgyorgyi, Tom, 469

Tabachnik, Robin, 384
Tabaka, Victoria, 436
Tabakov, Oleg, 412
**Tablets, The,** *477*
**Tabs,** *516*
Taccone, Anthony, 427
Tachiki, Sadahiko, 460
Tackaberry, Celia, 525
Tagg, Alan, 8, 387
Taikas, Pauline Achillas, 367
Takarazuka Revue Company, 366
**Takarazuka,** 4, *366, 367*
Takase, Kazuki, 456
Takayama, Akira, 364
Takazawa, Marie, 397
**Take Me Along,** 28
Takeshita, Vernon, 518
Takita, Kyoko, 397
Talbot, Kate, 506
Talbot, Susan, 455
**Talented Tenth, The,** 11, 16, *417*
Taleporos, Zoe, 386
**Tales of the Central Park Woods,** *468*
**Tales of the Lost Formicans,** 452, *472*
**Talking Pictures,** *536*
Talking Band, The, 457, 471

**Talking Things Over With Chekhov**, 11, *430*
Tallawi, Akram, 475
Talman, Ann, 379, 422
**Tamara**, 399, 445
Tan, Victor En Yu, 467, 472, 519
Tancredi, Dorothy, 436, 437
**Tango**, 40, *365, 366*
**Tango Apasionado**, 366
Tani, Masazumi, 367
Tanji, Lydia, 518
Tannenbaum, Lori, 531
Tannenbaum, Shirley, 530
Tanner, Dolores, 524
Tanner, Kerry, 513
Tanner, Tony, 41, 374
Tarson, Geoffrey, 539
Task, Jeanne, 511
Tasker, Jill, 414, 463, 464
Tassin, Christen, 377
Tate, Judy, 475
Tateishi, Lisa, 518
Tatlock, Michael, 513
Tatum, Marianne, 384
Tavares, Eric, 537
Tavariani, Tengiz, 428
Tavartkiladze, Kakhaber, 428
Taveras, Elvira, 465
Taylor, Bernadette, 393
Taylor, Beth, 560
Taylor, David, 478
Taylor, Dendrie, 512
Taylor, Holland, 439
Taylor, Irving, 394
Taylor, James, 3
Taylor, Kate, 535
Taylor, Kim, 560
Taylor, Lynne Flijian, 459
Taylor, Myra, 520
Taylor, Noel, 525
Taylor, Rebecca, 517
Taylor, Regina, 463, 475
Taylor, Robyn Karen, 387
Taylor, Sunny, 514
Taylor, Ty, 530
Taylor, Victoria, 478
Taylor-Corbett, Lynne, 525
Taymor, Julie, 422, 463
Tcharkviani, C., 427
Tchkhaidze, Revaz, 427, 428
Tchkhikvadze, David, 428
Tchkhikvadze, Ramaz, 427
Techman, Charles, 530
Tecson, David, 412
Tejera, Jose, 466

Temerson, Catherine, 479
Temperley, Stephen, 408
**Tempest, The**, 11, 52, *420*, 449, *474*
**Tenth Man, The**, 4, 48, *378*, *379*
Tenwinkel, John, 523
Terada, Takio, 367
**Terminal Hip**, 450, *463, 477*, 558
Terrell, John, 464
**Terrors of Pleasure: The Uncut Version**, *477*
Terry, Keith, 427
Terry, Megan, viii, 527
Terry, Susan, 380
Terry, W. Benson, 524
Tesich, Steve, 469
Tessier, Claude R., 434
Testa, Mary, 414
**Tete a Tete**, *539*
Teti, Tom, 520, 524
Tewes, Darryl, 408
Thaler, Terri, 513
*That Was the Week That Was*, 15
Thau, Harold, 369
Theater for a New Audience, 479
Theater for the New City, 412, 470
Theater Hall of Fame, 560
Theater Off Park, 471
Theater Union of the U.S.S.R., 383
Theater Virginia, 532
Theater West, 516
*Theater World* Awards, 559
Theater X, 523
TheaterWorks, 527
Thebus, Mary Ann, 472
**There's No Such Thing as an Unwanted Millionaire**, *468*
Theroux, Paul, 528
Therriault, Daniel, 479
Theta Theater Company, 479
Thibodeau, Marc P., 383
Thiergaard, Judith, 429
Thies, Howard, 455, 459, 559
Thigpen, Lynne, 464
**Thin Air**, *470*
**Thin Air: Tales From a Revolution**, *535*
**Thing's the Play, The**, *468*
**This is Not a Soap Box**, *463*

Thole, Cynthia, 370
Thomas, Blair, 508
Thomas, Colby, 478
Thomas, Dylan, 458
Thomas, Francine, 517
Thomas, Frozine, 42, 430
Thomas, John C., 422
Thomas, John Henry, 384
Thomas, John Norman, 382, 531
Thomas, Leonard, 423, 424
Thomas, Marie, 417
Thomas, Raymond Anthony, 425, 474, 524
Thomas, Richard, 9, 369, 405, 469
Thomas, Traci Lyn, 463
Thomasson, Peter, 503, 504
Thome, David, 436
Thompson, Adrienne, 470
Thompson, Barbara, 456
Thompson, Dale, 390
Thompson, David, 523
Thompson, Elizabeth, 475
Thompson, Evan, 380
Thompson, John Leonard, 540
Thompson, Kent, 523
Thompson, Lynn, 458
Thompson, Martha, 539
Thompson, Sada, 439
Thompson, Stuart, 395
Thompson, Tazewell, 456
Thompson, Tommy, 534
Thomsen, Richard, 472, 476, 511
Thomson, Anna Levine, 457
Thomson, Peter Gregory, 468
Thorne, Raymond, 395
Thornton, Cheryl, 476
Thorson, Linda, 364
**Three Johnsons and a Mule**, *464*
**Three Musketeers, The**, *534*
**3 Penny Opera**, 4, 6, 49, *372*, 556
**Three Poets: Komachi, Hrosvitha and Akhmatova**, 452, *470*
**Three Sisters, The**, *477*
**Threepenny Opera**, 49, *372*
Thuna, Leonora, 525
Thunder Bay Ensemble, 460
Thunhurst, William, 530
Thurber, James, 524
Tichenor, Austin, 522
Tichman, Nomi, 431

**Ticket to Plainfield, *469***
Ticotin, Nancy, 441
Tierney, Thomas, 530
Tighe, Kevin, 538
Tighe, Michael, viii
Tighe, Susanne, 406, 420
Tilford, Joe, 473
**'Till the Eagle Hollers, *470***
Tillinger, John, 6, 9, 369, 401, 406, 526
Tilney, Rebecca, 455
Time and Space Limited, 479
**Time Traveler, *479***
Timerman, Alec, 377
Tindall, Blaire, 388
**Tiny Dimes, *475***
Tipton, Jennifer, 404
Tiscornia, Nelly Fernandez, 535
Titcomb, David, 384
Tittle, Scotti, 367
**Titus Andronicus,** 11, 52, 53, *402, 403, 404*
Tobias, Fred, 368
Tobias, Patricia Wing, 468
**Tod, the Boy, Tod, *524***
Toda, Chiaki, 397
Todaro, Paul, 478
Todd, Albert, 383
Todd, Gina, 473
Todd, Linnea, 508
Tokar, Michael, 370
Tokoro, Harumi, 367
Tokyo Broadcasting System International, Inc., 377
Tokyo Engeki Ensemble, 460
Tolan, Kathleen, 30, 406, 467
Tolan, Peter, 400, 461
Tolbert, Amy, 367
Tom, Lauren, 437
Tomaine, Chris, 475
Tomasino, Matt, 479
Tomasovic, Thomas, 478
Tombello, Drew, 535
Tompos, Doug, 380
**Tone Clusters, *520***
**Tonight We Love, *458***
Tono, Agus, 470
Tony Awards, 59, 61, 554
**Tony 'n' Tina's Wedding,** 560
Topol, Richard, 414, 531
Torcellini, Jamie, 433
Toren, Suzanne, 529
Torme, Mel, 368
Toro, Natalie, 443
Torpey, Erin, 386

**Torrents of Spring, *525***
Torres, Gina, 524
Totah, Isa Nidal, 478
Touchstone Theater, 504
Touda, Ikuei, 367
Toussaint, Lorraine, 417
Tovar, Candace, 438
Tovatt, Ellen, 384
Tovatt, Patrick, 472
Towb, Harry, 433
**Tower of Evil, The,** 452, *457*
**Tower, The, *464***
Towers, Charles, 527
Towler, Laurine, 387
Townsend, Clista, 528
Toy, Christine, 522
Tracey, Bob, 530
Tracy, Jim, 479
Tradewell, Hiedi, 479
**Tradition 1A, *529***
Trainer, David, 537
Traister, Andrew J., 537
*Trance*, 422
*Trapp Family Singers*, The, 383
Trapp, Maria Augusta, 383
**Traveler in the Dark,** 452, *473*
**Travesties, *475***
Travis, Mark W., 478
Treadwell, Tom, 506
**Treasure Island, *509***
Treat, Martin, 459
**Treatment of Dr. Love, The,** *431*
Trevino, Vic, 512
Treyz, Russell, 466, 476
TRG Productions, 479
Triangle Theater Company, 479
**Tribute to Diana Vreeland,** *460*
Trichter, Judd, 401
Trigg, Richard, viii
Trilling, Ossia, viii
Trinidad, Carmen, 504
Tripplehorn, Jeanne, 381
Tritthart, Christine, 459
Trofimov, Gennady, 383
**Trojan Women, The,** *470*
Troob, Daniel, 505
Troster, Gavin, 478
**Troubador, *478***
Trouille, Clovis, 359
Troy, Doris, 475
Troya, Ilion, 477

**Tru,** ix, 4, 6, 28, 30, 62, *381*, 556, 558, 559, 560
**True Stories, *477***
True, Jim, 386
True, Sandra Cox, 511
Trujillo, Marc Allen, 466
Trulock, Dianne, 376
**Truly Blessed,** 4, 42, *389*
Trumbull, Robert, 476
Trusits, Marie, 456
Tseckares, Demetra, 521
Tsoutsouvas, Sam, 413, 474
Tsuji, Ann M., 467
Tsujimoto, Gary, 535
Tsypin, George, 558
Tubb, Dan, 408
Tubert, Susana, 467
Tucker, Gary, 528
Tucker, Robert, 362
Tucker, Shona, 463, 474
Tucker-White, Pamela, 473
Tucket, John, 468
Tufts, Clark, 455
Tull, Eric, 413
Tull, Patrick, 418
Tully, John, 523
**Tumbleweed in Cowtown, *507***
Tune, Tommy, 36, 44, 62, 375, 556, 559
Tunick, Jonathan, 50
Turai, Terrie, 393
Turenne, Louis, 378
Turkiashvili, Giorgi, 428
Turlish, Susan, 529
Turnbull, Jill, 367
Turnbull, Laura, 369
Turner, Caroline F., 531
Turner, Charles, 464
Turner, Glenn, 375
Turner, Kathleen, 6, 9, 30, 47, 386, 556, 559
Turner, Martin, 433
Turner, Richard V., 424
Turner, Susan Watson, 423
Turns, Ali, 465
Turpin, Bahni, 425
Turrin, Joseph, 473
Tursky, Vladimir, 383
Tuths, Evelyn, 429, 478
**Tutti Non Ci Sono, *459***
Twain, Mark, 18
**Twelfth Night,** 11, 52, *402, 403*, 560
**Twelve Days of Christmas, The, *468***

**Twenty Fingers, Twenty Toes,** *473*
**Twice Shy,** *413, 414*
**Twilight Tales II,** *478*
2 (Two), *483,* 484, 485-490, 558
**Two Centuries,** *470*
**Two Good Boys,** *531*
**II Samuel 11, Etc.,** 452, *475*
**Two Trains Running,** *526*
**Two War Scenes,** *458*
Twomey, Anne, 46, 364
Tyler, Edwina Lee, 460
Tyler, Jim, 368
Tyler, Royall, 466
Tynan, Kenneth, 56, 359
Tyree, Dianne, 522
Tyrone, Keith, 415
Tyson, Fred, 364
Tyson, Nikki, 531
Tyson, Pam, 463
Tyson, Pamala, 449, 474, 558
Tywang, Rene, 478
Tyzack, Margaret, 27, 61, 387, 556
**Tzigane,** *507*
Ubu Repertory, 479
**Ubu Roi,** 401
**Ubu,** 11, 48, *401*
Udell, Peter, 362
Ueda, Shinji, 367
Uggams, Leslie, 432
**Ugly,** *468*
Uhry, Alfred, 399, 560
Ullrick, Sharon, 513
Ulmer, John, 536
Ulrych, Petra, 513
Ultz, 17, 31, 419
**Umpy the Pumpkin,** *524*
**Unconditional War,** *528*
**Undercurrents,** *540*
Underwood, Jackie, 456
Underwood, Sandy, viii
**Unfinished Reach, The,** *466*
Unger, Jay, 517
**Unholy Trinity,** *524*
United Scenic Artists, 554
University of Virginia, 55, 56, 376
**Untitled,** *468*
**Up 'n' Under,** *458*
**Up Against It,** 11, 40, *406, 408, 409, 412*
Upstart Stage, 497
**Upstate Mourning,** *468*
Urban Blight, 37

Urbani, Vince, 524
Urbanito, Joe, 507
Urena, Fabio, 479
Urrutia, David, 528
Ursua, Rene, 504
Utermohlen, Mark, 524
Utzig, Gregory, 362, 410
Vachss, Andrew, 468
Vador, Ella, 522
Vago, Sandra, 534
Vail, Maria, 463, 464
Valando, Tommy, 429
Valdes-Aran, Ching, 464, 470, 475
Valentine, Karen, 469
Valentino, Lou, 473
Valenza, David, 534
Valenzuela, Luisa, 528
Valero, Wayne, 512
Valk, Kate, 479
Valle, Fred, 467
**Value of Names, The,** *472*
**Vampire Dreams,** *536*
**Vampire Lesbians of Sodom,** 399
Van Bellinghen, Carolyn, 514
Van Dam, Sander, 477
Van Dyck, Jennifer, 368
Van Dyke, Elizabeth, 425
Van Fossen, Diana, 458
Van Groningen, Chris, 466, 468
Van Hyning, Howard, 384
van Itallie, Jean-Claude, 473
Van Lindt, Bob, 469
Van Name, J.J., 529
Van Over, Maryday, 517
Van Patten, Joyce, 397, 445, 535
Van Peebles, Melvin, 450
Van Tieghem, David, 457
Vance, Courtney, 22, 23, 422, 558
Vance, Danitra, 20, 411, 524, 558
Vance, Rodney, 513
Vandergriff, Robert, 405
Vandertholen, John, 525
Vanoff, Nick, 379, 555
Varga, Harvey, 478
Vasconcello, Anthony, 407
Vasquez, Randy, 417
Vasseux, Jean-Claude, 469
Vassiliev, Vladimir, 383
**Vaudeville Nouveau,** *461*
Vaughan, Melanie, 527

Vaughan, Stephanie, 528
Vaughn, Robert, 369
Vawter, Ron, 461, 479
Vazquez, Cookie, 434
Velarde, Teresa, 512
Venable, Noe, 535
Veneziale, Renee, 443
Vennema, John C., 29, 429, 525
Venner, Tracy, 377
Venora, Diane, 53, 404
Ventilador, Val, 385
Venton, Harley, 48, 378
Ventriss, Jennie, 379
Ventura, Susana, 477
Vercoutere, Maurice, 536
Verdi, Josephine, 514
Verica, Tom, 468
Vernacchio, Dorian, 512
Vernan, Ron, 535
Veselka Festival, 477
Vialliancourt, Lise, 464
Vic, Cliff, 461
Vic, Joel, 456
Vichi, Gerry, 432, 464
Vickers, Larry, 390
Victory Gardens Theater, 502, 508
Vidal, Marta, 467, 509
Viertel, Thomas, 369, 405
Vietnam Veterans Ensemble Theater Company, 479
Villa, Marc, 365
Village Voice Off-Broadway (Obie) Awards, 557
Villagran, Patricio Strahovsky, 465
Villamor, Christen, 467
Vincent, Glyn, 470
Vincent, Paul, 509
Vincic, Yvonne, 524
Vineyard Theater, The, 472
Vinkler, Greg, 509
Vinovich, Stephen, 17, 368
**Violent Peace,** 452, *472*
Vipond, Neil, 421
Viracola, Fiddle, 372
**Virago,** *525*
Virginia State Theater, 527
**Virgule,** *517*
Virta, Ray, 458, 477
**Vital Signs,** *519*
Vitale, Angela, 475, 476
Vitalo, Marie, 475
Vitella, Sel, 373
Vivas, Nelly, 470

Viveiros, Tom A., 507
Viverito, Sam, 505
Vladlen, Dosortsev, 468
Vogelgesang, Fred, 384
**Volga Sunset Room, *507***
Volz, Jim, 523
von Bargen, Daniel, 365, 404, 559
von Kleist, Heinrich, 476
Von Mayrhauser, Jennifer, 459
von Mayrhauser, Peter, 419
Von Tilser, Alex, 393
von Ziegesar, Peter, 470
Vosburgh, David, 363
Vose, Holland, 411
Voulgaris, John, 455, 473
Vowell, Jaymee, 517
Voznesensky, Andrey, 383
Vroman, Lisa, 387, 388
Vuoso, Teresa, 424

Waara, Scott, 380
Wachsberger, Bob, 511
Wadbrook, Russell, 528
Waddell, Jack, 455
Waddell, Mary Jayne, 367
Wade, Adam, 424
Wade, Jeree Palmer, 463
Wade, Mark Anthony, 459
Wadsworth, Don, 530
Wadsworth, Oliver, 464
Wagner, Chuck, 440, 441
Wagner, Frank, 367
Wagner, Guy S., 403
Wagner, Kathryn, 455
Wagner, Robin, 6, 33, 380, 404, 556, 558, 559
Wahrer, Timothy, 437
Waites, Luigi, 527
Walch, James, 519
Walden, Stanley, 359, 359, 521
Waldheim, Julianne, 375
Wasser, Scott, 405, 478
Waldman, Robert, 414
Waldo, Terry, 455
Waletzko, Craig, 377
Walker, Bonnie, 377
Walker, Fuschia, 415
Walker, Janet Hayes, 473
Walker, Jonathan, 414
Walker, Lee, 516, 517
Walker, Mary, 525
Walker, Paul, 540
Walker, Peter, 440
Walker, Ray, 443
Walker, Rene, 460

Walker, Seth Jerome, 386
Walker, Sullivan, 526
Walker, Thomas, 477
**Walking the Dead, *456***
Wallace, Jack, 469
Wallace, Lee, 392
Wallach, Allan, 62, 553
Wallem, Linda, 400, 461
Walnut Street Studio Theater, 529
Walsh, Deirdre, 468, 469
Walsh, Elizabeth, 473
Walsh, Thomas J., 438
Walsh, Tony, 463
Walter, Jessica, 445
Walton, Amy, 511
Walton, Jim, 363, 523
Walton, Tony, 6, 35, 44, 375, 469, 507, 556
Wandachristine, 508
Wang, Szu-Ming, 518
Ward, Diane, 417
Ward, Douglas Turner, 30, 423, 424
Ward, Elsa, 408, 427, 467
Ward, Michael, 420
Warfield, Joe, 459
Waring, Wendy, 531
Warmen, Tim, 473
Warp and Woof Theater Company, 405
Warrack, David, 362
Warren, David, 467, 526
Warren, James, 438
Warren, Jennifer Leigh, 463
Warren, Joseph, 463, 477
Warren, Robert, 473
Washington Post Award, 560
Washington, Don Corey, 464
Washington, Kenneth, 538
Washington, Sharon, 459
Wasinger, Sonny, 512, 513
Wasser, Scott, 405, 478
Wasserstein, Wendy, 59, 360
Wasson, David, 429
**Watchman, *470***
**Water Music, *458***
Waterhouse, Jane, 522
**Watermelon War Song, *513***
Waters, Les, 6, 412, 518, 519
Watkins, Jeffrey, 504
Watkins, Marcia Lynn, 436
Watson, Ara, 509
Watson, Lisa L., 424
Watson, Miles, 463, 464
Watt, Douglas, 551, 552, 559

Watts, Susan, 527
**Waves, The, 450, *466***
Wavick, Wesley, 523
Way, Lillo, 455
**We Keep Our Victims Ready, *476***
We, 20
**We, Part III: Jonquil, *423***
**We, Part IV: Burner's Frolic, *423***
**Weather Outside, The, *474***
Weathers, Danny, 438
Weatherstone, James, 440
Weaver, Danyelle, 365
Weaver, Fritz, 369
Weaver, Lois, 460
Weaver, Sylvester A. Jr., 424
Webb, Carolyn, 473
Webb, Jeff, 507
Webb, Mitch, 364
Webber, Andrew Lloyd, 5, 34, 35, 359, 360, 387, 388, 556
Webber, Julian, 469
Weber, Jake, 403
Weber, Kym, 397
Weber, Margaret, 478
Weber, Patricia, 397
Weber, Paul Anthony, 516
Webster, Bryan, 469
Webster, Jeff, 479
Webster, Leigh, 433
Wedgeworth, Ann, 415
Wefel, Susan, 524
Wehrle, Margaret, 475
Weidman, John, 360
Weil, Scott, 468
Weill, Kurt, 49, 372, 394
Weill, Tim, 410
Weinberg, Hazel, 528
Weinberg, Jeff, 435
Weiner, Bernard, 484
Weiner, Leslie, 525
Weinstein, Jo, 533
Weir, Michael, 436
Weiser, Shari, 367
Weisman, Jael, 504
Weiss, Adrienne, 460, 475
Weiss, Christine, 469
Weiss, David, 410
Weiss, Jeff, 365
Weiss, Julie, 505
Weiss, Marc B., 511, 525
Weisser, Norbert, 512
Weissler, Barry and Fran, 376, 386, 556

Weitz, Paul, 458
Welby, Donnah, 477
Welch, David, 466
Welch, Jane, 425
Welch, Ken & Mitzi, 361
Welch, Laurie, 367
**Welcome to the Moon**, *468*
Weldon, Charles, 423, 424
Weldon, Duncan C., 364, 382, 556
Weldon, Kevin, 367
Wellman, Mac, 450, 457, 463, 464, 477, 535, 558
Wells, Alexander, 528
Wells, Christopher, 461, 534
Wells, Martin, 368
Wells, Tico, 524
Welsh, Dwight, 515
Welsin, Scott, 427
Welty, Doug, 474
**Wenceslas Square**, 560
Wenckheim, Nicholas, 456
Wendt, Roger, 362, 410
Wendy, Darlene, 367
Weppner, Christina, 459
Werch, Shifra, 507
Werner, Lori, 441
Werner, Stewart, 400, 416, 417
Wernick, Adam, 520
Wertenbaker, Timberlake, 452, 475, 519
Werthmann, Colleen, 531
Wesley, Richard, 16, 17, 417
Wesner, George, 367
West Coast Ensemble, 560
**West Side Story**, 5, 52
West, Cheryl, 456
West, Matt, 438
West, Norma, 534
West, Steven Major, 372
Westbeth Theater Cabaret, 479
Westbrook, Dawn, 533
Westenberg, Robert, 440
Weston, Jack, 379
Wetzsteon, Ross, 557
Weynand, David, 507
Whalen, Jay, 531
Wharton, Richard, 507
**What a Man Weighs**, *469*
Wheeler, Ed, 423, 424
Wheeler, Hugh, 34, 362, 369, 556
Wheeler, Thad, 390
Wheeler, William, 403
Wheelock, Helen, 506
Whelan, Susan, 374

**When a Door Is Not a Door,** *512*
**When I Was a Girl, I Used to Scream and Shout,** *511*
**When She Danced,** 6, 10, 11, 31, *413*, *414*, 558
**Whistle in the Dark, A,** *475*
Whitcomb, Sarah, 533
White Barn Theater, 429
**White Boys Can't Tap,** *471*
**White Chocolate for My Father,** *474*
**White Collar,** *475*
**White Rose, The,** *535*
White, Al, 526
White, Alton, 507
White, Amelia, 469
White, David A. III, 509
White, David R., 536
White, Diane, 508, 519
White, Doug, 513
White, Harrison, 410
White, Jennifer Dorr, 478
White, Lillias, 410, 558
White, Rebecca, 535
White, Richard, 473
Whitehead, Marilyn, 439
Whitehead, Michael, 393
Whitehead, Paxton, 10, 27, 378, 387
Whitehead, Robert, 376, 378, 559
Whitehill, B.T., 405, 409
Whitehurst, Scott, 524
Whitelock, Patricia Ann, 513
Whitfield, Debra, 466
Whitford, Bradley, 457
Whitley, Stephen J., 474
Whitlock, Isaiah Jr., 365, 382
Whitney, Belinda, 380
Whitney, Gregg, 370
Whitney, Julie, 470
Whitted, Earl, 474
Whittemore, Cari Dean, 408
Whittemore, Helen, 455
Whitton, Margaret, 18, 412
**Who's Afraid of Virginia Woolf?,** 560
Whole Theater, The, 523
Whyte, Kyle, 370
Wicker, Taylor, 367
Wickleffe, Dale N., 468
Widdoes, Kathleen, 457
Widman, Frank, 527
Widney, Chris, 464
Widney, Stone, 464

**Widow's Blind Date, The,** 6, 11, 24, *419*, *516*
Widulski, E.G., 470
Wiener, Sally Dixon, viii
Wierzel, Robert, 408, 410, 417, 504
Wiesel, Elie, 3
Wiest, Dianne, 469
Wiggins, Pamela, 473, 478
Wiggins, Tommy, 509
Wilbur, Ellen, 528
Wilcher, James "Red", 42, 430
Wilcox, Larry, 395
Wilde, Oscar, 474, 475, 477
Wilder, Jessica, 386, 387
Wildpret, Eric, 466
Wiley, Irene, 422
Wilker, Lawrence J., 392
Wilkinson, Colm, 441, 444
Wilks, Talvin, 524
Will, Ethyl, 368
Willardson, Peter L., 534
Willett, John, 372
William Inge Award, 558
Williams, Barry, 473
Williams, Celeste, 508
Williams, Curt, 423
Williams, Dayne, 464
Williams, Doug, 456
Williams, Ellis E., 415
Williams, Jacqueline, 472
Williams, Jonathan, 461
Williams, Josh C., 443
Williams, K.R., 430
Williams, Karen, 470
Williams, Kathleen, 384
Williams, Kevin, 559
Williams, Sally, 384
Williams, Sammy, 438, 439
Williams, Tennessee, 45, 46, 47, 364, 386, 452
Williams, Treat, 9, 29, 369, 405, 421
Williamson, Ruth, 522
Williford, Lou, 525
Willis, Gay, 440
Willis, John, 559
Willis, Lisa, 522
Willis, Mervyn, 475
Willis, Mirron, 464
Willis, Ray, 479
Willison, Walter, 374
Wills, Ray, 429
Wilma Theater, 530
Wilner, Lori, 472

Wilson, August, 5, 6, 21, 22, 30, 56, 62, 389, 526, 551, 552, 554, 555, 559
Wilson, Bernadette, 537
Wilson, Daniel, 530
Wilson, Edwin, 551, 552
Wilson, Elizabeth, 439
Wilson, Erin Cressida, 417
Wilson, Julie, 472
Wilson, K.C., 509
Wilson, Kim, 534
Wilson, Laurel Ann, 383
Wilson, Lee, 370
Wilson, Lizanne, 507
Wilson, Mary Louise, 404
Wilson, Michael, 517
Wilson, Nan, 470
Wilson, Pamela Ann, 436
Wilson, Rainn, 403
Wilson, Tena, 455
Wilson, Tyrone, 387
Wiltse, David, 525
Wimmer, Karen, 479
Winborn, Brent, 473
Wincott, Michael, 368
Winer, Laurie, 59
Winer, Linda, 552
**Wink-Dah**, *458*
Winker, James R., 512
Winsett, Betty, 455
**Winslow by the Sea**, *469*
Winslow, Pamela, 440
Winston, Stan, 470
**Winter's Tale, The**, 405
**Winter**, *507*
Wintersteller, Lynne, 37, 419
Winther, Michael, 378
Winton, Graham, 403, 421
Winwood, Estelle, 48
Wion, John, 384
**Wipeout**, *464*
Wise, Scott, 434, 435, 441
Wise, Steve, 520
Wise, William, 528
Wiseman, Joseph, 379
Wisniski, Ron, 409, 473
**Witch, The**, *476*
Witt, Forrest, 560
Witt, Phil, 429
Wittenbauer, John, 420
Witter, Terrence J., 391
Wittmer, Mary Lou, 459
Wittstein, Ed, 539
Witzel, Linda, 468
Wodehouse, P. G., 360
Woelzl, Susan, 384

Wojcik, Randy, 434
Wojda, John, 382
Wojewodski, Robert, 534
Wojewodsky, Stan Jr., 504
Wolf, Catherine, 392
Wolf, Jeffrey, 469
Wolf, Lorraine, 390
Wolfe, David, 375
Wolfe, George C., 6, 19, 31, 407, 411, 524, 558
Wolff, Art, 390
Wolinsky, Robert, 372
Wolk, James, 528
Wollner, Don, 469
Wolsk, Gene, 431
**Wolves**, *455*
**Woman Floating Out a Window**, *458*
**Woman, the Man and the Indian, The**, *513*
**Women in Comedy**, *461*
**Women of Manhattan**, *478*
**Women Preachers**, *477*
Women's Project and Productions, The, 452, 472
**Wonderful Town**, *475*
Wondisford, Diane, 422, 463
Wong, B.D., 420, 443
Wong, Janet, 437
Wong, Lily-Lee, 437
Wong, Nathan, 518
Wonsek, Paul, 458
Wood, Frank, 521
Wood, Martha, 532
Wood, Natalie, 52
Woodall, Oliver, 395
Woodall, Ron, 430
Woodard, Charlaine, 403
Woodeson, Nicholas, 418
Woodhouse, Sam, 535
Woodman, Jeff, 537
Woods, Allie Jr., 504
Woods, Beth, 367
Woods, Eileen, 367
Woods, Kathleen, 527
Woodson, John, 470
Woodworth, Phil, 477
Woolard, David C., 376, 429, 467, 518
Woolf, Steven, 534
Woolf, Virginia, 450, 466
Woolsey, Wysandria, 387, 388
Woosnam, Tom, 527
Wooster Group, The, 479
Wooten, C'Esther L., 474
Working Theater, 479

Working One-Acts '89, 479
Workman, Jason, 370, 559
**World Goes 'Round ... With Kander and Ebb, The**, *523*
**World Without End**, *463*
Worley, Jo Anne, 41, 373
Worth, Penny, 375
Worthington, Cornell S. II, 397
Wortman, Bryna, 472
WPA Theater, 450, 472
Wrenn-Meleck, Peter, 503
Wright, Barbara, 479
Wright, Doug, 48, 401, 472
Wright, Kathryn Ann, 434, 435
Wright, Kimberly, 527
Wright, Linda, 369, 406
Wright, Lyn, 475
Wright, Miller, 405, 416, 431
Wright, Robert, 36, 374, 556
Wright, Rowland, 474
Wright, Samuel E., 526
Wright, Sara, 513
Wright, Tim, 477
Wright, Travis, 367
Wright, Z, 362
Wrightson, Ann G., 504, 523
**Writing on the Wall, The**, *479*
Wroe, Craig, 420
Wujko, Phyliss, 367
Wyatt, Lorell J., 506
Wyche, Mimi, 422, 473
Wyche, Ronald, 430
Wydro, Ken, 475
Wykoff, Carrie, 506
Wylie, John, 374, 476
Wynkoop, Christopher, 415
Wynroth, Alan, 470
Wynters, Gail, 539
Wyrick, Eric, 384

Xifo, Raymond, 380

Yagami, Toni, 535
Yaji, Shigeru, 511, 512
Yakim, Mina, 364
Yale Repertory Theater, 389, 392, 526, 555
Yamada, Sylvia, 397
Yamada, Taku, 367
Yamaguchi, Eiko, 467
Yamamoto, Ronald, 387
Yamauchi, Wakako, 467, 518
Yaney, Denise, 416, 417
**Yankee Dawg You Die**, 400

INDEX

Yankee, Luke, 473
Yankovsky, Filip, 412
Yannon, Angela, 518
Yarden, Guy, 462
Yates, Gary, 508
Yates, William Jr., 539
Yeakle, Ellen, 515
**Year of Pilgrimage**, *533*
**Year of the Baby, The**, *475*
Yearsley, Alice, 373
Yekimov, Yuri, 412
Yellen, Sherman, 49, 359, 429, 474
Yellow Robe, William Jr., 458
Yelshevskaya, Liya, 412
Yelusich, Andrew V., 513, 514
Yesso, Don, 516
Yeston, Maury, 36, 374, 376, 556
Yezzi, David D., 431
Yglesias, Jose, 476
Yi, Harold, 397
Yionoulis, Evan, 520
Yokobosky, Matthew, 459
Yonekawa, Toshiko, 367
Yorinks, Arthur, 477
York Theater, 453
York Theater Company, 473
York, Rachel, 33, 380
York, Rebecca, 437
York, Y, 449, 464, 477
Yoshida, Miki, 456
Yoshida, Peter, 529
Yoshizaki, Kenji, 367
**You Can't Think of Everything**, *459*
**You Hold My Heart Between Your Teeth**, *508*
**You Can't Take It With You**, 10
**You Never Can Tell**, 560
**You're a Good Man, Charlie Brown**, 5
Youmans, James, 411, 467, 472

Youmans, William, 520, 527
**Young Richard**, *507*
Young Playwrights Festival, 11, 413, 414, 559
Young, Bruce, 439, 507
Young, Damian, 475
Young, Glenn, vii
Young, James, 438
Young, Jim, 373
Young, Marie, 384
Young, Susan, 469
Young, Taylor, 382
Youngstrom, Juda, 479
**Your Handsome Captain**, *479*
Yudman, Gary, 461
Yudson, Steve, 434
Yulin, Harris, 469

Zablotsky, Peter, 468
Zacek, Dennis, 508, 509
**Zachary**, *469*
Zachos, Ellen, 455
Zagnit, Stuart, 474
Zaharia, Keith, 390
Zahrn, Will, 509
Zakharov, Mark, 383
Zakharova, Alexandra, 383
Zakowska, Donna, 463
Zaks, Jerry, 469
Zaloom, Paul, 472, 477
Zammit, Eddie, 534
Zanders, Marcus, 528
Zane, Lisa, 538
Zangari, Vincent, 455, 456
Zangrando, Wendy Warren, 511
Zap, Sam, 444
**Zara Spook and Other Lures**, *520*
Zarich, Janet, 444
Zarley, Matt, 438, 531
**Zeke's Vision**, *533*
Zeleni, Bill, 468
Zelenich, Zenon, 475

Zelenin, Yury, 383
Zeliger, Carl, 468
Zemach, Amielle, 476
Zemach, Benjamin, 476
Zerbe, Anthony, 533
Zercher, Joanna, 436
Zerkle, Greg, 442, 531
Zhivova, Valeria, 383
Ziegler, Tom, 458
Zielinska, Sara, 504
Ziemba, Karen, 436, 523
Zien, Chip, 440
Zimbler, Jason, 362
Zimet, Paul, 457
Zimmer, Frederick, 478
Zimmerman, Cathy, 460
Zimmerman, Joe, 456
Zimmerman, Mark, 473
Zindel, Annette, 559
Ziola, Tammi, 527
Zippel, David, 33, 34, 379, 552, 556, 559
Zipprodt, Patricia, 366, 386
Zirkuli, Bernadette, 384
Zisa, John, 367
Zito, Christine, 478
Zivancevic, Nina, 477
Zizka, Blanka, 530
Zizka, Jiri, 530
Zola, Emil, 528
Zolli, Robert, 506
Zollo, Frederick, 425
**Zora Neale Hurston**, 11, *424*, *425*
Zorn, John, 477
**Zoya's Apartment**, 4, 30, *362*, 552
Zuber, Catherine, 504
Zukerman, Robert, 478
zum Brunnen, David, 524
Zust, Genei, 531
Zweigbaum, Steven, 380